THE WORLD'S GREATEST HANDLOADING BOOK

HANDLOADER'S DIGEST™

18th EDITION

Edited by Ken Ramage

Editorial Comments and Suggestions

We're always looking for feedback on out books. Please let us know what you like about this edition. If you have suggestions for articles you'd like to see in future editions. Please contact.

Ken Ramage/Handloader's Digest
700 East State St.
Iola, WI 54990
email: ramagek@krause.com

Manuscripts, contributions and inquiries, including first class return postage, should be sent to the Handloader's Digest Editorial Offices, Krause Publications, 700 E. State Street, Iola, WI 54990-0001. All materials received will receive reasonable care, but we will not be responsible for their safe return. Materials accepted are subject to our requirements for editing and revisions. Author's payment covers all rights and title to the accepted material, including photos, drawings and other illustrations. Payment is at our current rates.

CAUTION: Technical data presented here, particularly technical data on handloading, inevitably reflects individual experience with particular equipment and components under specific circumstances the reader cannot duplicate exactly. Such data presentations therefore should be used for guidance only and with caution. Krause Publications, accepts no responsibility for results obtained using this data.

Published by

700 East State Street • Iola, WI 54990-0001
715-445-2214 • 888-457-2873
www.krause.com

Our toll-free number to place an order or obtain a free catalog is 800-258-0929 or please use our regular business telephone 715-258-2214.

Library of Congress Number: 2002107607
ISBN: 0-87349-475-X

Handloader's Digest 18th Edition

Staff

Editor

Ken Ramage

Contributing Editors

Larry Sterett – Metallic Reloading
John Haviland – Bullet Casting
Kurt Fackler – Shotshell Reloading
Holt Bodinson – Handloading Components

About the Covers

Front Cover

Hornady's Lock-N-Load AP (Automatic Progressive) reloading press combines innovative design with high-tech manufacturing techniques to give the reloader a machine that will turn out large quantities of either rifle or handgun ammunition. The press illustrated is equipped with Custom-Grade New Dimension Pistol Dies.

This press features Hornady's new Lock-N-Load die bushing system that allows you to switch dies in a matter of seconds without the need to readjust them. Standard-thread dies screw into the bushing and are loaded and unloaded from the press with a simple twist. The locking action holds the dies in a solid, perfectly aligned position. The five-station die platform allows the flexibility to add individual seating and crimping dies, or a taper-crimp die to the progressive process.

The Lock-N-Load AP press comes with Hornady's Lock-N-Load powder measure with micrometer dial for precise charge settings. The measure automatically dispenses a charge with every pull of the press handle when a shell is present in the station. It's easily adjusted and mounts just like the dies.

Priming is handled by an innovative primer slide that automatically picks up primers while the shellplate is held secure and level by the shellplate retainer.

Because the press opening is offset, there's easy access to the shellplate. Changeover is easy and adjustment-free since the shellplate bolt and lock nut are independent of the rest of the press. The Lock-N-Load press automatically and smoothly advances in half-clicks at the top and bottom of each stroke. The rugged linkage delivers enough leverage to handle tough resizing chores, and the handle is offset to provide a clear view of your work.

Other Hornady tools and accessories, clockwise from the press:

The Cam-Lock Trimmer with micrometer-adjustable cutter uses standard Hornady shellholders and pilots—and may be adapted to power operation.

The Complete Case Care Kit includes lube, pad, accessory handle, chamfer/deburr too, primer pocket cleaners (lg. & sm.), and three case neck brushes to accommodate most commonly loaded calibers.

The Digital Reloading scale measures accurately to the tenth of a grain, up to 750 grains. The scale, powered by a nine-volt battery, comes with two check weights, powder pan and the ability to weigh in either grains or grams. An optional AC adapter is available.

Handloaders need to measure their brass, bullets and loaded cartridge length, and nothing does it better than a dial caliper. Hornady's is available in either inch or metric calibration, and includes a protective case.

Hornady's reloading handbooks round out the equipment package. The two-volume set includes hundreds of pages of loading data, plus detailed information on exterior ballistics and handloading reference.

Back Cover

The Lock-N-Load Classic single-stage press is just the ticket for simple reloading projects. Once installed and adjusted for the specific cartridge, dies are easily replaced without further adjustment thanks the Lock-N-Load bushing system. The compound linkage multiplies the handle leverage, reducing the effort needed for all reloading operations. The Classic features the easy-access angled frame and Hornady's proven PPS priming system. An automatic primer feed system is optional.

Other Hornady tools and accessories, clockwise from the press:

Hornady's reloading handbooks are invaluable. The two-volume set includes hundreds of pages of loading data, plus detailed information on exterior ballistics and handloading reference.

This particular press is set up with Hornady's Custom-Grade New Dimension rifle dies. This family of dies incorporates a number of improved features, and Hornady guarantees they will never break or wear out from normal use.

Particularly handy for measuring diameters of bullets, expander plugs and such, Hornady's micrometer delivers a finer reading than does the Dial Caliper.

Empty brass sits in a loading tray that is actually the lid of the Case Care Kit. This versatile and very necessary accessory kit includes case lube, pad, accessory handle, chamfer/deburr tool, primer pocket cleaners (lg. & sm.), and three case neck brushes to accommodate the most commonly loaded calibers.

Handloaders need to measure their brass, bullets and loaded cartridge length, and nothing does it better than a dial caliper. Hornady's is available in either inch or metric calibration, and includes a protective case.

Next, the Cam-Lock Trimmer with micrometer-adjustable cutter, uses standard Hornady shellholders and pilots—and may be adapted to power operation. Improved design features include a taller frame and redesigned handle, and a replaceable large-diameter cutting head.

Finally, just behind the press is the Lock-N-Load Powder Measure fitted to the Fast Load Powder Measure Stand that accepts Lock-N-Load bushings and features a longer arm, allowing full charging access to a 50-round Universal loading block.

For complete details on these items, and the rest of the Hornady bullet, ammunition and reloading offerings, contact the manufacturer directly.

Handloader's Digest Contents

Features:

Reports From The Field:

P. 22

P. 51

Handloader's Digest Contents

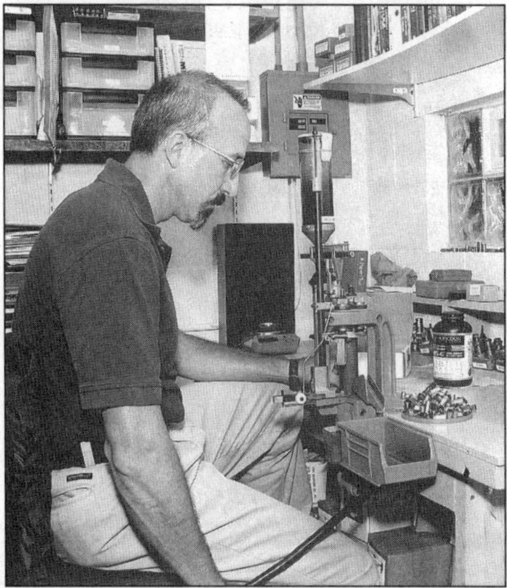

P. 76

P. 65

Harvey Prot-X-Bore Bullets

by Jim Foral

In the progress of arms and ammunition, there are but a handful of individuals whose names are readily recognizable, men who left behind major contributions and enduring legacies. Much more numerous are the lesser-known, those whose trend-generating gimmicks and short-lived innovations, for one reason or another, failed to make a lasting impact.

Foremost among this latter group was gun enthusiast Jim Harvey of Lakeville, Connecticut. Harvey was an inventor of fishing lures and imaginative products for the shooter. About 1956, Harvey introduced a line of 35- and 44-caliber rifle cartridges that he called the 'Maglaska' series. All modified 300 Magnum shells, the most powerful Maglaska cartridges were claimed to be more potent, in terms of muzzle energy, than the 458 Winchester Magnum. These were the days when new and purportedly useful wildcat cartridges were announced on a bi-weekly basis. Jim Harvey's also-ran cartridges had little to recommend them, and they never got off the ground.

In the early 1950s, Harvey made a practice of supplying smoothbore revolvers for use with shot cartridges. For a fee of $35-$45, plus the customer's perfectly good Colt Single Action or New Service, or Smith&Wesson N- or K-frame revolver, Harvey would ream out the rifling and thread the muzzle for a choke device of his own engineering. The very abundant and bargain-priced Colt and S&W 45 ACP double-action six-shooters could be adapted to a special cylinder-length 7mm Mauser case that held a payload of 130 pellets of #7 1/2 shot. Although .410 performance from a holster gun was claimed, demand for the conversion proved small.

More significantly, Harvey developed a high-speed revolver cartridge known as the 22 Kay-Chuck. There were two versions, both based on a shortened 22 Hornet case. Smith&Wesson rimfire K-22s were the guns most easily converted. The cylinders were rechambered for this small yet powerful cartridge, and the hammers were altered to centerfire. A 35-grain Sisk bullet, propelled by 9.5 grains of 2400, blew out of a 6-inch barrel at 2,200 fps. Jim Harvey's Kay-Chuck failed to gather a following and quietly withered away, but not before it inspired the 22 Remington Jet, which ushered in the day of the high-intensity handgun cartridge.

But Jim Harvey's claim to fame seems to be his less-than-memorable revolver bullet. 'Prot-X-Bore' was what Mr. Harvey chose to call his radical development. Fundamentally, it involved attaching a thin zinc washer to the base of a grooveless lead projectile. In effect, the zinc base of the Prot-X-Bore bullet was there to accomplish three primary objectives: *1)* It performed as an effective gas check. *2)* The zinc disk acted as a scraper, removing leading and other deposits and pushing them out the muzzle. *3)* The zinc band served as a dry metallic lubricant.

Harvey said his system offered distinct advantages over the lubricated cast bullets. A pure lead bullet is inarguably just the ticket for maximum expansion on game, and this was a major promotional point for the Prot-X-Bore. Ample testimonials to this effectiveness, printed in Jim Harvey's advertising, convinced the most skeptical.

Regarding accuracy, Jim Harvey was no different than anyone else who ever introduced a bullet with his name on it. In this department, the

Jim Harvey in 1952 ***(from one of his brochures).***

Prot-X-Bore was claimed to be without peer. Prot-X-Bore bullets required no sizing, and Harvey cautioned against the urge to do so. The special SFM *(Shoot From Mould)* moulds were precision-cherried to produce proper diameter bullets for the respective caliber when cast of pure lead.

The zinc-base bullets didn't appreciably wear a gun barrel. Harvey himself shot 10,000 38-caliber Prot-X-Bores through his S&W 38-44 with no sign of erosion, and he did it without cleaning the bore. Most importantly, however, the originator insisted that his bullets would not lead a revolver bore, and required no messy lubrication. Among the Prot-X-Bore evaluators, there were those who contended the Harvey bullets could dispense with conventional lubrication on account of the unique self-lubricating properties of zinc. In his extensive experiments with zinc alloy rifle bullets, published in *AMERICAN RIFLEMAN* for January of 1948, Col. E.H. Harrison failed to detect this so-called characteristic of the metal. Bullet diameter was especially crucial though, he determined. Slightly oversized projectiles required no lube, but the sub-caliber slugs left behind an extreme zinc fouling condition. These days, professionals in the industry are more inclined to believe Harvey's self-lubricating assertions were more salesmanship or loose observation, than fact.

Actually, the zinc-based bullet was nothing new. In the early 1860s, E.D. Williams developed a 579-grain grooved lead projectile fitted with a convexly-positioned zinc base. Its purpose was to scrape blackpowder fouling from the bores of the Springfield 58-caliber musket. Union soldiers were instructed to fire one of the Williams Clean Out bullets every tenth shot or so to prevent excessive residue build-up during prolonged shooting sessions, such as a firefight with the Rebels. The troopers found the Williams bullet to be as ineffective for its purpose as it was inconvenient to load from the muzzle. Most of the Williams bullets issued were dumped into the nearest creek.

Before the Prot-X-Bore bullets could be shot through a revolver barrel, the bore needed to undergo a conditioning, or seasoning, treatment. Prior to this seasoning, the handgun barrel needed to be thoroughly cleaned. Heavy copper fouling from jacketed bullets could be dissolved with a stronger ammonia solution, taking precautions to keep the liquid from settling onto blued surfaces.

Harvey suggested that all traces of previous leading deposits be removed by pouring a spoonful of mercury into the barrel, plugging each end with a finger, and rolling the quicksilver around the bore. Alternatively, Mr. Harvey sold a "One-Shot Cleaner" for the purpose. A capsule containing a special mercury amalgam was loaded behind a bullet and atop a light powder charge and then fired. The vaporized mercury alloy deposited itself along the entire length of the barrel, saturating leaded surfaces. The gun was then laid aside for an hour or so while the mercury did its work, after which time the bore could

Swaged bullet *(left)*, cast bullet *(right)* show difference in methods of attaching zinc bases.

be swabbed out normally. It is important to remember that the danger associated with using these toxic mercurial treatments was little understood in the mid-1950s.

Once cleaned, the bore was ready for conditioning to the zinc, and Harvey's instructions spelled out the procedure. This was accomplished by firing a number of moderate loads with zinc washer-based bullets. A microscopically thin wash of zinc was gradually deposited on all surfaces the washers contacted. Generally, fifty rounds were required to uniformly plate the entire length of a pistol bore, although particularly rough bores might require upwards of a hundred shots. Each bore was unique in its condition and requirements. Some may have needed a bit of lubrication such as standard cast bullet lube, or an Ipco wad.

When the bore had acquired a bright, hard coating of zinc, the barrel was said to be *sherardized*, a metallurgical term meaning to coat steel with a thin cladding of zinc. This zinc plating, it was claimed, would not build up. One writer insisted that a properly conditioned bore didn't even require cleaning. According to Jim Harvey, once the bore was *sherardized*, it was protected against rusting and leading. This is the protection Harvey's trademarked designation Prot-X-Bore alluded to. The zinc bases, or washers, were secured to the body of the bullet by an integral rivet head of lead. A conical die-formed head was extruded through the washer in the swaged version of Prot-X-Bore.

In the cast type, the fastener was moulded directly to the bullet by pouring lead through the washer. Lyman made the single-cavity moulds for Harvey's company, Lakeville Arms. Hensley and Gibbs produced a few four- and six-cavity moulds for the SFM bullets. Double-cavity moulds for some styles could be had from Lyman as well. The Lyman moulds were apparently serially numbered, and assigned cherry numbers 500-514. The vast majority were base-pour moulds, but evidence suggests the earliest were of the nose-pour type. The Prot-X-Bore line offered bullet styles especially lightweight for the caliber. There were short 106- and 125-grain 38-caliber zinc-base bullets–both hollowpoints–with a muzzle velocity potential (presumably in the 357 Magnum) of 1,800 and 1,600 fps respectively. Harvey promoted these as hunting and plinking bullets. The "target" bullet weighed 135 grains. In 44 caliber, there were stubby 158- and 170-grain hollowpoints for game and defense. In the 44 Magnum, 1,855 and 1,670 fps could be expected. The 220-grain solids or hollowpoints were the ones Harvey recommended for targets. A single 190-grain bullet was available in 45-caliber.

The bullet seating procedure for the Prot-X-Bore bullets was somewhat unusual. For starters, Harvey stressed the importance of seating and crimping as individual operations. If seated and crimped simultaneously, the exposed shoulder of the bullet could expand as much as .003/.005-inch. In some guns this could result in difficult chambering, barrel leading, bullet shaving, and

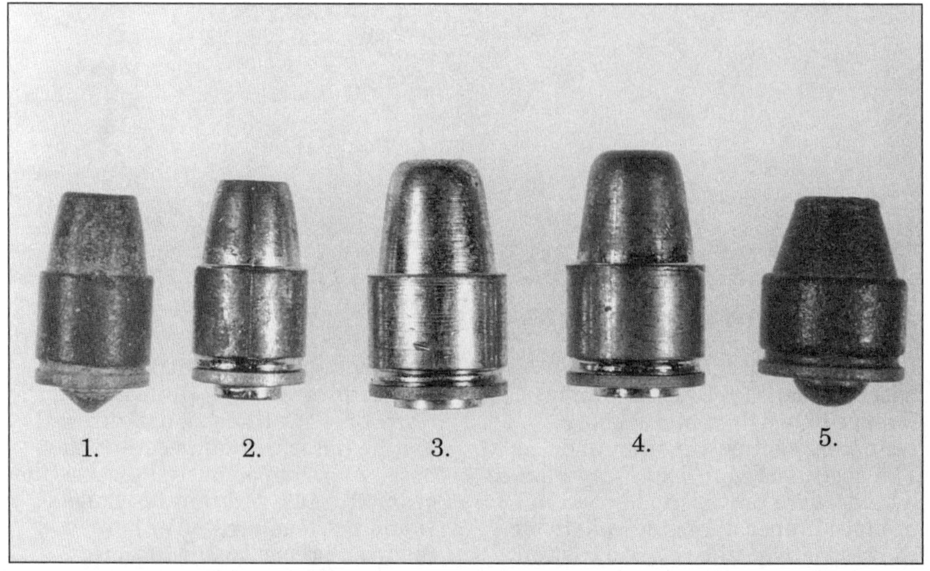

Harvey swaged and cast bullets *(l to r)*: *1)* 135-grain swaged; *2)* 358500 135-grain cast; *3)* #429507 220-grain cast; *4)* #429508 HP 220-Grain cast, and *5)* #452505 190-grain 45-caliber swaged.

other unpleasant complications. Constantly readjusting the seater die could be a time-consuming nuisance and Harvey recommended the convenience of a separate die for seating and another to administer the crimp. Since the Prot-X-Bore bullets had no crimp groove, the necessary crimp was swaged directly into the solid body of the soft untempered lead bullet. This novel Lakeville Arms method might sound unacceptably crude, but 45 years ago, there were no doubts concerning its effectiveness.

Early on, the Prot-X-Bore bullets presented unique troubles when used in semi-automatic pistols. Bore leading and bullet stripping were common complaints. Jim Harvey advised that a tin- or antimony-incorporating bullet might be helpful. Most people found the alloyed bullet, which required sizing, held the grooves of their shallow-rifled barrels and minimized leading in the hard-to-handle 38 Super and 9mm. Harvey also offered a Prot-X-Bore mould for a 124-grain projectile that incorporated two shallow lubricating grooves, features that didn't engender a strong public faith in the Prot-X-Bore system or its originator/promoter.

Casting these Harvey Prot-X-Bore bullets was not exactly a straightforward exercise. To begin with, I had a deuce of a time getting the molten pure lead to completely fill out the sharp corners of the moulds. Too, the washers sucked heat from the liquid metal, causing sunken, less than perfect bases. This was a common characteristic of all three of my moulds. A little tin, I felt, would have helped, but I was determined to follow Harvey's instructions. Turning up the heat was the solution, of course. This was my first experience casting bullets of unalloyed lead, and getting the square shoulders required a good deal more heat than I would have ordinarily expected. Allowing a larger than normal puddle of bullet metal to remain on the sprue plate helped retain the necessary heat.

The washer installation takes a few seconds, and the opened mould cools a bit. Inserting the zinc washer into its narrow slot in the quite hot mould isn't something easily accomplished with gloved fingers, and it is not nimbly or speedily done with tweezers. The most efficient method I found is to use bare fingers. After casting hundreds of these things, I've yet to be burned. Fiddling with the plug on the hollow-point 44 mould was an additional time-consuming step that compounded the difficulties. Consequently, the percentage of 'keeper' hollow-point bullets was frustratingly lower than when using the solid #429506. Others, who have tried it, volunteered that casting a shootable Prot-X-Bore bullet can be a "pain."

Actual handloading of the zinc-base bullets, apart from bullet seating, is pretty straightforward. In all cases, I adhered to Jim Harvey's loading information published in Lyman's *41st Edition Handbook* (1957), and his early brochures. This data for the 38 Special, 357 Magnum, 44 Special and 44 Magnum was developed by Hercules and tested by the H.P. White Lab. In assembling 38 and 44 Special and 44 Magnum handloads, I adjusted the seating die to first seat the bullet to the Harvey-advised depth, and seated the bullets. Then I readjusted the die to apply the crimp. In the case of the 38 Special and the 135-grain #358500, Harvey calls for seating the exposed shoulder out 0.050-inch, resulting in an overall cartridge length of 1.475 inches. The 220-grain #429506 (*HP*) and #429507 each needed to be seated to a depth of 0.275-inch in the 44 Special and Magnum. The edge of the case mouth is forced into the soft body of the bullet, and finished loads look very much like cartridges using conventional semi-wadcutters.

My 44 Magnum test gun was a Contender, one of the very early guns with the removable choke for shot capsules. To *sherardize* the 0.4288-inch bore, I fired 50 pure lead #429507s ahead of 8 grains of Unique. This is quite a mild load, for which Harvey gave a muzzle velocity of 1,000 fps. Zinc plating originated at the breech end, but didn't become apparent until the tenth zinc washer was pushed through. After 25 shots, land coverage was patchy and estimated at 75-80% complete, while the grooves were 100% plated. A thin, not particularly uniform, film of bright zinc covered the entire bore by the thirty-fifth shot. In addition to this, a peculiar dark gray fouling that I hadn't seen before began to accumulate. By the 50th round, this scaly fouling ran the length of the bore and was beginning to flake off at the breech end. Three passes with a dry brush removed most of it. Underneath was a nice silvery coating of zinc, just as Jim Harvey promised.

The fifty-shot group, incidentally, measured 5 inches at 25 yards. I

Cartridges showing proper seating depth *(l to r)*: 38 Special, 357 Magnum (not tested), 44 Special and 44 Magnum.

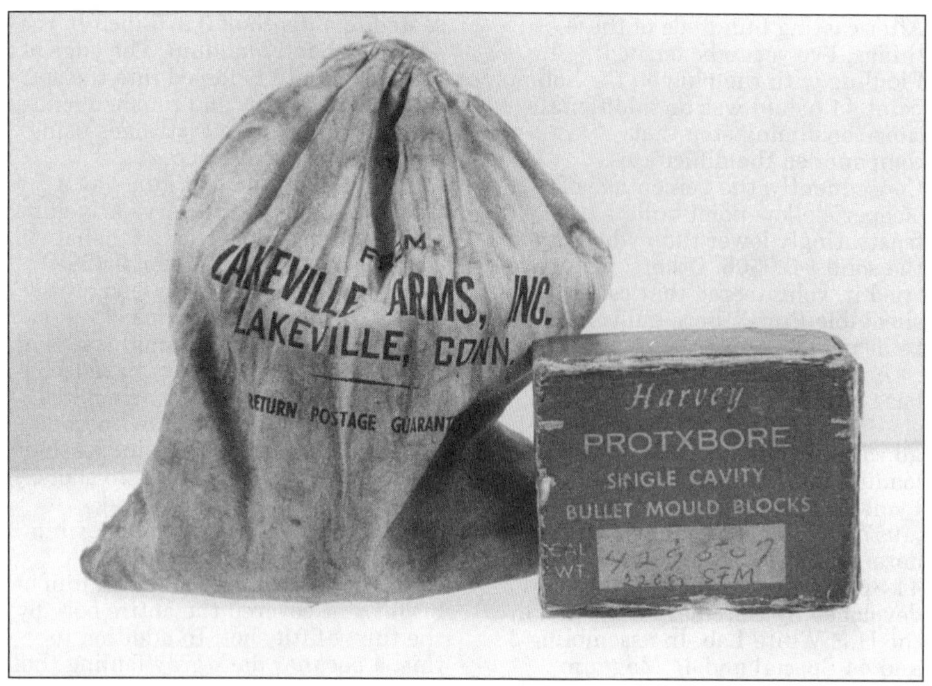

An original sack of Lakeville Arms 44-caliber zinc washers, and an original mould in box.

tried a few groups with 9 grains of Unique and both #429506 and #429507–and experienced significant leading and horrible accuracy. Too, there were spotty patches of the strange fouling. The residue and tiny particles of lead came out of the chamber with the bore brush.

I spent a couple afternoons at the range shooting various Harvey-published 44 Magnum loads, and recording the worst groups I've ever been forced to look at. Many shots never hit the 25-yard paper at all. Some printed on an adjacent target. The bore leaded noticeably with 21 grains of 2400, a grain below Harvey's maximum with the 220-grain bullet. The lead, in contrast to the zinc, was somewhat darker and non-reflective. Two of five shots hit the target. Harvey wrote that it was within the rules to use Ipco wads. For the 44 Magnum, I selected the pink soft gas check wads *(the modern Ipco counterpart) from CF Ventures (located, coincidentally, at 509 Harvey Drive, Bloomington, IN 47403).*

I went home, cleaned the gun and loaded twenty rounds with the same charge. Then I pressed in a CF Ventures wax wad. Briefly stated, the pink wads absolutely prevented leading with this load, but did not improve on the abysmal accuracy. I shipped a handful of swaged #452505 45-caliber 190-grain bullets to a friend. With an unspecified powder charge, he fired them through an 'unseasoned' 45 Colt SA. At 25 yards, no bullet hit a four-foot square target frame. At half that distance, no bullet cut the target.

My 38 Special was much less cantankerous. The K-38's bore was thoroughly zinc-conditioned with twelve shots. There was no leading or abnormal fouling when using 5.3 to 8.0 grains of Unique, and some original 136-grain Harvey swaged Prot-X-Bores. In the accuracy department, six-shot groups averaged 2.5 inches at 25 yards. Over the course of the summer, the cast 145-grain #358500s performed just as nicely, and delivered the same level of accuracy.

My S&W Model 624 44 Special was conditioned with the same 8-grain charge of Unique I'd used to prepare the 44 Magnum Contender. The zinc plating started in the leeward edges of the grooves and seemed to be reasonably complete after 40 shots. Shot straight from the mould, there was some minor leading associated with most loads using the .429-inch diameter #429507. The consistent 2.5-inch groups at 25 yards (at 800-950 fps) were acceptable, but not the best I felt possible.

The universally respected NRA technical staffer M.D. Waite tested this same bullet at low pressures and sub-900 fps velocities and pronounced it to be "finely accurate" in his 44 Special. No leading was mentioned in Waite's report. Trials with .046 Ipco wads suggest these graphite-incorporating wax wads may prevent or minimize leading up to 1,100 fps with the 220-grain bullets. I loaded fifty 44 Special cases with 16 grains of 2400, the Jim Harvey-suggested maximum load. Next I inserted CF Ventures' wax wads, and crimped the whole bunch. The first 16 grouped into 2 inches with no apparent leading in the already *sherardized* bore. *"This would make a crackerjack deer load,"* I recall thinking at that point. After the 24th shot, leading was beginning to accumulate. As the box of shells was emptied, things got steadily worse. I watched as a pretty 2-inch group degraded into one twice that size. When the 50-shot string was completed, there was a badly leaded revolver bore to scrub. Most of the serious leading, aside from what had built up in the corners of the grooves, was concentrated on the right side of the barrel. In this gun, the CF Ventures wad did little to control leading. The mysterious fouling encountered in the 44 Magnum did not present itself in the Special.

Those that might want to try out the Prot-X-Bore approach will need a mould–they show up at gun shows occasionally–and a supply of zinc washers. These days, there are two suppliers of zinc bases dimensionally correct for the Lyman/Lakeville Arms moulds *(Sport Flight Mfg. P.O. Box 1082, Bloomfield Hills, MI 48303 and 4-D Custom Die Co., 711 N. Sandusky St., Mt Vernon, OH 43050).*

The handgun sports had made significant advancements in the early 1950s. By the middle of the decade, it seemed clear the trend in revolver bullets was beginning to swing to a metal-jacketed variety, and Jim Harvey intended to be a part of it. In 1956, Harvey supplemented his handgun bullet line by offering a 1/2-jacket style that used a pure lead core and a soft 0.014-inch thick copper jacket. These 'Jugular' bullets were available in the usual variety of weights directly from Lakeville Arms, or components could be purchased separately for swaging at home, a practice Jim Harvey was instrumental in popularizing. Lakeville Arms also sold Harvey-designed swaging dies adapted to standard loading presses. These were rugged, simple-to-use tools with high production rates, and they were regarded very highly. Both the Jugular and Prot-X-Bore styles could be formed on these dies. In the mid-'50s, the more conservative handgunners were somewhat suspicious of the Jugular concept, particularly when it involved burning the Harvey-recommended load of 26 grains of 2400 behind a 220-grain Jugular in the brand new 44 Magnum cartridge. One writer assessed the Jugular bullet as *"the greatest advance in handgun shocking power since the 357 Magnum."* For a time, the Jugulars were quite popular, and helped guide the sport of handgunning into the modern era.

All in all, Prot-X-Bore was a disappointment for Jim Harvey and the shooters he aspired to service. Independent analysts felt they had isolated the reason for Prot-X-Bore's failure in many revolvers. Success with the zinc-banded bullets was totally dependant on precise fit between the zinc base and the grooves. Pure lead, at handgun pressures, needs but the slightest gap–less than 0.001-inch–to flow past the non-upsetable zinc washer, liquefy, and deposit itself in the form of lead streaks. If a gap existed, and in some guns it was unavoidable, the gas seal was not complete and leading resulted. The washers were stamped out to 'nut and bolt' tolerances on automatic machines, and there were bound to be some variances. The disks obtainable from Lakeville Arms, for example, were stamped out to nominal groove diameter. Each had a square side, the other being microscopically radiused. To assure positive scraping action, Harvey advised placing the sharp edge facing the bullet base. Harvey's washers occasionally had their holes a trifle off-center, which complicated things. Jim Harvey and his bullets gathered in a few avid followers, but not on the scale he'd hoped for.

Three original Lakeville Arms moulds made by Lyman. These are serially numbered.

A recovered #429507 bullet. Muzzle velocity @ 675 fps; shed its washer in range backstop. This shows the ring where bullet was crimped.

Various contemporary reports indicate that Prot-X-Bore worked well in some guns, generally at low to mid-range velocities. Other accounts contended the bullets caused leading. Elmer Keith's 1952 evaluation, reporting leading in the grooves of a 357 Magnum, soured multitudes and was certainly influenced Prot-X-Bores initial acceptance. Some said it was the tendency of the zinc washer to 'iron over' leading, rather than scraping it out the muzzle. Others had the opposite experience. It is entirely possible the shiny zinc plating was mistaken for leading, causing some users to give them up without fair trial. Unavoidably, the word circulated that the self-lubricating properties of the zinc band, and its sure-fire scraper function, was a misleading overstatement. NRA testing concluded that the zinc base was ineffective in eliminating, or even reducing leading. In any event, the consensus seemed to be that the zinc washer had no magical characteristics or special merit, and offered no particular advantages. Many found the extra casting and loading steps to be a nuisance, not worth the bother. Taken all in all, the shooter of the 1950s was underwhelmed, and the brief acceptance of Prot-X-Bore failed to last.

When Jim Harvey died in the early '60s, Lakeville Arms went out of business and Prot-X-Bore believers discovered that the source of zinc washers was abruptly shut off. Harvey's zinc-based principle withered and blew away. At the same time, commercially swaged 1/2- and 3/4-jacketed pistol bullets became widely available, got favorable press, and quickly fell into favor. And all the while, the variety and versatility of the properly put-up cast and lubricated lead alloy bullet was never in danger of being lost.

Retrospectively, the Prot-X-Bore system did have a following of sorts. Shooters of any generation would stand in line to try out the latest new-fangled idea, and the prospects of jacketed performance at cast bullet costs certainly had its appeal. ●

Are Benchrest Loading Techniques Worth the Trouble?

by Richard S. Gardiner

Townsend Whelen has often been quoted as saying that only accurate rifles are interesting. Unless you treasure exhibition-grade walnut, intricate scrollwork and gold inlays, you have to agree with that statement. Have you ever heard anyone brag that their favorite deer rifle is only capable of 3-inch groups at 100 yards? How often have you seen in print that some gun writer's newest wildcat 6.5 - 50 BMG Short prints nice, round 2-inch clusters? For that matter, are you truly happy with the accuracy of your own guns, or would a 1/4-MOA less make you more confident in your ability to take that distant 6x6 bull in the waning light of day?

What we are willing to allow as acceptable accuracy is something we all have to decide on. For my purposes, consistent 1.5-inch groups at 100 yards with premium big game bullets are sufficient. Although I would always prefer less, 10-ring accuracy with my stock DCM Garand keeps me from losing sleep. "Minute of Squirrel" with my Browning T-Bolt provides varied table fare for my household.

Just because I am willing to tolerate what some would consider mediocre accuracy in my guns does not mean that I am not always trying to find inexpensive methods to shave a bit more off my groups. We all know the easiest way to get our guns to shoot is to throw money at some custom gunsmith and have a new barrel installed–along with such labor-intensive modifications as action truing, lapping the bolt lugs, and pillar bedding. As a matter of course, I always sort my brass by weight, deburr the flash holes, and uniform the primer pockets. This is also labor-intensive, but low-cost. I continue to read the shooting press looking for cheaper methods to achieve better accuracy.

With this in mind, I followed the reports of Browning's development of the BOSS *(Ballistic Optimizing Shooting System)* closely. Here was the promise of an off-the-shelf rifle capable of undeviating sub-minute of angle accuracy. When Browning announced their National BOSS Shootout contest, my interest became even more intense. The final result of this contest should be indicative of what the system is capable of producing, assuming the shooter used sound technique, had properly prepared handloads and good glass.

The results of the Shootout were no surprise. Each of the finalists had aggregate averages consisting of three five-shot groups of well under one inch. Their methodology was what one would expect for this level of competition. The contestants uniformed primer pockets, deburred flash holes, turned case necks, weighed both cases and match-grade bullets, and checked loaded rounds for concentricity. What jumped out at me from the printed page like a P.E.T.A. guerrilla on opening day of dove season was the one contestant that simply trimmed his cases to length and had at it. Although not the benchrest Super Shoot, here was a contestant in national competition using the simplest of loading techniques.

Over the years, I have set up my handloading tools such that all case preparations, except the actual

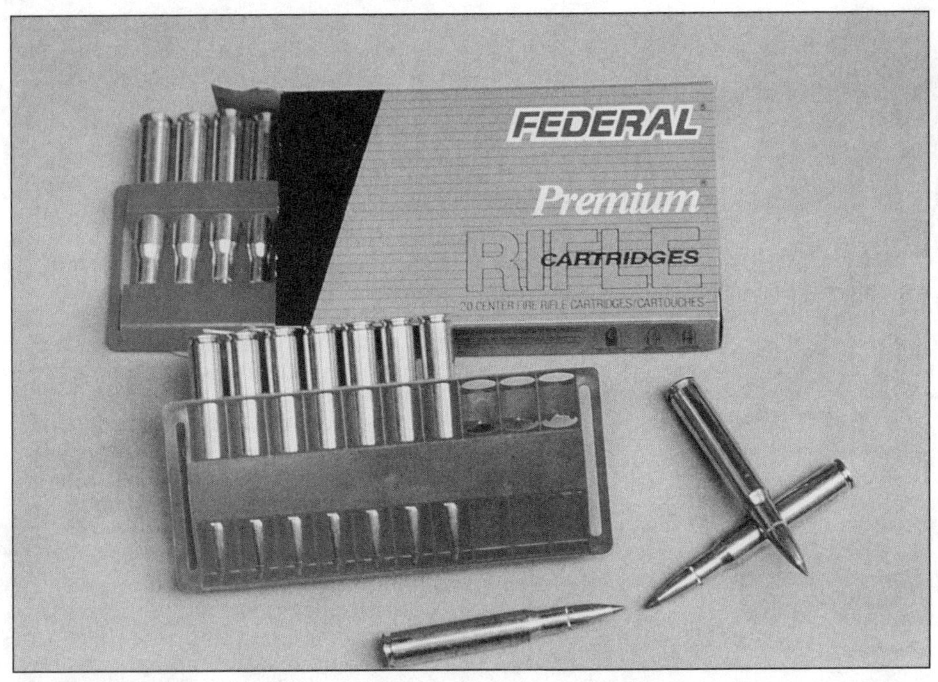

A good example of the new super premium factory ammunition offerings is this Federal Premium offering, using 150-grain Nosler Ballistic Tip bullets.

resizing, can be done in the family room while spending "quality time" watching television with my wife and kids. My case trimmer has been mounted on a block of wood. My primer pocket uniformer and flash hole deburring tool can be hand-driven and, although tedious to use, don't make enough noise to interfere with the family's enjoyment of mindless entertainment. Although I don't really relish this amount of case prep, I have always done it, believing it necessary to cheaply achieve the best accuracy from each rifle. Now the results of the National BOSS Shootout had me questioning whether or not that was true, particularly if a given rifle is not capable of sub-MOA accuracy to begin with. I intended to find out if my time would be better spent actually shooting.

Selecting a test platform for this was an easy choice. My gun room contains a push-feed Model 70 Winchester, purchased new in 1974, and chambered in 30-06 Springfield. Contrary to current trends, it has a Bausch and Lomb 2x7 Elite 3000 mounted in Tasco World Class rings on a one-piece base. The trigger has been set at 3.25 pounds. The only modification is that the receiver and first two inches of the barrel have been fiberglass-bedded and the rest of the barrel free-floated, sometime around 1976. This was necessary to reduce the average group size to below 2 inches. It has an egalitarian appetite and usually puts everything fed it into groups that measure 1.5 to 2.25 inches–day in and day out–without any accuracy gremlins. Its outstanding attribute is that the point of impact never shifts more than 1/4-inch from year to year. I consider this gun to be fairly typical of most bolt-action deer rifles.

To have confidence in the results, it was felt that the investigation planned should be done with once-fired cases from the same lot, like the average hunter/casual shooter may have on hand, but in a much larger quantity. While shooting up 250+ factory rounds is entertaining, it can be devastating to your budget unless you are as rich as Croesus. Loading up virgin brass and simply banging away would have given me my empties, but I originally started handloading to shoot more for less, and this did not appeal to my parsimonious nature. In my gun room, under the old catalogues, used targets, spilled powder and spent primers, I located 560 once-fired LC 67 cases from past CMP shoots.

You might question the usage of military brass for a couple of the customary reasons. Military brass is usually considered to be heavier than commercial. I picked up over 200 Remington 30-06 cases from varying lots at my gun club's annual hunter sight-in days last year and the majority of them weighed more than 195 grains, the average amount this batch of LC 67 brass scaled. It has been said that commercial cartridge cases are designed for reloading and that military cases are not. I have personally loaded some military cases as many as 15 times, and most of the old-timers I have talked to prefer them, at least in 30-06 and 45 ACP. I have also heard that military brass is "soft," as compared with commercial, to withstand the rigors of full-auto usage and are, therefore, prone to expand more at any given pressure. Does anyone really believe that the U.S. military uses sticky brass in its weapons, particularly those that can "cook off" a round? I hesitate to even guess what the pressure might be. I suspect that, if anything, military cases are actually harder than commercial brass.

However, there was some concern about the brass not having been fired in the rifle in question. As it turns out, my Garand has a chamber large enough that cartridges fired in it will not chamber in the Model 70. It was a simple enough matter to fire one LC 67 cartridge in the test gun and use the headspace gauge sold by Stoney Point to set the shoulder back far enough that the bolt handle would close with just the smallest amount of pressure, giving a zero headspace condition. The Precision Micrometer, a gauge RCBS makes available in assorted calibers, also could have been used to accomplish similar results. Alternatively, if I had neither on hand, I could have achieved the same effect by screwing my 1974-vintage sizing die into the press incrementally and repeatedly trying the case in the rifle. Prior to resizing, I lubed the exterior of all 560 cases with RCBS Case Lube-2 and the inside of the necks with a Lyman Case Neck Dipper. Since the RCBS lube is water soluble, you just hose the cases off in the sink after resizing and place them on newspaper in the sun to dry. No needless messing with solvent-soaked rags.

Prior to acquiring the Stoney Point headspace gauge, I was rather lazy when it came to keeping my empty cases sorted by manufacturer, lot, and number of times loaded. We have always been instructed to do so, but I assumed that it was just because of case capacity and differential work-hardening of the cartridge neck. I felt

These components were used to assemble author's test rounds.

that for normal paper-punching it was not worth the additional hassle, and used once-fired cases from the same lot only for hunting. I had always set my sizing dies using the "turn and try" method and had been satisfied with the lifespan of the brass. Using the Stoney Point gauge and same die setting, I have found that variations in different lots (*from annealing, case thickness, and elasticity*) can cause as much as nine one-thousandths of an inch disparity in the distance between the datum line on the shoulder and the case head after resizing. That works out to be about 1/8 of a revolution with a normal 7/8x14 sizer. This gauge has also proven to me that if you adjust your die for partial sizing, the shoulder of the case actually moves forward a couple of thousandths, making this method of setup questionable at best.

Military cases need one additional step to prepare them for loading that commercial cases do not. You have to remove the crimp, something that turns off many handloaders. Since I don't believe in removing metal from anything except as a last resort, I didn't ream out the crimp, but used an RCBS Primer Pocket Swage Set that I already had on hand. Dillon Precision also makes a pocket swager, but the one they manufacture is a separate tool. Swaging is quick and only has to be done once during the life of the case, and I am happy to do so if the brass is free.

Due to varied lengths of virgin and factory-loaded brass, regardless of the manufacturer, I always trim all my cases after they have been sized the first time. I set my Forster case trimmer to the usually recommended trim length of 3.484 inches and ran all the cases through it, finding some that barely had the neck squared and others that required considerable work. I keep a case on file that has already been trimmed and it takes less time to do the set-up using that case as a gauge than it does to describe it. Trimming such a large quantity of brass by hand became mighty monotonous and I am currently in the market for a power trimmer. All the necks were deburred (inside and out) using an ancient carbide tool once available from C-H. *(I believe I'll be buying an electric deburring tool, too.)* After cleaning the primer pockets with a home-made gizmo, I had enough brass prepared to the same minimal standards as the one shooter in the contest to begin running the comparisons I had in mind.

In the past, it was accepted as fact that a careful handloader could easily surpass factory ammo in both accuracy and terminal performance. With the factories loading Speer Grand Slams, Trophy Bonded Bear Claws, Nosler Partition and Ballistic Tips, Swift A-Frames, Barnes X-Bullets–and some I'm sure I forgot to mention–terminal ballistics can no longer be bested quite so effortlessly. We certainly can jazz up velocities in some of the older rounds by raising pressures above SAAMI standards, but I question the intelligence of trying for that last 50 fps. I feel that if standard velocities with the readily available premium bullets won't do what you want, you need a bigger gun, not more powder. Although I find the Hornady Light Magnum and

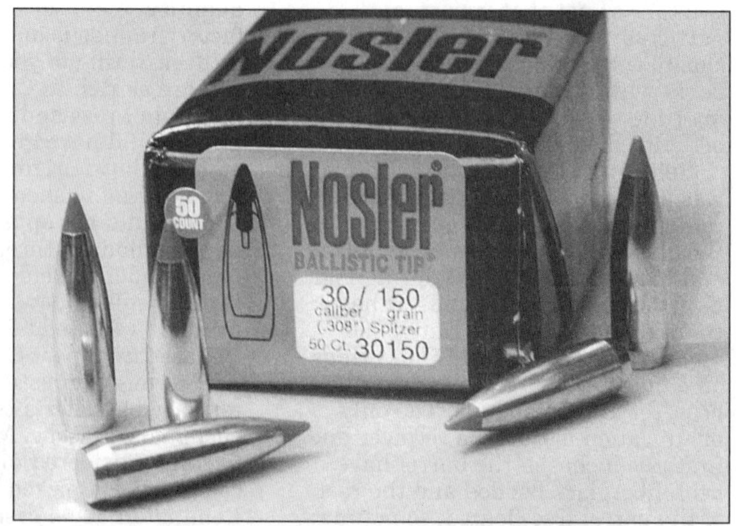

The vaunted 150-grain Nosler .308-inch Ballistic Tip.

Federal High Energy concept intriguing, the additional 80 to 120 fps that they actually chronograph over factory-equivalent handloads is really insignificant in terms of energy and bullet drop at normal ranges. I just can't get too excited about differences in drop figures of less than one inch at 300 yards. No animal that ever lived would notice an additional 100 ft-lbs of wallop at the same distance.

With careful handloading, the accuracy of factory cartridges can usually be topped, but by how much is often open to question. I thought that it might be interesting to try a box of the new super factory loads to see if any improvement over them could be gained by using modified benchrest loading techniques. It would give me a pretty good idea as to what to expect with this rifle. Plus, for part of this comparison, I needed to know the over-all length of a factory cartridge. I picked up a box of Federal Premium loaded with 150-grain Nosler Ballistic Tips, a brand usually noted for consistency, capped with a bullet that has earned a reputation for being very accurate. I was almost afraid to fire them because if you believe the advertising hype, I'd never handload another round.

The following results for the Federal Premium, like all reported in this article, are five shots in each group at 100 yards and are measured in inches. The average is pretty much what I have come to expect as standard with this rifle and the better factory ammunition. Please take note of the exact group sizes. The largest group shot is more than twice the size of the smallest. This would suggest that somewhere in the manufacture there is a lack of consistency on which we can improve, although the other three groups are quite good. Case expansion, as measured at the pressure ring immediately ahead of the solid web, was 0.006-inch.

When I shoot multiple groups off the bench, I try to allow at least one minute between shots. I clean my barrel about every 20 rounds so fouling will not affect the results. My usual procedure is to run one patch wet with Shooter's Choice bore cleaner down the barrel, followed by ten passes with a bronze brush. I follow that with an additional moistened patch and two dry. After that, Shooter's Choice Copper Remover is used as directed by the manufacturer. I then dampen a patch with a fast-drying solvent *(like RemAction Cleaner)* to evaporate any moisture still in the bore. Two cartridges are fired to foul the bore prior to shooting any more for record.

GROUP

#1	#2	#3	#4	Average
1.556	**1.168**	**2.238**	**1.084**	**1.571**

Standard Deviation = 0.523. Lot # 414452V094. Temperature 57° F to 64° F. Winds E-5 mph to NW-9 mph. Line of sight is N to S.

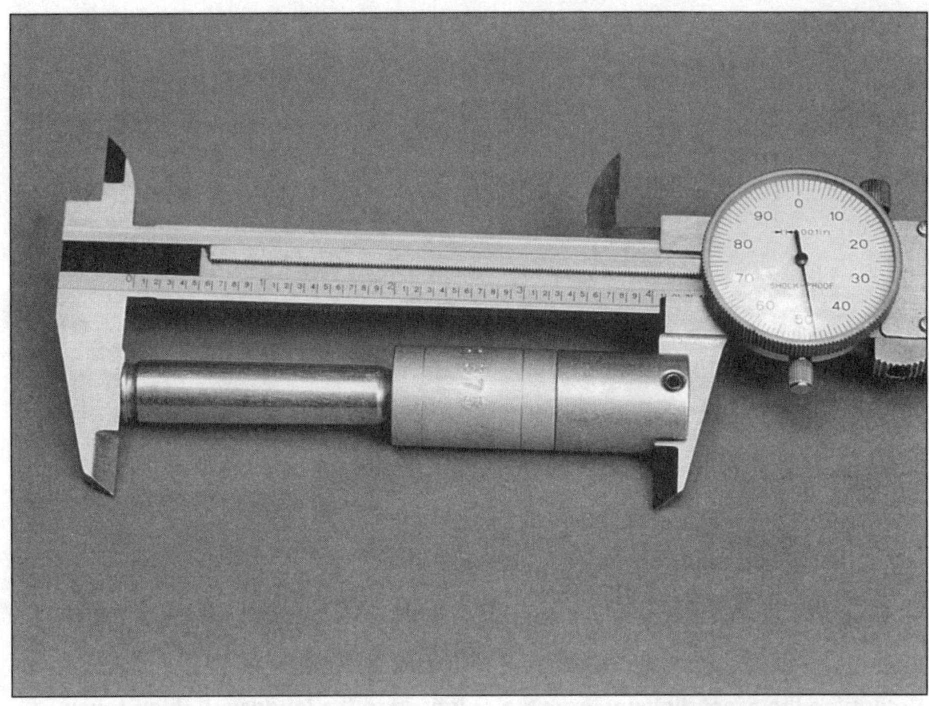

Use a once-fired case and this Stoney Point headspace gauge to precisely set your sizing die.

Picking a load to contrast with the Federal and run the rest of this comparison was your basic no-brainer. Since the Federal was topped off with 150-grain Nosler Ballistic Tips, that was the same bullet I would use, seated to the same overall length (3.264" + / - 0.004") as the Federal factory loads. As stated above, the Noslers' reputation for accuracy is beyond reproach. They have a high ballistic coefficient for flattening trajectories and lessening wind drift. The polycarbonate tip moves the center of mass towards the rear just like match-grade hollowpoints.

Originally, the plan was to shoot four groups with weight-matched bullets, but nine were deposited on the pan on my old Ohaus 5-0-5 balance before I came across the first one that varied 0.1-grain (0.06%) from the rest. I have weighed competition-grade bullets with greater diversity. I personally have never used Ballistic Tips for hunting because earlier lots had a reputation for being rather fragile, and more often than not, we measure the distances at which we shoot deer in northern Michigan in feet rather than yards. I prefer my venison without bone chips and bloodshot meat.

This particular rifle has shown a singular fondness for cases charged with IMR-4350 in all bullet weights of 150 grains and above. I have seen in print that 59.0 grains, when coupled with a 150-grain bullet, is a "factory equivalent" load. The Nosler manual states that this combination will produce a loading density of 97%, although I found it to require light compression. My understanding is that Nosler ballisticians figure case capacity by using a once-fired case prior to resizing and filling the case with water to the base of the bullet. That alone could explain this apparent discrepancy. IMR and other sources list this load as being compressed. High loading densities within certain parameters usually

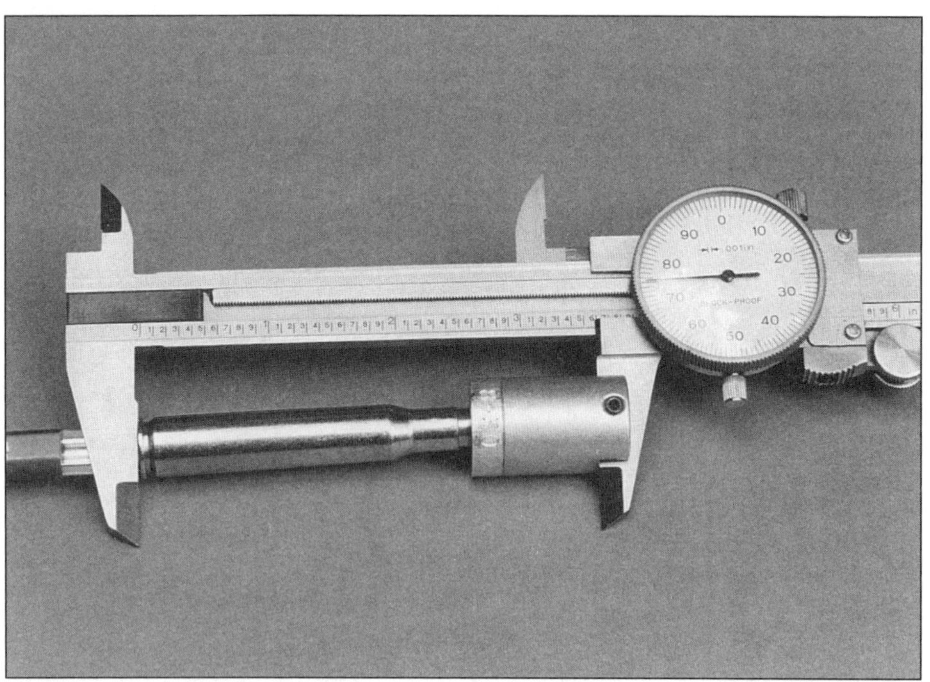

Determine the exact distance from the bolt head to the lands with this Stoney Point overall length gauge and bullet comparator.

produce good consistency. Despite the fact that IMR lists the pressure of this load as less than maximum and cases fall out of my rifle, you should always reduce charges by 10% and work upward if you choose to replicate this test. Using my components and my rifle, I measured case expansion at the pressure ring immediately forward of the case head at 0.005-inch, which was 0.001-inch less than the Federal Premium, and 0.001-inch more than the original LC 67 ball. Please be aware that these figures are only significant with this lot of components shot through my rifle. Because of the coarseness of IMR-4350, I weighed all charges, and simply dumped them into the case.

As I make it a practice to use magnum primers for all extruded powders slower than IMR-4320 and Reloder-15 and any globular propellants, I capped these loads with the CCI-250. I'm certain that results would have been pretty much the same with any magnum primer. I once ran a series of tests comparing magnum brisance primers with non-magnum caps and a case full of IMR-4350 and found the groups with the magnum primers to be more uniform, at least in cases of this capacity. However, you may find just the opposite. Just be certain to reduce loads by 10% and work upward if you elect to change primers.

Most benchresters prime each individual case with a separate hand tool to feel the primer "bottom" in the primer pocket. Some of the more advanced tools even have dial indicators for measuring each pocket and individual primer to guarantee identical seating depth.

The operative word with my search for accuracy has always been "cheaply." I prime all my cases with a Lee Auto Prime II that mounts on the press where the dies usually go. If you are not familiar with it, it has a built-in primer flipper and automatic primer feed. As you never have to touch a primer, the usual cause of primer contamination is removed from the procedure. Properly set up, each cap is seated to a positive stop in relation to the front face of the rim, precluding crushed primer pellets. Regardless of what is usually said about press-mounted priming tools, you can still feel the primer bottom out unless you have the tactile sensitivity of a chainsaw. I make it a practice to seat each primer, drop the ram 1/4 inch, and raise it again to the stop after giving the case about a half-turn. This seems to seat that tiny sparkplug more evenly. (Because you have up to 100 primers staring you in the face, *please* wear safety glasses.)

To determine whether or not benchrest case preparation techniques can actually make a significant change in the groups shot with your typical hunting rifle and if that difference is enough to spend the time to do the prep, it was decided to

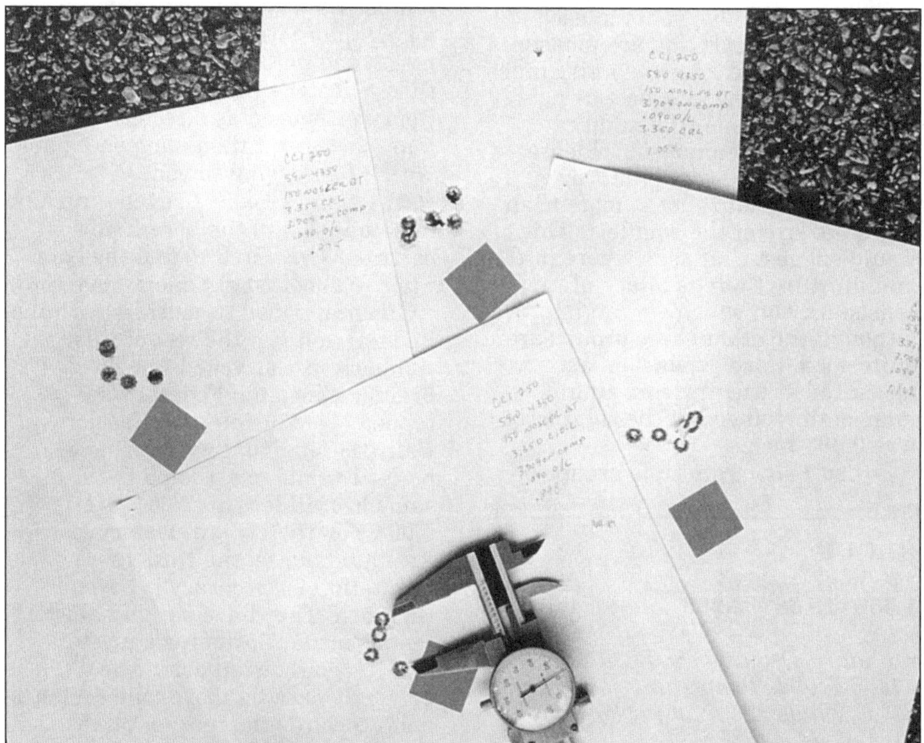

Adjustment of seating depth can deliver tighter groups.

first examine each operation separately.

There are three procedures common to the benchrest fraternity that I absolutely refuse to perform. No one has ever proven to me that turning case necks is beneficial unless you have a custom barrel with a tight chamber that is capable of 1/2-inch groups. Another is sorting loaded rounds by concentricity variation, again for the same reason. I simply seat each bullet about half way, give the case a half-turn, and finish seating it. Even with standard-grade dies, this seems to cure any cocked bullet problem, at least to my satisfaction. The tools to do these two processes also tend to get rather pricey. I refuse to even discuss squaring case heads, at least as far as hunting rifles are concerned.

The next series of groups consisted of 20 cases randomly selected and simply filled with the chosen load to see if any improvement could be gotten from using the rifle's preferred powder. Other than simple inspection to be sure than there were no faulty cases, nothing else was done.

GROUP					% Change
#1	#2	#3	#4	Ave.	from Fed.
1.710	1.842	1.494	2.082	1.782	+ 13.4 %

SD = 0.246. Temp. 57° F to 64° F. Wind E-5 mph to NW-9 mph. Line of sight is N to S.

As you can see, simply using a preferred powder and randomly selected charge does not necessarily make a difference. At this point, I could have attempted to juggle powder charges in an effort to decrease group size, but all I needed was a fairly accurate load to use as a control. An overall increase in group size over the factory loads of 0.271-inch may or may not be significant, depending on what you are trying to accomplish. If your goal is to come up with factory-equivalent ballistics and save considerable cash, you could stop right now. These handloads are accurate enough for any normal deer hunting that I know of, with the possible exception of sniping along *senderos* or across bean fields, and cost $ 0.70 less per shot than the manufactured cartridges. While the Federal Premium varied a full inch between the largest group shot and the smallest, these were only 0.59-inch apart, with a much smaller standard deviation. The largest group is actually smaller than the biggest one shot with the Federal Premium. This in itself would suggest that already something in the handloading process was more consistent, but it was too soon to hazard a guess as to exactly what it was. Be aware that standard deviation figures with samples of this size are really only significant when contrasting comparable group size averages.

All brass, both once-fired and virgin, is trimmed to ensure uniform length.

The next series of groups were shot after simply deburring the primer flash hole of twenty randomly selected cases. Most, if not all, cartridge cases produced in this country have the flash hole punched from the outside, instead of drilled. This raises a brass burr into the case. This burr is normally not concentric around the flash hole, let alone the same in all cases from any given lot, and has to cause variations in the primer flash intensity. Years ago, I used a quarter-inch drill to remove this burr and lightly chamfer the interior flash hole. Today, I prefer a tool specifically designed for this with a centering bushing and a flat face backing the cutter. This makes it next to impossible to ruin a case. These tools also drill out the flash hole to a uniform size. The easiest way to perform this step is to simply purchase a tool that can be chucked into an electric screwdriver or variable speed drill, and set it up in accordance with the manufacturer's instructions. These tools are available from many sources, such as Sinclair Products and Midway. All do a credible job. I have yet to break a decapping pin since I started removing this burr. Please note that beginning with this set of groups, the percent change is reported as "% change from Federal Premium / % change from randomly selected non-prepped cases."

GROUP					
#1	#2	#3	#4	AVE.	% Change
1.474	1.643	1.026	0.826	1.242	- 17.8 / - 30.3

SD = 0.380. Temp. 57° F to 63° F. Winds NW - 6 mph to WNW - 15 mph. Line of sight is N to S.

The result from this step is quite amazing. I did not expect the groups to be reduced this much by simply removing that little burr. I suspect group #4 is one of those anomalies that we cut out and keep in our wallets. If we were to remove it from the average, we would increase it to1.38 inches and lower the standard deviation to 0.319, but that is not enough difference to be able to reject it.

The next step was to fire a series using randomly selected cases and

Deburring the flash hole using an electric screwdriver.

uniformed primer pockets. I originally got interested in uniforming primer pockets, not because I believed that I would see any great increase in accuracy, but because I noticed with maximum specification primers and minimum specification pockets, the primers were often deformed trying to seat them the recommended one or two thousands below the case head. Crushing the primer pellet can't do accuracy any good, but seating them below the case head is mandatory. I once actually had a slam-fire in an M-1 Garand due to a high primer, causing spontaneous disassembly of the bolt. Note that this was with mil-spec ball.

When the primer pocket is punched into the case head, most pockets tend to be cupped inward, with a radius where the primer pocket wall meets the bottom. By uniforming the pockets, the bottom is reamed flat and square with the case head. This allows for more consistent contact with the primer anvil and the bottom, resulting in, my benchrest friends tell me, much more consistent ignition. I have come to prefer a carbide cutter with a positive factory-adjusted stop that can be either chucked in a drill or run by hand. These tools are available from Midway, Sinclair, K & M, and other sources. An added benefit is that they make an excellent primer pocket cleaner that does not dull with extended usage. If the pocket does not clean up completely the first time it is uniformed, it will after a couple of cleanings because brass expands in all directions. The results from this part of the comparison were:

GROUP

#1	#2	#3	#4	Ave.	% Change
1.296	2.329	2.030	1.256	1.728	+ 12.5 / - 3.0

SD = 0.535. Temp. 57° F to 63° F. Winds NW - 6 mph to WNW- 15 mph. Line of sight is N to S.

The contribution this procedure appears to make in the overall search for accuracy appears to be miniscule at best. Since the group size is not significantly different from those shot with randomly selected cases and the SD is virtually identical to the Federal factory load, I can only conclude that uniforming primer pockets, at least with my combination of components, is a waste of time. The results may be totally different in cases with much smaller capacity or with match-grade primers, so I will not condemn the practice in general, at least on the basis of this one test. However, I have just uniformed my last primer pocket.

The final step in the first part of my testing triad was to load 20 cases sorted by weight. Prior to doing any sorting, I randomly selected 100 cases for the next major part of the comparison so that I would not inadvertently create any unwanted variables in that section of the test.

When electronic digital scales first appeared on the reloading market, some better-known gun writers raved about how much time they would save when sorting brass by weight. That might be true if you insist on knowing the exact weight of each case down to the tenth of a grain. For what I wanted, that's nothing more than wasted effort. What I normally do is first weigh a sampling of each lot of brass consisting of about ten cases. Unless you have some pretty wild weight fluctuations, that will give you some idea of the minimum and maximum for each lot. For these LC 67 cases, I found that I had a range from around 193.2 grains to 198.2 grains, a variance of 2 1/2%, plenty close for most purposes. I then set my scale for a figure towards one end of the weight range, in this case 197.0 grains, and weighed the cases on a + / - basis. Then I set the balance to a higher weight, 198.0 grains, and again scaled the brass that fell above the lower weight. This gave me the twenty cases I needed for this section of the test and an additional twenty for later with a weight variation of 0.5%. In case you are wondering, the Federal Premium cases averaged 197.0 grains. The results are as follows and kind of interesting.

GROUP

#1	#2	#3	#4	Ave.	% Change
1.394	0.950	1.472	1.029	1.211	- 19.8 / - 32.0

SD = 0.260. Temp. 57° F to 63° F. Winds NW - 6 mph to WNW-15 mph. Line of sight is N to S.

I was not surprised by the results. A weight variation of 0.5% should relate to about 0.3 grains of water capacity between cases of this size with identical outside dimensions, while a 2.5% variation would be about 1.5 grains. The standard deviation turned out to be quite good. The groups probably should have been more consistent, but the wind may have been the limiting factor.

The first major part of my comparison testing was now over. I could have fired groups consisting of combinations of the above tested techniques, like weighed cases and deburred flash holes or randomly selected cases with both deburred flash holes and uniformed primer pockets, but I had a good indication what each step would contribute to overall accuracy. Furthermore, I was straining at the gate to get to the second major part of this comparison, the part that I have found in the past to contribute the biggest gain to overall accuracy.

When I first began handloading, the literature usually stated to simply seat your bullet to the same length as factory ammunition. It's still touted as the way for beginners to go and the method I used for the first third of this series of tests. This was simple enough, but sometimes seated bullets with certain streamlined profiles quite a distance from the lands, and didn't everyone know that seating them closer would result in improved accuracy? The handloading press had several different suggestions to accomplish this, including long seating and smoking a bullet in a dummy cartridge, then seating it deeper to the tune of the amount of soot that the lands rubbed off, plus another 1/32 of an inch or so. This quite often resulted in a stuck bullet, plus I was uncomfortable placing a round, live or otherwise, in a rifle in my gun room.

Another method that was commonly expressed was to hold a bullet against the lands with a dowel, drop a flat-faced rod down the barrel to contact the tip and mark it even with the rifle's muzzle. You then removed the bullet using the rod, closed your bolt, and measured the distance to the bolt face with the rod.

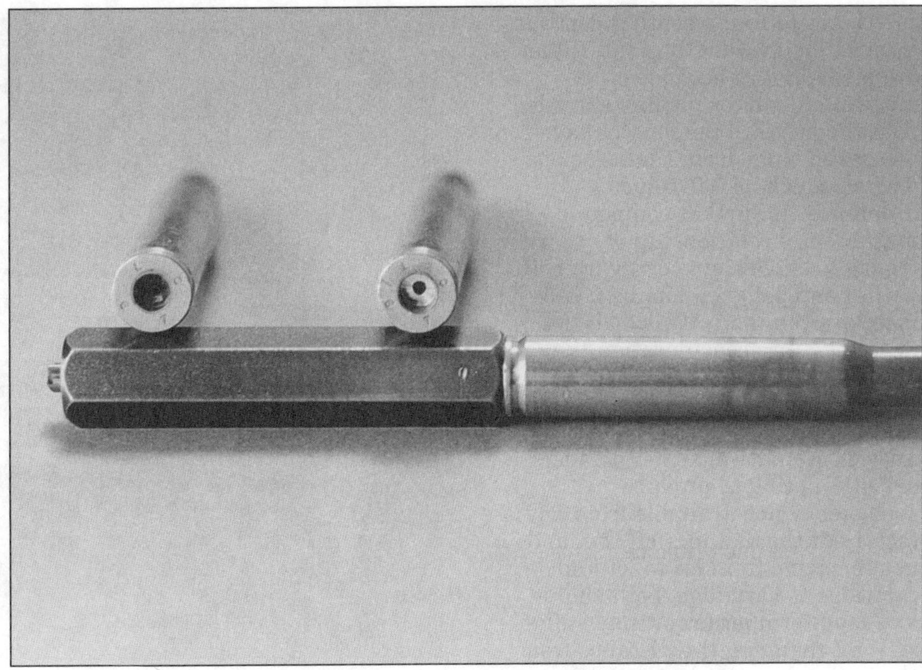

Uniforming primer pockets is not worthwhile, author finds.

After you measured the difference, you subtracted a given amount, and you had your overall length. You don't need to have the training of a nuclear physicist to realize neither method was particularly precise.

Both of the above-mentioned methods are as dead as high-capacity magazines. Today, we have a number of instruments on the market designed to precisely measure the distance of a bullet's ogive to the lands and help you determine optimum seating depth.

The above-mentioned RCBS Precision Micrometer is one of the easier ones to use, but is caliber specific. Sinclair and others make bullet comparators, but you still have to find some way to get a cartridge just long enough to touch the lands. Stoney Point manufactures a gadget they call the Overall Length Gauge and Bullet Comparator, with variations for both bolt guns or single shots and semi-autos or pumps. This tool goes under the heading of *"Why didn't I think of that?"* You have to make the initial expenditure for your basic tool, but then it is only necessary to buy a specially prepared case for each cartridge you load, and a precisely machined bushing for each bore size. This makes it inexpensive to use if you load multiple calibers, and the directions that accompany the component parts are extremely easy to understand. It simply takes a little bit of practice to get repeatable readings. You will need a precision dial caliper to use with this gauge. If you don't already have one, exactly how are you taking the measurements needed to safely pursue your hobby?

You owe it to yourself to buy one of these gauges, regardless of manufacturer. Have you ever had a previously accurate load go sour with the next box of bullets? Anyone that measures overall length of their

C.O.L. / D.O.L.	Group # 1	2	3	4	Ave.
3.355 / 0.085	2.207	1.098	1.923	0.993	1.555
			SD = 0.601		
3.350 / 0.090	1.054	1.102	0.975	0.898	1.007
			SD = 0.090		
3.345 / 0.095	1.444	1.019	1.595	1.540	1.399
			SD = 0.261		
3.340 / 0.100	1.033	0.710	1.470	1.129	1.085
			SD = 0.313		
3.335 / 0.105	1.475	1.647	2.285	1.465	1.718
			SD = 0.387		
			Overall Average		**1.353**
			Overall SD		**0.431**

C.O.L. = Cartridge overall length.
D.O.L. = Distance Off Lands.
Temp. 59° to 70° F. Wind from target to bench at 3 mph to 7 mph.

cartridges to find a seating depth is aware that the length of individual bullets will vary because of the amount of lead (or plastic) extruded past the jacket. I personally have measured slugs from the same box with as much as 0.075-inch difference. To further compound matters, the relationship of overall length to ogive shape can vary both within and between lots by 0.040-inch, or even more. This does not even take into consideration the difference in shape of the ogive between makers. By this time you are saying, "Why bother?" The answer is that we, as handloaders, are attempting to produce consistency not available from any factory. If the distance off the lands is not the same from lot to lot and cartridge to cartridge, both short- and long-term accuracy may suffer.

Why changing the distance from the bullet ogive to the lands makes such a difference in accuracy is open to conjecture. It is my feeling that it alters the barrel oscillations in basically the same way that the B.O.S.S. does, but from the other end of the barrel. When running a series of various seating depths like I did for the next third of this project, I noticed not only a change in the consistency of the load, but also a change in the point of impact. I found that it is quite easy to change the bullet-to-land distance 0.004-inch simply by varying pressure on the press handle at the positive stop. This could explain some of those weird fliers we all get from time to time, regardless of the quality of the bullet.

When I use one of these tools to measure the cartridge head-to-land engagement distance prior to adjusting my seating die, I normally will use from five to ten different bullets and average the readings, depending on how consistent the ogive shape is. With this batch of Nosler Ballistic tips my measurements varied less than 0.003-inch, definitely match-grade consistency. This amount of quality control is seldom seen outside competition circles and one more reason for the vaunted accuracy of this bullet.

After measuring the distance to the lands, I usually start a bullet seating depth test series beginning with a distance off the lands at least equal to the variance in the actual measurements of the ogive on the

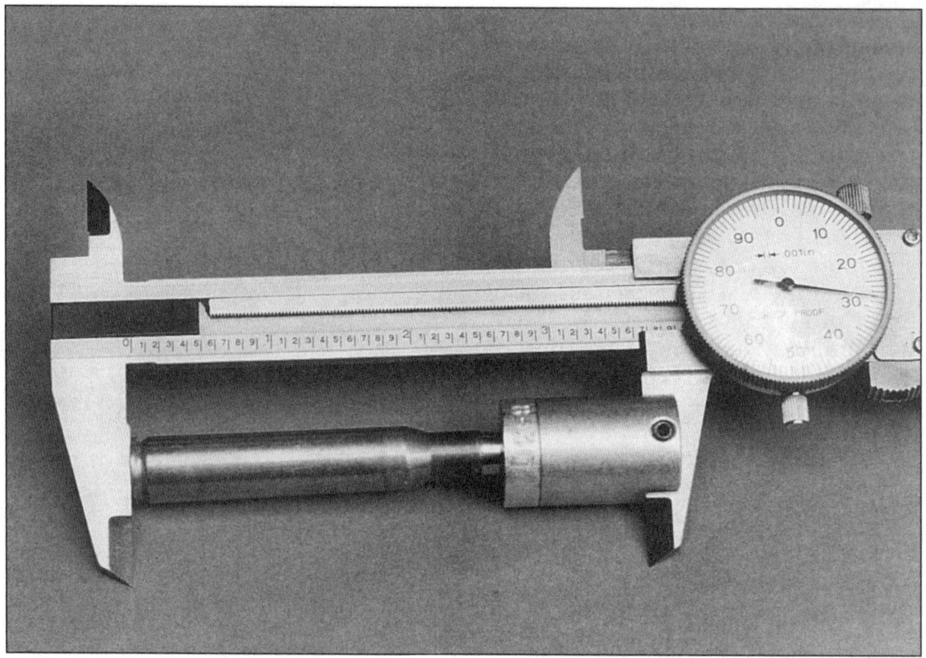

The 'free run' between the rifling lands and the bullet ogive in a loaded cartridge can be precisely measured by this bullet comparator from Stoney Point.

different bullets and increasing the depth by increments of 0.005-inch, as suggested by the people at Stoney Point. The literature that comes with the tool recommends 0.010-inch to 0.060-inch free run before contact with the lands. With bullets seated 0.005-inch off the lands, I ran into the only glitch in this whole comparison. My cartridge overall length was 3.440 inches, well over

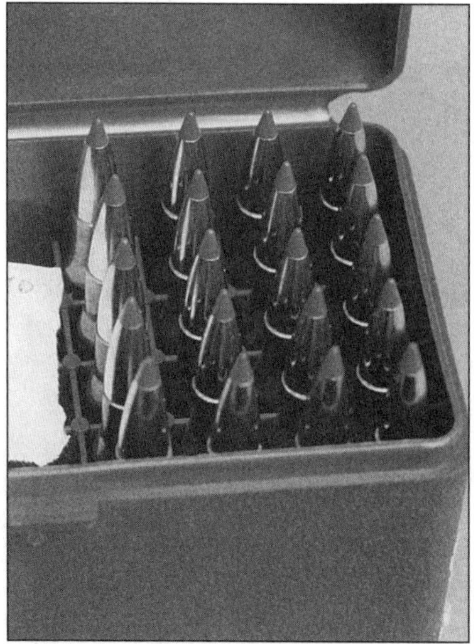

Four 5-shot groups were fired after the test ammunition was prepared, using selected case preparation techniques.

SAAMI maximum, and the magazine box on this gun measures only 3.410 inches. I suggest the throat in this rifle has eroded quite a bit over the years, since I have shot over 5,000 rounds through it. If I were loading for target work, this would have been no big deal as the cartridges could be single-loaded, but I was attempting to find out if my techniques would actually help the typical deer-hunting rifle.

With this in mind, I started this series with a maximum overall length of 3.355 inches, also over SAAMI specs, which would feed reliably in this gun. The 1/4 x 28 bullet-seating stem that RCBS uses in their dies will increase seating depth 0.0045-inch for every 1/8 turn. This is not as exact as on micrometer-adjustable match-grade dies, but with careful adjustment, good enough for my purposes–and less expensive. The results from this were both pleasing and eye-opening.

Examine these figures closely and take note of a few pertinent facts. Group size varied from less than 3/4 inch to over 2 1/4 inches; an actual difference of over 1.575 inches between groups. The overall standard deviation is probably not significantly smaller than that of the Federal Premium factory loads. That's not really important. What is important is the difference in averages that changing the seating depth by 0.005-

inch can make. What should really jump out at you is the consistency of the C.O.L. of 3.350 inches. Even though the smallest group in this part of the test was not shot using that seating depth, the size of the largest and smallest groups shot with the ogive 0.090-inch off of the lands is only 0.20-inch apart, and that is significant. The standard deviation is 0.090-inch, and it does not get much better than that. This section of the test should prove that one of the most important components of overall accuracy is finding a preferred seating depth for each rifle.

The people at Stoney Point claim that you only have to run a seating depth series once with each rifle and bullet "A" will have its most accurate D.O.L. the same as bullet "B". I have no reason to doubt this, but plan on finding out for certain sometime in the future. What I do know is that each rifle will have more than one seating depth that will give comparable accuracy. This particular gun will shoot good groups at a D.O.L. of 0.020-inch, but the cartridges must be single-loaded, which is what I do for my club's turkey shoots. The B.O.S.S. may also have more than one "sweet spot" for each load, according to Browning. If you are questioning why different factory loadings of the same bullet weight have a different "sweet spot", reread the above comments about changing ogive shape between makes–and even lots. Although I have not had a chance to play with a B.O.S.S.-equipped rifle, I would be surprised if different lots of the same factory ammunition did not have a slightly different "sweet spot".

The D.O.L. for the Federal Premium load was measured at 0.177-inch + / - 0.005. I suggest this variation is one of the reasons it was not as consistent as it could have been, but then they load it by the millions. What was amazing, at least to me, was when I seated my bullets to the same overall length as the Federal, the D.O.L. was exactly the same. This certainly says something about Nosler's quality control from batch to batch. I later measured a different lot of the Federal Premium and got identical figures. That also says something for Federal's quality control. This gave me confidence that any improvement I achieved over the factory load in the earlier part of this comparison was because of modified benchrest case preparation techniques, and not due to shooting cartridges with a D.O.L. which the rifle prefers.

I stated above that I had no intention of experimenting with combinations of various case preparation techniques. That is not quite true. For the last part of my testing, I wanted to shoot four groups consisting of completely prepped weight-matched brass with the bullet seated to its preferred depth. Since I had good data comparing the results from individual preparation techniques with both the groups obtained from the Federal Premium factory loads and unprepped cases, I wanted to see if the changes in accuracy were cumulative, and by how much. I felt this would give me a good idea as to whether or not I could stop performing some of the more onerous operations. For this series, I used the same basic load as in the first two parts of my test, but with the bullet seated 0.090-inch off the lands. You may question why I did not use the 0.100-inch figure, since it produced the smallest individual group in the last chart. The reason is consistency. Although the averages for those two D.O.L. are similar, again take note the greater consistency at the one depth.

GROUP

#1	#2	#3	#4	Ave.	% Change
1.075	0.962	1.192	1.196	1.106	- 26.8 / - 37

SD = 0.111. Temp. 57° F to 64° F. Winds E - 5mph to NW - 9 mph. Line of sight is N to S.

You will notice the groups shot with completely prepped cases actually average 0.099-inch larger than the groups shot using the same D.O.L. and randomly selected cases. That's about the thickness of three sheets of paper, and could have been caused by different shooting conditions, the way I felt that day, or, for that matter, the phase of the moon. The totally prepped cases did vary 2.6% more in their range of group sizes for my final test, but we are only talking 0.030-inch, entirely insignificant in the long run, and for all purposes, identical. I realize a benchrester will do handstands for that amount, but it will make absolutely no difference in any shot any hunter has ever taken. The slightly larger SD is also insignificant.

My average for this last set of groups is less than 1/2-inch smaller than the Federal Premium. I even have a hard time getting excited about that. At 300 yards, that's only 1.5 inches, and most people can't hold anywhere near that close. But, the difference between the factory load's worst group and the worst group from this last series is over an inch. At 300 yards, that may make a difference. Once your group size approaches calculated bullet drop, you have problems.

As stated earlier the throat in this rifle is probably eroded, but as long as the barrel will continue to stabilize the bullets, improved accuracy can be gained with good loading technique, particularly if one is willing to make an effort to find one of the best D.O.L. Remember, these groups were shot with a 7x scope. I can only speculate as to how much smaller they might have been if I had used a 24x or 32x target scope with an adjustable objective. Due to the size of the crosshairs alone, one MOA probably approaches the best this rifle and scope combination will do, except by accident. Unfortunately, this does not allow me to see if the above improvements in accuracy are cumulative. I suspect they may be, but to prove by how much would require a more accurate test platform.

Feel free to uniform primer pockets, deburr flash holes, weigh cases, and turn necks–or whatever, if you want. In the future, I will simply run a bullet depth seating series for any bolt gun I may own until I run into a rifle that approaches 0.5 MOA. For guns that must have the bullet crimped in place or have cartridge length limited for functional reasons, I will deburr the flash hole if I don't have enough cases to sort by weight, although you always have some leeway with seating depth. Until then, I'm going to go shooting. I guess my family will have to do without me when they watch television. ●

Remember This Neglected Reloading Step

by John Haviland

At best, failing to perform a seemingly insignificant reloading step can lead to poor reloads. At worst, it can turn your rifle into a pile of scrap metal and kindling wood.

Firing and resizing cartridge cases lengthens their necks. For safe reloads, case necks must be measured to make sure they are shorter than their maximum allowed length. Case necks that are too long must be trimmed back to the proper length.

A loaded cartridge with a too-long case neck may fit into the chamber of a rifle. However, that extra neck length is actually protruding into the throat of the rifle chamber. On firing, the extra neck length has no room to expand to release the bullet. The bullet is pinched – and pressures go wild.

"Pressures are going to rise dramatically if you fire a cartridge with a case neck two or three thousandths of an inch too long," warned Warren Cloninger, a ballistics technician with Blount Inc. *"You'll be lucky if all you have is a blown primer from shooting such a load. Over the years I've seen several blown-up rifles that were caused by shooting cases with necks too long."* On a less dangerous note, case necks of varying lengths produce inferior loads.

Long, long ago, when gasoline cost 29 cents per gallon, I started loading the 30-30 Winchester for a Winchester Model 94. I read the warning in the loading manuals that stated the tube magazine of the Model 94 required that bullets be crimped into place. I poured the correct amount of powder in a 30-30 case and put it in the shellholder of my press. Then I set my seating die to crimp the mouth of the case into the cannelure of a 170-grain bullet.

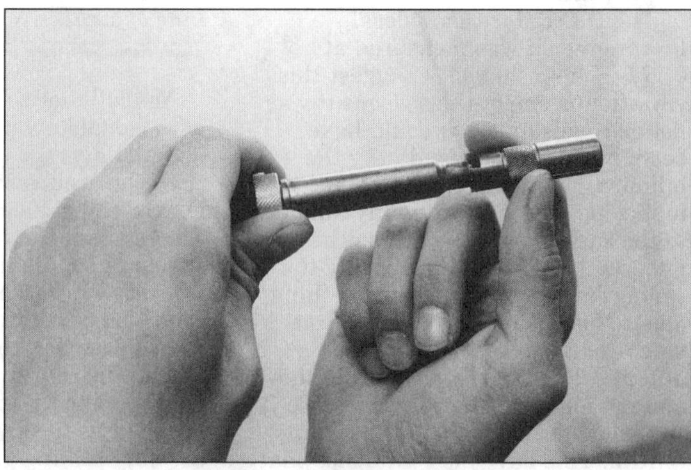

The Lee case trimmer is a simple tool that includes a shellholder for each different case head size and case-length gauges that screw into a cutter head.

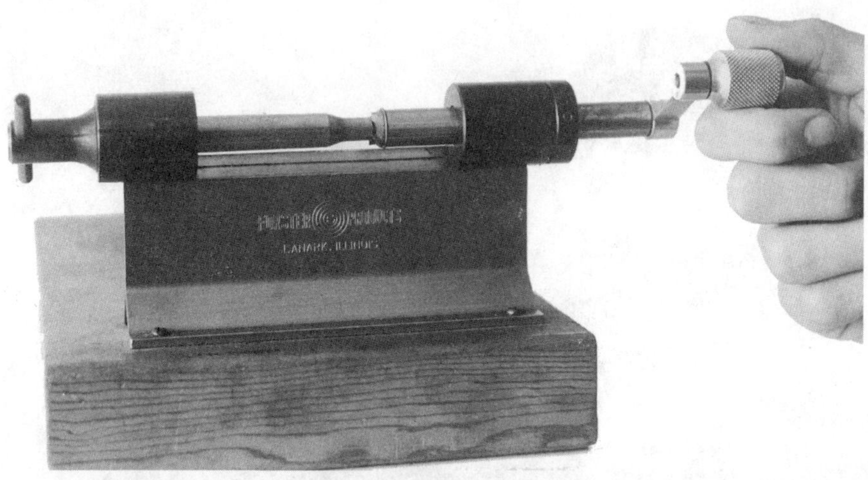

The lathe-like Forster trimmer is still manually operated. Yet it's a snap to clamp in a case, turn the handle to trim the case, and then pop it out.

All set to go, I started loading a batch of cases. However, I quickly discovered something amiss: One load had a perfect crimp, the next barely any crimp at all, and the next so much crimp the case mouth bulged. After scratching my chin in deep thought, I discovered the necks of the 30-30 cases, although shorter than maximum, varied in length. From that day forward, I have trimmed all my 30-30 cases every time they are resized. My problem disappeared.

Ways to Trim

Back when I lived in an apartment so tiny even the mice dined out, I had

Safety glasses are a must for protection from flying brass shavings from power equipment.

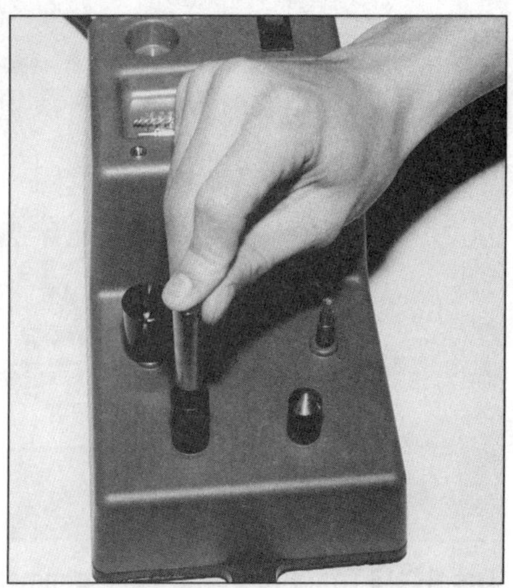

Deburring the outside of a case mouth with the RCBS Case Prep Center.

The RCBS Case Prep Center has five rotating stations to whittle down case-preparation time. This picture shows chamfering inside of a case mouth.

The RCBS Trim Pro power case trimmer is a breeze to use. It holds a case to be trimmed like a manual trimmer. But when the case is ready to trim, a motor handle is released that rotates the cutter and feeds into the case mouth rim.

precious little room for my reloading gear. I trimmed all my case necks with a Lee case trimmer. The hand tool included a shellholder for each different case head size and case-length gauges that screwed into a cutter head. On lonely winter nights, I sat in my cramped quarters and trimmed cases by manually turning the cutter head. When the cutter stopped cutting, I knew the case neck was the correct length. The index finger and thumb on my right hand developed some major muscle mass from the work of pressing and turning the cutter head of the tool. But I only reloaded a few hundred rifle cartridges a year, so the work wasn't too much of a pain.

To remove the rim of brass from the outside of the case mouth and beveling the inside of the mouth, I used a Forster deburr/chamfer tool. A couple of twists of the tool and the case was ready to load. I usually did this tedious job while watching television. The only problem was the brass shavings my wife found when she vacuumed the folds of the chair.

Years later, my wife bought me a Forster case trimmer to help me whittle down the pile of cases I had from my increased appetite for shooting. The lathe-like Forster was still manually operated. Yet it was a snap to clamp in a case, turn the handle (like hand-cranking an old International Harvester tractor) to trim the case, and then pop it out. Of course, my wife still raised Cain about the brass shavings in the folds of the chair in front of the TV.

To set the trimmer stop at a specific length required a method to measure case length. For a while, I trimmed a case in my Lee trimmer, then used it as a guide to set the stop on my Forster trimmer. That worked fine, but after a time I wanted to know exactly what case length I was cutting, so I bought a dial caliper.

Over the years, I have used the caliper to set my trimmer, as a gauge to tell whether or not cases required trimming, and a host of other parameters.

Power Trimming

In the years since I received my Forster trimmer, I've moved up in the world of consumerism. A house and a family of shooters to fill it have come along. Keeping my kids in ammo for their hunting rifles means I spend more time than ever trimming case necks.

One evening at the loading bench, I tired of cranking on the handle of my manual trimmer. I looked at my power drill, then at the trimmer. Why not? I removed the hand crank and clamped on the drill. I was trimming with power! The setup was a bit awkward, but as long as the drill's rpms were kept slow, it worked.

Last Christmas, Santa checked his list a second time and found I'd been more nice than naughty. Under the tree Christmas morning sat an RCBS Trim Pro power case trimmer and a

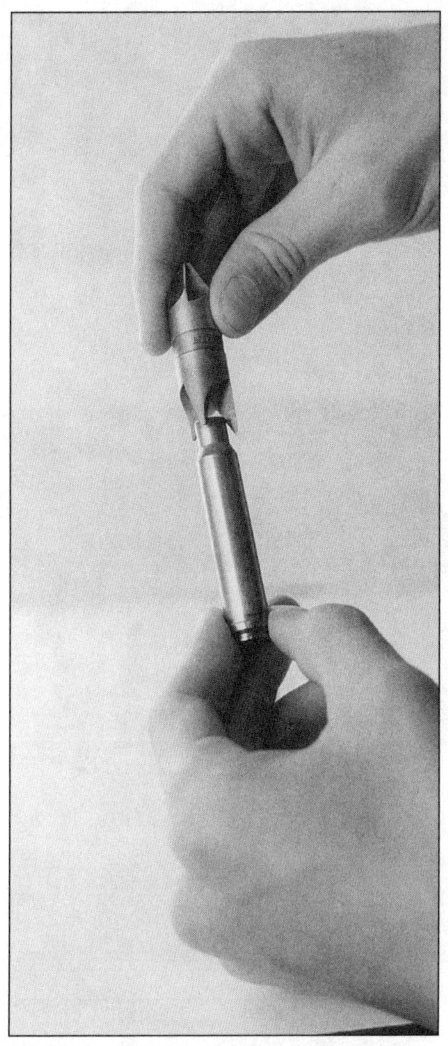

A Forster debur/chamfer tool removing the brass left over from trimming on the outside of the case mouth.

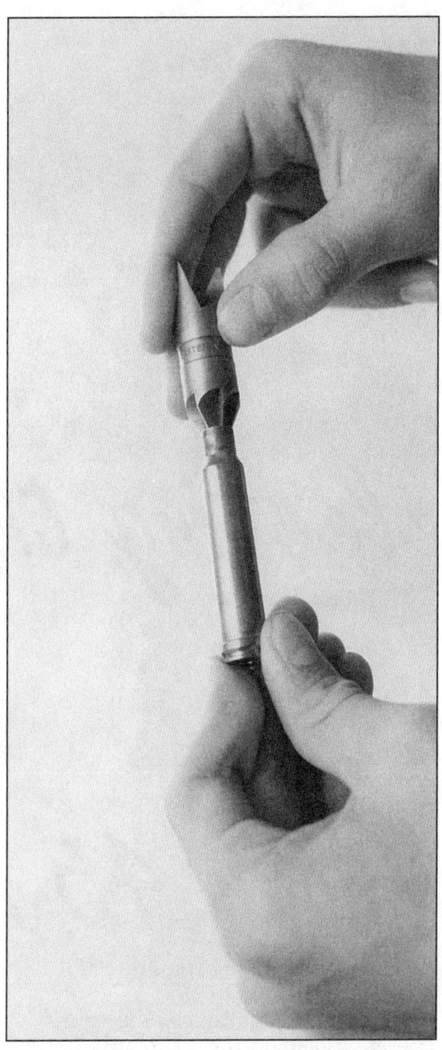

A Forster debur/chamfer tool removing the brass left over from trimming on the inside of the case mouth.

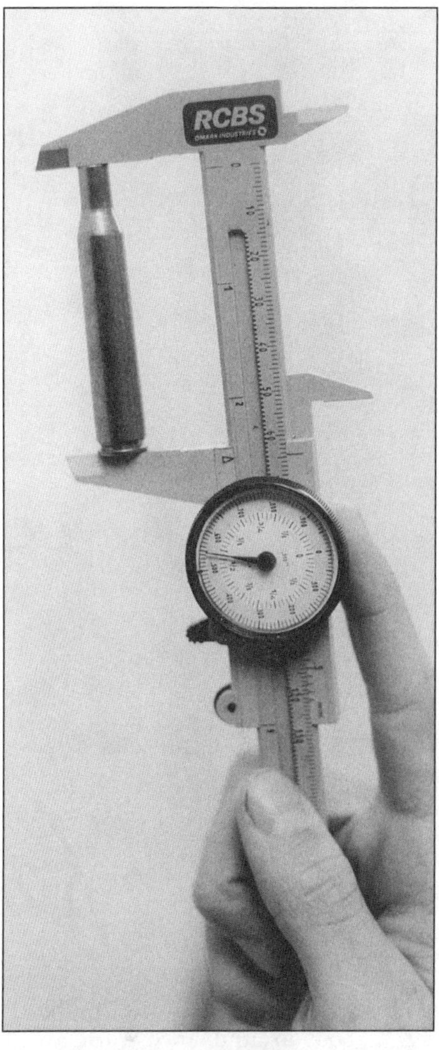

Although the neck of this 270 Winchester case is only .001-inch over maximum length, it's still enough to raise pressures to a dangerous level.

Case Prep Center.

The power trimmer is a breeze to use. It holds a case to be trimmed like a manual trimmer. But when the case is ready to trim, a motor handle is released that rotates the cutter and feeds into the case-mouth rim. Springs keep tension on the cutter. The electric motor produces a slightly higher-pitched whine when the case has been trimmed to the proper length. Another way to determine when a case is finished is when the gap of light disappears between the adjustment bushing and the cutter guide.

The difference in time between the manual and the power trimmer is not all that great, at least for a few cases. The power trimmer took 2 minutes and 5 seconds to trim 10 30-06 cases. The manual trimmer required an even 2 minutes. But my arm and wrist begin to lag after 10 minutes of keeping pace with the manual trimmer. The electric motor, though, keeps on turning.

A power trimmer must be anchored to keep it stationary. Because of a limited amount of counter space, I mounted mine on a board. When I want to use it, I anchor the board to my bench top with a C-clamp. The trimmer sits on a shelf when not in use.

The RCBS Case Prep Center is based on better living through electricity. The Prep Center's rotating stations accept tools to debur and chamfer the brass left on case mouths from trimming. Small and large primer-pocket cleaners, military crimp remover, primer-pocket uniformer, and flash-hole deburring tools can also be mounted on the Center's five stations.

The Prep Center is a great time-saver. Deburring, chamfering, and cleaning the primer pockets on 10 30-06 cases took 1 minute and 35 seconds on the Prep Center. My old hand tool took 2 minutes and 10 seconds just to debur and chamfer 10 cases. And my wife really likes the Prep Center because she no longer has to vacuum brass shavings out of the recliner in front of the television.

Hand-trimming tools are still fine for the casual reloader. But as my reloading has grown over the years, so have my tools to keep pace. These power tools have taken the drudgery out of trimming to help ensure the safety and quality of my reloads. ●

Selecting the Proper Diet for Your 45 AR

by J.R. Schroeder

Although the 45 Auto Rim has been around since World War I and has acquitted itself well in combat, hunting, and target use, comparatively little has been written about this fine handgun cartridge. Due to the recent importation of who knows how many S&W Model 1917 revolvers in this chambering, a closer look at handloading it is in order.

First off, the 45 AR is nothing but a rimmed 45 ACP case. This allows revolvers of this chambering to be loaded with single rounds that will eject in a conventional manner; 45 ACP cartridges, held in 2-, 3-, or 6-round clips, can be used as well.

Due to the fact that this cartridge, and many of the guns made for it, go back about 85 years, handloading for it has to be approached from three different levels – what I call Level One, Level Two, and Level Three.

The older guns – those manufactured from World War I to World War II by both S&W and Colt – while fine revolvers, are less capable of withstanding high-pressure loads than those of more recent manufacture. Even so, with proper handloads these older guns can easily outperform the only factory-loaded 45 AR round available. These guns, then, fall into Level One for loading data.

Level Two includes two Smith& Wessons. The Model 1950 is built on the large N-frame. It has a tapered barrel and adjustable sights. The second gun is the 1955 Model, which later came to be designated the Model 25-2. These two guns, metallurgically speaking, are much stronger than the Level One guns.

Although other wheelguns are capable of firing the 45 ACP cartridge loaded to 45 AR specs, only one other handgun can handle the true 45 AR case as well as the 45 ACP in clips – the S&W Model 625. Made of tough stainless steel, it is an N-frame with the smaller K-frame grip. This is the Level Three gun in the 45 AR series.

One fact needs to pointed out: This is not a treatise on how to magnumize the 45 AR. If you need a magnum, get a 357, 41, 44, 454 – or whatever, and leave the good old 45 AR to do what it does best – produce surprisingly good big-bore results

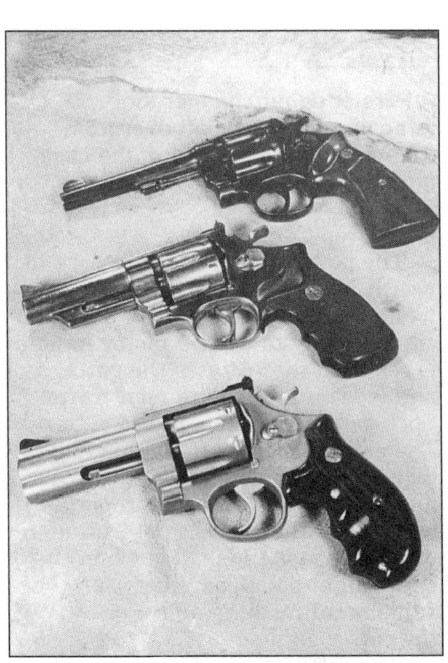

Due to the fact that the 45 AR cartridge, and many of the guns made for it, go back about 85 years, handloading for it has to be approached from different levels to ensure safety.

Older revolvers, like this Smith & Wesson Model 1917, are less capable of withstanding high-pressure loads than those of more recent manufacture. Even so, with proper handloads, these guns can easily outperform newer revolvers shooting factory loads.

with medium-bore recoil.

If the bullet you use has a crimping groove, by all means use it, whether the case be 45 AR or 45 ACP. Use a taper crimp die on all other bullets. If they have a front driving band and you are loading for Levels One or Two, seat the bullet just deep enough to allow a slight roll crimp over the front of the front band.

When seating and crimping the 250-grain bullet over Hercules 2400 power in Level Three, use a taper crimp die and seat the bullet just to the center of the front driving band.

Watch out for old balloon-head cases, some of which are still around. They hold more powder than the newer solid-web cases, but are weaker and should be relegated to the collector's corner. In line with this caution, some older books list loads heavier than those given here or in the modern loading manuals. Don't use those older loads.

To identify a balloon-head case, look down into it. If the center of the base area that contains the primer protrudes into the case, leaving a recessed perimeter around it, it is a

The 1950 Target Model 25 from Smith & Wesson, much stronger than the Model 1917, utilizes the large N-frame and has adjustable sights.

Introduced in 1988, the Smith & Wesson Model 625-2 is a tough stainless-steel gun capable of handling the 45 AR case, as well as the 45 ACP in clips. It features a 5-inch barrel and an N-frame within a smaller K-frame grip.

Author's Loads for the 45 AR

LEVEL 1

S&W Model 1917 — **5-1/2" Barrel**

—Bullet— (Wgt. Grs.)	(Type)	Load (Grs./Powder)	MV (fps)	Remarks
200	SWC Lyman #452460	7.0/Unique	886	Small-game load.
250	SWC Lyman #452424	6.0/Unique	825	Bad medicine on javelina.
250	SWC Lyman #452424	6.1/Unique	866	Bad medicine on javelina.

LEVEL TWO

S&W Model 1955 — **(Model 25-2) 4" Barrel**

—Bullet— (Wgt. Grs.)	(Type)	Load (Grs./Powder)	MV (fps)	Remarks
200	SWC H&G 68	7.2/Unique	980	Accurate/potent.
250	SWC Lyman #452424	6.2/Unique	877	Reasonable recoil.

LEVEL THREE

S&W Model 625 — **5" Barrel**

—Bullet— (Wgt. Grs.)	(Type)	Load (Grs./Powder)	MV (fps)	Remarks
200	SWC H&G 68e	7.5/Unique	1002	These three loads exceed
250	SWC Lyman #452424	6.5/Unique	933	velocity and energy levels
250	SWC Lyman #452424	13/2400	963	of 45 Colt factory loads.

Comparison Load: Remington 45 AR 230-grain lead round-nose, 810 fps.
All velocities derived from an average of 10 rounds fired over a Pro Tach chronograph set up 7 feet from the muzzle of the gun. These loads were used by the author during the preparation of this article and are listed here for information only. Their use by others is not recommended by the author or the publisher and no responsibility for damages resulting from such use will be assumed

balloon-head. The inside base of a solid-head case is flat across, with just a hole in it to allow the primer flame to reach the powder. Solid-head cases are considered safer to reload than balloon-heads.

All of this may sound like nitpicking, but it isn't anything of the kind. When you are attempting to gain higher velocities in a case having limited capacity to begin with, and are using large bore, heavy bullets, small changes in seating depths or case capacity can boost pressures in a hurry.

The 45 AR cartridge actually didn't come into being until some years after the revolver itself was introduced to utilize the 45 ACP cartridge. Born during a WWI shortage of Colt 45 Automatic Pistols, both Colt and S&W took existing 45 Colt revolvers and converted them to use the 45 ACP cartridge held in three-shot, half-moon clips. It wasn't until after WWI that the rimmed 45 AR was produced.

Cylinders of those first converted revolvers were usually bored to .454-inch to fit the old 45 Colt bullet. Bores of these guns vary some, but are quite often found to be of .451-inch diameter. This posed no problem with the 45 ACP metal-cased bullet, which is close to .451 and wouldn't expand in the chamber when fired. The old 45 Colt bullet was cast pretty soft, and it had a hollow base as well, so even though it did expand in the chamber, it easily swaged back down upon entering the smaller bore.

The cast bullets we use today are considerably harder than were the old 45 Colt bullets. They are solid-

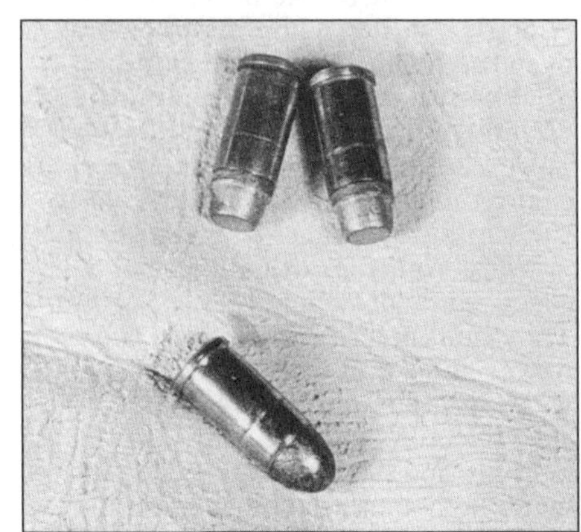

The 45 AR is nothing but a rimmed 45 ACP case. This allows revolvers chambered for this cartridge to be loaded with single rounds that will eject in a conventional manner.

based as well. They, too, will expand to chamber dimensions if fired with a stiff load, but they won't swage back down to bore diameter without possibly boosting pressures to the danger point in the Level One category. The later models, in Levels Two and Three, have chambers bored closer to bore diameter, so this problem is reduced to a great extent.

You may be asking, "Just how effective is the 45 AR in the practical scheme of things?" I have long carried and used a handgun in various calibers and configurations in my work as a Predator Control Officer along the Mex-Tex Border. It has been my responsibility to take numerous skunks, raccoons, foxes, and coyotes that were obviously sick, and possibly rabid. I have tried the 22 LR, 22 WMR *(Winchester Magnum Rimfire)*, and 357 Magnum, and have found all to be wanting in one respect or another. Either they couldn't provide the quick, humane, one-shot kill I demand, or as is the case with the 357 high-velocity round, they set up a hydrostatic shock effect on impact. This sometimes creates a brain hemorrhage in the animal. To test for rabies, a laboratory requires an intact, undamaged brain. Therefore, a shoulder shot is required, one that will anchor the animal in its tracks without damaging the head in any way.

Experience has proven, at least to my satisfaction, that a .451-inch flat-nosed or semi-wadcutter bullet, weighing from 200 to 250 grains and having a muzzle velocity in the 850-950 fps range, suits my needs admirably. That spells 45 AR in my book.

With regard to larger game, recently I put a whitetail deer in the freezer. I shot it from a blind, at 35 yards, with a 45 Colt handload that utilized the same 250-grain bullet I use in my 45 AR. Muzzle velocity of this load was 970 fps – almost identical to the 45 AR load in Level Three. The bullet completely penetrated the shoulders and the deer dropped in its tracks.

Over the years, the 45 AR has time and again proven itself to be plenty good enough for my needs. Loaded sensibly, it can do the same for you. ●

To get the most out of your 45 Auto Rim handgun, you must handload, and the age of your gun determines the proper loads for it.

Good for target shooting, hunting and self-defense, the 45 AR *(left)* produces big-bore results with medium-bore recoil. The 45 ACP can also be used in revolvers when loaded into two-, three- and six-round clips.

Heavy Bullets in the 30-30 Winchester

by R.H. VanDenburg, Jr.

In the annals of hunting and shooting literature over the last century, much has been written of the 30-30 Winchester. Much praised and much maligned, comments have ranged from "good for just about anything" to "good for nothing."

My own study of the cartridge and the guns chambered for it has led me to conclude that the better the woodsman, as opposed to the better the rifleman, the more likely the comments will be favorable. My remark is not intended to discredit either group, but to distinguish between them. The woodsman is more likely to know how, and prefer, to hunt close. The rifleman is more likely to seek out, and depend on, a more powerful and flatter-shooting cartridge.

The late Col. Townsend Whelen, in "Why Not Load Your Own", wrote:

"Way back in 1901 and 1902 I shot many mule deer, sheep and goats with my 30-30 and very successfully up to about 150 yards, but I also subsisted largely on grouse, rabbit, ducks, porcupine and beaver shot with reduced loads. The 30-30 is not to be despised as an all-around rifle."

Many years later, on his last elk hunt, the Colonel is reputed to have again chosen his 30-30. He took an Imperial bull.

In more recent times, two men who have written widely and well on the 30-30 and the Model 94 Winchester have been H.V. Stent and Sam Fadala. Both men seem to have a good grasp of the limitations and the versatility of the gun/cartridge combination. Both have written often of round balls and cast bullets, reduced loads and varmint bullets, hunting loads and heavy bullets, all in the 30-30, and of targets from mice to moose. Fadala seems to prefer the Winchester 94 in its rifle configuration; Stent is a fan of the Model 64, similar to the 94 carbine except for a pistol grip, a half-magazine, and a longer barrel.

Stent often recalled the exploits of F.H. *(Bert)* Riggall, a guide from Alberta, Canada. Riggall would load the 30-30 with 190-grain Winchester Silvertips originally intended for the 303 Savage. Unavailable as reloading components, then, as now, one had to purchase 303 Savage ammunition and pull the bullets. The load was 31 grains of IMR-3031 (then Du Pont). Intended for elk, Riggall reported scores taken with complete satisfaction. Both Stent and Fadala also wrote of their efforts to find suitable 180-grain bullets. It was along about this time that I joined up.

Previously, I had fired thousands of 30-30 rounds in competition *(silhouette)*, plinking, and hunting—from the 40-grain round ball to cast and jacketed bullets of 170 grains or so. I began my heavy bullet quest with the 190-grain Silvertip. Frankly, I was surprised at the ready availability of this ammunition and was shocked at the price–about a buck a round. Undaunted, I set out to duplicate the Riggall/Stent efforts. Stumbling block number one: Depending on the case make, the number of times it had been fired and its overall length, I sometimes could not get 31 grains of IMR-3031 into the case and seat the bullet without severely compressing the powder. This resulted in the

Minute-of-elk, or so. Group fired offhand at 50 yards measured about 2-1/2 inches.

bullet-seating stem damaging the very soft Silvertip nose.

While considering my options regarding the 190-grain bullet, I began to think about the 180. As Stent and Fadala had discovered, there was no end to 180-grain 30-caliber round-nose bullets. None, however, had an appropriately placed cannelure as required in tubular magazines, and few were designed to function at 30-30 velocities.

Imagine, then, my elation at discovering that Winchester had produced 180-grain ammunition for the 307 Winchester to be used in the beefed-up Model 94 Angle Eject. Imagine, also, my chagrin at discovering the product had been discontinued. A trip to the nearest trading post of any size quickly produced a box, but at 190-grain prices. Brief testing proved the bullets would work–even the cannelure was in the right place–provided case length was kept to minimum length. The next trip produced a couple more boxes, this time at one-half 190-grain prices—fifty cents per round.

Fadala had indicated, and the Speer manual concurred, that the Speer 180-grain Mag-Tip would be worth considering as it was designed to function at lower than normal rifle speeds. A good looking bullet, the Mag-Tip has a cannelure, but not in the right place, and even a circular groove ahead of the cannelure, but again not in the right place. There is a further restriction in that the nose shape does not conform to tubular magazine requirements. This would make the 94 a two-shot proposition, but I could live with that.

So I was left with two stumbling blocks. One, trying to get all that 3031-the traditional 30-30 powder-into the case while maintaining the overall cartridge length necessary to function in the Model 94; and two, to crimp the case at the correct length in the absence of a properly placed cannelure.

In the latter regard, Stent records simply applying a military-style crimp with a screwdriver, three stabs around the circumference of the neck after seating the bullet. It worked, and should. With a case full of powder, there is really no place for the bullet to go.

However, as luck sometimes has it, two products, both new, came to my attention that appeared to offer solutions. First, a new powder. A relative newcomer *(and now defunct/ED)* to the powder scene, Scot Powder Co., supplier of handgun and shotgun powders such as Royal Scot, Pearl Scot and its Solo series, introduced a rifle powder line called the Brigadier. Its four entries included 4197, 3032, 4065 and 4351. The powders are manufactured in Scotland by ICI's Nobel's Explosives Co. Made of nitrocotton rather than nitrocellulose, they are reputed to be

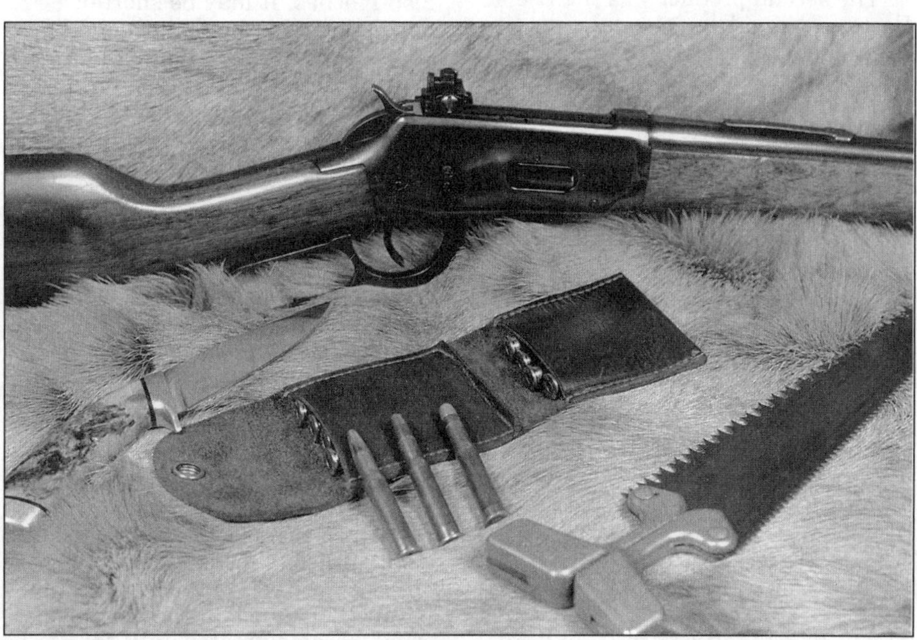

Model 94 Winchester and elk hunting aids.

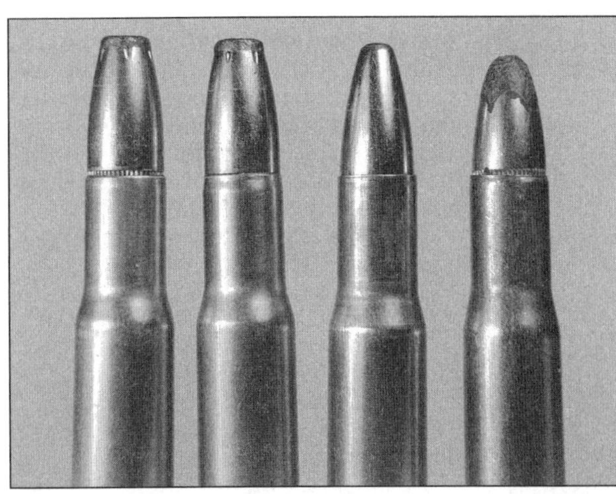

There are crimps, and there are crimps! *From left:* 180-gr. 307 Winchester bullet with roll crimp; same bullet with Lee factory crimp; 180-gr. speer Mag-Tip with Lee crimp; Remington 170-tgr. factory round.

cooler and cleaner burning than traditional powders. Anyone familiar with the old Du Pont line would immediately recognize the potential use of each.

After reading all I could find about 3032, I contacted the company president, Spencer Watson. Shortly thereafter, samples of each and the new Scot reloading manual arrived. Briefly put, 3032 is a grain or so faster than IMR-3031. I hoped it would allow me to produce the ballistics of the 31 grains of 3031 and the 190-grain bullet without compression and bullet deformation. I thought it should also do well with 180-grain bullets.

The second product was the Lee Factory Crimp Die, introduced by Lee Precision, Inc., makers of fine, but not costly, reloading dies and accessories. This die was designed to apply a factory-style crimp after the bullet had been seated using a regular seating die. Its advantages, the company claimed, were that, since a roll crimp was not used, neck length was not critical. This was relative, of course, and meant that as long as the case-neck length was shorter than the chamber-neck length, minor differences in length among cases was unimportant. Factory literature also indicated that non-cannelured bullets could be crimped without difficulty. The 30-30 Winchester was one of the first chamberings offered, and I bought the first one I saw.

The Lee Factory Crimp Die in action.

Now I was ready to begin anew. I worked with IMR-3031 and the newly arrived Scot 3032, and included W-748. Years of use had taught me that this is a fine 30-30 powder and works well with heavier bullets, but is anything but clean burning. Standard large rifle primers (CCI 200) were used with both 3031 and 3032. W-748, however, is usually paired with a magnum primer for improved ignition, although residue is still there and dirty. For it, I chose the CCI 250 large rifle magnum primer.

Case length still had to be contended with, but to a lesser extent. Maximum case length for the 30-30 is 2.040 inches. Many chambers accept even longer cases. Overall cartridge length is even more critical, though, usually given as 2.550 inches. It may be shorter, depending on bullet length and nose shape. The Hornady manual, for example, lists 2.550 inches for its 150-grain bullet, but only 2.530 for its 170. If cases are allowed to grow and crimps are applied in the normal fashion at the cannelure, feeding problems can develop. On the other hand, if a proper overall length is determined for each bullet and the crimp applied with the Lee die, or cases are kept trimmed and roll-crimped, no problems should develop. But it is important to determine the proper overall length for each bullet.

A couple of comments regarding the factory-crimp die are in order. First, its range of adjustment is slight. If cases were trimmed to 2.020 inches, no crimp could be applied. At 2.030 inches, a modest but very good crimp appeared. As the length grew beyond 2.030 inches, the degree of crimp became greater until the maximum crimp was applied. But the dies worked as advertised. From a length of about 2.030 inches on, excellent crimps were applied, regardless of the bullets used. Tests by others that I have read comparing the accuracy of roll-crimp versus factory-crimp ammunition in other calibers, revealed better accuracy when using the new Lee die. My tests will not be documented here, but they were made and I did get better results with the Lee die.

On the downside, especially when longer cases were employed, the factory crimp was not always removed by firing and a bullet could not be inserted in the fired case neck. As I sometimes use this trick to ensure that all is well, it was somewhat disconcerting. I did prove to my satisfaction, however, that it is a function of applying a solid factory crimp and not simply an overly long case for the chamber. I could take one of the offending cases, resize and reload it with a roll crimp, fire it and insert a bullet in the fired case mouth with ease. I do not see this as a problem, but rather something to be aware of.

Now, back to reloading. I began by firing several rounds of factory Remington 150- and 170-grain ammunition and chronographing the results. I wanted to familiarize myself with the recoil, the real (not published) velocity in my gun, and the level of ease or difficulty of cartridge extraction. Factory cases were measured at the pressure ring before and after firing, as were all reloads. Before firing, factory ammunition measured .415-inch just in front of the case web. Afterward, cases which fired 150-grain bullets measured .419. Those firing the 170-grain went .420. This .420 mark, I was to discover, was significant. Reloads could expand slightly, to perhaps .4202 or .4203, before extraction began to get sticky. At .421 extraction was very sticky and case life was poor. Ironically, accuracy was often excellent.

Although my quest dealt with the heavier bullets, I reloaded the 170-grain Speer flat-nose with each powder and fired it at each range session. It, along with the factory ammunition, gave me two good reference points.

Others were tried, but my tests were based on W-W Super cases. A sampling of resized, trimmed and weighed cases revealed the following:

Loads used in test. *From left:* 170-gr. Speer; 180-gr. 307 winchester; 180-gr. Speer Mag-Tip; 190-gr. 303 Savage Silvertip; Remington factory 150-gr.; Remington factory 170-gr.—all in 30-30 Winchester

Case	Average Weight
W-W Super	134.0 grains
Winchester	130.3 grains
R-P	126.0 grains

Clearly, the W-W Super cases will hold less powder, but probably provide better case life, assuming equal pressures.

Working with IMR-3031, the decades-old load has been 31 grains coupled with the 170-grain bullet. Interestingly, this is 1 1/2 grains over maximum in the latest Speer manual, yet less than tops in the Hornady. It works fine in my 94 with a velocity of 2120 fps. A load of 31.5 grains gets me to 2175 fps and is very reliable, while 32 grains put me over the magical 2200 fps, but with beginning signs of excess pressure. I like 31.5 grains. Going to 180-grain bullets, 30.5 grains produced 2082 fps with no excess pressure signs with the 307 Winchester bullet and 2054 fps with the Speer Mag-Tip. With the 190-grain Savage bullet, 29.5 grains gave me 2024 fps; a near duplicate of published 303 Savage ballistics (usually given as 1980 fps). Additional powder gave early pressure signs and seating difficulties.

Winchester-Western's 748 is a spherical, single-base powder that the company touts highly for the 30-30. It meters well and produces excellent ballistics. Unfortunately, the use of W-748 in the 30-30 is viewed differently by different reloading manual publishers. The Winchester manual (10th Edition, revised 1989) suggests 32 grains is tops and will push a 170-grain bullet out of a 24-inch barrel at 2145 fps. Speer's 11th Edition agrees with the 32 grains, but comes up with 2128 fps out of a 20-inch barrel. Actually these differences are well within the bounds of variables that naturally occur in loading ammunition. The only problem is that no such thing occurs when I load this combination. In my carbine it takes 36 grains to get to 2132 fps. On the other hand, the Hornady manual (3rd Edition) says 39 grains will produce 2300 fps in a 20-inch Model 94.

My carbine seems to prefer the Hornady data, coming very close to its numbers. However, I load the 170-grain bullet with 36.5 grains for 2,225 fps or so. Good load in my gun. Fadala encountered the same conditions and mentioned using 37 grains in his guns. Moving up to the heavier bullets, I ended up cutting the powder charge by 2 grains for each 10-grain increase of bullet weight. With the 180-grain bullets, 34.5 grains worked well, and 32.5 with the 190.

Scot's 3032 was the powder I was most anxious to try. I wasn't disappointed. It is simply the cleanest burning powder I have ever used. Oddly, instead of toying with reloading manual limits, this time I could not get close. The maximum load in the Scot manual for the 170-grain bullet is 33 grains for 2225 fps.

PENETRATION TESTS

—Bullet— (Wgt. Grs.)	(Type)	Inches of Penetration	Retained Weight (Grs.)	Percent of Orig.	Expansion (in.)
170	Speer FN	10	154.7	91.0	.492
180	Winchester FN	17	132.2	73.4	.515
180	Speer Mag-Tip	18	166.3	92.4	.547
190	Win. Silvertip	13	157.2	82.7	.566

Fired at 50 yards into wet newspaper. Expansion was measured at widest point.

Too much powder and the stretchy '94 receiver will produce incipient case separations like these.

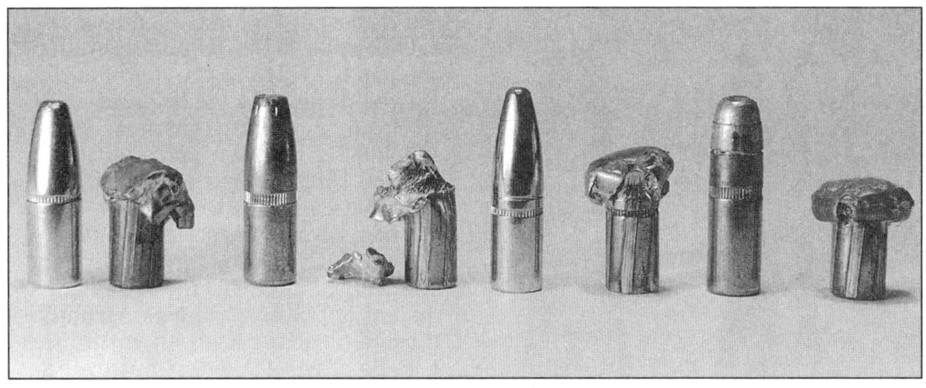

Before and After – bullets unfired and recovered from test medium. ***From left:*** **170-grain Speer; 180-grain 307 Winchester; 180-grain Speer Mag-tip; 190-grain 303 Savage Silvertip.**

In my gun, that load produced a lot more velocity than that, but at the expense of definitely excessive pressure signs. I ended up with 31 grains for the same 2225 fps.

As with 3031, a 1-grain cut as bullet weight increased worked well. With the 180-grain 307 bullet, 30 grains produced 2113 fps, and with the 180-grain Mag-Tip I got 2116. The 190-grain Silvertip was pushed to 2052 fps by 29 grains. Accuracy was excellent throughout, and 3032 tied or bettered the other two powders with all four bullets. The most accurate bullet of all tested was the 190-grain Silvertip, regardless of powder used; the 180-grain Mag-Tip was next.

Two good products for the 30-30 handloader. Too bad the propellant is no longer available.

All of this was great fun, of course, but bullet performance was of greater concern than slight variations in velocity or accuracy. Photographs of sectioned bullets hint at probable results. A trip to the range with boxes of wet newspapers was more definitive. At a measured 50 yards, samples of each were test fired into the paper medium. More photographs and measurements tell the results. Actually, on this day, the newsprint was not quite as wet as I would have liked and penetration figures are likely less than would occur in game. However, the figures are instructive.

Both the 180s penetrated farther than the 190. The Mag-Tip dug in a solid 18 inches, mushrooming as a bullet should. The 307 Winchester bullet penetrated almost as far, 17 inches, but the jacket forward of the cannelure broke off en route. The jacket behind the cannelure and the core remained intact. I view this not as something to worry about, but likely a case of the cannelure being applied a little too strongly. A different lot of bullets may not exhibit this trait at all. The Silvertip passed through 13 inches of wet paper before stopping in perhaps the quintessential expanded form. All reflect the potential to perform well on game at close range.

So, in the end, I had a new powder I am very pleased with, a crimping tool that works well with all bullets and, most especially, heavyweight bullets for my 30-30. They must work on game, for my first outing last fall duplicated Stent's experience his first time out with heavyweights. The game simply vanished-out of respect, no doubt. But this season...

Should you decide this is a path you would like to tread, I encourage you to use both factory 170-grain ammunition and 170-grain reloads as starting points. When extraction becomes the slightest bit sticky, back off a grain. I am positive I could back off another half-grain on each of the loads presented and neither the game nor I would ever know the difference. I also feel sure I could increase each load a half-grain without blowing anything up, but at decreased case life. I heartily recommend you cut all loads by 3 grains and work up from there. ●

PERFORMANCE TESTS

—Bullet— (Wgt. Grs.)	(Type)	Powder (Grs./Type)	MV (fps)	Extreme Spread	Accuracy	Remarks
170	Speer FN	31.0/IMR-3031	2120	28	B	
		31.5/IMR-3031	2176	10	A	
		36.5/W-748	2223	17	A	
		31.0/SCOT 3032	2225	42	A	
180	Win. FN	30.5/IMR-3031	2082	28	B	
		34.5/W-748	2154	63	B	
		30.0/SCOT 3032	2113	65	B+	
180	Speer Mag-Tip	30.5/IMR-3031	2054	51	B	
		34.5/W-748	2162	10	A	
		30.0/SCOT 3032	2116	9	A	Good load.
190	Win. Silvertip	29.5/IMR-3031	2004	30	A+	Second most accurate load.
		32.5/W-748	2050	11	B	
		29.0/SCOT 3032	2052	16	A+	Most accurate load.
170	R-P Factory		2118	47	C	
150	R-P Factory		2299	19	C	

Why Follow The Recipe?

by M.L. McPherson

It is tempting for us handloaders, intrepid souls that we are, to tinker with component choices in our loads. Primer and bullet substitutions are a common means of trying to improve performance. In fact, many metallic cartridge reloaders, including myself, have often disdained shotshell loading as "following a recipe" and therefore unworthy of serious pursuit. The unsaid suggestion was that metallic cartridge reloaders were free to safely substitute primers and bullets in pursuit of the "perfect" load.

Alas, this has never been true. As is well known among experts in the industry, bullet or primer substitutions can dramatically alter a load's ballistics. In many instances, such substitutions can alter the pressure more than using the same charge of a significantly different type of powder. No self-respecting handloader would even consider using IMR-3031 as a grain-for-grain substitute for IMR-4320, but many handloaders have routinely practiced primer and bullet substitutions that result in a greater difference in peak chamber pressure.

Most loading-data sources list specific recipes for metallic cartridge loads. This genre includes Speer, Hornady, Nosler, Barnes, Sierra, Winchester *(Olin)*, IMR, VihtaVuori, and Accurate Arms. As near as I can tell, only Alliant *(formerly Hercules)* and Hodgdon Powder offer semi-generic handloading data; one can use any similar bullet of the proper weight with the given load. In the case of Alliant, the generic data is given only for pistol and revolver loads – rifle loads are complete recipes.

In the instance of Hodgdon, at least, ballistic testing establishes which bullet of standard size and weight generates the highest pressures. Hodgdon's ballisticians then generate the published data using that bullet. Primer, case, powder, and charge limits are *(or should be)* specified in all data sources.

As a quick review of the following

***Accurate Study #* 1:**
Accurate Arm's Universal Receiver, used for all testing. Both the 270 Winchester and 30-06 Springfield barrels were equipped with conformal transducers.

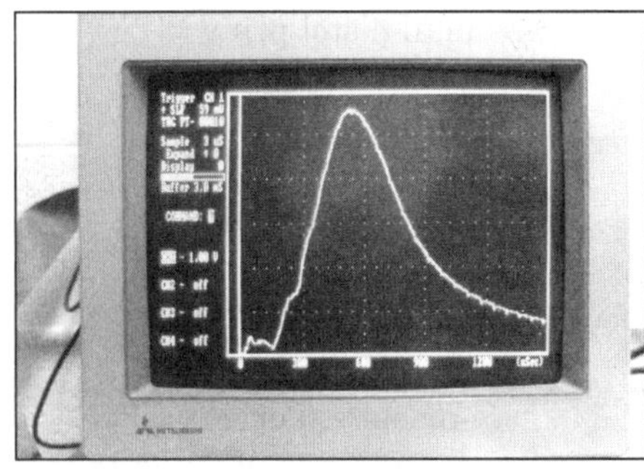

Accurate Study #3:
Example pressure curve with mild pistol primer and A2700 (ball-type) powder. Note the initial pressure rise, followed by the drop in pressure before the main pressure rise. This almost certainly indicates the primer was not properly igniting the powder charge. (The squiggles in the graph are an electronic glitch.)

data will clearly demonstrate, if the data call for a specific primer or bullet, safety requires that you use exactly those components when working up the load.

There is no way to determine which primer or which bullets might safely substitute for any other in any given application. If you think you see a trend in the following bullet-substitution data, rest assured that similar tests with different cartridges will generate different results. Often, the make and type of bullets that showed the highest pressures here show higher pressures in other calibers. However, this correlation is not dependable. As a demonstration of this fact, this test produced several surprises compared to preconceived notions based on prior experience. Also, the primer test demonstrated that the consequences of primer substitutions are not predictable. Even in this limited study, one can see that there is no obvious

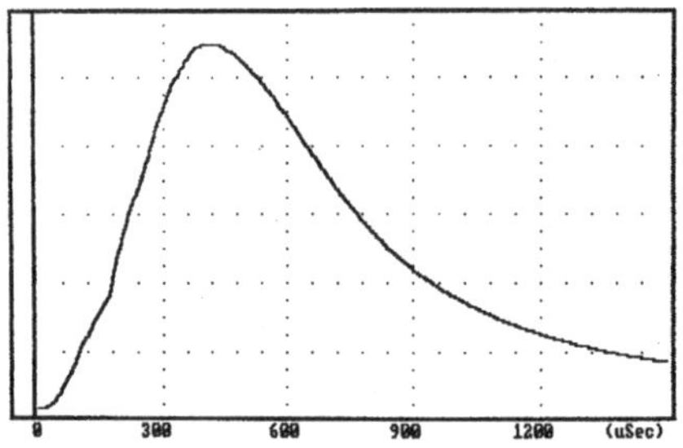

Accurate Study #4
Printout of pressure graph: 30-06 study, CCI-200 Primer.

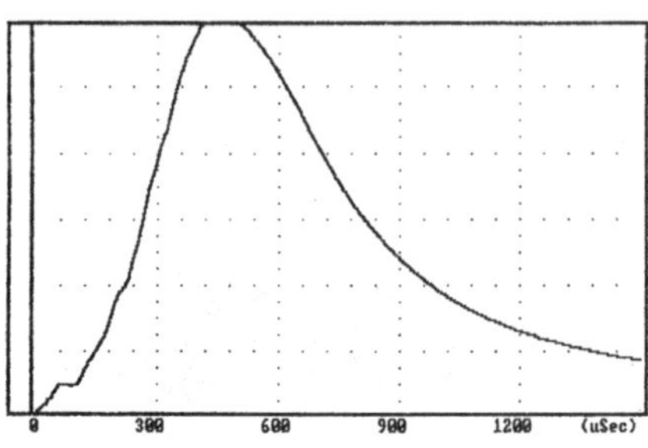

Accurate Study #5
Printout of pressure graph: 30-06 study, CCI-350 Primer. Note that this primer produced more pressure than the CCI-200.

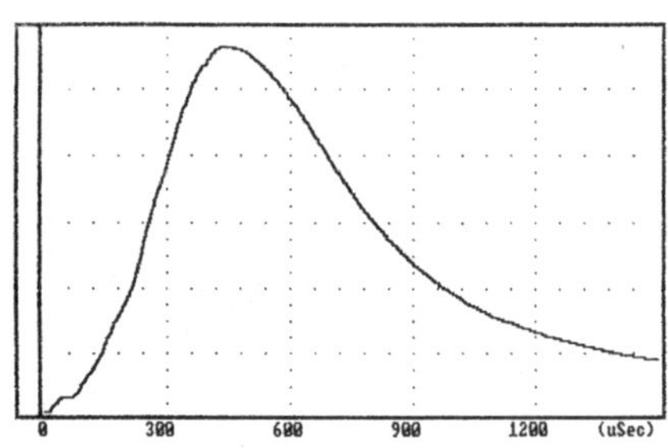

Accurate Study #6
Printout of pressure graph: 30-06 study, WinWLRM Primer.

Table 1

270 WINCHESTER BULLET SUBSTITUTION TEST, ACCURATE ARMS BALLISTICS LABORATORY

Bullet		Pressure			Velocity			%Difference from Lowest Pressure Standard Bullet		
gns.	Make and Style	psi	Extreme Spread	Standard Deviation	fps	Extreme Spread	Standard Deviation	Pressure	Velocity	Relative Energy to Peak Pressure
150	*Brn-X*	*72,400*	*8,900*	*3,000*	*2898*	*103*	*31*	*25.7*	*2.7%*	*-12*
150	Spr Sptz	69,500	2,400	1,200	2917	47	14	20.7	3.3%	-8
150	Nos BT	69,000	4,000	1,300	2923	35	10	19.8	3.5%	-6
150	**Spr GS**	**66,900**	**2,800**	**900**	**2930**	**34**	**11**	**16.1**	**3.8%**	**-7**
150	Hdy SP	66,200	3,700	1,200	2907	30	10	14.9	3.0%	-3
150	Sra SBT	63,300	2,500	900	2887	76	21	9.9	2.3%	0
150	Nos Part	62,600	1,600	600	2866	22	7	8.7	1.5%	-1
150	Spr BT	61,900	2,200	600	2907	20	6	7.5	3.0%	+3
150	Hdy RN	61,600	3,400	1,000	2866	29	8	6.9	1.5%	0
150	**Sra RN**	**57,600**	**2,900**	**1,300**	**2823**	**43**	**14**	**0.0**	**0.0%**	**+4**
150	*Brn Solid*	*54,700*	*3,100*	*900*	*2854*	*38*	*13*	*-5.0*	*1.1%*	*+12*
	Average	64,200	1,200	2889		13				
	Extreme	17,700	2,400	107		25				
	S. Dev.	5,300	700	33		7				
140	*Win FS*	*61,500*	*4,200*	*1,500*	*2927*	*52*	*17*	*6.8*	*3.796*	*-2*
160	*Nos Part*	*63,100*	*3,100*	*900*	*2831*	*29*	*8*	*9.5*	*0.3%*	*+2*

Bold entries signify highest- and lowest-velocity bullets. *Italics* entries signify exotic and non-150-grain bullets.

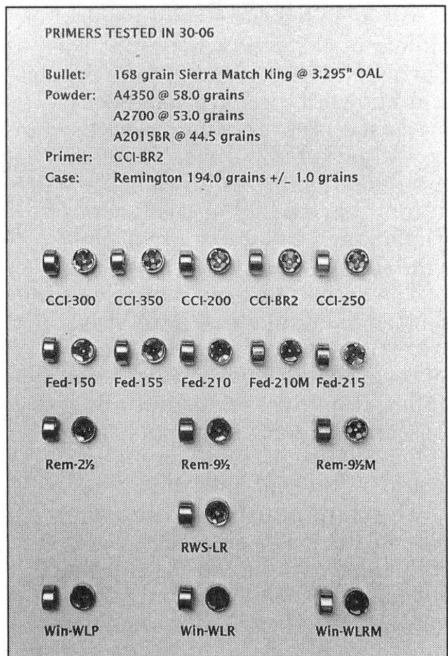

relationship between type of primer used and a load's peak pressure. Again, given different loads, we would expect different primer/pressure ranking orders.

As an adjunct to this data, consider the following accounts. In 1975, I developed a 357 Magnum load using SR4756 and 110-grain Speer JHP bullets. Initially I used the CCI #500 *(standard small pistol)* primer. Later I decided to try the CCI #550 *(small pistol magnum)* primer. In working up this new load, I fortunately reduced the initial test-load charge about 15 percent.

I had to drive those fired cases from the cylinder using a hardwood dowel and a rubber mallet! To achieve about the same velocity and pressure as the original load, I had to reduce the powder charge a full 30 percent. That fact suggests that an equal charge with the CCI-550 primer would have generated more than twice the pressure.

Since SR-4756 granules are comparatively fragile, it is possible the hotter primers were fracturing the individual powder disks. Such fracturing would increase the surface area and therefore the burning rate.

In a similar experience, Accurate Arms once had reason to test various powders in the 357 Magnum using several types of primers *(four pistol and one rifle)*. In that test, one particular ball powder produced 47 percent more pressure with a certain magnum small pistol primer, compared to the same brand of small rifle primer. *(This result is in direct contradiction to the oft' quoted remark that ball-type powders are not particularly sensitive to primer choice.)*

This test result seemingly makes no sense. After all, everyone "knows" that rifle primers are much hotter than pistol primers. Perhaps pre-ignition bullet movement explains this unexpected result. Consider that in the 38 Special, seating a 148-grain WC 0.1-inch deeper can double peak pressure. Obviously, in some instances, chamber pressure is highly dependent upon where the bullet is when the powder ignites. In Accurate's test, perhaps the rifle primer was hotter but was also driving the bullet farther out of the case before the powder ignited. On the other hand, perhaps the rifle primer was just a lot milder.

Don't Substitute Bullets

The first study we completed was as an adjunct to Accurate Arm's work with bullet substitutions. We set out to test one cartridge with a wide array of bullets of the same weight.

Table 2 – 30-06 Springfield

PRIMER SUBSTITUTION STUDY, ACCURATE ARMS BALLISTICS LABORATORY

PRIMER	PRESSURE				VELOCITY				
Make & Number	psi	Extreme Spread	% Difference From Lowest Standard Deviation	Pressure Load	fps	Extreme Spread	% Difference from Lowest Standard Deviation	Pressure Load	% Relative Energy to Peak Pressure
Win-WLRM	**63,900**	**2,700**	**1,100**	**20.3**	**2951**	**30**	**11**	**4.4%**	**-5%**
Win-WLR	61,600	2,600	1,200	16.0	2926	23	10	3.5%	-3%
CCI-350	59,400	7,700	700	11.9	2905	23	9	2.8%	-1%
Fed-215	59,400	3,200	1,300	11.9	2908	50	19	2.9%	-1%
Fed-210	59,000	4,700	1,800	11.1	2901	52	20	2.6%	0%
Rem-9 1/2M	58,900	6,000	2,200	10.9	2896	64	22	2.4%	-1%
Fed-210M	58,100	2,700	1,200	9.4	2892	35	14	2.3%	0%
CCI-250	57,700	1,100	400	8.7	2882	9	4	1.9%	0%
CCI-BR2	57,300	3,700	1,500	7.9	2886	39	18	2.1%	+1%
Rem-9 1/2	56,300	1,500	600	6.0	2867	12	4	1.4%	+2%
CCI-200	55,100	3,200	1,100	3.8	2858	36	14	1.1%	+3%
Win-WLP	*55,000*	*2,600*	*1,300*	*3.6*	*2859*	*46*	*19*	*1.1%*	*+4%*
RWS-LR	54,900	1,700	600	3.4	2850	30	11	0.8%	+3%
Fed-155	*54,400*	*1,400*	*600*	*2.4*	*2853*	*13*	*4*	*0.9%*	*+5%*
Fed-150	*53,600*	*2,100*	*900*	*0.9*	*2839*	*31*	*12*	*0.4%*	*+5%*
CCI-300	*53,400*	*1,800*	*700*	*0.6*	*2831*	*29*	*10*	*0.1%*	*+5%*
Rem-2 1/2	*53,100*	*1,200*	*600*	*0.0*	*2827*	*20*	*9*	*0.0%*	*+5%*

Bold entries indicate highest- and lowest-velocity loads. *Italics* entries indicate pistol primers.New primers tested with 58/A4350 and 168-grain Sierra Match King.

Accurate Study #8A/8B/8C/8D:
Various primer flashes, showing representative appearances. It is impossible to judge performance based on any feature of the unconfined flash's appearance. Equally, it is impossible to judge a _priori_ what type of primer will generate the most pressure with any given load. In some instances, the mildest-appearing primer might generate the most pressure.

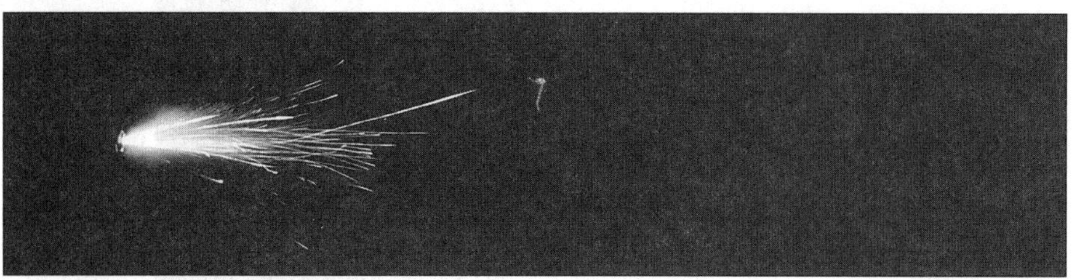

Accurate Study #8A:
Winchester Small Rifle primer.

Certainly this limited test cannot suggest any general trend, but it does clearly show that one cannot safely substitute bullets. Frankly, the results of this test suggest that if the loading data you are using specifies one brand and type of bullet, you had better stick to that bullet.

Our choice of the 270 Winchester for this test had several justifications. First, because the 270 is such a well-known cartridge, many handloaders would be able to relate their experiences with our 270 results. Our second reason was the wide selection of 150-grain 270 bullets available. This allowed us to make many comparisons that we believed would demonstrate our point -- that different bullets of the same size and weight generate significantly different pressures. Third, the 270 works at the upper end of "normal" pressures. We were looking for results that might get people's attention. The higher the base pressure, the more impressive any pressure excursions night be.

Our test load was as published in Accurate's data manual *(for the Sierra 150-grain SBT)*. The test ammunition used 184-grain Frontier 270 cases loaded with the CCI BR2 *(a match-grade non-magnum large rifle primer ballistically similar to the CCI-200)* and 53 grains of A4350. Cartridge overall length was 3.25 inches for all bullets. This is a maximum-fisted load for Sierra's SBT bullet. With that bullet, peak pressure in this test was 63,300 psi, while SAAMI's pressure limit for this cartridge is 65,000 psi.

(All pressures reported in this article are conformal transducer data. A reading of 65,000 psi in the 270 corresponds to about 52,000 CUP, 60,000 psi in the 30-06 corresponds to about 50,000 CUP.)

I loaded the ammunition for this and the following described primer-substitution test with utmost care. I fully prepped new cases from one lot, as if we would use the ammunition for bench rest competition. I loaded all the ammunition ahead of time so that I would have plenty of time to do it right. I made every effort to minimize all associated variables, both while loading and during shooting.

We included several unusual bullets in this study. First was the Barnes X, constructed of pure copper and known to produce somewhat increased pressure when compared to typical jacketed bullets. There are three likely reasons for this: They are harder, have a higher coefficient of friction, and take up more of the available powder space.

The second unusual bullet was the Barnes Solid, made of pure brass. While this bullet is harder than either a solid copper or a jacketed bullet, it produces substantially less friction. Our data suggests that bullet-to-bore friction is a major factor in internal ballistics.

The third unusual bullet was Winchester's 140-grain Fail Safe, ballistically similar to the Barnes X but featuring a friction-reducing coating that is evidently somewhat effective. *(Winchester does not offer a 150-grain 0.277-inch FS bullet, so we used the 140-grain version for comparison purposes.)*

Finally, we compared Nosler's 160-grain semi-spitzer partition *(the old stress-relieving grooved version)*. We tested this bullet because my experience with it suggested it

Table 3 — 30-06 Springfield
OLD PRIMERS VERSUS NEW PRIMERS

Primer		**Pressure**			**Velocity**		
Make & Number	Date of Manufacture	psi	Extreme Spread	Standard Deviation	fps	Extreme Spread	Standard Deviation
Fed-215	1970s	61,400	5,000	2,000	2927	43	16
Fed-215	1995	59,400	3,200	1,300	2908	50	19
Fed-210	1970s	61,100	2,000	900	2932	21	9
Fed-210	1995	59,000	4,700	1,800	2901	52	20
Rem-9 1/2M	1970s	58,800	3,000	1,300	2904	39	14
Rem-9 1/2M	1995	58,900	6,000	2,200	2896	64	22
Rem-9 1/2	1970s	58,500	1,600	700	2897	23	10
Rem-9 1/2	1995	56,300	1,500	600	2867	12	4
CCI-250	1979	57,000	1,400	600	2872	31	12
CCI-250	1995	57,700	1,100	400	2882	9	4
CCI-200	1974	57,500	4,800	1,900	2874	77	29
CCI-200	1980	54,500	2,600	1,000	2855	30	12
CCI-200	1995	55,100	3,200	1,100	2858	6	14

Additional Primers Tested

Primer		**Pressure**			**Velocity**		
Make & Number	Date of Manufacture	psi	Extreme Spread	Standard Deviation	fps	Extreme Spread	Standard Deviation
Alcan LRM	1970s	60,900	3,800	1,400	2906	33	13
Alcan LR	1970s	58,900	3,200	1,500	2925	54	22

Load: 58/A4350, 168-grain Sierra Match King

produced similar pressures, compared to Sierra's 150-grain SBT in the 270 *(at least when used with H4831 powder and CCI's 250 primers)*.

We tested nine standard 150-grain jacketed bullets, all we could get for this testing. This also represents most of the "standard" 150-grain 270 bullets that are commonly available.

Bold entries signify highest- and lowest-velocity bullets. Italics entries signify exotic and non-150-grain bullets.

Load details:

- New 184-grain Frontier cases; fully prepped via flash hole, primer pocket, case length, and case-neck preparations using various K&M and RCBS tools.
- 1995 production CCI-BR2 primers, seated with 0.003" +/- 0.001 pellet preload via K&M Services Deluxe Priming Tool.
- 53 grains of A4350 powder weighed to maximum accuracy via Lyman's AutoScale and verified via RCBS' Powder Pro digital electronic scale.

All powder was fresh and from the same lot and container.

Powder was installed into cases via Forster's Blue Ribbon funnel *(6" drop tube)* using a consistent swirl-charging technique. *(In this system, the powder is poured from the pan at a constant rate and against the side of the funnel's cone; conservation of momentum helps to form a consistent rapidly swirling stream as the granules funnel into the drop tube.)*

All bullets were seated via RCBS Competition seating die to 3.250 OAL.

Test gun was Accurate's Universal receiver and a SAAMI minimum specification barrel fitted with a comformal transducer. Each test represents ten shots for record with each bullet.

Fouling and warming shots were fired and the pressure barrel was not overheated during this testing.

You might note that, as shown by the SD numbers, there is a statistical correlation between bullets that create low pressures and those that produce consistent velocities. If we ignore the exotic bullets and Sierra's RN, this is a strong correlation. The five remaining bullets at the top of the list generated an average pressure of 67,000 psi with an average standard deviation in velocity of 13 fps. The remaining three bullets at the bottom of the list generated an average pressure of 62,700 psi with an average standard deviation in velocity of 7 fps.

Bullet – Bore Friction Significant

A quick look at data for the Barnes Solid suggests that bullet-to-bore friction is a significant factor in the amount of energy generated. The shank on this bullet is 0.555-inch long and 0.276-inch in diameter; from in front of the cannelure to the beginning of the ogive, it measures 0.266-inch. These dimensions are similar to the other round-nose bullets tested. Evidently, since this bullet cannot deform significantly in the gun's leade and has a much lower coefficient of friction than the other bullets tested, it transfers much less energy to the bore; therefore, if loaded to the same pressure as the others, this bullet would, evidently, have higher velocity and thus significantly higher energy.

We believe this test clearly demonstrated that one cannot substitute any bullet without running the risk of dangerously altering the internal ballistics **(safety)** of the load.

This test suggests good reason to always begin load development at the start charge, rather than near the maximum load. Owing only to lot-to-lot variation, your components might be sufficiently different from those used to develop the data to alter chamber pressure significantly.

We also conducted a similar safety study to analyze the relationship between choice of primer and

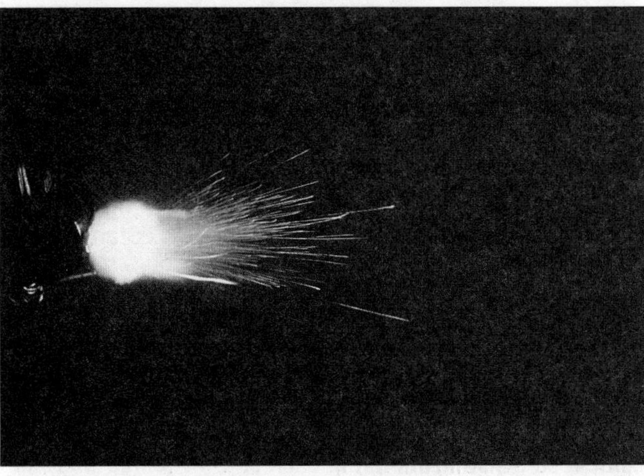

Accurate Study #8B: **Federal Small Rifle primer.**

Accurate Study #8C: **RWS Small Rifle primer.**

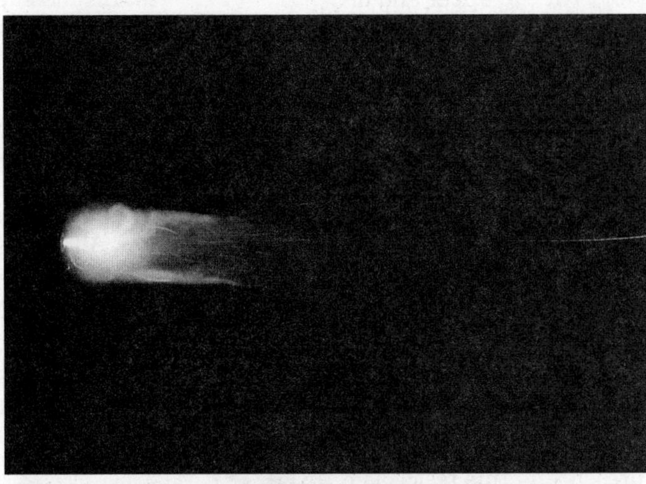

Accurate Study #8D: **CCI-250 Large Rifle Magnum primer.**

Table 4

OVERALL STATISTICAL RESULTS OF PRIMER STUDY IN THE 30-06

Pressure & Velocity Data Results (1990s Primers)

Load	Pressure			Standard Deviation			Velocity			Standard Deviation		
	Average	Spread	SD	Average	Spread	SD	Average	Spread	SD	Average	Spread	SD
58/A4350	57,100	10,800	2,900	1,100	1,800	500	2878	124	34	12	18	6
53/A2700	54,900	6,800	2,200	1,100	1,800	500	2744	82	26	13	22	7
44.5A2015BR	59,100	5,800	1,600	1,300	1,900	600	2741	31	10	10	16	5

internal ballistics. Here, we compared 30-06 loads using each of three powders with Sierra's 168-grain Match King. We chose this combination because both the 30-06 and this bullet are common and well understood. This is also in the middle of the "normal" range of rifle loads and is an example of a combination for which many handloaders might suspect they could safely substitute primers.

With all three powders, we chose loads slightly below the maximum recommended. We used Accurate 4350, a tubular single-base powder, because in this application, it is slow burning and a compressed charge. We chose Accurate 2700, a double-base powder, as an example of a middle burning rate ball-type propellant. Accurate A2015BR is a fast-burning tubular single-base powder. It was not feasible to test more powders.

In the test with A4350, we included several old primers just to see if those produced significantly different results, compared to their '90s-era counterparts. We also tested the obsolete Alcan rifle primers. With all three powders, we tested every 1990s production large rifle and large pistol primer we could obtain – 17 types.

A review of this data suggests several interesting points, not the least of which are the following: Pistol primers were generally more consistent than rifle primers in this test. Both this result and anecdotal reports suggest that a pressure barrel Universal receiver setup is likely a poor choice for measuring primer performance. The striker in these guns is very light *(typically less than 100 grains)* and evidently delivers marginal impact energy and momentum when used with rifle primers.

Experienced ballisticians say that the operator can alter test results by using more or less force when firing these guns, which use an automatic striker release system. When the operator pulls the tether, a hook pulls on a piston, which compresses a spring. Eventually, the hook goes over-center and automatically releases the piston, which falls and hits the striker. This design allows a violent pull of the tether to "overcock" the piston. When one yanks the tether, as the hook releases the piston, the piston is traveling fast enough to continue compressing the spring a small additional amount. It hits the striker harder and, therefore, the striker hits the primer harder. The proof of this is simple: A harder/faster pull typically generates more muzzle velocity. This result seems most unlikely if this mechanism routinely provided sufficient energy to thoroughly and consistently ignite all primers. Our test results support this conclusion, i.e., pistol primers require a lighter blow for proper ignition and one might, therefore, expect those to perform more uniformly with a milder blow, compared to rifle primers. Rifle primers might have compared better if the test gun could have delivered a stronger striker blow. All logic supports this hypothesis; it seems unlikely that primer manufacturers would go out of their way to deliberately produce rifle primers that were less consistent than pistol primers.

Accurate 2700 seems to be more sensitive to primer choice than either of the other powders tested. These average statistics might not appear to support this view, but note that with this ball-type powder, several ostensibly hot primers produced very mild pressures and low velocities, while several supposedly mild primers produced high pressures and velocities. There seems, also, to have been little uniformity regarding the consistency of any particular type of primer with this powder. However, I could be reading entirely too much into this extremely limited data, so judge for yourself.

Accurate 4350 and 2015BR both showed a preference toward mild primers. *(We define "mild" based upon generation of comparatively low velocity and pressure.)* With the milder primers these powders generally gave better uniformity in both velocity and pressure. This correlation was statistically strong with A2015BR.

With all three powders, the relationship between peak chamber pressure *(and, therefore, the area under the pressure curve)* and muzzle energy is reasonable. Primers that generated more pressure generated more velocity. If one graphs the peak pressure vs. velocity points on an X/Y graph, the points plot reasonably close to a straight line.

That is just about the only thing in all of this primer data that agrees reasonably with any preconceived notions we might have had. If you do not believe that many of our "reasonable" pre-notions were proven bogus, might I refer you to the CCI-350 *(large pistol magnum)* results vs. the CCI-250 *(large rifle magnum)* results, as just one example.

A quick review of the A4350 data shows that primers have changed in the recent past. If you switch to a different age lot of the same type of primer, you might expect to see a moderate change in pressure. With this in mind, one can easily understand the prudence of the often quoted: "Do not begin your load development with the maximum recommended load!" There is a reason for a recommended start charge – your safety! The consequences of primer substitution are completely unpredictable. ●

Handloading for the 30 Mauser C.96

by Don Horne

I suppose all firearms enthusiasts have, in the nether regions of their consciousness, a list of firearms that simply must be owned someday. If prevailed upon, said enthusiast may be able to justify owning them but the truth of the matter is that some firearms simply must be possessed. Cold, hard reasoning remains unused in the quest for "that" gun.

For myself, and many others, the C.96 or "Broomhandle" Mauser is one of "those" guns. It isn't smooth and svelte, nor does it kill like lightning or produce 1/4-inch groups. What it does do is stir visions of the Germany of Kaiser Wilhelm, Churchill in the Sudan and ragged bands of Chinese warlord soldiers brandishing Broomhandle Mausers. I simply had to own one.

In the last ten years several Broomhandles had come my way. All of them were recent imports, and ranged in condition from rough to rusted in half. None had bores any better than a gas pipe, or any more blue than a new coffee table. I didn't try to shoot any of them. Last winter a retired small-town farmer called saying he had three guns to sell. He had been to the local gun shop but found the shop uninterested. The clerk at the gun shop had given him my number, explaining my interest in "old, weird things". We talked, the telephone seemed to heat-up, and I told the farmer when and where to meet me. Next came the begging and pleading with the keeper of the purse strings. Having been given the green light, the meet took place, a deal was made, and a C.96 WWII war trophy followed me home. It is in 90 percent-plus condition, with a shiny bore, matching stock, and leather harness with cleaning tool.

Privy Councillor Dr. Ingenieur Paul von Mauser is most often given credit for the design of what came to be known as the Construction 96 *(hence C.96)* Mauser Military Automatic Pistol, but Mauser factory General Superintendent Herr Fidel Federle and his brothers Friedrich and Josef are also credited with the basic design.

Regardless of designer, the locked-breech, short recoil C.96 self-loading pistol became quite successful commercially, due at least in part to the high-velocity cartridge for which it was chambered. Hatcher, writing in *Textbook of Pistols and Revolvers* on page 106, refers to the "great advantage" of the Mauser pistol with its "rifle-like velocities". The Mauser's 86-grain bullet loaded to a velocity of 1400 fps may not be considered rifle-like today, but was quite a screamer as a pistol cartridge in its day. The 7.63 Mauser cartridge was a Mauser modification of the 7.65 Borchardt designed by Hugo Borchardt for the self-loading pistol bearing his name. While dimensionally identical to the Borchardt, the 7.63 Mauser was loaded to chamber pressures that produced muzzle velocities 300 fps higher. Mauser also changed the metric designation from 7.65mm to 7.63mm to avoid confusion with the 7.65mm Borchardt and a similarly named Mannlicher cartridge. Other known chamberings are the 9mm Parabellum, 9mm Mauser, and a cartridge called the 8.15mm, also

Table 3: Loads with 90-grain Sierra JHC

30 Mauser Load Chart

Bullet *(grains)*	**Powder**	**Charge** *(grains)*	**Velocity** *(fps)*	**Remarks**
Sierra/90				
	Unique	5.2	1192	poor functioning
		5.5	1210	good accuracy
	Red Dot	5.1	1256	mediocre accuracy
	AA#2	4.5	1081	poor functioning
	AA#5	5.9	1173	mediocre accuracy
	AA #7	6.7	909	mediocre accuracy,
		7.0	946	poor accuracy
		7.5	970	poor accuracy
		7.8	1,027	mediocre accuracy
		8.0	1,057	best accuracy with jacketed bullets
		8.3	1,120	poor accuracy
	Bullseye	5.0	1244	excellent accuracy
		5.6	1380	poor accuracy, too hot
	452AA	5.0	1247	poor accuracy
		5.3	1337	excellent accuracy
	231	5.1	1159	good accuracy
		5.5	1279	good accuracy
	HP38	5.0	1210	excellent accuracy
		5.3	1257	mediocre accuracy
	7625	5.0	1155	poor accuracy
		5.3	1223	mediocre accuracy

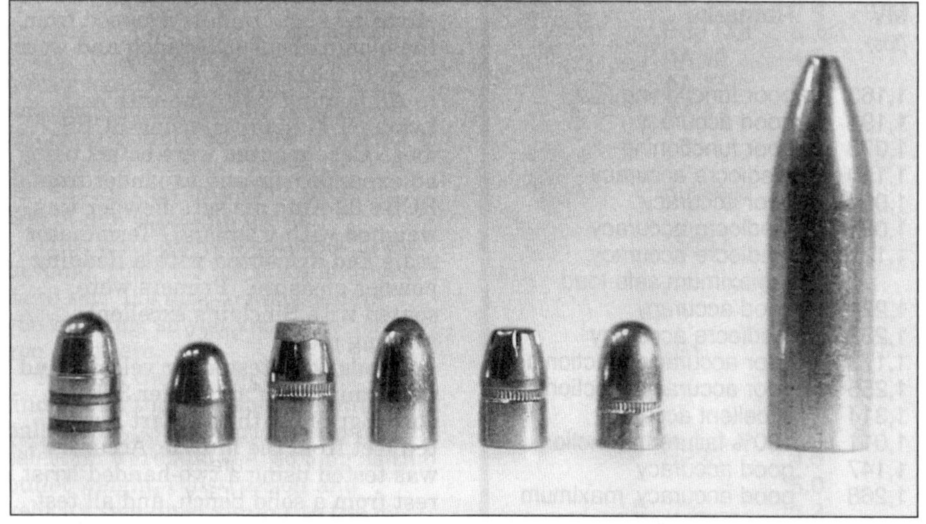

Bullets used in 30 Mauser tests *(from left)*: Lyman 83-grain #311227; Sierra 71-grain. RN; Sierra 90-grain JHC; Sierra 85-grain RN; Hornady 85-grain XTP; Hornady 86-grain FMJ; shown with Barnes 500-grain 458-caliber X bullet for comparison.

shooting was done at 25 yards.

A brief explanation of the remarks in the tables regarding accuracy is in order. Groups measuring 4 inches and over were classified as poor. Those measuring 3 to 4 inches were classed as mediocre. Good groups measured 2.5 to 3 inches, and those groups considered excellent were 2.5 inches, or less.

After test firing began, it was noted that all groups fired in the Mauser with the rear sight at its lowest setting printed at least 12 inches high at 25 yards. This was expected, inasmuch as the rear sight was graduated from 50 meters to 1000 meters. In an effort to find a load that printed closer to the point of aim at 25 yards, the 71-grain Sierra RN was tried. This bullet produced good accuracy, but still printed 12 inches high at 25 yards, and one of the loads failed to cycle the Mauser action. Further testing of light bullet loads was abandoned at this point.

After studying the test results in the tables, and looking back to the goals set at the beginning of the experiment, I concluded the exercise to be modestly successful. Goal One, to develop a load that duplicated military hardball, was met by the 86-grain Hornady FMJ loaded with 5.0 grains of Bullseye. This load produced 2.5-inch groups at 1,247 fps, which is the best possible shooting I am capable of with any hand-held firearm at this range. As a curious aside, Phil Sharpe recommended this load on page 403 of the 1953 edition of his *Complete Guide to Handloading.*

If the 86-grain Hornady FMJ was not available, the Hornady 85-grain XTP over 5.5 grains of Unique, or 5.0 grains of Bullseye would be a perfectly acceptable substitute, although these two loads were slightly less accurate than the 86-grain FMJ over 5.0 grains of Bullseye. Equaling the 86-grain FMJ over 5.0 grains of Bullseye, the Sierra 90-grain JHC over 6.6 grains of 800X produced equivalent accuracy, at slightly lower velocities.

Goal Two, to develop a cast bullet load that would duplicate ball ammo ballistics was met by Lyman 311227 cast of Linotype and loaded over 7.2 grains of AA #7. This load produced the best accuracy of any load in these trials. If AA #7 was not available, 5.0 grains of Bullseye with this bullet delivered slightly higher velocities, with groups almost as small as AA#7.

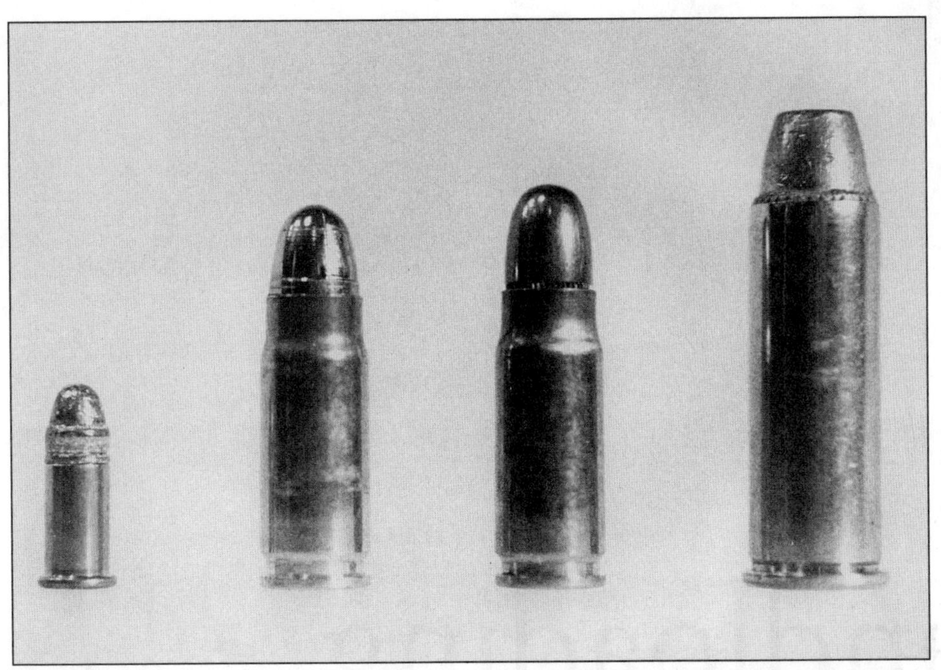

30 Mauser loaded round comparison *(from left)*: 22 Short; 30 Mauser with Lyman #311299; 30 Mauser with Hornady 86-grain FMJ; 44 Magnum factory round.

A word of explanation is in order concerning the compromise of one of the goals set for this project, namely, the requirement that acceptable handloads should shoot close to the point of aim at 25 yards. Much of my handgun testing is done at this distance because my bullet trap is 25 yards away from my carport. I can step out of my back door, walk ten steps, and shoot. A load that would shoot close to the point of aim at this range would have been welcome, but I realized from the start that it might not be possible with this gun with its sight configuration. Other loading projects with similar goals have been attempted over the years, most of which achieved varying degrees of success. Not so this time. In these trials I failed to find any load combination that would shoot to the point of aim at 25 yards.

A close friend brought his 1896 Broomhandle to me one time, asking me to install a higher front sight on his gun to center the point of aim at 25 yards. The higher front sight was made and sweated in place. After a bit of file work, the old Mauser printed nice, centered groups at the desired range. Don't panic. His gun was in rough condition, with obviously little collector value. Mine, however, was in what I considered much too good a condition to alter in any way.

I considered making a temporary aluminum front sight, which would clamp to the Mauser barrel via a split-collar arrangement, and so not make any permanent alteration to the pistol. *(Ugly, nasty thing.)* Probably would have worked, though. As I pondered these weighty philosophical issues it suddenly dawned on me that I had a ball shooting this gun, even when it shot a foot high at 25 yards. I had no intention of using the Mauser for Bullseye competition, silhouette shooting, or hunting. It was a fun gun, meant to satisfy those boyhood urges to own and fire a piece of firearms history.

As childhoods go, mine was idyllic. My father was a gun collector, and we lived on the East coast. Back then, there were always several gun shows every weekend within easy driving distance, and my father went almost every weekend, taking me with him. I spent my boyhood Saturdays roaming hotel ballrooms drooling over table after table of rare and exotic firearms. Dad collected cap and ball Colts and cased sets of English duelers. They were OK, but I always gravitated to the tables of strange auto pistols, many of which contained Broomhandles.

Promptly, the 25-yard range was left behind, along with my misplaced goal, and a cardboard image of an enemy machinegun crew was set up at 100 yards. The Mauser proceeded to wreak havoc with the cardboard gunners, and I saved the day with my very own Broomhandle Mauser. I had been waiting 40 years for that moment. It was great. I think I'll go do it again.

Table 4: Loads With Lyman #311227

30 Mauser Load Chart

Bullet *(grains)*	Powder	Charge *(grains)*	Velocity *(fps)*	Remarks
Ly #311227/83				
	AA #2	4.2	1,219	poor functioning
		4.6	1,239	good accuracy, will not function 100%
	AA #5	5.7	1,318	excellent accuracy
		6.0	1,370	poor accuracy
	AA #7	7.2	1,110	best accuracy of all loads tested
	Unique	5.2	1,298	poor accuracy
		6.0	1,455	poor accuracy, maximum load
	Bullseye	5.0	1,408	excellent accuracy
	Red Dot	5.1	1,415	poor accuracy

Handloading *the* 400 Cor-Bon

by Steve Gash

Good cartridge ideas have a way of popping up in different venues periodically. So it is with the 400 COR-BON cartridge, brought to fruition by an innovative company with the wherewithal to get it done.

The idea of necking down the 45 ACP is not new, and has been done numerous times before. Probably the best known is the 41 Avenger, designed by J. D. Jones of SSK Industries. The 10mm Centaur, designed by Charles Petty, is similar to the 400 COR-BON. Both are good cartridges, but neither is widely available. The 38/45, designed by Bo Clerke, has been around for many years, and has been a modestly popular wildcat on the target circuit. However, to the best of my knowledge, none of these rounds were produced as a factory cartridge.

The 400 COR-BON is also nothing more than the 45 ACP necked down to 10mm. It was introduced as a factory cartridge by the COR-BON Bullet Co., and has been around since at least July, 1996. This cartridge really pushes the envelope when it comes to velocity and power. According to COR-BON's product literature, their 400 COR-BON factory loads with the 135-grain Sierra JHC bullet have a muzzle velocity of 1450 fps, and a 155-grain Bonded Hollow Point moves out "at near 1330 fps." COR-BON correctly notes that this performance rivals the 357 Magnum and the hottest 10mm loads.

The stated design criteria were to *(a)* gain velocity and energy over both the 45 ACP and 10mm auto cartridges, and *(b)* to keep pressures low, thereby eliminating the need for special modifications to most 1911 Government Model pistols. A simple re-barreling is usually all that is needed.

New cartridges that don't require a whole new gun interest me, and so the high performance 400 COR-BON became a "must have" item in short order. Like most inveterate handloaders, I thought I'd just load this sucker to maximum warp, and blaze away. Little did I know that I would end up at the other end of the power spectrum, and be happy as a clam.

COR-BON's product literature lists numerous companies that produce replacement barrels in 400 COR-BON. I obtained mine from Accu-Match, International, Inc. *(952 East Baseline Road, Mesa, AZ 85204).* I got a 5.5-inch barrel with a screw-on compensator, but they make un-compensated models, as well. The barrel came with a National Match bushing, a no. 2 link, and link pin.

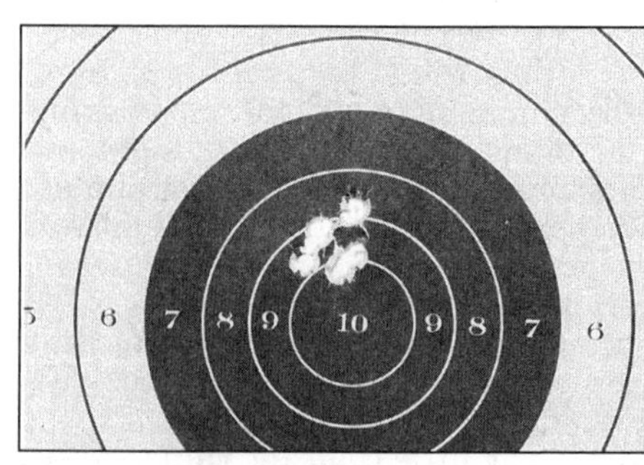

Representative 400 COR-BON group, shot with 155-grain Hornady XTP and 10.3 grains of Winchester Action Pistol; velocity, 1330 fps; range, 25 yards.

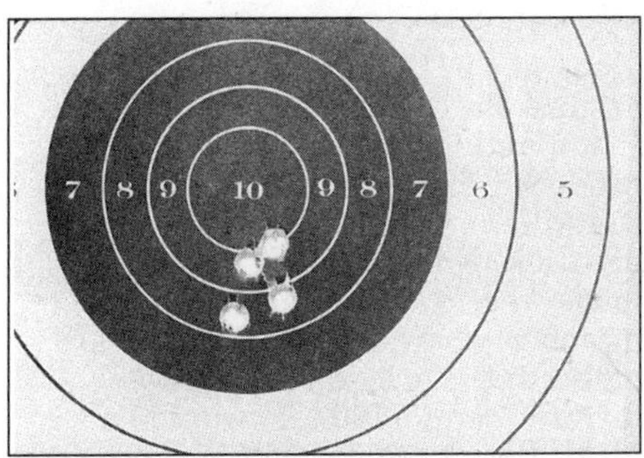

Representative 400 COR-BON group, shot with 165-grain Sierra JHC and 9.8 grains of VihtaVuori N-350 powder; velocity, 1274 fps; range, 25 yards.

Representative 400 COR-BON group, shot with 175-grain cast SWC bullet and 7.3 grains of Hodgdon's Universal Clays powder; velocity, 1179 fps; range, 25 yards.

The receptacle of the new barrel was a 1992-vintage Colt "Combat Elite" pistol. This is one of the first "enhanced" models, and has downed many an NRA falling plate in the past five years. It is very accurate in it's 45 guise, so I had great expectations for the 400 barrel. Installation of 1911 barrels isn't my favorite pastime *(did I say "simple" re-barreling?)*, but eventually, it was done, and it works.

A set of Hornady's "Custom-Grade New Dimension" dies was used for all reloading chores, and they are excellent dies. A Lyman T-Mag II turret press speeded things up considerably. About the only fly in the 400's soup is that you have to lube the cases before sizing. Carbide dies are available, but they're rather expensive. My first test loads were assembled in some 45 ACP cases that I necked-down. While these worked OK, it was a pain. Starline, Inc. *(1300 West Henry Street, Sedalia, MO 65301)* produces ready-made 400 COR-BON cases, with the correct head-stamp, and this is the way to go. Uniform and tough, these are superb cases in every respect. 400 COR-BON factory loads are put up in Starline cases.

COR-BON says that the best results are with bullets weighing 165-grains or less. I can only assume that this admonition is due to the goal of very high velocities, or perhaps the very short neck *(0.15-inch)* on the 400 COR-BON case. The factory literature states that the 400 COR-BON headspaces off the shoulder, and that one should monitor this dimension carefully during case forming or sizing.

Colt Combat Elite pistol with Accu-Match International 5.5-inch compensated 400 COR-BON barrel, and Tasco 1x22 pistol scope.

I took a three-fold approach to load development. First, I wanted some master-blaster JHP bullet loads to tame the toughest "varmint." Secondly, I would need a load with cast semi-wadcutter bullets that make "major" power factor *(PF)* for IPSC-type shooting. Lastly, I needed a low-recoil load for lead semi-wadcutters that makes a PF of 125-130 for NRA action shooting. As it turned out, each of these objectives was easy to achieve—especially the NRA load.

All tests were shot from a rest with a 2x scope or a 1x dot sight at 25 yards. Some of these groups were not great, but I am not the world's best benchrester with a pistol, and in these trials I was more interested in getting to the particular velocity goal for the load in question. This is also the reason that some group sizes were not recorded. With the final loads selected, accuracy for my intended purposes was quite acceptable. Jacketed bullets chosen to test were those that have given me such good results in the 10mm auto and 40 S&W, namely, the 155-grain Hornady XTP, and the Sierra 165-grain JHC. And of course, I had to try some of the light 135-grain Sierra JHC bullets.

COR-BON'S literature states that they use non-canister powders that are not available to the handloader, and that *"it is not possible to duplicate factory"* velocities with handloads. Based on my tests, one can come pretty close, at least with 165 grain bullets. The 135-grain JHC bullet was a different story. The COR-BON box for their 135-grain factory load *(dated 3-20-97)* lists a velocity of 1450 fps. Could be, but in my 5.5-inch comp barrel, this load clocked a blistering 1544 fps *(!)*, with an SD of only 6. Recoil was very sharp, and the velocity of the fired cases made them a lethal weapon. This is **hot** ammo; a few primers were extruded into the firing pin hole, and sheared off. But it is accurate. More than one

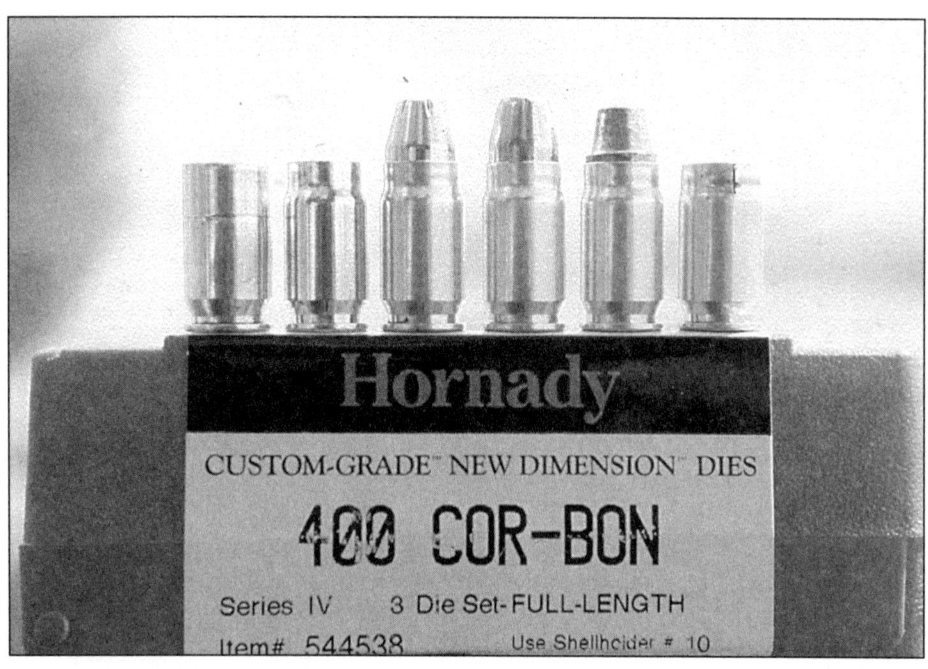

Hornady dies were used for handloads: *(from left)* parent 45 case; loaded rounds with 155-grain Hornady XTP, 165-grain Sierra JHC, and 175-grain cast SWC; and a fired 400 case; note split neck.

group shot with it was less than 2 inches at 25 yards. A 1911 loaded with a magazine of this stuff would quell the most determined adversary.

Loading data supplied by COR-BON along with their product information lists 135-, 150/155-, and 165-grain bullets. My test loads were based on the COR-BON data, but also included several powders not shown by COR-BON. Powder selection boiled down rather quickly to a few slow burners that have worked well in another bottle-necked pistol case of my acquaintance, the 357 SIG. Given the spectacular performance of that 9mm cartridge, I had great expectations for the new 10mm number.

Winchester's Action Pistol, Alliant's Power Pistol, N-350 from VihtaVuori, AA-5 and A-7 from Accurate Arms, and Hodgdon's Universal Clays were tried for the jacketed and major power loads, and Winchester 231 was used to develop the minor power plate loads. Starline cases and Winchester large pistol primers were used for all loads reported in the tables. I should mention that the standard deviations *(SD)* of the better loads were under 25 fps. This gives coefficient of variation *(CV)* of about 2% for the high velocity loads, and about 3% for the lighter loads.

Table 1 shows the results of the load trials. Although I don't use lightweight 10mm bullets much, my trials with the 135-grain Sierra JHC bullet were a real eye-opener. This bullet shot great; perhaps now we know why COR-BON uses them in their factory loads. I was able to exceed 1400 fps with it with three powders: WAP, N-350, and Power Pistol. Accuracy was outstanding with WAP and N-350, with groups under an inch. Power Pistol was no slouch with a 1.46-inch group average. Energies of the top loads approximated 600 fpe but, as the COR-BON folks predicted, I couldn't even come close to the factory load velocity of 1544 fps.

Hornady XTP bullets just seem to shoot well, no matter what the weight or caliber, and the 10mm 155-grainers were no exception. At velocities above 1300 fps, accuracy and uniformity were very good. With 10.3 grains of Winchester Action Pistol, velocity was a sizzling 1320 fps, and 25-yard groups averaged 2.26 inches. A charge of 10.3 grains of Alliant's new Power Pistol boosted the 155-grain XTPs along at 1330 fps, exactly as claimed for factory loads. This load was slightly less accurate – but accurate enough. Energies of both of these loads were above 600 fpe.

The 165-grain Sierra JHC bullets were slightly more accurate than the lighter Hornadys, and also fast. With 9.8 grains of N-350, this bullet raced along at 1271 fps, and shot 1.26-inch groups. Both 9.8 grains of Power Pistol and 9.9 grains of WAP produced 1250 fps, but the load with the Alliant powder was more accurate. Energy levels with these loads were 573 fpe and up. In action matches where jacketed bullets are allowed, those loads with power factors around 180-190 would be ideal. Recoil is relatively modest, for the power level, due to the effectiveness of the comp.

COR-BON literature suggests that a "tight bullet crimp be used." I experienced no problems using jacketed bullets without a cannelure, but for maximum reliability, it might be advisable to roll a crimping cannelure on jacketed bullets to be used for defense or hunting loads. I can tell you that if you try to put too much crimp on a jacketed bullet load, the case will buckle at the shoulder, usually enough that the round won't chamber.

There is an interesting feature of the 400 COR-BON case that is, I presume, by design. Note in the accompanying photo that fired cases have a rather large neck, with a little "turn-in" right at the case mouth, like a left-over crimp. The neck diameter of a fired case is about 0.448-inch, while the neck of an expanded new case is 0.419-inch. The COR-BON case drawing shows a neck diameter of 0.423-inch; my loaded rounds mike 0.424-inch. This amounts to quite a bit of resizing, but everything seems to work. I experienced only a few split necks after many reloadings; such a split is also shown in the photo.

Due to my good experience with Hodgdon's Universal Clays in the 357 SIG, I concentrated on it for major power loads with cast semi-wadcutter bullets in the 400 COR-BON, and was not disappointed. A PF of 175 was easy to obtain with both 155- and 175-grain SWC bullets. With the 155-grain E&E bullets, a charge of 7.3 grains *(or higher)* of Universal Clays made major. Probably the best load with this bullet and powder was 7.5-grains at 1170, and a PF of 181, and great accuracy; groups averaged 1.28-inches. I also tried AA-5 with this light bullet. SDs were high, but the accuracy was good. A charge of 9.5 grains of AA-5 produced a velocity of 1142 fps, 1.89-inch groups, and a PF of 177.

Turning to the 175-grain Lane SWC bullets, Universal once again came out on top. A charge of 6.5 grains produced a PF of 188, but accuracy wasn't as good as with 7.3 grains. At a velocity of 1179 fps, this load grouped well (1.34 inches), recoil was indistinguishable from the lighter load, and, with a PF of 206, it smacks a steel target with authority. As with the lighter bullets, AA-5 registered high velocities and great accuracy. A load of 8.0 grains had a velocity of 1003, grouped into 1.36 inches, but barely made major at 175.5. A better choice is 9.0 grains of AA-5, which gave a velocity of 1121 fps, a PF of 196, and a group average of 1.16 inches. With a SD of only 23 *(CV = 2.05%)*, this load is a keeper.

The plan for the minor power loads was simple. In the 45 ACP, I shoot 175-grain SWCs at 734 fps, for a PF of 128. So a 10mm 155-grain at 830 fps, or a 175-grain at about 740 would be the ticket.

Winchester 231 is a very uniform powder in light loads. After loading up and down the spectrum, I settled on 4.3 grains with the 155-grain bullets. This load clocked 815 fps, grouped into 1.25 inches, and had a PF of 126. Good enough.

With the 175-grain bullets, a charge of 4.0 grains of 231 gave a velocity of about 730 fps. Groups ran about 1.50 inches, and the PF was about 127.8. Recoil in the comp gun with this load is about like a 22 rimfire; it is so low that one can use all of the allotted time aiming, rather than trying to find the dot again!

Ah, plate load perfection. Or so I thought. The problem is that, while this load will cycle the gun with a 6-lb. recoil spring, the force of this light recoil spring will not reliably strip a cartridge off of the magazine – more on this later.

If I had to pick the best powders for this cartridge, I'd have to go with Action Pistol or Power Pistol for the high-power loads, although AA-7 also worked well. Of course, good old WW 231 was the easy pick for the light loads. Hodgdon's Universal Clays is pretty darn good with anything, though. Universal Clays is, well, unique.

The COR-BON case drawing shows a cartridge overall length *(COL)* of 1.225 inches. I used 1.220 inches for the Sierra 135s, 1.235 inches for the Hornady 155s, 1.240 inches for the Sierra 165s, and 1.200 inches for all cast bullet loads, and experienced no feeding problems that could be attributed to cartridge lengths.

Table 1. 400 COR-BON Load Data

Jacketed Bullet Loads

Bullet: Sierra JHC 135-gr. **COL =1.220-in.**

Powder	Charge	Vel.	Group	Power Factor	M.E. (ft-lbs)	Comments
UNIV.	8.0	1208	1.66	163.1	438	good load
	8.5	1325	0.75	178.9	526	very accurate
WAP	10.0	1293	1.08	174.6	501	uniform ballistics
	10.5	1338	1.25	180.6	537	with WAP
	10.7	1409	0.95	190.2	595	working max.
N-350	9.8	1371	1.65	185.1	564	
	10.3	1420	0.85	191.7	605	highest vel. recorded
P.P.	10.0	1346	1.73	181.7	543	
	10.5	1419	1.46	191.6	604	working max.
AA-7	13.0	1258	1.18	169.8	475	
	13.5	1332	0.94	179.8	532	good load
	14.0	1380	2.54	186.3	571	

Bullet: Hornady XTP 155 -gr. **COL =1.235-in.**

Powder	Charge	Vel.	Group	Power Factor	M.E. (ft-lbs)	Comments
UNIV.	7.5	1115	1.95	172.8	428	good everyday load
WAP	9.4	1152	2.25	178.6	457	
	10.0	1221	2.22	189.3	513	good major power load
	10.3	1320	2.26	204.6	600	max. do not exceed
N-350	9.4	1165	2.21	180.6	467	both good loads
	9.7	1278	2.32	198.1	562	
P.P.	9.4	1177	n.r.	182.4	477	mild
	10.0	1260	1.10	195.3	547	
	10.3	1330	2.56	206.2	609	max. do not exceed
AA-7	13.0	1145	2.06	177.5	451	mild
	13.2	1208	0.71	187.2	502	accurate load
	13.7	1271	2.74	197.0	556	max.

Bullet: Sierra JHC 165 -gr. **COL = 1.240-in.**

Powder	Charge	Vel.	Group	Power Factor	M.E. (ft-lbs)	Comments
UNIV.	7.3	1097	1.52	181.0	441	mild, good load
WAP	9.1	1104	n.r.	182.2	447	mild
	9.6	1145	1.16	188.9	480	good load
	9.9	1250	2.28	206.3	573	
N-350	9.1	1127	n.r.	186.0	465	mild
	9.5	1237	1.77	204.1	561	
	9.8	1274	1.26	210.2	595	good load, max.
P.P	9.6	1227	1.18	202.5	552	
	9.8	1250	1.54	206.3	573	
AA-7	12.7	1158	0.85	191.1	491	most accurate load
	13.2	1210	1.08	199.7	537	

Which brings us to the topic of proper functioning with the various power level loads in a compensated pistol. The Accu-Match compensator is very efficient; a load that will cycle the gun without the comp on won't even think about ejecting a case with the comp screwed on. With the high-performance jacketed bullet loads, and with the major power lead SWC loads, a 15-lb. recoil spring in my pistol with the comp gave 100% functioning.

For the minor power loads, it was

Table 1: 400 COR-BON Load Data, ***continued***

Cast Bullet Loads:

Bullet:E&E SWC 155-gr. COL =1.200-in.

Powder	Charge	Vel.	Group	Power Factor	M.E. (ft-lbs)	Comments
UNIV.	7.3	1139	1.58	176.5	447	
	7.4	1180	2.16	182.9	479	
	7.5	1170	1.28	181.4	471	good major power load
	8.0	1255	1.54	194.5	542	recoil sharp
A-5	9.0	1090	1.87	169.0	409	high SDs w/ AA-5
	9.5	1142	1.89	177.0	449	major power, max.
WW-231	4.0	802	n.r.	124.3	221	very mild loads, &
	4.2	794	n.r.	123.1	217	good functioning w/
	4.3	815	1.25	126.3	229	6-lb. recoil spring
	5.0	957	n.r.	148.3	315	

Bullet: Lane SWC 175 -gr. COL =1.200-in.

Powder	Charge	Vel.	Group	Power Factor	M.E. (ft-lbs)	Comments
UNIV.	5.8	878	1.38	153.7	300	
	6.2	996	2.36	174.3	386	
	6.5	1072	2.16	187.6	447	
	7.3	1179	1.34	206.3	540	max. do not exceed
AA-5	8.0	1003	1.36	175.5	391	
	9.0	1121	1.16	196.2	488	good load, mild press.
WW-231	3.8	694	n.r.	121.5	187	too light
	4.0	730	1.61	127.8	207	use 6-lb. spring
	4.2	776	1.93	135.8	234	use 8-lb. spring
	4.5	795	0.95	139.1	246	use 8-lb. spring
	4.6	860	1.79	150.5	287	use 10-lb. spring

COR-BON Factory Load: COL = 1.216-in.

Bullet	Vel.	Group	Power Factor	M.E. (ft-lbs)	Comments
135-gr. JHP	1544	1.99	193.0	662	hot, but accurate; some pierced primers

Note: *All loads were fired in a Colt Combat Elite pistol with Accu-Match International 5.5-in. bbl. with screw-on compensator. All handloads used Starline cases and Winchester large pistol primers. Group sizes are the average of at least three 5-shot groups at 25 yards. Range temperatures were 50-55 degrees F. n.r. = not recorded.*

a different story. None of the wimp loads would work at all with the 15-lb. spring. The lowest velocity that would function reliably with a 10-lb. spring was 860 fps with the 175-grain SWC bullet. This velocity was achieved with 4.6 grains of WW-231. This load shot well, but at a power factor of 150, it was neither fish nor fowl. At 795 fps with 4.5 grains of 231, an 8-lb. spring would usually eject fired cases. My chosen NRA action load with a 175-grain SWC and 4.0 grains of 231 at about 730 fps would cycle the gun with a 6-lb. spring *(with the comp)*, but this light recoil spring would not strip a cartridge off of the magazine.

The solution to this conundrum is to install lighter magazine springs. The standard factory spring for 7-round magazines is 9.5-lb. As most gun owners know, if you need a gun spring, you call the W. C. Wolff Co. *(P.O. Box 1, Newton Square, PA 19073)*. Wolff makes reduced power magazine springs in 6-, 7-, and 8-lb. ratings. The nice folks at Wolff will tell you that these are only for 7-round magazines, not the 8-round mags that now come with Colt pistols. Could be, but when I installed a Wolff 6-lb. spring in a 8-round Colt factory magazine, the 6-lb. recoil spring would strip a cartridge off of it slicker than scum off of a Louisiana swamp. If one has to have the absolute minimum recoil with a minor power load, this is the way to go. I use it, and it works. One has to be careful not to mix the magazines with light springs with those with full-power springs, or malfunctions will result. Different-colored base pads are the easy solution. All this is no big deal, but it is a factor to consider when building up and using one of these comp pistols. The recoil of this compensated pistol is still very light, and double-taps were indeed fast. In fact, the reticle hardly seems to move on the target. The handling characteristics of this shooting system are excellent, it is quite pleasant to shoot with either major or minor loads, and it is sufficiently accurate that any misses are strictly operator error.

Overall, I think that a 400 COR-BON cartridge in a tricked-out pistol – with the appropriate loads – is a prime candidate for both NRA action matches and IPSO/USPCA-type shooting, or in a uncompensated version for practical class matches. Minor power loads are accurate, and have negligible recoil. Major power loads are easy to whip up, and the bottleneck cases sure don't hurt feeding, either. In a carry gun, full-power JHP loads would certainly ruin a bad guy's day in a hurry. The 400 COR-BON cartridge is powerful, versatile, accurate, and reliable; and the guns, dies, and components are readily available. This adds up to a pretty alluring combination, don't you think? ●

SELECTING The RIGHT BULLET For BIG GAME

by Thomas C. Tabor

Even if you shoot the best-made rifle and scope, practice until you are able to shoot the eyelid off a prairie dog at 400 yards off-hand, you could fail miserably when that *once in a lifetime trophy* appears out of nowhere—if you don't select your hunting bullet wisely.

Ironically, the same shooters that expend enormous amounts of money to surround themselves with the best possible hunting equipment sometimes pinch pennies when it comes to purchasing their hunting bullets or ammunition. Buying a generic brand of aspirin to save a dime or two is one thing–risking your hunting success by purchasing poorly-constructed bullets is quite another matter and a choice you will-in all likelihood-come to regret.

While many hunters are simply trying to save a little money by purchasing bargain-bin bullets, other shooters make the same mistake, but for different reasons. At one time or another, they may have had some degree of success with a particular

The Swift A-Frame is a heavy-jacketed bullet with an integral barrier built into the jacket to separate the front and base lead cores.

This mushroomed Norma Oryx 180-grain bullet was retrieved from a mule deer shot with a 308 Norma Magnum at 350 yards. The Oryx performed flawlessly and retained 170 grains of its weight.

This Nosler Partition 180-grain bullet was retrieved from an African Nyala bull shot at 200 yards with a 300 Winchester Magnum rifle. The shot was broadside and went through the lungs. The Partition retained 51 percent of its original weight.

bullet and, as a result, have ever since wrongfully attributed their hunting achievement to that ammo. I have several friends that fall into this category and, when questioned about their choice of ammunition, their response usually goes something like this: *"If the bullet worked -- why change? It put meat on the meat-pole, didn't it......how could you improve on that?"*

In many cases the bullet these individuals cherish so dearly probably didn't have to work too hard to accomplish its goal. It may have been the result of a perfect broadside shot, requiring little in the way of penetration. Perhaps the shot was simply a fluke, where a piece of exploded bullet jacket mysteriously and miraculously found its way to just the right spot. What's the old cliche........ *"sometimes even a blind hog finds a root"*. Perhaps the trophy animal in question wasn't really much of a trophy at all, but rather a yearling whitetail with about as much meat on its scrawny carcass as a grain-fed jackrabbit. No matter what the circumstances were, what if conditions were not perfect? What if that tiny whitetail turned out to be a 300-pound mule deer buck in its prime that was heading to the high country in a real hurry, or a muscle-toned bull elk sporting massive seven points to a side antlers and tipping the scales at close to a half a ton, or a crusty old bull moose determined to survive no matter what? What if the only option you had was to drive your bullet through a shield of armor-like bone just to reach the animal's vitals? Would the end result have been the same—and would the hunter have come away with the same positive opinion of the bullet's performance?

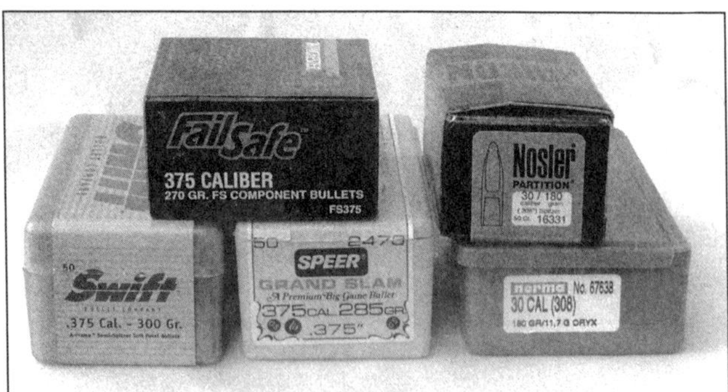

These are just a few of the quality hunting bullets currently on the market.

These are examples of typical bullet blowup. *(Left-Right)*: *1)* Remington factory loaded Core-Lokt bullet - Blacktail buck deer shot in the head at 50 yards; *2)* Remington factory loaded Core-Lokt bullet - Blacktail buck deer shot through the shoulder at 125 yards; and *3)* Federal factory-loaded softpoint bullet - mule deer shot through the shoulder at 150 yards.

Dangerous game, like this Cape buffalo, requires a bullet that will hold together and penetrate deeply. If your bullet doesn't reach the vital organs of the animal, your life could be in jeopardy. Bullet selection for Cape buffalo is a controversial issue, but many hunters prefer a combination of full-metal-jacketed bullets to ensure deep penetration, and top-quality softpoint bullets.

Selecting a good hunting bullet can be a bit of a challenge, and many of the bullet manufacturers have done nothing but add to that confusion. Virtually every bullet advertisement, except for those specifically dedicated to shooters of paper, carries some sort of assurance that their bullets are of *'premium hunting quality'*. Of course, the ads almost always contain a huge, awe-inspiring picture of the perfect expanded bullet. Ironically, the manufacturers seldom divulge under what conditions that perfectly-mushroomed bullet was formed.

Producing a quality hunting bullet is not an easy task. One of the most difficult and crucial challenges a manufacturer faces lies in the process of bonding the bullet's outer jacket to its lead core. If not done properly, the bullet will surely come apart upon impact. Aside from bonding, if the jacket material is too heavy–or too hard–the bullet may hold together, but not expand adequately. On the other hand, if the jacket is not heavy enough and tough enough—the bullet could come apart, losing its ability to penetrate.

In essence, the issue of expansion is a two-edged sword. We need good frontal expansion to produce a significant degree of tissue damage and shock, by transferring the bullet's energy into the target. As the frontal area of the bullet increases, friction and drag will increase as well. Eventually this slows the forward movement of the bullet and it stops, but hopefully not until the bullet has reached its objective—the vitals. The best-case scenario would be for the bullet to hold together, retain a high degree of its original weight, expand to about double its original diameter, yet drive deep enough to reach the vitals of the animal no matter what it has to penetrate along the way.

Without doubt one of the worst

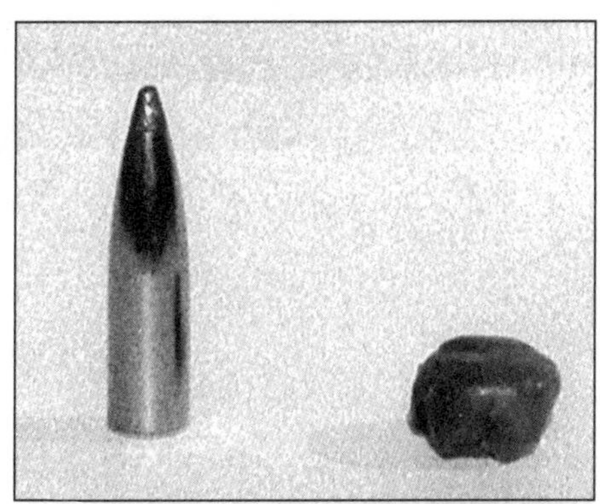

This Nosler Partition 180-grain bullet was retrieved from an African Blue Wildebeest bull shot at 200 yards with a 300 Winchester Magnum. The shot was broadside and went through the lungs. The Partition retained Nosler's typical 60 percent of its original weight.

possible scenarios in big game hunting is for a bullet to shed its jacket upon impact. When this occurs it usually results in a dramatic explosion that results in the once-dynamic projectile being transformed into worthless small pieces of shrapnel.

Most hunting bullets today possess either a single lead core, or two lead cores. In the case of the dual core bullets the cores may be either partially, or completely separated from one another. A gilding metal jacket, most often made of a copper-zinc alloy, serves to hold the bullet together.

Lead is used for bullet cores because it is heavy, soft, relatively inexpensive, stable and easily manipulated. The hardness of the lead will vary depending upon how much antimony the manufacturer adds. In some cases, particularly the dual-core *(partition-style)* bullets, the hardness of the lead may vary within the bullet itself, with softer lead sometimes used for the bullet tip. The softer tip section encourages frontal expansion, while the structural strength of the harder lead in the base helps retain weight.

The 'X-Bullet,' made by Barnes, is the exception to the above. Whereas most bullets possess some sort of an inner lead core, the X-Bullet is formed solely from a copper alloy, with no internal lead.

Jacket metal thickness will vary, sometimes substantially, from one bullet design to another. In addition, the jacket may be heavier at the rear of the bullet, tapering to thinner metal at the tip. Designing bullet jackets in this manner also promotes frontal expansion and retained weight.

Bullets possessing dual internal cores, like the Nosler Partition *(not to be confused with Nosler Solid Base and Ballistic Tip bullets)*, Swift A-Frame and Speer Grand Slam have become very popular for hunting big game, and justifiably so. These are fine hunting bullets that will almost always hold together upon impact, deliver good expansion and retain a large percentage of their original weight.

Even though Speer's Grand Slam contains two core compartments, its

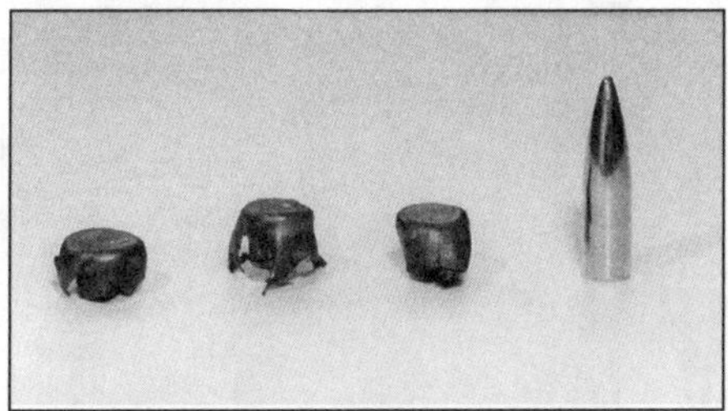

These Nosler Partition 180-grain bullets were all shot from a rifle chambered in 300 Winchester Magnum. *(l to r)*: *1)* Blue Wildebeest bull shot in the shoulder/lungs at 200 yards - 60 percent retained weight; *2)* Black Wildebeest bull shot through the chest at 150 yards - 61 percent retained weight; and *3)* mule deer buck shot between the shoulder blades from above at 60 yards - 61 percent retained weight.

The author's wife took this fine mule deer buck at 350 yards with a 308 Norma Magnum and a handloaded 180-grain Norma Oryx bullet. The retrieved bullet responsible for this kill can be seen in the photo. When retrieved on the far side of the buck, it retained 94 percent of its original weight.

design differs from the partition-style Nosler and the Swift A-Frame. Speer utilizes a swaged ring, made from the jacket metal, to encircle the juncture of the two cores *(as can be seen in the drawing)*. The Nosler Partition and the Swift A-Frame cores are separated from one another by a thick barrier, integral to the jacket.

I found the dual-core bullets, the Nosler and Swift in particular, to be exceptionally tough bullets that hold together well and produce very consistent results over a broad range of velocities and conditions. On impact they do often sacrifice some, or all, of the lead in the front core compartment. Even when the frontal lead is lost, these bullets will still retain around 60 percent of their original weight. The goal these manufacturers have set for themselves is consistency of performance, no matter what types of game, or field conditions, are encountered. Velocity and energy levels will drop off as the range to target increases. Consequently, for the hunters faced with varying conditions, a dual-core *(partition-style)* bullet is certainly an excellent choice. I like to think of these bullets as proven standbys you can always count on, regardless what shooting conditions are encountered. They will produce good expansion, excellent penetration—and do this consistently and uniformly with about 2/3 of their original weight each and every shot.

Like the word 'premium,' another term often misused in the bullet business is 'bonded core.' This term refers to adhesion between the jacket material and the lead core. Bonding two distinctly different metals together is no easy task. If you question how difficult that might be, ask a welder to weld a piece of steel to a piece of aluminum sometime, or a piece of copper to a lead fishing sinker. Undoubtedly, after explaining the basics of metallurgy to you, he will send you packing.

In years past, successfully bonding lead to copper was almost an impossibility; however, great advances have been made in this area. Nevertheless, a wise shooter should view all 'bonded core' claims with a bit of skepticism. This term, by itself, provides no assurance that the bonding process used will result in keeping your bullet together.

One of the best bonded-core bullets I have used was introduced in the U.S. only recently by the Swedish company, Norma. Norma essentially

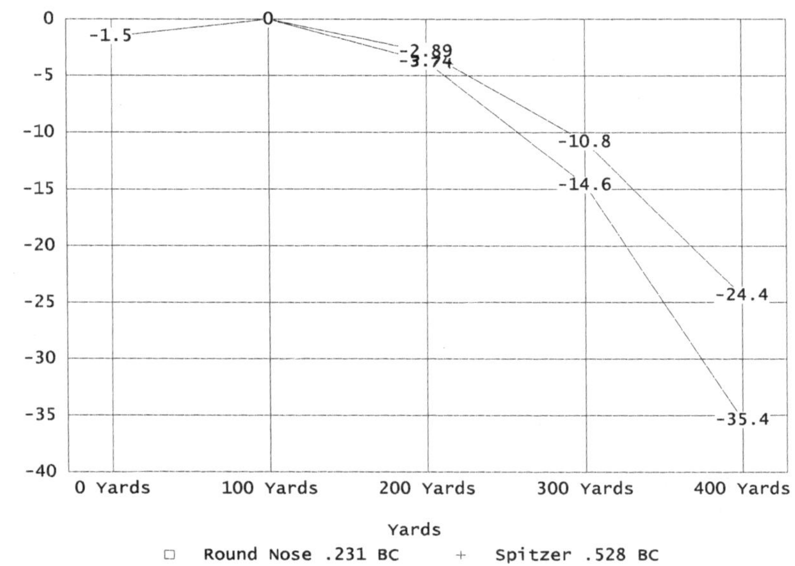

Graph #1: **In this example a 180-grain, 30-caliber blunt-nose bullet has been compared to a streamlined spitzer-style bullet of the same caliber and weight. The difference in trajectory should be enough incentive for any hunter to avoid using a round- or flat-nose bullet.**

The moose is one of the largest of North American game and requires a good quality, deep-penetrating bullet.

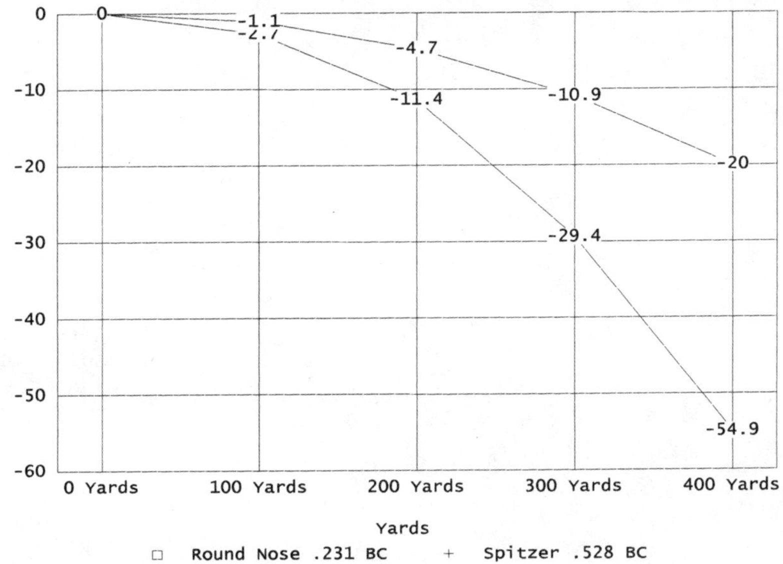

Graph #2: **Using the same example of two like-weight bullets *(180-grain .308-inch diameter)*, one with a ballistic coefficient value of .231 and the other of .528, we see a dramatic difference in how even a moderate 20 mph cross-wind affects the bullet's horizontal drift.**

took a leave of absence from the U.S. marketplace for several decades, but has returned. Several new products have been added during their absence and one in particular has the potential of serving the American big-game hunter extremely well.

Norma's newly developed bullet called the 'Oryx' is a true bonded-core bullet that will hold together, even when sent out the muzzle at magnum velocities. The Oryx is available both in the Norma line of loaded ammunition and as a reloading component. I have used the Oryx in my own handloads to take several animals under varying conditions, and find this particular bullet to perform flawlessly: excellent retained weight, good expansion delivering extensive tissue damage—all coupled with deep penetration. The 180-grain Oryx left the muzzle at over 3,000 fps from my 308 Norma Magnum. Because the Oryx has been available in the States only for a short time, my testing and use is relatively limited. However, I found its performance to be exceptional based the three mule deer taken thus far. Certainly more testing is required on heavier game, but indications are the Oryx will out-perform many of the other so-called 'premium hunting bullets' and, compared to the competition, the Oryx is priced very competitively. Currently the Oryx is offered in a limited number of calibers and weights; however, the company is promising to increase their selections.

Even though the impact performance of a big-game bullet is ultimately important, it is certainly not the only consideration. In order for a bullet to do its thing in an animal, it must first reach the target consistently and accurately under varying field conditions. Not all bullets are created equal when it comes to how the natural elements will affect their flight. Some bullets will shoot flatter, some will better resist cross-wind drift and some will retain a greater amount of energy at long range.

In my opinion, one of the most misplaced beliefs common in the hunting world today is that a round- or flat-nose bullet will some*how 'buck the brush'* and hold together better than a bullet of pointed design. Believing this myth, some shooters have significantly sacrificed bullet performance in other areas, to no real benefit. A few years back, I conducted extensive experimentation along these lines involving three vastly different cartridges: 300 Winchester Magnum, 30-30 Winchester and a 22-250 Remington. The tests were conducted in an effort to determine what effect there would be on the flight of a bullet after

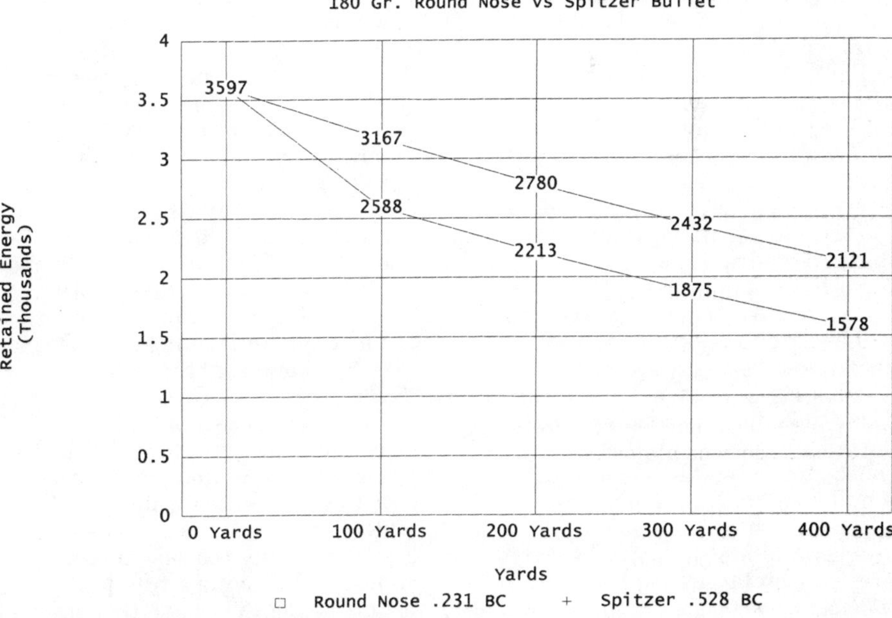

Graph #3: **Clearly a pointed streamlined bullet, like a spitzer *(top line)*, retains a greater degree of energy than a round- or flat-nose bullet *(bottom line)*. While some people feel the reduction of energy is more of a concern in the case of long-range shooting, it is interesting to note that the largest deviation between these two bullets occurs in the first 100 yards.**

This Blue Wildebeest was taken with a 300 Winchester Magnum handloaded with a Nosler Partition bullet. The retrieved bullet can be seen in one of the accompanying photos.

encountering an obstacle, like a small tree limb. Going into the testing I believed, as so many others do, that the round-nose bullets would out-perform the pointed spitzer-style bullets. I couldn't have been more wrong!

For the tests, hardwood doweling was used to simulate the tree limbs and brush of a real hunting situation. The doweling was arranged so the bullets would be forced to encounter at least one dowel during its flight to the target. In virtually very case there was no major difference in flight deflection between the bullet styles *(pointed vs. blunt nose)*, and while there was some measurable differences between the cartridges, it was not significant overall. In all cases the effect of encountering the doweling was essentially non-consequential. This is not to say that a bullet can clip off a limb just beyond the muzzle, then travel several hundred yards and still be precisely on target. If, however, a bullet *(blunt- or pointed-nose style)* encounters a limb of, say, 1/4-inch diameter within 30 or 40 feet of its intended target—even a pointed bullet will experience little deflection.

Ironically, the testing revealed a flaw in the chambering that many people believe to be the ultimate in 'brush bustin' - the 30-30. Factory-loaded ammunition was used and, in virtually every instance, whether the bullets came into contact with the doweling or not, the bullets literally exploded upon impact. At the slightest contact, the bullets came apart, and did so quickly and violently. Even at the slow velocities generated by the 30-30, the jackets were ripped loose and the lead cores were instantly fragmented. This is the perfect example of why a shooter must choose his bullets wisely if they are to perform well while hunting.

A complete report on my testing can be found in Handloader's Digest, 12th Edition under the title of *"Bullets Can Bust Brush"*.

In areas other than bullet deflection, when we compare the performance of round- or flat-nose bullets with pointed, spitzer-style bullets, drastic differences can be seen. For safety reasons, a person using a rifle having a tubular magazine does not have the option of shooting a pointed bullet, but for other types of rifle designs, there is seldom any legitimate justification for using a bullet other than one of pointed, streamlined styling. **Graphs 1 through 3** provide a spectacular comparison between two 180-grain, 30-caliber bullets *(blunt vs spitzer)* started at the same velocity. As can clearly be seen the spitzer-style bullet dramatically out-performs the blunt-nose bullet in all categories: energy retention, trajectory and wind drift.

The bullet's ballistic coefficient and sectional density values determine how your bullet will resist the effects of nature's influences. Sectional density value *(SD)* is displayed as a 3-digit number. Essentially, the SD of a bullet is determined by taking the bullet weight *(in pounds)* and dividing it by the area of the bullet base *(in square inches)*. Without getting into extensive and boring details of how SD affects your bullet's flight, let's just say that the higher the SD number, the better the bullet will retain velocity, the higher its retained energy will be and the greater its penetration will be.

A long thin projectile will penetrate better than a short fat one. So, assuming two bullets are started at the same muzzle velocity, one a 100-grain 243 Winchester bullet and the other a 100-grain 30-06—the 243 will, in all likelihood, out-penetrate the 30-06. The lesson of this story is a simple one—don't try to shoot too light a bullet in any caliber. For that matter, under normal circumstances a shooter should avoid using extremely heavy bullets as well. For any caliber there is a common range of weights that are best suited for that particular bore diameter and a wise shooter should stay somewhere within that normal range.

Next, and possibly even more important than sectional density, is the bullet's ballistic coefficient *(BC)*. The BC value of a bullet is also shown as a 3-digit number. The official definition for ballistic coefficient would go something like this: The ballistic coefficient of a bullet is the ratio of its weight *(in pounds)* to the product of the square of the bullet's diameter, and its form *(shape)* factor. Pretty confusing, huh? Well, let's just say the higher the BC value -- the better your bullet will resist the effects of wind drift, retain more of its original energy and resist the effects of the gravitational pull. A pointed spitzer-style bullet will always possess a much higher BC value than a bullet of the same weight with flat- or round-nose design. Again, the graphics provide a pretty dramatic representation of how a bullet with a good BC value will out-perform a bullet that carries a lower value.

There will always be a difference of opinion as to whether a hunting bullet should deliver total penetration, or whether it is better for the bullet to remain inside the target animal. Certainly no one could make a valid argument against the benefit of transferring as much as possible of the bullet's energy to the target and, if the bullet should exit, that some energy will be lost. The important thing is that your bullet must be capable of reaching the vitals, no matter what the conditions are, and that the bullet does enough damage along the way to disrupt the bodily functions of the animal.

Unfortunately, every hunting situation is different. For example, the size of the animal, the distance the bullet must travel to the target and how much bone and resistance it will encounter along the way will all have a direct bearing on how deep your bullet will penetrate. In addition, as the bullet flight distance increases, the energy of the bullet will drop off, affecting its ability to penetrate. **Graph #3** illustrates such energy loss.

Just because a bullet exits its target is not necessarily a bad thing as long as the bullet performs well along the way. If the bullet stays intact, retains a significant degree of its original weight, experiences good expansion and, of course, makes contact with the animal's vitals - you can't really ask for much more.

Good bullet selection is even more important today than in years past simply because of the current trend of faster, flatter-shooting cartridges. It's difficult enough to keep a bullet intact at the speeds of the old-time cartridges like the 30-06 and 30-30, but when we load the same bullet into the 300 Winchester Magnum, boosting its velocity by 300 or 400 fps - disaster can easily occur if a good quality bullet isn't selected.

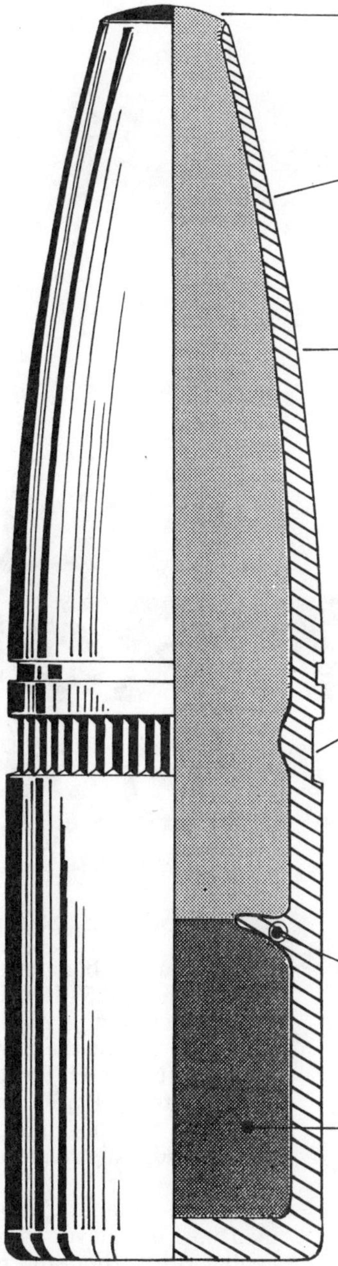

Speer's Grand Slam bullets contain a dual lead core. The back portion of the core is formed from 5% antimony lead alloy, while the tip section is made from much softer lead. The jacket thickness is thinner at the tip to encourage good frontal expansion. A swaged ring of jacket metal is used as a partial barrier to separate and secure the two core sections.*(Speer)*

There are a lot of good quality hunting bullets available today, but you can't always accept the claims of manufacturers solely on their own merits. You should do your homework and carefully evaluate what features are necessary to provide good performance under a wide range of field conditions. If you approach your bullet selection in this manner, when that 'once-in-a-lifetime' trophy presents itself - you will be ready. ●

The 257 Roberts, Not Dead Yet

by Scott E. Stoppelman

A while back, my Dad announced he was going to have a new custom rifle built on a Mauser 98 action and stocked in nice walnut. The chambering, 250 Savage. The intended use of this rifle was hunting deer, and possibly elk. Elk? Yes I thought it a bit light, too. But you see Pop suffers from bursitis in both shoulders so he wanted a rifle that was capable, but one that wouldn't slap the shoulder as much as a more likely elk cartridge would.

Over the years many hunters have come to recognize the ability of some of the smaller calibers, in the hands of a good rifleman, to cleanly harvest big game. I asked Pop why not a 257 Roberts, or maybe a 25-06 Remington. Well, the 257 is okay says he but the 25-06 might kick a bit too much for his shoulder. At any rate, as Pop's hunting days are about over his choice of calibers and cartridges is rendered somewhat moot.

A short time later it occurred to me that I had never owned a 25-caliber rifle either, and reasoned it was likely time to rectify the situation.

Already having good rifles in 280 Remington, 30-06, 375 H&H–and others in between that pretty well covered big to very large game–a rifle just for deer *(and possibly antelope)* was clearly necessary. To me the choice was easy; the chambering would be a 257 Roberts. It's just enough better than the 250 Savage to make it more attractive, and nearly as good as the 25-06–which makes it a very good round, indeed.

Classic lines, clean 24-inch barrel and excellent optics make for an attractive package. Unlike several other 700 Classics seen, this one has highly polished wood and metal.

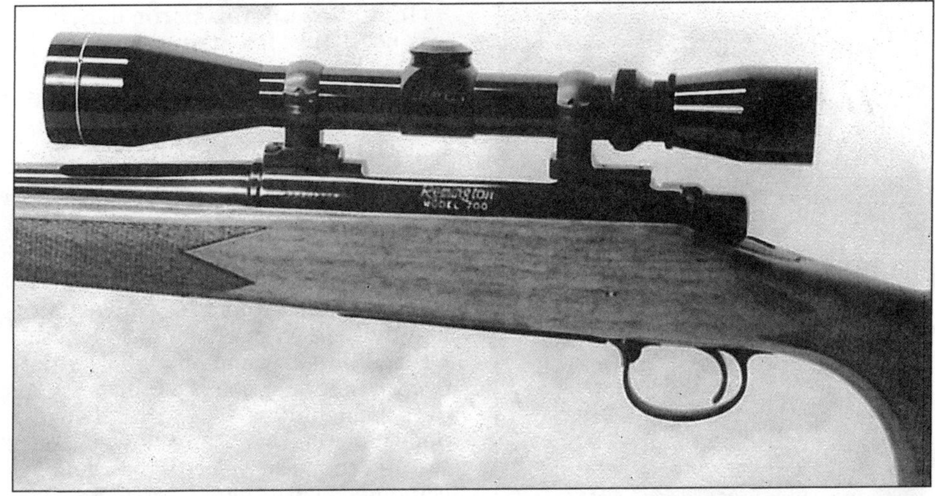

Left side of Model 700 Classic rifle with now-discontinued Leupold Vari-X II 3-9x40 scope.

A Brief History

Now as many already know, the 257 was developed back in the 1920s by a well-known wildcatter named Ned Roberts. Basically, the round is a 7x57 Mauser necked down to .257-inch diameter. It remained a wildcat round for some years, available only as a custom proposition until around 1934 when the Remington company changed the shoulder angle a little and offered it in their Model 30 rifle, a modified 1917 Enfield.

The Roberts seems to enjoy a reputation for good, and sometimes excellent, accuracy depending upon who is doing the shooting–and the writing. It also depends somewhat on what one considers good, or excellent, accuracy. To my way of thinking 'good' accuracy is four- or five-shot groups of about 1-1/2 to 2-1/2 inches at 100 yards. Groups smaller than this should be considered 'excellent'. These parameters of accuracy pertain only to hunting-type rifles of normal weight and length of barrel with hunting-type sights, whether iron or glass. The benchrest and match-type shooters demand much higher performance from their equipment.

Early Problems

One problem that cropped up early on for the Roberts was that Remington saddled its new round with a built-in velocity inhibiter. What they did was offer it in a rifle with an action large enough for the longest cartridges of the day, but then blocked the magazine to just accept the short S.A.A.M.I. overall length of 2.77 inches. Then, adding insult to injury, chamber throats were often cut deep enough to accept a much longer overall cartridge length, thus depriving their own round of its natural capabilities. Many owners of early 257 rifles had to deal with this irritation by having gunsmiths unblock their magazines to allow bullets to be seated out far enough that they wouldn't have to make such long jumps to the rifling, which may affect accuracy. Also, the ammo makers keep the pressure limit for the cartridge at 45,000 C.U.P., which seems a little odd as the same rifle for which it was initially offered is a very strong rifle, and already chambered in 30-06 which had a S.A.A.M.I. limit of 50,000 C.U.P. Most modern rifles have solved this problem to some degree.

All of this in mind while looking for a Roberts, older rifles were not eagerly sought after, but the current selection of modern factory rifles in 257 is very small, indeed. Ruger seems to be the only manufacturer still offering rifles so chambered. Their No. 1 rifle is offered in this chambering, as is the M77R Mk. II and the Ultra Light with its 20-inch barrel.

Almost all of the major makers have, at one time or another, offered the Roberts as a standard chambering, but it isn't a real hot seller these days and so doesn't appeal much to the corporate bean counters. This is too bad as the Roberts really is a very good round and a lot of shooters are missing out on enjoyable, low-recoil shooting. These days, however, the trend is towards making cartridges more powerful, not less.

Starting Up

So a new Ruger M77R Mk. II was purchased and topped with a new Weaver 6x scope. Dies and various loading components were gathered, and a new loading project was begun. Now a new loading project is always fun, but this one proved to be a bit frustrating at times. This is not meant to be a harsh criticism of Ruger *(I know it borders on sacrilege to criticize a Ruger product)*, but this particular gun should never have left the factory. I own several Ruger guns and they are all first-rate.

Right side of Model 700 Classic with bolt partially withdrawn illustrates the long action used. The difference in length between long and short actions has never been a problem for the author.

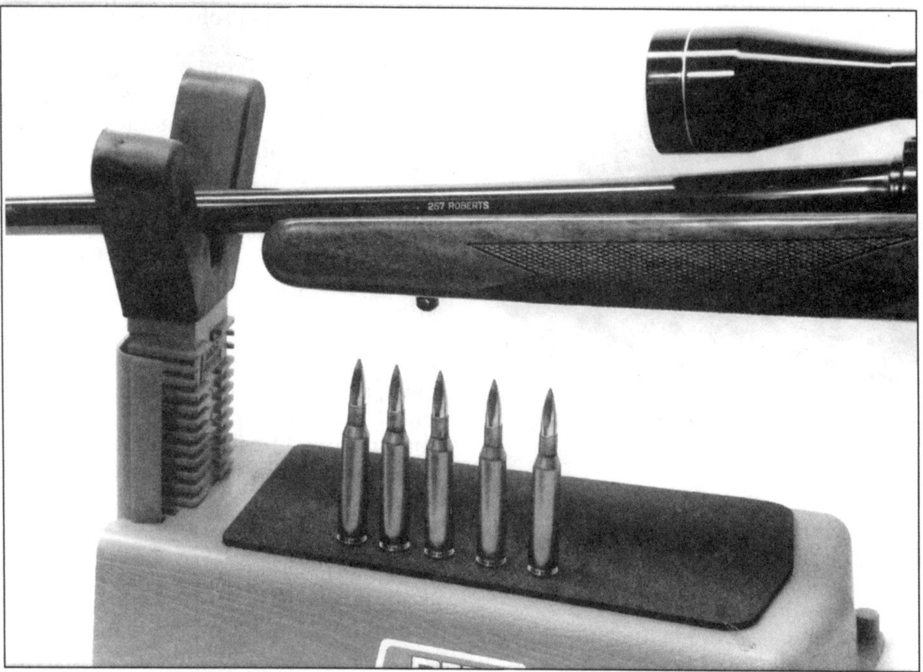

Groups fired using 100-grain Sierra match bullets show consistent good performance. Barrel twist rate of 1:10 inches seems to shoot this weight bullet just a shade better than the heavyweights.

Antelope Hunt

As stated earlier, the main quarry of this rifle /cartridge was to be deer and pronghorn antelope. Shortly after finishing the main body of this piece, I did have a chance to test the round during a Montana antelope hunt.

The first morning of the hunt found my hunting partner and myself glassing a large area of hills and coulees in eastern Montana, not far from Fort Peck Lake. Both of us had spotted a band of 'prairie goats' well over half-mile away in the gray morning light.

When the critters went below a low hill we began our stalk. After following the coulees to stay below the ridge tops for about a half hour we knew we were close. As we belly-crawled up to a ridge top we spooked a bunch of sharptail grouse that in turn spooked the antelope, which were indeed just over the top of the ridge milling around. Scared the heck out of us, too! They ran a few hundred yards, then stopped to look back as they often do–and thus gave us our chance.

Knowing my rifle was sighted in about dead-on at 200 yards *(which would put me about 6 inches low at 300 yards)*, I held just a little over the top of a good-looking buck's back and sent a 115-grain Nosler Ballistic Tip his way. The buck dropped at the shot but was fighting to get back up so I fired a second round, which missed low, and then a third shot which entered the chest and finished the job. Upon inspection of the carcass, we found the first bullet had broken the animal's back, which would account for the dramatic drop to the grass. The bullet that entered the chest did a pretty thorough job of tearing up the lungs and heart but, again, little was found of the bullet. I have since switched to the Nosler Partition, as I know they always hold together for deep penetration.

At any rate there were no surprises here as the cartridge did for me what it has been doing for others for many years: getting the job done without a lot of fuss, just results.

To begin with, this particular rifle was poorly bedded–it sure doesn't help when the front action screw bottoms out in its hole before it pulls the action down tight into the stock. I chose not to send the rifle back to the factory; instead, I had a local 'smith make the necessary repairs. While he had the rifle, I opted to have the throat cut a little deeper, so I could seat the longer bullets to an OAL of about 3.1 inches. The action and magazine are of standard length, but the throat would only allow an overall length of about 2.9 inches with some bullets, less with others, depending on their shape. As I wanted the most velocity the round could offer with the Nosler 115-grain Ballistic Tip bullet, it seemed the extra expense would be justified. This was followed by the mandatory trigger job most factory rifles require, thanks to our litigious society. Then the action and first two inches of barrel were glass-bedded, and the rest of the barrel free-floated.

All of this should have made the rifle a very accurate shooter, but–alas–it did not. It would shoot the occasional good group with the heavier bullets that I prefer, but nothing consistent. It did do somewhat better with bullets of 100 grains but I really wanted a rifle that would shoot the heavier bullets. Many combinations of powder, bullets and primers were tried but it just did not want to group the way it should.

In the meantime, while still wringing out the Ruger, I got a call at work one day from a fellow shooter that I now refer to as my "new best friend", about a Remington Classic in 257 Roberts for sale at a local gun shop. These Classics can be a little scarce at times and, not wanting to miss out on a good thing, the proper amount of "green" changed hands and the Classic had a new owner.

Remington's Classic 257

This rifle is very attractive, with its satin-finished dark walnut stock, clean 24-inch barrel, and overall classic lines sans white line spacers, grip cap or forend tip. Made in 1982 as a limited run in this chambering, this was hardly a new gun–but it appeared to have been carried or shot very little. So a new Leupold Vari-X II 3-9x scope was added and the process started all over again. This rifle, like the Ruger, was built on the standard-length action and magazine but has a longer throat that allows my preferred bullet to be seated out

257 Roberts Selected Loads

Bullet/Grs.	Grs./Powder	OAL	MV	Group	Comments
Sierra 117 FB	42.0 /IMR4350	3.06	2725	3 in 5/8"	Ruger
Speer 120 BT	46.0/IMR4831	3.08	2800	4 in 7/8"	Ruger
Nosler 100 BT	50.0/R-22	3.1	3185	4 in 1"	Ruger
On occasion the Ruger would shoot like this; repeatability was the hard part.					
Nosler 115 BT	43.0/IMR4350	2.94	2750	4 in 3/4"	Rem. Very accurate.
Nosler 115 Par.	47.0/IMR7828	2.88	2800	4 in 1"	Rem.
Nosler 115 BT	48.0/R-22 *(210 Match primer)*		--	4 in 4"	Rem.
Nosler 115 BT	49.0/IMR7828 (210 Match primer)		--	4 in 4"	Rem.
Nosler 115 BT	48.5/R-22 (WLR primer)	--	2915	4 in 3/4"	Rem. Favorite hunt load.
Sierra 100 MBT	44.0/IMR4350 (210 Match primer)		--	4 in 5/8"	Rem. Most accurate load.
Sierra 100 MBT	45.0/IMR4831 (210 Match primer)	--		4 in 3/4"	Rem.
Rem. 120 PSP	47.0/R-22	2.85	--	4 in 1 3/4"	Rem.
Nosler 115 BT	37.0/Varget (CCI 200 primer)			4 in 1 1/4"	Rem. Good accuracy.

The loads chronographed were measured 15 feet from the muzzle, and not corrected. All loads listed used R-P cases. One can see the variation in groups when using different primers.

to and OAL of about 3.0 inches. That may be just enough, so the rifle won't be throated further until it proves necessary. This rifle required bedding as well, and the trigger worked down from its stiff seven pounds, but it already shows more promise than did the Ruger *(A pity, it was neat little rifle, I suspect the barrel just wasn't up to the task.)*. With 100-grain Sierra Match bullets and Federal 210 Match primers, loaded in Remington cases, the Classic will, with either IMR 4350 or IMR 4831, group five rounds a little under an inch at 100 yards when I do my part from sandbags. I shoot groups of four so I can get 5 groups out of a box of 20.

Results with the heavy bullets did almost mirror the results of the Ruger, but things did change dramatically as time went on. The Nosler reloading manual suggests that in the quest for the best accuracy, one need look no further than IMR 4350. The Ruger didn't bear this out but it appears to be truer with the Classic, in particular with 100-grain bullets. With heavier bullets, excellent results have been achieved with H 4831, IMR 7828 and, in particular, with Reloder 22 from Alliant. Though these are fairly slow powders, they are showing pretty uniform results with the heavier bullets. Now groups of an inch or less are becoming more common.

The two powders that stood out the most in the Classic were IMR 4350 and Reloder 22. A note here on primers: With powders slower than 4350, my load tests show that standard large rifle or magnum primers work best. When I tried some Federal 210 Match primers with those powders, groups opened noticeably. It pays to experiment, and good record keeping is critical to avoid confusion.

Barrel Twist

Barrel twist in both the Ruger and the Remington is one turn in ten inches *(1:10)*. There has long been some question as to whether this is the optimum twist rate for bullets heavier than 100 grains, at least in this caliber. However, I can find no reference of any barrel maker using a faster rate of twist in this caliber, including rifles chambered in 25-06 Remington and 257 Weatherby. And

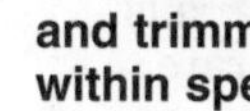

Case length needs to be checked with an accurate dial caliper, after sizing and trimming, to make sure it is within spec.

Measuring overall cartridge length with bullet seated. Known as O.A.L, this round measures 2.975 inches, which fits the Remington long action nicely.

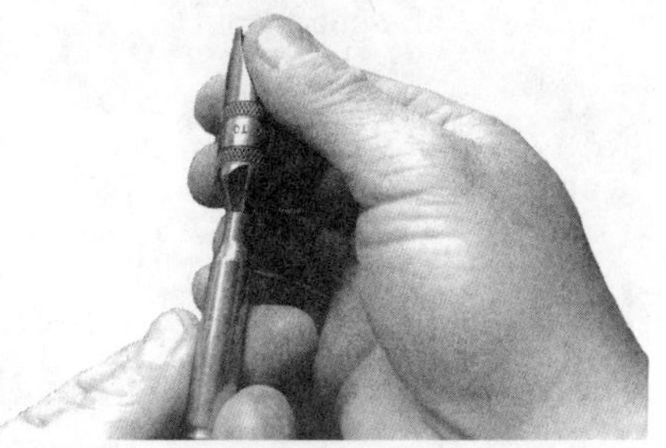

Case mouths must be deburred and chamfered after trimming to facilitate bullet seating.

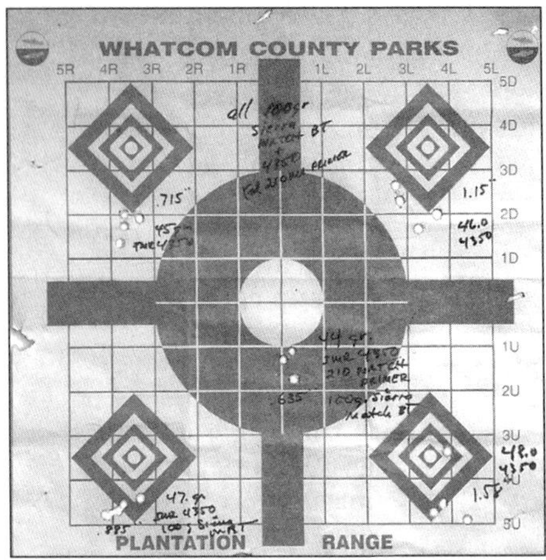

Groups fired using 100-grain Sierra match bullets show consistent good performance. Barrel twist rate of 1:10 inches seems to shoot this weight bullet just a shade better than the heavyweights.

Case set up and ready for trimming to safe length in lathe-type trimmer.

you don't hear complaints about these cartridges shooting poorly. Perhaps then the answer is the particular cartridge's ability to drive the heavy bullet fast enough to be fully stabilized in a marginal twist. Some rifles do better than others, so about all one can do is experiment with different bullet brands and different powders.

At any rate, if a hunting rifle will usually group its shots into something under 2 inches at 100 yards, it is adequate.

Hunting Applications

Which raises the question of suitable game for this cartridge. As a varmint round, the Roberts is an excellent choice. Loaded to high-velocity with light bullets, it is a proven winner at that game. The Roberts has always been an excellent choice for deer and antelope, despite the current trend of using magnums to shoot deer at ranges which most of us have no business shooting at anything except paper targets. At reasonable ranges, out to 300 yards, this round is perfectly capable of downing even big-bodied mule deer. Some have opined that it is even an adequate elk round. Certainly it will take an elk with a good bullet, put exactly where it belongs–but so will just about anything. Since I already have several more suitable elk rifles in the safe I would leave that argument alone.

Inevitably the question arises as to which is the better round for hunting, the 257 Roberts, or one of the 6mms–like the 243 Winchester, the 6mm Remington, or others. It's hard to see where there could be a whole lot of difference on game when all are using 100-grain bullets. Where the Roberts and other 25s have at least a slight advantage is in their ability to use bullets of up to 120 grains, and having that little bit of extra diameter won't hurt either.

In the accuracy department the likely winner would be the 243 Winchester by virtue of its case design, it being fairly well accepted that shorter, fatter cases tend to be more accurate when capacities are similar. Both the 257 and the 6mm Remington are based on the venerable 7x57 Mauser case, whereas the 243 Winchester is of course based on the 308 Winchester – one of the more accurate cartridge designs around.

An excellent combination of reloading components. Electronic scale shows 48.5 grains of Alliant's Reloder 22, which will be topped with a quality bullet like the Nosler Partition. This load chronographs at over 2900 fps. Primers are Winchester standard large rifle.

Velocities For The 257

Velocities with a handloaded 257 can be pretty impressive. Even with the 22-inch barreled Ruger, 100-grain bullets tripped the chronograph at almost 3200 fps and did over 2900 fps with bullets up to 117 grains. That doesn't lag very far behind a factory-loaded 25-06 or 270. Does that mean that it is as good as a 270? No, not really, but the real-world difference isn't that much.

The Remington Classic showed about the same speed with similar loads, even though it has two more inches of barrel. I've noticed before that if nothing else, Ruger barrels are fast, if not the most accurate.

Finished round as it comes from the Lee seating die mounted in the author's well-used RCBS Rock Chucker press.

Of course to realize these kinds of velocities and keep pressures down to a sensible level, requires the judicious handloading of near-maximum charges of the aforementioned slower-burning powders. Another option nowadays is the use of select factory loads that are in the honest +P range. Hornady offers its 117 BTSP bullet in its Light Magnum Load. Federal loads the 120-grain Nosler Partition in its High Energy line. Both are loaded to reportedly much higher velocities than normal factory loads *(most of which are fairly anemic)*. But even in the standard velocity range the Roberts still has power in the 30-30 Winchester category, a cartridge that has always been adequate for deer-sized game. Plus, it has the added benefit of a flatter trajectory, making shots over 150 yards easier to make.

Components

There is no shortage of bullets from the various makers for the handloader, ranging from 60 to 120 grains, both flat base and boattail, for any application that can be imagined.

Cases are another matter, as Remington is usually the only supplier of empty unprimed brass.

I did recently receive a batch of Winchester +P cases but have not yet had the time to compare them to the Remington cases that I have been using; therefore, all loads listed here utilize Remington cases. Normally, the only way to get other brands of brass is to shoot factory loads, and then reload them.

A reminder about safety: While working with test loads for the 700 Classic I had five blown primers using the Remington cases. All of these came from the same lot of brass, and when I purchased more new brass from a different source there were no further problems. When the first one blew, I got a nice warm blast of gas and particles in the face. Fortunately, I was wearing safety glasses for all but the first of these little wakeup calls.

Final Thoughts

In retrospect it's possible I lost patience with the Ruger too soon, although over 600 bullets were launched from it before I gave up. The 700 Classic is a very handsome rifle and has my preferred barrel length of 24 inches, as opposed to the 22-inch tube of the Ruger. It also is the opinion of many that when it comes to quality factory barrels, Remington's are hard to beat. Some will agree with this, others will have perhaps had a different experience. Every 700 I have ever owned has had a very good barrel. At any rate, it's been a real learning process loading for the 257 Roberts. Having owned many rifles that would group loads into an inch or less without much fuss has perhaps spoiled me a bit when it comes to making a rifle shoot. The Roberts, at least on the basis of loading for these two rifles, appears to be a bit load sensitive. But if we have a good platform to begin with, then it is usually just a matter of time before it all comes together. That's where the reward is.

Yes, the Roberts is a dandy little cartridge, and while it may not be enough cartridge to be considered an all-around, do-everything cartridge for all North American game, as a potent light recoiling round for deer, antelope, varmints and such, it fills the bill quite nicely and I look forward to spending time afield with it. ●

Favored components: 115-grain Nosler Ballistic Tips and Reloder 22; Sierra 100-grain Match Kings, with IMR 4350.

***(Left to right)*:** **7x57mm Mauser, 257 Roberts, 243 Winchester and the 250-3000 Savage.**

Reloading the 45 Colt Cartridge

by R. H. Vandenburg, Jr.

In his famous treatise, *"Sixguns"*, the late Elmer Keith had this to say about the 45 Colt cartridge: *"If I had to shoot only factory ammunition the rest of my life, I would take the 45 Colt as my game and defense cartridge."*

The operative phrase above is *"factory ammunition"* as Keith had long before decided that, despite the 45 Colt's excellence, he could improve on it by handloading the 44 Smith & Wesson Special. His reasoning was simple. The best guns chambered for each cartridge used the same frame and cylinder. Consequently, the 44-chambered revolvers had thicker cylinder walls and would therefore withstand being loaded to higher pressure and velocity than the 45. Further, because both cartridges could use bullets of the same weight, 250 grains, the longer 44 would offer higher sectional density, better retain its velocity and accuracy and provide greater penetration on game.

The guns in which they were chambered limited both cartridges. Indeed, the Colt revolver in which the cartridges were chambered had changed little since its inception in 1873. The 45 cartridge began as a blackpowder round the same year and survived the transition to smokeless powder. Pressures were kept quite low, in keeping with gun design, and to this day don't exceed 14,000 psi. Still, it was a big cartridge, firing a heavy bullet and was capable of the best performance of any factory handgun round–hence Keith's proclamation. The 44 Special, dating from 1907 and prized as a target round, was also a blackpowder round initially and was chambered in a number of revolvers, many of the top-break design. In time, Smith & Wesson, in particular, began to chamber the cartridge in large, solid-frame, double-

Cowboy Action shooters need to carry guns, ammo and accesssories. Here's a clever solution.

action revolvers. It was here Keith began his experimenting, eventually pushing 250-grain lead alloy bullets of his own design to a reported 1200 fps. In spite of Keith's bullet designs improving the performance of the 45 Colt as well, the 44 Special had gained the upper hand.

As every handgunner worthy of the name knows, it was Keith's experimenting with heavy handloads in the 44 Special that led Smith & Wesson *(arms)* and Remington Arms *(ammunition)* to announce, in 1956, a major improvement in handgun cartridges–the 44 Remington Magnum. Because the new cartridge was loaded to a much higher pressure level than any other handgun cartridge on the market, new guns, often larger and with improved steels and heat-treating, had to be developed.

The irony should not be lost on anyone that these same, and further, developments in steels, heat-treating and design created an environment where today, the 45 Colt is capable of surpassing the 44's performance. To many knowledgeable handgunners, the 45 Colt is, once again, simply the best big-bore revolver round in existence.

To reach such a lofty level of performance, however, requires the use of modern revolvers such as those from Ruger or Freedom Arms. Thompson/Center Contender single-shot pistols are also capable of such performance. Because the great preponderance of guns chambered for the cartridge are of the older Colt design and strength, no major factory loads 45 Colt ammunition over the 14,000 psi level. Handloading is how we achieve better performance and therein, as they say, lies the rest of the story.

For the last 40 years or more, handgunners have been subjected to written reports of how *(a)* the 45 Colt is the most difficult handgun cartridge to load for or *(b)* the 45 Colt is no different, or more difficult, to load for than any other handgun cartridge. My personal experiences have caused me, at times, to take up residence in the former camp. However, I'll be the first to admit that if one uses only modern guns, the latest dies and load data, and both cases and a shellholder that aren't on their last legs, one could rightfully wonder what the commotion was all about.

To understand the perplexities of those in the former camp, we must go back to the guns themselves. Almost all of the early guns chambered for the cartridge were Colt single-action revolvers. Initially the cartridge dimensions called for a barrel groove diameter of .454-inch and a fairly loose-fitting chamber, befitting its blackpowder origin. After World War II, factory barrels were changed to a nominal groove diameter of .452-inch. Although factory blackpowder ammunition was no longer being manufactured, chamber dimensions appear to have remained the same. This created the condition of a loose-fitting cartridge in a chamber with a mouth often measuring .457-inch or more and a barrel groove diameter of .452-inch. With regard to cast bullets only, this made determining proper bullet diameter difficult, to say the least. Bullets that were close to groove diameter didn't align themselves properly in the throat area and allowed propellant gases to get around the bullets before they entered the barrel, melting the lubricant and the bullet bearing surfaces. The results were uneven bullets, barrel leading and inaccuracy. Larger bullets of .454-inch diameter still didn't correspond with chamber throats, but were an improvement.

As other manufacturers–notably Ruger–entered the scene, their barrels were cut to .452-inch with higher lands and their chambers and chamber throats were cut to somewhat smaller dimensions than

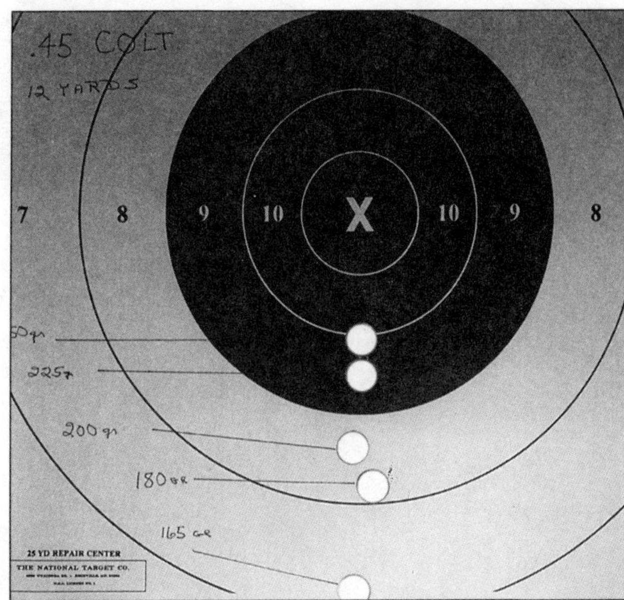

Even at close range bullet placement relative to point of aim is still important. Here, a traditional 6 o'clock hold produced this at typical Cowboy Action distance.

The Mexican flavor fits right in, as well.

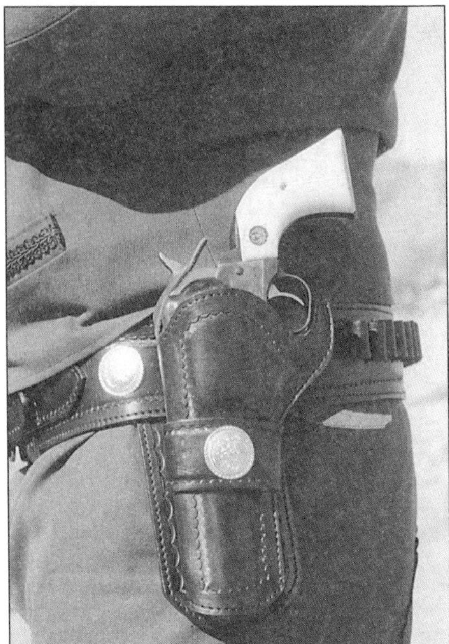

Fancy dress and rigs are part of Cowboy Action shooting.

earlier models. Here the bullet mould manufacturers began to design moulds to drop bullets to be sized .452-inch. This was fine for the new guns, but only exacerbated the problems with the older guns. Along about this time we began to see jacketed bullets for the 45 Colt. They invariably had diameters of .451-, .4515- or .452-inch, depending on manufacturer. They didn't lead barrels, generally had soft jackets and cores and often performed much better than ill-matched cast bullets, but rarely up to the cartridge's potential.

Throughout all of this period, which took up much of the latter half of the 20th century, 45 Colt factory ammunition performed very well. It wasn't until quite recently that we've seen jacketed bullets in factory ammunition. For most of the period, 45 Colt ammunition consisted of a soft lead 250-grain bullet, often with a cupped *(or hollow)* base, sized to .454-inch. When fired, the bullet, or at least the base, would expand under pressure to meet the dimensional demands of chamber throats and barrels. When I got my first 45 Colt six-gun, a Colt Single Action Army, in the early 1970s, I used factory ammunition as a benchmark for measuring the effectiveness of my handloads. Accuracy was outstanding; it took years to learn how to overcome the handloading pitfalls that stood in the way of even approaching such performance.

Often the pitfalls were not just the dimensional incompatibility of chamber throat, barrel and bullet–but of the loading die sets themselves. Early loading dies were naturally built around the early cartridge dimensions and their .454-inch bullets. As the guns began to change, the dies did not-for the most part. It was not unusual to find that a sized and expanded case wouldn't hold a jacketed bullet at all, or at least not tightly enough to allow pressure to build up properly. Results were erratic. Loading manuals of the day often recommended using a 45 ACP sizing die to alleviate the problem. These dies were built around a .451-inch jacketed or .452-inch cast bullet and typically sized cases a good .005-inch more than 45 Colt sizers. This did nothing to help case fit in a sloppy chamber. Also, the 45 ACP expander buttons were typically .450-inch, whereas 45 Colt expanders often measured .453. Over time, however, things began to change and modern 45 Colt loading dies produce properly sized and expanded cases without a hitch. That is, unless one chooses to use .454-inch bullets in an older, or perhaps modern replica, six-shooter. In this case a larger expander button may be called for and is sometimes included with the die set.

Over the years I experienced most of these problems. In addition to using 45 ACP dies to close down at least the case necks, I accumulated quite a collection of expander buttons. A custom-turned one of .448 inch kept company with others of .4495-, .450-, .4528- and .453-inch. My most recent die acquisition sizes cases to perfection. I have reduced my expander button use to the .4495 for all jacketed bullets and all cast bullets sized .453 or less. For cast bullets sized .454 or slightly larger, I've gotten best accuracy with the .4528 expander. I have to admit that unless I'm building heavy hunting loads, the .450 expander works as well as the .4495. I've also turned to a straight-line bullet seater for my heavy hunting loads and am amazed at the concentricity of the finished rounds. For more ordinary use, the latest die set performs adequately without the straight-line seater. All bullets are seated in one operation and crimped in another, regardless of the die set used. Since crimps are extrem-ely import-ant in the loading of revolver ammu-nition, it's imper-ative that all cases are trimmed to the same length so that each crimp will exert the same force.

In the development of the load data that follows, two six-guns were employed. One, the

Period dress adds to flavor and feel of Cowboy Action shooting.

45 COLT LOAD DATA

Traditional (R-P cases; CCI 300 primers)

Bullet	Powder	Amount (grains)	Velocity (fps)	Remarks
Speer 225 JHP	Blue Dot	13.0	922	
	Unique	9.0	803	
Sierra 240 JHP	Unique	9.0	851	Best jacketed bullet load
	W-W231	8.2	784	
Hornady 250 JHP	W-W231	8.0	770	
	Unique	8.5	818	
	Universal	8.8	826	
	2400	16.5	806	Ruger only
Cast #454190	Bullseye	5.0	661	Best groups in Colt
	Bullseye	6.5	793	
Cast #452424	Unique	8.5	868	Best all-round
	Unique	9.0	885	
	True Blue	9.4	876	Good load
	2400	16.5	881	Ruger only

Note: *All groups fired in a 4 3/4-inch Colt Single Action except 16.5/2400 load for Ruger only.*

aforementioned Colt single-action *(Second Generation)* has a 4 3/4-inch barrel. The chamber throats measure about .455-inch. With its .452-inch barrel groove diameter, .454-sized cast bullets of moderate softness perform best. The second gun, a Ruger Bisley Vaquero, was purchased as a platform for launching 300-grain project-iles. With the re-discovery of the potential of the 45 Colt in modern guns capable of withstanding much higher pressures than the SAAMI-approved 14,000 psi, heavy bullets have become the rage and I didn't want to be left behind. In his time Keith experimented with various bullet weights, including weights up to 300 grains. He accomplished that by casting bullets in the Lyman #457191 mould for the 45-70 and 45-90, squeezing them down to .454-inch and stuffing them in 45 Colt cases. One Keith story that always brings a smile involved his recounting celebrating the 4th of July one year by dropping the hammer on such a load in a Colt single-action and blowing the gun to smithereens. Fortunately no one was hurt and, although I smile, the lesson was not lost. Keith rightly reasoned that the optimum bullet weight for the 45 Colt–given the guns and powders then available–was about 250 grains. I reserve my heavy bullets and high pressures for the Ruger. This gun has a 5 1/2-inch barrel with an internal measurement of .4515-inch. Chamber throats, on the other hand, measured .4505-inch, on average. Not unusual, oddly, for new Rugers. Although the combination would never work for hard cast bullets, accuracy was excellent with softer jacketed ones. While the Colt is box-stock save for the replacement of the hammer and a couple of springs over the years, the Ruger has been fairly extensively modified. Although, unless you really know your Rugers, most of the modifications will not be readily apparent. Germane to our discussion is that the cylinder throats have been opened up to .453-inch. The gun has turned out to be quite accurate with 300-grain heavy hunting loads that turn in 50-yard groups of 2-2 1/2 inches. The Colt is hard-pressed to do that at 25 yards.

Smokeless powder still smokes, as two of the good guys go into action.

When we get to the actual loading of the 45 Colt cartridge we must stay within certain parameters. For guns of the Colt single-action type, from Colt or its many clones, we must adhere to the SAAMI-approved 14,000 psi. This category would also include Smith & Wesson revolvers such as the Model 25. Our more heavy-duty loads can be built around such modern single-action revolvers as the Ruger Blackhawk and Vaquero, the fine Freedom Arms guns and double-action revolvers such as the Ruger Redhawk and Super Redhawk. Most new loading manuals carry separate data for this category and typically restrict loads to a maximum of 30,000 psi. Such loads are perfectly safe in suitable guns but will destroy the older design in short order, sometimes immediately!

In developing the accompanying loading data, I ended up with three

Heavy Hunting (Starline cases; Federal 155 primers)

For Heavy Modern Guns Only

Bullet	Powder	Amount *(grains)*	Velocity *(fps)*	Remarks
Sierra 240 JHP	H110	27.7	1365	
	2400	23.0	1366	
Barnes 250 "X"	2400	20.0	1280	
Swift 265 JHP	H110	23.5	1151	
	2400	20.0	1159	
Nosler 300 Partition	H110	23.0	1170	Accurate
Hornady 300 JHP	H4227	22.3	1142	
LBT 300 WFN	H110	23.0	1207	Excellent

Note: *All loads fired in a 5 1/2-inch Ruger Bisley Vaquero. All loads are considered maximum in my gun.*

categories: traditional, Cowboy Action and heavy hunting. Before I started I needed to make certain I could identify which loads, regardless of bullet, were loaded to which pressure level. For this I began with the cases. I had a new lot from Winchester, Remington and Starline. Although the maximum overall length of 45 Colt cases is 1.285 inches and the "trim to" length is 1. 275 inches, I found all the new cases were somewhere in between, leaving just enough brass to *"true up"* the cases to the prescribed 1.275-inch length. The new Winchester cases averaged 103.6 grains in weight. As they seemed to be the most spacious and the name Winchester more synonymous with the Old West, I set these aside for my Comboy Action loads. The Remington cases averaged 105.2 grains. They were assigned to the traditional category. The Starline cases were the heaviest at 110. 9 grains and were reserved for my heavy hunting loads. Now not only would each loaded cartridge be readily identifiable as to pressure level, I can dump all fired cases in the case tumbler and, after cleaning, easily separate them by group.

Primers were less of a concern. Large pistol primers were used throughout, the standard variety for traditional and Cowboy Action loads and the magnum variety for my heavy hunting efforts.

Powders were another matter. There doesn't seem to be any end to the list of usable powders for such an endeavor, although powders for the heavy hunting loads are severely restricted. Back when I started loading for big-bore handguns we had, for the most part, Bullseye, Unique and 2400–all from Hercules. To a far greater extent than one might imagine, it worked quite well. I long ago settled on 8.5 grains of Unique with a 250-grain cast lead bullet for my 45 Colt traditional load. Other powders over the years often worked as well, but no better. I reasoned that any shortcomings I might be experiencing were due to mismatched revolver parts and loading dies than brand or burning rate of powder. Velocity from my Colt averages 868 fps – about perfect for the sights and for any practical use to which I might put the gun.

What with the flood of new powders, Bullseye doesn't get called on much anymore for use in the 45, but it wasn't always that way. In Lyman's Handbook of Cast Bullets, copyright 1958, on page 159 is a picture of a bullet from the Lyman mould #454190. It is captioned *"Regular standard bullet for the .45 Colt. Suggest 5 grains of Bullseye."* On the very next page is a picture of a bullet from the #454424 mould captioned *"Designed by Elmer Keith for the .45 Colt with 5 grains of Bullseye."* I doubt that Keith ever

Cowboy Action (Winchester cases; Winchester LP primers)

Bullet	Powder	Amount *(grains)*	Velocity *(fps)*	Remarks
160 RNFP	Titegroup	6.0	814	
	Titegroup	6.5	881	
	Clays	5.0	664	
180 RNFP	Universal	6.5	702	
	W-W231	6.0	680	
200 RNFP	Unique	6.7	693	
	W-W231	7.0	727	Best 200 gr. load
	W-W231	8.0	803	Good
225 RNFP	Titegroup	5.6	710	
	W-W231	6.5	702	
250 RNFP	Clays	4.8	682	Size .454"
	Titegroup	5.5	702	
	Unique	7.7	840	
	Universal	7.2	715	
250 gr. Ly#454190	Bullseye	5.0	661	Most accurate

Note: *All loads fired in a 4 3/4-inch Colt Single Action. All RNFP bullets from Magma moulds.*

Bullets used in typical loads, *from left:* jacketed Speer 225 gr. JHP; Sierra 240 gr. JHP; Hornady 250 gr. JHP; Cast Lyman 250 gr. 454191, 250 gr. 452424, 250 gr. 452664.

Cowboy Action bullets are usually round nose, flat point. *From left:* 160, 180, 200, 25, and 250 grain. the 225 gr. is from Lyman mould 452374 and is designed for the .45 ACP. The rest are Magma moulds for Cowboy Action shooting.

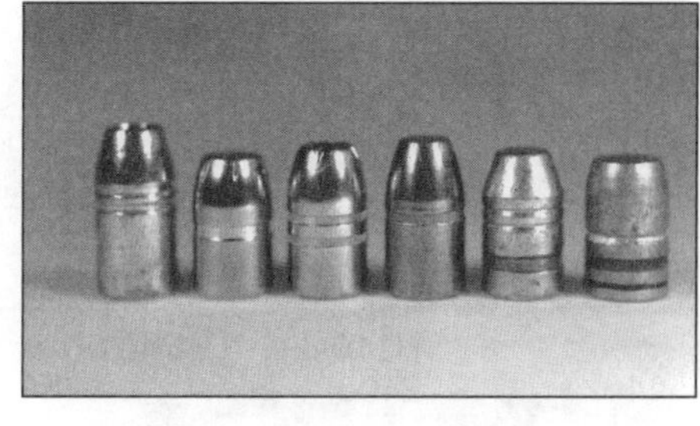

Heavy hunting bullets include, *from left:* 250 gr. Barnes "X", 265 gr. Swift "A" frame, hollowpoint, 300 gr. Hornady XTP, 300 gr. Nosler Partition Protected Point, 300 gr. Lazercast and 300 gr. LBT WFN.

used the 5-grain load, for elsewhere in the book he recommended 6.5 grains when using Bullseye. The point is that in my Colt the best 25-yard groups have come from bullets cast in my #454190 mould and seated over 5.0 grains of Bullseye. Velocity is abysmal, less than 700 fps, but five-shot groups frequently sneak under 2 inches. For paper punching, I've yet to beat it.

2400 is also an excellent powder rarely recommended for the 45 Colt these days. Perhaps better suited for Rugers than Colts as a steady diet, there are a lot of folks who think 16.5 grains of 2400 under a 250-grain cast bullet is as good as it gets.

Another very popular powder for both traditional and Cowboy Action loads is Winchester's 231. More than a few feel it has no equal in the big Colt. Its virtual clone, Hodgdon's HP38, occupies the same position in the minds of many. Hodgdon's new Titegroup, promoted as not being position-sensitive in the case, is also developing a following. Most powders, when used in small quantities, react poorly when positioned away from the primer at time of firing. Titegroup is, I think, better suited for Cowboy Action or other target loads than getting maximum velocity with 250-grain bullets in the traditional class.

In the heavy hunting class, 2400 and Hodgdon's new Lil'Gun are fine with bullets up to 300 grains but cannot generate the velocities of H110. So far, it and it's near twin–Winchester's 296–are king of the hill.

In the traditional category, bullet weight centers around 250 grains. Cast bullets such as Lyman's #454190 and #452664 list at a nominal 250 grains. Their #452424 *(it used to be #454424)* and #452490 *(gas-check design)* are shown as weighing 255 grains. There are several other manufacturers of bullet moulds, all with a variety of 250 grain or so offerings. The list includes RCBS, Redding-SAECO, NEI, Lee and Magma, to name a few. Jacketed bullets run from a 225-grain Speer to a 240-grain Sierra to several 250-grainers. All have hollow points and, if used for hunting, should be reserved for light deer and smaller game.

In the Cowboy Action group things get

Carbines in handgun calibers are part of the game.

Different cases used for each type of load: Winchester for Cowboy Action; R-P for traditional; Starline for heavy hunting.

Guns used in load developement: Ruger Bisley Vaquero *(top)*; Colt Single Action Army.

interesting. The governing body of Cowboy Action shooting, the Single Action Shooting Society *(SASS)* limits handgun bullets to cast, no gas checks or fillers, and to a velocity of 1000 fps. The latter is hardly a problem as matches are multi-shot events and are scored by elapsed time with penalty points for misses. This means reducing recovery time between shots is important and contestants accomplish this by reducing velocity and often bullet weight. This has led to some yeoman efforts in mould design with bullet weights in the 45 Colt ranging from 160 grains or so through 180, 200 and 225 to 250 and 255 grains. Throughout this report I worked with all of these weights and spoke to a number of Cowboy Action shooters and commercial cast bullet manufacturers. In spite of the wide range of bullet weights available, it appears most people have settled into one of two camps. First is the "light bullet" camp. In speaking to numerous shooters in this group the 200-grain bullet was almost always the preferred weight. This was backed up by sales from custom bullet manufacturers. The reason for this choice is shown in one of the accompanying photos. Of the lighter weight bullets, the 200-grain shoots closest to point of aim while still giving the benefit of reduced recoil. Lighter bullets would, more than likely, require reducing the height of the front sight, limiting the gun for other work.

Gifted pistolsmith Milt Morrison, "Easy Money" to his Cowboy friends, likes W-W 231 as his powder with 200-grain bullets. "Enough to get about 800 fps," he says. That would be about 8 grains, but many use less. Milt was quick to add he chose 231 "because that's what I use for everything." When I asked "Sweetwater" Bill Hall, president of the Sand Creek Raiders, a Cowboy Action club near Denver, Colorado about his load, he quickly responded, "A 200-grain bullet with 6.7 grains of Unique. It chronographs at 720 fps." (His gun was a Ruger and I'm not surprised I only clocked 693 fps out of my Colt. It's close enough.) I couldn't help but laugh and exclaim, "That's a horrible load. Unique needs to operate at a higher pressure than that." Bill's answer gets to the essence of Cowboy Action shooting: "I like it because it smokes more. Sort of in keeping with the old guns and ammo without contending with blackpowder."

In talking to one cast bullet manufacturer, who also confirmed that the 200-grain bullet was the most popular, I asked about bullet hardness. He was quick to point out his bullets are hard! I didn't make his day, I don't suppose, when I told him he was doing it all wrong. For traditional or Cowboy Action shooting, bullets should be soft. Wheelweights generally end up, after a seasoning period, at a Brinnell Hardness number of 10 or so. That's plenty, even too hard for most Cowboy loads. *(I measured his bullets on my LBT tester at 19.)* Harder bullets won't obturate, compounding

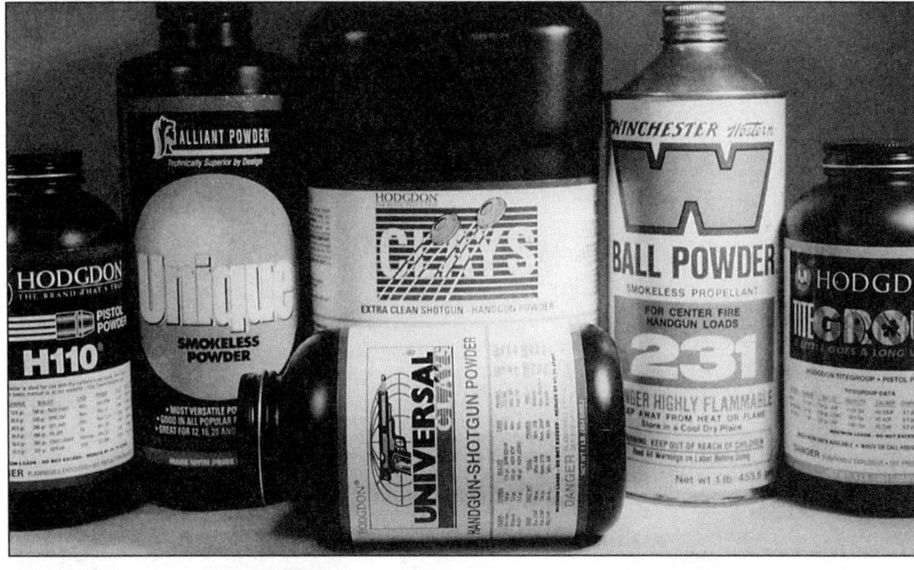

Some of the more popular 45 Colt powders.

all those early problems, especially with some Colts and imported clones. He didn't flinch, "My customers demand hard bullets and my IPSC customers need them. Besides it would be impractical for me to try to operate my business with more than one alloy." Fair enough, and since his business is thriving and his customers are happy, who can complain? Still, we can make bullets more suitable to the pressure they are being subjected to if we're willing to do the work. Less leading and greater accuracy will be our reward.

The other camp of Cowboy Action shooters uses 250- or 255-grain bullets because, dammit!, that's what 45 Colt bullets are supposed to weigh! Mike Daly of Hodgdon Powder Company and author of their "Cowboy Action Data" booklet, is an unapologetic member of the camp. In a recent phone conversation he said "45 Colt Cowboy loads should have 250-grain bullets sized .454." Mike went on to say that bullets of less weight or smaller diameter were less accurate. His personal Cowboy load is 4.8 grains of Hodgdon's Clays for 675 fps. (I recorded 682 fps in my gun.) Another point of view comes from Allan Jones, editor of the Speer reloading manuals. In the latest, number 13, is an excellent chapter on Cowboy Action guns and loads. However, at the end of the chapter Allan offers his own opinion, ending with; "Would a self-respecting cowboy or woodsman in 1885 carry a 45 Colt single action with 165 grains loaded to 700 feet/sec when he could get 255-grain bullets shooting 900 feet/sec in the same revolver? How would you feel if you placed high in a match with 'real' ammo? Even if I came in fourth behind three guys shooting 'mouse' loads, I'd feel pretty good about it." No mincing of words there.

Costumes need not be elaborate.

When we get to heavy hunting loads, we're looking at bullets that generally weigh more than 250 grains, up to 300. Jacketed bullets in this class include a 260-grain Partition from Nosler, a 265-grain from Swift and several 300s from Nosler, Hornady and Sierra. Barnes adds a 250-grain "X" bullet. Most of these bullets are hollowpoints and, while they can be very effective, they should not be used where extreme penetration is called for. Nosler has a fine 300-grain Protected Point, flat with a wide meplat that should be suitable for heavier work. The real workhorses, where deep penetration is demanded, are cast. We show no disrespect to Elmer Keith when we acknowledge that others have built upon what he started and now offer designs that improve upon even his work.

My personal favorite is a 300 WFN *(Wide Flat Nose)* from a LBT mould. It is hard cast, BHN 16-17. Mine are supposedly .452 but measure about .453 on my micrometer and are a perfect fit in my Bisley Vaquero. Twenty-three grains of H110 propels them to about 1200 fps out of the 5 1/2-inch Ruger. They'll do anything I need doing.

In the accompanying table are a variety of loads for traditional, Cowboy Action and heavy hunting. All stem from published data. Few are maximum and most can be adjusted somewhat but I consider the heavy hunting loads to be maximum in my gun. Several of the Cowboy Action recipes are published starting loads and should not be reduced.

In the end, I join those who proclaim the 45 Colt the most versatile and useful handgun round we have. Long may it live. ●

Two-gun cowboys compete in the gunfighter class.

Feeding FOUR 25s

by Wilf MacGlais

Four 250 Savages have come my way over the years. My first–a Model '99 takedown–was traded off for a prodigal creature that I had fraudulently been led to believe was a bird dog. My second 250–a pre- war Model 70 Winchester in near-new condition–was purchased some 30 years back from a none-too-bright lad who had come by it a short time before *(there is a moral here for all of us)* by inheritance. For some years now I have reluctantly conceded that the fellow to whom I traded away this one could very well be making disparaging comments about my mental prowess. In a fit of nostalgia that can only be ascribed to the eccentricities of mid-life crises, I traded off a mint condition Steyr 22 rimfire for my third 250. There was, I am pleased to say, no trade involved in the acquisition of my fourth.

The idea of putting together a 250 Savage came to me when I found myself with a pair of reworked "relic" Mauser actions on hand, and few niches to fill. The resultant home-brewed job was based upon the DWM action previously mentioned. The welding-on of a new Brownell bolt handle, drilling for scope mount bases, polishing, bluing, and magazine shortening block, were all handled in my own cluttered hobby shop. Carved from a Calico Hardwoods full fiddleback Bastogne walnut blank, the stock, too, is my own creation.

Originally fitted to a Mk. X 7mm Magnum *(hence the recoil pad)*, the stock needed only a bit of routing out and glass-bedding to suit the 250. A Timney trigger, F.N. *(deluxe)* bolt head safety, Redfield Jr. mount, 6-24x Bausch and Lomb varmint scope, and Flaig-installed Douglas air-gauged #5 barrel completed the package.

All the bullets shown here perform well in all four cartridges. Magnum primers were used in the 25-06 and 25 Niedner.

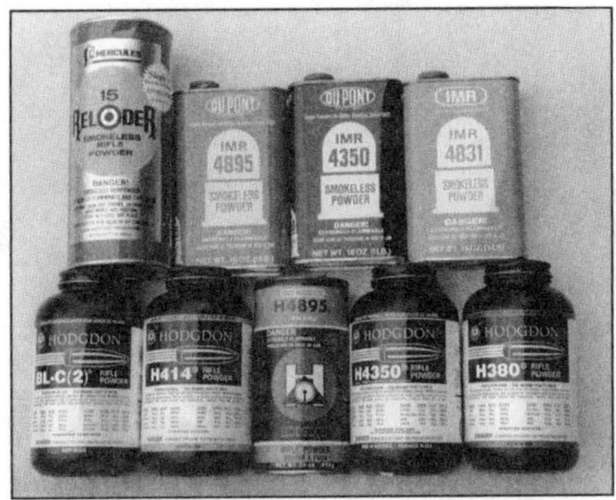

Powders in author's loads: H414 gave best results in the 250 Savage. H4831, best performer in the 25-06 and 25 Niedner, is a bit slow in 257 Roberts loads.

250-3000 Savage Loads

Bullet	Charge	Power	Velocity	Remarks
75 gr.	44	H414	3460	Best accuracy
	37.7	RLA-15	3300*	
	38	BL-C2	3299	
	42	H-380	3393	
87 gr.	41	H-380	3210	
	37	H4895	3208	
	42	H-414	3297	Best accuracy
	37.6	RL.15	3208	
100 gr.	40	H-414	3102	Best accuracy
	36	RL 15	3000	
	34	H-335	2921	
	35	H-4895	2988	

Anyone who cannot do most of the conversion work himself will be better *(though perhaps less satisfactorily)* served by starting with a new commercial action or by paying one of the astute pirates that haunt the gun shows a premium price for a 250 rifle. Sad to say, in spite of its near-new condition, were I to put this rifle on a table at any nearby gun show, I would probably be hard put to recover even a major fraction of my investment. Fortunately the story does not end here.

The strength of the Mauser action, combined with a heavy 1:12 twist barrel, enables this rifle to perform well over a wide load spectrum. Given proper feeding, my 250 will produce tight groups with a wide variety of loads ranging from 22 Hornet through 243 Winchester levels.

At the lower end, 75-grain bullets pushed by 32.8 grains of Reloader 15 in the 250 virtually duplicate the velocity of the Hornet factory load at 150 yards, while slightly bettering the Hornet's trajectory and energy numbers. The 75-grain Hornady hollowpoint bullet, when pushed along at 3200 fps by 42 grains of H4350 in the 250 and our 55-grain Speer-bulleted 223 Remington load moved at the same muzzle velocity by 25.3 grains of H335, show identical mid-range trajectories of 5.5 inches, while 10 mph cross-wind deflection for both loads is 10.5 inches at 300 yards. [1]

Author's doomed Husqvarna, with its discarded "California-style" stock.

When pushed at a muzzle velocity of 3460 fps by 44 grains of H414 our 75-grain 250 load is shaded by the top 53-grain 22-250 load by only one inch in mid-range trajectory and two inches in 10 mph cross-wind deflection at 300 yards.

One hot 75-grain Sierra hollowpoint 243 Winchester load shades our top 75-grain 250 Savage load by only one inch in mid-range trajectory and 1 1/2 inches in 10 mph cross-wind deflection at 300 yards. The top 100-grain 243 and 250 loads show nearly identical trajectories and cross-wind deflections at 300 yards. A 100-grain 250 Savage load listed in my old Herter's manual slightly betters the trajectory and wind deflection numbers of my 243—it also stiffens up bolt lift in my 250.

Given the opportunity, either the 243 or the 250 Savage will be your best bet for reaching over into the next county for a big mule deer. It is here that the 250 has the advantage–its decibel levels won't be disturbing the residents over there, either.

The 243 vs. 250 controversy is probably best summed up in the preface to the 250 Savage in Hodgdon's excellent Manual #26... *"There isn't two cents worth of difference in their performance."* As both a former and a present 243 owner, I say Amen to that.

A more recent project is a 257 Roberts–my first. This one is based upon a Steyr-produced "Model 1912" Chilean military Mauser action *(also purchased as a "relic")*. The key word here is project. At the time that this

The 25 Niedner "keeper".

1 This is a function of their virtually identical ballistic coefficients.

Performance of the 257 Roberts cartridge, plus the light-gathering power of the Bausch and Lomb's large objective lens, make this a great poor light coyote-getter.

one was put together I already owned–in addition to the 250 Savage–a 25- 06 and a 25 Niedner. Once it was drilled for scope mount bases and fitted with a new bolt handle, the beautifully finished Steyr action *(not to be confused with their M.S. action)* was shipped off to Flaig's to be fitted with a Douglas air-gauged barrel. A concerned call to Flaig's a couple of months later brought disturbing news–their shop had been closed down.

We will spare the reader two long sad stories by saying only that my Steyr action now sports a Shilen barrel and an attractive stock carved from one of Presliks' modestly-priced Claro blanks. We should also mention that it performs very well indeed.

Another long, sad, oft-told *(but not here)* story is that detailing the 257's "failure" and reasons for same. Any handloading 257 owner *(including yours truly)* will soon disabuse all willing listeners of the notion that it is, or has ever been, a failure.

With 48 grains of H 380 behind it, the 75-grain Sierra bullet produces 3560 fps in the 257 at a mild 48,300 C.U.P. Muzzle velocity of the top 87-grain 257 load is an impressive 3375 fps at 47,600 C.U.P. Top listed 87-grain 25-06 loads are only 95 fps faster, while running a bit over 50,000 C.U.P. [2] Only when one moves up to the 100- and 120-grain bullets does the difference in the performance of these two cartridges becomes worth mentioning.

In spite of the above, I number myself among those who believe that ballistic tables have yet to bring down their first mouse, therefore my handloads seldom push the upper limits. Hunters with undeveloped stalking and shooting skills frequently go awry as a result of their acceptance, as gospel, of the frequently-found fiction suggesting that favorable down-range ballistic numbers are a remedy for ineptitude.[3] More often than not the tyro's misconceptions lead to: *(a)* His turning to a rifle that produces more recoil than he is able to handle comfortably; *(b)* Shots taken at impractically long distances; *(c)* Poorly placed bullets, i.e., wounded and lost game.

Two extreme *(not to say ludicrous)* examples of the bullet placement argument come to mind: *(a)* Wally Johnson's tale of the foolhardy teenager *(the ultimate redundancy)* who brought down a Cape buffalo with a single 22 Hornet bullet behind the ear. *(b)* The even more bizarre tale, *(Capstick's, I believe)* of the bull elephant who bled to death after having a major artery punctured by a 22 rimfire bullet.

A far less dramatic, but closer to home, parable stars the late scofflaw son of the woman to whom my uncle was married. With the aid of a salt lick, a comfortable platform in a huge oak tree, and a powerful spotlight, his "take" from 1927 through 1941 totaled well over 200 deer. Showing no regard for age or gender, he shot them all between the eyes from a distance of around 25 yards. As with the elephant, the rifle used was a 22 rimfire.[4]

For reasons that date back to the Model 70 Winchester mentioned earlier, my 25-06 is the only one of the four that is not *(excepting its stock)* a home-brewed product. Among the several goodies that the heir from whom I bought the Model 70 had come into was a dense, full fiddleback Bastogne walnut gunstock blank for which I paid a bit less than 50 of today's dollars. In spite being a "steal," the blank would not prove a bargain. It worked out so thin in the receiver area that I was left with only one option–a small-ring receiver–and that proved expensive.

Unable to find a small-ring Model '98 "relic" action, I purchased an Ackley-barreled Husqvarna "improved Model '98" Mauser-actioned custom rifle, and discarded its California-style stock.

It could be said that my 25-06 shoots tight groups with all bullets as long as they are 87-grain spitzers pushed by either 56.8 grains of H 4831 or 48.5 grains of IMR 4320. Even with these loads, groups spread out to two minutes of angle after the first half-dozen shots, forcing one to turn to the cleaning kit.[5] At this juncture I am resigned to the possibility that before long, all that will remain of the original rifle is its Husqvarna action.

Were I given to naming my sporting accouterments in the manner of Col. Whelen, I would give my 25 Niedner a name in keeping with its resurrection from the discard drawer. In the mid-1960s I ordered a Zastava-made 25-06 barrel from Herter's mail order house. Said barrel was paired with a new F.N. deluxe commercial Mauser action, but the combination proved so inaccurate that the barrel was pulled

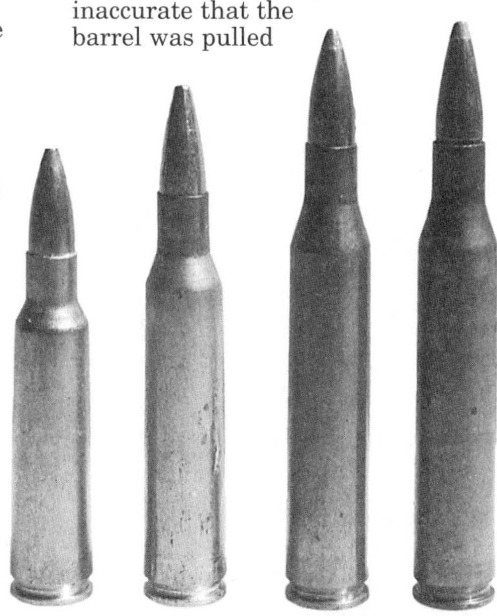

**Left to right:
250 Savage, 257 Roberts, 25 Niedner and 25-06.**

2 Pressure data is from Hodgdon's manual #26.
3 The author pleads guilty to taking this fork in the road back in the 1930s.
4 None of the above is meant to suggest that a non-resident hunter who has big money invested in a hunt should attempt the "shot of a lifetime" with a "peashooter."
5 This rifle's 26-inch barrel is slow, as well, with top velocities running as much as 40 fps slower than those from my Niedner's 24-inch barrel.

Author's home-brewed 250 Savage.

and set aside–for over 25 years.

Not until I used the Herter barrel's chamber for a Cerro Safe test run would I discover the reason for its poor accuracy. Though the shank of the barrel was stamped 25-06, the chamber cast measured out to the 25 Niedner dimensions illustrated in the wildcat section of the old Herter loading manual. The only dimensional differences–.075-inch in the length from base to shoulder/neck juncture–proved enough to cause hard bolt closure, erratic pressures, and poor accuracy.

The "ailing" barrel was subsequently paired with a VZ 24 action, bedded in a stock I carved from one of Preslik's English walnut blanks, and topped with a Redfield mount and my Redfield 12x M.S. test scope.

A variety of test loads were made up, using unfired Frankford arsenal 30-06 brass progressively necked down in a 280, a 270, and finally the 25-06 die. Unlike my Husqvarna, this rifle has produced tight groups with all loads tried to date. Though less than 50 rounds had been put through the Herter barrel during its unsuccessful early tests, the first three-shot group from my "new" 25-06 cut a cloverleaf one inch below the fouling shot on my 100-yard target. When the shooter does his part, this rifle regularly produces groups running a minute of angle, or less. Like my 250 Savage and 257 Roberts, this one is a keeper! ●

In the better bolt-action rifles, the 250 Savage cartridge can be loaded to near-243 (second from right) levels. It also performs well when loaded down to X-Hornet (far left), 223, and 22-250 levels.

257 Roberts Loads

Bullet	Charge	Power	Velocity	Remarks
75 gr.	50	H-4350	3422	
	48	H-380	3560	Best accuracy
	41.3	RL.15	3400*	
	52	H 414	3555	
87 gr.	40.2	RL. 15	3200*	
	46	H4350	3066	Best accuracy
	50	H 414	3363	
	47	H 380	3364	
100 gr.	49	H4831	3010	Best accuracy
	44	H 380	3108	
	45	H 414	3098	
	43.5	IMR4350	3000*	
120 gr.	39	RL. 15	2809	
	44	IMR 4831	2757	Best accuracy
	40	H 380	2700	
	42	IMR4350	2760	

25-06 and 25 Niedner Loads

Bullet	Charge	Power	Velocity	Remarks
75 gr.	60.1	IMR 4831	3700*	Best accuracy
	56.2	H 414	3700*	
	51	H380	3573	
	50.3	RL.15	3700*	
87 gr.	58.8	IMR 4831	3600*	
	60.3	H 4831	3600*	
	54.8	IMR 4350	3500*	
	47	RL15	3343	
100 gr.	55.9	H 4831	3300*	
	52.8	IMR 4350	3300*	Best accuracy
	52	H 4350	3296	
	53	H450	3134	
120 gr.	51	H 4831	3040	Best accuracy
	50	H 450	2995	
	48	IMR 4350	2984	
	44.4	IMR 4064	3000*	
115 gr.	52	H 4831	3042**	Excellent long-range deer and antelope load Barne's X

R.P. cases used in all but 25 Niedner loads, which used necked-down unfired Frankford arsenal 30-06 brass. CCI B.R. primers were used in 250 Savage and 257 Roberts loads and Winchester magnum rifle primers used in 25-06 and 25 Niedner loads. Accuracy notations do not apply to my particular 25-06 ***(see text)****. Approach all loads from below.*
Listings without asterisk are from Hodgdon's manual #26. Those with one asterisk are from Speer's manual #4. The two-asterisk Barnes X load is from Barnes' #2.

Reloading *In* Volume

by Patrick Sweeney

We all know that to get better you have to practice. All things being equal, the more you practice, the better you get. With that thought in mind, you decided to invest in a progressive press in order to produce more ammo with which to practice, but you have discovered an annoying problem: despite having a progressive press you don't have much more ammo to show for it; thus your practice is languishing. What's the problem?

The basic problem is that you haven't changed your reloading process or habits. Reloading with a single-stage press is a batch-crafting process, while getting the volume a progressive offers requires a production-flow process. The bottlenecks in the batch process are slowing you down.

The common bottlenecks are: An uncomfortable work space, not enough components in the room, not enough components on the bench, components spread out too much, and too much attention to detail. I'll show how my plain old Dillon 550B *(the slowest one of the Dillon line)* is capable of turning out reloaded handgun ammunition at the rate of almost 500 rounds an hour. I'll also explain why some cartridges will have a slower rate, and the special problems rifle reloaders face.

Workspace Comfort

Work at the right height. Get lots of light. Use a stiff, heavy bench. If reloading is work, you won't do much. Nothing dampens your enthusiasm for getting out and shooting like facing a reloading process more akin to laborious coal mining than a relaxing ammo-making session. You don't have to reload from a recliner to be comfortable, but you do have to pay attention to the effect your space has on you. First, do you load standing or sitting? Regardless of which one you choose, the press and bench have to be the correct height, or loading will be so tiring that you'll quickly quit. When I type, I have the keyboard at a height so my forearms are level. When I load, *(I load sitting)* the bench is the same height that a keyboard would be. The press handle has to go down to cycle the press, and if you sit too high you'll have to lean on the downstroke. Sit too low and you'll have to reach over the edge of the bench to get anything, and the upstroke of the press handle would be up and not away from you.

Have plenty of light. I loaded in a dark and cavernous basement for a long time, and when I finally saw the light I couldn't believe how less fatiguing it was to work in a well-lit space.

If at all possible, place your bench against a solid wall. The support the wall offers *(once the bench is pressed against it)* can be amazing. If your bench isn't against a wall, the flex of the bench under the load of cycling the handle can make your job harder. I've even seen *(and loaded on for a while)* benches that moved around the room. Get a stiff, heavy bench, and slide it against the wall.

Not Enough Components In The Room

Keep lots of brass on hand. Buy your components in bulk. Wait a minute, you're trying to get in more practice, but you're still using the

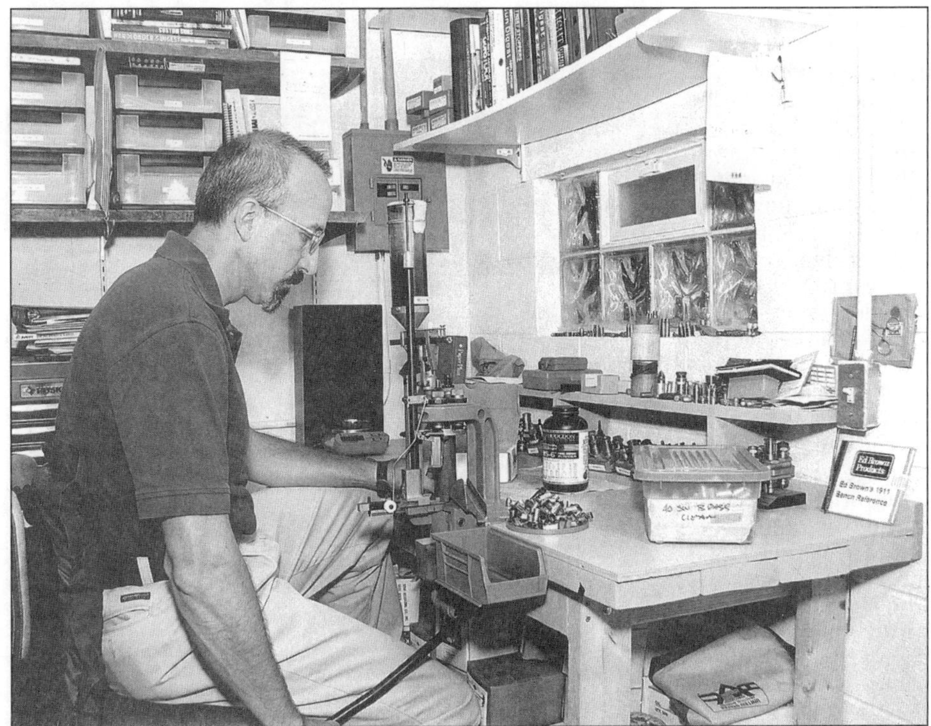

A comfortable bench, with everything in reach. On the shelf are loading manuals; on the bench all the components needed for an hour's loading, minimum.

same 200 handgun empties you've been using all along? Get more. When you get home from shooting your 200 rounds *(less than an hour's practice in some shooting disciplines)*, the first thing you have to do is sort the empties and toss them into your brass cleaner. Until they're clean you're at a standstill. How much brass do you need? At least three times a practice session, up to as much as you have room for. For the 200 rounds needed by a practice session shooter, you should have a minimum of 600 empties. More is better. With the extras in your loading flow, you can toss the new empties in the brass tumbler *(or not)* and still be able to reload.

The larger volume of brass on hand lets you get ahead in cleaning. If you have clean brass, and components on hand, you can load it all. A rainy weekend could easily produce four or five thousand rounds of ammunition, all salted away for future practice.

And when it comes to the reloading, buying one-pound cans of powder, and the cute little 100-bullet boxes are the kiss of death. The per-shot cost of buying components in small amounts will crush your wallet, and the bottleneck of loading 100 at a time will crush your enthusiasm. Buy eight-pound kegs of powder, bullets by the thousand, and primers by the 5,000 sleeve. "But I'll never shoot that much!" is the usual response. Do the math. As an example, let's use a reloader shooting the 45ACP, loading the old standard IPSC load of 5.8 grains of WW-231 and a 200-grain lead semi-wadcutter. An eight-pound keg gets you 9,655 rounds. The 5,000 primers loads half those. Each 1000-bullet box loads a tenth of that. How much will you shoot in a year? If it is available, you could go through the 9,655 rounds in a year. Two trips a month of 400 rounds each totals 10,400 rounds. You wanted to practice more, right?

As for the primers, using a single filling tube is fine, but have plenty of primers and the flipper tray close at hand.

Not Enough Components On The Bench

Keep a volume of components on the bench sufficient for the full loading session. When you sit down to reload, what is on the bench next to the press? If you sit down with 100 primers, bullets and cases, and carefully pour your powder hopper one-quarter full, there's your problem.

If you want volume, you have to have components, and not where getting them breaks your routine. Put a 500-bullet box on the bench next to the press. If you load from a bullet tray, grasp a handful of bullets and dump them on the tray. Refill as needed. I started long before bullet trays were thought of, so I just use the bench top. Having a box of bullets on hand is a psychological lure to load the whole box. "*Hey, there's just a hundred left, I might as well finish them.*"

Fill the powder hopper, both for safety and for volume loading. If you're in the habit of only putting "just enough" powder in the hopper, and sit down with a big box of bullets, you'll run out of powder and may have produced some squib rounds.

On the right side of the press keep a pile of brass. I use the lid from a coffee can to keep them from rolling off the bench. I keep the main brass bin close at hand so I can refill the bench supply by reaching and scooping.

The primers and the flipper tray go to the side of the bullets, out of the main work area, but within reach for a quick refill.

Components Widely Scattered

Don't store things any farther away than necessary. Where is your brass supply? Down the hall in the closet? Where are your bullets? Across the room? If so, your reloading sessions will entail entirely too much walking. In an ideal reloading room, the brass and

You should have a clean space to work in. I used to be messy, but I've learned from experience, and now run a neat and tidy loading bench.

primers are on shelves right next to the loading bench. That way you won't have to go any farther than needed to get more. I load seven cartridges in high volume, another ten or so in medium volume, and a dozen more once a year or so. The Big Seven (9mm, 38 Super, 38 Special, 357 Magnum, 40 S&W, 45ACP and 223) are stored closest. The rest are stored where they fit. But when I load, the whole storage bin comes to the bench. Don't be walking back and forth across the room for each handful of brass to replenish the bench supply.

And when you store your brass, think of the movie *The Graduate*. "Plastic." I use shoebox plastic storage containers, bought at the local surplus and overrun store for less than a dollar each. Clean brass stays clean and dust-free; they are easy to label, don't rust, and add little weight to the shelves' load.

The primers stay with the brass, simply to keep them away from the powder.

As for the bullets, use them to make your bench heavier. I built my bench with a reinforced bottom shelf, and I stacked the bullet boxes on the bottom shelf and underneath against the legs. There is approximately half a ton of lead holding the bench down, with that much again stacked against the legs. That bench isn't going anywhere.

The powder is the exception that proves the rule. Store your powder across the room. When you go to load a cartridge, bring one container of the powder you're going to use and leave it on the bench as a reminder of just which one is in play. If you are going to change powders, dump the powder out of the hopper into the can or keg, and carry it back to the shelves. Then **(and only then)** bring the new one over. Never, NEVER, have two cans of powder open on your bench. Or even on your bench. The least bad thing that can happen is that you'll get a powder measure full of powder confused, dump it in the wrong can, and have to discard the whole can as a result.

My bench won't move. Not with a wall behind it, a ton of bullets on the shelf, and more leaning against the legs.

Attention To Unnecessary Detail

Inspect after the loading session. Don't sort head-stamps. Don't trim brass. Don't weigh bullets. There are things you must pay attention to, but going overboard will make you crazy and slow you down. On a Dillon press with the powder safety bar, you do not have to look into every single case to make sure there is powder in it. If you simply must, rig a mirror to look. Don't rise up out of your seat on every round to peer into the case. Or, get a press with enough stations in the toolhead that you can use a powder check sensor. I use a 500B, I don't have a sensor, and I don't use a mirror. The powder safety bar has never failed me.

Don't inspect each primer as the round comes off the press. Inspect the first few off the press, and inspect a few in each hundred to make sure nothing has fallen into the primer seat cup. Then do your inspection after you've loaded.

Don't sort brass by head-stamp. Yes, I know, it is heresy to say so, but very few applications require sorted brass. Which ones do? Those requiring performance at the edge of the envelope. If you're trying to tune your Slow Fire Bullseye load, then

The bench top with only the essentials, but plenty of those. Note that only the specific powder and primer being used are on the bench, or within reach.

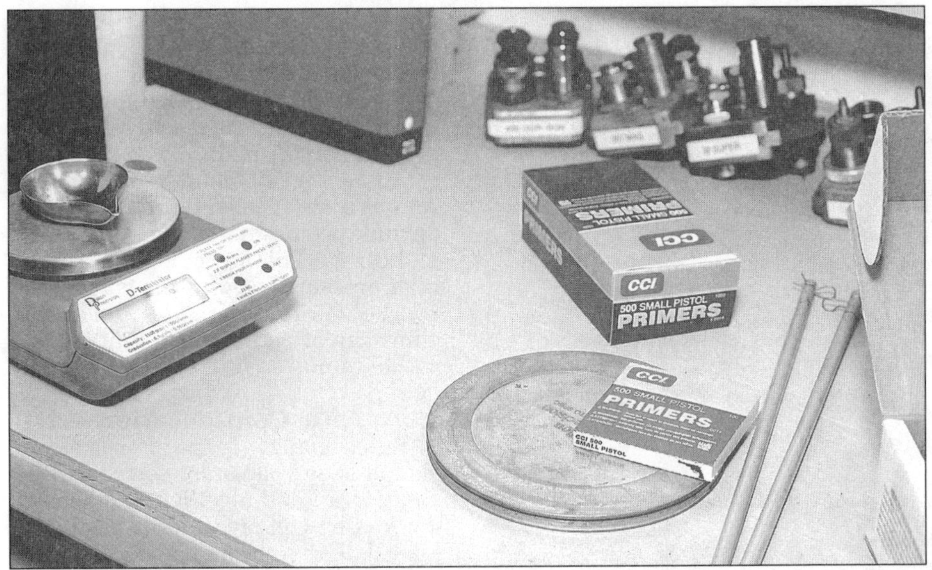

Primers, a flipper tray, tubes and the scale to check things occasionally (always when first setting up!).

using a single batch of brass can help. If you're loading your 44 Magnum with 315-grain hard cast bullets up to J. D. Jones' velocities, then using a single batch is a good idea. As a parallel, trimming handgun brass is a waste of time unless you are loading the examples I just gave. The only handgun brass I've ever trimmed in 25 years of reloading *(once I gave up on the idea)* was a batch of 44 Magnum brass I trimmed to load those aforementioned 315-grain bullets.

When you open a box of bullets, weigh a few to make sure they are the correct ones. I've opened boxes marked with one weight or style bullet, only to find some other in it. Once you've determined they are the correct ones, load them. Again, unless you're doing the most exacting work, the weight variations will not matter.

Details That Do Matter

Keep your loading data close at hand. Label your production. Keep the area clean. If your logbook is across the room, you might be tempted to depend on memory. Back when I loaded one load in each of three or four different cartridges, I could remember everything. Today, I have so many loads and such a busy day that sometimes I have to look at my driver's license to see who I am and where home is. So write down the load specs., check it, and be sure you store it where it belongs. And part of proper storage is labeling. If you don't label your ammo properly, you could get to a match and find you've brought the wrong stuff. Or find out the hard way you've brought ammo unsuited for the firearm you have with you. As for cleanliness, if your bench is littered with spent primers, spilled powder, scattered random brass and all sorts of tools, books and papers, how can you be expected to work? The litter will distract you, tire you and make it hard to find what you're looking for. I used to be messy, but I feel much better now.

Not All Cartridges Are The Same

Once I started working out the methods of increasing volume, I discovered that some cartridges just couldn't be loaded as quickly as others. The two things that slow you down are case size compared to the press and your hands, and operating pressure. The fastest cartridge to reload is the 45 ACP. It is a big case, easy to grab and manipulate. The bullets are big, and set in the case quickly and straight. And with a good press, the sizing effort needed is minimal and quickly handled.

A set of slower cartridges are the 38 Special, 357 Magnum and the 9mm. The two revolver cases are long and skinny. If you whip the toolhead up too quickly, the vibration may make the cases rock enough that you'll catch the mouth of one on the sizing die or the bullet seat die. If caught, it will get crushed. The 9mm is a small case, and if your hands are average or larger, just picking it up and getting it into the press requires a tad more effort. Effort slows you down. Smaller is worse yet. I once loaded a batch of 32 ACP ammo. Once I was done with them, the 9mms seemed as big as garbage cans, the 45s like 55-gallon drums.

High-pressure cases slow you down. The sizing effort required to run a 44 Magnum case into the sizing die can slow things appreciably. If your brass is mixed, then sizing force varies from the mild effort of the hot 44 Special-level loads to the stand-on-the-handle force needed to resize a J. D. Jones load.

Long-for-their-weight bullets slow you down, especially in the medium bores. A slightly tipped short bullet will still run up in the seating die, get straightened and be seated. A

Label everything. Containers of brass, ammo, loading dies — everything. Memory can be a weak reed to lean on; that's why mankind invented writing.

Trust the press. the powder safety linkage on my Dillon has never failed, and never let me load a squib or drop a double charge. I do not feel the need to inspect every round.

longer bullet may not. As a result, you have to go slower, and guide the bullet with your fingertips.

The 40 S&W and the 10mm are slower, for different reasons. The 40 is just enough smaller than a 45 that it can be a bit more fiddly to handle. And as a short case, there is time during the run-up for the bullet to tip and catch. The 10mm is often run at high pressures *(That's the whole point of the 10mm, right?)* and sizing effort can often approach that of the 44 Magnum.

Rifle Considerations

Rifles change things. For one, you should keep your brass sorted. Use a single brand all together, and keep track of how many times it has been loaded. Cycle through a whole batch before reloading any of it a second time. That way your brass will have a known number of loadings. It would be a shame to have your brass mixed in its number of loadings, and find out at a match or hunting trip that the round you just fired was fired one time too many.

You must trim rifle brass. If you expect to load in volume, give up the hand-crank trimmers. Buy the Dillon power trimmer, wear earmuffs, and trim quickly. The Dillon trimmer is a sizing die with a power trimmer on top, and resizing your brass also trims it. Yes, it seems expensive, but after a few weekends of trimming brass by hand *(and hating every minute of it)* the cost won't seem so excessive. I set my trimmer and a sizing die on a separate toolhead, and run my brass through the press twice. *(Once to size and trim, and once to then load.)* I still load at the rate of 200 rounds per hour.

A straight-line seating die speeds things up considerably. Especially when using flat-base bullets. A rifle bullet must be hand-seated straight, and stay straight all the way up into the seating die. Rather than guide it with your fingertips, use a straight-line seater. The seater has a window, and you drop the bullet into the window. The die holds the bullet in line for the case, and as the case comes up the bullet is seated straight. When I switched to flat-based bullets for the 223 *(they were offered dirt-cheap, so I bought them)* I was getting one or two crushed cases per hundred rounds. The straight-line seater eliminated the crushed cases and improved accuracy, too. ●

Non-Toxic Shot In the 21st Century

by Kurt Fackler

Some say shotshell evolution started and stopped a bit over a century ago. That perhaps state-of-the-art shotshells could have just as well rattled around inside a basket on the running board of a Model-T as wedged between the back seat of your millennium-fresh, yet mud-crusted and wet-dog aroma-infused rig. Well, that dog on the upholstery has not changed, but shotshells have.

You can still load as if it was 1901. Everything to load a vintage shotshell is available today. However, with a vast array of exciting, refined products and their sub-categories of pellets, wads, hulls and powders, you have the ability, if not the wherewithal, to create high-performance specialized loads for almost every shooting situation. Cars still have four wheels, and shotshell cases still have primers igniting charges of powder. The rapidly-expanding gasses produced by combustion push a seal of wadding that, in turn, pushes a payload of pellets through a constricted space (barrel). However, the pieces that comprise a car, and the pieces that comprise a shotshell have evolved to a point where performance, fit and finish are all enhanced, with no diminishment of the joy for the user.

The United States Fish and Wildlife Service began a program in the late 1970s with the objective of eliminating toxic lead pellets used in shotshells. The scenario was and is that waterfowl, living in water and eating goodies off the bottom, would eat spent pellets out in the swamps. Said pellets would be ground by an autonomic action within the bird *(please refer to your high school biology text)*, and the toxic lead bits would eventually sicken and kill the bird from lead poisoning. Factoring the arsenic from herbicides aside, policy was set and lead shot put on a path of extinction.

Non-toxic pellets perhaps seem confusing, but really break down to a few elemental pellet varieties whose compositions have specific requirements for loading inside of shotshells. We will take a look at what is available and provide a material overview, hopefully helping you decide which non-toxic pellet is best for your shooting conditions and reloading procedures.

Today, all major shotshell manufacturers are incorporating non-toxic pellets into their shotshell line-ups. Most manufacture steel shot loads, an evolved example of the non-toxic species, and at the same time more recent arrivals to the non-toxic

Available to waterfowlers in the 21st century are several types of non-toxic pellets approved by the U.S. Fish and Wildlife Service. Shown are: Kent's TungstenMatrix; Bismuth Cartridge Company's Bismuth/tin pellets; Fiocchi's steel pellet loads and Federal's Tungsten and Tungsten Poly. Not shown is Remington's Hevi-shot.

Steel shot, not a waterfowler's friend when first introduced in the 1970s, has come a long way. Modern specialized components, firearms and loading procedures, available to handloaders today, have made steel into a modern-day bargain with performance exceeding many lead loads of old.

community, including tungsten in several forms, bismuth/tin alloy, poly resins and nickel.

Remington has struck a deal recently with Environmental, a manufacturer of the non-toxic pellet called Hevishot, to unite in a collaborative effort between shotshell manufacturer and pellet manufacturer. Remington will be using the proprietary Hevishot non-toxic pellets under a licensing agreement, inside the Remington brand shotshells. Bismuth Cartridge Company, and Kent Cartridge Company, are making a stand with proprietary, competitive pellets of their own.

Some non-toxic pellets are available, as a component, to handloaders. Using these pellets, you have an opportunity to apply the magic of one shell at a time manufacturing. Some non-toxic manufacturers prefer, at this time, their pellets to remain shrouded behind little plastic cylindrical walls in box lots of 10 to 25 packaging that renders handloading redundant, expensive and really, somewhat unreasonable considering the usefulness of the containers as loaded ammunition.

Steel Shot

Steel shot was the first non-toxic answer. In the earliest years only an enthusiastic crowd of government-funded research consultants applauded the introduction of laws mandating the use of steel shot. Lethal range of steel shot, loaded at low-velocity with heavy payload, was seemingly somewhere between 20 feet and 20 yards.

The similar hardness of the pellets and barrels did unspeakable damage to the latter. Things evolve, though, and the speedy evolution of steel shot into today's lethal and reasonably-priced waterfowl load can be directly attributed to America's handloaders and the fiercely competitive industry that supports them. Prototype loads were cooked up and tested in the labs, used in the field, then published long before mass-produced steel shot ammunition achieved a performance standard considered a reasonable option.

The first steel shot components developed were protective wads. There was once a time when plastic shotcups were used to protect soft lead pellets from deformation; conditions incompatible with long-range patterns. When a pellet is squashed, and thrown out a barrel at high velocity, the result is much like when you hold your hand out the window of a car, playing airplane. Next time you are playing airplane, make a fist instead of a flat airfoil. Yup, the fist tends to be stable, not as much fun to apply aerodynamics. Yeah, similar effect with pellets.

Steel shot wads are manufactured with thicker petals and of special proprietary polymers. In the Tuff Wads, designed and manufactured by Ballistic Products, special attention was paid to designing the wad's base, inside and out, to take advantage of ultra-slow burning powders and large volume, low-density payloads.

Steel shot *(which is actually a stage name for dead-soft iron pellets' but steel looks so much nicer in print)* is about 70 percent the density of the lead shot it replaced. We learned early that velocity was the critical element to produce lethal steel loads. We learned that American handloaders needed to take a new look at their shotshells and accept the mantra: even though the load is lighter, it is about the same number of pellets as my old lead load.î Poor training, disseminated by manufacturer's advertising groups, lead shooters to believe they should look for parity of payload weight—not volume, not velocity. However, after a few smacks with the rolled-up newspaper, and a decade of admonishment, things got better and steel became a viable non-toxic field pellet.

As with everything, there is a point of diminishing returns and that rule applies to shotshells. By using modern slow-burning shotgun powders and modern wads 1600 fps steel shot loads can be delivered reliably. Greater speeds can be attained, with a price of variability in pressure/velocity by combining extraordinarily light payloads with great piles of slow-burning powder. Like a top-fuel dragster, these loads can burn brightly, but would you want to commute with it, or in our case, bet your hunt on it?

The art of loading steel shot has been evolving the longest of the non-toxic class. Steel's years in the field are exemplified by a huge wide selection of components, loads, shot sizes and performance gains. Steel shot has also groomed shooters over

Using steel shot requires using specialized wads that protect barrels from contact, maximize potential energy of slow-burning powders and deliver long-range patterns.

There's plenty of help out there for non-toxic shot handloaders. Powder manufacturers, reloading press manufacturers and component manufacturers publish instructional books and manuals. Most have tested data, others have specific loader information and component compatibility information. Knowing the components that make up your loads will help you make better overall loads.

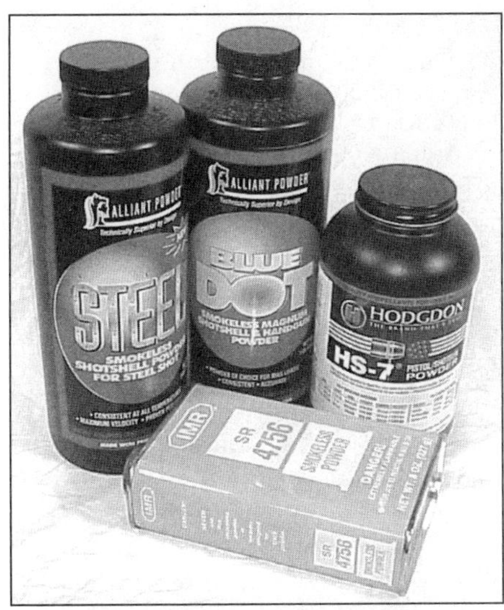

Non-toxic pellets require special powders to perform properly. Alliant, with their powder "Steel" has even developed a formula specifically tailored to the high-volume, less-density requirements of steel pellet. Alliant Blue Dot, Hodgdon HS-7 and IMR's 4756 have remained enduring favorites as non-toxic loading has evolved.

the last 20 years or so, to understand its dynamics—the leads and ranges most effective using steel. Furthermore, modern shotguns and chokes have become steel shot friendly pushing effective patterns to longer lethal ranges.

Pellet size applications have been refined, and re-defined. Powders, such as Alliant Steel, have sprung up to serve steel-shot handloaders. There are several comprehensive steel-shot loading manuals, some with lab-tested load recipes and specific instructions for assembling superb field loads available for handloaders. These include step-by-step instructions as well as becoming a handloader's link to a technical staff and ballistic laboratory. You may like handloading steel shot. Steel shot reacts well to using small, performance-enhancing products such as specialized buffer, shot wrappers and specialized two-piece wad—columns creating stable and balanced loads. It is an economical modern non-toxic solution, more effective today than many of the lead shot loads it has replaced.

Bismuth

Bismuth as it is known, Bismuth/Tin as it is comprised, showed up in the mid-1990s. Bismuth is offered for handloading and available through retail outlets across the United States. Ducks can eat bismuth all day. In fact they can find it at our local grocery stores. Bismuth is an active ingredient in stomach medicines usually pink in color.

Bismuth/tin was the first non-steel pellet approved by a seemingly reluctant USFWS for use on migratory waterfowl. The rules that had been set into place were, it seemed, predisposed toward steel shot as a final solution. Hats off to the Bismuth Cartridge Company for a vanguard effort through a tangled jungle of regulation.

Because it is softer than barrels, bismuth does not harm barrels—eliminating the need for a shotcup barrier between pellets and barrel. Furthermore, the malleability of bismuth pellets allows shooters to drag small-bore shotguns, once relegated to wall-hanger status, back out into active field duty.

Because bismuth is a crystalline element, it does have a propensity for breaking during initial setback of firing, particularly with large pellet, high-volume high-velocity loads. Handloads, as well as the factory-made loads, address pellet breakage by buffering the pellets inside of full-length shotcups. Buffer is comprised of tiny plastic flakes that occupy the spaces between pellets inside a load. When the load is fired, the buffer provides increased surface area contact between the pellets, reducing breakage of bismuth pellets and similarly, in lead loads where buffer reduces the number and magnitude of deformed pellets.

In the field, bismuth shoots a lot like lead. It's dense enough to carry the patterns to reasonable range and is the handloaderís non-toxic choice for small-bore shotguns. Young shooters, or anyone who feels like it, can again carry a .410 bore, 28 gauge or 20 gauge to the duck blinds and anticipate excellent performance without fearing damage to their shotguns. Furthermore, fine old double barrels, squirreled away when harder non-toxic pellets were the rule of the day, are being brought out into the light of day again and, with dignity, taking their rightful place in the field.

Bismuth and TungstenMatrix are the only currently available non-toxic pellets using full-choke effectively—without concerns of damage or blemishes. Bismuth and TungstenMatrix offer another advantage of softness: Once a pellet has found its target, we need it to transfer all of its forward energy-right now-making the hit lethal. A pellet that does not deform may continue, without transferring much energy, right through to the other side leaving only minor tissue damage. Like jacketed bullets in high-velocity small-caliber rifles, energy transfer is at the crux of a criticism of hard, non-toxic pellets; that perhaps they penetrate a little too efficiently. Clearly, a great hunting load is more than holes in pattern paper.

Bismuth Cartridge Company offers their non-toxic pellets as a handloading component. The pellets are soft and therefore barrel contact will not harm shotguns. Happily, old doubles and small-bore shotguns, once tucked away, are returning to the field using with a huge variety of handloads and factory-loaded ammunition—in every available gauge.

Bismuth is also available in a wide variety of loaded ammunition, including new turkey and upland loads, as well as waterfowl loads in all gauges from 10 on down to the little .410 bore.

Hevi-Shot

Hevi-shot, an exciting, denser-than-lead non-toxic pellet, was introduced to shotgunnners a couple of years ago. It is a combination of tungsten nickel, iron and certain binding polymers. The pellets

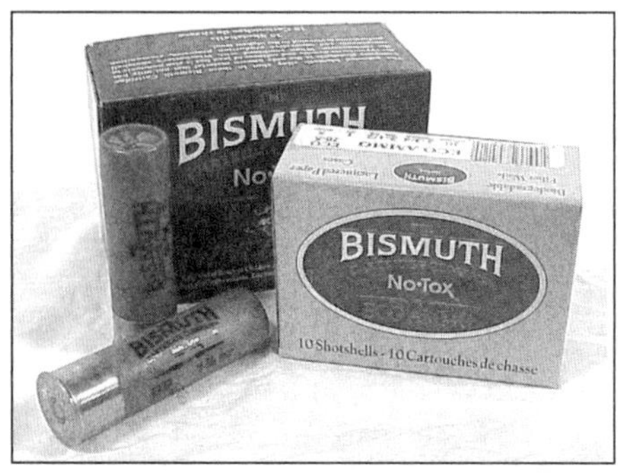

Bismuth Cartridge Company offers their non-toxic pellets as a handloading component. The pellets are soft and therefore barrel contact will not harm shotguns. Happily, old doubles and small-bore shotguns, once tucked away, are returning to the field using with a huge variety of handloads and factory-loaded ammunition—in every available gauge.

Federal Cartridge Company manufactures two types of non-toxic pellets. Tungsten is a Tungsten/Iron combination, dense like lead, but hard like steel. Federal uses a specialized overlapping wad to protect steel-approved shotguns. The pellets deliver excellent energy downrange. Federal's other offering is Tungsten-Poly pellets; which will not harm nitro-approved shotguns and maintains lead-like density. Neither pellet is available as a component.

actually exceed the density of lead, by about 10 percent, and in doing so, have demonstrated ballistic advantages as pellets surpass a nontoxic pellet's ìdense as lead barrier. Denser than lead and high velocity deliver incredible energy. Furthermore, Hevi-shot has collected awards for its ability to hold patterns.

Hevi-shot is effective. Hevi-shot is effective like Frankenstein's monster is effective in that they both are sporting a greenish hue, seem oddly put together, and are unstoppable. Superior to Frankenstein's monster, Hevi-shot is unaffected by the strangeness of fire. In fact, put in close proximity with fire inside the shotshell, the two become quite compatible, delivering solid hits and undisputedly nice patterns. You really have to see results to believe in Hevi-shot. Judged by conventional wisdom, without shooting, Hevi-shot could receive a mid-term grade advisory pinned to its lapel.

Here's a graphic example of how to relate energy from pellets with different densities. On the left, steel shot #1, an excellent choice for pass shooting high-flying ducks. On the right, is Hevishot #4s. They are also an excellent choice for pass shooting ducks. The larger steel shot pellets are a similar weight to the smaller, denser, Hevishot pellets.

Hevi-shot pellets are oblong, strange and in the larger sizes, such as BB, will sometimes have seemingly grown little evil heads. But, unconventional things come from the Environmental's lightning-powered laboratory in Sweet Home, OR: Hevi-shot delivers lethal energy within these patterns to extended ranges. In fact, turkey hunters, the kings of one-shot killing patterns, are choosing to turn from lead to Hevi-shot for the most lethal pattern in the woods.

Using Hevi-shot you just don't need to oversize the pellets to retain lethal energy. Downrange energy has become a relative term depending on the shooter; we have become accustomed to steel shot in the last twenty years or so and use it as a yardstick to measure performance. Maybe you remember, and maybe you don't, the sizes once used for taking game with lead pellets. If you do not, Hevi-shot brings back a scale unused since the days of lead: #6 pellets are effective for ducks over decoys. #2s can be used for geese. In fact, we highly recommend you try the smaller sizes before going for the larger sizes.

Hevi-shot is as hard, or harder, than shotgun barrels. Hevi-shot requires the use of protective shotcups in every load and, like steel, we would not recommend using it in the smaller gauges. Several shotcups manufactured exclusively for the specific demands of Hevi-shot are available.

Steel is about 70 percent as dense as lead and Hevi-shot is 10 percent denser than lead. Neither can be substituted for any other type of pellet in shotshells; I do not care how many calculations you have extrapolated on volume and weight. Attempting to calculate pellet substitutions is putting yourself and your equipment at risk, not to mention your hunt. Each pellet type produces a unique internal ballistics scenario.

TPS *(Tungsten Propulsion System)* wads, load data and buffers are manufactured specifically for the high density and barrel protection necessary for using Hevi-shot.

Tungsten Matrix

Developed in Britain in the 1990s, Tungsten Matrix is a serious player in the non-toxic ammunition game, but unfortunately, manufacturer Kent Cartridge of Kearneysville, WV, has made a decision not to include handloaders in the fun and TungstenMatrix is not available for handloading. However, because TungstenMatrix is a viable performer, we need to spend a moment comparing this non-toxic

Most major manufactures offer steel shot non-toxic loads. The performance of the loads in the field gets better every year. Amongst formidable competition of new non-toxic pellets, modern, high-performance steel shot loads have become an excellent value for waterfowlers. Steel shot is available in a wide variety of sizes and grades.

Almost all ammunition boxes will list certain features important for selecting the right ammunition for your shooting conditions. These are 12 gauge, 2-3/4", 1-1/8 oz. #4 steel. A good choice for ducks over decoys. Usually, velocity will be listed in terms of feet-per-second. Dram equivalent, with regards to non-toxic ammunition, is largely irrelevant to hunters. Any effective non-toxic load for hunting will be a "max" dram equivalent.

option to the others available to us.

TungstenMatrix is soft, like lead and bismuth, not requiring a protective barrier between pellets and barrels. The loaded ammunition is geared toward standards expected by performance handloaders, but without the specific options and tweaking only made possible by loading one shell at a time.

The pellets, because of similar characteristics to lead, have huge potential, and much of that is realized during Kent's ammunition manufacturing process. Kent uses the best possible components, many of which are familiar to handloaders, and assembles the loads following a philosophy placing high performance above other manufacturing constraints. Kent has TungstenMatrix loads available in 10 gauge, all lengths of 12 gauge and most of the small bores. For Kent's manufacturing efforts, we get some very decent shells. Still, we would appreciate making some ourselves.

Federal Cartridge Company offers two other non-toxic pellets inside loaded ammunition. One is a Tungsten-polymer pellet offering malleability and density characteristics very similar to lead. You can find Federal's Tungsten Poly loads in most shotshell configurations.

Federal also manufactures shotshells with tungsten-iron pellets. These loads utilize a proprietary

Kent claims TungstenMatrix "looks like lead, shoots like lead." It does. Unfortunately, Kent does not offer TungstenMatrix to reloaders, who would then be able assemble more specialized loads in all gauges.

overlapping shotcup specifically designed to maximize barrel protection. The pellets are hard and the pellets are dense. Federal's tungsten-iron pellets, like Hevi-shot, carry a huge amount of energy throughout their effective range. The ammunition manufactured with these two non-toxic pellet types are available in 10 and 12 gauge - in their various lengths for waterfowl and turkey. Neither of Federal's USFWS-approved pellets are available for handloading.

Hevi-shot is hard and dense and cannot come into contact with shotgun barrels. The pellets also place extraordinary demands on the shotcup designed to contain them. Shotcups and protective sleeves, designed specifically to contain the dense, fast-moving payloads are available to handloaders.

So, at this point you would probably like to see our recommendation for USFWS-approved non-toxic pellets. Can't do that. Depending on equipment you use, conditions in which you will be shooting on any particular day you will make a choice. The more you know, the more refined your decisions will become.

Steel has evolved into an effective hunting pellet with a tremendous amount of data and components available to tailor-make your loads. Over the past 20 years we have become used to using steel effectively. Bismuth and TungstenMatrix allow you to use your fine old doubles and small-bores. Hevi-shot and Tungsten-iron deliver unbelievable energy—to ranges we thought not possible with lead, let alone non-toxic pellets. However, you will have to take measures to properly protect your firearms. Maybe your choice should depend on game you are chasing this day. Options-loads suited for the hunt-are what make handloading worthwhile, creative and exciting. ●

Hevi-shot, manufactured by Environmetal, is available to handloaders and is being loaded into ammunition by contract with Remington. The pellets are actually denser than lead, which has proven to be an enormous ballistic advantage for hunting waterfowl. Yes, the pellets are ugly, but they work, patterning well beyond expectation. Leave everything you have learned about pellets and patterns behind and try them.

The Starline Story

by Patrick Sweeney

If it were not for empty brass, none of us would be reloaders. Yes, you can load and fire a firearm without brass *(it's called "muzzleloading")*, but the modern phenomenon known as handloading would not be possible without empty, reloadable brass. Without brass, a firearm designed around cartridges cannot be used. Done any plinking with your 8mm Nambu lately?

There used to be thousands of Colt single-action revolvers quietly resting on their memories, until the cowboy action shooters started playing with them, and caused the manufacture of brass for chamberings that hadn't had a run of new brass since W.C. Fields was sober.

One of the leaders of the new brass movement is Starline. Robert Hayden and Frank Snow started Starline in 1976 with one product, a 38 Special case. Why a 38? In 1976, there was still lots of surplus 45 and 9mm ammo. Competition handgun shooting was either Bullseye or PPC, and if you wanted to load ammunition for them you needed brass. Your choices then were to use miscellaneous collected brass, or to buy a bunch of factory ammo and shoot it. Starline offered another choice. The 38 Special was quickly followed by 357 Magnum cases and then 44 Magnum. The Starline product line quickly grew. If you are plugged into the ammunition manufacturing circuit, the names should be familiar. Robert and Frank are two of the three founding members of Sierra Bullets, which Starline is adjacent to in Sedalia, Missouri. They determined that the manufacturing of ammunition and components had one small flaw in it back in 1976: the only people making brass cartridge cases were making it solely to load their brand of ammo. Today, and for some years now, the operation is run by Barbara Hayden, Robert's wife.

In addition to making brass for consumers, Starline also makes brass for custom loaders, high-volume reloaders, and the big guys, too. Why would an ammo plant place an order with an outside vendor? Look at it this way: If you were the production manager for an ammo maker, and knew that to tear down the line and make the brass you need for a small order was going to throw your schedule off by weeks, would you make it or buy it? Especially if buying it put you ahead of schedule? Back when I was working as a gunsmith, the then-owner of the shop came agonizingly close to getting into custom reloading. The tooling was there, the name and product was there, and the profit margin was there. A few days hesitation was there, and it didn't happen. What was so neat about it was that the shop had their brass made with their head-stamp: "Nevins." Starline made that brass.

Today there are 60 cartridges listed in the Starline brass catalog, and more than that considering special orders or industrial products that the rest of us have no need for. Everything from the tiny 32 S&W Long to 480 Ruger in handgun brass, and rifle brass besides. Do you have an old Winchester rifle in 40-65? Starline has new brass for you. Starline brass even includes blanks for the cowboy action shooters who

Some of the Starline brass I've been using lately, *L-R:* 9x19, 9x21, 38 Super, 38 SuperComp, 357 SIG, 400 Cor-Bon, 40 Super and 460 Rowland.

shoot mounted, and those who practice fast draw.

Some of the Starline cases I've been using lately have been 400 Cor-Bon and 40 Super, some 45 Super and the quite robust 460 Rowland. They are all hot numbers, and reloads that brush up against the redline can prove to be hard on your brass. I haven't blown any cases yet, but the fact that I have a ready supply means I can work away to my heart's content, secure in the knowledge that I'm not experimenting with a limited supply of irreplaceable brass. *(I've been through that before, and it wasn't fun.)*

"We make everything right here," says Barbara Hayden. "We bring in the brass, run the machines, ship the cases." I've used a bunch of it, and have always found it top notch. "We constantly measure and test, gauge and inspect, to make sure our customers get the best."

And sometimes the odd. For those with the slightly strange, or limited-production handguns, often Starline can keep your gun running. Some ten years ago, there was a bunch of different cartridges developed for autopistol competition, chamberings now less enthusiastically loaded. The 9x21 was an attempt to get 38 Super ballistics out of a 9mm Parabellum handgun. There were a large number of competition handguns made in 9x21, and if you have one now, Starline is your source for brass. *(After the majority of IPSC competition shooters went to the 38 Super case, you could buy raceguns in 9x21 cheap.)* Another victim of those experimental days was the 356 TSW, another attempt at gaining Super load performance from a 9mm handgun. There were some very choice competition guns chambered for it. The last time I noticed, a box of the Federal ammo *(factory-loaded, back then)* at a gun show carried a sticker price of $52! For that, Starline will ship you just about 500 empties.

Competition shooters aren't the only ones looking for good brass. One pistol that can be very tough on brass is the broomhandle Mauser. The chambers can be rough, the bores pitted, and the chamber shoulder of the 7.63 Mauser can be generous. When ammo was only corrosive, expensive and non-reloadable, the many 1896 pistols didn't get shot much. Starline now has the brass. While it still gets worked hard by pitted chambers and generous shoulder locations, it is reloadableñand it is inexpensive compared to surplus ammo.

And even if you aren't looking for the wild or woolly, the weird or rare, Starline has the goods. Plain old 38 Special, 9mm Parabellum, several 45s, and 44 Magnum brass crowd the warehouse shelves of Starline. Everything is made in-house, starting with coiled brass sheets from which the discs to begin the cartridge-making process are punched. Why make brass that others make? Why not focus on just the strange stuff? "Because the customers want it." After all, if you're buying a bunch of 32-20, 38-40 and 44-40 for your cowboy action shooting, you might as well round out the order with some 45 ACP for your IDPA or IPSC guns, right? That's how I make sure I have enough on hand.

How good is Starline brass? Good enough that national champions use it, both for practice and match use. At many competitions, brass that hits the ground is "lost brass," and immediately belongs to the range. *(There simply isn't time to go scrounging for brass, and still finish the match at a reasonable hour.)* Starline brass is so well thought of that competitors like Jerry Barnhart and Doug Koenig shoot it and leave it. Only reloaders can understand that shooting a case once and leaving it on the ground is a compliment.

How did Starline end up with so many offerings? By listening to their customers. As they got requests for this chambering or that cartridge, they kept track. When it seemed they had requests enough to make a new cartridge a viable project, they ran a batch *(or ten)* and added it to the lineup. And for those who want something out of the ordinary, you can order your own brass. With your own head-stamp. The odd calibers might be an extra charge *(and just what am I going to do with 100,000 8mm Nambu empties with my name on them?)* but for a custom head-stamp on regular production brass, you aren't going to find it too expensive. You will have to find room for that 100,000-piece minimum order, though.

If you aren't looking for your own headstamped brass, but do want Starline to make brass you need, the process is simple. Write or e-mail them, tell them what chambering you desire, and approximately how many a year you will be using. If your buddies also need some, say so, and include their use in the total. Starline is always trying to figure out what their customers want, and will work with you as best they can. ●

Starline uses many headstamps: Two stars with a line in between two stars in the designation, and the name of the cartridge and originator. *L-R:* 357 SIG, 400 Cor-Bon, 40 Super and 460 Rowland.

THE LATEST RELOADING TOOLS AND ACCESSORIES

by Larry S. Sterett

Some of the old-line firms are gone, but there are many new products available to the handloader.

Barnes Bullets

Barnes' Reloading Manual No. 3 was mentioned in the last edition, as was the new Barnes Ballistics Program Version 2.0. Currently the firm is busy keeping up with production of bullets, including the new Taurus HEX Copper Bullets.

Battenfeld Technologies

Battenfeld has a new lightweight hand-held Vibra-Prime Automatic Primer Tube Filler that's a gem. Battery operated; it will fill primer tubes, large or small rifle or pistol, in seconds for transferring to Dillon or RCBS progressive presses. Place the primers in the tray, jiggle until the primers have flipped, open the gate and pull the trigger. It's simple and it's fast.

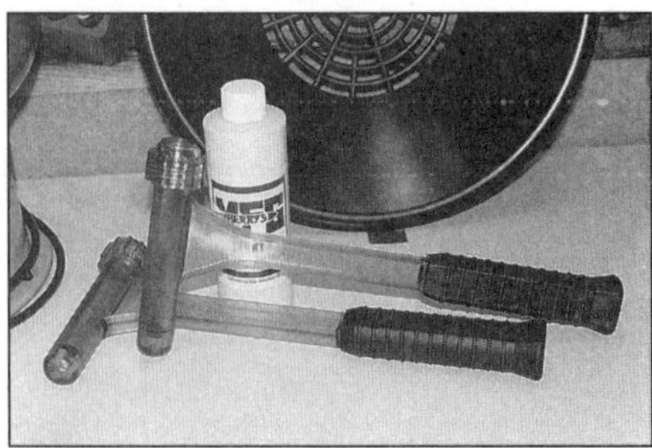

Berry's new inertia Deluxe Bullet Puller features a rubberized grip and comes with three collets.

Berry's Manufacturing

Berry's is known for its plastic ammo boxes, powder funnels, ammo trays, and plated swaged bullets for reloading. In addition to a couple of new round nose bullet designs, one each for the 9xl8mm Makarov and 45-70 Govt., the firm has a new Deluxe Bullet Puller. Featuring an overmolded head and large rubberized grip, the Puller comes complete with three collets, and will handle most cartridges when a bullet has to be pulled to check a powder charge.

Corbin Manufacturing & Supply

Long known as the swaging people, Corbin Manufacturing & Supply has a new high precision, all-

One of the links on the Corbin S-Press showing the location of the roller bearings at both ends of the link.

Corbin's new S-Press is specifically designed for reloading metallic cartridges using regular 7/8 x 14 dies, but is capable of swaging bullets up to .458 size.

The Hollywood Universal I loading press can be changed to a 12-station turret press by changing the die head, and by adding other parts the single shellholder can be increased to four different sizes. Hollywood parts are again available, in addition to new Senior and Turret

steel reloading and bullet-making press. Designed to eliminate the need for an arbor press often used with straight-line dies in precision reloading, the new S-Press features four sets of Torrington needle-bearings in the linkage to provide smooth operation. The S-Press weighs 22 pounds, and accepts standard 7/8 x 14 dies and RCBS-type button shellholders. *(Optional arbor press anvils will permit the press to use non- threaded dies if desired.)* Supplied with a side-vented primer port, a primer catcher tray that travels with the ram, and a CNC-style floating punch holder for bullet swaging punches, the S-Press replaces the 1980s Corbin Series II-style swaging press. With a 4-inch ram stoke for reloading and a 2-inch high-powered swaging stroke, the new O-frame press has an 180,000-psi tensile strength and is capable of swaging bullets up to .458-inch diameter. Finished with a gold and black metal polymer powder coat to resist heat, abrasion, wear and most chemical solvents, the S-Press is a professional-quality tool suitable for reloading or swaging. It will handle most cartridges, but the ram travel is not long enough to handle the 50 BMG, nor will it accept dies for this cartridge.

Forster Precision Products

The Lanark, Illinois, firm has six new chamberings added to their Bench Rest die set line, plus an optional 'short-throw' handle for the Co-Ax loading press. The new cartridges covered include 300 Winchester Short Mag, the 338 Lapua, and the 7mm and 300 Remington Short Ultra Mag and the 7mm and 375 Remington Ultra Mag cartridges. Complete die sets - or individual dies - are available, including the Ultra Seating dies. A Kwik-Fill Sandbag Filler, with long drop tube, is also available to help fill the bags needed to check out those handloads.

Hollywood Engineering

Handloaders who have been around for a while will recall the ultimate reloading presses were those produced by Lyle S. Corcoran of the Hollywood Gun Shop. A half-century ago they had the Senior, "Junior," Universal I, II, and III, and later an automatic 12-gauge model that could churn out 1,800 loaded shotshells per hour ... provided the hoppers and magazines could be kept filled. Bullet swaging dies were available in most popular rifle and handgun calibers, and so were many other loading items, powder measures, lead core cutters, and a multitude of loading dies–including the 23 calibers of the Wildcat C.C.C. *(Controlled Combustion Cartridge)* series from the 218 Bee C.C.C. to the 375 Magnum C.C.C.

The Hollywood presses were massive and almost indestructible, but they were not low-priced. The Universal III, which had a 12-station turret die head, four-position shellholder head and four-position primer rod head, minus dies, shellholders or primer rods was $88.50 in 1952, and worth it, while the single-stage Senior with one set of dies was priced at $37.50.

Over the years some of the press models, such as the Junior and Universal *(a couple were renamed the A and B models.)*, were discontinued and the names changed. By the mid-1960s the firm was still at the same address in Hollywood, but was now Hollywood Reloading, Inc. Only the Senior, which had doubled in price without the dies, a Senior Turret model, and an automatic at $895.00 for metallics–plus two shotshell tools in a choice of 20, 16, or 12

The Collet Resizing Die from Innovative Technologies will work on more than 15 belted cartridge cases, ironing out the pre-belt bulge and extending the reloading life of the case.

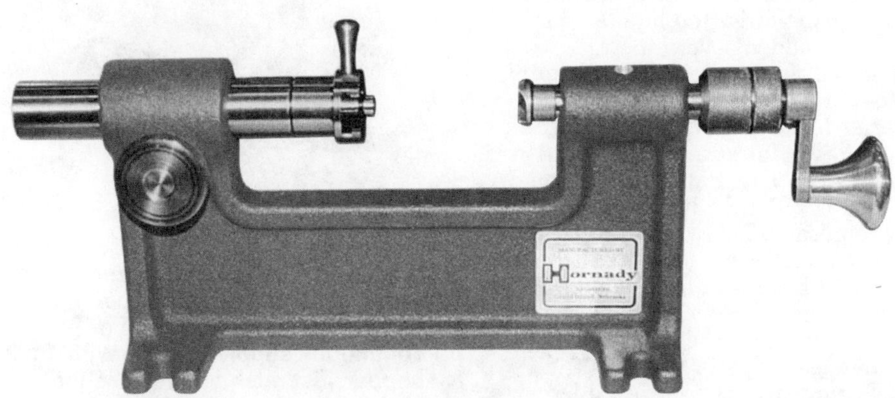

Hornady's Cam-Lock Trimmer makes the job of trimming brass cartridge cases much easier, and extra cutters can be obtained.

Lyman's new Pro Magnum Tumbler will handle up to 900 38 Special cases at a time, or a smaller number of larger cases.

gauge–were available. All the loading die sets, including the 50 BMG at $35.00 and most of the big British calibers from the 360 No. 2 up to the 600 Nitro Express for $25.00-$35.00 were still available.

The good news is some Hollywood tools are again available. It's now Hollywood Engineering and the firm is in Sun Valley, not Hollywood. Only the Senior and Senior Turret presses are available, but parts for the older models—Universal, etc.—are still available as are swaging dies, lead core cutters, loading die sets, including those of the C.C.C. and 50 BMG cartridge. For handloaders owning an older Hollywood press who have lost their instructions, copies are available for a fee, and old tools can be reconditioned and repaired. *(The Hollywood was unique for its time in featuring 1-1/2 x 12 threaded die stations with bushings to handle regular 7/8 x 14 die sets. The larger holes permitting the use of shotshell dies, big-bore English caliber or 50 BMG die sets, or regular 7/8 x 14 die sets using the bushings. It's good to have them available again.)*

Hornady Manufacturing

The big news from Hornady was the introduction of the exciting new 17 HMR rimfire cartridge, plus 405 Winchester and 458 Lott loads, and a more powerful 444 Marlin load in their ammunition line, in addition to some other new loads. However, the firm hasn't forgotten handloaders and has added several new chamberings to their line of loading dies. In the two-die Custom Grade Series I, the 270 WSM, 7mm WSM, 300 WSM, 7mm Remington SA Ultra, 7mm Rem. Ultra Mag., 300 Rem. SA Ultra, 375 Rem. Ultra Mag. calibers have been added, while in the Series II three-die sets, the 405 Winchester and 458 Lott have been added. Shell holders have been added for the 405 Winchester and the 338 Lapua cartridges.

For maximum accuracy all metallic cases require trimming to the correct length and the Hornady Cam-Lock Trimmer makes the job easy. Now a Cam-Lock Premium Extra Cutter can be obtained. With a Cam-Lock Trimmer, pilots, Premium Cutter, and a Neck Turning Tool with micro-adjustable cutter, a handloader should be set to handle all case trimming needs.

Innovative Technologies

Handloaders who reload several different cartridges based on the 300/375 H & H Magnum belted case head size may find the Magnum Collet Resizing Die manufactured by Innovative Technologies *(1480 Guinevere Drive, Dept GDH, Casselberry, FL 32707)* useful. Conventional resizing dies do not always fully restore belted cases to their original size, resulting in a

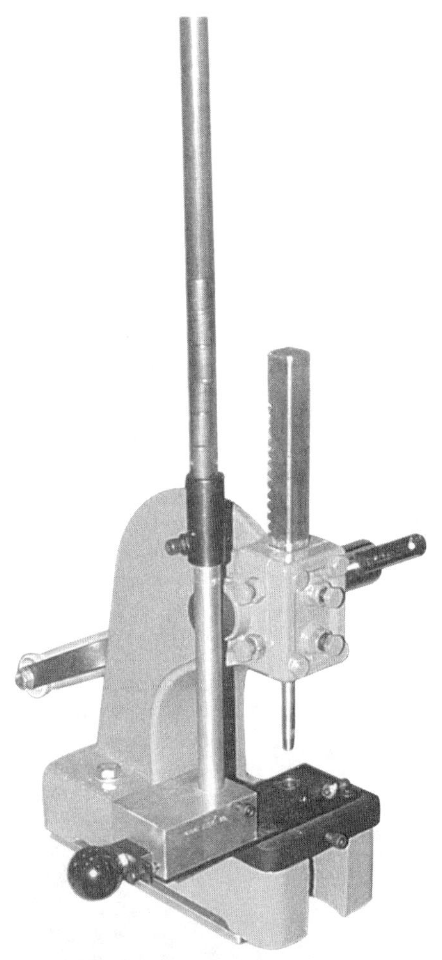

Magma Engineering's new Case Master Jr. Rimless Case Sizer features a shovel handle for easy operation and the hopper will provide a continuous supply of case. With a full hopper, just push and release the plunger head on the left, move the handle to its stop, and return, and the case is sized to the original head size.

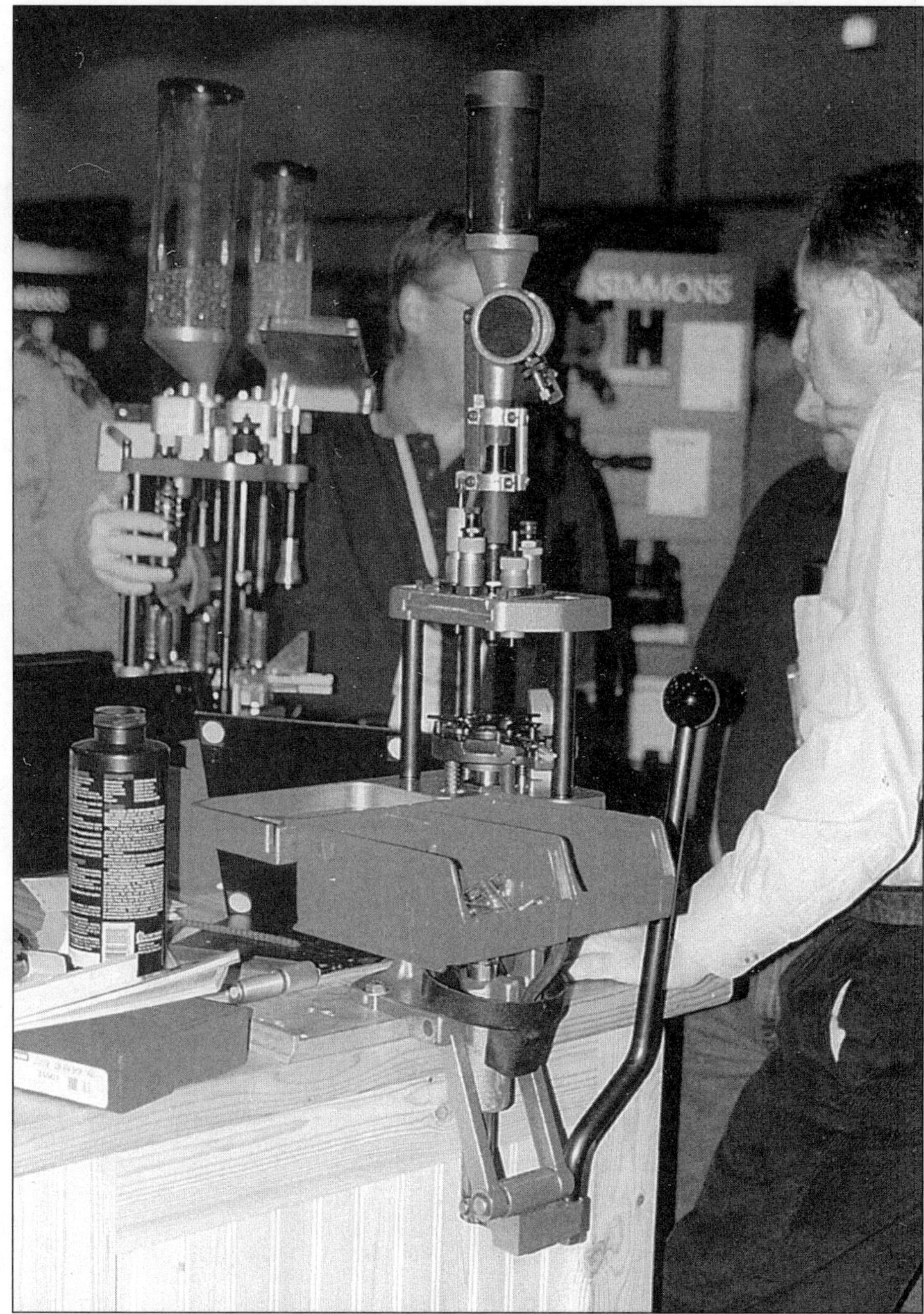

The RCBS Piggyback III can increase loaded metallic output by a factor of eight by simply changing a single-stage press into a five-station, manual-indexing progressive unit, as shown in the foreground.

'bulge' above the belt. This die uses a collet, which fits over the cartridge case up to the belt. The collet, with case, is then inserted into the sizing die where the top of the die serves as a gauge to determine when "complete" brass resizing is required. By allowing the case to go farther into the die the 'bulge' can be reduced, permitting up to 20 firings per case. This unit will work on more than 15 different belted magnum calibers, and can even resize loaded ammunition according to the manufacturer. Currently available only from the manufacturer, the die is not inexpensive, costing just under a C-note, delivered.

King & Co.

Handloaders wanting a specific set of loading dies and not being able to find it may want to contact King & Co. *(P. O. Box 1242, Bloomington, IL 61702)*. This firm states it is the nation's largest die service, buying and selling and even trading 7/8 x 14 dies, new and used. It could be well worth the price of a letter and a SASE *(self-addressed, stamped envelope)*.

Lee Precision, Inc.

Lee Precision has four new bullet moulds available, all flat-nose designs, including a 158-grain 38, a 200-grain 45, a 300-grain 45 for the 454 Casull and a 400-grain for the 480 Ruger and 475 Linebaugh cartridges. The Lee Turret Press is now available with a four-hole turret, and updating kits are available, as are extra four-hole turrets. Owners of Lee turret presses with the three-hole turret can change them to four-hole. The Lee three-die carbide pistol die set has been upgraded to a Deluxe Pistol Die Set in six calibers by including a free crimp die along with the free shellholder. The cartridges for which the Deluxe dies are available include the 9mm Luger, 38 Special, 40 S & W, 44 Special, 45 Colt, and 45 ACP. Others may be added later.

Lyman Products

Lyman Products has been in the reloading business longer than most of the firms covered in this report, starting back in the days of blackpowder and Ideal 'tong' tools. Among the latest from Lyman is the Pro Magnum Tumbler, which features a two-gallon capacity capable of handling up to 900 38 Special cases at a time. Available in two versions, 110 or 220 volts, it has a heavy-duty motor designed to deliver fast cleaning.

Three new chamberings, 300 SWM, 7mm Rem Ultra Mag and 375 Remington Ultra Mag, have been added to the Lyman line of 2-die sets, with three taper-crimp dies added to the blackpowder die line. Blackpowder cartridges require charge compression for proper ignition. The Taper Crimp dies, available in .40, .45 Short and .45 Long sizes, will provide the firm neck tension required for such blackpowder cartridges as the 40-65, 45-70, 45-100, 45-110 and 45-120. Neck-size dies in the same three calibers, plus 38-55, are also available. These dies allow the case neck to be sized to retain the bullet, without overworking the case body. *(Cases that are repeatedly fired in the same rifle tend to provide better accuracy when neck-sized only.)*

The new RCBS Grand shotshell press is available in 12 or 20 gauge, and a conversion unit is available. The powder and shot stations are case-activated.

Magma Engineering Company

Magma Engineering, the firm that produces the Master Caster and Mark 6 Bullet Master casting machines, the Lube Master, the Case Master Rimless Case Sizer, and more than 100 styles of bullet moulds, now has a Case Master Jr. Rimless Case Sizer. Manually operated, the Jr. features a shovel-style handle for ease of operation. The cases pass completely through the carbide die, insuring a completely round circumference.

Magma has five new bullet moulds, mainly for shooters handloading for cowboy action shooting, with one each in the 32-20, 38-40, 41, 44, and 45-caliber sizes. One, for the 38-40, is a round-nose design, the other four produce flat-nose bullets. Cast bullet handloaders could also benefit from the Meister Slug kits Magma features. Available in six sizes, from .30 to .45, each kit contains soft lead slugs, driving pins, forceps, and lubricant to permit determining the barrel bore groove diameter. For reloading, the shooter should then select a bullet that matches, or is one thousandth over the slug diameter.

MTM Molded Products Co.

MTM is known to handloaders for its line of molded plastic ammunition boxes in which to store their reloaded rifle, handgun or shotgun cartridges. The firm also produces loading blocks or trays, primer flippers, powder funnels, a handloaders log, load labels, and boxes to hold die sets. For handloaders who take a small press, powder measure, and components, etc. to the range with them, one of the new MTM Utility Plus Dry Boxes may be just the answer. Six models are available, and the SPUD 6 or 7 models should be about right. These boxes offer a top-access lid compartment, a lift-out tray, plenty of depth for a small press, etc.– and each features thick-wall construction, heavy-duty latches, padlock tabs, crush-proof O-ring sealing, handles, and a hands-free nylon carrying strap.

RCBS

RCBS has a couple of new 'big' units, one each for metallic reloaders and shotshell loaders. Piggyback units have been available before, but the latest, Piggyback III, is a conversion unit that can increase loaded cartridge output from 50 rounds per hour to over 400 by changing a single-stage press into a 5-station, manual-indexing, progressive unit which allows the use of a separate crimp die, a powder checker, etc. It will handle all handgun cases from 32 and up, and rifle cases up to the 223 Remington. Case insertion and removal can be performed at each station. Interchangeable die plates permit fast and simple cartridge conversions and the Piggyback III utilizes the APS Priming System. The kit comes with a bullet tray, loaded cartridge box and empty case box, ready for easy installation.

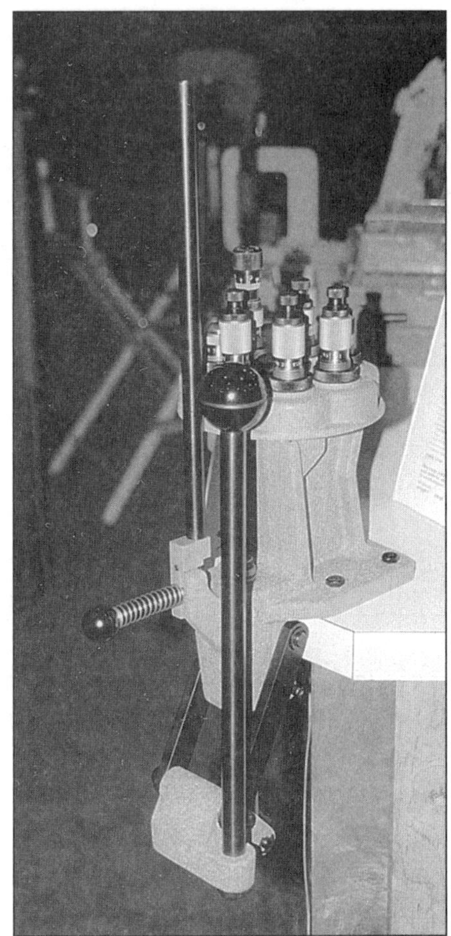

Redding's T-7 Turret press with the Redding Slide Bar Automatic Primer Feeding System.

Shotshell reloaders will appreciate the new RCBS Grand press, available in 12 and 20 gauges, with Conversion Units available to permit loading

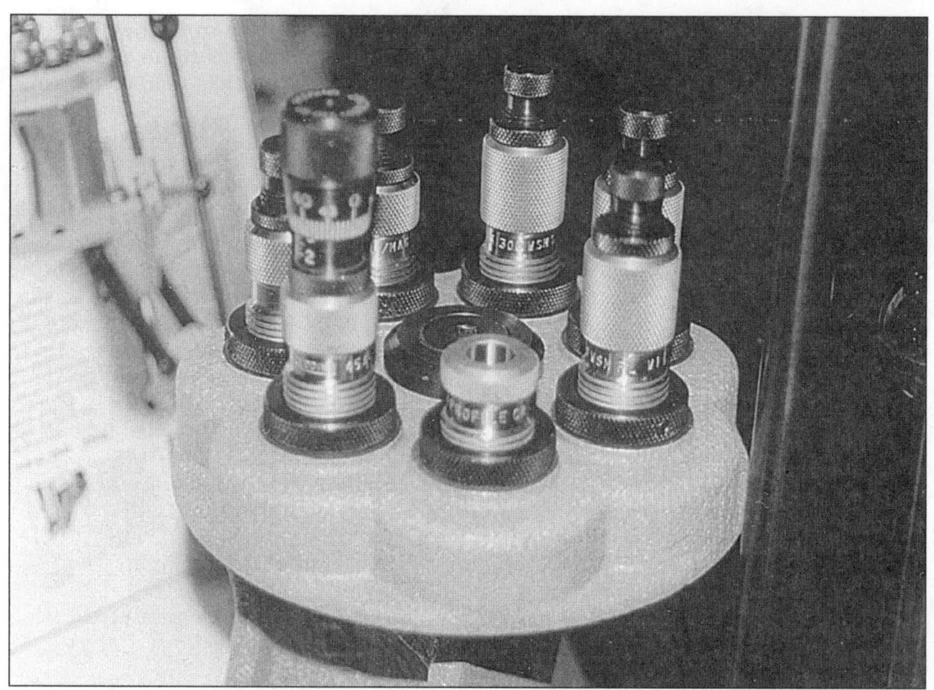

The head or turret of Redding's new T-7 press will hold seven dies, as shown, or a powder measure and six dies, or even three 2-die sets.

both gauges on the same press, *(the Grand has a lifetime warranty.)* The shot and powder hoppers hold 25 pounds of shot and 1-1/2 pounds of powder respectively, and both have convenient forward drains for rapid component removal or changing. The powder station is directly in front of the press, and powder and shot bushings can be changed in less than one minute when needed.

The massive green-colored frame is large and open, permitting easy access to all 8 stations. Both the powder and shot systems are case-activated. No hull? Then no powder or shot; no need to manually shut off either of these stations–no spillage of powder or shot can occur. Cases can be removed at any station, and universal case holders allow the case to be sized down to the rim using a steel sizing ring. Primers are fed one at a time, and fired primers drop down a tube into an easily emptied container. The wad guide tilts out for convenient feeding of wads. Progression of the hull through the stations is automatic, but it can easily be altered to permit manual indexing, if desired.

Redding Reloading Equipment

Redding has several new items, including a 'Big Boss' reloading press and a T-7 Turret press. Both presses feature cast iron frames and one-inch diameter rams with nearly four inches of travel. The 'Big Boss' frame has 36 degrees of offset to provide easy access and an offset ball handle for ease of operation. It and the T-7 are also designed to accept the new optional Slide Bar Automatic Primer Feeding System *(which comes with a safety shield and tubes for small and large primers.)*. Both presses feature compound linkage for additional power, and the new seventh station on the T-7 allows for a powder measure or an additional die. *(The Big Boss press will be available as an option in the latest Redding Reloading Kits, Pro-Pak or Deluxe.)*

Other new Redding products include "E-Z Feed" shellholders featuring a tapered design to permit easier case entry, and a knurled exterior for ease in handling. The E-Zs are available individually, or in a set of six of the most popular sizes, and will fit Redding presses or most other popular brands.

Redding is now packaging Type S bushing dies with their Competition seating dies. Either a full-size or neck-size is packaged, depending on the die set selected. A deluxe version of the Pro Series die sets, known as the "Competition Pro series," is now available for use in progressive reloading presses. This three-die set includes a Titanium Carbide sizing die, Competition seating die, and a Profile Crimp die that headspaces on the case mouth.

Reloading Innovations, Inc.

Reloading Innovations has a new system that's ideal for shotshell reloaders who shoot skeet, trap, etc. extensively. Called the Ultimate Loading System, it consists of a

The Shell Caddy by Reloading Innovations is a method of stacking and storing those shotshell reloads in neat 25 round, reusable plastic boxes.

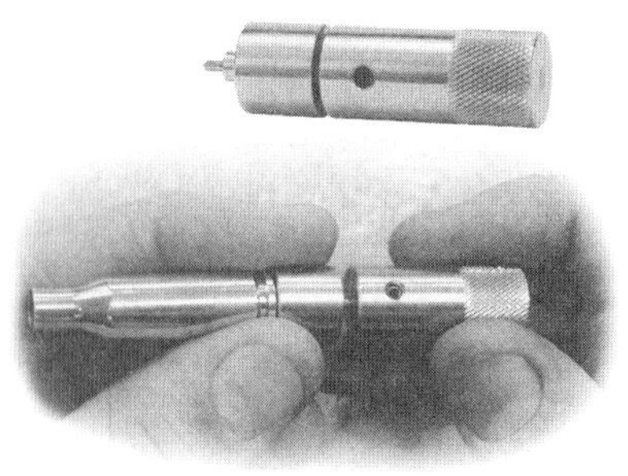

Sinclair's new Flashhole Reamer will open the flash holes in PPC and BR brass cases just enough to permit the decapping pin to pass though without sticking.

Sinclair's Bullet Comparator is manufactured using actual rifle throating reamers to allow more accurate measurement. The six-caliber stainless steel comparator shown will handle 17-, 22-, 6mm, 30-, 27-, and 33-caliber.

special angled metal loading stand to hold the Shell Caddy line of reusable plastic 25-round shell boxes, a Shell Caddy pouch which holds a box of shells, plus some spare rounds and a few accessories, and the Shell Caddy 'Shooters Carrying Case,' which will hold ten boxes of shells, up to 200 empty hulls, and additional accessories. It's available as a complete system, or the loading *(stacking)* stand and Shell Caddy boxes can be purchased separately per pack of ten. The stands are available in a choice of red or black, and the Shell Caddy boxes in red, black, or green–each with space provided on which load information may be written.

It's not new, but with many surplus bolt-action military rifles in 6.5mm Carcano, 7.35mm Terni, 7.5mm French, and 7.5mm Swiss being available in the past few years, why isn't a plentiful supply of Boxer-primed reloadable brass available? Norma has brass in some of these

Swift's new ***Reloading Manual, Number 1***, is a hardbound volume that provides reloading data on 47 popular hunting cartridges.

calibers, but not all, and Norma brass is not always easy to locate. Back in 1959 the Pasadena, California, firm of Santa Fe had virgin unprimed Boxer cases available in 30-06, 7.5mm Swiss, and 6.5mm Swedish, with the 6.5mm Carcano, 7.35mm Terni, etc. scheduled for 1960. Unfortunately, it never came to pass, but the demand is still there, and especially for the French 7.5mm, Italian 6.5mm and 7.35mm, Russian 7.62x54mm, and the Swiss 7.5mm. It would enable owners of such rifles to do considerably more shooting.

Sinclair International

Handloaders concerned with maximum accuracy from their rifle and handgun reloads realize the flash holes in the case primer pockets can make a difference, especially on cases such as the 220 Russian, 6mm BR, etc. These cases have small flash holes *(approximately 0.060-inch)* and the decapping pins can stick in them. Sinclair International has a new reamer which will open the flash holes just enough to reduce the sticky pin problem. Consisting of a reamer holder and a guide sleeve, this stainless steel tool is knurled for easy turning to make each flash hole the same diameter. Sinclair also has a new handle for their DB-1000 Flashhole Deburring Tool, making it more comfortable to use when a lot of cases are being deburred. The handle will fit all the Sinclair Deburring Tools in this series, whether it is standard *(0.080-inch)*, small *(0.060-inch)* or on one of the 17-caliber cases.

Swift Bullet Company

Swift, manufacturer of the famed A-Frame and Scirocco bonded bullets, has a new hardbound loading manual, their first. Contained within the more than 400 pages is loading data and ballistics information on 47 popular hunting cartridges. Each cartridge will be provided a dimensioned drawing, plus a sectioned loaded cartridge illustration, and a big game sketch.

The Pail Hopper by Vertsatile Rack solves the problem of how to handle the mass of empty hulls and wads necessary to do some serious shotshell reloading. The kit can be used to convert the plentiful five-gallon buckets into hoppers.

The latest VihtaVuori Reloading Manual, No.3, has reloading data for nearly nine dozen handgun and rifle cartridges, including a few not often seen in the U.S., such as the 7x33mm SAKO and the 9.3x53R Finnish.

There's a plentiful supply of 'comp' loading data manuals and guides available to handloaders for the asking. Your local gun dealer should have several of these, if not all. The amount of data presented varies form a few calibers or gauges to rather extensive coverage-and its's all useful.

Swift currently produces more than a dozen different caliber A-Frame bullets from .25 to .470, in 32 different weights from 100 to 500 grains. The Scirocco rifle line currently includes three calibers, 270, 7mm, and 30. Swift also has two calibers of hollowpoint A- Frame handgun bullets from 240 to 325 grains, with four of these included in their saboted muzzleloading bullet line. The new manual includes the test components used with each of the cartridges for which loading data is provided.

Versatile Rack Co.

Shotshell reloaders who have a problem keeping the empty hulls and wads orderly on the loading bench may want to check into the Pail Hopper at their local dealer. Versatile Rack Co. has a kit that converts those plentiful five-gallon plastic pails, often available for a dollar or two each at discount stores, into a handy hopper holding enough hulls or wads–or even metallic cases–for several hours reloading. The pails can even be used to transport empties from the range, and a patent- pending flow pan ensures a constant flow of the components. Having the hulls in a hopper on one side and a hopper full of wads on the other side for a progressive shotshell reloader should definitely save time.

Hood

Benchrest shooters and some other handloaders often feel the need for a compact, lightweight, portable loading press to take to the range with them. Such a press is the Hood model, available in two sizes and three variations. The more compact version features a 2-1/2" stroke, weighs 6-1/2 pounds, and folds into a 1-1/2" x 4" x 10-1/4" package for transporting. It's available to accommodate Wilson-type inline seater and neck dies, or regular full length 7/8 x 14 dies, or with one 7/8 x 14 station, and one blank station for use with a Wilson-type seater die.

Extremely rigid for its size, its portability can be surpassed by few other table presses and possibly only by such hand tools as the Lee Hand Press and Lyman Tong Tool.

New & Noteworthy Reloading Information

With new bullets, powders, wads, and other components being introduced, handloaders never have enough information. However, there is an abundance of loading data available, much of it free for the asking.

One of the most interesting new handloading volumes this handloader has used in some time is the Manual of Reloading No. 5, by Rene Malfatti. This large *(as tall as the GUN DIGEST, but not quite as thick)*, softbound manual contains more 160 pages of loading data and even more pages of textual material on handloading. Each of the cartridges for which data is provided is illustrated with a photograph, along with the specifications, a history, and comments. The rifle cartridges covered range from the 17 Remington to the 50 BMG, with handgun calibers from the 32 ACP to the 50 A. E. Among the cartridges not always found in other current reloading manuals are the 5.6x57mm, 6x62mm Freres, 6.5x57mm, 7x64mm, 30-284, 32 Remington, 8x60mmS, 351 Winchester SL, 7.65mm Long *(Re: 1918 Pedersen device, the French M1935 pistols, etc.)*, 8mm Nambu, 41 A.E., and 11mm M1873. Components are, for the most part, those with which U. S. handloaders are familiar: CCI, Federal, Hirtenberger, Lapua, Norma, Remington, R.W.S., Sierra, Speer, and Winchester–although the powders are principally Vectan varieties.

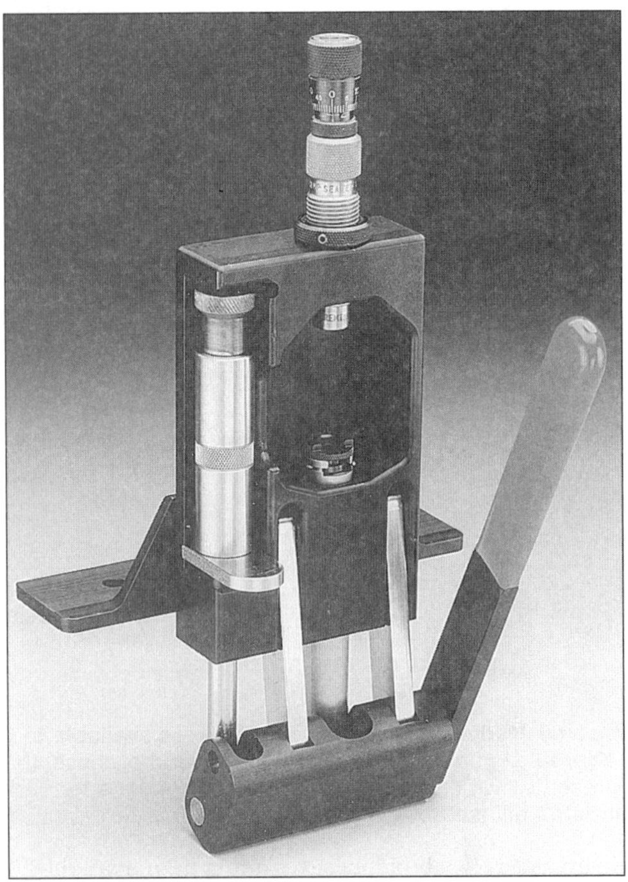

Handloaders who like to reload at the range should find the Hood press to their liking. The unit weighs 6 1/2 lbs. and is shown here operating with two different die types: *(left)* a Wilson-type straight-line die and , *(top)* in the center die station, a standard 7/8 x 14 die.

The textual portion is lavishly illustrated with photographs, drawings and tables. Many of the photos and drawings present sectioned views of cartridges, dies, bullets, primers, etc. The coverage of handloading is extensively thorough, and among the many topics discussed are primers, differences of Boxer and Berdan primers, powders, comparison of powders—Accurate Vectan, IMR, Hodgdon, W.W., Norma, R.W.S., VithaVuori, —pressures, exterior ballistics, tools for reloading, bullet casting, and much more. In addition projectiles (bullets)–European and U.S.– cast, swaged and jacketed are listed and illustrated. Most, if not all, known loading die calibers are listed, including the French Lynx and the Australian Simplex brands. Many cartridge cases that are not currently available as factory-loaded ammunition are listed and illustrated, including such oldies as the 11mm Werndl, 10.75x58R Berdan, 11mm Gras, 450 Webley, 350 Rigby, and 600/ 577 REWA. *(These have Boxer primer pockets and include the Le Hussard and Bertram Bullet brands.)*

Completing this volume are tables of conversion units, including grain/ gramme, bushing volumes, a bibliography, listings of photographs, cartridges, accessories and eight tables listing the dimensions of both metric and English caliber metallic cartridges, handgun and rifle. Shotshells, reloading or otherwise, are not covered in this manual.

Available direct from the publisher, Editions Crepin-Leblond, any U.S. bookstore handling foreign books, and possibly from your local book dealer, this is a worthy addition to the handloader's reference shelf. The text is in French, but most of the loading data is in English and can easily be deciphered.

Thompson/Center Arms is the manufacturer of the most famous single-shot pistol of all times, the T/C Contender. Most reloading manuals now devote space to loading data for the many cartridges for which the Contender is, and has been, chambered. Loading data specially for the Contender is featured in a spiral-bound T/C manual that features over 5,197 tested and proven loads for Contender cartridges, from the 17 Bumble Bee to the 45-70 Gov't. All for the price of less than three sawbucks.

VihtaVuori has a new 60-page reloading guide available that provides loading data for two dozen handgun cartridges *(from the 7mm TCU to the 50 A.E.)* and four-dozen rifle cartridges *(from the 17 Remington to the 50 BMG)*. A burning rate chart for 108 different powders is provided, along with a discussion on powders, storage recommendations, and other useful information. The regular hardbound *Reloading Manual, 3rd Edition*, can be purchased at most gun shops handling handloading supplies and the VihtaVuori line of powders. The first six of the total eleven chapters in this volume cover VihtaVuori powders, rifle and handgun competition, VihtaVuori Powders for Small Arms, Reloading Components and Cartridge Properties, Exterior Ballistics, and Reloading Process. Chapters 9-11 are devoted to Ballistic Measuring System, and Unit Conversions, ending with an excellent illustrated Glossary followed by several pages for notes. Chapters 8 and 9 provide reloading data for nearly six dozen rifle cartridges, from the 17 Remington to the 50 BMG, and 28 handgun cartridges from the 25 ACP to the 50 E. C. Most of the rifle cartridges are familiar, but some on which reloading data is not often found include the 5.6x35R Vierling, 220 Russian, 5.6x57mm, 6.3x53R Finnish, 6.5x57R, 7x33mm SAKO, 7x54mm Finnish, 8.2x53R Finnish, and 9.3x53R Finnish. Each cartridge has a dimensioned drawing, followed by specs and a few paragraphs of history. The test components are listed preceding the actual loading data, which includes both Starting Load and Maximum Load columns.

The data for handgun cartridges does not include any but current production cartridges, including the 9x21mm and the 9x23mm Winchester cartridges. Format is the same as with the rifle cartridge loading data. There is no data on handloading of shotshells.

Micro Tech, LLC., the Duster Wads firm, has a 28-page guide of loads using their wads in 12-, 20-, and 28-gauge shotguns, plus .410-bore *(no 16-gauge loads in this guide)*. Major hull, primer and powder brands are included, and there are several useful tables, such as the one illustrating the space occupied by one ounce of shot in the various shells, from the .410-bore to the 12 gauge.

Nosler, the Ballistic Tip and Partition bullet manufacturer, has a new Reloading Guide, their number five, available. Featuring the newest bullets and the latest cartridges *(as of the date the Guide went to press)*, this hardbound volume is a welcome addition to the wealth of data available to handloaders.

Graf & Sons, Inc., distributors of the Rex line of Hungarian smokeless powders, has a 16-page booklet of loading data featuring Rex, Alliant, and Hodgdon powders. Data is provided for five handgun calibers, and the 12, 16, 20, and 28 gauges, plus .410-bore. There are only four 16-gauge loads listed and only with Universal powder in Cheddite hulls, but it's better than no data. Three 'recommended bushings' tables for use with Rex powders are also provided, along with other miscellaneous information.

Western Powders has a new 64-page *Handloading Guide, Edition II*, featuring Ramshot powders. Featured are nine handgun calibers from the 9mm Luger to the 54 Casull, and 23 rifles calibers from the 222 Remington to the 45-70 Gov't. Several pages are devoted to loads for the 12-gauge shotshells using the Ramshot Competition powder. Bushing charts for MEC, Hornady, and P/W also provided, along with a number of blank tables and worksheets for the reloader to record his or her own data; these sheets are thorough, providing spaces for not only the components used, but location, temperature, humidity, wind, maximum group size, comments, etc.

Hodgdon has the most extensive line of complimentary "reloader's manuals," with at least three: *Pyrodex, Cowboy Action 4th Edition*, and *Basic 2002*. They also have their more comprehensive *2001 Shotshell Manual* and *No. 27 Data Manual*, which are available for purchase. The cowboy action manual features data for the new Triple Seven powder, plus regular smokeless and Pyrodex loads for the more common chamberings used in CAS handgun, rifle, and shotgun events. The thin Pyrodex loading guide deals mainly with the use of pellets and loose powders in muzzle-loading arms, but does provide data for the use of pellets in four 44 and 45 metallic cartridges, along with lots of other useful information.

The handy 76-page *Basic* manual is divided approximately into two parts: metallic cartridges and shotshells. The first half provides data for reloading over six dozen rifle cartridges and more than three dozen handgun cartridges. The rifle calibers range from the 17 Remington to the 50 BMG, including the 338-06, 356 Winchester and 376 Steyr, while the handgun calibers covered range from the 223 Remington to the 500 Linebaugh and include the 9mm Makarov, 44 Auto Mag, 460 Rowland, and 480 Ruger. The second half covers shotshells, from the 10 gauge to the .410-bore, and includes the 16 gauge. Bushings tables for Lee, MEC, P/W and Hornady/Spolar are provided, along with a chilled shot table, shot chart, powder reference table, wad chart, and some excellent notes on recoil.

Accurate Arms' *2002 Reloaders Guide* features 64 pages of data based on the Accurate line of powders. The guide is thumb-tabbed in black for handy reference in seven categories, from Introduction to Shotshell. Loading data is provided for 29 handgun cartridges, including the 300 Whisper, 357 SIG, and 50 A.E., and 13 cowboy cartridges. *(The 480 Ruger didn't make this edition.)* In the rifle section data is provided for 54 different cartridges, from the 17 Remington to the 50 BMG, including 450 Marlin, 45/120 Sharps 3 1/4", and 50/140 Sharps 3 1/4". Under the Shotshell Data section, in addition to cowboy action loads, charts on MEC, Lee, Hornady, and P/W bushings for the respective presses, load data is provided on regular--field and target-- 12, 16, 20 and 28 gauge shells, plus the .410-bore. There are also Quick Guides to shotshell primers and wads and wad assemblies.

Alliant Powder's large magazine-size *Reloaders' Guide* features shotshell reloading data for the 10, 12, 16, 20 and 28 gauges, plus the .410- bore for the various Alliant powders, plus 12 gauge data with the Promo powder, which is available in 8-pound containers only. Sections are also devoted to 12-gauge International loads, steel shot loads, buckshot loads, and rifled slug loads. Loading data is provided for 23 regular handgun cartridges from the 25 Auto to the 454 Casull, with separate sections covering cowboy action and silhouette calibers. Centerfire rifle reloading data is provided for nearly five-dozen cartridges from the 17 Remington to the 458 Winchester Magnum–but there are some missing, such as the 30-40 Krag and 450 Marlin. *(Data for the 458 Lott, which is now factory-loaded by Hornady, is not covered in any of the 'comp' manuals.)* There are also several pages of useful reference data and precautions provided, including tables on shot sizes, the number of shells which can be loaded per pound of powder, bore diameters, choke definitions, ballistic data, etc.

Just as new and improved components for reloading become available, so too do new products—tools, accessories, manuals, etc.—designed to make handloading safer, faster, and even more enjoyable… and the resulting cartridges and shotshells more accurate to bag more game, break more clays and produce smaller groups. Handloading has come a long way from the era of the tong tool, casting bullets over an open fire, and waterglassing or paraffinning the top wad in a brass shotshell. ●

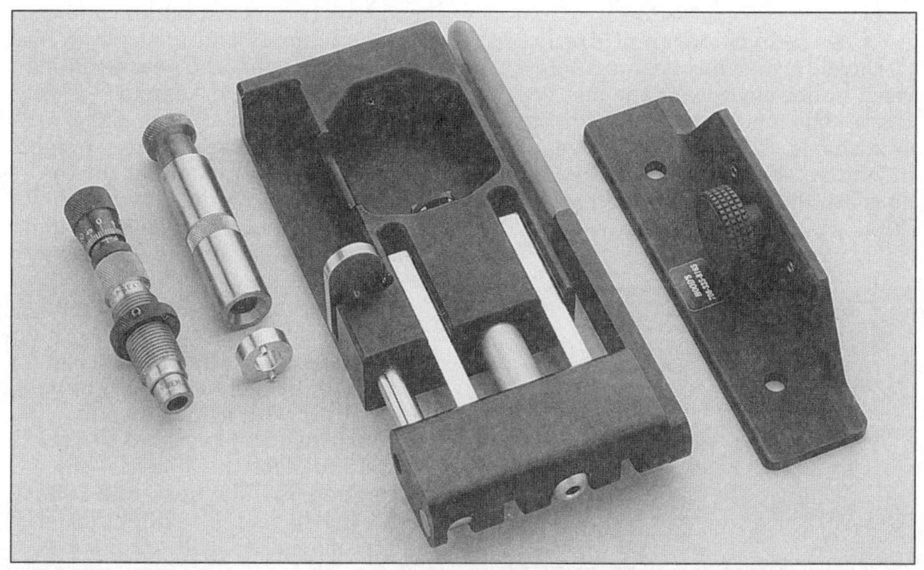

Dismantled and folded for transport, the two-piece Hood press weighs 6 1/2 lbs. and measures a compact 10-1/4 x 4 1/2 inches. Integral workstations support two types of die systems: 7/8 x 14 *(left)* and straight-line *(right)*.

BULLET CASTING REPORT

by John Haviland

You'd think lead alloy bullets and all the work that goes into casting them would have gone the way of ironed shirts and polished shoes. But according to many companies making bullet-casting equipment, bullet casting is gaining popularity for a variety of reasons, including cowboy action and blackpowder rifle shooting, and interest in historical firearms.

To keep up with the growing demand, a variety of companies offer moulds for bullet designs that have been around for a century, moulds for new bullet designs and casting and sizing and lubricating machines for the casual caster and reloader who want to speed up the process.

Ballisti-Cast Manufacturing

Ballisti-Cast makes automatic and manual casting machines, and lube/sizers. Peter Niess, of Ballisti-Cast, says more people are taking up blackpowder shooting. "Right now we're trying to gathering information on what customers want and stock some inventory," he says.

The Mark II is a gear-driven casting machine that has a melting pot capable of holding 100 pounds of lead alloy. It goes along with the Mark V Luber that automatically sizes and lubricates up to 5,500 bullets an hour.

For someone casting for his own needs, but who wants to quickly finish the job, The Mark IV takes a 45 pound melting pot and operates with a manual lever to cast bullets. The Mark VI lube/sizer is also manually operated, with tubes that feed bullets into the die. Hard or soft lube is fed with pressure from an air cylinder.

Ballisti-Cast recently bought the Hensley and Gibbs line of bullet moulds. Moulds include plain-, bevel-base and gas-check bullets starting at a 50-grain design for the 25 ACP and include every conceivable style, diameter and weight—up to a 525-grain bullet for the 50 caliber. Thirty-one moulds are offered for the 45-70. Muzzleloader bullets run from 32 to 54 caliber. Moulds for percussion revolvers include 36 and 44 caliber.

Colorado Shooter's Supply

Dave Farmer has been making Hoch bullet moulds for the last 18 years. His moulds are on a custom order basis. "I really don't keep any inventory," Farmer says, "although I do sell some moulds through Midway. What we do is help anybody who has an idea about what they would like in a bullet design and would like to try it out," Farmer says. "They tell us and we build the mould for them."

A 223 Remington cartridge loaded with a cast bullet and Unique powder costs only four cents a round.

Farmer says he has seen an increase in the popularity of blackpowder rifle cartridge shooting, and a corresponding upsurge in cast bullet interest. "I get a lot of calls from those shooters," he says.

Lee Precision

Interest in cast bullet shooting has remained steady for Lee in some areas and really taken off in others. Cast bullets in cartridges like the 270 Winchester and 30-06 has remained steady for Lee. "Cast bullets for Cowboy Action Shooting has been big with Lee for years and years and it's growing all the time," says a spokesman for Lee. "Most of the Cowboy shooters use a lighter-weight bullet, in 44-40 for example, for the reduced recoil." Moulds for the 45-70 are the most requested from Lee and those requests come from long-range target shooters.

"Handgun hunting has also really taken off," the spokesman says. Interest has grown considerably in handgun bullets of heavy weight and large caliber with a wide meplat. Lee has four new moulds of that design: a 358-158-RF for the 38 S&W, 38 Special and 357 Magnum, 452-200-RF for the 45 Colt, C452-300-RF for the 45 Colt and 454 Casull and a 476-400-RF for the 480 Ruger and 475 Linebaugh.

Lee has a new bullet hardness tester planned for introduction in the coming months. "With the hardness tester, people can check the hardness of their bullets and then load for the correct velocity for that hardness. That will really make it easier to get good performance out of cast bullets," the spokesman says.

NEI

"I'm ten weeks behind on orders," says Walt Melander, the owner/operator of NEI. "What does that tell you about the popularity of cast bullets?"

Melander says the interest in cast bullets is across the board. "Cowboy action shooting has certainly renewed interest in cast bullets and so has long-range blackpowder rifle competition." he says.

NEI has several new moulds, including one for the 50 BMG, 405 Winchester and 40-caliber pistol.

NEI keeps several hundred mould designs in stock, from a 39-grain 22 caliber to a 3,000-grain bullet to fit a four-bore.

Last winter I started thinking the cost of 22-caliber jacketed bullets was too high for the short ranges I normally fired them. After all, a bullet at high speed from the 223 and 22-250 Remingtons was a bit much for the 75 to 150 yards I shoot at ground squirrels. So I set to work casting bullets from NEI 45- and 55-grain moulds and fired them to collect the data in the accompanying tables.

I started with the 223 zeroed at 100 yards with 55-grain bullets. From the solid rest of a Harris bipod, and with the Swarovski scope turned up to 12-power, the gophers were easy targets out to 125 yards. Much past that range, though, I had to hold

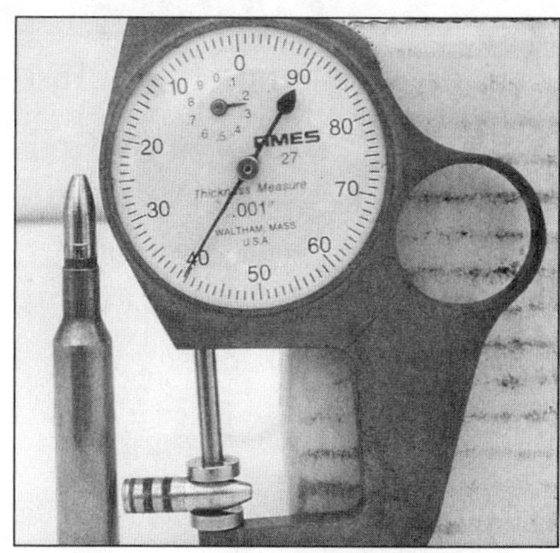

The cast bullets from an RCBS 243-95-SP mould measure .240-inch on the nose, just right for a perfect fit in the 6mm Remington.

Hoch 38-55 nose-pour mould.

Rooster Laboratories cast bullet lubes. *From left:* Zambini, High Velocity Rifle and Black Powder. SPG lube is the choice for bullets in blackpowder cartridges. It also works well with all cast bullets.

Table 1 – 223 Remington

Bullet	Powder/Grs.	MV	Group/In.
NEI 45 Gr.			
2.05" OAL	BLC(2)/18	1,994	1.78
	Green Dot/6.5	2,109	1.90
	H4198/13	1,949	.85
	H4895/17	1,934	1.95
	IMR4227/9	1,709	2.21
	TAC/15	2,010	.83
	Unique/6.5	2,091	1.96
	X-Ter./14	1,922	2.43
NEI 55 Gr.			
2.05" OAL	BLC(2)/17	1,760	1.08
	H4198/12	1,655	.92
	H4198/14	1,916	.67
	TAC/14	1,630	2.14
	W748/19	2,020	2.56
	X-Ter./12	1,549	1.65

Table 2 – 22-250 Remington

Bullet	Powder/Grs.	MV	Group/In.
NEI 45 Gr.			
2.23" OAL	Green Dot/8	2,131	3.09
	H4198/15	1,869	1.29
	TAC/19	1,792	1.00
	Varget/22	2,095	1.78
NEI 55 Gr.			
2.27" OAL	Green Dot/8	2,009	1.32
	H4198/15	2,033	1.00
	R7/13	1,823	1.17
	TAC/18	1,983	1.96
	Varget/20	2,082	1.02

Table 3 – 6mm Remington			
(Remington 600, 18 1/2-inch barrel & 4x Nikon)			
Bullet	**Powder/Grs.**	**MV**	**Group/In.**
RCBS-243-095-SP			
2.89" OAL	Green Dot/9	1,527	.71
	BLC(2)/21	1,570	1.92
	H4198/21	1,968	2.08
	H4895/21	1,663	.56
	IMR4227/18	1,887	2.03
	Reloder7/19	1,820	.97
	TAC/21	1,730	.88
	W748/24	1,753	.88
	XMR4064/24	1,747	1.97

over some. The explosive effect of the bullets on the little gophers carried pretty well out to 150 yards. So for about two cents a cast bullet, and that much more for powder, I had a great gopher load.

Lyman

A couple years ago I came out ahead on a trade for an Ideal #358318 mould *(Ideal was sold to Lyman in 1925)* originally intended for the 35 Winchester. The mould dropped round-nose bullets cast of wheel-weights that weighed 247 grains. Loaded ahead of Varget powder, the bullets had a muzzle velocity of 2,000 fps fired from my 35 Whelen and grouped right at one inch at 100 yards. I got to thinking the bullet would make a pretty good white-tailed deer load for hunting in the brush. The first animal I found, though, was a bull elk lying in its bed. The bullet plowed through the lungs and then took out a shoulder bone on the way out. The elk rolled over dead.

Lyman has several new rifle bullet moulds this year. They include bullet #2660673 for the 6.5 mm, #311299 30 caliber and #378674 for 38-55. The 6.5 is a 150-grain bullet intended for silhouette shooting. The 30-caliber is a .311-inch diameter of the same mould number that has been available for decades in a 205-grain weight in .314-inch diameter for the 303 British. So many shooters requested the same design to fit a 30-caliber that Lyman decided to accommodate them. The 38-55 bullet weighs 335 grains and has a smaller-diameter nose for the new rifles with smaller-diameter bores.

Lyman still makes moulds for handguns from 30 to 45 caliber in nearly 50 weights and styles. Rifle bullets span from 22 to 50 caliber in 43 weights and styles. Muzzle-loading designs include Plains, Minie' and Maxi Ball.

With the growing shift to hard lubes, Lyman has introduced the 4500 Lube Sizer, which includes a built-in lube heater. "It unclips, or you can just unplug it if you're using soft lubes," says Karen Griffith, of Lyman.

Griffith says she has seen a definite increase in the number of bullet casters. "Blackpowder rifle cartridge has become real popular, especially long-range cartridges like 40-65, 40-70, 45-70 and 45-90. Of course you still have all your diehard pistol shooters who run through a lot of cast bullets," she added.

The Lyman *Reloading Handbook, 48th Edition* will be out soon. The Handbook features reloading data for jacketed and cast bullets for a variety of rifle and handgun cartridges. The section on bullet casting will be especially helpful for all those new bullet casters.

Magma Engineering

Magma Engineering developed the first automatic bullet-casting machine designed for use by an individual who needs volume casting. The company also produces manual bullet casting machines, automatic case sizers, bullet-lubricating and -sizing machines and lead alloy melting pots for use on Magma machines, or for hand casting.

The Bullet Master Mark 6 automatically casts up to 4,000 bullets an hour, the Lube Master sizes and lubes up to 6,000 bullets an

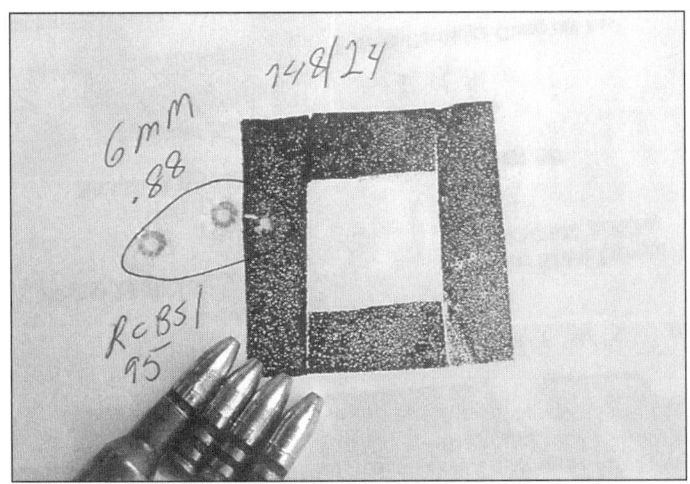

A variety of powders shoot accurately in the 6mm Remington with the RCBS 243-95-SP bullet. W748 shot well under one inch at 100 yards.

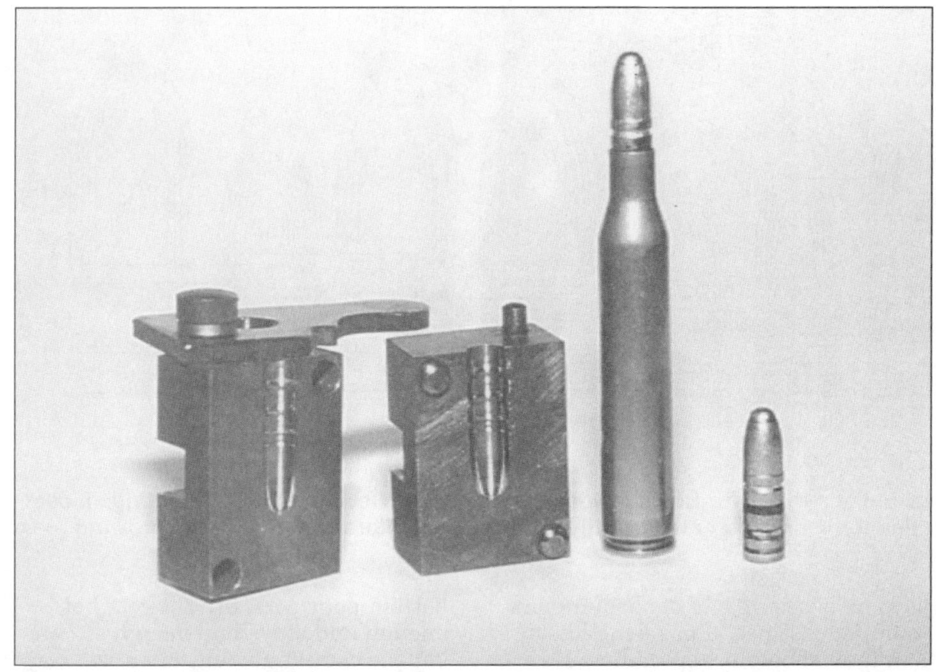

This old Ideal #257325 shoots well in nearly all 25-caliber rifles, from the 25-35 Winchester to the 25-06. Old moulds like this have become quite the collector's item.

hour. Machines like these have revolutionized cast bullet shooting by allowing small shops that cast bullets to spring up all over the country. By selling locally, these shops save transportation costs that big companies must charge to ship their swaged lead bullets. That has nearly done away with the swaged lead handgun bullets that are so soft they leave a handgun bore full of stripped lead unless fired at the lower velocities. The local sporting goods store sells cast bullets for the handguns with a Brinell hardness number (BHN) of 17 at $12 for 250, 240-grain 44-caliber bullets. These bullets do not lead the bore of my Ruger Super Blackhawk 44 Magnum and shoot just as accurately as any jacketed bullet that costs more than twice as much. These high-output machines have also allowed big companies like Federal Cartridge to sell cartridges loaded with cast bullets, like the Federal Hunting cartridges for the 357, 41 and 44 Magnums.

Most of us require only a fraction

A 55-grain bullet cast from an NEI mould shoots accurately from the 22-250.

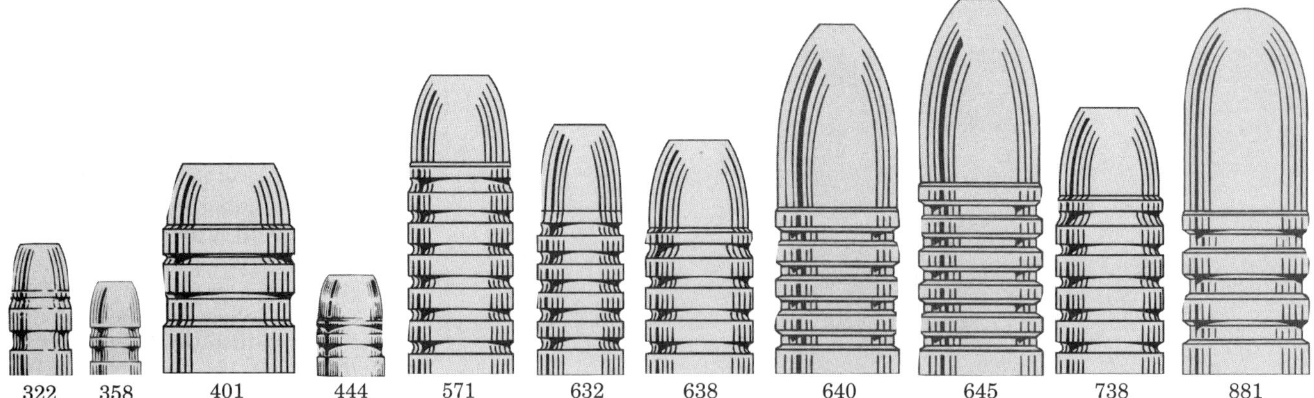

SAECO has an extensive line of traditional bullet moulds for Blackpowder Cartridge and Cowboy Action Shooting. Most of these bullets have been in the SAECO line for years and have recently returned to the forefront due to the growing popularity of these two shooting games.

of the production of these machines. The Magma manual Master Caster casts 500 bullets an hour and, along with the manual Star Lube-Sizer, is plenty of output for most of us.

For hand-casting or to accompany its machines, Magma makes moulds in more than 100 styles and calibers. "Everybody has their own idea of the perfect bullet and mould. But I don't come out with a new mould design when just one person wants it. But when we get quite a few requests for a bullet, we'll cut a cherry and make the mould," says Bob Clausen, of Magma.

Clausen says Cowboy Action Shooting has created a strong and steady demand for cast bullets. "Also, people who bought guns a few years back with the whole Brady thing, didn't really shoot them," Clausen says. "But since 9/11, shooting range owners have been telling me people are really shooting their handguns and that's good for cast bullets."

Midway

Midway no longer publishes its *Essential Bullet Casting Catalog*, but will incorporate it into its regular semi-annual catalog that includes every shooting item in the universe as we know it.

A Midway spokesman says he is seeing lots of shooters new to bullet casting. "I'm seeing lots of handgun shooters, especially guys that are into Cowboy Action shooting," he says. Interest has also increased in cast bullets for blackpowder cartridge rifles like the 40-65 and 45-70. "These guys take pride in making their own ammunition and part of that comes from casting their own bullets," he says.

Rapine

Ray Rapine says he is barely keeping up with bullet mould orders from his current list. Cowboy Action Shooting and long-range blackpowder cartridge shooting are the main reasons. "I'm also getting quite a few orders for hollow base bullet moulds for Colt 1859s and such that have been converted to cartridges and need that hollow base to expand to fit the larger bore," he says.

Rapine had a customer in his shop who hadn't had very good luck casting heavy bullets for his blackpowder cartridge rifle and Rapine was taking the time to teach the customer how to cast good bullets. "The first thing you want to start with is a good pot, like my RSS-20 stainless steel," Rapine says. "Unlike bottom-pour pots, my pot gets hot enough and stays hot enough so you get the correct amount of bullet shrinkage, which is important for good bullets," he says.

RCBS

RCBS has one new mould, a 6.5mm-140-SIL. This bullet has a long bore-riding forward portion and a single lube groove and is intended for silhouette shooting. The 6.5 joins the RCBS 7mm and two 30-caliber Silhouette moulds. The short groove-diameter portion of these bullets makes them ideal for cartridges with relatively short necks like the 260 Remington, 7mm-08 and 300 Savage.

Kent Sakamoto, of RCBS, says the Cowboy Bullet Moulds for the 25-20 and .30-30 rifles and 32-20, 38 Special, 38-40, various 44s, the 45 S&W Schofield and 45 Colt are real popular.

I recently bought an RCBS-243-095-SP mould for practice and small game bullets to shoot out of my 6mm Remington. I figure every time a bullet drops from the mould I save nearly a dime over a store-bought jacketed bullet.

The RCBS bullet is a true bore-riding bullet and shot very well in

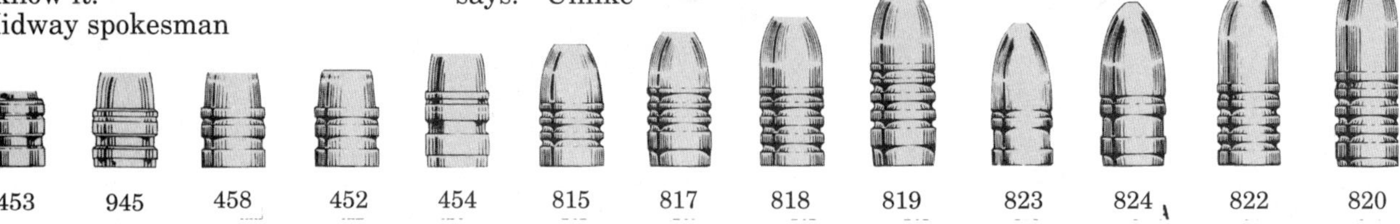

Patrick Ryan, of Redding/SAECO, says most of the bulletcasters he sees concentrate on quality bullets, like these 45-caliber bullets for blackpowder rifles.

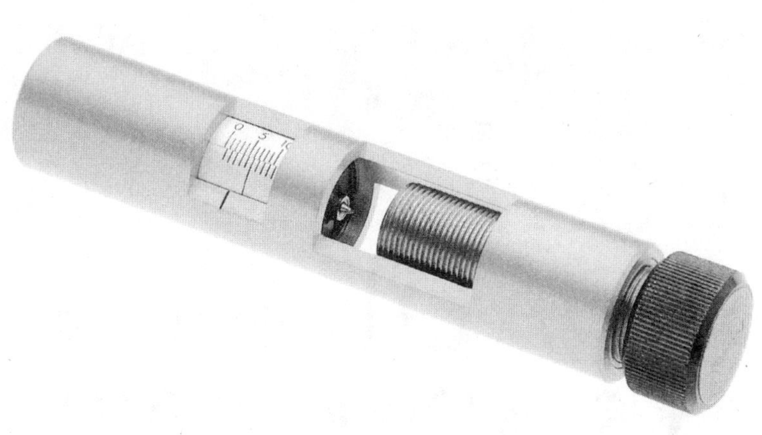

The SAECO lead hardness tester facilitates the conversion of scrounged and scrap lead alloy into bullets of known hardness so they can be loaded to the appropriate velocity for the material.

the 6mm Remington. In fact, half the loads fired grouped under one inch at 100 yards. The following is the 100-yard, five-shot accuracy evaluation of the RCBS bullet fired from my little 6 mm:

A good part of that accuracy was the near-perfect dimensions of the bullet as it dropped from the mould. The diameter of the forward section measured .240-inch. When the nose of a bullet was pressed into the bore, the lands left a light engraving on the sides. The bullet's body diameter measured .2448-inch as it dropped from the mold, and .2445-inch after it was run through a .244-inch sizing die. That diameter provided a slip-fit in the chamber throat. My 6mm rifle is only slightly worn on the rifling lands at the front of the throat and the bore supported 72 percent of the bullet's length.

SAECO

Patrick Ryan, of Redding/SAECO, says most of the bullet casters he sees concentrate on quality bullets, like for blackpowder rifles. "I think most of the handgun shooters who shoot a high volume of cast bullets are buying their bullets from commercial casters," Ryan says. "The bullets are so inexpensive it is really not worth your time to cast them yourself."

SAECO makes moulds for six different styles of bullets:

* ***Style A*** is a cylindrical bullet, similar to original factory bullets for most blackpowder cartridges. The diameters at the front and base bands are the same.
* ***Style B*** is a cylindrical bullet similar to Style A, except the front 'wiper' band has been deleted.
* ***Style C*** is a two-diameter bullet, with the front three bands slightly larger than bore diameter, while the rear three bands are groove diameter.
* ***Style D*** is a two-diameter bullet, same as Style C, but without a front 'wiper' band.
* ***Style E*** is a tapered bullet with the front band near bore diameter, tapering to slightly larger than groove diameter. This style bullet was furnished by most of the old-time barrel makers, such as Harry Pope.
* ***Style F*** is a Hudson bullet. This two-diameter bullet has front bands near bore diameter with the two rear bands slightly larger than groove diameter.

Bullet Lubrication

Duane Benton, the owner of ***Rooster Laboratories***, says the best cast bullet lubricant should have a high melting point to withstand the high temperature of burning powder and the friction created as the bullet slides down the bore. The lube should also last the length of the bore. "The whole idea is to leave a film of lubricant in the bore for the next bullet to ride on," Benton says. "Only hard lubes can do that and my Zambini and HVR (High Velocity Rifle) both have a melting point of 220 degrees."

Benton says hard lubes are also the best because the lube won't melt out and "kill" the powder charge, are clean to handle and don't pick up abrasive dirt. "For every pound of hard lube I sell to a person who casts his own bullets, I sell 1,000 pounds to commercial bullet casters. The commercial casters can't fool around with the mess of handling and shipping bullets with soft lubes."

On the other hand, ***SPG*** bullet lubricant is the lube for blackpowder bullets because the mushy, almost runny lube keeps blackpowder fouling soft. Steve Garbe grew up shooting muzzle-loading and blackpowder cartridge rifles–and to this day considers the 30-06 as newfangled technology.

Garbe fired 30,000 rounds developing his SPG lubricant, which is commonly found in the winner's circle of Black Powder Cartridge Silhouette. "We're seeing lots of new shooters in mid- and long-range silhouette shooting," says Sheryll Garbe, Steve's wife. "A lot of them are shooting the 38-55 and 40-65 and they're calling for information loading and cast bullets."

Garbe steers them toward SPG publications. *The Black Powder Cartridge Reloading Primer* contains reloading data for 20 popular blackpowder cartridges and information on blackpowder cartridge reloading. The quarterly *Black Powder Cartridge News* contains product reviews, reloading how-to and hunting stories. "The Black Powder Cartridge News has grown so much that it's now half our business," Sheryll Garbe says. ●

The Latest HANDLOADING COMPONENTS & ACCESSORIES

by Holt Bodinson

Accurate Arms

The appearance and growing popularity of the short magnum rifle cartridges have spurned on the powder companies to develop and market a compatible line of high-performance propellants. MAGPRO is Accurate Arms' response in the form of a ball powder with a burn rate tailored specifically to the fat, squat little magnums. From the loading data we've seen on the 300 WSM, MAGPRO is capable of delivering factory-level velocities.
www.accuratepowder.com

Alliant Powder

Possibly the biggest news of 2002 was Alliant Technologies' acquisition of Federal Cartridge, CCI/Speer, Estate Cartridge, RCBS, Weaver, Simmons, Redfield, Ram-Line and Outers from Blount. As the largest supplier of ammunition in the world, Alliant is uniquely positioned to bring its vast resources and experience to bear on the civilian ammunition market. This is a company to watch. Meanwhile at Alliant Powder, there is a new varmint/benchrest rifle powder--Reloader 10X--designed specifically for the 223 and similar-sized varmint and target cartridges. Don't miss Alliant Powder's latest, free "Reloader's Guide" that includes updated data for the short magnums, the full spectrum of shotshells, and additional sections on cowboy action and silhouette loads.
www.alliantpowder.com

A-Square

A-Square is under new ownership and management. The company's up-beat president, James Smith, assures us that the complete A-Square line of cartridges, cases and bullets is back in production.

Ballistic Products

Here's the mother lode for shotshell reloaders. If a wad, case, projectile, tool or loading manual isn't contained within the 60 or so pages of their entertaining catalog, it probably doesn't exist, nor have a right to. Always on the cutting edge, the company now offers bulk Hevi.Shot in #s BB, 2,4,6, 7 1/2 and 9, plus special 10- and 12-gauge wads, and, most importantly, a well-researched and informative loading manual entitled "Handloading Hevi.Shot." The new Hevi.Shot manual joins the company's already excellent series of manuals on handloading non-toxic steel and Bismuth shot. There's even data on loading non-toxic shells for the English 2-, 2 1/4- and 2 1/2-inch shells.

Promised are specialized manuals devoted to the 20 and 28 gauges. These folks have manuals on everything from the "Mighty Ten Gauge" to loading for "Fine Doubles and Vintagers," and they're essential reading. There's a new universal spreader wad being offered, called the "X-stream," that fits into the shot

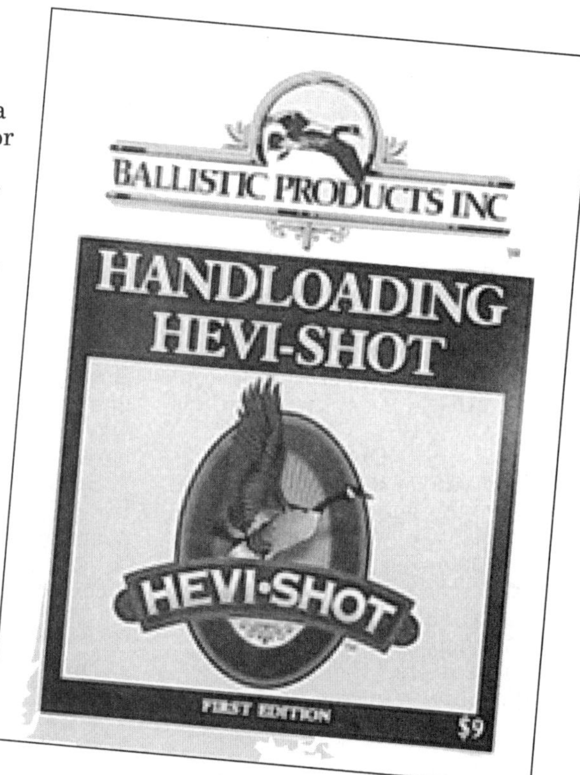

Hevi•Shot is in--Ballistic Products has bundled some great recipes in their new reloading manual.

Barnes new reloading manual includes new data for the company's XLC and VLC bullets.

column of every gauge from 20 through 10. Remember the Alcan "Air Wedge" wad? Ballistic Products has its own version--the GS2 Air Wedge. This is a 1/4-inch spacer/sealer wad, for the 12-gauge shell, that facilitates adjustment of wad columns. If you load shotshells, go to www.ballisticproducts.com

Barnes

Barnes new "Reloading Manual #3" is what a reloading manual should be. Pictures of suitable bullets accompany each cartridge together with clear graphic displays of comparative bullet trajectories and energy levels, recommended powder data, and application preferences. In addition, each caliber chapter, such as the 6mms, is followed by a complete ballistics section for all available Barnes bullets. The new manual also includes never-before-published reloading data for their lines of dry film-lubricated "X" bullets (XLC) and copper-jacketed, lead-core varmint bullets (VLC). There's even a thread-pitch table for every brand of seating die that equates degrees of seating stem rotation with thousandths of an inch. Neat!

New in the bullet line this year are a 168-grain .308 XLC modeled after a match bullet; two, hot varmint bullets, a 58- and a 72-grain 6mm VLC; and a 195-grain .458 Expander muzzleloader bullet. www.barnesbullets.com

Cast Performance Bullet Company

Looking for an LBT bullet design, an odd-caliber bullet, a lead bullet sized to different diameters, or a 500-grain Springfield Trapdoor bullet cast from a 20:1 alloy? Cast Performance probably can supply it. These are quality hand-cast products. In fact, they're so good, Cast Performance bullets are factory-loaded by Federal in its Cast Core Premium Handgun Hunting Cartridge line. www.castperformance.com

CCI-Speer

Now part of the Alliant Ammunition Group, CCI-Speer has developed some intriguing products. Speer is now offering the complete line of Trophy Bonded Bear Claw bullets in diameters from .224 to .458, plus 165- and 180-grain .308 Deep-Shok bullets. Previous to this, both bullet lines were loaded exclusively by Federal and unavailable as separate components. With the increasing popularity of the 454 Casull, 50 Action Express, 475 Linebaugh and 480 Ruger in handgun hunting circles, Speer is offering a 300-grain HP .45; 300-grain HP .50; and a 325-grain SP .475 in its Gold Dot component line-up. Finally, Speer's truly non-leading, dry-film lubricant has been added to all of their extensive lead bullet designs. www.cci-ammunition.com & www.speer-bullets.com

GPA

This is a new monolithic copper alloy, HP or solid bullet that was announced at the SHOT Show by ROC Import. According to their literature, it will be available in every caliber from 6mm to .600. See them at *www.roc-import.com*

Hodgdon's TRIPLE SEVEN muzzleloading propellant contains no sulfur, produces high velocities and cleans up quickly with water.

Hodgdon's RETUMBO propellant is formulated to bring out the best in the largest capacity magnum cases.

Lyman's "Black Powder Handbook and Loading Manual" is the most comprehensive treatment of the subject ever published.

Graf & Sons

This popular handloader's heaven is importing a new line of shotgun/pistol powders manufactured in Hungary by Nitrokemia under the trade name "REX." Presently the REX line is available in four burn rates corresponding roughly to Bullseye through Universal. www.grfs.com

Hodgdon

What powder powers the new 17 HRM? It's Hodgdon's Lil' Gun. Never at a loss to give handloaders a new

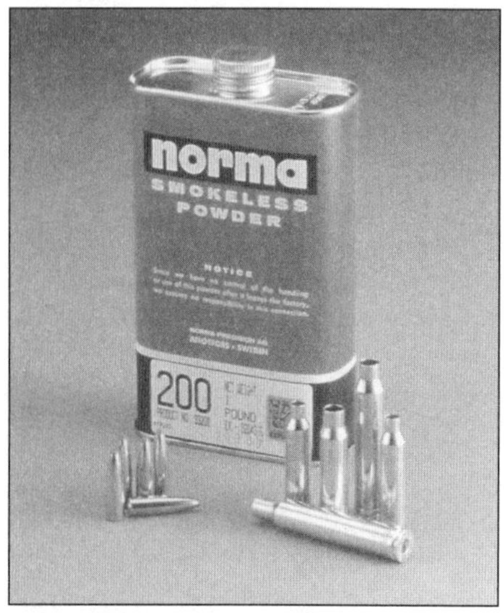

Noted for their quality, Norma reloading products should be more plentiful in 2003.

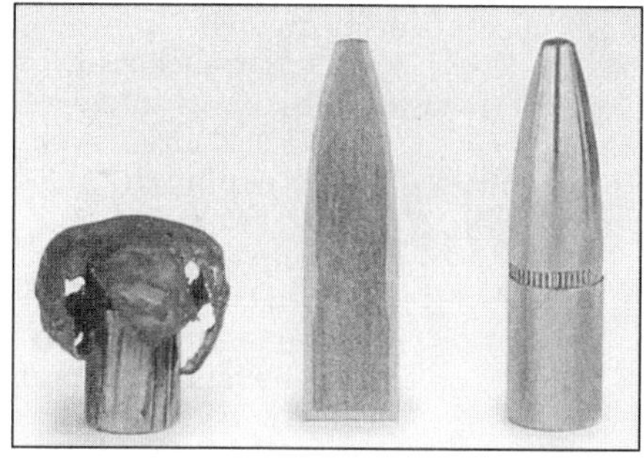

Remington's classic Core-Lokt bullet has been improved with the addition of a bonded-core and redisigned jacket. It's the new Core-Lokt Ultra.

propellant, Hodgdon is introducing RETUMBO magnum rifle powder for super-big capacity cases like the 30-378 Weatherby. The loading data looks exciting, with very high velocities at sane pressures in the big boomers. If you're into muzzleloading, you'll enjoy Hodgdon's new TRIPLE SEVEN powder that contains no sulfur, is odorless, cleans up completely with one to three water-soaked patches and, volume-for-volume, delivers velocities that exceed all other blackpowder substitutes. If you're more traditional and shoot a 45-caliber muzzle stuffer, there's a new Pyrodex 45-caliber/50-grain pellet available for you. Finally, Hodgdon has produced a new 81-page shotshell manual that covers all gauges from .410 through 10, including the 2- and 2 1/2-inch cases for English 12-gauge doubles. www.hodgdon.com

Hornady

Hornady's line of SST (Super Shock Tipped) game bullets has been expanded with the addition of nine new bullets from 6mm to .338 while there are nine new ammunition offerings featuring the SST projectiles. Other new handloading components include a 300-grain .411 FP bullet for the 405 Winchester and a .475 gas check. www.hornady.com

Huntington

Looking for a unique or hard-to-find reloading component? Huntington is the place to find it. Do you need 22 Rem. Jet, 6.5 Rem. Mag., 30 Rem., or 416 Rem. Mag. cases? Huntington commissioned Remington to make special runs of these great, but often neglected, cartridges this year. From quality brass makers like Hirtenberger and Horneber,

Norma's new Oryx big-game bullet features a bonded core and is available in Norma ammunition or as a reloading component.

Huntington has secured ample supplies of cases for the 5.6x50mm, 5.6x50R, 6.5x57mm, 6.5x68S, 8x68S, 5.6x35R, 6.5x61mm, 7x66 Vom Hofe, 7x72R, 280 Ross, 8mm Lebel, 8x56 MS, 9x56 MS, 9x57mm, 9.3x64mm, 9.5x57 MS, 10.75x68mm, 11.2x72 Schuler and any classic English big-game case you can think of. There's also a fresh supply of 8mm Nambu cases on hand. I'm just touching the tip of the iceberg. See them at www.huntingtons.com

Lapua/VihtaVuori

Lapua's debuting a number of new products including 750-grain and 800-grain "Bullex-N" match bullets for 50 BMG shooters; brass and a wide selection of hunting and match bullets for the 338 Lapua Magnum; and five new VihtaVuori high-energy powders for shotshell reloading under the "Total Knockdown" label. www.lapua.com

Lyman

Lyman's series of handloading manuals have always been among the most original and invaluable references in the field. Not tied to any particular brand of powder or projectile, Lyman manuals have a breadth of data that is refreshingly unique. This year's release of the 2nd Edition Black Powder Handbook & Loading Manual carries on the tradition, covering not only every possible aspect of muzzleloading but blackpowder cartridges as well. The loading and ballistics data section contains thousands of combinations

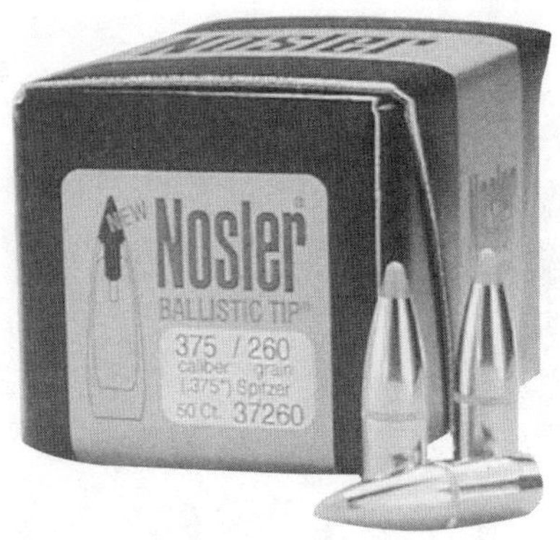

Have a 375 H&H languishing in the closet? Nosler's 260-grain .375 BT is specifically designed for light to medium big game.

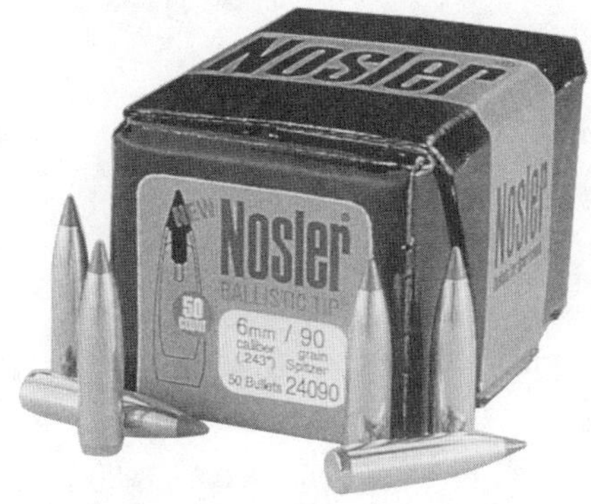

Nosler's expanding Ballistic Tip line now includes a 95-grain .243 BT that should bring out the best in the 6mms.

for every caliber, barrel length and barrel twist typically available. The powders tested include GOEX, Elephant and Pyrodex. Don't miss this manual. It's that good. www.lymanproducts.com

MAST Technology

Here's the home of the famous Bell Brass. The two new commercial offerings this year are 11mm(43) Mauser and 338 Lapua. If you follow military matters, MAST was just awarded the contract to manufacture M-781, 40mm practice grenade ammunition at the Lake City Army Ammunition Plant. See their complete list of tough brass cases at www.bellammo.com.

Norma

Norma's upping the ante with their announcement of the release of the Oryx hunting bullet. The Oryx is a flat-based, semi-spitzer, bonded-core bullet with a gilding metal jacket to reduce fouling. The company indicates fired weight retention runs 90-95 percent. Oryx bullets are already loaded in Norma ammunition and will be available this year as components in: 6.5mm/156 grain; 7mm/156 grain; .308/180 and 200 grain; 8mm/196 grain; and 9.3mm/286 grain. www.norma.com

Northern Precision

Northern Precision is the place to look for a unique variety of .308, .358, .375, .429, .416 and .458 handmade bullets. They include a 198-grain .416 or 265-grain .458 "Varminter;" bonded-core big-game bullets; and more recently a full line of .358-inch diameter projectiles. Catalogued this year are even primer-propelled .375 "poly balls" for short-range indoor target shooting with your Holland & Holland. Tel: (315) 493-1711

Nosler

Have a 375 H&H languishing in the gun cabinet? Filling in their ever-expanding line of terrific performing Ballistic Tips, Nosler has released a 260-grain .375 BT specifically designed for light to medium big game. With a ballistic coefficient of .473, the new .375 BT combines flat trajectory with tremendous down-range energy. For the smaller-bore enthusiast, there's a new 95-grain .243 BT designed specifically for light big game in the deer and antelope class. And for the high-power and service rifle competitor, there are new 69-grain and 80-grain .224 match bullets made on benchrest-quality J4 jackets. Both bullets are hollowpoint boattail low-drag designs with ballistic coefficients of .359 and

"Trueshot" is Oregon Trails' latest line of high quality gas-checked and plain-based handgun and rifle bullets.

Made with benchrest-quality J4 jackets, Nosler's 69-grain .224-inch match bullet is ideal for high-power and service rifle events.

.440 respectively. A 1:9 twist is recommended for the 69-grain, and a 1:7 for the 80-grain bullet. www.nosler.com

Oregon Trail/Trueshot

Offering a wide selection of pistol and rifle bullets cast from a great alloy, sized and lubricated correctly, Oregon Trail has earned an enviable reputation in the shooting community. Their former line of "Laser-Cast" gas-checked and plain-based rifle and pistol bullets is now called "Trueshot." It includes such specialized designs as gas-checked 310-grain 44-caliber and 360-grain 45-caliber revolver bullets as well as exceptionally accurate 30- and 32-caliber rifle bullets.

Responding to a request from dedicated IDPA and Limited shooters for a 40-caliber bullet that would feed reliably in 1911 autoloaders and meet major power factors with safe pressure margins, Trueshot has developed the solution--the 40-1911 185-grain RN SWC. The new bullet feeds flawlessly in 10mm and 40 S&W guns without having to resort to freeboring. See them at www.trueshotbullets.com.

Responding to the needs of IDPA and Limited competitors, Oregon Trail designed a 185-grain 40-caliber bullet that works flawlessly in the Model 1911.

Schroeder Bullets

Having trouble locating old or odd-size bullets and brass? Then send for Schroeder's new catalog. In it is everything from .287-inch diameter 280 Ross bullets to 6mm Lee Navy brass. And if you really want a wildcat, try Schroeder's 5mm centerfire conversion kit for the Remington Model 591/592 5mm Rimfire Magnum. It makes into the perfect urban varminter.
Tel: (619) 423-8124.

Sierra

If you enjoy shooting the 8mm in any guise, you'll find Sierra's new 200-grain 8mm HPBT MatchKing a sterling performer. Designed originally for the 8x57mm and marketed exclusively in Europe, the new MatchKing is being made available to any aficionado who wants to wring out the best from an 8mm case. Periodically, Sierra publishes a very informative and technical newsletter called the "X-Ring" that any handloader will find useful. The current issue, as well as back issues, is available at the company's web site: www.sierrabullets.com

Sierra's 200-grain 8mm HPBT MatchKing is designed to deliver target accuracy in the 8x57mm and other 8mms.

Swift Bullets

The bonded-core, polymer-tipped Scirocco line is being expanded this year with the addition of a 130-grain .270 bullet with a ballistic coefficient of .430, and just possibly a 210-grain .338 as well. Finally Swift is issuing a handloading guide for their complete lines of premium bullets. The first edition, that covers 50 popular hunting cartridges, will be published as a hardbound limited edition, so get your orders in early. Tel: (785) 754-3959.

Widener's

This is a great catalog supply house for components and ammunition--some of which are unique. They always stock a wide selection of surplus military bullets, powder, and loaded ammunition with extensive listings of Israel Military Industries products. Excellent prices -- good service. www.wideners.com

Winchester Ammunition

There are lots of new components this year, including all of the WSM cases and bullets; 9x23mm and 454 Casull brass; and the Platinum Tip shotgun and muzzle-loading sabot projectiles. www.winchester.com ●

TODAY'S SHOTSHELL RELOADERS

by Kurt D. Fackler

Modern shotshell reloading presses are all good. Every shotshell press available today, when properly set up and adjusted, is fully capable of delivering finished shells rivaling the best factory-assembled. The trick is recognizing unique loading capabilities designed into each machine, making one more useful than all the others for you. Your favorite load types, with each machine, represent a fixed investment to every type of reloading press. Consider: time setting up–or adapting–the press and/or number of loads. There is represented with each a potential number of shells produced per hour, as well as start-up costs—a monetary investment for the costs of acquiring a press. Value is achieved when you find the machine most compatible with the complexity of your load recipes, output expectations and pocketbook.

Like choosing a car that fits your styles and needs, there's a reloading press right for you: whether you are a budget-conscious shopper looking for a utilitarian bargain or an upscale buyer looking for a feature-laden model. Within these categories there are presses ready produce a finished shell every pull of the handle, or offering the flexibility and tight tolerances to craft complex, high-performance hunting loads.

Shotshell reloading presses can be accurately placed into one of two categories: single-stage or progressive. A single-stage reloader works one shell at a time, from depriming to final crimp. A progressive machine, by our definition, is a reloading press designed to work on multiple shells at once; once ramped up, producing a shell with every pull of the handle. Henry Ford would have preferred a progressive reloader for its mechanical efficiency, while perhaps Stradivarius, when not building violins, would have enjoyed building his shotshells one at a time on a single-stage press.

Progressive machines lend themselves well to target shooters and ironically, because the machines are usually about double the initial cost of a single-stage, the budget-conscious shooter. Progressive machines are, by Webster's definition, engines—converting energy into motion. One gear turns another gear and so forth. When a machine becomes a system, adjustments have to be right, because part "A" not only affects part "B", it also goes on down the line to parts C, D, E and so forth. Precise mechanisms naturally are more costly than simpler ones. The "art" expressed by a progressive reloader is a quality, bargain-priced shotshell with every pull of the handle. Large-volume clay target shooters, (individuals who, when not occupying space in the basement reloading, will be found at the range shooting), are progressive reloader candidates. Every shell he makes takes him another step toward recouping his investment, not to mention the performance gains found with

This photo illustrates some of the differences between a hunting wad and a target wad. Target wads emphasize the cushion section, delivering a lighter payload, and proper fit within the shotshell. The demands on the wad are not significant, so details are intricate. The hunting wad is designed to deliver heavy payloads at high velocity. The entire structure is designed around this effort. Using a hunting wad for targets is overkill, while using light target wads for hunting is going well beyond design intent.

Pellet payloads are conventionally metered by volume – either through a bushing or a charge bar, in all types of reloaders described herein. Once a critical size is being used for a load, however, you should switch to weighing pellets. As illustrated, large pellets do not flow as well as smaller ones do, creating conditions for inconsistent drops.

specialized components.

The unique demands of hunting loads—the wad columns, the specialized shot drops, the large volume powder charges—usually require personal attention. While volumetric bushings can do an excellent job of dropping metered amounts of small-sized shot, large pellets and heavier payloads tend to

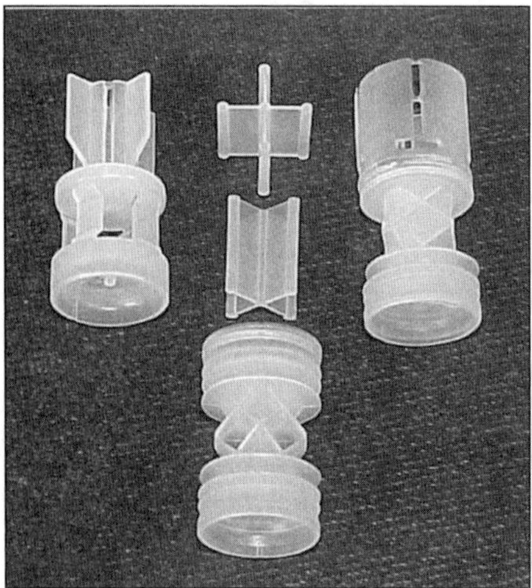

Sometimes target loads present a challenge for reloaders too, as illustrated by these more exotic clays/light field spreader loads.

Hunting and specialized loads require more complex wad columns. Because the wad station becomes a several step affair, it's a wise choice to choose a machine that indexes manually, or a single stage. Progressive machines (automatic indexing) become a complicated hindrance in this case.

get become jammed in the bushing spaces—leading to inaccurate (short) drops. Once jammed up, the shell has to be cleared, increasing the likelihood of other sequential problems for other shells in line. Rule of thumb concerning the progressive: Keep the loads simple and conventional. The archetype load for your progressive machine is the 1-1/8 oz. clay target load, using a plastic wad.

Progressive machines depend on a consistent flow of components and are designed with modern shotshell architecture of primer/powder/plastic wad/shot (volumetrically measured). Deviations from this architecture mean you are working outside of the machine's design intent. Progressive reloaders, by design, do not offer great flexibility for components or shell types. They want to be set up to hum right along—producing hundreds of rounds with one shell type, one wad type and one crimp adjustment.

Single-stage reloading presses are for the craftsman; the person wanting the performance gains of complex shells suited perfectly to shooting conditions. Single-stage shotshell presses allow full concentration on the one product. This isn't to say that a rhythm

Most slug and buckshot loads are best assembled on a single-stage machine. The buckshot is too large to be metered, by volume, through a bushing and slugs require careful hand-placement into the shotshell.

cannot be developed as you load, producing quite a few shells over the course of an evening – just not as many as a fully-automated press.

To a handloader, single-stage loaders are synonymous with versatility and high performance. You take each shell and lovingly place each component, in exactly the configuration necessary to create your special load. Each shell is going to receive all your attention. You can back up, remove the shell for inspection, and even hand-drop shot charges—particularly if the load requires high-volume or large-pellet payloads. On a single-stage press, you can load slugs, buckshot and all types of non-toxic shotshells as well. Special loading procedures play a large role in manufacturing hunting loads. In fact, this attention to detail delivers the superior performance expected of handloads versus off-the-store-shelf ammunition. To produce a cost-effective number of shells for retail sales, manufacturers make accommodations for high-speed loading machines; a compromise is made between "what works in the

An accurate (grain) scale is a handloader's best friend. 473.5 grains equals one ounce. Besides measuring shot and powder and verifying bushing accuracy, grain scales of sufficient capacity can be used for quality control. Weigh samples of each component used in the load. Added together, they should represent the weight of a finished shell. If the weight is significantly different, something may be wrong with the load and it should be checked for an error.

machine" and "what works best in the field." The handloader gets the advantage every time, as results in the field are his only yardstick of success.

Speed versus versatility presents a dilemma to a handloader. The solution: Own both a progressive and a single-stage reloader. You deserve this indulgence. Which one to use on which day? When you go to the range, crank out a box of shells on the progressive. As time permits during the evening, craft a couple boxes of specialized loads on your single-stage machine. The single-stage loader stays busy during clays shooting months, as well. We like to salt our collection of clays loads with a few exotic ringers, European shooter style—suited to personal tastes for particular target conditions.

Now perhaps you've realized you need not one, but two new reloading presses. Which is right for you? It's hard to go too far wrong with the shotshell presses available this year. All have been available for a few years, and in some cases much longer. Notable changes are those of refinement rather than reinvention – making already good machines even better.

Dillon

The progressive Dillon Shotshell Reloader, SL900, is a modified-for-shotshell version of the feature-laden Dillon XL650 progressive metallic cartridge reloader frame. Once loaded up with Dillon's option packages, such as the nifty low-powder sensor, it is a unique and quality unit for manufacturing large quantities of single-purpose shotshells for trap, skeet or sporting clays. Other features include an electric case-feeder and case-activated powder drop with a fully adjustable powder bar. The SL900 is available in 12, 20 and 28 gauge with an interchangeable tool head—allowing the handloader to switch gauges without losing die setup adjustments. The SL900 is sold in your choice of gauge, and options can be purchased with the machine. The SL900 is fast–and refined as a reloading press for the person who wants to make a pile of target loads. Others, who want to handload for hunting, or use a wide variety of target components, may find the focus a bit confining.

Hornady

Hornady offers the APEX 90 as an example of an exception to the rule. Apex 90 is, by best definition, a multi-station reloader. You can send one load through at a time in order to pay proper attention, or you can just as easily load progressively using all the stations at once for increased productivity. The APEX 90 uses a manually-indexed table. Operating the APEX as a multi-station loader requires a bit of concentration, as there is choreography of steps, involving powder metering, wad insertion and shot drops. However, there is a great advantage in the ability to work optionally as a single- or multi-station loader: During set-up, one shell at a time is taken through each stage, the tooling adjusted at each until fit and finish is perfect. This is easier than a fully progressive, self-indexing machine

MEC's collet resizer, as seen up close. The fingers press the bottom part of the shell into a diameter compatible with shotgun chambers. Every time a shell is fired, it expands–conforming tightly to the shotgun's chamber. Unless a shotshell is resized as it is reloaded, it will be very difficult to chamber.

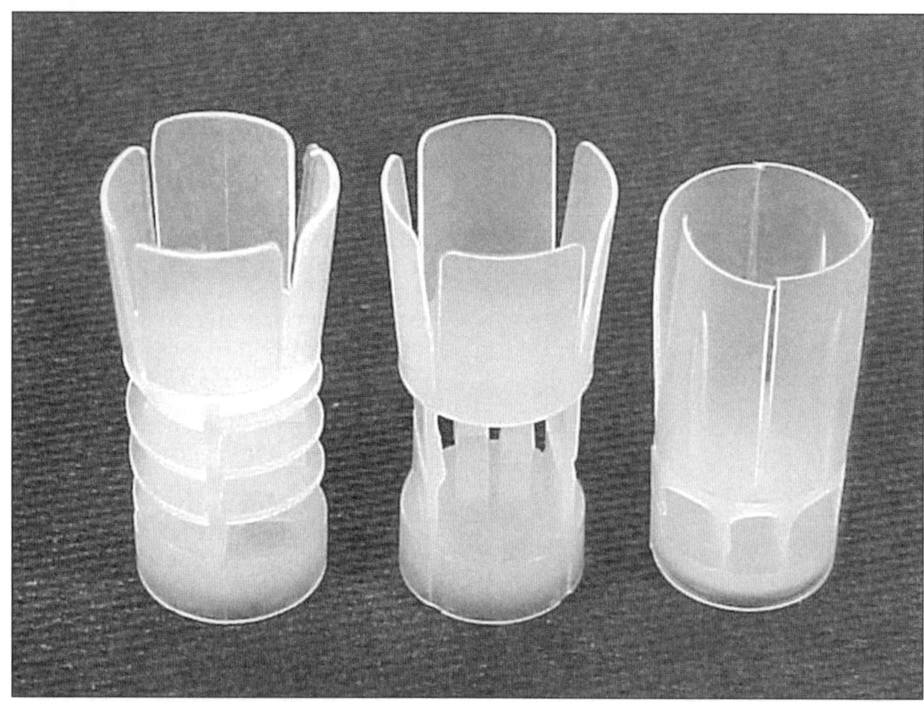

Manufacturers use high-speed automated loading equipment when they produce shotshells. Some shotshell manufacturers offer reloaders the same wads used in ammunition. You can benefit by using the same wads, as these wads are excellent candidates for high-speed, progressive reloaders. Examples shown are the Federal 12SO 1-oz. Target Wads, Winchester WAA12 Super Lite Pink Wads and Remington's RP12 1-1/4 oz. field and target wads.

where one must learn to synchronize and set up all the stages at once. The APEX 90 is capable of loading many different types and lengths of shotshells, including hunting and non-toxic loads. The APEX 90 is available in 12, and 20 gauge.

MEC

MEC (Mayville Engineering Company) has been busy manufacturing reloaders since 1956. MEC presses represent value hard to ignore by veteran and new reloader alike. The reloaders produced by MEC are a labor of love, and represent an intrinsic part of the company's history. Reloading presses represent only a small part of what this engineering company manufactures. However, the resources and experience of MEC are used to our benefit. MEC manufactures quite a variety of models: cleanly, simply, purposefully designed. The models available for sale and used by handloaders are the same reloaders used and owned by the engineers who designed them. On weekends, these engineers turn into camouflaged sportsmen and women, pockets full of shells, grins on their faces. MEC is very cognizant of their machine's role in creating shotshells; you will recognize it in conversations with their technical support staff.

MEC Progressive Reloaders

MEC's top-of-the-line progressive reloader is the 9000-H, the 'H' designating it as hydraulically operated. Press the actuator button, get a shell. Another fully progressive machine (meaning that a single action initiates the entire operation) is the 9000 operated, quaintly, manually. Pull the lever, get a finished shell. The 9000 loaders are available in 12, 16, 20, and 28 gauge, and .410 bore.

The MEC 650 is a multi-station reloader. Reasonably priced, this reloader has been a favorite for many years with shooters for its simplicity of design, reliability and performance. The 650 does all the jobs at once—however, you index the shell by manually spinning the base, then you pull the handle and get a finished shell. There is also the MEC 650 Grabber – it has a resizing collet used to squash shell brass back down to size for easy fit into shotgun chambers. The resizing collet looks like a circle of little fingers, with a ring on the outside of the bunch. As the ring is forced upward on the outsides of the fingers, the shell is constricted to shape. As a shooter, you will appreciate resized shotshells. Resized shells do not jam up in autoloaders and drop easily into and out of double barrels. The 650 and the 650 Grabber are available in 12, 16, 20, and 28 gauge, and .410.

MEC also manufactures a tool called the Super-Sizer, which resizes empty shotshells as a separate, off-the-press operation. Because shells already resized work more easily through all types of progressive reloaders, we make it a habit to run hulls through a Super-Sizer before reloading sessions.

The Super-Sizer is available in 10, 12, 16, 20, and 28 gauge, and .410 bore.

Single-Stage MEC Reloaders

MEC manufactures the Sizemaster, Steelmaster and 600 Junior Mark V single-stage reloaders. The Sizemaster and Steelmaster are built on the same frame, the Steelmaster differentiating itself by being painted black and outfitted with MEC's Steel Shot accessories. The price is comparable to the Sizemaster and the steel shot hardware works well with most lead loading applications. Both have MEC's Power Ring Collet resizing.

Steelmaster and Sizemaster are available in 10, 12, 16, 20, 28 and .410.

The 600 Junior is the final MEC in the lineup. It is an incomparable value for its price. We have yet to see one actually worn-out. Some of these reloaders have been around since the mid-1950s. The 600 Junior Mark V represents nearly a half-century of refinements and improvements. The shell is resized as it is deprimed in a clever die. The shell is then moved sequentially through each station until it is closed at the final crimp station. Once adjusted properly, the final crimp works extremely well. Unfortunately, though, too often reloaders don't spend the time to adjust the final crimp station and the shells don't look as nice as they could. Take the time read the instruction manual and make sure you fully understand the section regarding cam adjustment. Readjust the final crimp station every time you change hulls and you will be thrilled with the shells produced by the little

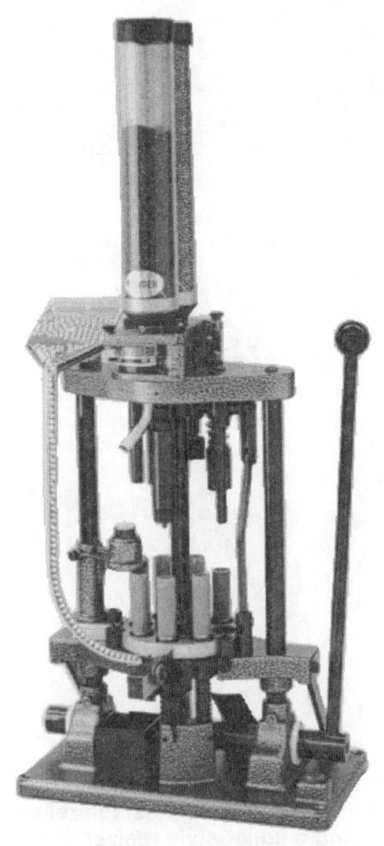

The Ponsness/Warren Model 950 resizes the hulls with tooling located above the hull, as opposed to full-length sizing dies used in the Model 900 series. The Model 950 is a progressive reloader.

MEC. The 600 Junior Mark V is available in 10, 12, 16, 20, 28 and .410.

Lee Precision

Lee Load-All 2 represents the price leader for single-stage reloaders. For about the price of two boxes of non-toxic ammo, you can purchase a Lee-Load All 2 to try your hand at reloading shotshells. Several safety features found on the Lee will be extremely helpful to the novice. For instance, the charge bar will not function if a powder metering bushing is not in place. The Load-All also comes with a set of 24 shot and powder bushings to help a handloader get off to a good start. The Load-All is a great way to get started, but size and structure limit it a bit when it comes to the more visceral practice (re: leverage requirements) of magnum shotshell reloading. Compact, price-leader and fun, Lee Load All has introduced a legion of reloaders to the art. The Lee Load All 2 is available in 12, 16 & 20 gauge.

Ponsness/Warren

Ponsness/Warren manufactures both progressive and single-stage reloaders with a high degree of quality materials and finish. If a quality tool is your sole objective, Ponsness/Warren is a good place to stop. The machines are delivered well-adjusted, nicely finished and with nary a problem.

Progressive Machines

For 2002, Ponsness/Warren makes two types of fully-progressive reloaders, the Platinum 2000 (950) Reloader with shell base holder system and a version of same with a full-length shell sizing-die system (Platinum 2000 (900)). Pressed into P/W's signature sizing-die, the shell is fully resized and factory dimensions are maintained throughout each reloading station until the last, when the shell is extracted from the die.

Both the Platinum 900 and the Platinum 950 are fully progressive machines, turning out a shell for every pull of the handle. New features on both machines include Ponsness/Warren's proprietary die removal system. Manufactured of a material P/W calls 'grivory,' the die removal system allows the operator to remove an individual shell during loading for examination, because it fouled—or whatever reason you may have. The shell removal system can be retrofitted to earlier model P/W progressive reloaders. Ponsness/Warren confidently guarantees the strength of the 'grivory' part with an unconditional lifetime warranty against any wear. The Platinum loaders also feature new large-capacity shot and powder hoppers and an improved brass primer feed system, which can also be retrofitted to certain previous models.

Ponsness/Warren has made an effort to bring the speed of progressive shotshell reloading to non-toxic and 10 gauge in the LS-1000 models. The LS in the description refers to the machine's capability of loading either lead or steel shot. Undisclosed in the name is that it will also load bismuth.

The Ponsness/Warren Model 900 series utilizes the full-length dies. The shell is pressed into the full-length die at the first station where it is held throughout the process. After the shell is crimped and a taper applied, the finished shotshell is pressed out of the die at the final station.

The LS Series, available in 10 or 12 gauge, features full-length sizing dies and oversized bushings that seem to handle large volumes of non-toxic pellets with consistency better than the standard sizes found in the other machines. The LS's shortcoming, shared by any fully-progressive machine when loading shotshell for hunting: It requires a regular sequence of events and components, assembled in order, to properly function. However, if your goal is assemble a large batch of hunting loads, and you are willing to work within a few limitations set by the machine, the LS will play.

Ponsness/Warren also manufactures a single-stage reloader: the Model 375C. The 375C reloaders, available in 10, 12, 16, 20 28 and .410, have pretty well set the standard of excellence for handloading hunting shells. Residing in a heavy, cast frame, the

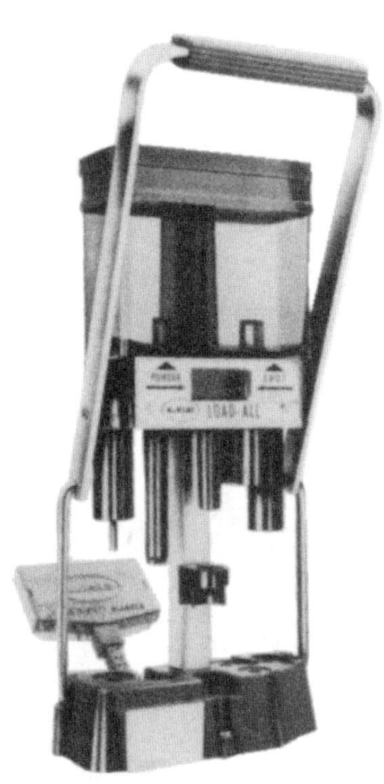

The Lee Load-all 2 removes barriers and excuses. For about the same price as four boxes of hunting loads, you get a durable little press that includes about everything, including bushings, to start loading shotshells.

machined tooling works the shotshell while it resides inside of a full-length resizing die. Once the components are in place, the 375C applies a tapered crimp then neatly presses the finished shell out of the die. The long actuating handle and engineered leverage make all stages, including resizing, easy operations. Tapered crimps will make any shell feed seamlessly through a semi-automatic, particularly good news if the firearm has a history of requiring factory-loaded shells to cycle properly. A shotgun will either take shells loaded in the 375C, or it needs to visit the gunsmith. Gauge changes are simplified with exchangeable tooling heads. Two Allen screws on top of the posts hold the tooling head in place. Remove them, slide in another tooling head with another gauge's tooling in place. Cinch down the Allen screws, change the full-length sizing die and viola! Gauge converted. Furthermore, dies remaining in the exchanged tooling head will not need adjustment when the tooling head is exchanged again. Ponsness/Warren is proud that any type of pellet—lead, bismuth, steel and Hevishot—can be loaded through the 375C. Other than recommending that shot payloads are manually weighed on a precision reloading scale, we concur–the system works as advertised.

RCBS

RCBS, a well-known and respected reloading press manufacturer for metallic cartridges, has added a dedicated shotshell reloading press to its line of impressive products. The Grand, named after the famous trap-shooting event, is a fully progressive reloader drawing on RCBS's years of industry experience to design and manufacture a machine to please a market already familiar with features they want to see on a reloader.

The Grand relies on smart engineering and quality parts to make the entire loading process user-friendly. It simply does not like to make you look bad, and in fact will make you look pretty good, with a neat floor and piles of nicely finished shotshells.

RCBS realizes that to achieve a final product, the shell first has to be taken through each reloading stage, without forcing the user to act on anticipated problems. For instance, RCBS has smartly integrated a case-activated shot and powder drop system. If there is no shell present at the powder drop stage, no powder will be dropped. Same with shot. Smart equipment makes the user look smarter, too. Experienced handloaders will tell you that dropping a charge of powder or shot all over the machine, all over the bench and floor too, holds the number-one ranking of annoyances, were there a top-ten list of handloaders' annoyances. Probably number two on that same list would be primers not properly positioned – leading to powder falling through the shell and out the vacant primer hole. RCBS got out in front of this, too, with a reliable automatic priming system. The RCBS priming system does not allow double-stacked primers, upside-down primers or skipped primers. RCBS's unique case-holding system allows shells to be fully resized by the tool's resizing ring – from the top on down to the case rim.

MEC's Steelmaster, like the Sizemaster, is a single-stage reloader offering a collet-style resizer and automatic primer feeding. The Steelmaster, however, is set up at the factory for requirements of steel shot handloading. You can use the Steelmaster for loading all other types of pellets, too.

Shells can be removed for inspection or weighing at any stage. The user-friendly theme is applied also to powder and shot delivery systems. The powder-drop station is placed purposefully directly in front of the user. This way, powder drops can be monitored and the shell removed, if desired, for further inspection or powder weight verification (accomplished with a reloading scale) before the shell is placed back into sequence. Powder and shot bushings are quickly and easily accessed from the top.

The RCBS Grand is fully progressive (self-indexing as well as multi-stationed), at the user's option. A single shell can even be run through the Grand for a full-conversion to single-stage reloading (remember, powder and shot are activated by the shell). The user can opt, also, to manually index one or a table-full of shells. This is accomplished by removing the one-piece indexing unit.

The Grand is competitively priced, especially when one considers the extraordinary features and ease of use—even for beginners—and adaptability to many different types of loads. If a person only wants one new reloader, the Grand deserves to make the "must-see" list. The RCBS Grand is available in 12 or 20 gauge.

Spolar Power Load Inc.

Spolar reloaders are an exercise in metal arts. Making few, if any compromises from the late Frank Simpson's original hand-made machine, Spolar manufactures the Gold Premier out of billet T6-6061 aircraft aluminum. Machined billet means that of a given big chunk of aluminum, all the little bits that don't look like a reloader are machined away—leaving a solid, one-piece part. Spolar's tolerances are held to aircraft standards and sealed ball bearings with oil-impregnated bronze bushings are found at pivot points.

Using these quality materials and expert craftsmanship, it is Spolar's objective to create a fine loading experience for the user of this fully progressive machine. The Spolar Gold is available in 12, 16, 20 and 28 gauge. The machine features two final crimp stations—allowing for perfect crimp seating and the ability to remove shells from any station, at any time. The handle can be mounted right- or left-handed–or not at all–with Spolar's proprietary hydraulic option. A shell counter and 25 lb. capacity shot tube are standard equipment, as is an extra-large 400 unit-capacity primer tray crafted of billet aluminum.

The Spolar Gold is designed to turn out huge numbers of quality, competition-grade shotshells. It is exotic, handmade and beautiful to look at. It is not your reloading price-leader, but we think you could still like it.

Bushings, Inspection, etc.

Most shotshell presses use the same sized-shot and powder bushings. As long as the bushing manufacturer's recommended charts are followed and verified, you can share bushings between Ponsness/Warren, RCBS, Hornady and Spolar. MEC bushings can be used in these machines with a special sleeve adapter, but only MEC bushings will fit into a MEC reloader. Lee Load-Alls are supplied with a complimentary set of Lee bushings. The quickest, easiest method of controlling the quality of the shotshells you are loading is to subject every finished shell to a weight test on a reloading scale. Take several finished shells, verified correct, and weigh them. Make note of the finished weight, in grains. Deviations from this weight can mean a problem with either shot or powder charge. You may decide, at this point, to disassemble the shell and weigh the individual components to determine the source of the variation.

Visually inspect shells, as well, for defects. Start with the primer. Is it seated correctly? Is the base of the shell concave in the area? It should be flat to sight and touch. Check the shell for folds, cuts bulges or creases—any sign indicating a problem. Move up to the crimp. Is the crimp tightly closed, flat and recessed about 1/8-inch from the top? If so, it is right.

As you become acquainted with a machine you will learn to account for its peculiarities. Every system requires adjustments to operate properly, and every machine listed here will require the same. All the manufacturers include comprehensive instruction/operator's manuals with their reloading presses. It behooves you, once you finish unpacking and admiring your new reloader, to take an hour or so to read the manual. On down the line, you will be glad you did and your press will deliver decades of enjoyment, not to mention those tailor-made shotshells. ●

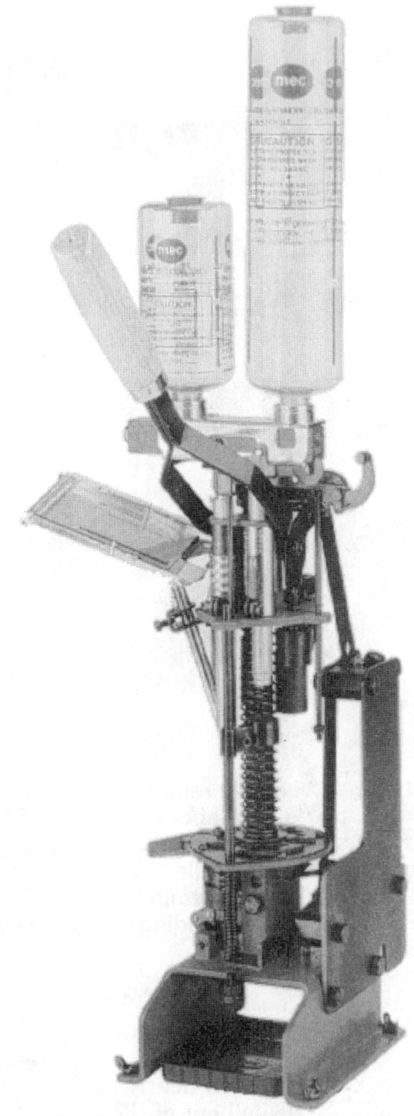

MEC's high-speed progressive reloader. A reliable machine, depended on by generations of target shooters. The 9000 is also available as a hydraulically-activated unit, the 9000H.

INTERESTING PRODUCT NEWS FOR THE ACTIVE SHOOTING SPORTSMAN

The companies represented on the following pages will be happy to provide additional information – feel free to contact them.

The Gun Digest® Book of Modern Gun Values

11th Edition

edited by Ken Ramage

Identify, evaluate and price any of the commonly encountered firearms made from 1900 to present. This specialized, heavily illustrated, expanded edition helps you easily identify and value older firearms found in gun shops, auctions, advertisements-or that old family gun you've just inherited. More than 7,500 post-1900 models are gathered by type then listed alphabetically. All prices are fully updated to mid-year. Includes more photos, and new sections covering mechanical inspection and (full-color) condition evaluation. New reference section lists books and associations for collectors.

Softcover • 8-1/2 x 11 • 640 pages • 3,000+ b&w photos • 8-page color section

Item# MGV11 • $24.95

To order call

800-258-0929 Offer GNB2

M-F 7am - 8pm • Sat 8am - 2pm, CST

Krause Publications, Offer GNB2
P.O. Box 5009, Iola WI 54945-5009
www.krausebooks.com

Shipping & Handling: $4.00 first book, $2.25 each additional. Non-US addresses $20.95 first book, $5.95 each additional.

Sales Tax: CA, IA, IL, NJ, PA, TN, VA, WI residents please add appropriate sales tax.

FOR THE SERIOUS RELOADER...

Rooster Labs' line of top-quality, innovative products...for individual and commercial reloaders...now includes:

- **ZAMBINI** 220° Pistol Bullet Lubricant (1x4 & 2x6)
- **HVR** 220° High Velocity Rifle Bullet Lube (1x4)
- **ROOSTER JACKET** Water-based Liquid Bullet Film Lube
- **ROOSTER BRIGHT** Brass Case Polish...Brilliant!
- **CFL-56** Radical Case Forming Lube...for the Wildcatter
- **PDQ-21** Spray Case Sizing Lube...quick, no contamination
- **BP-7 BLACK POWDER** Bullet Lube (1x4 hollow)

Rooster LABORATORIES®

P.O. Box 414605, Kansas City, MO 64141
Phone: 816-474-1622 • Fax: 816-474-7622
E-mail: roosterlabs@aol.com

CUSTOM COMPONENTS FOR HIGH-PERFORMANCE AMMUNITION

For over 20 years, Ballistic Products has provided handloaders with custom components for high-performance shotshell ammunition. BPI provides reloading guides and components for sporting clays, targets, small bore, upland, 10-gauge and slug ammunition.

Non-toxic shot redefined handloading. Ballistic Products stayed at the forefront of the evolution by developing reloading guides and specialized components for each type of non-toxic shot as it is developed. Guides such as the "Status of Steel", "Handloading Bismuth" and "Handloading Hevi-shot" will give you the background information you need to load high-performance non-toxic loads. Each manual details wad selection, load design and patterning, along with a large selection of top-performing recipes.

Call to request your free product catalog today.

BALLISTIC PRODUCTS, INC.

PO Box 293, Corcoran, MN 55340
Phone: 763-494-9237

SHOOTER'S MARKETPLACE

6x18x40 Varmint/Target Scope

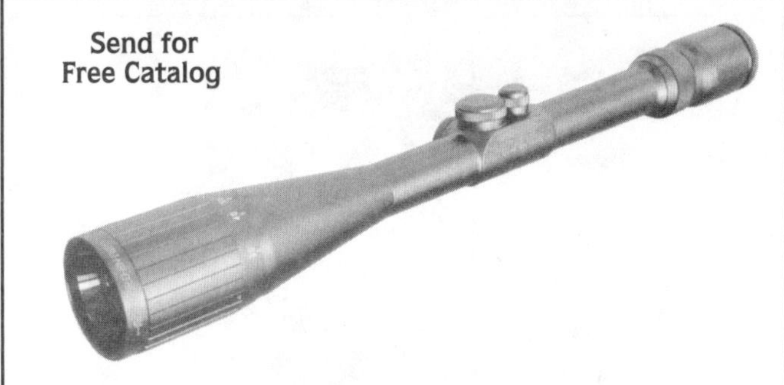

The Shepherd 6x18x40 Varmint/Target Scope makes long-range varmint and target shooting child's play. Just pick the ranging circle that best fits your target (be it prairie dogs, coyotes or paper varmints) and Shepherd's exclusive, patented Dual Reticle Down Range System does the rest. You won't believe how far you can accurately shoot, even with rimfire rifles.

Shepherd's superior lens coating mean superior light transmission and tack-sharp resolution.

This new shockproof, waterproof scope features 1/4 minute-of-angle clicks on the ranging circles and friction adjustments on the crosshairs that allow fine-tuning to 0.001 MOA. A 40mm adjustable objective provides a 5.5-foot field of view at 100 yards (16x setting). 16.5 FOV @ 6X.

SHEPHERD ENTERPRISES, INC.

Box 189, Waterloo, NE 68069

Phone: 402-779-2424 • Fax: 402-779-4010

E-mail: shepherd@shepherdscopes.com • Web: www.shepherdscopes.com

High Quality Optics

One of the best indicators of quality is a scope's resolution number. The smaller the number, the better. Our scope has a resolution number of 2.8 seconds of angle. This number is about 20% smaller (better) than other well-known scopes costing much more. It means that two .22 caliber bullets can be a hair's breadth apart and edges of each still be clearly seen. With a Shepherd at 800 yards, you will be able to tell a four-inch antler from a four-inch ear and a burrowing owl from a prairie dog. Bird watchers will be able to distinguish a Tufted Titmouse from a Ticked-Off Field Mouse. Send for free catalog.

SHEPHERD ENTERPRISES, INC.

Box 189, Waterloo, NE 68069

Phone: 402-779-2424 • Fax: 402-779-4010

E-mail: shepherd@shepherdscopes.com • Web: www.shepherdscopes.com

Combination Rifle and Optics Rest

The Magna-Pod weighs less than two pounds, yet firmly supports more than most expensive tripods. It will hold 50 pounds at its low 9-inch height and over 10 pounds extended to 17 inches. It sets up in seconds where there is neither time nor space for a tripod and keeps your expensive equipment safe from knock-overs by kids, pets, pedestrians, or even high winds. It makes a great mono-pod for camcorders, etc., and its carrying box is less than 13" x 13" x 3 1/4" high for easy storage and access.

Attached to its triangle base it becomes an extremely stable table pod or rifle bench rest. The rifle yoke pictured in photo is included.

It's 5 pods in 1: Magna-Pod, Mono-Pod, Table-Pod, Shoulder-Pod and Rifle Rest. Send for free catalog.

SHEPHERD ENTERPRISES, INC.

Box 189, Waterloo, NE 68069

Phone: 402-779-2424 • Fax: 402-779-4010

E-mail: shepherd@shepherdscopes.com • Web: www.shepherdscopes.com

Gunsmithing: Guns of the Old West

by David R. Chicoine

Learn to repair, improve and upgrade your antique and replica firearms from the Old West. This gunsmithing manual provides step-by-step detailed illustrations for more than 40 popular original and replica Old West guns. You'll be able to keep your favorite cowboy action shooting guns functioning properly, and you'll know when to have an experienced gunsmith perform the repairs.

Softcover • 8½x11 • 352 pages • 300 b&w photos

Item# GUWS • $27.95

To order call **800-258-0929**

Offer GNB3

M-F 7am - 8pm • Sat 8am - 2pm, CST

Krause Publications
Offer GNB3
P.O. Box 5009, Iola WI 54945-5009
www.krausebooks.com

Shipping & Handling: $4.00 first book, $2.25 each additional. Non-US addresses $20.95 first book, $5.95 each additional.

Sales Tax: CA, IA, IL, KS, NJ, PA, SD, TN, WI residents please add appropriate sales tax.

SHOOTER'S MARKETPLACE

Cartridges of the World™

10th Edition, Revised and Expanded

by Frank C. Barnes, Edited by Stan Skinner

Stay up-to-date with the new, re-introduced, and improved cartridges from all corners of the earth. In recent years, cartridge companies have been expanding their offerings to meet demand. This new edition covers more than 1,500 current, obsolete, and wildcat cartridges listed with illustrations, historical notes, and loading data. Cartridge and firearm experts offer exciting articles on shooting, bullets, cartridge identification, military ammunition, and reloading.

Softcover • 8½x11 • 528 pages
600+ b&w photos
Item# COW10 • $27.99

To order call **800-258-0929**
Offer GNB3
M-F 7am - 8pm • Sat 8am - 2pm, CST

Krause Publications
Offer GNB3
P.O. Box 5009, Iola WI 54945-5009
www.krausebooks.com

Shipping & Handling: $4.00 first book, $2.25 each additional. Non-US addresses $20.95 first book, $5.95 each additional.
Sales Tax: CA, IA, IL, KS, NJ, PA, SD, TN, WI residents please add appropriate sales tax.

BLACK HILLS GOLD AMMUNITION

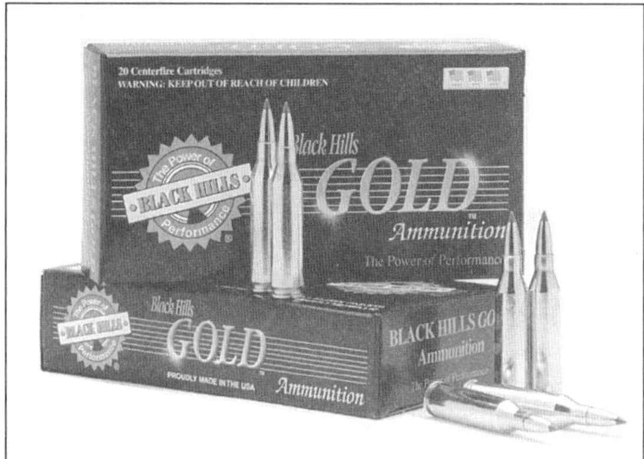

Black Hills Ammunition has introduced a new line of premium performance rifle ammunition. Calibers available in the Black Hills Gold Line are .243, .270, .308, .30-06, and .300 Win Mag. This line is designed for top performance in a wide range of hunting situations. Bullets used in this ammunition are the Barnes X-Bullet with XLC coating and the highly accurate Nosler Ballistic-Tip™.

Black Hills Ammunition is sold dealer direct. The Gold line is packaged in 20 rounds per box, 10 boxes per case. Black Hills pays all freight to dealers in the continental United States. Minimum dealer order is only one case.

BLACK HILLS AMMUNITION
P.O. Box 3090, Rapid City, SD 57709
Phone: 1-605-348-5150 • Fax: 1-605-348-9827
Web: www.black-hills.com

NYLON COATED GUN CLEANING RODS

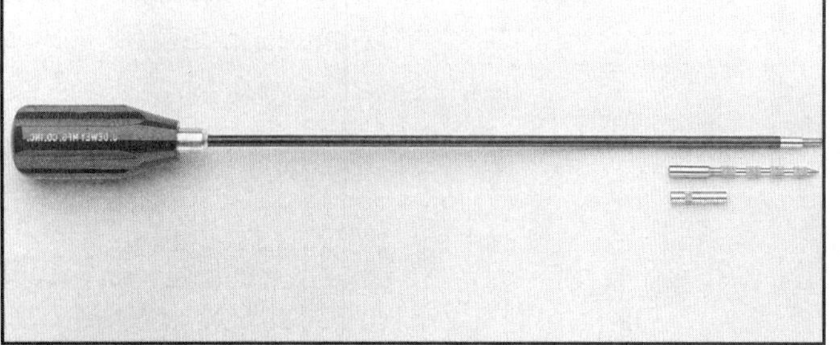

J. Dewey cleaning rods have been used by the U.S. Olympic shooting team and the benchrest community for over 20 years. These one-piece, spring-tempered, steel-base rods will not gall delicate rifling or damage the muzzle area of front-cleaned firearms. The nylon coating elmininates the problem of abrasives adhering to the rod during the cleaning operation. Each rod comes with a hard non-breakable plastic handle supported by ball-bearings, top and bottom, for ease of cleaning.

The brass cleaning jags are designed to pierce the center of the cleaning patch or wrap around the knurled end to keep the patch centered in the bore.

Coated rods are available from 17-caliber to shotgun bore size in several lengths to meet the needs of any shooter. Write for more information.

J. DEWEY MFG. CO., INC.
P.O. Box 2014, Southbury, CT 06488
Phone: 203-264-3064 • Fax: 203-262-6907
Web: www.deweyrods.com

CLENZOIL FIELD & RANGE®

This is what museums, collectors, and competitive shooters are switching to in serious numbers.

Clenzoil Field & Range® is a remarkable one-step bore cleaner, lubricant, and long-term protectant that contains absolutely no teflon or silicone, so it never gets gummy or sticky.

A regional favorite for many years, Clenzoil is finally available nationwide. Clenzoil is signing up dealers daily, but your local shop may not carry it yet. If that's the case, you may order 24 hours a day by calling 1-800-OIL-IT-UP. Dealers may join the growing Clenzoil dealer network by calling 440-899-0482.

Clenzoil is a proud supplier to ArmaLite, Inc. and Ithaca Classic Doubles.

25670 First Street, Westlake, OH 44145
Phone: 440-899-0482 • Fax: 440-899-0483

HANDLOADER'S DIGEST CATALOG

18TH EDITION

Section 1: Metallic Cartridges

C-H/4-D Heavyweight Champion

Frame: Cast iron
Frame Type: O-frame
Die Thread: 7/8-14 or 1-14
Avg. Rounds Per Hour: NA
Ram Stroke: 3 1/4"
Weight: 26 lbs.
Features: 1.185" diameter ram with 16 square inches of bearing surface; ram drilled to allow passage of spent primers; solid steel handle; toggle that slightly breaks over top dead center. Includes universal primer arm with large and small punches. From C-H Tool & Die/4-D Custom Die.
Price: **$220.00**

C-H/4-D No. 444

Frame: Aluminum alloy
Frame Type: H-frame
Die Thread: 7/8-14
Avg. Rounds Per Hour: 200
Ram Stroke: 3 3/4"
Weight: 12 lbs.
Features: Two 7/8" solid steel shaft "H" supports; platen rides on permanently lubed bronze bushings; loads smallest pistol to largest magnum rifle cases and has strength to full-length resize. Includes four rams, large and small primer arm and primer catcher. From C-H Tool & Die/4-D Custom Die.
Price: **$195.00**

C-H/4-D No. 444-X Pistol Champ

Frame: Aluminum alloy
Frame Type: H-frame
Die Thread: 7/8-14
Avg. Rounds Per Hour: 200
Ram Stroke: 3 3/4"
Weight: 12 lbs.
Features: Tungsten carbide sizing die; Speed Seater seating die with tapered entrance to automatically align bullet on case mouth; automatic primer feed for large or small primers; pushbutton powder measure with easily changed bushings for 215 powder/load combinations; taper crimp die. Conversion kit for caliber changeover available. From C-H Tool & Die/4-D Custom Die.
Price: . . . . **See chart for pricing.**

FORSTER Co-Ax Press B-2

Frame: Cast iron
Frame Type: Modified O-frame
Die Thread: 7/8-14
Avg. Rounds Per Hour: 120
Ram Stroke: 4"
Weight: 18 lbs.
Features: Snap-in/snap-out die change; spent primer catcher with drop tube threaded into carrier below shellholder; automatic, handle-activated, cammed shellholder with opposing spring-loaded jaws to contact extractor groove; floating guide rods for alignment and reduced friction; no torque on the head due to design of linkage and pivots; shellholder jaws that float with die permitting case to center in the die; right- or left-hand operation; priming device for seating to factory specifications. "S" shellholder jaws included. From Forster Products.
Price: **$309.00**
Price: Extra shellholder jaws **$27.80**

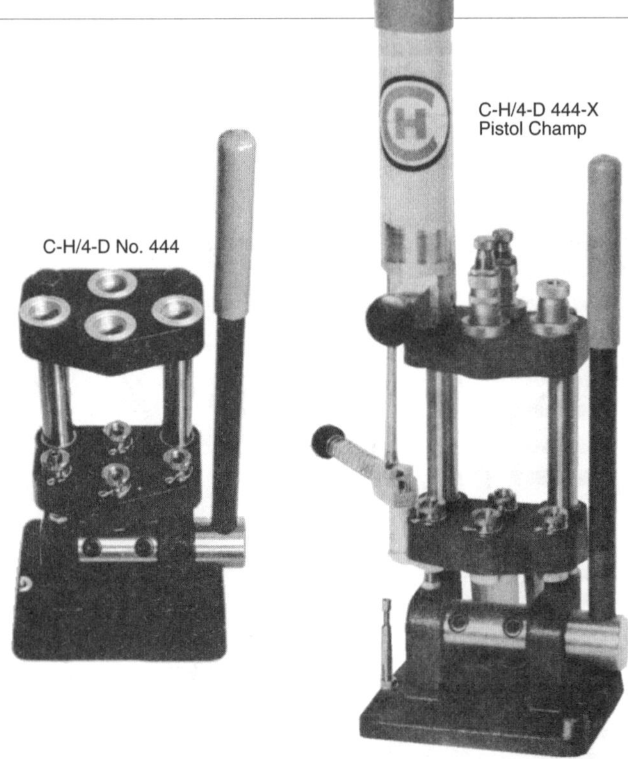

C-H/4-D No. 444

C-H/4-D 444-X Pistol Champ

C-H/4-D				
	No. 444 Pistol Champ		444-X Conversion Kit	
Caliber	Carbide Sizer	Steel Sizer	Carbide Sizer	Steel Sizer
10mm/40 S&W	$308.50	$292.00	$92.50	$62.80
30 M1 Carbine	316.50	292.00	92.50	62.80
32 S&W/H&R Mag.	308.50	292.00	84.50	62.80
38 Spl/357 Mag.	308.50	292.00	84.50	62.80
41 Magnum	308.50	292.00	84.50	62.80
44 Magnum	308.50	292.00	84.50	62.80
45 ACP	308.50	292.50	84.50	62.80
45 Colt	308.50	292.00	84.50	62.80
9mm Luger	308.50	292.00	84.50	62.80

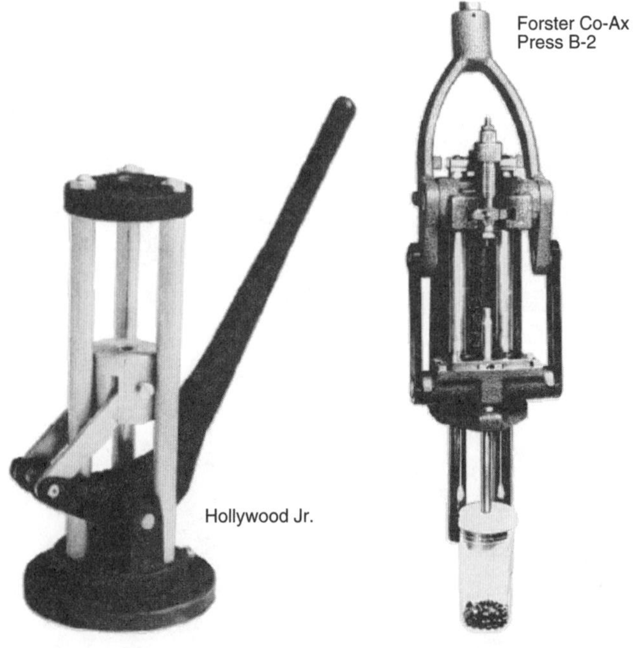

Forster Co-Ax Press B-2

Hollywood Jr.

Hollywood Senior

Hollywood Senior Turret

HOLLYWOOD Senior Press

Frame: Ductile iron
Frame Type: O-frame
Die Thread: 7/8-14
Avg. Rounds Per Hour: 50-100
Ram Stroke: 6 1/2"
Weight: 50 lbs.
Features: Leverage and bearing surfaces ample for reloading cartridges or swaging bullets. Precision ground one-piece 2 1/2" pillar with base; operating handle of 3/4" steel and 15" long; 5/8" steel tie-down rod for added strength when swaging; heavy steel toggle and camming arms held by 1/2" steel pins in reamed holes. The 1 1/2" steel die bushing takes standard threaded dies; removed, it allows use of Hollywood shotshell dies. From Hollywood Engineering.
Price: **$600.00**

HOLLYWOOD Senior Turret Press

Frame: Ductile iron
Frame Type: H-frame
Die Thread: 7/8-14
Avg. Rounds Per Hour: 50-100
Ram Stroke: 61/2"
Weight: 50 lbs.
Features: Same features as Senior press except has three-position turret head; holes in turret may be tapped 1 1/2" or 7/8" or four of each. Height, 15". Comes complete with one turret indexing handle; one 11/2" to 7/8" die hole bushing; one 5/8" tie down bar for swaging. From Hollywood Engineering.
Price: **$700.00**

Hornady Lock-N-Load Classic

HORNADY Lock-N-Load Classic

Frame: Die cast heat-treated aluminum alloy
Frame Type: O-frame
Die Thread: 7/8-14
Avg. Rounds Per Hour: NA
Ram Stroke: 3 5/8"
Weight: 14 lbs.
Features: Features Lock-N-Load bushing system that allows instant die changeovers. Solid steel linkage arms that rotate on steel pins; 30° angled frame design for improved visibility and accessibility; primer arm automatically moves in and out of ram for primer pickup and solid seating; two primer arms for large and small primers; long offset handle for increased leverage and unobstructed reloading; lifetime warranty. Comes as a package with primer catcher, PPS automatic primer feed and three Lock-N-Load die bushings. Dies and shellholder available separately or as kit with primer catcher, positive priming system, automatic primer feed, three die bushings and reloading accessories. From Hornady Mfg. Co.
Price: Classic Reloading Package **$115.95**
Price: Classic Reloading Kit **$274.95**

Huntington Compac Tool

HUNTINGTON Compac Tool

Frame: Aircraft aluminum
Frame Type: NA
Die Thread: 7/8-14
Avg. Rounds Per Hour: NA
Ram Stroke: NA
Weight: 37 oz.
Features: Small and lightweight for portability; performs all standard reloading operations; sufficient leverage to full-length resize, decap military brass and case-form. Accepts standard shellholders. Is bench mountable. Dimensions: 31/2" x 9". From Huntington Die Specialties.
Price: **$79.98**

Lee Hand Press

FORSTER
Co-Ax "S" and "LS" Shellholder Calibers

PISTOL	
22 Rem. Jet	25 Auto
30 Luger	38 Special
32 Auto	351 Win.
32 Colt N.P.	25-20 Win.
32 S&W	351 Win. S.L.
9mm Luger	32-20 Win.
38 Special	41 Rem. Mag.
380 Auto	44-40 Win.
32 Short Colt	45 Auto
32 Long Colt	45 Colt
9mm Win. Mag.	45 Win.
32 Rem.	38-40 Win.
30 Rem.	303 Savage
38 Auto	45 Auto Match
38 Short Colt	44 Rem. Mag.
38 Long Colt	10mm

RIFLE	
17 Rem.	7mm Wea.
218 Bee	280 Rem.
221 Rem.	284 Win.
222 Rem.	300 Savage
222 Rem. Mag.	30-30 Win.
223 Rem.	30-40 Krag
5.6x50	300 Win. Mag.
30 Carbine	303 British
32-20 Win.	307 Win.
219 Zipper	308 Win.
22 Savage	308 Nat'l M
224 Wea.	308 Norma
220 Swift	30-06
22-250 Rem.	300 H&H
225 Win.	300 Wea.
240 Wea.	8mm Rem. Mag.
243 Win.	8mmx57
6mm Rem.	8mmx68S
6mm PPC	32 Win.
25-06 Rem.	32-20 Win.
250 Savage	38-40 Win.
25-35 Win.	338 Win.
257 Roberts	340 Wea.
257 Wea.	35 Rem.
264 Win. Mag.	350 Rem. Mag.
6.5x54 Mann.-Schoe.	356 Win.
6.5 Rem. Mag.	358 Win.
6.5 Swede	358 Nor. Mag.
270 Win.	375 Wea.
270 Wea.	375 H&H
7x64 Brenneke	38-55 Win.
7mm-08	444 Marlin
7mmx57	44-40 Win.
7mm BR	458 Win. Mag.
7mm Rem.	375 Win.
	32-40 Win.

LEE Hand Press

Frame: ASTM 380 aluminum
Frame Type: NA
Die Thread: 7/8-14
Avg. Rounds Per Hour: 100
Ram Stroke: 31/4"
Weight: 1 lb., 8 oz.
Features: Small and lightweight for portability; compound linkage for handling up to 375 H&H and case forming. Dies and shellholder not included. From Lee Precision, Inc.
Price: **$24.98**

LEE Challenger Press

Frame: ASTM 380 aluminum
Frame Type: O-frame
Die Thread: 7/8-14
Avg. Rounds Per Hour: 100
Ram Stroke: 3 1/2"
Weight: 4 lbs., 1 oz.
Features: Larger than average opening with 30° offset for maximum hand clearance; steel connecting pins; spent primer catcher; handle adjustable for start and stop positions; handle repositions for left- or right-hand use; shortened handle travel to prevent springing the frame from alignment. Dies and shellholders not included. From Lee Precision, Inc.
Price: **$45.00**

LEE Loader

Kit consists of reloading dies to be used with mallet or soft hammer. Neck sizes only. Comes with powder charge cup. From Lee Precision, Inc.
Price:.................................. **$19.98**

LEE Reloader Press

Frame: ASTM 380 aluminum
Frame Type: C-frame
Die Thread: 7/8-14
Avg. Rounds Per Hour: 100
Ram Stroke: 3"
Weight: 1 lb., 12 oz.
Features: Balanced lever to prevent pinching fingers; unlimited hand clearance; left- or right-hand use. Dies and shellholders not included. From Lee Precision, Inc.
Price: **$24.98**

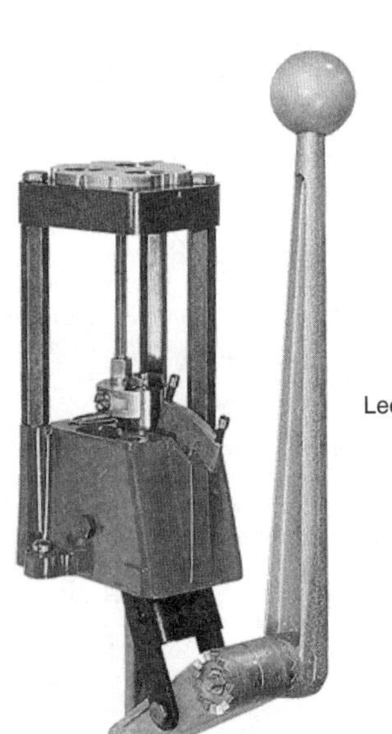
Lee Turret

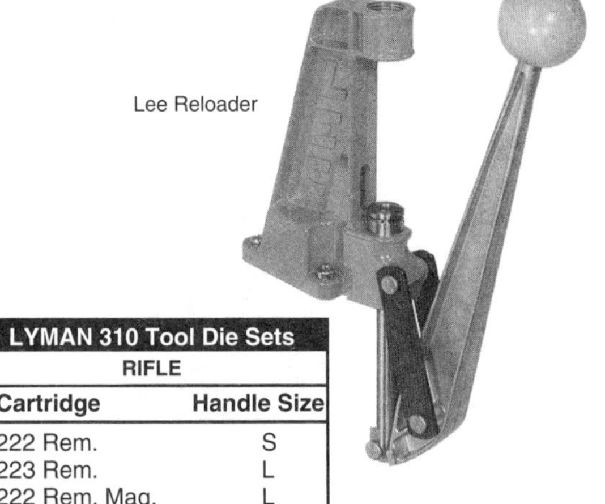
Lee Reloader

LYMAN 310 Tool Die Sets

Cartridge	Handle Size
RIFLE	
222 Rem.	S
223 Rem.	L
222 Rem. Mag.	L
243 Win.	L
6mm Rem.	L
270 Win.	L
30 M1 Carbine	S
30-30 Win.	L
30-06	L
7.62mmx63	L
300 Savage	L
308 Win.	L
38-40	S
44-40	S
45-70 Gov't.	L
PISTOL	
Cartridge	**Handle Size**
9mm Luger	S
38 Auto	S
38 Spl./357 Mag.	S
44 Rem. Mag.	S
45 ACP	S
45 Colt	S

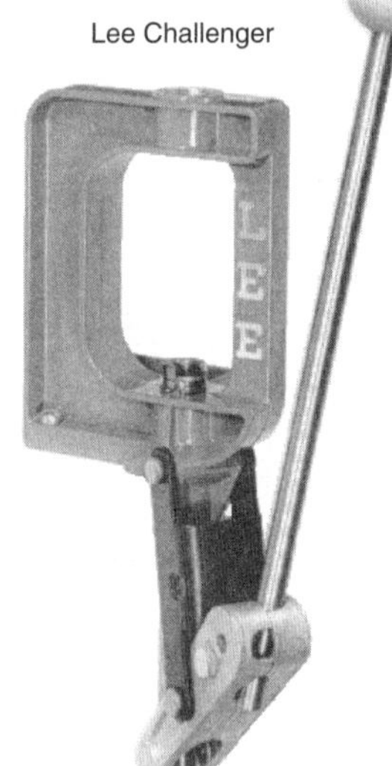
Lee Challenger

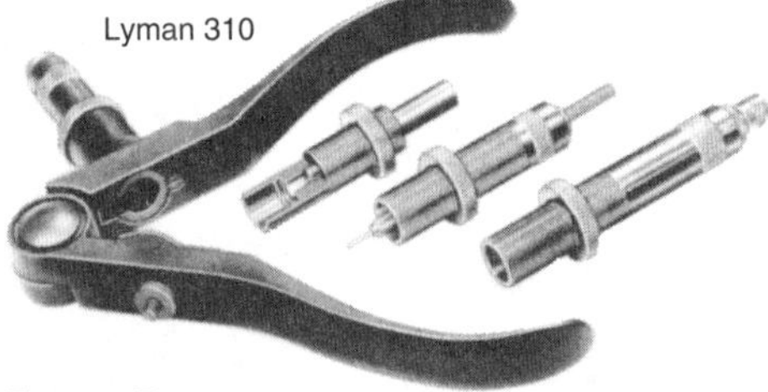
Lyman 310

LEE Turret Press

Frame: ASTM 380 aluminum
Frame Type: O-frame
Die Thread: 7/8-14
Avg. Rounds Per Hour: 300
Ram Stroke: 3"
Weight: 7 lbs., 2 oz.
Features: Replaceable turret lifts out by rotating 30°; T-primer arm reverses for large or small primers; built-in primer catcher; adjustable handle for right- or left-hand use or changing angle of down stroke; accessory mounting hole for Lee Auto-Disk powder measure. Optional Auto-Index rotates die turret to next station for semi-progressive use. Safety override prevents overstressing should turret not turn. From Lee Precision, Inc.
Price: **$69.98**
Price: With Auto-Index **$83.98**
Price: Extra turret...................... **$10.98**

Turret handle disconnector

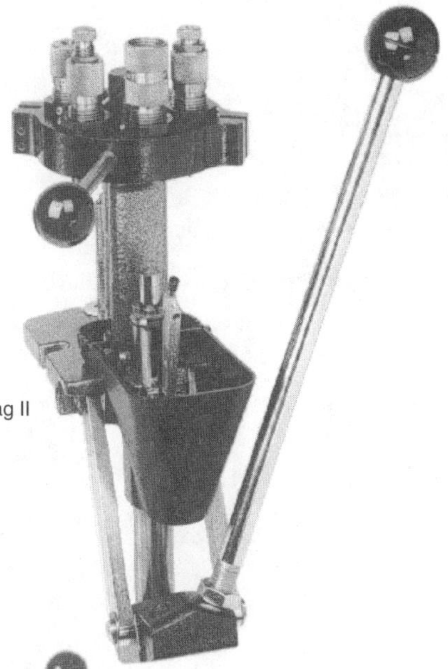

Lyman T-Mag II

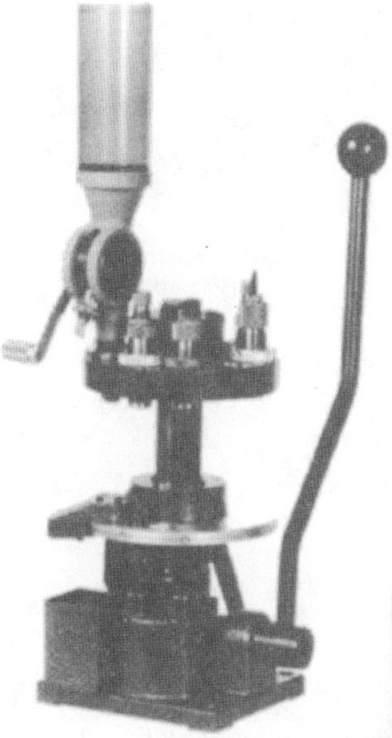

Ponsness/Warren Metal-Matic P-200

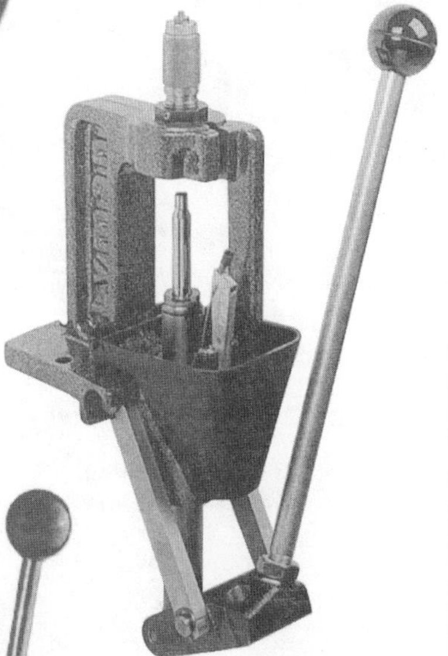

Lyman Orange Crusher II

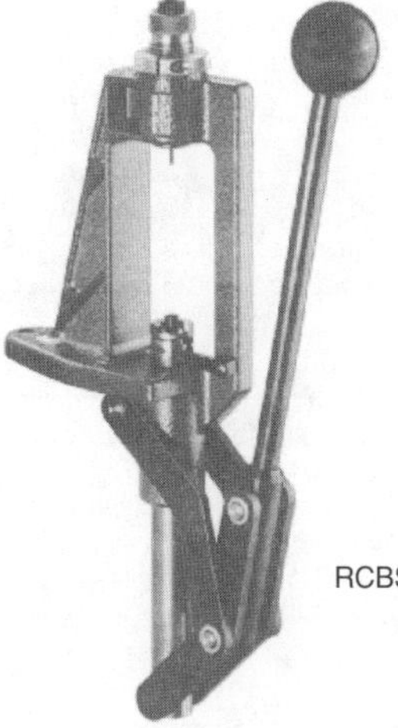

RCBS Partner

LYMAN 310 Tool
Frame: Stainless steel
Frame Type: NA
Die Thread: 7/8-14
Avg. Rounds Per Hour: NA
Ram Stroke: NA
Weight: 10 oz.
Features: Compact, portable reloading tool for pistol or rifle cartridges. Adapter allows loading rimmed or rimless cases. Die set includes neck resizing/decapping die, primer seating chamber; neck expanding die; bullet seating die; and case head adapter. From Lyman Products Corporation.
Price: Dies. $45.00
Price: Press. $47.50
Price: Carrying pouch $9.95

LYMAN AccuPress
Frame: Die cast
Frame Type: C-frame
Die Thread: 7/8-14
Avg. Rounds Per Hour: 75
Ram Stroke: 3.4”
Weight: 4 lbs.
Features: Reversible, contoured handle for bench mount or hand-held use; for rifle or pistol; compound leverage; Delta frame design. Accepts all standard powder measures. From Lyman Products Corporation.
Price: **$34.95**

LYMAN Orange Crusher II
Frame: Cast iron
Frame Type: O-frame
Die Thread: 7/8-14
Avg. Rounds Per Hour: 75
Ram Stroke: 37/8”
Weight: 19 lbs.
Features: Reloads both pistol and rifle cartridges; 1” diameter ram; 41/2” press opening for loading magnum cartridges; direct torque design; right- or left-hand use. New base design with 14 square inches of flat mounting surface with three bolt holes. Comes with priming arm and catcher. Dies and shellholders not included. From Lyman Products Corporation.
Price: **$116.50**

LYMAN T-Mag II
Frame: Cast iron with silver metalflake powder finish
Frame Type: Turret
Die Thread: 7/8-14
Avg. Rounds Per Hour: 125
Ram Stroke: 313/16”
Weight: 18 lbs.
Features: Reengineered and upgraded with new turret system for ease of indexing and tool-free turret removal for caliber changeover; new flat machined base for bench mounting; new nickel-plated non-rust handle and links; and new silver hammertone powder coat finish for durability. Right- or left-hand operation; handles all rifle or pistol dies. Comes with priming arm and primer catcher. Dies and shellholders not included. From Lyman Products Corporation.
Price: **$164.95**
Price: Extra turret. **$37.50**

Section 1: Metallic Cartridges

PONSNESS/WARREN Metal-Matic P-200

Frame: Die cast aluminum
Frame Type: Unconventional
Die Thread: 7/8-14
Avg. Rounds Per Hour: 200+
Weight: 18 lbs.
Features: Designed for straight-wall cartridges; die head with 10 tapped holes for holding dies and accessories for two calibers at one time; removable spent primer box; pivoting arm moves case from station to station. Comes with large and small primer tool. Optional accessories include primer feed, extra die head, primer speed feeder, powder measure extension and dust cover. Dies, powder measure and shellholder not included. From Ponsness/Warren.
Price: **$215.00**
Price: Extra die head **$44.95**
Price: Powder measure extension............. **$29.95**
Price: Primer feed **$44.95**
Price: Primer speed feed **$14.50**
Price: Dust cover **$21.95**

RCBS Partner

Frame: Aluminum
Frame Type: O-frame
Die Thread: 7/8-14
Avg. Rounds Per Hour: 50-60
Ram Stroke: 3 5/8"
Weight: 5 lbs.
Features: Designed for the beginning reloader. Comes with primer arm equipped with interchangeable primer plugs and sleeves for seating large and small primers. Shellholder and dies not included. Available in kit form (see Metallic Presses-Accessories). From RCBS.
Price: **$63.95**

RCBS AmmoMaster Single

Frame: Aluminum base; cast iron top plate connected by three steel posts.
Frame Type: NA
Die Thread: 11/4"-12 bushing; 7/8-14 threads
Avg. Rounds Per Hour: 50-60
Ram Stroke: 51/4"
Weight: 19 lbs.
Features: Single-stage press convertible to progressive. Will form cases or swage bullets. Case detection system to disengage powder measure when no case is present in powder charging station; five-station shellplate; Uniflow Powder measure with clear powder measure adaptor to make bridged powders visible and correctable. 50-cal. conversion kit allows reloading 50 BMG. Kit includes top plate to accommodate either 1 3/8" x 12 or 1 1/2" x 12 reloading dies. Piggyback die plate for quick caliber change-overs available. Reloading dies not included. From RCBS.
Price: **$212.95**
Price: 50 conversion kit.................... **$100.95**
Price: Piggyback/AmmoMaster die plate **$26.95**
Price: Piggyback/AmmoMaster shellplate **$29.95**
Price: Press cover.......................... **$13.95**

RCBS Reloader Special-5

Frame: Aluminum
Frame Type: 30º offset O-frame
Die Thread: 1 1/4-12 bushing; 7/8-14 threads
Avg. Rounds Per Hour: 50-60
Ram Stroke: 3 1/16"
Weight: 7.5 lbs.
Features: Single-stage press convertible to progressive with RCBS Piggyback II. Primes cases during resizing operation. Will accept RCBS shotshell dies. From RCBS.
Price:.................................... **$115.95**

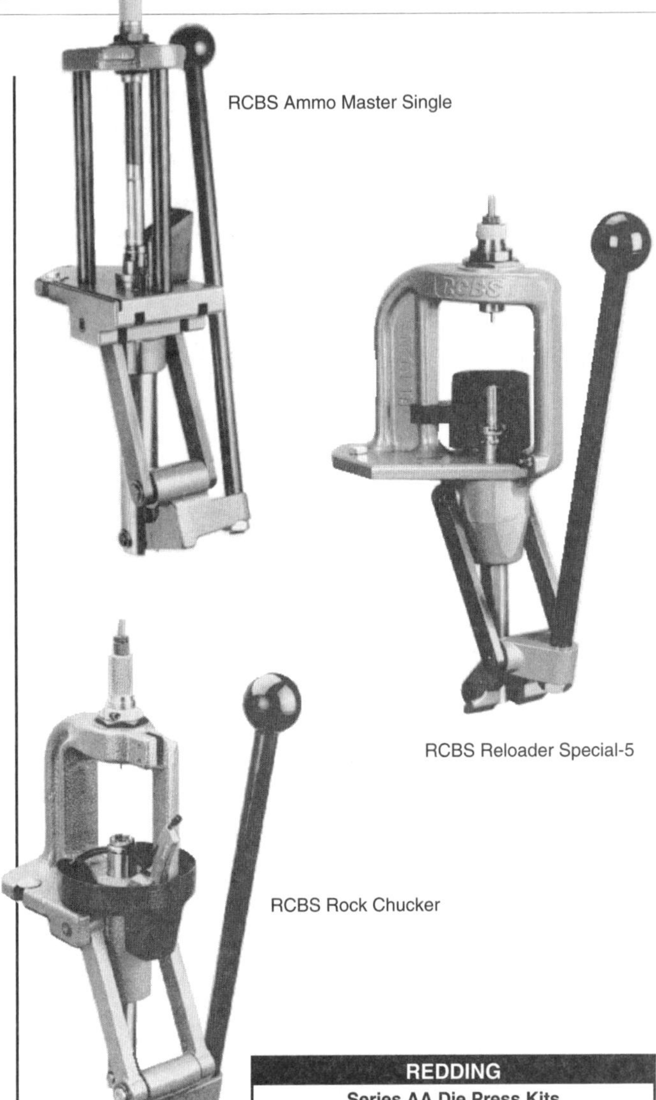

RCBS Ammo Master Single

RCBS Reloader Special-5

RCBS Rock Chucker

REDDING	
Series AA Die Press Kits	
RIFLE	
221 Rem. Fire Ball	7mm Rem. Mag.
22 Hornet	7mmx57 Mauser
220 Swift	280 Rem.
222 Rem.	284 Win.
22-250 Rem.	7.62x39
223 Rem.	30-30 Win.
243 Win.	30-40 Krag
6mm Rem.	30-06 Sprfld.
250 Savage	300 Wea. Mag.
25-06 Rem.	300 Win. Mag.
257 Roberts	308 Win.
6.5mmx55	303 British
Swed. Mauser	8mmx57 Mauser
264 Win. Mag.	338 Win. Mag.
270 Win.	35 Rem.
7mm-08 Rem.	375 H&H Mag.
PISTOL	
30 M1 Carbine	38 Spl./357 Mag.
32 S&W Long	41 Mag.
32 H&R Mag.	44 Spl.
380 Auto	44 Mag.
9mm Luger	44-40 Win.
38 Spl.	45 ACP & AR
357 Mag.	45 Colt

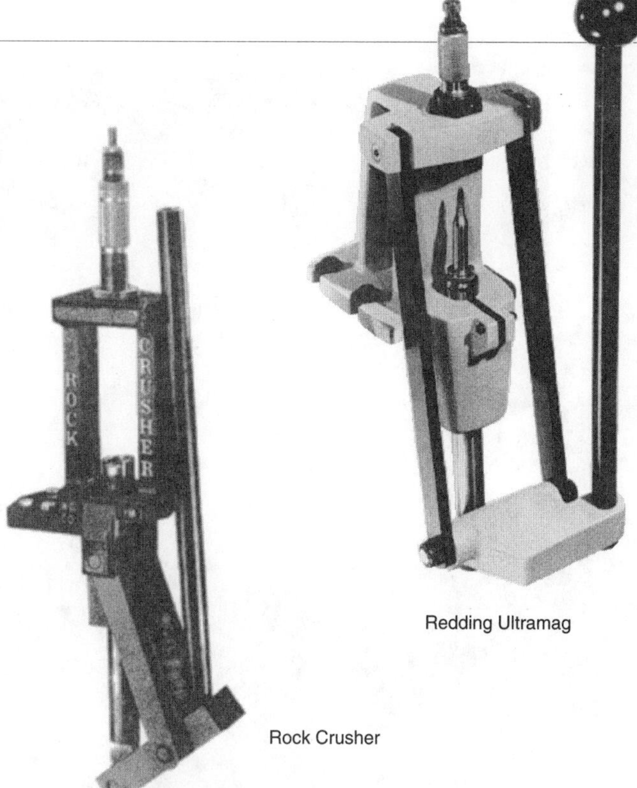

Redding Ultramag

Rock Crusher

Sharp Shooter
Port-A-Press

Redding The Boss

RCBS Rock Chucker
Frame: Cast iron
Frame Type: O-frame
Die Thread: 1 1/4"-12 bushing; 7/8-14 threads
Avg. Rounds Per Hour: 50-60
Ram Stroke: 3 5/16"
Weight: 17 lbs.
Features: Designed for heavy-duty reloading, case forming and bullet swaging. Provides 4" of ram-bearing surface to support 1" ram and ensure alignment; ductile iron toggle blocks; hardened steel pins. Comes standard with Universal Primer Arm and primer catcher. Can be converted from single-stage to progressive with Piggyback II conversion unit (see Metallic Presses-Accessories). From RCBS.
Price: **$145.95**

REDDING Model T-7 Turret Press
Frame: Cast iron
Frame Type: Turret
Die Thread: 7/8-14
Avg. Rounds Per Hour: NA
Ram Stroke: 3.4"
Weight: 23 lbs., 2 oz.
Features: Strength to reload pistol and magnum rifle, case form and bullet swage; linkage pins heat-treated, precision ground and in double shear; hollow ram to collect spent primers; removable turret head for caliber changes; progressive linkage for increased power as ram nears die; slight frame tilt for comfortable operation; rear turret support for stability and precise alignment; six-station turret head; priming arm for both large and small primers. Also available in kit form with shellholder, primer catcher and one die set. From Redding Reloading Equipment.
Price: **$298.50**
Price: Kit **$339.00**

REDDING The Boss
Frame: Cast iron
Frame Type: O-frame
Die Thread: 7/8-14
Avg. Rounds Per Hour: NA
Ram Stroke: 3.4"
Weight: 11 lbs., 8 oz.
Features: 36° frame offset for visibility and accessibility; primer arm positioned at bottom of ram travel; positive ram travel stop machined to hit exactly top-dead-center. Also available in kit form with shellholder and set of Redding A dies. From Redding Reloading Equipment.
Price: **$139.50**
Price: Kit **$180.00**

REDDING Ultramag
Frame: Cast iron
Frame Type: Non-conventional
Die Thread: 7/8-14
Avg. Rounds Per Hour: NA
Ram Stroke: 41/8"
Weight: 23 lbs., 6 oz.
Features: Unique compound leverage system connected to top of press for tons of ram pressure; large 4 3/4" frame opening for loading outsized cartridges; hollow ram for spent primers. Kit available with shellholder and one set Redding A dies. From Redding Reloading Equipment.
Price: **$315.50**
Price: Kit **$355.50**

SHARP SHOOTER Port-A-Press
Frame: 6061 aluminum
Frame Type: O-frame
Die Thread: 7/8-14
Avg. Rounds Per Hour: NA
Ram Stroke: 2 1/2"
Weight: 8 lbs.
Features: Lightweight, compact three-station turret press; measures 12" high, 5" wide and 6 1/2" deep; built-in bench clamp to attach to any bench; removable turret. From Sharp Shooter Supply.
Price: **$250.00**
Price: Extra turret **$10.50**

DILLON RL 550B
Frame: Aluminum alloy
Frame Type: NA
Die Thread: 7/8-14
Avg. Rounds Per Hour: 500-600
Ram Stroke: 37/8=
Weight: 25 lbs.
Features: Four stations; removable tool head to hold dies in alignment and allow caliber changes without die adjustment; auto priming system that emits audible warning when primer tube is low; a 100-primer capacity magazine contained in DOM steel tube for protection; new auto powder measure system with simple mechanical connection between measure and loading platform for positive powder bar return; a separate station for crimping with star-indexing system; 220 ejected-round capacity bin; 3/4-lb. capacity powder measure. Height above bench, 35=; requires 3/4= bench overhang. Will reload 120 different rifle and pistol calibers. Comes with one caliber conversion kit. Dies not included. From Dillon Precision Products, Inc.
Price: **$329.95**
Price: Instruction manual **$5.95**

DILLON RL 1050
Frame: Ductile iron
Frame Type: Platform type
Die Thread: 7/8-14
Avg. Rounds Per Hour: 1000-1200
Ram Stroke: 25/16=
Weight: 62 lbs.
Features: Eight stations; auto case feed; primer pocket swager for military cartridge cases; auto indexing; removable tool head; auto prime system with 100-primer capacity; low primer supply alarm; positive powder bar return; auto powder measure; 515 ejected round bin capacity; 500-600 case feed capacity; 3/4-lb. capacity powder measure. Loads all pistol rounds as well as 30 M1 Carbine, 223 and 7.62x39 rifle rounds. Height above the bench, 43=. Dies not included. From Dillon Precision Products, Inc.
Price: **$1,399.95**

DILLON Square Deal B
Frame: Zinc alloy
Frame Type: NA
Die Thread: None (unique Dillon design)
Avg. Rounds Per Hour: 400-500
Ram Stroke: 25/16=
Weight: 17 lbs.
Features: Four stations; auto indexing; removable tool head; auto prime system with 100-primer capacity; low primer supply alarm; auto powder measure; positive powder bar return; 170 ejected round capacity bin; 3/4-lb. capacity powder measure. Height above the bench, 34=. Comes complete with factory adjusted carbide die set. From Dillon Precision Products, Inc.
Price: **$277.95**

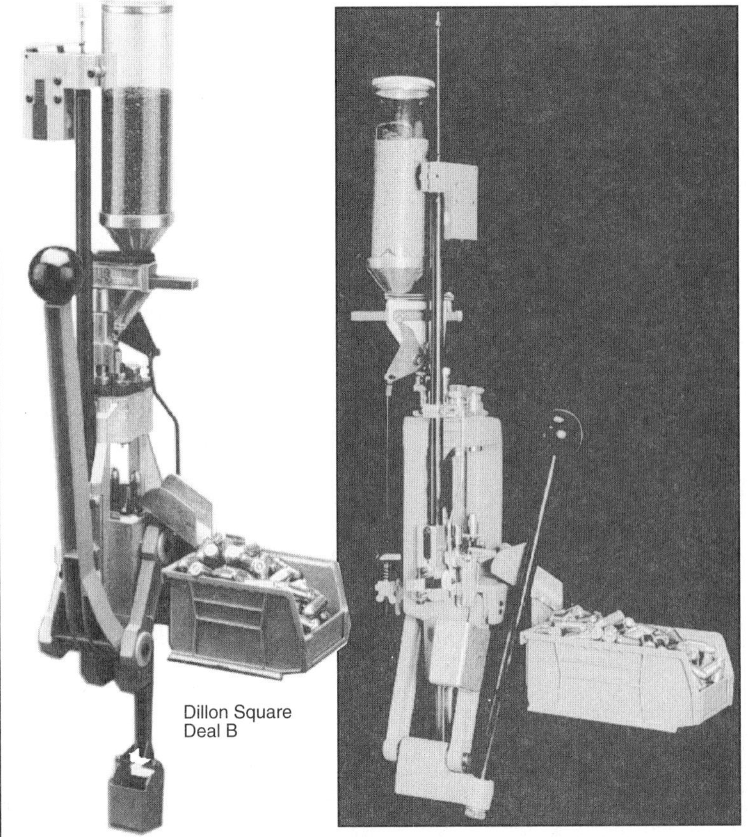

Dillon Square Deal B

Dillon RL 550B

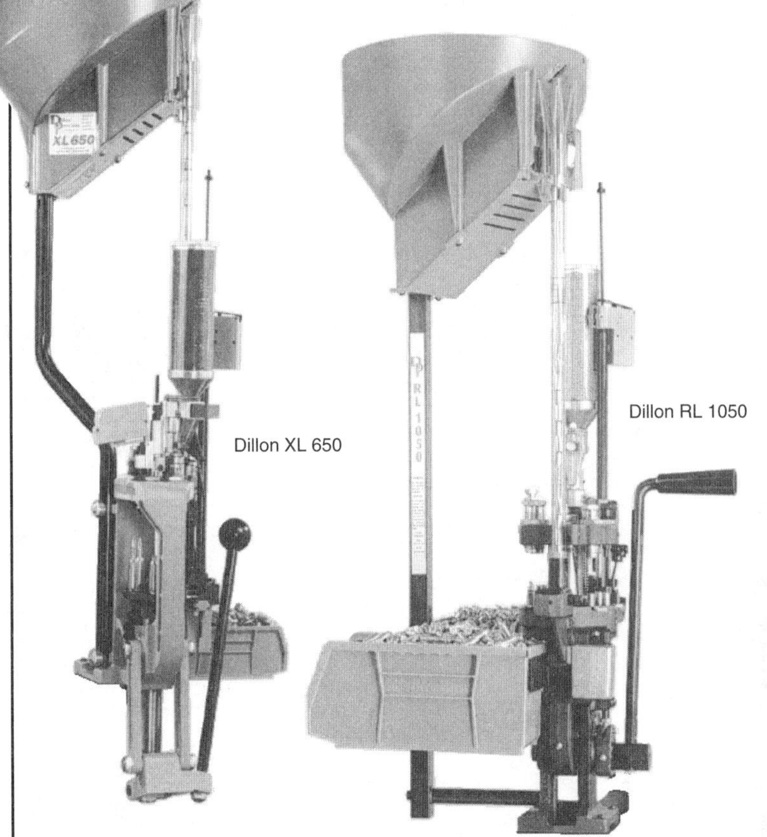

Dillon XL 650

Dillon RL 1050

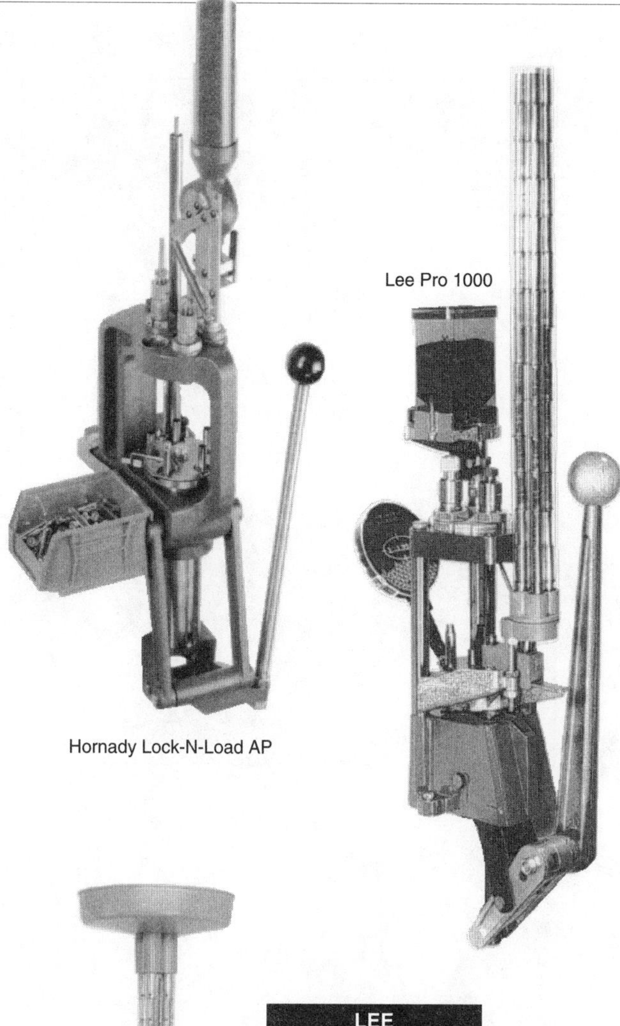

Lee Pro 1000

Hornady Lock-N-Load AP

LEE
Load-Master Pistol Calibers
32 S&W Long
32 H&R Magnum
9mm Luger
380 Auto
38 Special
357 Magnum
40 S&W
10mm Auto
44 Special
44 Magnum
45 ACP
45 Colt

LEE
Load Master Rifle Calibers
222 Rem.
223 Rem.
22-250
243 Win.
6.5x55
270 Win.
30-30 Win.
308 Win.
30-06

Lee Load Master

DILLON XL 650

Frame: Aluminum alloy
Frame Type: NA
Die Thread: 7/8-14
Avg. Rounds Per Hour: 800-1000
Ram Stroke: 49/16=
Weight: 46 lbs.
Features: Five stations; auto indexing; auto case feed; removable tool head; auto prime system with 100-primer capacity; low primer supply alarm; auto powder measure; positive powder bar return; 220 ejected-round capacity bin; 3/4-lb. capacity powder measure; 500-600 case feed capacity with optional auto case feed. Loads all pistol/rifle calibers less than 31/2= in length. Height above the bench, 44=; 3/4= bench overhang required. From Dillon Precision Products, Inc.
Price: **$443.95**
Price: Video instruction manual **$5.95**

HORNADY Lock-N-Load AP

Frame: Die cast heat-treated aluminum alloy
Frame Type: O-frame
Die Thread: 7/8-14
Avg. Rounds Per Hour: NA
Ram Stroke: 33/4=
Weight: 26 lbs.
Features: Features Lock-N-Load bushing system that allows instant die changeovers; five-station die platform with option of seating and crimping separately or adding taper-crimp die; auto prime with large and small primer tubes with 100-primer capacity and protective housing; brass kicker to eject loaded rounds into 80-round capacity cartridge catcher; offset operating handle for leverage and unobstructed operation; 2= diameter ram driven by heavy-duty cast linkage arms rotating on steel pins. Comes with five Lock-N-Load die bushings, shellplate, deluxe powder measure, auto powder drop, and auto primer feed and shut-off, brass kicker and primer catcher. Lifetime warranty. From Hornady Mfg. Co.
Price: **$379.95**

LEE Load-Master

Frame: ASTM 380 aluminum
Frame Type: O-frame
Die Thread: 7/8-14
Avg. Rounds Per Hour: 600
Ram Stroke: 31/4=
Weight: 8 lbs., 4 oz.
Features: Available in kit form only. A 13/4= hard chrome diameter ram for handling largest magnum cases; loads rifle or pistol rounds; five-station press to factory crimp and post size; auto indexing with wedge lock mechanism to hold one ton; auto priming; removable turrets; four-tube case feeder with optional case collator and bullet feeder (late 1995); loaded round ejector with chute to optional loaded round catcher; quick change shellplate; primer catcher. Dies and shellholder for one caliber included. From Lee Precision, Inc.
Price: Rifle **$320.00**
Price: Pistol **$330.00**
Price: Case collator **$14.98**
Price: Adjustable charge bar **$9.98**

LEE Pro 1000
Frame: ASTM 380 aluminum and steel
Frame Type: O-frame
Die Thread: 7/8-14
Avg. Rounds Per Hour: 600
Ram Stroke: 31/4=
Weight: 8 lbs., 7 oz.
Features: Optional transparent large/small or rifle case feeder; deluxe auto-disk case-activated powder measure; case sensor for primer feed. Comes complete with carbide die set (steel dies for rifle) for one caliber. Optional accessories include: case feeder for large/small pistol cases or rifle cases; shell plate carrier with auto prime, case ejector, auto-index and spare parts; case collator for case feeder. From Lee Precision, Inc.
Price: **$199.98**

PONSNESS/WARREN Metallic II
Frame: Die cast aluminum
Frame Type: H-frame
Die Thread: 7/8-14
Avg. Rounds Per Hour: 150+
Ram Stroke: NA
Weight: 32 lbs.
Features: Die head with five tapped 7/8-14 holes for dies, powder measure or other accessories; pivoting die arm moves case from station to station; depriming tube for removal of spent primers; auto primer feed; interchangeable die head. Optional accessories include additional die heads, powder measure extension tube to accommodate any standard powder measure, primer speed feeder to feed press primer tube without disassembly. Comes with small and large primer seating tools. Dies, powder measure and shellholder not included. From Ponsness/Warren.
Price: **$375.00**
Price: Extra die head **$56.95**
Price: Primer speed feeder **$14.50**
Price: Powder measure extension **$29.95**
Price: Dust cover **$30.95**

RCBS Pro 2000
Five-Station progressive press for pistol and rifle cases.
Price: **$491.95**
Price: Star wheel **$5.95**
Price: Tube priming conversion kit **$88.95**
Price: Low primer detector **$25.95**
Price: Dust cover **$13.95**

STAR Universal Pistol Press
Frame: Cast iron with aluminum base
Frame Type: Unconventional
Die Thread: 11/16-24 or 7/8-14
Avg. Rounds Per Hour: 300
Ram Stroke: NA
Weight: 27 lbs.
Features: Four or five-station press depending on need to taper crimp; handles all popular handgun calibers from 32 Long to 45 Colt. Comes completely assembled and adjusted with carbide dies (except 30 Carbine) and shellholder to load one caliber. From Star Machine Works.
Price: With taper crimp **$10257.00**
Price: Without taper crimp **$995.00**
Price: Extra tool head, taper crimp **$425.00**
Price: Extra tool head, w/o taper crimp **$395.00**

Fully-automated Star Universal

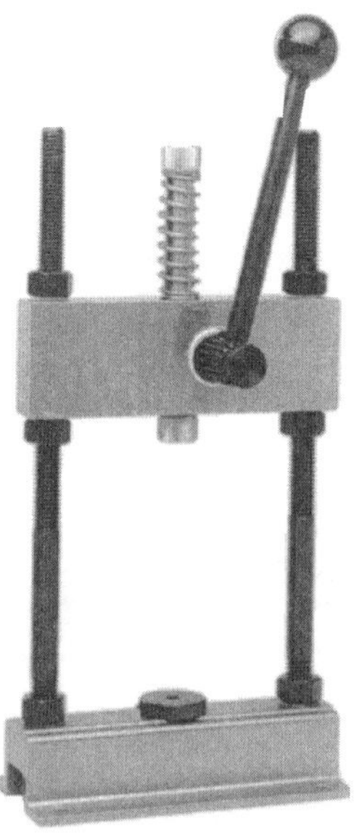

B-Square Super Mag Arbor

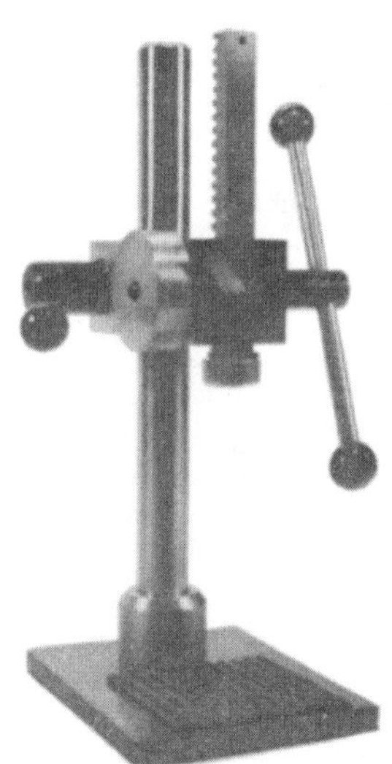

Hart Arbor Press

METALLIC PRESSES/PROGRESSIVE

Bald Eagle Lightweight

Sinclair Arbor Press

Jones Arbor Press

K&M Services Arbor Press

BALD EAGLE Lightweight Press
Frame: 2024-T6 aircraft aluminum
Mechanical Advantage: 1:5
Weight: 1.25 lbs.
Features: Spring-loaded plunger which elevates and returns handle to original position. Uses Wilson-style seater die. Main support is 65/8" high; base is 3"x5". Finish is black hardcoat. From Bald Eagle Precision Machine Co.
Price: **$60.00**

B-SQUARE Super Mag Arbor Press
Frame: Stress-proof steel with 60/61T6 aluminum base and head
Ram Stroke: 11/2"
Weight: 81/2 lbs.
Features: Features twin posts for "no-spring"; capability to full-length size up to 30-06 in Wilson die; fully adjustable press head; spring return ram and replaceable brass caps; 41/2" handle adjustable for right- or left-hand use. Dimensions: height, 12"; width, 4". From B-Square Company.
Price: **$99.95**

HART Arbor Press
Frame: Steel and aluminum
Ram Stroke: 3.5"
Weight: NA
Features: Bronze bushings; vertical adjustment from 1" to 7"; handle offers 2" stroke per revolution; locking handle for securing vertical adjustments. Deluxe version available with spring return on ram. From Robert W. Hart & Son, Inc.
Price: **$110.95**
Price: Deluxe press **$129.95**

JONES Arbor Press
Frame: Aluminum alloy
Ram Stroke: NA
Weight: 4 lbs.
Features: Hardened and polished steel guide post; adjustable head; open base for catching spent primers; adjustable for right- or left-hand use; easy takedown for transportation and storage. From Neil Jones Custom Products.
Price: **$135.00**
Price: 50-caliber **$155.00**

K&M Arbor Press
Frame: Aluminum
Ram Stroke: .900"
Weight: 42 oz.
Features: T-bar and rectangular bar constructed for strength. Ram adjustment made by socket head cap screws which allows sliding ram unit on T-Bar. Overall height 9 1/2" with 3 3/4x5" rectangular base. Portable press for home or range designed to be used with hand dies. Toggle link/crankshaft design provides smooth operation. Ram bushings of Oilite bronze. From K&M Services.
Price: **$78.00**
Price: Force Measurement **$98.00**

SINCLAIR Arbor Press
Frame: Stainless steel with steel base
Ram Stroke: 3 1/2"
Weight: 4 1/2 lbs.
Features: Designed for use with hand dies; compact and portable; steel base eliminates need to clamp down for use. From Sinclair International, Inc.
Price: **$88.00**

BULLET SWAGING SUPPLY

Conversion Unit
Converts RCBS Rock Chucker, Lyman Orange Crusher and Pacific 007 presses into swaging press. Consists of modified ram for swaging, a punch holder and ejector pin. One hole must be drilled in base of press for ejector pin. Includes BSS 3-die set. From Bullet Swaging Supply, Inc.
Price: **$75.00**
Price: With 3-die set **$325.00**
Price: For RCBS Big Max..... **$350.00**

C-H/4-D

"H" Ram
Can be used with any Hollywood or Dunbar press and will accept any universal shellholder head. Available with standard 5/16" center hole or 3/8" center hole used at priming station and H-Mag press. Does not include shellholder. From C-H Tool & Die/4-D Custom Die.
Price: **$7.65**

Press Top Bushing
Designed to work with most O- and C-type presses to allow use of dies threaded larger than 7/8-14. From C-H Tool & Die/4-D Custom Die.
Price: 1 1/4"-12x7/8"-14........ **$12.95**
Price: 1 3/8"-12x7/8"(or 1")-14 .. **$13.95**
Price: 1 1/2"-12x7/8"(or 1")-14 .. **$14.95**

Shellholder Adaptor
Fits all Herters and Lachmiller presses which use one or two set-screws to hold shellholder. Adapts them to standard snap-in shellholder. From C-H Tool & Die/4-D Custom Die.
Price: **$14.25**

Shellholder Extension
For use when trimming short cases in file trim die. Extends shellholders 3/4". From C-H Tool & Die/4-D Custom Die.
Price: **$12.00**

Universal "C" Press Ram
Features relieved clearance for primer and floating shellholder action for alignment. Shellholder not included. From C-H Tool & Die/4-D Custom Die.
Price: **$16.45**

Universal Shellholders
Detachable shellholders to fit all popular presses. From C-H Tool & Die/4-D Custom Die.
Price: **$6.00**

DAKOTA

Shellholders
Shellholders for Dakota Arms proprietary cartridges, 7mm, 300, 330, 375, 416 and 450 Dakota. From Dakota Arms.
Price: **$15.00**

DILLON

AT 500 Auto Eject Upgrade
To upgrade AT 500 press to RL 550B. Includes cartridge chute/bracket and cartridge bin. From Dillon Precision Products.
Price: **$15.95**

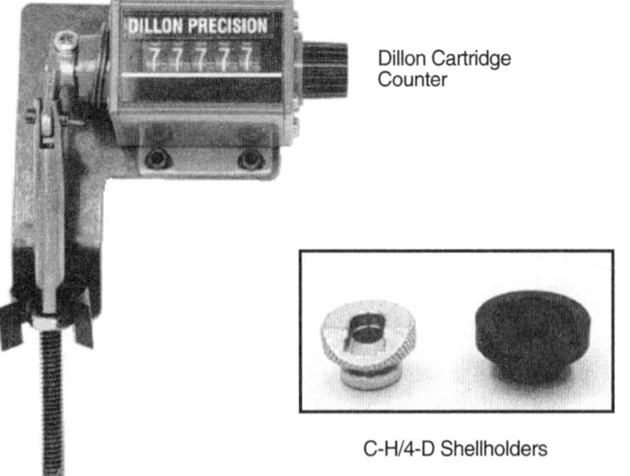

Dillon Cartridge Counter

C-H/4-D Shellholders

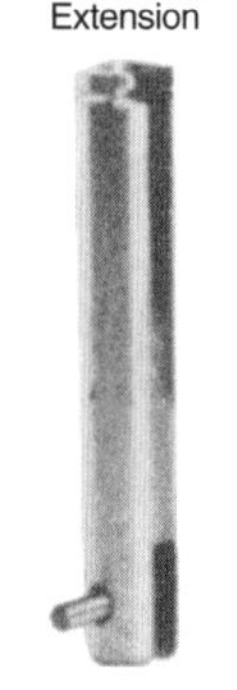

C-H/4-D Shellholder Extension

Dillon 550B Conversion Kit

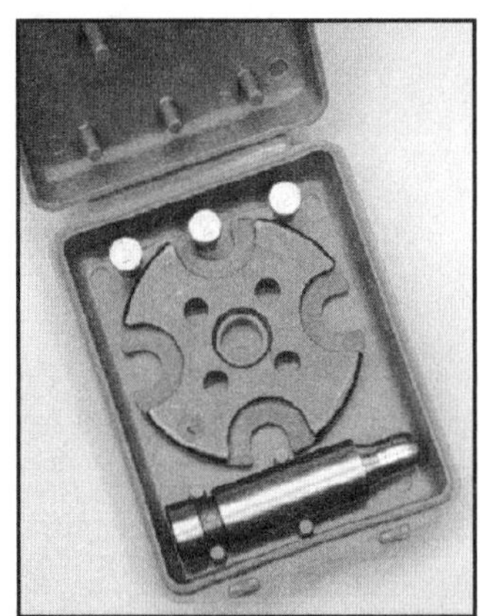

DILLON RL 1050
Caliber Conversion Kits
32 S&W
380 Auto
9mm
9x25 Dillon
38 Super
38/357 Mag.
40 S&W
10mm
41 Magnum
44 Magnum
45 ACP

DILLON Square Deal B
Caliber Conversion Kits
32 S&W
380 ACP
38 Special
357 Magnum
38 Super
9mm
40 S&W
10mm
41 Magnum
44 Spl.
44 Mag-

DILLON RL 550B
Caliber Conversion Kits

RIFLE				PISTOL
17 Rem.	257 Wea. Mag.	32 Rem.	6mm Rem.	30 Mauser
218 Bee	25 Rem.	32 Win. Special	6.5-06	30 Luger
219 Zipper	264 Win. Mag.	33 Win.	6.5x52 Carcano	32 S&W Mag.
219 Donaldson	270 Win.	338 Win.	6.5x54 Mann.-Sch.	32 H&R Mag.
220 Swift	270 Wea. Mag.	340 Wea. Mag.	6.5x55 Swedish	32 Short Colt
221 Rem. Fireball	280 Rem.	348 Win.	6.5 Jap.	32 ACP
222 Rem.	284 Win.	350 Rem. Mag.	6.5 Rem. Mag.	380 ACP
22-250	30 M1 Carbine	356 Win.	6mm PPC	9mm
222 Rem. Mag.	300 Win. Mag.	357 Herrett	7mm-08	38 S&W
223 Rem.	30-06	358 Win.	7.62x39 Russian	38AMU
224 Wea. Mag.	300 H&H	358 Norma Mag.	7.65x53 Mauser Rim.	38 Super
225 Win.	300 Savage	35 Rem.	7.62x54 Russ.	38/357 Mag./Max.
22 Hornet	300 Wea. Mag.	35 Win.	7mmx57 Mauser	10mm/40 S&W
22 Rem. Jet	303 British	35 Whelen	7x64 Brenneke	41 AE
22 Sav. Hi-Power	30-30 Win.	375 Win.	7.7 Japanese	41 Mag.
240 Wea. Mag.	30-338 Win.	375 H&H Mag.	7mm BR	44 Special
243 Win.	30-40 Krag	375 Super Mag.	7mm Express	44 Mag.
244 Rem.	307 Win.	375 Wea. Mag.	7mm Int'l.	45 ACP
250 Savage	308	38-40 Win.	7mm Rem. Mag.	45 Auto Rim
25-06	308 Norma Mag.	38-55 Win.	7mm Merrill	455 Webley
25-20 Win.	30 Herrett	416 Rem. Mag.	7mm Int'l Rimmed	45 Long Colt
25-35 Win.	30 Merrill	444 Marlin	7mm TCU	45 Win. Mag.
256 Win. Mag.	30 Rem.	44-40 Win.	7mm Wea. Mag.	454 Casull
257 Roberts	32-20 Win.	45-70 Gov't.	8mm Mauser	50 AE
257 Ackley Imp.	32-40 Win.	458 Win. Mag.	8mm Rem. Mag.	

AT 500 Auto Powder Upgrade
To upgrade AT 500 press to RL 550B. Accurate to within 0.1-grain. Magnum rifle powder bar optional. From Dillon Precision Products.
Price: **$66.95**
Price: Magnum rifle bar **$19.95**

DILLON
AT 500 Auto Prime Upgrade
To upgrade AT 500 press to RL 550B. Includes priming housing and shield; large and small primer slides; large and small pickup tubes, tube lips and magazine tubes; operating rod; primer track bearing; housing screws; spring retaining pin. From Dillon Precision Products.
Price: **459.95**

AT 500 Early Warning Primer Upgrade
To upgrade AT 500 press to RL 550B. Features easy slip-on attachment. From Dillon Precision Products, Inc.
Price: **$15.00**

Accessory Roller Handle
Accessory press handle for Dillon XL 650, RL 550B and AT 500. From Dillon Precision Products, Inc.
Price:....................... **$24.95**

Auto Powder Measure System
For RL 550B and XL 650 presses. Powder measure to fit extra tool head allowing for quick caliber changeovers. From Dillon Precision Products, Inc.
Price: **$49.95**

Bench Wrenches
Has all correct sizes for Dillon dies, powder systems and press adjustments. From Dillon Precision Products, Inc.
Price: **$4.95**

Cartridge Counter
Attaches to all Dillon presses or any "crimp only" crimp die. Counts number of rounds of loaded ammo. From Dillon Precision Products, Inc.
Price: **$15.95**

Low Powder Sensor
Provides audible and visual signal when powder level in reservoir drops to 1000 grains. Made of clear polycarbonate with LED light. Two AAA batteries included. From Dillon Precision Products, Inc.
Price: **$29.95**

Press Covers
Packcloth nylon machine cover for all Dillon presses. Features D-ring for locking, heavy-duty zipper and optional master lock. From Dillon Precision Products, Inc.
Price: RL 550B/Square Deal B with lock **$22.90**
Price: RL 550B/Square Deal B cover only **$19.95**
Price: RL 1050/XL 650 with lock **$37.90**
Price: RL 1050/XL 650 cover only **$34.95**

Dillon Tool Head Assembly

DILLON XL 650
Caliber Conversion Kits

RIFLE	Price	RIFLE	Price
17 Rem.	$49.95	308 Norma Mag.	$100.00
22 Hornet	49.95	256 Win. Mag.	49.95
7.62x39	49.95	8mm Rem. Mag.	100.00
22 Rem. Jet	49.95	257 Roberts	49.95
218 Bee	49.95	338 Win. Mag.	100.00
7.62x54	100.00	257 Ackley Imp.	49.95
220 Swift	49.95	340 Wea. Mag.	100.00
30M1 Carbine	49.95	257 Wea. Mag.	100.00
30-06	49.95	6mm Rem.	49.95
222 Rem.	49.95	350 Rem. Mag.	100.00
300 Wea. Mag.	100.00	6.5 Rem. Mag.	100.00
222 Rem. Mag.	49.95	375 H&H Mag.	100.00
300 Win. Mag.	100.00	6.5x55	49.95
22-250	49.95	38-40 WCF	49.95
300 H&H Mag.	100.00	264 Win. Mag.	100.00
30-338 Win. Mag.	99.95	444 Marlin	49.95
32-20	49.95	270 Wea. Mag.	100.00
223-5.56mm	49.95	44-40 WCF	49.95
303 British	49.95	270 Win.	49.95
224 Wea. Mag.	49.95	458 Win. Mag.	100.00
30-30 Win.	49.95	7mm Rem. Mag.	100.00
243 Win.	49.95	45-70 Gov't.	100.00
308-7.62 Nato	49.95	7mm Wea. Mag.	100.00
25-06	49.95		
PISTOL	**Price**	**PISTOL**	**Price**
221 Rem. Fireball	49.95	7mm TCU	49.95
30 Luger	49.95	44 Mag.	49.95
30 Mauser	49.95	9x21	49.95
38 Super	49.95	45 ACP	49.95
32 ACP-7.65mm	49.95	9mm	49.95
38/357 Mag.	49.95	45 AR	49.95
32 H&R	49.95	9x18 Makarov	49.95
10mm/40 S&W	49.95	454 Casull	49.95
32 Short Colt	49.95	9x25 Dillon	49.95
41 Mag.	49.95	45 Long Colt	49.95
32 S&W	49.95	380 ACP	49.95
44 Special	49.95	45 Win. Mag.	49.95

RL 550B Caliber Conversion Kits
Contains shellplate, powder funnel and locator buttons. See chart for available calibers. From Dillon Precision Products, Inc.
Price: All calibers **$27**
Price: 50 AE . . . . **N/A**

RL 1050 and XL 650 Powder Check System
Automatically checks cases for over or under powder charges. From Dillon Precision Products, Inc.
Price: . . . . **N/A**

DILLON
RL 1050 Caliber Conversion Kits
Includes dies (optional), shellplate, locator buttons, swage backup rod/expander, case feed adapter, case feed plunger and powder funnel. See chart for available calibers. From Dillon Precision Products, Inc.
Price: With dies **$124.90**
Price: No dies **$74.95**
Price: 9x25, 223 with carbide dies **$159.95**
Price: 30 M1 with carbide dies . **$137.00**

Square Deal B Conversion Kits
Carbide sizer die, expander/powder funnel, seat die, crimp die, shellplate and locator buttons. See chart for available calibers. From Dillon Precision Products, Inc.
Price: **$67.95**

Tool Head Conversion Assembly
A separate stand-alone unit used in conjunction with Dillon caliber conversion kit to change calibers easily on Dillon progressive presses. RL 550B Assembly: Includes toolhead, powder measure, powder die, cartridge counter and toolhead stand; dies optional. RL 1050 Assembly: Comes with toolhead, powder measure and cartridge counter. XL 650 Assembly: Toolhead, toolhead stand, powder measure and cartridge counter. From Dillon Precision Products, Inc.
Price: RL 550B without dies . . . **$77.45**
Price: RL 1050 . . . . **$169.95**
Price: XL 650 . . . . **$78.45**

Tool Heads
For Dillon RL 550B, Square Deal B and XL 650 progressive presses for caliber changeovers. Keeps dies in alignment to eliminate time-consuming die adjustment when changing calibers. Tool head stand extra. From Dillon Precision Products, Inc.
Price: RL 550B **$12.45**
Price: Square Deal B **$19.95**
Price: XL 650 . . . . **$15.95**
Price: Tool head stand **$11.95**

Universal Mounting Hardware
Designed for use with all Dillon presses for bench mounting press. Includes four Grade 5 hex bolts, four lock nuts, four flat washers and two wood screws. From Dillon Precision Products, Inc.
Price: RL 550B **$3.95**

Hanned Line
Convert-A-Ball Dies

Hollywood
Auto Primer Feed

Forster Conversion Kit

XL 650 Caliber Conversion Kits
Comes complete with shell plate, locator buttons, powder funnel and casefeed adapter parts. See chart for available calibers. From Dillon Precision Products, Inc.
Price: . . . . **See chart.**

XL 650 Case Feed Assembly
To change to large pistol, small pistol, large rifle or small rifle. Comes with case feed bin, case feed tube and attachment bar. From Dillon Precision Products, Inc.
Price: **$173.95**
Price: Extra case feed plate **$33.95**

XL 650 Powder Dies
Designed for the XL 650 press. Allows moving powder measure from tool head to tool head without changing the "belling" adjustment. From Dillon Precision Products, Inc.
Price: **$6.95**

FORSTER
"E-Z Just" Shellholder/Primer Conversion Kit
For Co-Ax presses manufactured prior to 1983. Converts old shellholder/primer system to the current "S" jaw/primer catcher system. From Forster Products.
Price: **$74.50**

HANNED LINE
Convert-A-Ball Die
Converts military ammo with FMJ bullets into flat tips. Standard thread allows use with any standard reloading press. Two versions available: short version for 7.62x39mm or 308 NATO; long version for 7mm Mauser, 7.62x54R Russian, 303 British, 30-06, 7.65x54mm French and 8mm Mauser. From The Hanned Line.
Price: Short **$49.95**
Price: Long **$56.95**

HOLLYWOOD
Auto Primer Feed
Fits Hollywood Senior Turret press for automatic priming of cases. Available for standard rifle/pistol cases as well as 50-caliber and shotgun primers. From Hollywood Engineering.
Price: Rifle/pistol **$35.00**
Price: 50-cal./shotgun **$45.00**
Price: Primer tube with spring . **$15.00**
Price: Tube only **$10.00**
Price: Primer tube spring **$5.00**

HORNADY Shellplates

SHELLPLATE NO. 1
5.6x57
22/250
240 Wea.
243 Win.
244/6mm
6mm Int.
6mm/284
6mm BR
250 Sav.
25-06
257 Rbts.
25-284
6.5-06
6.5x57
270 Win.
7x57 (7mm Mau.)
7mm-08
7mm Rem BR
7x64
7mm Exp./280
284 Win.
300 Sav.
308 Win.
30-06
7.7 Jap.
8mm Mau.
8mm-06
8x60S
35 Whelen
358 Win.
9.3x57
9.3x62
44 Auto Mag.
45 ACP/WM

SHELLPLATE NO. 2
219 Zipper
5.6x52R
22 Sav. HP
25/35 Win.
30-30 Win.
30 Herrett
32 Win. Spl.
8.15x46R
357 Herrett
375 Win.
7x30 Waters
32-40

SHELLPLATE NO. 3
22 Hornet
22 K-Hornet

SHELLPLATE NO. 4
220 Swift
225 Winchester
7mm Merrill
30 Merrill

SHELLPLATE NO. 5
257 Wea.
6.5 Rem. Mag.
264 Win. Mag.
270 Wea.
7mm Rem. Mag.
7mm Wea.
300 H&H
300 Win. Mag.
300 Wea.
308 Norma Mag.
8mm Rem. Mag.
338 Win. Mag.
340 Wea.
350 Rem. Mag.
358 Norma Mag.
375 H&H
416 Rem. Mag.
458 Win.

SHELLPLATE NO. 6
22 PPC
22 Rem. Jet
256 Win.
6mm PPC
7.62x39
38 Spl.
357 Mag.
357 Max.

SHELLPLATE NO. 8
30 Luger
9mm Luger
38 Super Auto

SHELLPLATE NO. 10
10mm Auto
40 S&W

SHELLPLATE NO. 11
303 British

SHELLPLATE NO. 14
33 Winchester
378 Wea.
460 Wea.
45-70 Gov't.
416 Wea.

SHELLPLATE NO. 16
17 Rem.
17/222
17/223
221 Rem.
222 Rem.
222 Rem. Mag.
5.6x50 Mag.
223 Rem.
6mm/223
6x47 Rem.
6.5mm TCU
7mm TCU
7mm/223 Ingram
7x47 Helm
380 Auto
6mm TCU

SHELLPLATE NO. 22
30 M1 Carbine
32 ACP

SHELLPLATE NO. 26
35 Rem.

SHELLPLATE NO. 29
41 Mag.

SHELLPLATE NO. 30
6.5x68
7.5 Swiss
357/44 Bain & Davis
44 Spl.
44 Mag.

SHELLPLATE NO. 32
45 Long Colt

SHELLPLATE NO. 36
32 S&W Long
32 S&W Short
32 H&R

HOLLYWOOD
Priming Rod
For use with shellholder extension and Universal shellholder and button inserts. Height will depend on combination of use. Specify press, small or large, flat or oval, pistol or rifle. For all Hollywood presses. From Hollywood Engineering.

Price: **$30.00**
Price: 50 BMG............... **$35.00**
Price: 20mm **$45.00**
Price: Shotgun............... **$30.00**

Senior and Universal Turret Head Plates
Turret head plates for the Hollywood Senior press can be ordered in four configurations: eight, 1 1/2-12 threaded holes for large dies; four 1 1/2-12 threaded holes; four, 7/8-12 holes; or eight, 7/8-14 holes. Turret plates are also available for the old Hollywood Universal press. Available as standard turret or solid aluminum 10-hole turret threaded 1 1/2-12 for use with all large dies. From Hollywood Engineering.

Price: Senior **$125.00**
Price: Senior Turret **$100.00**
Price: Universal, standard.... **$150.00**
Price: Universal, 10-hole **$200.00**

Hornady Shellholder

Hornady Lock-N-Load Bushing System

Hornady Case Activated Powder Drop

Shellholder Extension
Shortens stroke on Hollywood presses. Makes loading small cartridges easier and assists in case forming and heavy press work. Must have special priming rod. From Hollywood Engineering.

Price: **$25.00**

Universal/Standard Shellholder
Will accept all button inserts. Must have Hollywood priming rods for use on Hollywood presses. From Hollywood Engineering.

Price: Standard calibers **$7.00**
Price: Universal shellholder.... **$10.00**
Price: Shellholder inserts **$7.00**
Price: 50 BMG............... **$35.00**
Price: 20mm **$45.00**
Price: Shotgun............... **$30.00**

HORNADY
Auto Primer Shutoff
Standard on the Hornady Lock-N-Load AP press, primer shutoff also available as accessory. Allows removing primer tubes from auto primer feed without spilling primers. Weight: 4 oz. From Hornady Mfg. Co.

Price: **$34.99**

Automatic Primer Feed
For Lock-N-Load Classic and 0-7 single-stage presses. Comes with large and small primer tubes. Weight: 1 lb. From Hornady Mfg. Co.

Price: **$32.95**

Case Activated Powder Drop
Progressive press accessory for Hornady, RCBS and Redding powder measures. Allows powder to be dispensed automatically with each pull of the lever only when a case is present in the station. No adjustments needed when changing powder measures. Uses Lock-N-Load bushing system. From Hornady Mfg. Co.

Price: **$44.95**

Lock-N-Load Bushings
Unique bushing system to allow quick caliber changeovers on press. Threaded 7/8-14 to house and store any die or powder measure. Bushing with die or measure lock solidly into Hornady Classic or AP press. A press conversion bushing for use with other brands of reloading presses using 11/4-12 bushings also available. From Hornady Mfg. Co.

Price: 2 pack **$9.33**
Price: 3 pack **$13.52**
Price: Press conversion bushing **$16.63**

Lock-N-Load Classic Kit
Includes Lock-N-Load Classic single-stage press; three die bushings; primer catcher; auto prime system; auto prime feed; deluxe powder measure; magnetic scale; primer turning plate; large and small primer pocket cleaners; accessory handle; three case neck brushes; powder funnel; chamfer/debur tool; die wrench; loading block; Unique case lube; and the abridged Hornady Handbook; and Hornady Handbook of Cartridge Reloading video tape. From Hornady Mfg. Co.
Price: **$274.95**

Shellholder 007 and L-N-L Classic
Machined from solid steel. Available for all popular calibers. Fits Hornady and most other standard presses. Weight: 1/4-lb. From Hornady Mfg. Co.
Price: **$11.42**

Shellholder Extension
Used for forming long cases into short cases. Fits all rams designed for universal shellholders. Extension shellholder number corresponds with standard, removable-head shellholder number. Available in #1, #2 and #16. Weight: 1/4-lb. From Hornady Mfg. Co.
Price: **$10.71**

Shellplates Pro-Jector and L-N-L AP Press
Retainer spring shellplate to hold cases in place during loading operation. Available for over 170 calibers. From Hornady Mfg. Co.
Price: **$29.15**

HOWELL

Rotary Bullet Feeder
For most standard progressive reloading presses. Feeds 22-, 25-, 30-, 33-, 9mm, 38-, 41- or 45-caliber bullets, nose or base first, at a rate of 100 bullets per minute. Capacity for 700 to 900 bullets. 14", 16" and 20" bowls available. Powered by 110-volt completely enclosed assembly. Comes set up and ready to run for one or two calibers. From Howell CNC & Machine.
Price: 14", one size base first . . **$995.00**
Price: 14", two sizes base first **$1,225.00**
Price: 14", one size nose first. **$1,150.00**
Price: 14", two sizes nose first **$1,375.00**
Price: 14", one size nose or base first **$1,475.00**
Price: 14", two sizes nose or base first **$1,750.00**
Price: 16", one size base first. **$1,350.00**
Price: 16", two sizes base first **$1,625.00**
Price: 16", one size nose first. **$1,500.00**
Price: 16", two sizes nose first **$1,750.00**
Price: 16", one size nose or base first **$1,750.00**
Price: 16", two sizes nose or base first **$2,150.00**
Price: 20", one size base first. **$2,375.00**
Price: 20", one size nose first. **$2,673.00**

HUNTINGTON

Aluminum Primer Catcher
Designed for RCBS reloading presses to replace plastic primer catcher standard on Rock Chucker, Jr. or Reloader Special-5. Cast from aluminum and designed to attach to press with rubber band. From Huntington Die Specialties.
Price: **$9.98**

Aluminum Wedge Block
For the old RCBS Jr. press. Allows the press to be tipped back at a more comfortable angle. From Huntington Die Specialties.
Price: **$9.98**

LEE

Anniversary Reloading Kit
Includes Lee Challenger press; Lee Perfect powder measure; Lee Safety scale; powder funnel with powder data manual; case cutter and lock stud for trimming cases; chamfer tool; tube of sizing lube; Lee Auto-Prime tool with shellholders for over 115 cartridges; primer pocket cleaner. From Lee Precision, Inc.
Price: **$109.98**

Bullet Feed Kit
Designed for use on the Lee Pro 1000 or LoadMaster progressive presses to automatically feed bullets in line with case mouths for seating and crimping. Available in eight sizes from 30-caliber to 45. Comes complete for one caliber. From Lee Precision, Inc.
Price: **$29.98**
Price: Feed die and fingers for additional calibers **$14.98**

LEE

Case Collator
For use with Load-Master or Pro 1000 presses. Made of durable plastic, the collator fills the four case feed tubes. From Lee Precision, Inc.
Price: **$14.98**

Case Feeder
For the Lee Pro 1000 and Load-Master presses. Transparent four-tube case feeder for large or small pistol and rifle cases. Large pistol case feeder will handle 38 Special, 357 Magnum, 41 Magnum, 44 Special, 44 Magnum, 45 ACP, 45 Colt, 10mm Auto and 7.62x39 Russian cases. Small feeder handles 9mm Luger, 380 Auto, 32 Auto, 32 S&W Long, 32 H&R Magnum, 38 Auto and 38 Super. Rifle feeder takes 222, 223 and 30 M1 cases. Extra case feeder tubes available. From Lee Precision, Inc.
Price: All sizes. **$25.00**
Price: Extra tubes, 7-pack **$7.98**

Challenger Press Kit
Includes Lee Challenger press; ram prime; powder funnel; case sizing lube; dies for one caliber with shellholder; powder dipper and load data. Available in 2-die rifle sets or 3-die carbide pistol sets. Special kit price with purchase of Lee die set. From Lee Precision, Inc.
Price: 2-die kit. **$68.98**
Price: 3-die kit. **$73.98**
Price: With Lee die set **$41.98**

Lee Case Feeder

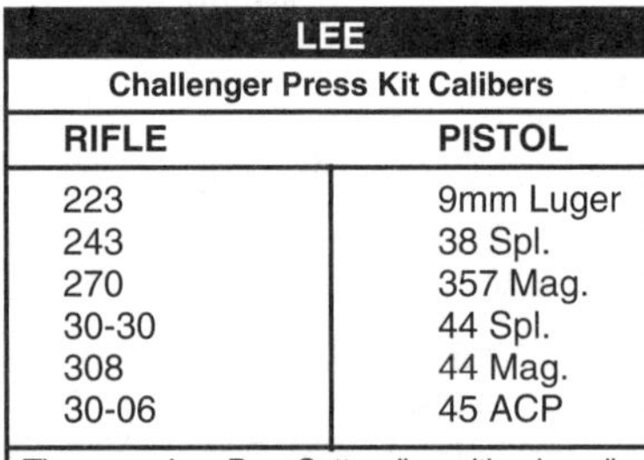

LEE
Challenger Press Kit Calibers

RIFLE	PISTOL
223	9mm Luger
243	38 Spl.
270	357 Mag.
30-30	44 Spl.
308	44 Mag.
30-06	45 ACP

These are Lee PaceSetter dies with crimp die.

LEE
Hand Press Kit Calibers

RIFLE	PISTOL
223	9mm Luger
243	38 Spl.
270	357 Mag.
30-30	44 Spl.
308	44 Mag.
30-06	45 ACP

These are Lee PaceSetter dies with crimp die.

Lee Load-Master Shellplate

LEE Shellplate Carrier Calibers	
SHELLPLATE #	CALIBER
1	38 Spl., 357 Mag.
2	45 ACP
4	222, 223, 380 Auto, 32 S&W Long, 32 H&R Mag.
7A	30 M1 Carbine
9	41 Mag.
11	44 Spl., 44 Mag., 45 Colt
19	40 S&W, 9mm Luger, 38 Super, 38 Auto, 41 AE
19L	10mm Auto

LEE Turret Kit Calibers
PISTOL
9mm Luger 38 Spl. 357 Mag. 41 Mag. 44 Spl. 44 Mag. 45 ACP 45 Long Colt 223 (with rifle charge die)

Deluxe Pistol Reloading Kit
Includes Lee Turret press; Auto Disk powder measure; Safety scale; primer pocket cleaner; cutter and lock stud for trimming cases; chamfer tool. From Lee Precision, Inc.
Price: 2-die kit. **$115.98**

Hand Press Kit
Includes hand press; ram prime; powder funnel; case sizing lube; dies for one caliber and shellholder; powder dipper; and load data. Available in 2-die rifle sets or 3-die carbide pistol sets. Special kit price with purchase of Lee die set. From Lee Precision, Inc.
Price: 2-die set. **$65.98**
Price: 3-die set. **$67.98**
Price: With Lee die set **$34.98**

LEE
Load-Master Pistol Kit
Comes with Lee Load-Master press, carbide die set for one caliber, Pro Auto-Disk powder measure and a case feeder. Comes factory set up for one caliber. From Lee Precision, Inc.
Price: **$330.00**

Lee Load-Master Turret

Lee Hand Press Kit

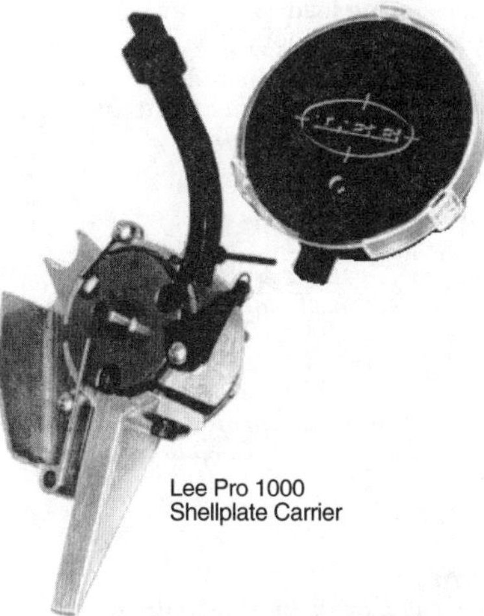

Lee Pro 1000 Shellplate Carrier

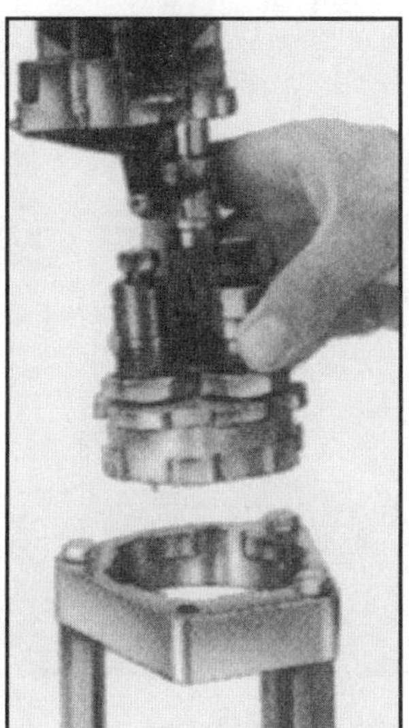

Lee Deluxe Pistol Reloading Kit

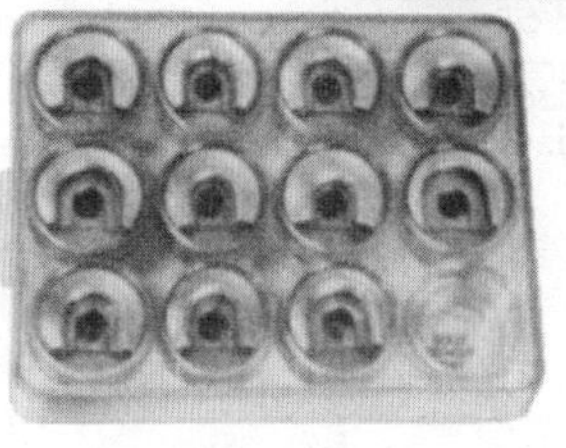

Lee Shellholder Set

Lee Turret Press Kit

Load-Master Rifle Kit
Includes Lee Load-Master press, Lee Pace-Setter dies, Perfect powder measure, Universal charge die and case inserter. Comes factory set up for one caliber. From Lee Precision, Inc.
Price: **$320.00**

Load-Master Shellplate
Five-station shellplate for Lee Load-Master. From Lee Precision, Inc.
Price: **$29.98**

Load-Master Turret
Five-station turret for Lee Load-Master press with 20 locking lugs for quick caliber changeover. From Lee Precision, Inc.
Price: **$14.98**

Load-Master Loaded Round Catcher
Accessory for Lee Load-Master. Made of tough plastic. Capacity for 100 45 ACP rounds. From Lee Precision, Inc.
Price: **$14.98**

Multi-Tube Adapter
Designed for use with Lee Bullet Feed Kit. High-capacity 100-round magazine supplies Lee Bullet Feeder during reloading operation. Unit includes adaptors for large and small bullets and comes with four large and small feed tubes. From Lee Precision, Inc.
Price: **$25.00**

Pro 1000 Shell Plate Carrier
To change calibers entire shellplate carrier can be replaced. Includes shellplate, Auto Prime, case ejector, Auto Index and spare parts. From Lee Precision, Inc.
Price: **$53.98**

Pro 1000 Shellplates
Three-station shellplates for Lee Pro 1000. If converting to caliber of different primer size, Pro 1000 primer attachment must be ordered. From Lee Precision, Inc.
Price: **$20.00**

Pro 1000 Turret
Turret for the Lee Pro 1000 press. From Lee Precision, Inc.
Price: **$10.98**

Ram Prime
Primes on press up-stroke. Includes punches for large and small primers. From Lee Precision, Inc.
Price: **$11.98**

Shellholder Box
Plastic transparent box to hold eleven shellholders. From Lee Precision, Inc.
Price: **$2.60**

Shellholder Set
Eleven shellholders to fit over 115 of the most popular cartridges. From Lee Precision, Inc.
Price: **$19.98**

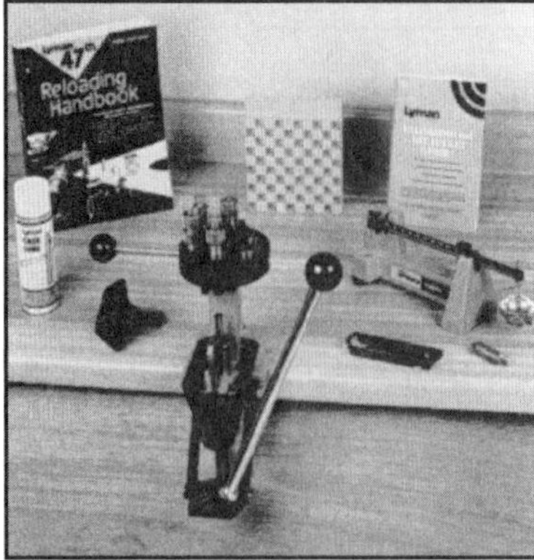

Lyman T-Mag II Pro Kit

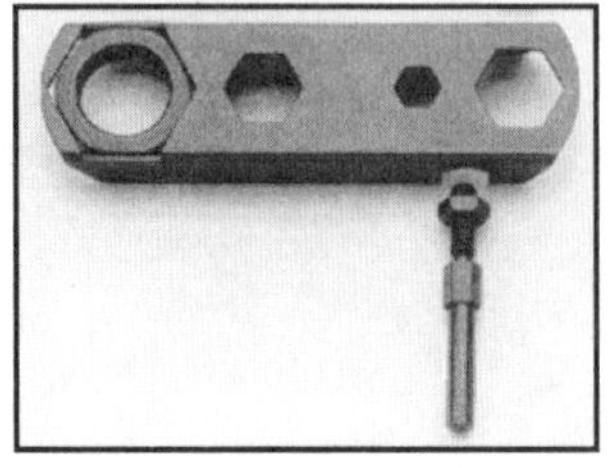

Lyman Bench Wrench

Turret Press Kit
Includes Lee Turret press; Auto-Index with factory installed and adjusted carbide dies for one caliber; shellholder. From Lee Precision, Inc.
Price: **$109.98**

LYMAN

Auto-Primer Feed
For T-Mag II and Orange Crusher presses. Specify older presses when ordering. Comes with two tubes, large and small. Weight: 3 lbs., 1 oz. From Lyman Products Corporation.
Price: **$19.25**

Bench Wrench
Steel combination wrench designed to fit all Lyman die lock nuts and T-Mag II turret support post. Also fits new style Lyman and RCBS 7/8x14 nuts. From Lyman Products Corporation.
Price: **$4.50**

Detachable Shellholder
Precisely machined and hardened for Orange Crusher, O-Mag, T-Mag II or Special-T presses. From Lyman Products Corporation.
Price: **$5.75**

Crusher II Pro Kit
Kit contains Orange Crusher press; Model 505 powder scale; case lube kit; loading block; powder funnel; primer tray; *Lyman 47th Edition Reloading Handbook*. Weight: 25 lbs. (500 scale); 24 lbs. (AccuScale). From Lyman Products Corporation.
Price: **$164.95**

Primer Catcher
Heavy-duty plastic. Locks securely to Orange Crusher, T-Mag II, Special-T and Spar-T presses. From Lyman Products Corporation.
Price: **$5.75**

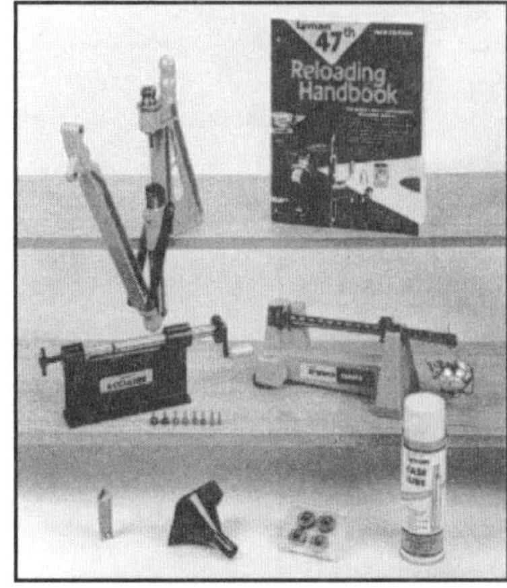

Deluxe Pistol Reloaders Kit

Lyman Shellholder Set

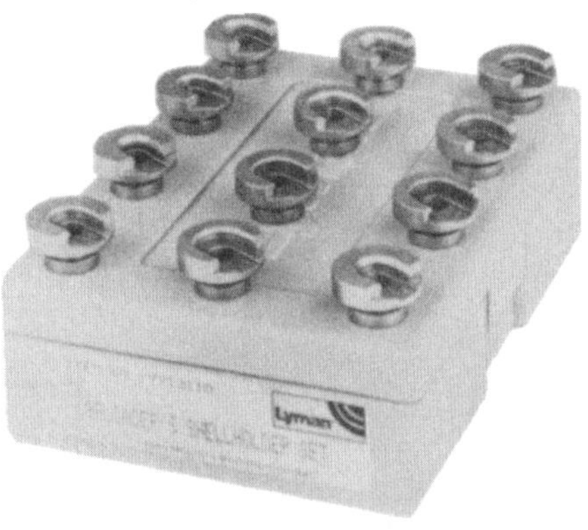

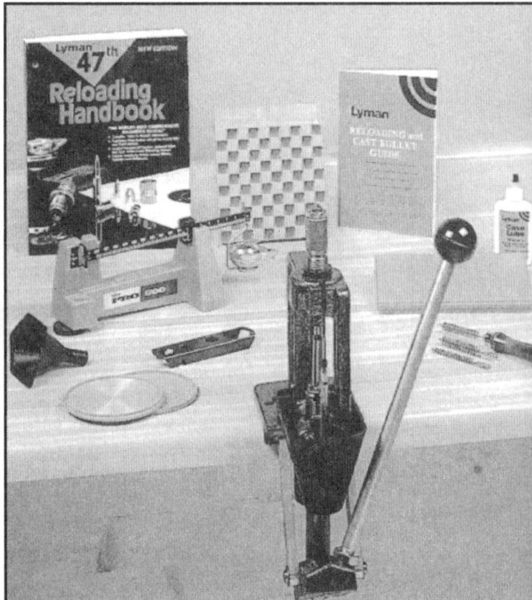

Lyman Orange Crusher Starter Kit

Lyman Expert Kit

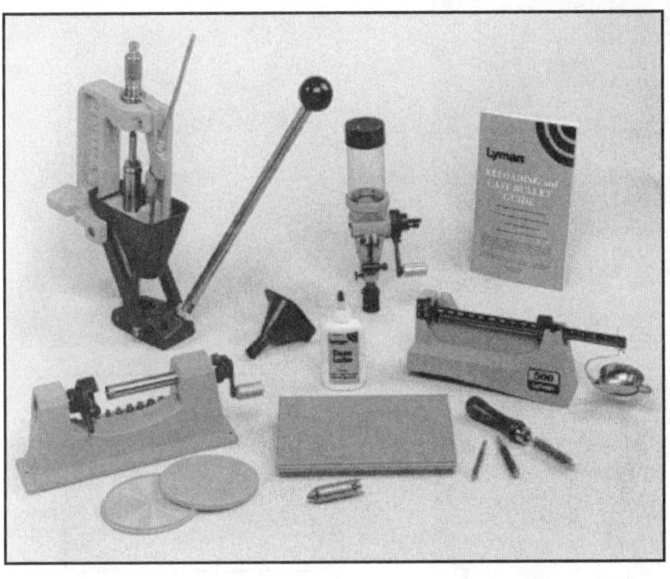

Midway Reloading Stand

Expert Kit
Includes choice of T-Mag II or Orange Crusher press; Universal case trimmer with expanded pilot multi-pack; M-500 reloading scale; #55 powder measure; Universal priming arm; primer tray; auto primer feed; detachable shellholder; primer catcher; quick-release turret system (T-Mag only); deburring tool; case lube kit; powder funnel; extra decapping pins; 7/8-14 adaptor for mounting powder measure; instructions; and *Lyman Reloading and Cast Bullet Guide*. T-Mag kit available with or without dies and shellholder. T-Mag Rifle Set includes rifle die set (223, 22-250, 243, 270, 308, 30-30, 30-06) and shellholder to load one cartridge, 30 lbs; Carbide Pistol Set includes carbide 3-die set (9mm, 38/357, 10mm/40 S&W, 44 Mag., 45 ACP) and shellholder to load one caliber, 31 lbs. Orange Crusher Expert Kit comes in no-cal. version only and does not include dies or shellholder. From Lyman Products Corporation.
Price: T-Mag rifle set **$389.95**
Price: T-Mag pistol set **$378.95**
Price: T-Mag no-cal. **$364.95**
Price: Crusher II no-cal. **$329.95**

Shellholder Set
Includes 12 standard shellholders for most popular pistol/rifle cartridges in organizer/storage box. From Lyman Products Corporation.
Price: **$24.95**

J to X Shellholder Adaptor
Adaptor available to allow use of X shellholder with older Lyman presses using J-type shellholders. From Lyman Products Corporation.
Price: Adaptor **$8.95**

310 Tool Set Pouch
Rugged nylon camouflage pouch with military-type belt clip holds 310 tool handles and dies for field use. From Lyman Products Corporation.
Price: **$9.95**

Universal Priming Arm
Seats all sizes and types of primers. Supplied with two priming sleeves, large and small. From Lyman Products Corporation.
Price: **$9.75**

PONSNESS/WARREN

Dust Covers
Sturdy canvas cover for Metallic II and Metal-Matic presses. From Ponsness/Warren.
Price: Metallic II **$30.95**
Price: Metal-Matic **$21.95**

Metallic II Die Head
Extra die heads for changing and mounting a different caliber. From Ponsness/Warren.
Price: **$56.95**

Metallic II Powder Measure Extension
Raises powder measure above dies. Complete with housing, spring and large and small primers. From Ponsness/Warren.
Price: **$29.95**

P-200 Die Head
Extra die heads for changing and mounting a different caliber. From Ponsness/Warren.
Price: **$44.95**

P-200 Primer Feed
Fits all Metal-Matic presses. Includes large and small primer tubes and steel primer tube shield. From Ponsness/Warren.
Price: **$44.95**

P-200/M-II Primer Speed Feeder
Feeds primers to primer feed. Available for large or small primers. From Ponsness/Warren.
Price: **$14.50**

PRIME RELOADING

Hydro Punch
Hydro punch for removing Berdan or Boxer primers from crimped or non-crimped cases. Available for over 120 calibers from 22 Hornet to 55 Boyes. Body constructed of brass, integral reservoir of non-ferrous metal. For rare or vintage calibers, send two sample fired cases. From H.J. Kohne.
Price: . . . . . . **Contact manufacturer.**

RCBS

Accessory Base Plate-2
Heavy .820" thick aluminum casting measuring 9 7/8"x5 1/2" with holes drilled and pre-tapped for mounting reloading tools. For use with RCBS rotary case trimmer, powder measure stand, Lube-a-Matic, Reloader Special-5 press, Rock Chucker, Partner press, auto and standard priming tools. Fasteners included. From RCBS.
Price: $26.95

APS Priming System
Revolutionary new priming system utilizing pre-loaded flexible primer strips that are automatically indexed with each pull of the handle. The APS tool can be bench mounted or press mounted. The 25-capacity primer strips are color coded by primer type and can be hooked together for continuous feeding. The bench-mounted tool is a free-standing unit with its own handle while the press-mounted tool fits into conventional presses. From RCBS.
Price: Bench-mounted tool **$95.95**
Price: Press-mounted tool. **$60.95**

APS Primer Strips
Available as fully loaded color-coded strips with 25 primers per plastic strip or empty, ready for use with the APS Primer Strip Loader. From RCBS.Unprimed
Price: $2.95

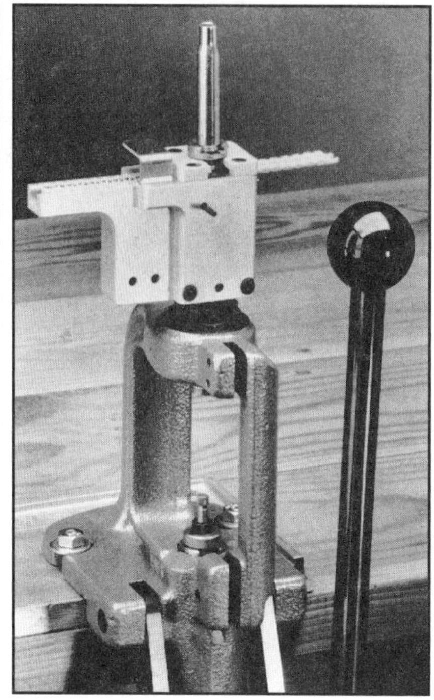
RCBS APS Press Mounted Priming System

APS Primer Strip Loader
For loading primers into empty APS plastic strips for reuse. Each push of the handle orients and seats 25 primers into the strip. Compact in size for easy storage. From RCBS.
Price: **$26.95**

Lock-Out Die
Detects a no-powder or double charge condition in the progressive reloading process and locks up or halts ram travel at the case mouth. For use with pistol calibers. From RCBS.
Price: **$42.95**

Partner Reloading Kit
Comes with Partner press. Includes: 5-0-2 scale; case loading block; case lube kit; Primer Tray-2; deburring tool; powder funnel; and Speer Reloading Manual. From RCBS.
Price: **$167.95**

Piggyback 3
Converts RCBS Rock Chucker, Reloader Special-3 and Reloader Special-5 single-stage presses to progressive units. Features automatic indexing, priming, powder charging and loaded round ejection. Case detection system disengages powder measure when no case is present in powder charging station. Comes with clear powder measure adaptor to view and correct bridged powders. Five-station shellplate, reloading dies and powder measure not included. From RCBS.
Price: **$280.95**

Redding Shellholder

Powder Checker
For use with progressive presses to confirm each case receives the correct powder charge. A moving rod indicates the presence of powder and provides a quick visual comparison for the amount of powder dropped. Located between the powder charging and bullet seating stations. Black oxide finish. From RCBS.
Price: **$27.95**

Reloading Accessory Kit
Package includes: powder measure/Piggyback stand, powder trickler, primer pocket brush combo, case loading block, stainless steel dial caliper and small and medium size case neck brushes.
Price: **$105.95**

Reloading Starter Kit
Comes with Reloader Special-5 press. Includes: 5-0-5 scale; case loading block; case lube kit; Primer Tray-2; powder funnel; and Speer Reloading Manual. Dies and shellholders must be purchased separately. From RCBS.
Price: **$267.95**

RCBS

Shellholders
Price: **$5.95**
Price: Extended shellholder **$8.95**
Price: Shellholder ram, C press . **$21.95**
Price: Adaptor, H press **$14.95**
Price: Adaptor, Herters **$16.95**

Rock Chucker Reloading Kit
Comes with Rock Chucker press. Includes: 5-0-5 reloading scale; Uniflow powder measure; *Speer Reloading Manual*; Trim-Pro manual trimmer; case trimmer kit; hex key set; case loading block; case lube kit; automatic primer feed; Primer Tray-2; powder funnel; and deburring tool. From RCBS.
Price: **$415.95**

REDDING

Boss Pro-Pak
Contains Boss reloading press; Model #2 powder/bullet scale; powder trickler; set of Series A reloading dies; pad-style case lube kit; deburring tool for cases from 17- to 45-caliber; Model #18 case preparation kit; powder funnel; and *Hodgdon Loading Data Manual*. From Redding Reloading Equipment.
Price: **$324.00**

Competition Shellholder Sets
Five-piece set in .002" increments (+.002", +.004", .006", +.008" and +.010") allows headspace control adjustments on press. Finished in black oxide and clearly marked. From Redding Reloading Equipment.
Price: **$51.00**

E-Z Feed Shellholder
Universal snap-in design precision machined and heat-treated. From Redding Reloading Equipment.
Price: **$8.40**

Extended Shellholders
Required when trimming short cases under 11/2" OAL. From Redding Reloading Equipment.
Price: **$13.80**

Reloading Press Kits
Each Redding press available in kit form to include the press, choice of one set of Series A reloading dies and matching shellholder. From Redding Reloading Equipment.
Price: Boss press kit **$180.00**
Price: Turret press kit **$339.00**
Price: Ultramag press kit. **$355.50**

THOMPSON

Tool Mount
Interlocking steel plates allow use of multiple reloading tools from a single mounting point. The base plate is permanently affixed to the reloading bench while the accessory plate is attached to the tool in use-powder measure, case trimmer, lubrisizer, etc. The plates are 1/8" thick, 53/8" long and 21/2" wide. Complete installation instructions included. From Thompson Tool Mount.
Price: **$35.00**

Vega Tool Re-Manufactured Shellholders

Redding Competition Shellholder

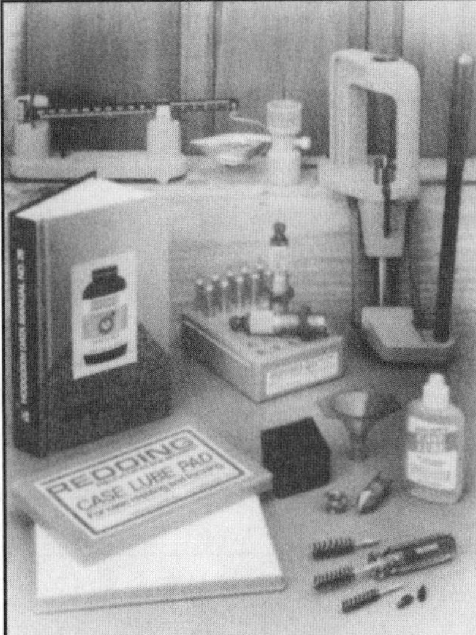

Redding Boss Pro-Pack

Thompson Tool Mount

Section 1: Metallic Cartridges

BALD EAGLE

Unchambered Die Bodies

Stainless steel 7/8-14 short, medium, long, and tong tool dies. These unchambered sizing dies accept Wilson sizing bushings for adjusting neck tension on loaded rounds. Concentric inside and out. From Bald Eagle Precision Machine Company.

Price: **$50.00**

C-H/4-D

20mm Lahti Dies

Dies threaded 1 1/2-12 with expander for use with U.S. 20mm projectiles. Expander for original projectiles available. Shellholder with 5/8-18 thread and priming tool also offered. From C-H Tool & Die/4-D Custom Die.

Price: **$385.00**
Price: Shellholder **$40.00**
Price: Priming tool **$60.00**

50 BMG Bushing Neck Sizer Die

Neck size die with bushings in .001" increments in sizes from .538 to .552. Bushings interchangeable with Neil Jones arbor die. Comes complete with one bushing. From C-H Tool & Die/4-D Custom Die.

Price: **$210.00**
Price: Neck sizer and seater **$400.00**
Price: Bushing **$15.00**

50 BMG Dies

Chrome-plated steel two-die set threaded 11/2-12 for reloading 50 BMG caliber. Set includes full-length size and crimp seater. From 4-D Custom Die.

Price: **$215.00**
Price: Shellholder **$15.00**

50 BMG Straight Line Seater

Features sliding sleeve to hold bullet in alignment with case with normal run-out of .002"-.004". From C-H Tool & Die/4-D Custom Die.

Price: **$210.00**
Price: Neck sizer and seater die combo $400.00

Blank Crimping Die

Crimp die for loading blank cartridges. Straight-walled cases need only one die. Rimless calibers require shoulder to control headspace thus require shoulder die. Dies available for most popular calibers; odd calibers at extra cost. From C-H Tool & Die/4-D Custom Die.

Price: **$79.95**
Price: Shoulder die, 9mm, 45 ACP . . . **$19.95**

Bullet Sizing Die

Custom 7/8-14 threaded die to size down oversize bullets in .004" increments. From C-H Tool & Die/4-D Custom Die.

Price: **$54.95**

Bushing Neck Sizer Die

Bushing neck size die with bushings in .001" increments. Available in three body lengths: short (1" to 1 1/2" shoulder); medium (1 1/2" to 2" shoulder); long (2" to 2 1/2" shoulder). Bushings available from .239" to .400". From C-H Tool & Die/4-D Custom Die.

Price: **$49.95**
Price: Body only **$30.00**
Price: Bushing **$10.00**

Custom Reloading Dies

Die sets, forming dies, trim dies, etc. are stocked for hundreds of calibers or can be made to order for an additional tooling charge. Die groups A through H standard 7/8-14 thread; groups J and K, 1-14 thread; group N dies 11/2-12 threading. All dies except N are for use with shellholders or shellplates having industry standard dimension of 0.125" from case head to top of shellholder. From C-H Tool & Die/4-D Custom Die.

Price: . . . . **See chart**

Expander Die Bodies

Available in any length and top thread. Specify length, top thread, body diameter and minimum inside diameter. From C-H Tool & Die/4-D Custom Die.

Price: 7/8-14 O.D. **$11.00**
Price: 1-14 O.D.. . . . . **$22.00**

Bald Eagle Unchambered Die Bodies

"M"-Type Expander Plugs

Designed for loading cast bullets or jacketed bullets. Expander has plug .001" smaller than bullet diameter and a taper to bell case mouth slightly to prevent "lead shaving." From C-H Tool & Die/4-D Custom Die.

Price: To 45-cal. **$11.00**
Price: 46-50-cal. **$16.50**
Price: 51-70-cal. **$22.00**

Speed Seater Die

To facilitate seating of wadcutter-type bullets. Die opening is larger in diameter than main body, gradually tapering to seating stem. From C-H Tool & Die/4-D Custom Die.

Price: **$16.00**

Small Base Die Sets

For reloading cartridges to minimum dimensions. Available for 223 Remington, 30-06 and 308 Winchester. From C-H Tool & Die/4-D Custom Die.

Price: Set. **$35.00**
Price: Sizer die **$19.25**

Taper Crimp Die *(Pistol)*

Precision-honed, hardened and polished inside with non-glare satin finish outside. For autoloading calibers that headspace off the case mouth. Available in all C-H/4-D calibers. From C-H Tool & Die/4-D Custom Die.

Price: . . . . **See chart.**

Taper Crimp Die *(Rifle)*

Available in all C-H/4-D die offerings. Eliminates case trimming and is useful for handloading semi-auto rifle ammo. From C-H Tool & Die/4-D Custom Die.

Price: . . . . **See chart.**

Tapered Expanders

Gradual taper for expanding the case neck to larger caliber. Will expand neck .050" to .060". Sizes through 45-caliber, fits any expander body with 9-16 top thread. Larger sizes require special die bodies. From C-H Tool & Die/4-D Custom Die.

Price: To 45-cal. **$10.00**
Price: 46-50-cal. **$15.00**
Price: 51-70-cal. **$25.00**

Titanium Nitride Die Coating

Titanium nitride coating makes die harder than carbide with low coefficient of friction and requires less sizing effort. Available in any C-H/4-D standard die offerings. From C-H Tool & Die/4-D Custom Die.

Price: Per die. **$30.00**

C-H/4-D Custom Die Prices

DIES	GROUP A	B	C	D	E	F	G	H	J	K	N	S
Die Set	$35.00	$37.00	$40.00	$44.00	$57.20	$60.50	$83.60	$119.90	$130.90	$141.90	$214.50	$385.00
Neck Size Die	23.15	16.15	26.25	29.05	28.00	39.60	55.00	77.00	99.00	99.00	143.55	257.65
Seating Die	19.25	17.35	22.00	24.40	21.90	29.70	40.70	55.00	71.50	71.50	107.25	192.50
File Trim Die	29.70	29.70	29.70	29.70	29.70	29.70	40.70	55.00	71.50	71.50	104.50	187.55
Case Form Die	29.70	29.70	29.70	29.70	29.70	29.70	40.70	55.00	71.50	71.50	104.50	187.55
Taper Crimp Die*	12.00	12.00	12.00	12.00	12.00	22.00	29.70	41.80	52.80	52.80	66.00	118.45
Taper Crimp Die**	12.00	14.00	16.00	20.00	36.50	36.50	49.50	66.00	88.00	88.00	126.50	227.05
Reamer Die/Reamer	77.00	77.00	77.00	77.00	77.00	77.00	88.00	99.00	110.00	110.00	143.00	265.00

*Straight Wall; **Bottleneck/Straight Taper

Universal Decapping Die
Comes in two sizes-large and small. Small die decaps calibers 22 Hornet through 6mm-06. Larger die accommodates all calibers from 25-20 to50-110 Winchester and with 1/4" diameter decap rod and .070" decap rod will decap military 308 and 30-06 cases with crimped-in primers. From C-H Tool & Die/4-D Custom Die.
Price: 7/8-14 . . . . **$17.95**
Price: 1-14 . . . . **$26.95**

DAKOTA
Dakota Dies
Reloading dies for the Dakota Arms proprietary cartridges, 7mm, 300, 330, 375, 416 and 450 Dakota. From Dakota Arms, Inc.
Price: **$109.00**

DILLON
Custom Carbide Rifle Dies
Three-die carbide sets include size/decap, seater and crimp die. Design features include radiused carbide mouth; long tapered carbide ring; heavy headed decap pin; vented seating stem. All have large radiused mouths and wrench hex adjustments. Rifle die calibers: 223 Remington, 30 Carbine and 308 Winchester. Pistol die calibers: 380 Auto, 9mm, 38 Super, 38/357, 10mm/40 S&W, 41 Mag., 44 Spec., 44 Mag., 45 ACP, 45 C and 9x25 Dillon. From Dillon Precision Products, Inc.
Price: 223 . . . . **$103.95**
Price: 308 Win. **$113.95**
Price: Extra decap pin, ... **$2.00**

Forster Ultra Bullet Seater Die

Dillon's Dynamic Carbide Pistol Dies

Dynamic Carbide Rifle/Pistol Dies
Die sets with sizer/decap and seat die. Crimp die available separately. Carbide sizer and decapper feature larger lead-in radius for smoother reloading and a floating decap assembly with snap ring for release of spent primers. Seater die and crimp die allow disassembly without loosing adjustment. Seating die "flip-flop" stem allows changing bullet nose configuration without removal of die from press. Die sets do not include expander die; designed to work with a powder-through expander. Die calibers: 380 Auto, 9mm, 38 Super, 38/357, 10mm/40 S&W, 41 Mag., 44 Spl./44 Mag., 45 ACP, 45 Colt and 9x25 Dillon. From Dillon Precision Products, Inc.
Price: Pistol **$49.95**
Price: 9x25 Dillon **$103.95**

Three Die Rifle Set
Includes sizing/depriming seating and taper crimp dies. Size die features full-length to minimum tolerances, carbide expander ball and stuck case remover. For calibers 223 Rem., 308 Win., 30-06 Springfield and 7.62x39. From Dillon Precision Products, Inc.
Price: **$49.95**

FORSTER
Bench Rest Die Set
Two-die set that includes both the Bench Rest Sizing die and Bench Rest Seater die. From Forster Products.
Price: **$76.00**

Bench Rest Seater Die
Straight-line, chamber-type, non-crimping style die that holds bullet and case in alignment in close-fitting channel. Adaptable to standard loading presses. From Forster Products.
Price: **$42.40**

Bench Rest Sizing Die
Precision die with polished interior. Special attention given to headspace taper and diameter. The new expander button floats on the stem near the stem top to allow the expander to enter the case neck while it is in the neck sizing portion of the die to assure alignment. From Forster Products.
Price: **$35.30**

Ultra Bullet Seater Die
Bullet seating die with micrometer seating depth adjustment. Head is graduated in .001" increments with .025" bullet movement per revolution. Available in 51 calibers. Kit to upgrade Forster Bench Rest seater die available. From Forster Products.
Price: Ultra Seater Die. **$67.50**
Price: Die set with seater die. **$101.30**

FREEDOM ARMS
454 Casull Dies
RCBS Carbide 3-die set for .452" bullets. From Freedom Arms, Inc.
Price: **$53.00**

GOODWIN
Reloading Dies
Precision machined steel reloading dies made in England by James Goodwin for unusual and hard-to-find calibers. Reloading dies threaded 7/8-14. Special shellholders available. From Jack First, Inc.
Price: Die set. **$150.00**
Price: Shellholder **$15.00**

HARRELL'S PRECISION
Vari-Base Sizing Die
410 stainless steel resizing die that incorporates interchangeable screw-in neck and base reforming buttons that allow reforming fired PPC cases to concentric, near chamber dimensions. From Harrell's Precision.
Price: **$100.00**
Price: Die and one bushing **$75.00**
Price: Base buttons. **$12.50**

Forster Benchrest Die

FORSTER PRODUCTS
BENCH REST DIE SETS

CARTRIDGE		
17 Remington	250 Savage (250/3000)	30 Herrett
22 Hornet	257 Ackley (40°)	7mm T.C.U.
22 BR Remington	257 Roberts	30-30 Winchester
22 P.P.C. Sako	257 Weatherby Magnum	300 Winchester Mag.
221 Fireball	264 Winchester	300 Weatherby Mag.
222 Remington	6.5x57 Mauser	303 British
222 Remington Magnum	6.5x55 Swedish	308 Winchester
223 Remington	6.5x55 SKAN	308 Nat'l. Match
5.6x50 Rimmed	270 Winchester	30-06
220 Swift	7x64 Brenneke	30-06 Ackley (40°)
22/250 Remington	7mm-08	8mm Remington Mag.
243 Winchester	7x57 Mauser	8x57 Mauser
6mm BR Remington	7mm BR Remington	8x68S
6mm P.P.C. Sako	7mm Remington Mag.	338 Winchester Mag.
6mm Remington (224)	7mm STW	340 Weatherby Mag.
224 Weatherby Magnum	270 Weatherby Mag.	357 Herrett
240 Weatherby Magnum	7mm Weatherby Mag.	375 H&H
25/06 Remington	280 Remington	

Section 1: Metallic Cartridges

HOLLYWOOD

38-45 Dies

Comes as a complete set for reloading and case-forming or each die separately. A tungsten carbide sizer die is also available. From Hollywood Engineering.

Price: Complete set. **$200.00**
Price: Reloading die set **$46.00**
Price: Case-form die set **$100.00**
Price: Carbide size die **$180.00**

50-Caliber Seater/Necksizer Die

Hardened steel and plated die threaded 1 1/2-12. Comes complete with seater die, necksizer bushing, seater plug, inside lock nut, wrench for lock nut. From Hollywood Engineering.

Price: **$195.00**

Carbide Die Sets

Hollywood offers carbide decap rods, taper crimp dies and neck sizer dies for all their standard die calibers. They also offer full-length carbide sizer dies, full-length bottleneck sizer dies, full-length carbide sets and full-length bottleneck carbide sets for Hollywood, RCBS, Dillon and Star presses. From Hollywood Engineering.

Price: . . . . **See chart.**

Machine Gun Dies

Hardened steel and plated dies to fit any press with 11/2-12 threaded holes. Available for 50-caliber and 20mm. From Hollywood Engineering.

Price: 50-cal. **$195.00**
Price: 20mm **$295.00**

Standard Pistol/Rifle Die Sets

Two- and 3-die sets in most popular calibers. Dies made of steel and threaded 7/8-14. From Hollywood Engineering.

Price: **$46.00**

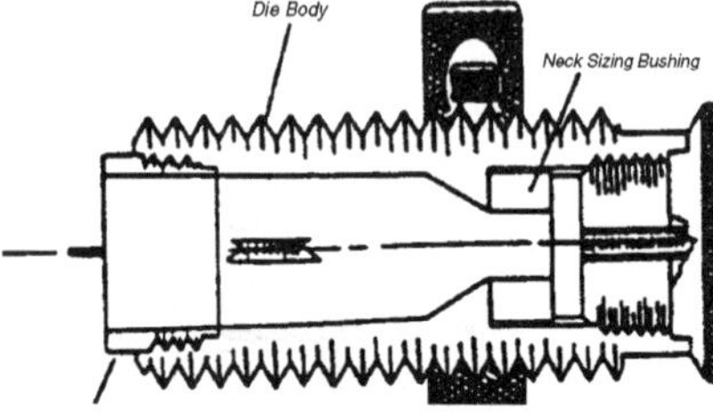

Harrel's Precision
Vari-Base Reloading Die

STANDARD PISTOL/RIFLE STEEL DIES

3-DIE SETS

22 Jet CF	32 S&W	38 Long Colt	44 Webley
221 Rem.	32 S&W Long	38 Spl.	44-40 Rev. Old
25 ACP	32 Short Colt	357 Mag.	44-40 Rev. New
256 Win.	32 Long Colt	38-40 Rev.	45 ACP
30 Mauser	32-20 Rev.	41 Short Colt	45 Long Colt
7.63 Mauser	9mm Short	41 Long Colt	44 Auto Rim
7.65 Mauser	9mm Luger	41 Mag.	455 Webley
7.65 Luger	380 ACP	44 American	45 Colt Blank
7.7 Jap. Nambu	38 Super Auto	44 S&W Spl.	45 Colt Short
31 Jap.	38 S&W	44 Mag.	
32 ACP	38 Short Colt	44 Russian	

2-DIE SETS

22 Hornet	25 Mag. Belted Cut.	7x64-06 Case	338 Win.
22 K-Hornet	25-6mm Donaldson	7x65mm Mauser	340 Wea. Mag.
218 Bee	25-06	7.35mm	348 Win.
218 Bee CCC	25-06 CCC	7.5mm Swiss	348 CCC
218 Mashburn	25-06 Imp.	7.5mm Schmidt Rubin	348-8mm Alaskan
22 Lovell	25-20 Repeater	7.7mm Japanese	35 Rem.
22 R2 Lovell	25-20 Single Shot	7.7-06 Case	35 Newton
221 Rem.	25-35 Win.	7.62 NATO	35 Newton
222 Rem.	250-3000 Savage	7.62mm Russian	35 Whelen
222 Rem. Mag.	250-3000 CCC	7.92mm German Sht.	35 Whelen Imp.
219 Zipper	250 Donaldson	30 M1 Carbine	35 Ackley Mag.
219 Zipper Imp.	250 Ackley Mag.	30 Rem.	35 Win. S.L.
219 Gib. Wasp	256 Newton	30 Newton	350 K&K
219 Don. .404	256 Japanese	30 Newton Special	350 Rem. Mag.
219 Don. .407	256 Spencer	30 CP Newton Belted	351 Win.
22 Sav. High-Power	256 Win.	30 Ackley Mag.	358 Norma
22 Sav. High-Power CCC	256 Mag. QT	30-30 Win.	358 Win.
22 Varminter	257 Roberts	30-30 CCC	9x56mm Mann.-Schn.
22 Varminter CCC	257 Roberts CCC	30-30 Krag CCC	9x57mm Rim.
22 Arrow	257 Imp. Roberts	30-40 Krag	9.3x62mm
22-06 CCC	257 Wea. Mag.	30-06	9.3x72mm Rim.
Lindahl Std. Chuck	6.5mm Rem. Mag.	30-06 CCC	9.3x74-357 Rim.
Lindahl Super Chuck	6.5mm Mann.-Schoen.	30-06 Ackley Imp.	9.3x74-367
22 Gebby Jr. Var.	6.5mm Japanese	30-06 8mm Ackley Imp.	9.3x74mm Rim. Imp.
22 Gebby Sr. Var.	6.5mm Carcano	30-06 8mm Standard	9.5mm
22 Rhetts	6.5mmx53 Rim.	300 Savage	9.5x57mm Mann.-Schn.
220 Swift	6.5mmx55 Krag	300 H&H Mag.	375 Mag. CCC
220 Swift CCC	6.5mmx55 Mauser	300 H&H CCC	375 Mag.
220 Wea.	6.5mmx57mm	300 Wea. Mag.	375 Mag. Flanged
220 Imp.	6.5mmx68mm	300 Win. Mag.	375 Mag. Wea.
22 Mag. CCC	264 Win.	303 British	375-06 CCC
223 Rem. Mag.	270 Win.	303 Savage	376-357 Imp. Flanged
224 Wea. Mag.	270 CCC	308 Norma	375-9mm Flanged
225 Win.	270 Mag. CCC	308 Win.	375-9.3mm Imp. Flngd.
228 Ackley	270 Ackley Mag.	32 Win. Spl.	38 WCF
240 Gebby Super Var.	270 Wea. Mag.	32 Rem.	38-55
240 Gebby Var. Belted	280 Ross	32-20 Win.	38-56
240 Cobra	284 Rem.	32-40	401 Win. Auto
243 Win.	284 Win.	8mm Mauser .318	405 Win.
6mm Rem.	7mm Mauser	8mm Mauser .323	44 WCF
244 Gibson	7mm CCC	8mm Lebel	444 Marlin
244 Rem.	7mm Mag. CCC	8x56mm Mann.-Schn.	45-70
244 H&H	7mm Rem. Mag.	8x57mm Mauser Rim.	45-90
25 Rem.	7mm Wea. Mag.	8x57mm Rimless	458 Win. Mag.
25 Souper	7mm Cradle	8x57mm Jr. Mauser	458 MCW Mag.
25 Donaldson Ace	7x57mm Mauser	8x60 Rim.	50-110
25 Krag CCC	7x57mm Rim.	8x68mm	11mm (43 Mauser)
25 Barr Belted Mag.	7x61mm Sharp & Hart	8.15x46mm Rim.	
	7x64mm German	33 Win.	

HOLLYWOOD Carbide Pistol/Rifle Dies

Caliber	Die Type	Price
DECAP RODS/TAPER CRIMP/NECK SIZER		
Standard	Decap rod, no carbide ball	$20.00
50	Decap rod, no carbide ball	55.00
Standard	Decap rod, carbide ball to 30-cal.	30.00
50	Decap rod, carbide ball	60.00
Standard	Decap rod, carbide ball 30-cal. and over	60.00
22-30	Taper crimp	50.00
30-50	Taper crimp	80.00
All	Neck Sizer	97.00
FULL-LENGTH SIZER(HOLLYWOOD, RCBS, DILLON, STAR)		
25 ACP, 32 ACP, 380 ACP, 38 S&W Short		65.00
30 M1, 32 S&W Long, 38/357, 38 Super ACP, 38 Special, 41 Mag., 44 Spl. Mag., 44 Rem. Mag., 45 ACP, 9mm Luger		75.00
10mm, 45 Long Colt		80.00
44 Auto Magnum		120.00
45-70		140.00
FULL-LENGTH BOTTLENECK SIZER (HOLLYWOOD, RCBS, DILLON, STAR)		
223, 308, 22-250, 38-40, 44-40		150.00
25-20 SS, 25-20 WCF, 32-20		130.00
30-06, 25-06, 7mm		155.00
50-caliber		425.00
FULL-LENGTH DIE SET (HOLLYWOOD)		
25 ACP, 32 ACP, 380 ACP, 38 S&W Short		50.00
30 M1,, 32 S&W Long, 38/357, 38 Super ACP, 38 Spl., 41 Mag., 44 Spl. Mag., 44 Rim. Mag., 45 ACP, 9mm		95.00
10mm, 45 Long Colt		100.00
44 Auto Magnum		155.00
45-70		160.00
FULL-LENGTH BOTTLENECK DIE SETS(HOLLYWOOD)		
223, 308, 22-250, 38-40, 44-40		170.00
25-20 SS, 25-20 WCF, 32-20		150.00
30-06, 25-06, 7mm		175.00
50-caliber		520.00

POR:Price on request.

Vickerman Seater Die
Steel die for standard and large pistol/rifle calibers and 50 BMG. Threaded 7/8-14 and 1 1/2-12. From Hollywood Engineering.
Price: Standard, 7/8" **$60.00**
Price: Large, 1 1/2" **$160.00**
Price: 50 BMG **$160.00**

HORNADY

50-BMG Die Set
New Dimension specialty two die set threaded 1 1/2-12. From Hornady Mfg. Co.
Price: .... **Call for price & availability**
Price: Shellholder **$25.50**
Price: Lock ring.................. **$13.00**

50 BMG File-Type Trim Die
New Dimension specialty trim die threaded 1 1/2-12. From Hornady Mfg. Co.
Price:......................... **$117.00**

Micro-Just Seating Stem
Micro-adjustable seating stem to fit any Hornady New Dimension Seating die. Allows precise bullet seating depth in .001" increments. From Hornady Mfg. Co.
Price:.......................... **$14.95**

Neck-Size Die
Steel die finished in hard satin chrome. Resizes only the case neck. Standard 7/8-14 thread with blued steel lock ring. Interior heat-treated and polished. Weight: 1 lb. From Hornady Mfg. Co.
Price:.......................... **$17.99**

GOODWIN DIES *Die Sets*

Dies		
240 Flanged	400-360	45-75 Win.
242 Vickers	360-2 1/2" NE*	45-90 Win.
6mm Lee Navy	360 #2 NE*	450 3 1/4" NE
244 Holland	369 Purdey*	500-450 3 1/4"
255 Rook	9.3x62 Mauser	500-450 #2
6.5x68	9.3x64	577-450 Martini Henry*
26 BSA	9.3x72R	455 Colt
280 Ross*	9.3x74R	455 Webley*
30 Newton	375-2 1/2" NE	455 Webley Auto
300 Sherwood	375 Flanged*	461 #1 Gibbs
7.62 Nagant Rev.	9.5x56	461 #2 Gibbs
351 Win. SL	38-56	500-465 NE
375-303	38-72	470 3 1/4"
310 Cadet	40-60 Win.	475 NE
318 Richards	40-82 Win.	475 #2
7.65 French Long*	400 Purdey	476 NE
8mm Lebel Rev.	400-375	50-70
8mm Lebel Rifle*	450-400 3"*	50-95 Win.
8x50R	450-400 3 1/4" NE*	50-110 Win.
8x57S	401 Win. SL	50-140 Win.
8x60R Port.	10.75x68 Mauser	500 Jeffrey
8x68S	10.75x73 Jeffrey*	500 3" NE
8.15x46.5R	405 Win.	577-500 Magnum
32 Win. Spl.	416 Rigby	505 Gibbs
33 Win.*	425 Westley Richards	577 Snider*
333 Jeffre	11 Gras	577 2 3/4"
9x56	43 Egyptian	577 3" NE
35 Win.	11 Mauser*	
400-350	45-60 Win.	

*Shellholder available.

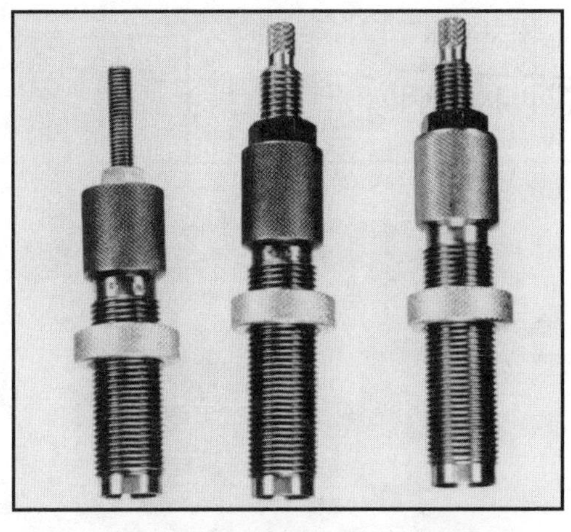

Goodwin Reloading/Case-Form Dies

Hornady

RIFLE/PISTOL DIES

Cartridge	Die Group	Shellholder	Cartridge	Die Group	Shellholder	Cartridge	Die Group	Shellholder
RIFLE								
17 Rem.	III	16	6.5x55/Scan.	I	19	300 Wea.	I	5
17/222	IV	16	6.5/06	IV	1	308 Norma Mag.	IV	5
17/223	IV	16	6.5mm TCU	III	16	7062 Russian	IV	23
218 Bee	III	7	6.5 Rem. Mag.	IV	5	705 Swiss	III	30
219 Zipper	IV	2	6.5 Mann.	IV	20	32/20 Win.	III	7
221 Rem.	III	16	6.5 Carc.	IV	21	7.62x39	I	6
222 Rem.	I	16	6.5 Japanese	IV	34	7.7 Japanese	III	1
222 Rem. Mag.	III	16	6.5x57	IV	1	303 British	I	11
22 Hornet (.224)	I	3	6.5x68	IV	30	7065 Beig.	III	24
22 K-Hornet (.224)	IV	3	264 Win. Mag.	I	5	32 Win. Spl.	III	2
22 RCFM-Jet (.224)	IV	6	270 Win.	I	1	32/40 Win.	IV	2
22 PPC (.224)	IV	6	270 Wea.	III	5	8mm Mauser	I	1
5.6x50 Mag. (.224)	IV	16	7x30 Waters	III	2	8mm/06	IV	1
5.6x52R (.227)	IV	2	7x57 (7mm Mauser)	I	1	8mm Rem. Mag.	III	5
5.6x57 (.224)	IV	1	7mm/08	I	1	8x60 S	IV	1
223 Rem. (.224)	I	16	7mm Rem. Mag.	I	5	8x68 S	IV	30
22/250	I	1	7mm Rem. BR	III	1	8.15x46 R	IV	2
220 Swift	I	4	7mm TCU	I	16	338 Win. Mag.	I	5
22 Savage HP	IV	2	7mm Merrill	IV	4	33 Win.	IV	14
Wea.	IV	17	7x65 R	IV	13	340 Wea.	I	5
225 Win.	III	4	7mm Wea.	I	5	348 Win.	IV	25
240 Wea.	III	1	7x64	IV	1	35 Rem.	I	26
243 Win.	I	1	7mm/223 Ingram	IV	16	35 Whelen	I	1
244/6mm	I	1	7x47 Helm	IV	16	357/44 B&D	IV	30
6mm Int.	IV	1	7x61 S&H	IV	35	350 Rem. Mag.	IV	5
6mm/223	III	16	7mm Express/280	I	1	357 Herrett	III	2
6mm/PPC	I	6	284 Win.	III	1	358 Win.	III	1
6mm TCU	III	16	7.35 Carc.	IV	21	358 N. Mag.	IV	5
6mm/284	IV	1	30/30 Win.	I	2	375 H&H	III	5
6x47 Rem.	IV	16	300 Savage	I	1	378 Wea.	IV	14
250 Savage	III	1	30 Luger	III	8	9.3x74 R	IV	13
25/06	I	1	30 Merrill	IV	4	9.3x57	IV	1
257 Roberts	I	1	30 Herrett	III	2	9.3x62	IV	1
25/20 Win.	IV	7	303 Savage	IV	33	10.3x60	IV	25
25/35 Win.	III	2	308 Win.	I	1	416 Rem. Mag.	IV	5
256 Win.	IV	6	30/40 Krag	III	11	416 Rigby	IV	38
257 Wea.	III	5	30/06	I	1	416 Wea.	IV	14
25 Rem.	IV	12	300 H&H	III	5	460 Wea.	IV	14
25/284	IV	1	300 Win. Mag.	I	5			
PISTOL								
25 ACP	II	37	38 Smith & Wesson	IV	28	44 Auto. Mag.	IV	1
30 M1 Carbine	I	22	38-357-357 Max.	II	6	44/40 Win.	IV	9
32 ACP	II	22	357 Win.	I	2	444 Marlin	II	27
32 S&W Long/ShortH&R Mag.	II	36	10mm Auto.-40 S&W	II	10	45 Auto. Rim	II	31
9x18 Makarov			38/40 Win.	IV	9	45 ACP/AR/WM	II	1
9mm Luger/9x21	II	8	41 Action Express	IV	8	45 Long Colt	II	32
380 Automatic	II	16	41 Mag.	II	29	45/70 Gov't	I	14
38 Super Automatic	II	8	44 Spl/44 Mag.	II	30	458 Win.	I	5

Hornady Custom Grade New Dimension Dies

Hornady Custom New Dimension Die Prices

Die Series	2-Die Rifle	3-Die Rifle	Custom Pistol
Series I Set	$29.95	$31.65	
Full-Length Die	21.40	24.24	
Seat Die	15.05	15.05	
Expander	12.57		
Series II Set			$41.95
Full-Length Die			$24.23
Seat Die			$18.51
Expander			$12.57
Series III Set	$39.95		
Full-Length Die	$26.57		
Seat Die	$15.05		

Custom Grade New Dimension Series I, II, III, IV Dies
Benchrest quality dies made of high-quality hand-inspected steel. Dies are lathed to industry-established dimensional tolerances for maximum cartridge size; inside surface hand polished and protective coating applied. Features redesigned and improved one-piece expander spindle for improved alignment and lock assembly for more precise fit; elliptical expander to reduce friction and case neck stretch; stronger, all-steel construction; in-line bullet seating system with floating sleeve and stem and built-in crimper; hardened steel decap pin; no-lube Titanium Nitride pistol size die; and wrench flats. Available in most standard rifle/pistol calibers (Series I, II, III). Custom dies (Series IV) also offered on special order. From Hornady Mfg. Co.
Price: .... **See chart.**

Taper Crimp Die
All steel and precision engineered. Add to three-die pistol set to apply crimp to autoloading pistol cases. Available for 9mm, 38, 9x21, 10mm, 40 S&W, 45 ACP, 45 Auto Rim, 45 Winchester Magnum. Weight: 1 lb. From Hornady Mfg. Co.
Price: **$14.80**

JONES

Micro-Adjustable Bullet Seating Hand Die
A straight-line seating die with bushings available in .001" increments to precisely support and align the neck of the case. Adjustable threaded cap and stem allow depth adjustment increments of .00125" and .050" per revolution. Manufactured of steel with black oxide finish. Die and bushings available for all popular calibers including wildcats. State loaded neck dimension of cartridge for proper bushing size. Comes with one bushing. From Neil Jones Custom Products.
Price: **$100.00**
Price: 17-cal. and cal., add **$12.00**

Micro-Adjustable Neck Sizing Hand Die
A precision neck-sizing die that features an adjustable cap threaded to provide .050" of movement per revolution and scribed increments of .00125". Used with Jones neck/shoulder bushings, the case neck is sized and the shoulder moved back in precisely controlled steps as case is forced into die. Shoulder bushings available in all sizes and shoulder angles including wildcats. Made of steel with black oxide finish. Tension adjustable decapping punch suitable for all calibers from 22 on up. For use on arbor press and with Jones bushing style No. 2. Comes with bushing and die base for arbor press use. From Neil Jones Custom Products.
Price: **$100.00**

Jones Micro Form Die

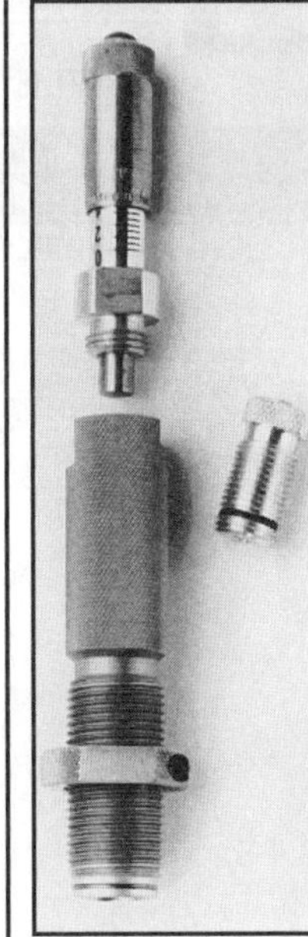

Hornady Micro-Just Seating Stem

HORNADY New Dimension Series I, II, III Dies

SERIES I 2-DIE	SERIES I 3-DIE	SERIES III 2-DIE	SERIES II 3-DIE
22 Hornet	30 M1 Carbine	17 Rem.	25 ACP
222 Rem.	375 Win.	218 Bee	32 ACP
223 Rem.	444 Marlin	221 Rem.	32 S&W Long/Short
22/250	45-70 Gov't.	222 Rem. Mag.	H&R Mag.
220 Swift	458 Win.	225 Win.	9mm Luger
243 Win.		240 Wea.	9x18
244/6mm Rem.		6mm/223	9x21
6mm PPC		6mm TCU	380 Auto
25-06		6mm Rem. BR	38 Super Auto
257 Roberts		25-35 Win.	38/357
6.5x55 Scan.		250 Savage	357 Maximum
264 Win. Mag.		257 Wea.	10mm Auto/40 S&W
270 Win.		6.5mm TCU	41 Mag.
7x57		270 Wea.	41 Action Exp.
7mm Exp./280		284 Win.	44 Spl.
7mm-08		7x30 Waters	44 Mag.
7mm Rem. Mag.		7mm Rem. BR	45 ACP
7mm TCU		30 Herrett	45 Win. Mag.
7mm Wea.		7.5 Swiss	45 Auto Rim
30-30 Win.		30 Luger	45 Long Colt
300 Savage		30-40 Krag	
300 Wea.		300 H&H	
308 Win.		7.7 Japanese	
30-06		7.65 Belgian	
300 Win. Mag.		32 Win. Spl.	
303 British		32/20 Win.	
7.62x39		8mm Rem. Mag.	
8mm Maus. (8x57 JS)		357 Herrett	
338 Win. Mag.		358 Win.	
340 Wea.			
35 Rem.			
35 Whelen			
375 H&H			

Price: 17-cal. and cal., add **$12.00**

Micro Form Die
Case-forming system consisting of micro-adjustable die body and a series of forming bushings. Bushings are manufactured with a larger lead angle than regular sizing bushings to reduce neck diameters and/or move the case shoulder. Number of bushings required depends on the caliber and if the shoulder is moved. Price does not include No. 6 style bushing. From Neil Jones Custom Products.
Price: **$100.00**
Price: Bushing **$12.00**

Threaded Neck-Sizing Die
Designed for use in conventional reloading press. Manufactured with standard 7/8-14 thread but uses interchangeable hardened steel bushings available in increments of .001" for precision neck-sizing. Single die with proper bushings will accommodate all cartridges with same head diameter. Expansion mandrels to open up case necks to larger caliber also available. Price does not include No. 2 style bushing. From Neil Jones Custom Products.
Price: **$100.00**
Price: 17-cal. and cal., add **$12.00**
Price: Extra bushing **$10.00**
Price: Expansion mandrel **$14.00**
Price: Decap punch **$10.00**

Threaded Seating Die
For use in conventional reloading press. Same design features as Jones micro-adjustable seating die with direct in-line alignment of case neck and floating seating punch adjustable in increments of .001". Available in most calibers and cartridges. Comes with one No. 5 style bushing. From Neil Jones Custom Products.
Price: **$100.00**
Price: 17-cal. and cal., add **$12.00**

LEE

Carbide Factory Crimp Die
For handgun ammunition. Carbide sizer sizes cartridge during crimping operation. Adjusting-screw sets desired amount of crimp. Trim length is not critical. From Lee Precision, Inc.
Price: **$17.98**
Price: 9mm **$19.98**

Carbide Speed Die
For use in single-station press. Eliminates need to change dies between operations. Comes with shellholder, powder dipper and load data for one cartridge. Available for 9mm Luger, 38 Special, 357 Magnum, 44 Magnum, 45 ACP. From Lee Precision, Inc.
Price: **$19.98**

Carbide/Steel Pistol Dies
Three-die pistol sets. Carbide dies contour ground to provide stepless sizing. Set includes sizer/ decapper, powder-through-expander and bullet seater. Each die has enlarged mouth to align with cases, even damaged cases. Steel dies have same features as carbide except case must be lubricated. Come with free shellholder. From Lee Precision, Inc.
Price: Carbide **$30.98**

Price: Steel **$27.98**

Collet Rifle Dies
No-lube neck size-only dies. A collet squeezes case neck against precision mandrel with minimum run-out. Not recommended for autoloaders, slide- or lever-action firearms. See chart for available calibers. From Lee Precision, Inc.
Price: **$34.98**

Decapping Die
No-lube decap die removes crimped-in primers on press. One size fits all cases. From Lee Precision, Inc.
Price: **$9.98**

Factory Crimp Die
Standard with Lee PaceSetter die sets. Crimps the bullet in place without possibility of case buckling. From Lee Precision, Inc.
Price: **$11.98**

Limited Production Rifle Dies
Limited Production two-die set includes full-length sizer, bullet seater/roll crimper, shellholder, powder dipper and load data for single cartridge in transparent storage container. This set does not include a factory crimp die. See chart for available calibers. From Lee Precision, Inc.
Price: **$29.98**

PaceSetter Rifle Die Set
Three-die rifle set includes full-length sizer, bullet seater/roll crimper, factory crimp die, shellholder, powder dipper, load data and instructions for single cartridge in transparent storage container. Two price levels-one for standard stocked die sets and another for Ltd. production die sets. See chart for available calibers. From Lee Precision, Inc.
Price: Standard.................. **$27.98**
Price: Limited Production **$29.98**

RGB Series Rifle Die Set
Rifle two-die set with full-length sizer and bullet seater/roll crimper only with load data for one cartridge in transparent plastic storage container. See chart for available calibers. From Lee Precision, Inc.
Price: **$14.98**

LEE
Rifle Charging Die
For use on standard threaded presses to charge small-capacity rifle cases using Lee Auto-Disk powder measure. Similar in operation to powder-through-expanding die, except does not expand case mouth. From Lee Precision, Inc.
Price: **$11.98**

Steel Rifle Dies
All Lee dies feature one-piece reaming, wrench flats, collet held decapper, finger adjustable bullet seater, elevated expander, O-ring locks. Dies offer unbreakable decapper, floating bullet seater, heat-treated to maximum hardness and progressively machine-honed inside surface. Lee dies come in five configurations: RGB, PaceSetter, PaceSetter Ltd., Limited Production and Collet dies. From Lee Precision, Inc.
Price: .... **See individual listings.**

LEE

RIFLE DIES

Caliber	RGB Series	PaceSetter 3-Die	PaceSetter Ltd.	Limited Production	Collet Necksize	Factory Crimp	Taper Crimp
RIFLE							
17 Rem.	NA	NA	NA	A	A	NA	NA
22 Hornet	NA	NA	A	NA	A	A	NA
218 Bee	NA	NA	A	NA	NA	A	NA
22 PPC	NA	NA	NA	A	A	NA	NA
221 Fireball	NA	NA	NA	A	NA	NA	NA
222 Rem.	A	A	NA	NA	A	A	A
223	A	A	NA	NA	A	A	A
22-250	A	A	NA	NA	A	A	NA
220 Swift	NA	NA	NA	A	A	A	NA
243 Win.	A	A	NA	NA	A	A	NA
6mm PPC	NA	NA	NA	A	A	NA	NA
6mm Rem.	NA	NA	A	NA	A	A	NA
25-20	NA	NA	A	NA	NA	A	NA
25-35	NA	NA	NA	A	NA	NA	NA
250 Savage	NA	NA	NA	A	A	A	NA
257 Roberts	NA	NA	A	NA	A	A	NA
25-06	NA	NA	A	NA	A	A	NA
260 Rem.	NA	NA	NA	A	NA	NA	NA
264 Win. Mag.	NA	NA	NA	A	NA	NA	NA
6.5 Carcano	NA	NA	NA	A	NA	NA	NA
6.5 Japanese	NA	NA	NA	A	NA	NA	NA
6.5 Rem. Mag.	NA	NA	NA	A	NA	NA	NA
6.5x55	A	A	NA	NA	A	A	NA
270 Wea..	NA	NA	NA	A	NA	NA	NA
270 Win.	A	A	NA	NA	A	A	NA
7mm BR	NA	NA	NA	A	A	NA	NA
7mm TCU	NA	NA	NA	A	NA	NA	NA
7-30 Waters	NA	NA	NA	A	NA	A	NA
7x57 Mauser	NA	NA	A	NA	A	A	NA
7x64 Brenneke	NA	NA	NA	A	NA	NA	NA
7mm-08	NA	NA	A	NA	A	A	NA
7mm Express	NA	NA	A	NA	A	A	NA
7mm Rem. Mag.	A	A	NA	NA	A	A	NA
284 Win.	NA	NA	NA	A	NA	NA	NA
7mm Wea.	NA	NA	NA	A	NA	NA	NA
7.35 Carcano	NA	NA	NA	A	NA	NA	NA
7.5 Schmidt Rubin	NA	NA	NA	A	NA	NA	NA
7.5X54 MAS							
7.62x39 Russian	A	A	NA	NA	NA	A	A
7.62x54 Russian	NA	NA	A	NA	NA	A	NA
30 Herrett	NA	NA	NA	A	NA	NA	NA
30/40 Krag	NA	NA	A	NA	NA	A	A
30-30 Win.	A	A	NA	NA	A	A	A
303 Savage	NA	NA	NA	A	NA	NA	A
308 Win.	A	A	NA	NA	A	A	A
300 Savage	NA	NA	A	NA	NA	A	NA
30-06	A	A	NA	NA	A	A	A
300 Win. Mag.	A	A	NA	NA	A	A	NA
300 H&H	NA	NA	NA	A	A	NA	NA
300 Weath. Mag.	NA	NA	A	NA	A	A	NA
7.65 Arg. Mauser	NA	NA	A	NA	NA	A	A
7.7 Japanese	NA	NA	A	NA	NA	A	A
303 British	A	A	NA	NA	A	A	A
32-20	NA	NA	NA	A*	NA	A	NA
32-40	NA	NA	NA	A	NA	NA	NA
32 Win.	NA	NA	NA	A	NA	NA	NA
33 Win.	NA	NA	NA	A	NA	NA	NA
8mm Rem. Mag.	NA	NA	NA	A	NA	NA	NA
8x57 Mauser	A	A	NA	NA	A	A	NA
8mm Lebel	NA	NA	NA	A	NA	NA	NA
338 Win.	NA	NA	A	NA	A	A	NA
348 Win.	NA	NA	NA	A	NA	A	NA
350 Rem. Mag.	NA	NA	NA	A	NA	NA	NA
356 Win.	NA	NA	NA	A	NA	A	NA
358 Win.	NA	NA	NA	A	NA	A	NA
35 Rem.	NA	NA	A	NA	A	A	NA
35 Whelen	NA	NA	NA	A	A	NA	NA
38-40	NA	NA	NA	A*	NA	A	NA
38-55	NA	NA	NA	A*	NA	A	NA
38-56	NA	NA	NA	A	NA	NA	NA
375 H&H	NA	NA	A	NA	A	A	NA
375 Win.	NA	NA	NA	A*	NA	A	NA
416 Rem.	NA	NA	NA	A	NA	A	NA
43 Mauser	NA	NA	NA	A	NA	NA	NA
43 Spanish	NA	NA	NA	A	NA	NA	NA
44-40	NA	NA	NA	A*	NA	A	NA
444 Marlin	NA	NA	NA	A*	NA	A	NA
45-70 Gov't.	NA	NA	NA	A*	NA	A	NA
458 Win. Mag.	NA	NA	NA	A*	NA	A	NA

A:Available; NA:Not available. *Special Order. **Custom die $30.00.

LEE

PISTOL DIES

Caliber	RGB Series	—PaceSetter— 3-Die	Ltd.	Limited Production	Collet Necksize	Factory Crimp	Taper Crimp
—PISTOL—							
25 ACP	A	NA	NA	A*	A*	NA	NA
30 M1 Carbine	A	NA	NA	A	A	A	NA
30 Luger	NA	A	NA	NA	A	NA	NA
30 Mauser	NA	A	NA	NA	A*	NA	NA
7.62 Tokarev	NA	A	NA	NA	A	NA	NA
32 ACP	A	NA	NA	A	A	NA	NA
32 S&W Long	A	NA	NA	A	A	A	NA
32 H&R Magnum	A	NA	NA	A	A*	A	NA
32-20	NA	A	NA	NA	A*	NA	A**
38-40	NA	A	NA	NA	A*	NA	A**
9mm Luger	A	A	A	A	A	A	A
9mm Makarov	A	NA	NA	A	A	NA	NA
38 Colt N.P.	NA	NA	NA	A	A*	NA	NA
38 Super/38 ACP	A	NA	NA	A	A	A	
380 Auto	A	NA	NA	A	A	A	A
38 S&W	A	NA	NA	A	A*	NA	NA
38 Special	A	A	A	A	A	A	A
357 Magnum	A	A	A	A	A	A	A
40 S&W	A	NA	NA	NA	NA	NA	A
10mm Auto	A	NA	NA	A*	A*	A	A
41 AE	NA	NA	A	A*	NA	NA	NA
41 Magnum	A	NA	NA	A	A	A	NA
44 Special	A	A	NA	A	A	A	A
44 Magnum	A	A	A	A	A	A	A
44-40	NA	A	NA	NA	A*	NA	A**
45 Colt	A	NA	NA	A	A	A	A
45 ACP	A	A	A	A	A	A	A
45 Auto Rim	A	NA	NA	A	A*	A	NA
455 Webley MII	A	NA	NA	A	A*	A	NA
45 Win. Mag.	A	NA	NA	A	A	A	A
454 Casull	A	NA	NA	A	A	A	A
45 HP Italian	A	NA	NA	A	A*	A	A

A:Available; NA:Not available. *Special Order. **Custom die $30.00.

Taper Crimp Die
Hardened steel die designed to overcome crimp problems caused by incorrect bullet seater dies. See chart for available calibers. From Lee Precision, Inc.
Price: **$9.98**

Universal Charging Die
Charges both rifle and pistol cases. Includes connecting rod and adaptors to actuate measure with the case. Measure positively resets when ram fully lowered. Comes with drop tubes for most cartridges from the 380 ACP to the 300 Winchester Magnum. Does not expand case mouth. From Lee Precision, Inc.
Price: **$24.98**

LYMAN

AA Rifle 2-Die Sets
All-steel die set consists of full-length resizing die, with decapping stem and neck expanding button, and a bullet-seating die. Best for reloading jacketed bullets in bottlenecked cases. For reloading cast bullets, add a neck-expanding die. From Lyman Products Corporation.
Price: **$29.50**

AA Rifle 3-Die Set
For reloading straight-wall cases. Full-length sizing die with decapping stem, AA two-step neck expanding (M) die and bullet seating die. Also good for loading cast bullets. From Lyman Products Corporation.
Price: **$39.95**

Carbide Pistol 3-Die Set
Tungsten carbide full-length resizing and decapping die, two-step neck expanding die and bullet seating chamber and screw. Comes with extra seating screws for loading all popular bullet designs for given caliber. Two-step expander prevents cast bullet distortion and assures precise case neck tension. Loads both magnum and special length cases. Resizing ring eliminates need for case lubing. From Lyman Products Corporation.

LYMAN AA Rifle 2-Die/ Small Base Die Parts

DIE/DIE PART	PRICE
2-Die Set	$24.95
Sizing die body	15.50
Decapping rod	2.00
Expanding die body	10.00
Expanding button	3.95
Expanding plug	5.00
Seating die body	13.50
Seating screw	3.95
Decapping rod	2.00
Decapping pin lock nut	.25

Lyman Carbide 4-Die Pistol Set

LYMAN AA Standard Rifle 3-Die Parts

DIE/DIE PART	PRICE
AA Standard 3-Die Set	$32.00
Sizing die body (steel)	15.50
Sizing die body (carbide)	22.95
Decapping rod	2.00
Neck expanding die body	10.00
Expanding plug	5.00
Seating die body	13.50
Bullet seating screw	3.95

LYMAN AA Standard Pistol 3-Die Parts

DIE/DIE PARTS	PRICE
AA Standard Pistol 3-Die Set	$28.50
Sizing die body	15.50
Deacapping rod	2.00
Neck expanding die body	10.00
Expanding plug	5.00
Seating die body	13.50
Bullet seating screw	3.95

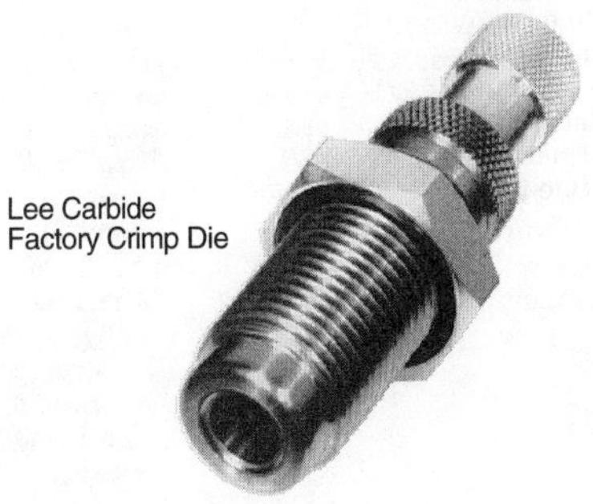

Lee Carbide Factory Crimp Die

Section 1: Metallic Cartridges

Lyman

RIFLE/PISTOL DIES

Cartridge	Die Group	Shellholder	Cartridge	Die Group	Shellholder	Cartridge	Die Group	Shellholder
RIFLE						PISTOL		
17 Rem.	AA-2	26	30 M1 Carbine	AA-3	19	45-70 Gov't	AA-3	17
22 Hornet	AA-2	4	30-30 Win.	AA-2	6	50-70 Gov't	AA-3	22
222 Rem.	AA-2	26	30-06	AA-2, SB-2	2	25 ACP	S-3	32
222 Rem. Mag.	AA-2	26	308 Win.	AA-2, SB-2	2	7mm TCU	S-3	26
223 Rem. (5.56mm)	AA-2, SB-2	26	300 Sav.	AA-2	2	30 Luger	S-3	12
22-250	AA-2	2	300 Wea. Mag.	AA-2	13	30 Mauser	S-3	12
220 Swift	AA-2	5	300 Win. Mag.	AA-2, SB-2	13	32 ACP	C-4, C-3, S-3	23
5.6mmx50R	MR-2	1	7.62x39mm	AA-2	3	32 S&W Long	C-4, C-3, S-3	9
243 Win.	AA-2, SB-2	2	7.62x54 Russian	AA-2	17	32 H&R Mag.	C-4, C-3, S-3	9
6mm Rem..	AA-2, SB-2	2	303 British	AA-2	7	380 Auto	C-4, C-3, S-3	26
25-06 Rem.	AA-2	2	7.65mm Arg. Maus.	AA-2	2	38 S&W	C-4, C-3, S-3	21
250 Sav.	AA-2	2	32-20 Win.	AA-3	10	38 Super Auto	C-4, C-3, S-3	12
257 Roberts	AA-2	2, 8	32 Win. Spl.	AA-2	6	9mm Luger	C-4, C-3, S-3	12
25-20 Win.	AA-3	10	8mmx57 Maus.	AA-2	2	38 Special	C-4, C-3, S-3	1
6.5mmx55 SCAN	AA-2	27	8mm Rem. Mag.	AA-2	13	357 Rem. Max.	C-4, C-3, S-3	1
6.5mmx57 Maus.	MR-2	2	338 Win. Mag.	AA-2	13	9mm Makarov	C-3	12
6.5mmx57R Maus.	MR-2	14B	35 Rem.	AA-2	8, 2	9x23 Win.	C-3	12
6.5mmx55Swed. Maus.	AA-2	27	35 Whelen	AA-2	2	40 S&W	C-4, C-3	15
270 Win.	AA-2, SB-2	2	358 Win.	AA-2	2	10mm Auto	C-4, C-3	15
7mm STW	AA-2	13	9.3mmx62	MR-2	2	41 Mag.	C-4, C-3, S-3	30
7mm TCU	ND-2	26	9.3mmx64	MR-2	30	41 Action Exp.	C-4, C-3, S-3	12
7mm Rem. Mag.	AA-2, SB-2	13	9.3mmx72R	MR-3	30	44 Mag.	C-4, C-3, S-3	7
7mmx57 Maus.	AA-2	2	9.3mmx74R	MR-2	14B	44 Spl.	C-4, C-3, S-3	7
7mmx57R Mauser	AA-2	14B	375 H&H	AA-2	13	445 Super Mag.	C-4, C-3, S-3	
280 Rem.	AA-2	2	375 Win.	AA-3	6	44-40 Win.	AA-3	14B
7mm-08 Rem.	AA-2	2	38-55 Win.	AA-3	6	45 ACP	C-4, C-3, S-3	2
7x30 Waters	AA-2	6	40-65	AA-3	17	45 Win. Mag.	C-4, C-3, S-3	2
7mm Wea. Mag.	AA-2	13	416 Rigby	AA-2	17	45 Colt	C-4, C-3, S-3	11
7mmx64 Brenn.	MR-2	2	44-40 Win.	AA-3	14B	50 AE	C-4	7
7mmx65R Brenn.	MR-2	14B	444 Marlin	AA-3	14B			

AA-2:2-die set for bottleneck cases; AA-3:3-die rifle set for straight-wall cases; MR-2:Metric rifle 2-die set; MR-3:Metric rifle 3-die set; SB-2:Small base 2-die set for jacketed bullets; C-4:4-die carbide set; C-3:3-die carbide set; S-3:Standard AA 3-die set.

Price: **$41.50**

Carbide Pistol 4-Die Set
Features one-piece decapping rod design made of hardened tool steel. Includes separate taper crimp die for reloading semi-auto cartridges; powder charge/expanding die with special hollow expander plugs for two-step neck expansion and powder charging. Top of expand/powder die threaded to accept Lyman #55 powder measure, AccuMeasure or any other brand threaded measure. Neck size die and seating die make up the quartet. From Lyman Products Corporation.
Price: **$54.00**

Multi-Expand/Powder Charge Die
Simultaneously expands case mouth and drops powder charge from measure. Includes expander/powder drop tubes for 32, 9mm, 38/357, 10mm/40 S&W, 41, 44 and 45 Auto plus non-expanding universal drop tube. Works with all presses and powder measures with standard die thread. From Lyman Products Corporation.
Price: **$25.75**

Neck Size Rifle 2-Die Set
Works only neck of case to retain fire-formed dimensions. Includes special sizing die with decapping stem and expander button and a standard bullet-seating die. From Lyman Products Corporation.
Price: **$31.50**

Ram Prime Die System
Designed for primer feeding on top of press. Standard die threading to fit all presses. Includes large and small primer punches. From Lyman Products Corporation.
Price: **$12.95**

LYMAN

Small Base Rifle 2-Die Set
Designed for loading jacketed bullets in cartridges sized to minimum dimensions. Set includes special small base full-length resizing die with decapping stem and expander button and a standard bullet-seating die. From Lyman Products Corporation.
Price: **$31.50**

Specialty Die Sets
Die sets for 475 Wildey and 50 Action Express. Four-die sets for both calibers include taper crimp die; case forming set for 475 Wildey allow cases to be formed from 284 Winchester cases. From Lyman Products Corporation.
Price: Die set. **$59.95**

Taper Crimp Die
Applies proper crimp to pistol and rifle cases. Heat-treated to R50 minimum surface hardness and interior hand polished to 8 rms finish. From Lyman Products Corporation.
Price: **$14.95**

Two-Step Expanding (M) Die
Designed for cast and jacketed bullet loads. Prevents case stretching to extend case life. Expands inside of case neck to just under bullet diameter then expands case mouth to bullet diameter or slightly over. From Lyman Products Corporation.
Price: **$12.95**

Universal Decapping Die
For all calibers 22 through 45 except 378 and 460 Weatherby. Solid one-piece construction of hardened tool steel. Works well for military crimped primers. From Lyman Products Corporation.
Price: **$12.00**

N.D.F.S

Die Service for Obsolete Cartridges
This English company manufactures custom three-die sets with standard threading for obsolete blackpowder cartridges. From N.D.F.S.
Price: . . . . **Contact manufacturer.**

RCBS

50 BMG Dies

Two-die set contains a full-length sizer and seater die with built-in roll crimper. Dies are produced in two diameters: 13/8"-12 for use with Big Max press and AmmoMaster 50 kit; 11/2"-12 for use with AmmoMaster 50 kit and other presses. Trim die and neck sizer die also available. From RCBS.

Price: Die set. **$264.95**
Price: Trim die **$129.95**
Price: Neck sizer die. **$161.95**

Carbide Rifle/Pistol Dies

RCBS Group B and Group C three-die sets include: carbide sizer die with decapping assembly, expander die, and seater die. Tungsten carbide inner ring resizes without the need for case lubing. From RCBS.

Price: Group B three die carbine **$44.95**
Price: Group c three die carbide **$62.95**

Neck Expander Die

For use when reloading cast bullets. Die expands case neck and slightly flares case mouth to prevent lead shearing. From RCBS.

Price:. **$20.95**
Price: Die body **$17.95**
Price: Plug. **$7.13**
Price: Plug rod **$3.95**

Case-Forming Dies

Contact RCBS for extensive listing of available case-form dies. From RCBS.

Price: . . . . **Contact manufacturer.**

Competition Rifle Dies

Two die sets feature: full-length sizer with raised expander ball for extra leverage and smooth neck expansion; maximum concentricity between die neck and body; seater die with micrometer bullet-seating head with 0.001" click adjustments; side window with sliding guide for bullet insertion and alignment; bullet-seating sleeve for correct alignment; extended shellholder for shorter rounds; and black oxide finish. Sets come with set-screw wrench, hexagonal lock rings. From RCBS.

Price: Full length Set. **$95.95**
Price: Full length sizer die. **$36.95**
Price: Seater die **$61.95**
Price: Extended shell holder **$9.95**
Price: Decapping pin **$1.95**
Price: Seater Plug Assembly **$8.95**
Price: Bullet Guide. **$5.95**

Lock-Out

Detects no powder or double charge in progressive reloading. From RCBS.

Price:. **$42.95**

RCBS

RIFLE/PISTOL DIES

Caliber	Die Group	Shellholder/ Shellplate #	Caliber	Die Group	Shellholder/ Shellplate #
17 Rem.	A	10	307 Win.	A	2
218 Bee	D	1	308 Norma Mag.	D	4
22 Hornet	A, Comp.	12	308 Win.	A, Comp., RS	3
22K-Hornet	D	12	7.5mm Schmidt-Rubin	D, Comp.	2
22 PPC	D	32	7.62x39	A, RS	32
22 Rem. Jet	D	6	7.62x54R Russian	A	13*
22 Sav. High-Power	D	2	7.65x53 Belgian Mauser	D	3
22-250	A, Comp., RS	3	7.7x58 Japanese Arisaka	D	3/2
220 Swift	A	11	32 Automatic	B	17
221 Rem. Fire Ball	A	10	32 H&R Mag.	B	23
222 Rem.	A, Comp., RS	10	32 S&W Long	B	23
222 Rem. Mag.	D	10	32 Win. Special	A	2
223 Rem.	A, Comp., RS	10	32-20 Win.	B	1
224 Wea. Mag.	D	27	32-40 Win.	D	2
225 Win.	D	11	8mm Rem. Mag.	D	4
5.6x50 Rimmed	D	6	8mm-06	D	3
240 Wea. Mag.	D	3	8mmx57 Mauser	A, Comp., RS	3
243 Win.	A, Comp., RS	3	8mmx68S Mag.	D	34*
6mm PPC	D	32	33 Win.	D	14*
6mm Rem.	A	3	338 Win. Mag.	A	4
25 Auto	B	29**	340 Wea. Mag.	D	4
25-06	A	3	348 Win.	A	5*
25-20 Win.	D	1	35 Rem.	A	9
25-35 Win.	D	2	35 Whelen	A	3
250 Sav.	A	3	350 Rem. Mag.	D	4
256 Win. Mag.	D	6	356 Win.	A	2
257 Roberts	A	3,11	357 Herrett	D	2
257 Roberts Improved	D	3,11	357 Mag.	B	6
257 Wea. Mag.	D	4	357 Rem. Maximum	B	6
264 Win. Mag.	A	4/26	358 Norma Mag.	D	4
6.5 Rem. Mag.	D	4	358 Win.	A	3
6.5mm T/CU	D	10	9mm Luger	B	16
6.5mm-06	D	3	9mm Makarov	B	16
6.5x50 Japanese Arisaka	D	15	9mmx21	B	16
6.5x52 Carcano	D	9	9.3x62 Mauser	D	3
6.5x54 Mannlicher-Scho.	D	9	9.3x72R	F	30
6.5x55 Swedish Mauser	A, Comp., RS	2	9.3x74R	D	4
6.5x57	D	3	375 H&H Mag.	A	4
270 Wea. Mag.	A	4	375 Win.	C	2
270 Win.	A, Comp., RS	3	378 Wea. Mag.	D	14*
280 Rem.	A	3	38 Colt Super Auto	B	39
284 Win.	D	3	38 S&W	E	6
7mm BR Rem.	A	3	38 Special	B	6
7mm Rem. Mag.	A, Comp., RS	4/26	380 ACP	B	10
7mm T/CU	A	10	38-40 Win.	E	35*
7mm Wea. Mag.	A	4	38-55 Win. & Ballard	F	2
7mm-08 Rem.	A, Comp.	3	40 S&W	B	27
7mmx57 Mauser	A	11/3	10mm Auto	B	27
7mmx64 Brenneke	A, Comp.	3	41 Action Express	B	16
7mmx65 Rimmed	D	26	41 Mag.	B	30
7-30 Waters	A	2	416 Rem. Mag.	D	4
30 M-1 Carbine	C	17	416 Rigby	D	37*
30 Herrett	D	2	44 Mag.	B	18
30 Luger	D	16	44 Special	B	18
30 Mauser	D	16	444 Marlin	C	28
30 Rem.	D	19	44-40 Win.	B	35*
30-06 Springfield	A, Comp., RS	3	45 ACP	B	3
30-30 Win.	A, RS	2	45 Auto Rim	B	8*
30-338 Win. Mag.	D	4	45 Colt	B	20
30-40 Krag	A	7	45 Win. Mag.	E	36*
300 H&H Mag.	A	4	45-70 Gov't.	C	14*
300 Sav.	A	3	458 Win. Mag.	C	4
300 Wea. Mag.	A	4	460 Wea. Mag.	D	14*
300 Win. Mag.	A, RS	4/26	50 Action Express	E	33*
303 British	A, RS	7	50-70 U.S. Government	F	31**
303 Sav.	D	21			

Comp.:Competition Dies; RS:Reloader Special Dies.
* Auto 4x4 shellplate not available.
** Auto 4x4 and five-station shellplates not available.
When two shellholder numbers are shown, the most popular is shown first.

Section 1: Metallic Cartridges

Precision Dies

RCBS Group A, E and F two- or three-die sets featuring: sizing dies with strict tolerances; satin matte finish; fine body knurling for non-slip adjustment; hardened die body; and thread adjustable expander-decapping assembly that locks in place. From RCBS.

Group A
Price: Full-length die set **$31.95**
Price: Sizer die. **$25.95**
Price: Neck die set. . . . . **$33.95 to 48.95**
Price: Neck sizer die . . . . **$27.95 to 33.95**
Price: Small base die set . . . . **$33.95 to 48.95**
Price: Small base sizer die . . **$27.95 to 33.95**
Price: Seater die **$21.95**
Price: Expand-Decapping unit. **$5.95**
Price: Trim die **$29.95**

Group E
Price: 3-Die set **$71.95**
Price: 3-Die roll crimp set **$59.95**
Price: Carbide sizer die **$47.95**
Price: Steel sizer die. **$34.95**
Price: Expander die **$20.95**
Price: Roll crimp die. **$27.95**
Price: Taper crimp seater die. **$27.95**
Price: Decap unit **$5.95**
Price: Trim die **$41.95**

Group F
Price: 3-Die roll crimp set **$69.95**
Price: Steel sizer die . . . .
Price: Expander die **$25.95**
Price: Roll Crimp seater die. **$5.95**
Price: Decap unit **$5.95**
Price: Trim die **$41.95**

Lube die

Decap and lube cases in one step. Designed for progressive presses.
Price: **$31.95**

Universal Decap Die

Precision machined die to decap uncleaned, unlubed cases from 22- to 45-caliber. Includes die body, decap assembly with lock nut, die lock ring and plastic storage box. From RCBS.

RCBS
Competition Rifle Dies

RCBS Group A Dies

DIE/DIE PART	PRICE
Full-Length Die Set	$29.00
Full-Length Sizer Die	23.00
Neck Die Set	30.50
Neck Sizer Die	23.00
Small Base Die Set	30.00
Small Base Sizer Die	23.00
Seater Die	19.50
Expander-Decapping Unit	5.20
Expander Ball	3.33
Expander-Decapping Rod	1.75
Decapping Pin (5)	1.75
Guide Bushing	1.75
Seater Plug	4.13
Trim Die	19.50

RCBS Group C Dies

DIE/DIE PART	PRICE
3-Die Carbide Set, Roll or Taper Crimp	$56.00
3-Die Set, Roll/Taper Crimp	37.13
Carbide Sizer Die	42.00
Sizer Die	19.63
Expander Die	13.88
Seater Die, Roll/Taper Crimp	17.88
Decapping Unit	5.59
Decapping Pin Holder	2.75
Decapping Rod	1.75
Decapping Pin (5)	1.75
Expander Assembly	5.53
Guide Bushing	1.75
Seater Plug	4.13

RCBS Group E Dies

DIE/DIE PART	PRICE
3-Die Set	$53.13
Sizer Die	30.88
Expander Die	18.63
Seater Die	24.50
Decapping Unit	5.59
Decap Pin Holder	2.75
Decapping Rod	1.75
Decapping Pin (5)	1.75
Expander Assembly	5.53
Guide Bushing	1.75
Seater Plug	4.13

RCBS Competition Dies

DIE/DIE PART	PRICE
Full-Length Die Set	$85.88
Full Length Sizer Die	28.75
Seater Die	53.63
Extended Shellholder	8.75
Expander-Decap Assembly	6.58
Guide Bushing	3.18
Expander-Decap Rod	3.18
Expander Ball	3.05
Decapping Pin Holder	2.75
Decapping Pin (5)	1.75
Seater Plug Assembly	7.38
Bullet Guide	5.13

RCBS Group B Dies

DIE/DIE PART	PRICE
3-Die Carbide Set	$39.63
3-Die Set, Roll/Taper Crimp	29.63
Carbide Sizer Die	28.88
Sizer Die	16.38
Expander Die	11.75
Seater Die, Roll/Taper Crimp	15.50
Decapping Unit	5.59
Decapping Pin Holder	2.75
Decapping Rod	1.75
Decapping Pin (5)	1.75
Expander Assembly	5.53
Guide Bushing	1.75
Seater Plug	4.13
Trim Die	19.50

RCBS Group D Dies

DIE/DIE PART	PRICE
Full-Length Die Set	$48.50
Full-Length Sizer Die	34.00
Neck Die Set	55.75
Neck Sizer Die	39.88
Seater Die	26.75
Expander Decapping Unit	5.20
Expander Ball	3.33
Expander Decapping Rod	1.75
Decapping Pin (5)	1.75
Guide Bushing	1.75
Seater Plug	4.13
Trim Die	35.38

RCBS Group F Dies

DIE/DIE PART	PRICE
3-Die Set	$61.25
Sizer Die	42.50
Expander Die	22.38
Seater Die	27.63
Decapping Unit	5.59
Decapping Pin Holder	2.75
Decapping Rod	1.75
Decapping Pin (5)	1.75
Expander Assembly	5.53
Guide Bushing	1.75
Seater Plug	4.13

RCBS Reloader Special

DIE/DIE PART	PRICE
Die Set	$17.00
Expander-Decapper Unit	4.18
Expander Ball	2.80
Expander Decapping Rod	1.75
Decapping Pin (5)	2.00
Collet	1.86
Collet Closer	1.86
Seater Plug	3.94

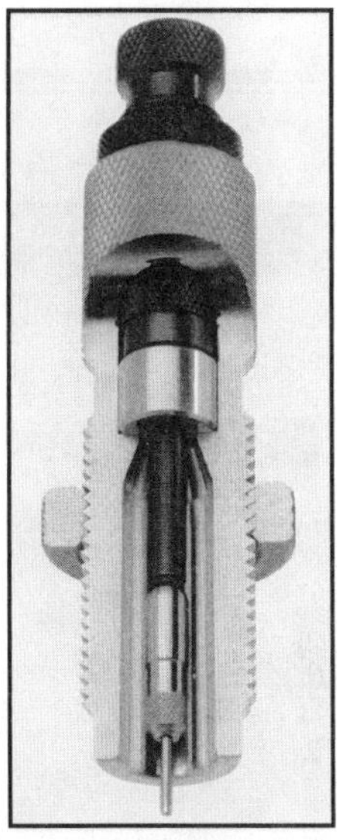

Redding Type S

REDDING Competition Die Calibers	
221 Rem.	260 Rem.
222 Rem.	6.5/284 Win.
223 Rem.	6.5x55 Swedish
22 PPC	264 Win. Mag.
22 BR Rem.	270 Win.
22-250 Rem.	7mm IHSMA
22-250 Rem. Imp. 40°	7mm TCU
220 Swift	7mm BR Rem.
6mm PPC	7mm-08 Rem.
6mm BR Rem	7mmx57 Mauser
6mm TCU	280 Rem.
243 Win.	280 Rem. Imp. 40°
243 Win. Imp. 40°	284 Win.
6mm Rem.	7mm Rem. Mag.
6mm/284 Win.	7mm STW
250 Savage	308 Win.
257 Roberts	30-06 Spfd.
257 Rob. Imp. 40°	300 Win. Mag.
25-06 Rem.	30-338 Win. Mag.
6.5/308 Win.	300 Wea. Mag.

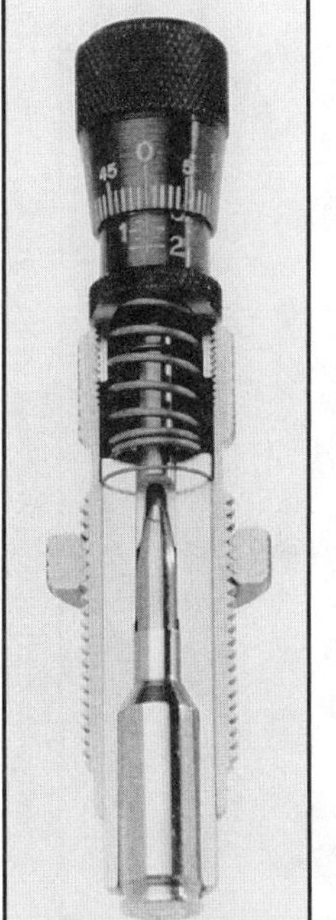

Redding Benchrest Competition Resizing Die

REDDING Pistol/Rifle 2-Die Prices

Die Set/Die Part	Series A	Series B	Series C	Series D
Full-LengthSet	$45.95	$ 63.00	$ 82.50	$ 94.50
Deluxe Set	$75.90	$102.90	$129.00	$150.00
Neck Sizing Die	$33.00	$44.40	$54.00	$61.50
Neck Die Set	$45.90	$63.00	$82.50	$94.50
Full-length Sizing Die	$33.00	$44.40	$54.00	$61.50
Decap Rod Assembly	$10.50	$10.50	$10.50	$10.50
Decap Rod	$6.90	$6.90	$6.90	$6.90
Size Button	$6.00	$6.00	$6.00	$6.00
Seating Die	$28.50	$38.40	$48.00	$52.50
Seat Plug	$6.90	$6.90	$6.90	$6.90
Form & Trim Die	$28.50	$38.40	$44.40	$52.50

REDDING Pistol/Rifle 3-Die Prices

Die Set/Die Part	Series A	Series B	Series C	Series D
3-Die Set	$45.90	$63.00	$82.50	$94.50
Sizing Die	$26.40	$34.80	$31.40	$49.50
Decap Rod Assembly	$10.50	$10.50	$10.50	$10.50
Seating Die	$24.00	$33.00	39.90	45.90
Seat Plug	$6.90	$6.90	$6.90	$6.90
Expander Die	$17.40	$24.00	$28.50	$33.00
Expander	$9.00	$9.00	$9.00	$9.90
Trim Die	$28.00	$38.40	$44.40	$52.50

Redding Taper Crimp Die

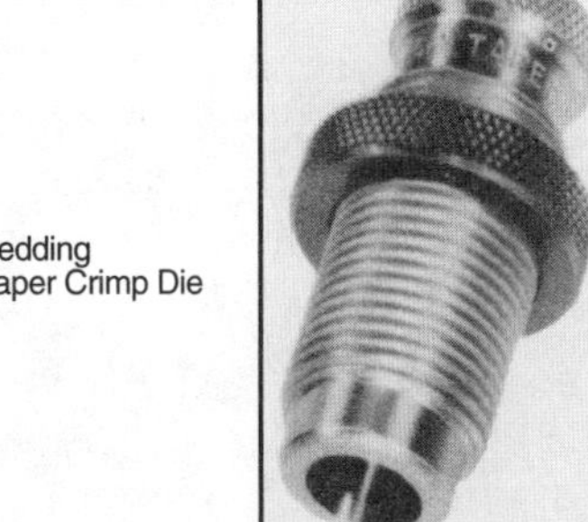

Redding Steel Rifle/Pistol Dies

Price: **$12.95**

REDDING

Bushing-Style Neck-Sizing Die

Designed to control amount of neck sizing for precision reloading. Two models available, Type S or Benchrest Competition. Both models will accept interchangeable sizing bushings that come in .001" increments and cover a size range from .235 to .340 or 22-caliber through 30. The dies are available in 42 calibers without the bushings and have an adjustable decapping rod to allow positioning of the bushing to resize only a portion of the neck length if desired. The Benchrest Competition die features micrometer adjustments. Bushings are of steel or titanium nitrite treated steel. From Redding Reloading Equipment.

Price: Type S neck sizing die
Category 1 .... **$57.00,**
Category 2 .... **$69.90**
Price: Benchrest competition bullet seating die
Category I.................... **$105.00**
Category II.................. **$127.50**
Price: Steel bushing **$13.50**
Price: Titanium nitrite steel bushing...................... **$24.00**

Bushing-Style Body Dies

Designed to full-length resize the case body only and bump the shoulder position for proper chambering without disturbing the case neck. No internal parts and intended for use only to resize cases which chamber with difficulty after repeated firings. From Redding Reloading Equipment.

Price: **$57.00**

Case Forming Dies

Made on a custom basis only to form brass cases from one caliber to another. From Redding Reloading Equipment.

Price: .... **Contact manufacturer.**

Competition Bullet Seating Die

Straight-line bullet seater with seating depth micrometer. Seating stem precision ground to exactly match bullet diameter. Micrometer calibrated in .001" increments for precise seating depth and has a "zero" set feature to zero micrometer to specific rifle. From Redding Reloading Equipment.

Price:.......................... $105.00

Custom Made Dies

Die sets for cartridges not listed can be custom made by Redding; send them chamber reamer drawing or dimensions and shoulder angle or cartridge for price quote. From Redding Reloading Equipment.

Price: 2-die set **$123.00**
Price: 2-die set with tapered expander.................... **$129.00**
Price: Full-length sizer or neck sizer. . **$81.00**
Price: Deluxe die set.............. **$190.50**
Price: Deluxe die set with tapered expander.................... **$196.50**
Price: 3-die set **$138.00**
Price: Taper crimp die **$60.00**
Price: Form die.................... **$60.00**
Price: Form & Trim die **$60.00**

REDDING

RIFLE/PISTOL DIES

RIFLE

Caliber	Die Group	Shellholder
17 Rem.	B	10
17 Mach IV	D	10
218 Bee	B	3
219 Zipper	C	2
219 Donaldson Wasp	D	2
22 Hornet	A	14
22 K Hornet	B	14
22 B.R. Rem.	C	1
22 Rem. Jet	D	12
22 Savage H.P.	C	2
220 Swift	A	4
22-250 Rem.	A	1
22-250 Imp. 40	C	1
221 Rem.	A	10
222 Rem.	A	10
222 Rem. Mag.	C	10
223 Rem.	A	10
224 Wea. Mag.	D	12
225 Win.	C	4
5.6x50 R Mag.	CM	12
5.6x57 RWS	CM	1
5.7MM Johnson (22 Spitfire)	CM	22
240 Wea. Mag.	C	1
243 Win.	A	1
243 Win. Imp. 40°	D	1
243 Imp. 30°	CM	1
6mm Rem.	A	1
6mm Rem. Imp. 40°	D	1
6mm TCU	B	10
6mm Wasp	CM	2
6mm BR Rem.	B	1
6mm PPC Rem.	B	12
6mm/223 Rem.	C	10
6mm/284 Win.	C	1
6mmx47(6mm-222 Rem. Mag.)	C	10
25 Rem.	D	5
25-06 Rem.	A	1
25-06 Rem. Imp. 40°	D	1
25-20 Win.	B	3
25-35 Win.	C	2
25/284 Win.	D	1
250 Sav.	A	1
250 Sav. Imp. 40°	D	1
256 Win. Mag.	B	12
257 Roberts	A	1
257 Roberts Imp. 40°	B	1
257 Wea. Mag.	B	6
264 Win. Mag.	A	6
6.5mm BC	CM	1
6.5 Rem. Mag.	D	6
6.5mm TCU	CM	10
6.5mm-06	C	1
6.5mmx50 Japanese	C	4
6.5mmx52 Curano	C	1
6.5mmx54 Mann.	C	24
6.5mmx55 Swed. Mauser	A	1
6.5mmx57 Mauser	D	1
6.5mmx68S	D	19
6.5mm/257 Roberts	CM	1
6.5mm/257Roberts Imp. 40°	CM	1
6.5mm/284 Win.	D	1
6.5mm/300 Wea. Mag.	D	6
270 Win.	A	1
270 Win. Imp. 40°	D	1
270 Wea. Mag.	B	6
270-257 Roberts Imp 40°	CM	1
280 Rem.	A	1
280 Rem. Imp. 40°	C	1
284 Win.	A	1
7mm Rem. Mag.	A	6
7mm B.R. Rem.	B	1
7mm TCU	B	10
7mm INT-R	C	2
7mm IHMSA	C	1
7mm Wea. Mag.	B	6
7mm STW	D	6
7mm-08 Rem.	A	1
7mm-08 Rem. Imp. 40°	D	1
7-30 Waters	B	2
7mmx47(7mm-222 Rem. Mag.)	CM	10
7mmx57 Mauser	A	1
7mmx57 Imp. 40	D	1
7mmx61 Sharp & Hart	D	6
7mmx64 Brenn.	C	1
7mm/300 Wea. Mag.	C	6
7mm-350 Rem. Mag.	CM	6
7.5mm Schmidt Rubin(Swiss)	C	2
7.62x39	A	12
7.62 Russian (7.62x54R)	B	15
30 Herrett	D	2
30 Rem.	D	5
30-06	A	1
30-06 Imp. 40°	C	1
30-20 TC	C	3
30-30 Win.	A	2
30-30 Imp. 40°	D	2
30-40 Krag	A	8
30-338 Win. Mag.	C	6
30-8mm Rem. Mag.(30 Super)	CM	6
300 H&H Mag.	B	6
300 Sav.	C	1
300 Win. Mag.	A	6
300 Wea. Mag.	A	6
303 Sav.	B	21
308 Win./307 Win.	A	1, 2
308 Norma Mag.	B	6
308x1.75	CM	1
7.65mmx53 Mauser(Belgian)	B	1
7.7mmx58 Japanese	C	1
303 British	A	8
32 Win. Spl.	B	2
32 Rem.	C	5
32-40 Win.	B	2
7.92mmx33 Kurz Mauser	D	1
8mm Rem. Mag.	C	6
8mm Lebel	CM	26
8mm-06	D	1
8mm-06 Imp. 40°	D	1
8mmx56 Mann.	D	1
8mmx57 Mauser	A	1
8mmx60S	D	1
8mmx64S Brenn.	D	4
8mmx68S	C	19
8.15x46R	D	2
33 Win.	D	18
338 Win. Mag.	A	6
338-06	C	1
338-06 Imp. 40°	D	1
338/284 Win.	CM	1
340 Wea. Mag.	B	6
348 Win.	C	20
35 Rem.	A	1
35 Win.	C	8
35 Whelen	B	1
35 Whelen Imp. 40°	D	1
350 Rem. Mag.	B	6
357 Herrett	D	2
358 Win./356 Win.	B	1, 2
358 Norma Mag.	B	6
358 STA	CM	6
9mmx56 Mann.	CM	1
9mmx57 Mauser	C	1
9.3mmx62 Mauser	C	1
9mmx74R	D	6
375 H&H Mag.	A	6
375 H&H Mag. Imp. 40°	D	6
375 Wea. Mag.	D	6
378 Wea. Mag.	D	18
416 Rem. Mag.	C	6
416 Wea. Mag.	D	18
460 Wea. Mag.	D	18

PISTOL

Caliber	Die Group	Shellholder
25 ACP (25 Auto)	D	27
270 REN	CM	14
30 M1 Carbine	A	22
30 Luger	C	13
30 Mauser	B	13
32-20 Win./30-20 TC	C	3
32 Short Colt	CM	10
32 Long Colt	CM	10
32 ACP	B	22
32 S&W (Short)	CM	10
32 S&W (Long)	A	10
32 H&R Mag.	A	10
32 S&W/32 H&R Mag.	A	10
32-20 Win.	B	3
38 Super Auto.	B	5
380 Auto.	A	10
9mm Luger	A	13
351 Win. S.L.	D	5
357/44 Bain & Davis	CM	19
38 S&W	D	12
38 Spl.	A	12
357 Mag.	A	12
38 Spl./357 Mag.	A	12
357 Maximum	C	12
40 S&W	B	5
10mm Auto.	B	5
40 S&W/10mm Auto.	B	5
38-40 Win.	C	9
375 Win.	B	2
38-55 Win. & Ballard	C	2
38-56 Win.	D	18
41 Long Colt	C	1
40-65 Win.	D	18
40-82 Win.	D	18
401 Win. S.L.	D	2
405 Win.	D	8
41 Mag.	A	21
41 Action Exp.	D	13
44 Russian	C	19
44 Special	A	19
44 Mag.	A	19
44 Spl./44 Mag.	A	19
44-40 Win.	A	9
444 Marlin	B	19
45 ACP & AR	A	1, 17
45 Win. Mag.	D	7
45 Colt	A	23
455 Webley	C	6
45-70 U.S. Gov't	B	18
45-90 Win.	D	18
458 Win. Mag.	B	6

Form & Trim Dies

Made to chamber dimensions to eliminate resizing when file trimming. Pistol trim dies require extended shellholder. From Redding Reloading Equipment.

Price: Series A **$28.50**
Price: Series B **$38.40**
Price: Series C **$44.40**
Price: Series D **$52.50**

Neck Sizing Die

Designed for bottleneck cases to neck size only. Available individually or come standard in Deluxe die set. From Redding Reloading Equipment.

Price: Series A **$33.00**
Price: Series B **$44.40**
Price: Series C **$54.00**
Price: Series D **$61.50**

REDDING

Taper Crimp Dies

For handgun cartridges that headspace on case mouth and conventional roll crimp is undesirable. Also available for some revolver cartridges. Rifle calibers include: 223 Remington, 7.62x39, 30-30, 308 Winchester and 30-06. From Redding Reloading Equipment.

Price: Series A **$26.40**
Price: Series B **$31.80**
Price: Series C **$36.60**
Price: Series D **$41.40**

Pistol/Rifle Steel Dies

Two- and three-die sets carefully machined to close and uniform tolerances and finish machined on precision lathes. All die parts made of high-grade steel alloy. Knurled outside surface allows hand adjustments. Standard (2-die) and Deluxe (3-die) sets are for bottleneck cases, the Deluxe set containing a separate neck size die. Three-die sets are for straight wall cases and include an expander die. Series A dies are pistol and rifle die sets for most popular calibers; Series B, die sets for slightly less popular calibers; Series C, popular wildcats and less popular rifle/pistol calibers; Series D, represent obsolete calibers and wildcats. Redding will also manufacture custom dies upon request. From Redding Reloading Equipment.
Pistol/rifle 2-Die Prices

Price: .... **See Charts**

Profile Crimp Die

For handgun cartridges that do not headspace on case mouth. Provides tighter more uniform roll-type crimp. From Redding Reloading Equipment.

Price: **$26.40**

Titanium Carbide/Pro Series Pistol Dies

No-lube standard three-die set available also in Pro Series for progressive reloading presses. Pro Series bullet seating die designed for bullet seating only with no crimping. A Profile crimp die is supplied for final crimp except for cartridges that headspace on the case mouth. For these a taper crimp die is substituted. All Pro Series dies have large radius at mouth for easy case entry. From Redding Reloading Equipment.

Price: Titanium carbide die set **$93.00**
Price: Titanium sizer die **$63.00**
Price: Pro Series die set **$120.00**
Price: 9mm, either set add.......... **$12.00**

PONSNESS/WARREN

Bullet Seating Die

Die body threaded 7/8-14 to fit all presses. Uses retaining sleeve to seat bullets precisely. Sleeves available in diameters .224" through .358 to handle calibers 22 through 35. From Ponsness/Warren.

Price: Die body **$32.95**
Price: Sleeve.............. **$14.95 to 21.95**

SCOTT

Benchrest Dies

Precision-made titanium nitride full-length resize dies for the benchrest shooter. Come in 6mm PPC or 6mm-22 BR calibers. From Dwight Scott.

Price: **$125.00**

STAR

Carbide Pistol Dies

Precision machined four and five carbide die sets threaded 11/16-24 to fit the Universal Star press. Available in most popular calibers. One set standard with press. From Star Machine Works.

Price: **$31.50**

WILSON

Full-Length Sizing Die

Designed for use on heavy-duty arbor press. Non-adjustable, straight-line die for reforming and resizing cases which have been fired numerous times. Available in most hunting and benchrest calibers. From Sinclair International, Inc.

Price: **$19.95**

Neck Sizing Die

Precision hand die used with either small mallet or arbor press to control and/or change incrementally cartridge case neck reduction through a series of interchangeable bushings. Bushings available in increments of .001", from .236" through .343". All neck dies size neck to 3/16" from mouth end. Available with or without one bushing. From L.E. Wilson, Inc.

Price: With bushing **$62.50**
Price: Without bushing **$50.00**
Price: Bushing **$12.50**

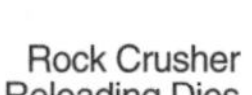
Rock Crusher Reloading Dies

Ponsness/Warren Bullet Seating Die

METALLIC DIES/PISTOL & RIFLE

ALEX

Stuck Case Extractor

Removes stuck cases separated above the case head from reloading dies. One extractor will work on nearly all cartridges of the same caliber. Available in calibers 22, 6mm (243), 25, 7mm (270), 30, 338, 35, 375, 44. From Alex, Inc.

Price: **$18.00**

C-H/4-D

Die Boxes

Plastic see-through boxes for die storage. Available in two sizes: 5x4$\frac{1}{4}$x1$\frac{1}{2}$ or 6x4$\frac{1}{4}$x1$\frac{1}{2}$. From C-H Tool & Die/4-D Custom Die.

Price: Small. . . . . **$.99**
Price: Large. **$2.00**

Die Wrench

Tightens 1-1$\frac{1}{8}$≤ die hex lock ring on any progressive loading press. From C-H Tool & Die/4-D Custom Die.

Price: **$7.95**

Lock Ring

Solid steel lock ring with nylon ball lock for ease of loosening. Fits all makes of dies with $\frac{7}{8}$-14 threads. From C-H Tool & Die/4-D Custom Die.

Price: $\frac{7}{8}$" **$2.25**
Price: 1$\frac{1}{2}$x12" **$6.00**
Price: $\frac{1}{2}$x20" **$1.25**
Price: $\frac{9}{16}$x18" **$1.35**
Price: $\frac{5}{8}$x18" **$1.45**
Price: $\frac{3}{4}$x16" **$1.55**
Price: 1x14" **$5.00**
Price: 1$\frac{1}{4}$x14" **$6.00**

Stuck Case Puller

Removes stuck cases from sizing dies. From C-H Tool & Die/4-D Custom Die.

Price: **$7.65**

Titanium Nitride Expander Ball

Coated expander ball eliminates need for case neck lubrication. Available in 22, 243/6mm, 270, 284/7mm, 308 and 323/8mm. 7mm and larger have 10-32 inside threads; others have 8-32 threads. Also fits RCBS, Redding, Hornady dies. From C-H Tool & Die/4-D Custom Die.

Price: **$8.95**

FORSTER

Lock Ring

Cross-bolt design for easy tightening and loosening with a screwdriver. From Forster Products.

Price: **$3.60**

Stuck Case Remover

Works on any sizing die and will extract cases which have the decap rod and expander ball stuck in die. Includes two extractor nuts, two punch rods and washer to protect top of die. From Forster Products.

Price: **$18.30**

HORNADY

Die Wrench

Fits flats on New Dimension die spindle assembly, lock rings and die body. From Hornady Mfg. Co.

Price: **$5.00**

Lock-N-Load Bushings

Bushings threaded $\frac{7}{8}$x14 for Hornady Classic and AP Lock-N-Load presses or conversion bushing for use with other brands of reloading presses. From Hornady Mfg. Co.

Price: 2 pack **$8.95**
Price: 3 pack **$12.95**
Price: Press conversion bushing **$10.95**

MicroJust Seating Stem

Incremented in .001≤ for precision bullet seating depth. Replaces standard seating depth adjustment stem of any New Dimension seating die. From Hornady Mfg. Co.

Price: **$14.95**

RCBS-Type Carbide Expander

Designed to fit RCBS dies. Includes carbide expander, elliptical expander, spindle, deprime pin and collar lock. Weight: 1 lb. From Hornady Mfg. Co.

Price: **$23.00**

Stuck Case Remover

Consists of #7 drill and $\frac{1}{4}$≤-20 tap and remover body that fits shellholder on any standard press. Weight: $\frac{1}{4}$-lb. From Hornady Mfg. Co.

Price: **$13.65**

Sure-Loc Lock Rings

Solid steel rings threaded $\frac{7}{8}$-14 lock solid without touching die threads. Weight: 4 oz. From Hornady Mfg. Co.

Price: **$2.49**

LYMAN

New Style $\frac{7}{8}$-14 Hex Nut

Designed for use with the Lyman bench wrench. From Lyman Products Corporation.

Price: **$2.25**

$\frac{7}{8}$-14 Adapter

Used to mount small diameter 310 and obsolete Tru-Line dies to modern presses. From Lyman Products Corporation.

Price: **$5.75**

AA Die Boxes

Tough plastic box for individual dies with snap lock hinged cover. Also available to hold two- or three-die die sets. From Lyman Products Corporation.

Price: **$2.00**
Price: **$2.50**

Die Rack Organizer

Plastic rack that holds four die sets with shellholder and unloaded cartridge for checking overall length. From Lyman Products Corporation.

Price: **$8.75**

Hex Nuts

Heavy-duty die check nut. Must be used with other brands of standard threaded dies when used in Spar-T press. From Lyman Products Corporation.

Price: **$2.00**

Split-Lock Ring

Steel split ring fits all standard threaded dies. From Lyman Products Corporation.

Price: **$2.50**

MARMIK

50 BMG Stuck Case Remover

Steel fixture to remove stuck cases from resizing die and used in combination with drill bit, tap and cap screw. From MarMik, Inc.

Price: **$4.00**

50 BMG Steel Polishing Plug

Case-shaped plug to polish and/or enlarge interior of 50 BMG die bodies. From MarMik, Inc.

Price: **$5.00**

MTM

Multiple Set Die Box

Holds four rifle or pistol die sets with space provided for shellholders and last round loaded with each set of dies. Label on inside of box lid. From MTM Moulded Products Company.

Price: **$10.20**

RCBS

Die Storage Box

Thick plastic box with built-in cradle to hold from one to three dies. From RCBS.

Price: **$3.63**

Die Wrench

Heat-treated steel construction die wrench with pivoting handle. From RCBS.

Price: **$3.00**

Stuck Case Remover

Williams-type tool removes stuck cases from sizing dies. Case head is drilled and tapped, stuck case remover placed over die and hex head screw is turned with wrench until case is freed. Comes with drill, tap and wrench. From RCBS.

Price: **$13.25**

Stuck Case Remover-2 Kit

Extracts cases from dies with removable guide bushings or dies with raised expander ball. Kit contains two extractor nuts and two punch rods. From RCBS.

Price: **$5.38**

REDDING

Carbide Size Button Kit

Upgrade die sets with carbide size button kit. Available for bottleneck cartridges 22- through 30-caliber. Die button free floating on decap rod allowing it to self-center in case neck. Includes: carbide size button, retainer and spare decapping pin. From Redding Reloading Equipment.

Price: **$21.00**

Die Spacer Kit

For use with combination die sets and reloading dies to compensate for case length or make no-crimp adjustment without removing lock ring. Kit includes three spacers: .062≤ for no-crimp or partial resizing; .125≤, 44 Spl./44 Magnum spacer; .135≤, 38 Spl./357 Magnum spacer. From Redding Reloading Equipment.

Price: **$7.80**

Stuck Case Removal Kit

Williams-type device to drill and tap case head. Place remover over die, turn hex head screw with wrench until case pulls free from size die. From Redding Reloading Equipment.

Price: **$16.50**

Tapered Size Buttons

To expand necks of bottleneck cartridges up to desired size. Available in 6mm, 25, 6.5, 270, 7mm, 30, 8mm, 338, 35 and 375. From Redding Reloading Equipment.

Price: Button only. **$12.00**
Price: Decap rod assembly with tapered button **$16.50**

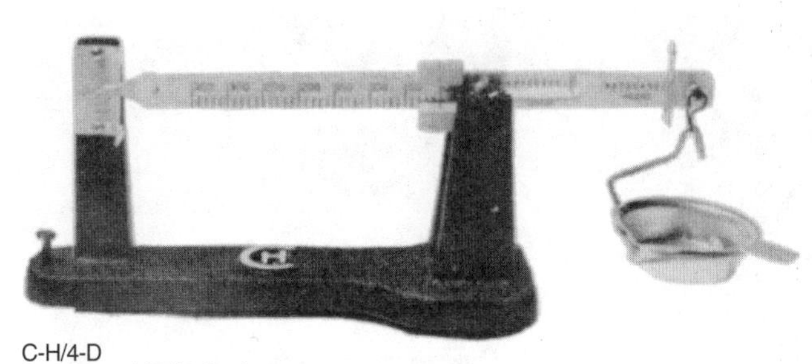
C-H/4-D
Powder and Bullet Scale

Dillon D-Terminator

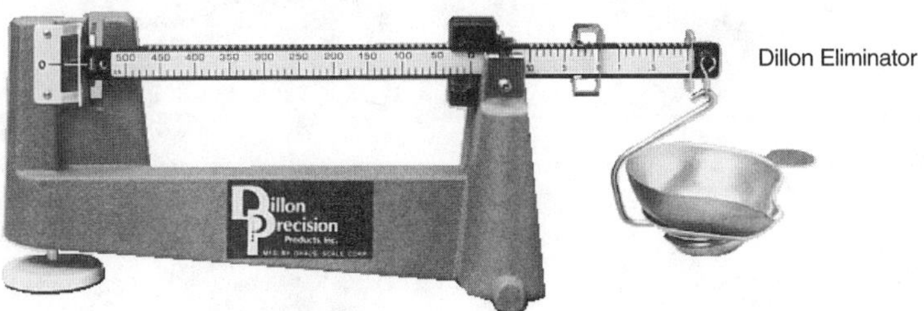
Dillon Eliminator

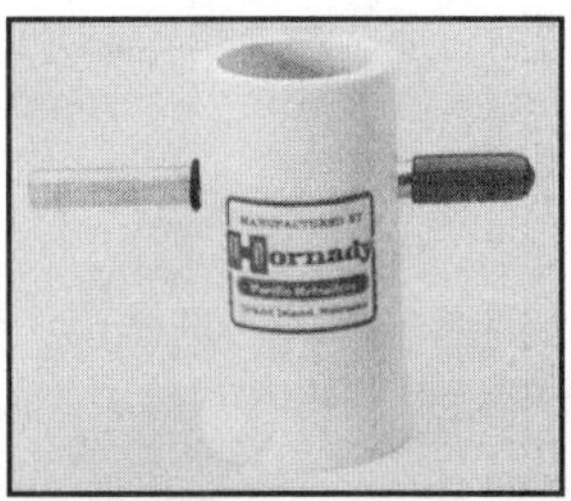
Hornady Powder Trickler

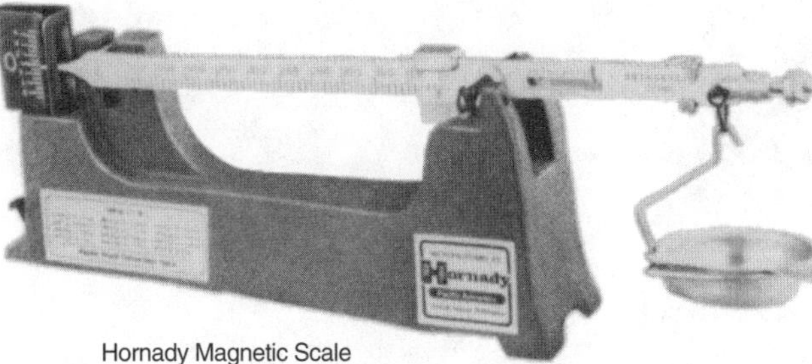
Hornady Magnetic Scale

C-H/4-D

Powder and Bullet Scale
All metal powder and bullet scale. Features magnetic damping, 510-gr. capacity and beam graduated in 10-grain, 1-grain and .1-grain increments; leveling screw on base. From C-H Tool & Die/4-D Custom Die.
Price: **$54.45**

Powder Dripper
Features extra large base with insert for weighting with shot or bullets for extra stability; knurled knob. From C-H Tool & Die/4-D Custom Die.
Price: **$7.25**

DENVER INSTRUMENT

Apex 402
Electronic scale with 1500-grain capacity and precision weighing to +/-0.1-grain. Response time of 2 seconds. Full range TARE function and flourescent display. Made of cast aluminum. Optional battery pack allows portability. Weight: 12 lbs. From Denver Instrument Co.
Price: **$555.00**

DILLON

D-Terminator Scale
Electronic scale accurate to within 0.1-grain/0.01-grain. Features 1500-grain/9.5-gram capacity and large LCD readout. Uses one 9-volt battery and comes with AC adaptor. From Dillon Precision Products, Inc.
Price: **$119.95**

Eliminator Scale
Accurate to 0.1-grain and employs triple-poise balance beam with magnetic damping. From Dillon Precision Products, Inc.
Price: **$48.95**

FORSTER

"Big Red" Powder Trickler
Two-piece construction trickler with ballast for additional stability. From Forster Products.
Price: **$14.20**

HORNADY

Magnetic Scale
Two models available, one to weigh in grains (Model M), the other in grams (Model G). Features magnetic damping; 1/10-grain accuracy; 510-grain capacity; conversion table for grains to ounces. Weight: 3 lbs. From Hornady Mfg. Co.
Price: **$57.95**
Price: With trickler................ **$66.90**

Powder Trickler
Features large-capacity plastic reservoir with lead counterweight to prevent tipping, brass tube and cushioned knob. Weight: 1/2-lb. From Hornady Mfg. Co.
Price: **$8.95**

Scale Plus Kit
Includes Hornady magnetic scale, powder trickler and powder funnel. Weight: 33/4 lbs. From Hornady Mfg. Co.
Price: **$70.11**

LEE

Safety Scale
Features 110-grain capacity; magnetically dampened approach to weight; razor blade pivot for sensitivity; sensitive and readable to 1/20-grain; tough phenolic resin beam. From Lee Precision, Inc.
Price: **$29.98**

LYMAN

Autoscale
Electronic powder scale that uses optoelectronics to sense the position of the balance arm, eliminating friction-caused weighing errors. Powder is dispensed through two barrels. High-speed barrel controls rapid feeding up to 10 grains per second; final load is controlled by the slow barrel with accuracy to +1/20-grain. 9-volt transformer fits any household outlet. Designed for large grain rifle powder only. From Lyman Products Corporation.
Price:110V. **$274.95**
Price: 220V **$285.00**

Electronic Scale Carry Case
Moulded carry case for storing or transporting. Separate compartments for adaptor, powder pan and calibration weight. From Lyman Products Corporation.
Price:. **$22.00**

Conversion Chart
Conversion Chart: Ounces to grains chart. Adhesive backing, mounts anywhere.
Price:. **$2.40**

LE-300 Electronic Scale
Offers 300-grain weight capacity. Converts to metric gram mode. Small and compact. From Lyman Products Corporation.
Price:. **$166.50**

LE-500 Electronic Scale
Features 650-grain working capacity; auto-touch calibration; accuracy to .1 grain; grain or gram readout; compact size, 31/2 x 53/8=. Comes with powder pan, four AAA batteries and storage/carry case. From Lyman Products Corporation.
Price:. **$183.25**

LE-1000 Electronic Scale
Offers 1,000-grain weight capacity with digital display. Converts to metric (gram) mode. Compact frame for storability and transportability. Powered by AC power adaptor or 9-volt battery. Calibration weight and dust cover included along with power adaptor. Optional carrying case available. 220-volt version for same price. From Lyman Products Corporation.
Price:. **$259.95**

Model 500 Powder Scale
Provides 505-grain capacity and accuracy to 1/10-grain. Features positive pan positioning and magnetic damping. Also available in 32-gram capacity metric model. Dust cover and conversion chart available separately. Weight: 2 lbs. From Lyman Products Corporation.
Price:. **$67.95**

Model 1000 Scale
Large capacity scale holds up to 1,005 grains and is accurate to 1/10-grain. Features magnetic damping, precision ground knife edge on agate bearings and positive pan positioning. Comes with conversion table and dust cover. From Lyman Products Corporation.
Price:. **$99.95**

Powder Dribbler
Features large powder reservoir and tip-free base. From Lyman Products Corporation.
Price:. **$10.50**

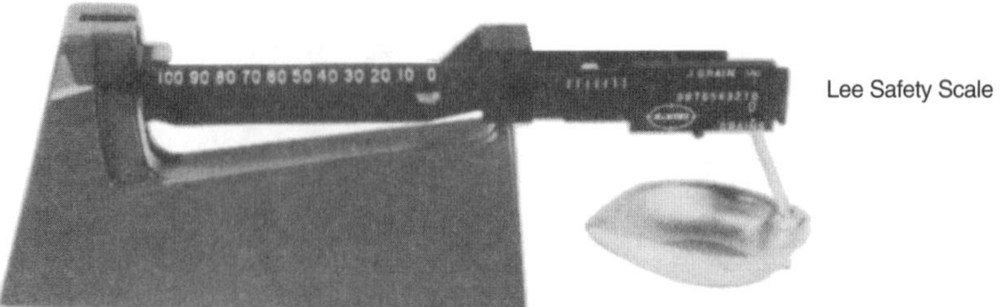

Lee Safety Scale

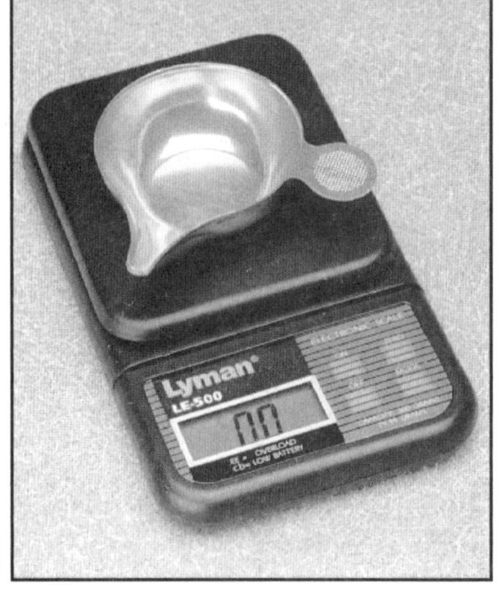

Lyman LE-500 Scale

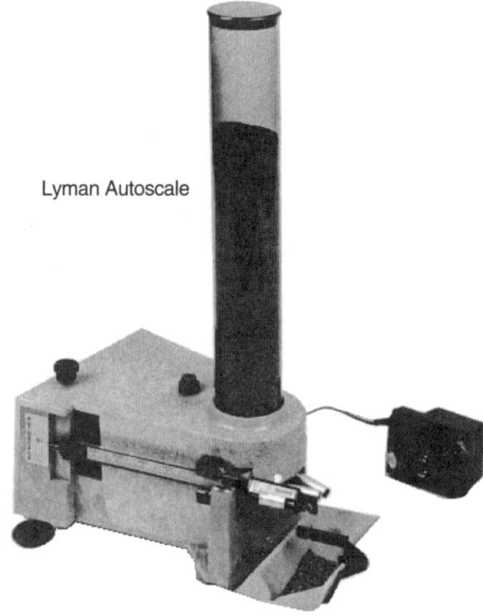
Lyman Autoscale

Lyman LE-1000 Electronic Scale

Lyman LE-300

Pro 500
Features high impact styrene base with built-in compartment for storage of check weights; large leveling wheel; large damper for fast zeroing; improved scale pan platform; 505-gr. capacity; accuracy to 1/10-grain. Weight: 12 oz. From Lyman Products Corporation.
Price: **$44.95**
Price: Metric **$47.50**

Pro 1000
Features high impact styrene base with built-in compartment for counter weight; large leveling wheel; large damper for fast zeroing; improved scale pan platform; 1005-gr. capacity; accuracy to 1/10-grain. Weight: 1 lb. From Lyman Products Corporation.
Price: **$62.50**

Scale Weight Check Set
To check scale accuracy. Deluxe 10-piece set has 210.5 grains total weight. Shooters weight set totals 60.5 grains. From Lyman Products Corporation.
Price: Deluxe set. **$31.00**
Price: Shooters set **$22.50**

PACT

BBK Scale
Features 750-grain, 50-gram capacity for powder or bullet weighing; accuracy to .1-grain to 300 grains, .2-grain from 300 to 750 grains. Includes two precision check weights, powder pan and one 9-volt battery. From PACT.
Price: **$89.99**
Price: Carry case. **$16.95**

Electronic Scale
Features 750-grain/50-gram working capacity; auto-touch calibration; accuracy to .1-grain up to 300 grains, .2-grain from 300 to 750 grains. Comes with powder pan, one 9-volt battery and two precision check weights. From Midway Arms, Inc.
Price: **$89.99**

Digital Precision Powder Dispenser
Delivers exact powder charges to PACT digital scale with simple keyboard charge entry. Infrared data port allows communications between dispenser and scale for exact calibration. From PACT.
Price: **$149.95**

Digital Scale
Features 1500-gr. or 100-gram capacity for powder or bullet weighing; accuracy to .1-gr.; automatic error detection software; large LCD readout. Comes with two precision calibration weights and AC adapter. Now available with infra-red data port to allow printing data and to drive a new Electronic Trickler. From PACT.
Price: Deluxe set. **$149.99**
Price: Powder pan. **$3.99**
Price: Storage case **$16.99**
Price: Infra-Red Data Port. **$25.00**

RCBS

5-0-2 Scale
505-grain capacity single-beam scale with die cast metal base. Features two-poise design: large poise reads up to 500 grains in 5-grain increments; the small poise to 5 grains in 0.1-grain increments. Magnetic damping system works on force-field principle so beam stops with minimal pointer swing. Weight: 11/2 lbs. From RCBS.
Price: **$65.95**
Price: Scale cover **$6.95**

5-0-5 Powder Scale
The 5-0-5 features a three-poise system. Calibrations on left side of beam are in 10-grain increments; two poises on right side adjust in 1- and 0.1-grain increments. Scale is magnetically damped; self-aligning agate bearings support hardened steel beam pivots with a guaranteed sensitivity of 1/10-grain. Capacity is 511 grains. Ounce-to-grain conversion table on the base for shotgun reloaders. Available in metric. Weight: 11/2 lbs. From RCBS.
Price: **$88.95**
Price: Scale cover **$6.95**

10-10 Powder Scale
Features a lockable micrometer poise for settings of 0.1 to 10 grains; approach-to-weight system to help avoid overloads; magnetic damping; non-stick/non-spill aluminum pan; self-aligning agate bearings; hardened steel pivot knives and plastic cover. Capacity is 1,010 grains. Attachment weight is included. From RCBS.
Price: **$140.95**

Partner Digital Scale
Compact, lightweight design featuring 750-grain capacity; 0.1-grain accuracy from 0-350 grains, 0.2-grain from 350-750 grains; four-digit LED readout; measures in grams or grains. Comes with 9-volt battery. From RCBS.
Price: **$168.95**

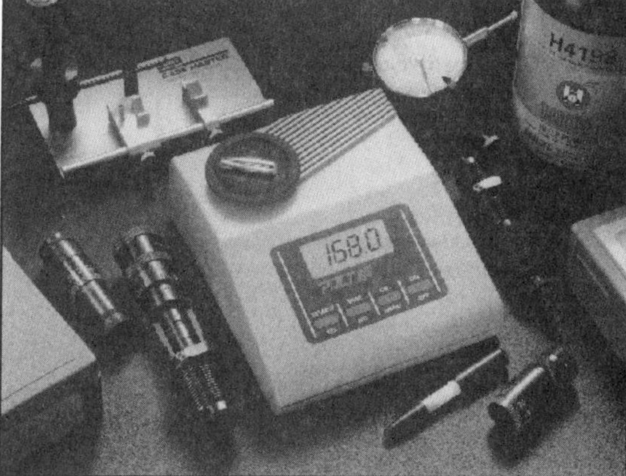

PACT Digital Scale

RCBS Model 5-0-2

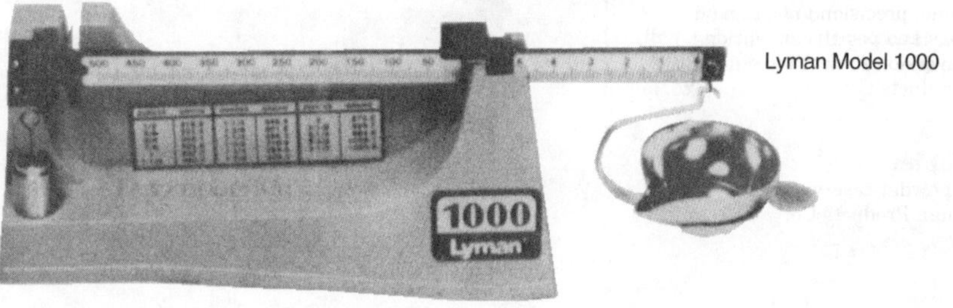

Lyman Model 1000

Section 1: Metallic Cartridges

PowderMaster Electronic Powder Dispenser
Features wireless infrared data transfer system to calibrate trickler with RCBS Powder Pro digital scale; rubber push-button charge weight data entry; dual feed augers; accuracy to 0.1-grain; clear plastic powder reservoir; special hopper design to eliminate static and powder bridging. From RCBS.
Price: **$251.95**

Powder Pro Electronic Digital Scale
Four digit LCD readout scale that features weight readout in .1-gr. increments up to 999.9 grains and in 1-gr. increments from 1000 to 1500 grs. Measures in grams or grains; pushbutton automatic zeroing. Compact design with recessed platform designed to accommodate trickler. Comes with scale pan, two calabration weights and AC transformer.
Price: 110 . . . . **$234.95**
Price: 220 . . . . **$241.95**

Powder Trickler
All-metal trickler with knurled plastic knob. Wide base to prevent tipping. From RCBS.
Price: **$12.95**

Scale Check Weights
For testing the accuracy of scale read-outs. Comes as standard set of 60.5 grains for powder charges (2x20, 1x10, 1x5, 2x2, 1x1 and 1x.5); or deluxe set of 510.5 grains for bullets, cases and powder (1x200, 2x100, 1x50, 2x20, 1x10, 1x5, 2x2, 1x1, 1x.5, 1 forceps). From RCBS.
Price: Standard. **$26.95**
Price: Deluxe. **$45.95**

REDDING

Model No. 2 Powder/Bullet Scale
Features magnetic dampened beam swing; hardened and ground knife edges that ride in milled stainless steel bearing seats; 505-grain capacity; accuracy to 1/10-grain; pour spout pan; two counterpoise system; 1/10-grain over/under graduations. From Redding Reloading Equipment.
Price: **$84.00**

No. 5 Powder Trickler
Solid all-metal trickler with metal tube and knurled knob. Features low center of gravity for stability. Weight: 1-lb. From Redding Reloading Equipment.
Price: **$22.50**

Model No. RS-1 Powder/Bullet Scale
Two counterpoise system with 1/10-grain over/under graduations and sensitive to less than 1/20-grain. Capacity for 380 grains and comes with pour spout pan. From Redding Reloading Equipment.
Price: **$55.50**

VIBRASHINE

Electric Powder Trickler
Features clear dispensing tube; push button switch; adjustable height and position on dispensing tube. Handles all conventional ball, stick or flake powders. From VibraShine, Inc.
Price: **$24.95**

RCBS Powder Pro

RCBS PowderMaster

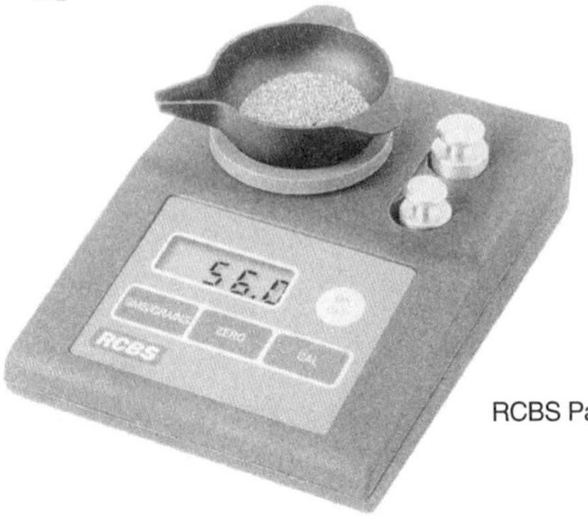

RCBS Partner

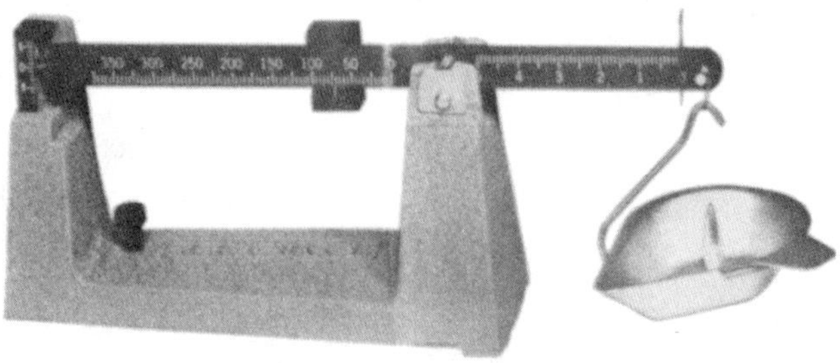

Redding Model No. RS-1

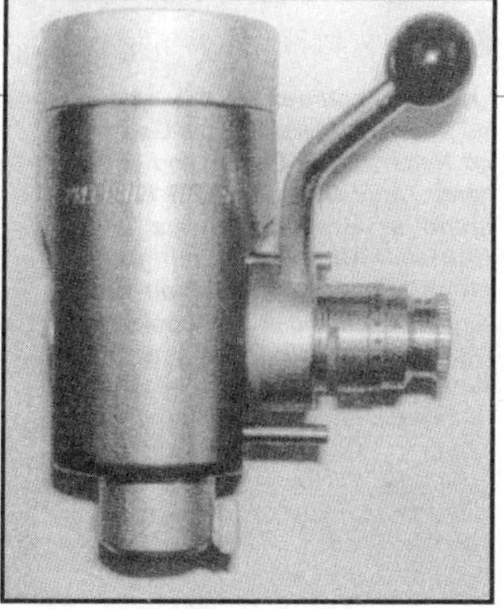
Bruno Powder Measure

BONANZA

Bench Rest Powder Measure

Features high carbon precision cast body and charge arm. Working surfaces designed to automatically compensate for dimensional changes due to wear. Powder is metered from the charge arm to minimize charge variation and powder shearing. Throws charges of $2^1/_2$ grains Bullseye to 95 grains 4320 without use of extra drums. Vernier scale located on charge arm permits minute changes in capacity. Small outlet in hopper serves as built-in baffle, and hopper cover can serve as primer turner. Two drop tubes for large and small capacity cases supplied with measure. Powder removal from hopper is done directly through charge arm into powder container. Mounts to bench or can be used with measure stand. Long drop tube also available. Weight: $3^1/_2$ lbs. From Forster Products.

Price: **$107.00**
Price: Measure stand **$23.40**
Price: Long drop tube **$16.50**

Bulls-Eye Pistol Powder Measure

Machined steel body with hard brass fixed-charge rotors. Rotors drilled to measure Hercules Bullseye powder in set grain weights (2.5, 2.7, 3.0, 3.5, 4.0, 4.5, 5.0, 5.3, 5.5, 6.0, 6.5, 7.0, 7.5, 8.4). Blank rotors with pre-drilled pilot hole available for customer alteration. Comes with quick detachable bracket for use on bench or as hand-held charger. Rotor not included. Weight: $1^1/_2$ lbs. From Forster Products.

Price: **$27.70**
Price: Rotor **$10.00**

BRUNO

Powder Measure

Made on CNC equipment; features body of non-magnetic stainless steel with bearing and bronze inserts. Culver-type clicks. Precision machined to exacting tolerances. Powder measure comes complete with pill bottles, adapter and drop tube. From Bruno Shooters Supply.

Price: **$279.99**

Harrell's "Culver" Type Powder Measure

Harrell's Schuetzen Pistol Measure

C-H/4-D

#502 Micrometer Measure

Aluminium cast non-sparking body; polished steel drum designed for right- or left-hand use; front or back micrometer positioning; up or down stroke powder charge drop. Powder hopper holds approximately $^1/_2$-lb. powder; optional 10≤ production hopper holds one pound. Micrometer adjusts up to 25 grains for more dense pistol powders and up to 100 grains for rifle. Base threaded $^7/_8$-14 to fit any standard press or stand. Also available as pistol/rifle combo. From C-H Tool & Die/4-D Custom Die.

Price: **$58.85**
Price: Combo, pistol/rifle **$75.85**
Price: 10" production hopper **$7.15**
Price: Micrometer **$17.55**

Pushbutton Powder Measure

Can be used with any single-station or turret press. Bells and expands case as it dispenses. Seventeen bushings available for over 215 powder/load combinations. Comes with or without hollow expander. Powder bushing not included. From C-H Tool & Die/4-D Custom Die.

Price: With expander **$43.45**
Price: Bushing. **$3.30**

HARRELL'S

"Culver" Type Measure

Precision hand-tooled measure made to exacting tolerances. From Harrell's Precision.

Price: **$200.00**
Price: Bottles. **$5.00**
Price: Extra drop tubes. **$3.00**

Schuetzen Pistol Measure

Designed specifically for throwing small charges from 2 to 25 grains. Each click is .03-grain. From Harrell's Precision.

Price: **$200.00**

C-H/4-D AUTO CHAMP & 444-X PUSHBUTTON POWDER MEASURE BUSHING CHART

Bushing	Bullseye	Red Dot	700X	Unique	2400	4227	Herco	H-110	230	630	4756	296	7625	231	HP38
1	2.4	NR	0.9	NR	NR	NR	NR	NR	2.1	4.2	NR	NR	NR	3.2	2.7
2	2.6	NR	1.0	NR	NR	NR	NR	4.0	2.6	4.5	NR	NR	NR	3.5	3.1
3	2.7	1.0	1.1	NR	4.0	NR	NR	4.5	2.9	4.6	NR	NR	NR	3.6	3.2
4	3.0	1.2	1.2	NR	4.4	NR	NR	5.1	3.1	5.0	NR	NR	NR	3.8	NR
5	3.5	1.5	1.5	NR	4.8	NR	NR	5.5	3.6	5.5	3.0	NR	3.2	4.1	3.4
6	3.8	1.8	2.4	NR	5.1	NR	NR	6.0	3.9	5.9	3.3	NR	3.7	4.4	4.0
7	5.0	3.0	3.5	4.0	6.6	6.6	4.2	7.8	5.1	7.8	4.5	NR	4.6	5.4	NR
8	5.9	4.2	4.9	5.5	8.6	8.5	5.4	10.2	6.5	10.2	5.9	10.0	6.3	7.0	NR
9	7.0	5.0	6.2	6.7	10.5	10.2	6.7	12.2	8.0	12.0	7.0	12.0	7.2	8.4	NR
10	8.2	6.2	7.0	.7.8	12.5	12.3	7.8	14.2	9.7	14.2	8.1	14.0	8.7	10.0	NR
11	9.3	6.7	7.7	8.9	14.0	13.6	9.0	16.2	11.0	16.3	9.1	15.9	9.8	11.5	NR
12	10.8	7.9	9.0	10.3	16.7	15.6	10.0	18.7	NR	18.7	10.4	18.5	11.4	13.3	NR
13	11.5	8.5	10.0	11.0	17.5	17.0	11.0	20.0	NR	20.0	11.1	19.7	12.0	NR	NR
14	12.3	9.3	10.5	11.7	18.9	18.3	11.9	NR	NR	22.0	12.0	21.3	13.0	NR	NR
15	NR	10.0	11.8	12.7	21.5	20.7	13.5	24.5	NR	24.5	13.8	24.2	14.7	NR	NR
16	NR	10.7	12.5	14.0	22.5	22.1	14.2	26.1	NR	26.3	14.7	25.5	15.6	NR	NR
17	NR	12.9	15.0	16.7	27.2	26.3	16.6	NR	NR	31.0	17.3	30.3	18.5	NR	NR
No Bushing	NR	14.9	18.0	20.5	32.5	31.7	20.9	NR	NR	37.7	21.3	37.0	22.6	NR	NR

C-H/4-D #502 Micrometer Measure

HART

Drop Tubes for Lyman Measures

Drop tubes 7/32" I.D. for Lyman 12≤, 3≤ and 5≤ measures. Will work with any caliber from 22 to 45. From Robert W. Hart & Son, Inc.

Price: For 12" **$7.47**
Price: For 3" **$6.83**
Price: For 5" **$7.30**

Pill Bottle Adaptor

Adaptor for Redding or Lyman powder measures to allow use of Hodgdon powder bottle or Libby pill bottle as powder reservoir. From Robert W. Hart & Son, Inc.

Price: For 5". **$19.95**

HOLLYWOOD

50-Caliber Powder Measure

Identical to standard measure except for enlarged drum hole to throw 240-280 grains powder. Features 23≤ transparent cylinder; 2 1/8" adapter for 3 1/2" cylinder; one 50-caliber drop tube and cylinder cover. Threaded 7/8-14 for use in standard presses; spanner lock nut allows attachment to tool head. Comes with one 50-caliber drop tube. From Hollywood Engineering.

Price: **$275.00**

Standard Powder Measure

Ductile iron body with ground, hardened steel drum. Adjustable from 2 1/2 grains Bullseye to 93 grains 4350. Disc baffle assures constant powder pressure on metering chamber. Hard-coated conical bearing surfaces for precise cutoff. Threaded 7/8-14 to fit most presses; large lock-spanner ring secures measure to press. Comes with one drop tube (22-270 or 7mm-45), cylinder cover and powder disk. From Hollywood Engineering.

Price: **$125.00**
Price: Drop tube **$12.00**

HORNADY

Deluxe Powder Measure

Micrometer adjustable measure for rifle or pistol powders. Comes complete with two powder-drop tubes (22-30 cal. and 30-45 cal.), large capacity hopper, bench stand and lock ring. Handle can be mounted for right- or left-hand operation. Standard 7/8-14 threads for mounting on bench stand or press. Weight: 5 lbs. From Hornady Mfg. Co.

Price: **$69.50**
Price: 17-cal. drop tube. **$5.10**
Price: Extra metering assembly. **$15.75**

Pistol Powder Measure

Includes five standard, high-precision, interchangeable bushings, Nos. 7, 8, 9, 11 and 13 for wide load choices. Bushings fit into sliding charge bar. Threaded 7/8-14 for stand or press mounting. Comes complete with stand and lock ring. Weight: 3 lbs. From Hornady Mfg. Co.

Price: **$40.30**
Price: Blank bushing **$4.20**

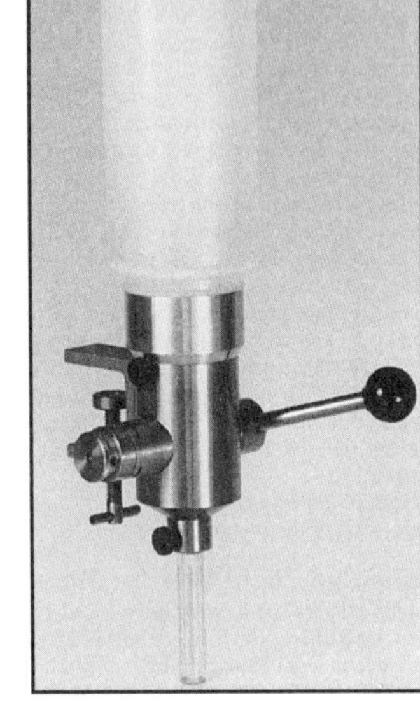

Jones Micro Measure

Hornady Pistol Measure

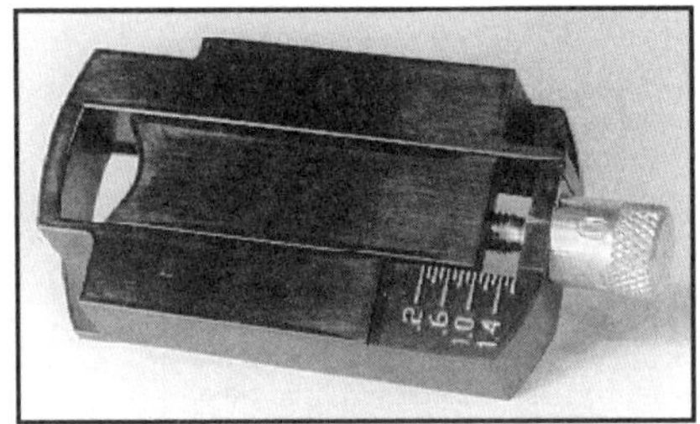

Lee Adjustable Charge Bar

Hornady Pistol Powder Measure Bushing Chart

Bushing	700-X	4227	SR7625	SR4756	PB	Bullseye	2400	Red Dot	Unique	Herco	Blue Dot	HP38	Trap 100	HS5	HS6	HS7	H110	H4227	R1	R123	231	296	680
1	2.0	NA	NA	NA	NA	2.6	NA	1.7	NA	NA	NA	3.0	2.3	4.1	3.9	4.0	4.2	3.6	1.9	NA	3.0	NA	NA
2	2.1	NA	NA	NA	NA	2.8	NA	1.8	NA	NA	NA	3.2	2.5	4.5	4.2	4.4	4.5	3.9	2.0	NA	3.3	NA	NA
3	2.3	NA	NA	NA	NA	3.4	NA	2.4	3.4	NA	NA	4.0	3.1	5.6	5.2	5.5	5.6	4.9	2.6	NA	4.1	NA	NA
4	2.7	NA	NA	NA	NA	3.4	NA	2.4	3.4	NA	NA	4.3	3.4	6.1	5.8	6.0	6.1	5.3	2.9	NA	4.5	NA	NA
5	2.9	NA	3.1	NA	2.9	3.7	NA	2.6	3.6	NA	NA	4.3	3.4	6.1	5.8	6.0	6.1	5.3	2.9	NA	4.5	NA	NA
6	3.0	NA	3.5	NA	3.1	3.9	NA	2.7	3.9	NA	NA	4.5	3.6	6.4	6.0	6.2	6.4	5.5	3.1	NA	4.6	NA	NA
7	3.2	NA	3.6	NA	3.2	4.1	NA	2.8	4.3	3.6	NA	4.8	3.9	6.9	6.3	6.7	6.9	6.0	3.2	NA	4.8	NA	NA
8	3.5	NA	4.1	NA	3.3	4.4	NA	3.2	4.5	3.8	NA	5.0	4.0	7.4	7.0	7.3	7.4	6.5	3.7	NA	5.3	NA	NA
9	3.7	NA	4.2	3.7	3.4	4.5	NA	3.3	4.6	3.9	NA	5.2	4.2	7.7	7.4	7.6	7.7	6.7	3.8	NA	5.5	NA	NA
10	4.0	7.3	5.0	4.5	4.0	5.1	NA	3.6	5.3	4.3	NA	6.1	4.9	8.5	7.9	8.4	8.6	7.5	4.3	NA	6.3	NA	NA
11	4.3	7.5	5.1	4.6	4.6	5.2	7.3	3.7	5.4	4.5	NA	6.4	5.1	8.9	8.2	8.8	9.0	7.7	4.5	NA	6.4	NA	8.8
12	4.6	8.0	5.5	4.8	4.8	NA	7.9	3.9	5.8	4.8	NA	6.8	5.3	9.4	9.0	9.3	9.5	8.2	4.8	NA	6.9	NA	9.5
13	5.0	8.8	6.0	5.6	5.3	NA	8.7	4.4	6.5	5.3	NA	7.6	5.8	10.3	9.7	10.1	10.4	9.0	5.3	NA	7.6	10.3	10.5
14	5.5	9.4	6.4	6.0	5.8	NA	9.3	4.7	6.8	5.7	NA	8.1	6.4	11.1	10.5	11.0	11.1	9.6	5.7	NA	8.1	11.0	11.2
15	5.8	9.9	6.8	6.4	6.0	NA	9.8	4.9	7.2	5.9	NA	8.5	6.7	11.8	11.1	11.6	11.8	10.2	6.0	NA	8.5	11.6	11.9
16	6.1	10.3	7.1	6.7	6.4	NA	10.3	5.2	7.5	6.2	8.9	8.9	7.0	12.4	11.5	12.3	12.4	10.7	NA	NA	8.9	12.2	12.6
17	6.5	11.5	7.9	7.6	7.0	NA	11.4	5.8	8.4	6.8	9.7	9.8	7.7	13.7	12.8	13.5	13.7	11.8	NA	NA	9.9	13.6	13.8
18	NA	12.1	8.1	7.8	7.3	NA	12.0	6.1	8.7	7.3	10.1	10.2	8.0	14.1	13.3	13.9	14.0	12.2	NA	10.1	NA	14.0	14.3
19	NA	12.3	8.6	8.3	7.6	NA	12.7	6.3	9.2	7.7	10.8	10.6	8.4	15.0	13.9	14.6	14.9	12.9	NA	10.8	NA	14.7	15.1
20	NA	13.4	9.1	8.8	8.0	NA	13.4	6.7	9.7	8.1	11.4	11.4	8.8	15.7	14.9	15.6	15.6	13.6	NA	11.5	NA	15.6	16.0
21	NA	14.7	9.9	9.7	8.9	NA	14.7	7.4	10.6	8.7	12.5	12.6	9.7	17.6	16.2	17.1	17.5	15.1	NA	12.5	NA	17.1	17.5
22	NA	15.7	10.4	10.2	9.4	NA	15.5	7.7	11.4	9.5	13.2	13.2	10.4	18.3	17.0	17.7	17.9	15.9	NA	13.2	NA	17.9	18.3

JONES

Custom Products Micro Measure

Tool steel body 100% machined assuring no rough surfaces. Features micrometer-adjustable brass drum with capacity of 16 to 114 grains and click value of approximately .1-grain; cutting edges designed to slice through most difficult of powders; bottle/adaptor assembly allows changing powders by changing bottles; bottom cutout and plug on reservoir makes it possible to return powder to reservoir without removing bottle from adaptor; baffle assures constant volume of powder on measure drum at all times. Can be mounted directly to bench or attached to powder measure stand. Optional 7/8-14 clamp adaptor or adaptor/baffle for Lyman 55 and other measures available. Comes complete with two 3" drop tubes and one powder bottle. Weight: 5 lbs. From Neil Jones Custom Products.

Price: **$279.00**
Price: Adaptor/baffle Lyman 55 . . . . . . **$20.00**
Price: Adaptor/baffle other measures . **$20.00**
Price: Powder bottle **$6.00**
Price: Padded cover. **$20.00**
Price: Drop tubes, 6". **$8.00**
Price: Drop tubes, 3". **$6.00**
Price: 7/8-14 clamp adaptor. **$5.00**

LEE

Adjustable Charge Bar

Adjusts between .28 and 1.6cc. Zero backlash micrometer made of nylon with solid brass. From Lee Precision, Inc.

Price: **$9.98**

Auto-Disk Powder Measure

Fixed-capacity measure. Cast body with polycarbonate see-through hopper. Cartridge case actuates measure while case neck is being flared. Designed for use with Lee powder-through-expanding die. Six-cavity glass-reinforced plastic powder disks. Comes with all four disks for 24 charge weights. From Lee Precision, Inc.

Price: **$27.98**

Auto-Disk Pull Back Lever

For Lee Pro-1000 and Load-Master to eliminate powder binding and reduce chance of missed or double charges. From Lee Precision, Inc.

Price: **$2.98**

Deluxe Auto-Disk Measure

Fixed-capacity measure. Chrome-plated casting with tough polycarbonate hopper and machined metering surfaces. Works best with ball powders. Designed for use with Lee powder-through-expanding die. Comes with all four disks for 24 charge weights. From Lee Precision, Inc.

Price: **$35.98**

Double Disk Kit

Conversion unit designed for standard, deluxe and Safety measures. Allows two disk stacking for fine charge adjustments up or down to .1-grain with different combinations of disks. Complete listing of disk combinations, four extra disks screws and risers included. From Lee Precision, Inc.

Price: **$14.98**

Micro Disk

For Auto-Disk powder measure. Designed to measure small charges below range of standard disks. Six cavities range from 1.1 to 2.5 grains of Bullseye. From Lee Precision, Inc.

Price: **$9.98**

Perfect Powder Measure

Drum-type micro-adjustable measure adaptable to Lee Pro-1000 and Load-Master progressive presses. Features soft elastomer wiper to strike off metering chamber not cut the powder; a self-lubricating nylon cone-shaped drum adjusts to zero clearance; micrometer adjuster in cubic centimeters with O-ring lock; positive powder shutoff for hopper removal or stoppage of flow; tapered drop tube. Charges of from 2 grains to over 100 grains can be thrown. Optional Universal charging die makes measure case-actuated for automation. Adaptors fit most all cartridges. Steel measure stand included. From Lee Precision, Inc.

Price: **$29.98**

Powder Measure Kit

Contains fifteen graduated and proportioned powder dippers. Slide card lists number of grains of every powder type each measure will dispense. From Lee Precision, Inc.

Price: **$8.98**

Lee Perfect Measure

Lee Micro Disk

Pro Auto-Disk

New design with elastomer wiper and teflon-coated metal casting to prevent powder cutting and help eliminate powder leakage. Large capacity hopper with shut-off valve attaches with brass thumb nuts for disk change ease. The swivel adaptor allows die set transfer without rotation of the measure and ensures precise postioning with firm clamps. Comes with adjustable charge bar. From Lee Precision, Inc.

Price: **$45.00**

Pro Disk Update Kit

To update the Lee Auto-Disk to Pro Auto-Disk. Includes oversize hopper and valve assembly with elastomer wiper, swivel adaptor, pullback lever, chain and attachments, solid knurled thumb nuts. From Lee Precision, Inc.

Price: **$19.98**

Safety Disk Powder Measure

Fixed-capacity measure. Lever-operated with built-in powder baffle and see-through drop tube. Includes measure stand, four, six-cavity disks, and mounting screws. From Lee Precision, Inc.

Price: **$27.98**

Swivel Adaptor

Screw attaches to die for transfer of Pro Disk measure between die sets with precise positioning. From Lee Precision, Inc.

Price: **$5.98**

Lee Swivel Adaptor

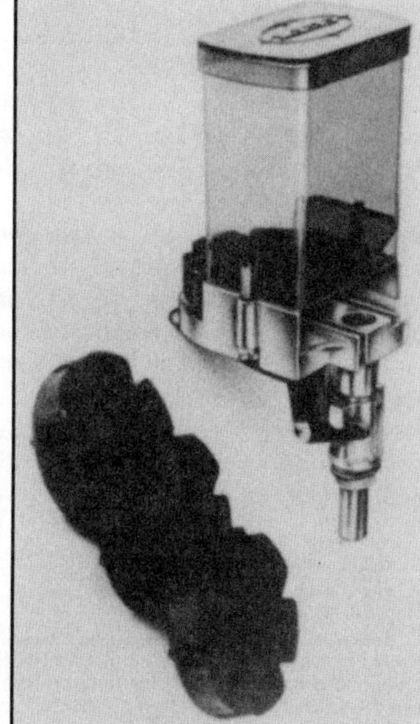

Lee Auto-Disk

Section 1: Metallic Cartridges

LYMAN

AccuMeasure and Rotor Set

Small-capacity measure designed for pistol and small-caliber rifle cases. Features 15 interchangeable brass rotors for over 700 load combinations. Comes with three of the most popular rotors. Additional 12 available separately. From Lyman Products Corporation.

Price . . . . **:$35.00**
Price: 12 additional rotors **$46.00**
Price: Single rotor **$7.25**

No. 55 Powder Measure

Features three-slide micrometer adjustable cavity with extra-fine adjustments of width and depth for consistent charges; 2400-grain capacity reservoir; attached knocker to assure complete charge; bench or press mountable. Includes 7/8-14 thread adapter for press or stand mounting. Optional 7,000-grain reservoir available. Weight: 2 lbs., 10 oz. From Lyman Products Corporation.

Price: **$71.50**
Price: 7,000-grain reservoir **$8.75**

Powder Measure Stand

Bench mountable stand threaded 7/8-14 for any standard threaded powder measure. Weight: 3 lbs., 6 oz. From Lyman Products Corporation.

Price: **$17.95**

RCBS

Little Dandy Pistol Powder Measure

Designed for pistol shooters and small-caliber rifle shooters. Twenty-eight interchangeable, fixed-charge powder rotors available to load up to 400 combinations. No re-adjustment after rotor changeover. Can be used hand-held, bench-mounted or mounted to powder measure stand. From RCBS.

Price: **$27.50**
Price: Powder rotor **$8.00**
Price: Measure cover **$7.13**

Little Dandy Rotor Knob

High-strength aluminum, knurled outer edge knob attaches to Little Dandy rotor with a setscrew. Makes the handle easier to turn. From RCBS.

Price: **$2.75**

Powder Measure Stand

Elevates any powder measure with standard 7/8-14 thread for positioning powder scale pan or case in a loading block under the drop tube. Bolts to loading bench or table. From RCBS.

Price: **$20.63**

Uniflow Powder Measure

Features large capacity 5" acrylic powder hopper, drop tubes for 22- to 45-caliber, precision-ground measuring cylinder surface and honed main casting. Adjustable cylinder for throwing charges from 0.5-grain Bullseye to 110 grains of 4350. Comes with stand plate for bolting to loading bench. 17-caliber drop tube optional. From RCBS.

Price: **$72.50**
Price: 17-cal. drop tube. **$6.13**
Price: Measure cover **$7.13**

Uniflow Powder Baffle

Enhances charge uniformity and consistency with Uniflow powder measure. From RCBS.

Price: **$5.25**

UPM Micrometer Adjustment Screw

Install on the RCBS Uniflow Powder Measure and record precise settings for powder charges. Dial in same number for that charge each time. To install, replace the Uniflow's standard metering screw. Available in large or small size. From RCBS.

Price: **$33.25**

RCBS LITTLE DANDY ROTOR CHARGE TABLE

Rotor #	00		0		01			02		03			04		05		06			07	19	20	21	22	23	24	25	26
11	12		13		14			15		16			17		18						NR	NR	NR	NR	NR	NR	NR	NR
Bullseye	1.7	2.2	2.5	2.7	3.0	3.2	3.5	3.7	4.0	4.5	5.0	5.5	6.0	6.5	7.2	7.8	8.4	9.0	9.7	NR	12.1	NR	NR	NR	NR	NR	NR	NR
231	NR	NR	2.7	3.0	3.3	3.6	3.9	4.2	4.5	5.0	5.6	6.2	6.8	7.2	7.9	8.6	9.3	10.0	10.6	11.3	12.3	NR	NR	NR	NR	NR	NR	NR
HP38	NR	NR	2.8	3.0	3.4	3.6	4.0	4.2	4.5	5.1	5.5	6.2	6.8	7.5	7.9	8.8	9.4	10.3	10.9	11.7	7.8	8.3	8.7	9.1	NR	NR	NR	NR
Red Dot	NR	NR	1.7	1.9	2.2	2.3	2.5	2.6	2.9	3.2	3.6	4.0	4.3	4.7	5.1	5.5	6.0	6.5	6.9	7.4	8.7	9.2	NR	NR	NR	NR	NR	NR
700-X	NR	NR	2.0	2.2	2.4	2.6	2.8	3.0	3.2	3.6	4.0	4.4	4.8	5.1	5.7	6.2	6.8	7.3	7.7	8.2	8.8	8.9	9.6	10.0	10.5	10.7	11.4	NR
Green Dot	NR	NR	1.9	2.1	2.3	2.5	2.8	3.0	3.1	3.5	3.9	4.4	4.8	5.1	5.5	6.1	6.6	7.0	7.5	8.0	10.3	10.9	11.4	12.0	12.4	13.4	13.9	14.5
SR4756	NR	NR	NR	NR	NR	NR	NR	3.5	3.7	4.2	4.7	5.1	5.6	6.2	6.8	7.3	7.9	8.5	9.1	9.7	NR	NR	NR	NR	NR	NR	NR	NR
HS-5	NR	NR	4.2	4.5	5.0	5.3	5.9	6.2	6.6	7.4	8.2	9.0	NR	NR	NR	NR	NR	NR	NR	NR	10.1	10.7	11.3	11.8	12.4	13.1	NR	NR
Unique	NR	NR	2.3	2.5	2.8	3.0	3.3	3.5	3.7	4.2	4.7	5.2	5.7	6.0	6.6	7.2	7.8	8.4	9.0	9.5	NR	NR	NR	NR	NR	NR	NR	NR
SR7625	NR	NR	2.5	2.7	3.0	3.2	3.5	3.8	4.0	4.5	5.0	5.5	6.0	6.5	7.2	7.7	8.3	9.0	9.6	NR	16.7	17.6	NR	NR	NR	NR	NR	NR
HS-6	NR	NR	NR	NR	NR	NR	5.4	5.7	6.1	6.9	7.6	8.4	9.1	10.1	11.0	12.0	13.0	13.9	14.8	15.7	16.8	17.7	18.6	NR	NR	NR	NR	NR
HS-7	NR	NR	NR	NR	NR	4.9	5.4	5.7	6.1	6.8	7.5	8.3	9.1	10.1	11.0	11.9	12.9	13.9	14.8	15.8	9.5	10.1	10.5	11.1	11.7	12.3	13.0	13.6
Herco	NR	NR	NR	NR	NR	NR	3.1	3.3	3.5	4.0	4.4	4.8	5.3	5.7	6.3	6.7	7.3	7.9	8.4	9.0	12.8	13.5	14.2	14.9	15.7	16.6	17.5	18.3
Blue Dot	NR	NR	NR	NR	NR	NR	NR	NR	NR	NR	5.9	6.5	7.1	7.7	8.4	9.1	9.8	10.6	11.3	12.0	17.9	18.8	19.8	20.8	NR	NR	NR	NR
630	NR	NR	NR	NR	5.0	5.3	5.8	6.1	6.5	7.3	8.1	8.9	9.7	10.8	11.7	12.7	13.7	14.8	15.8	16.9	15.4	16.2	17.0	17.9	18.9	19.8	20.8	21.8
2400	NR	NR	NR	NR	NR	NR	NR	NR	NR	NR	7.0	7.7	8.4	9.3	10.2	11.0	11.9	12.8	13.6	14.6	17.6	18.5	19.5	20.5	21.5	22.5	23.7	24.8
H110	NR	NR	NR	NR	NR	NR	NR	NR	NR	NR	NR	8.9	9.7	10.7	11.7	12.6	13.6	14.6	15.6	16.6	18.0	19.0	20.0	21.0	22.1	23.2	24.3	25.5
296	NR	NR	NR	NR	NR	NR	NR	NR	NR	NR	NR	9.1	9.9	10.9	11.9	12.9	13.9	14.9	15.9	17.0	11.5	12.2	12.8	13.5	14.2	15.0	15.8	16.5
SR4759	NR	NR	NR	NR	NR	NR	NR	NR	NR	NR	NR	NR	NR	NR	NR	NR	NR	NR	10.1	10.7	15.1	16.0	16.8	17.6	18.6	19.5	20.5	21.5
IMR 4227	NR	NR	NR	NR	NR	NR	NR	NR	NR	NR	NR	NR	NR	9.1	9.9	10.8	11.6	12.6	13.3	14.3	17.9	18.9	19.9	20.9	21.9	23.1	24.2	25.3
680	NR	NR	NR	NR	NR	NR	NR	NR	NR	NR	8.2	9.1	9.9	10.9	11.9	12.9	13.9	14.9	15.9	16.9	14.4	15.2	16.1	16.8	17.8	18.7	19.6	20.4
IMR 4198	NR	NR	NR	NR	NR	NR	NR	NR	NR	NR	6.5	7.2	7.9	8.5	9.4	10.2	11.0	12.0	12.7	13.5	15.7	16.6	17.4	18.3	19.3	20.3	21.3	22.3
H322	NR	NR	NR	NR	NR	NR	NR	NR	NR	NR	NR	NR	NR	NR	NR	NR	NR	13.0	13.8	14.7	15.9	16.8	17.7	18.5	19.5	20.5	21.6	22.6
Re-7	NR	NR	NR	NR	NR	NR	NR	NR	NR	NR	NR	NR	NR	NR	10.4	11.3	12.2	13.2	14.0	14.9	13.9	15.0	16.0	16.5	16.9	18.3	19.0	19.6
AA-2	NR	NR	3.1	3.3	3.9	4.2	4.6	4.8	5.1	5.6	6.2	6.8	7.6	8.4	9.4	10.0	10.5	11.2	12.1	12.9	17.1	18.0	18.9	19.8	20.8	21.9	23.0	24.3
AA-5	NR	NR	4.0	4.3	4.8	5.1	5.6	5.9	6.3	7.1	7.8	8.6	9.3	10.3	11.3	12.2	13.2	14.2	15.2	16.1	18.0	19.0	20.0	20.9	22.0	23.1	24.3	25.7
AA-7	NR	NR	4.2	4.6	5.1	5.4	6.0	6.3	6.6	7.5	8.3	9.1	9.9	11.0	12.0	13.0	14.0	15.0	16.0	17.0	17.8	18.8	19.8	20.7	21.8	22.9	24.1	25.4
AA-9	NR	NR	4.2	4.5	5.0	5.3	5.9	6.2	6.6	7.4	8.1	9.0	9.8	10.8	11.9	12.8	13.8	14.9	15.8	16.8	12.1	12.8	13.3	14.1	15.0	15.5	16.4	17.0
Olin 473AA	NR	NR	2.8	3.1	3.4	3.7	4.0	4.2	4.5	5.0	5.5	6.1	6.6	7.4	8.1	8.7	9.3	9.9	10.9	11.4	10.0	10.4	11.1	11.6	12.3	12.8	13.3	14.2
Olin 452AA	NR	NR	2.4	2.5	2.8	3.0	3.2	3.4	3.7	4.1	4.6	5.0	5.5	6.0	6.6	7.3	7.8	8.2	8.8	9.5	16.8	17.8	18.9	19.6	20.7	21.7	22.7	23.9
Olin 540	NR	NR	3.9	4.3	4.7	5.0	5.6	5.9	6.2	7.0	7.7	8.5	9.2	10.2	11.1	12.1	13.0	14.0	14.9	15.9	17.7	18.7	19.7	20.5	21.6	22.8	24.0	25.0
Olin 571	NR	NR	4.1	4.4	4.9	5.2	5.8	6.1	6.5	7.2	8.0	8.8	9.6	10.7	11.8	12.7	13.7	14.7	15.6	16.8								

NR=No known recommended load. WARNING: The powder charge weights shown for individual rotors are to be used for general reference only. Lot to lot variations in powder density, temperature, humidity, operating techniques and manufacturing tolerances, all introduce variations in charge weights from the values listed. Each rotor-powder combination used must be checked on accurate scale to determine actual charge weight prior to loading ammunition. From RCBS.

Lyman No. 55

RCBS
Little Dandy

RCBS Uniflow

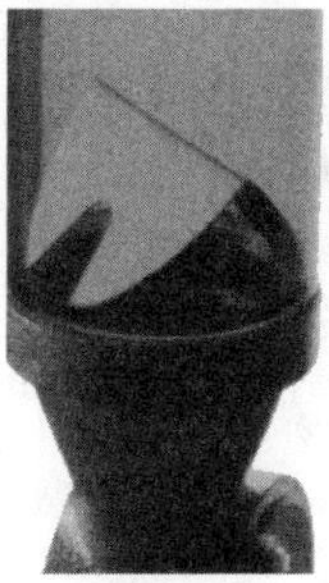

RCBS Uniflow
Powder Baffle

BR-30 Zero Backlash
Micrometer

3R Powder Baffle

Redding Competition
Model BR-30

Redding Match-Grade
Model 3BR

Redding Model 3

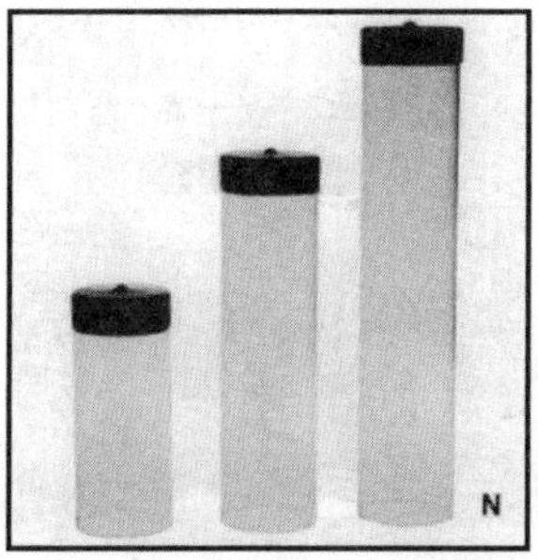

Redding Reservoirs
on RS-6 Bench Stand

REDDING

Bench Stand

For bench-top mounting all Redding powder measures or any other measure with 7/8-14 threads. Stand is not threaded but fitted with lock ring for rotating measure to any desired position or for dumping of reservoir. From Redding Reloading Equipment.

Price: **$27.00**

Competition Model BR-30 Powder Measure

Strictly a competition model with specialized drum and micrometer to limit overall charge range from low of 10 grains to maximum of about 50 grains. Has all same features of Redding Match-Grade model plus a reduction in metering cavity diameter and a change in the metering plunger shape to alleviate irregular powder settling and enhance charge uniformity. Unique rotating slightly heavier handle provides more uniform stroke. From Redding Reloading Equipment.

Price: **$180.00**

Master Model 3 Powder Measure

Precision machined cast iron frame with hand-honed fit between frame and hard surfaced drum. Features micrometer metering chamber; cast mounting bracket for shelf or bench attachment; large capacity clear powder reservoir; see-through drop tube for all calibers 22 through 50; threaded to fit measure stand. Comes with Universal metering chamber or with both Universal and pistol chambers. From Redding Reloading Equipment.

Price: With Universal chamber **$120.00**
Price: Pistol chamber **$33.00**
Price: Measure with both chambers. . $144.00

Match-Grade Model 3BR Powder Measure

Has all the features of Redding's Master Model 3 measure plus the match-grade conversion features. Match-grade features include micrometer metering chamber; zero backlash micrometer which takes up minute tolerances in screw thread so parts can't work loose and are self-adjusting; powder baffle positioned above metering chamber; positive lock system to allow micrometer setting changes without movement of micrometer body. Two metering chambers available. Universal chamber with charge range of approximately 5 to 100 grains; pistol metering chamber with range of 0 to 10 grains. Measure also offered with both chambers. From Redding Reloading Equipment.

Price: Measure with
Universal chamber. **$150.00**
Price: Pistol chamber **$45.00**
Price: Measure with both chambers . **$189.00**

Powder Measure Reservoirs

Replacement reservoirs available in three sizes with or without caps. Smallest is same size as supplied with any Redding measure. Intermediate is 7½" overall length with the largest being 10". Fit any Redding powder measure using 2⅛" O.D. reservoir. From Redding Reloading Equipment.

Price: Original size, no cap. **$6.00**
Price: Original size, with cap **$7.50**
Price: Intermediate, no cap **$9.00**
Price: Intermediate, with cap. **$10.50**
Price: Large, no cap **$12.00**
Price: Large, with cap. **$13.50**

Section 1: Metallic Cartridges

Supercharger PowderMeasuring Kit No. 101
Contains Redding Model RS-1 powder/bullet scale; Model No.3 powder measure; Model No. 5 trickler; and RS-6 bench stand. From Redding Reloading Equipment.
Price: **$195.00**

Supercharger Powder Measuring Kit No. 102
Contains Redding Model No. 2 powder/bullet scale; Model No. 3BR powder measure; Model No. 5 powder trickler; and RS-6 bench stand. From Redding Reloading Equipment.
Price . . . . :**$219.00**

Supercharger Powder Measuring Kit No. 102BR
Contains Redding Model No. 2 powder/bullet scale; No. 3BR powder measure; Model No. 5 powder trickler; and RS-6 bench stand. From Redding Reloading Equipment.
Price: **$256.50**

ROCK CRUSHER

Maxi Measure
Designed for loading very large caliber cases, 50 BMG on up. Made of machined steel and aircraft aluminum with solid brass drop tube. Design eliminates charge density variations by connecting hopper to charge reservoir which in turn is transferred to adjustable measuring chamber. Hopper is 1/2-gallon polypropylene bottle with capacity of 11 lbs. and capable of throwing charges of 700 grs. within .5-gr. Adjustable drop tube is solid brass with adjust range of 0 to 700 grains. Non-adjustable models available on special order. From The Old Western Scrounger.
Price: **$278.95**

SINCLAIR

Bottle Adaptors
Designed for Redding, RCBS Uniflow and Lyman 55 measures to replace the powder hopper with commercial powder bottles and screw them directly onto measure. Requires drilling and tapping small hole in RCBS or Lyman measure casting to attach adaptor; Redding adaptor uses factory screws. From Sinclair International, Inc.
Price: **$18.50**

Measure Bracket
Bracket designed for attaching C-clamp type measures to corner of tool box for loading in the field. From Sinclair International, Inc.
Price: **$14.00**

Powder Measure Stand
Adjustable powder measure stand allows both height adjustments and bench thickness allowances. Solid stainless steel shaft with powder-coated mounting plates. Three-point of contact plates threaded 7/8-14 in standard models. Also available with custom threading. From Sinclair International, Inc.
Price: **$29.75**

Powder Measure Tote Bag
Vinyl bag with cotton lined interior for transporting powder measure to the field. From Sinclair International, Inc.
Price: **$9.50**

Powder Bottles
16-oz. bottles to use in conjunction with Sinclair bottle adaptors. Helpful when working from larger keg and must keep powder lots separate. Come either in solid bottom configuration or with removable plug. From Sinclair International, Inc.
Price: Solid bottom **$3.50**
Price: Removable plug **$4.95**

Powder Drop Tubes
Clear Plexiglass tubes for Redding, RCBS Uniflow and Lyman measures for better visibility and greater powder compression in high density cases. Available in two lengths, 4≤ and 6≤ for Lyman and RCBS; or 3≤ or 5≤ for Redding. Attachment adaptor required for Redding measure. From Sinclair International, Inc.
Price: **$9.00**

SLAP

Powder Buddy
Accurate trip meter fitted to any powder measure or progressive/semi-progressive press to show a count from 1 to 99999 of each powder throw. Helps prevent double charging or no powder charge. All-metal construction. From SLAP Industries.
Price: **$29.95**

VEGA TOOL

Vega Schuetzen Meter
A remanufacture of the now obsolete Belding & Mull measure with new improvements to include: measure threaded for stand mounting; subreservoir made of brass; operating lever redesigned for more positive and crisp feel. From Vega Tool Company.
Price: **$229.95**

WELSH

Precision Powder Measure
Custom machined aluminum body with stainless steel liner and drum. Powder adjustment via Starrett micrometer. Dimensions: 3.25"x8". Comes with or without powder bottle system. From Bud Welsh.
Price: **$232.00**

CARL WERNER

Powder Measure Bracket
Swivel brackets attach permanently to metal tool box for mounting powder measure. Deluxe adapter for Redding measures also available. From Carl Werner.
Price: Standard **$22.00**
Price: Deluxe **$30.00**

SLAP Powder Buddy

Maxi Measure

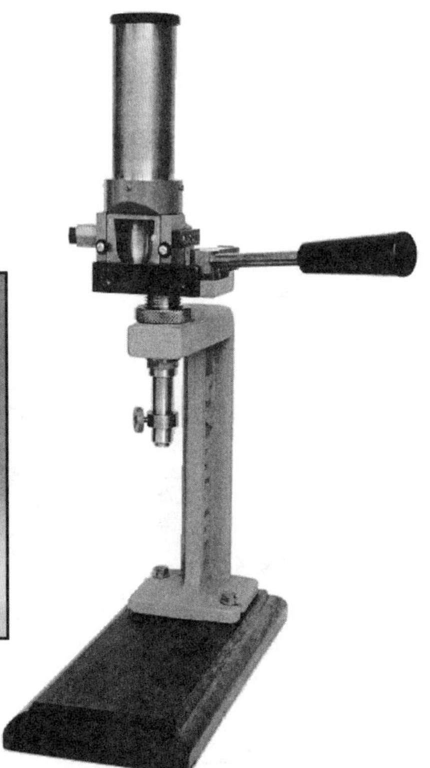

Vega Tool Schuetzen

C-H/4-D

Powder Funnel

High-quality anti-static funnel with drop tube to fit 22- to 45-caliber cases. From C-H Tool & Die/4-D Custom Die.

Price: **$2.00**

FORSTER

"Blue Ribbon" Long Drop Tube Funnel

For use with 4831 and other slow-burning powders where full capacity loads are needed. Long tube adds from 3 to 8 more grains of powder depending on case for a larger volume by weight. From Forster Products.

Price: $14.30

"Blue Ribbon" Powder Funnel

Made from Cycolac and designed with four mouth tabs to prevent rolling. One size for 22- to 45-caliber; another for 17-caliber. From Forster Products.

Price: Both sizes **$4.30**

Large Powder/Shot Funnel

Same funnel as used on Bonanza Bench Rest and Bulls-Eye powder measures. Made of tough plastic. From Forster Products.

Price: **$6.00**

HORNADY

Powder Funnel

Tapered tube design to reduce powder spills; fits all cases inclusive of 45-caliber. Anti-static treated transparent plastic. Weight: 1/4-lb. From Hornady Mfg. Co.

Price: **$2.95**

17 Caliber Powder Funnel Adaptor

Aluminum adaptor for Hornady powder funnel seals around mouth of 17-caliber cases to help prevent powder leakage. From Hornady Mfg. Co.

Price: **$4.95**

LEE

Powder Funnel

Large plastic funnel fits all cases from 22- to 45-caliber. Hole in flange permits mounting to Lee turret press, shelf or bench. From Lee Precision, Inc.

Price: **$2.49**

LYMAN

Powder Funnel

Plastic funnel for cases from 22 Hornet through 45-70. From Lyman Products Corporation.

Price: **$3.00**

MTM

Powder Funnels

Two see-through plastic models available. Universal model fits all calibers from 222 to 45. Adaptor 5-in-1 kit includes funnel and standard length adapters for 17 Remington, 222 Remington and 30 through 45 calibers. Long universal drop tube also available. From MTM Moulded Products Company.

Price: Universal **$2.83**
Price: Adaptor kit **$4.09**

PRECISION RELOADING

Aluminum Funnels

All aluminum one-piece construction funnels eliminate static cling of powder and buffer. Available in three sizes: 2 1/2-oz. with mouth OD of 2 5/8" and spout OD 7/16"; 1/2-pint, with mouth OD 4", spout OD 1/2"; and 3/4-pint, 5≤ mouth OD, 5/8" spout OD. From Precision Reloading, Inc.

Price: 2 1/2 oz. **$1.89**
Price: 1/2-pint **$2.49**
Price: 3/4-pint **$3.49**

RCBS

Powder Funnel

Specially-designed drop tube to avoid powder spills around case mouths, a non-stick, anti-static surface and square lip to prevent rolling. Available in one size for 22- to 45-caliber and another for 17. From RCBS.

Price: **$3.38**
Price: 17-cal. **$4.63**

REDDING

Powder Funnel

Lexan funnel fits all cartridge cases 22- to 45-caliber. Anti-static prevents powder sticking. From Redding Reloading Equipment.

Price: **$4.80**

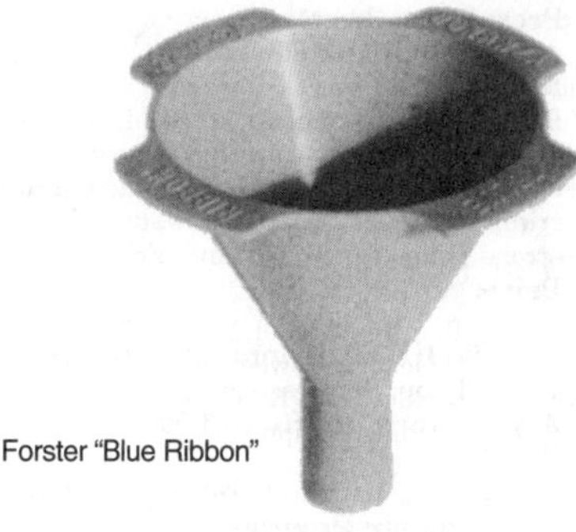

Forster "Blue Ribbon"

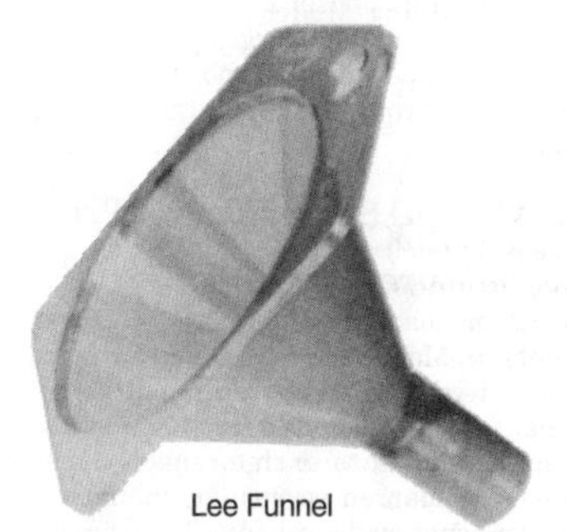

Lee Funnel

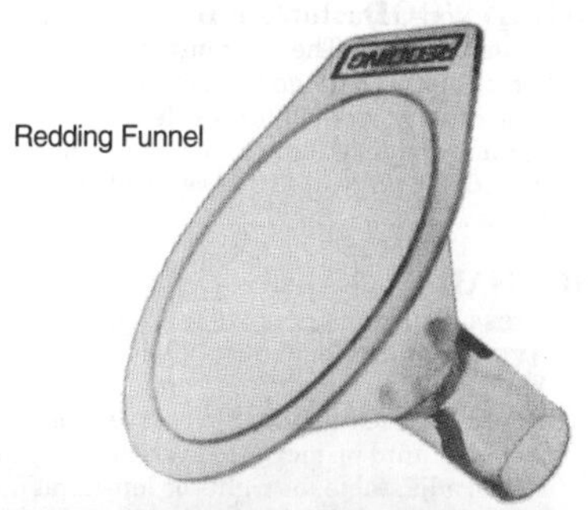

Redding Funnel

Hornady 17-Caliber Funnel Adaptor

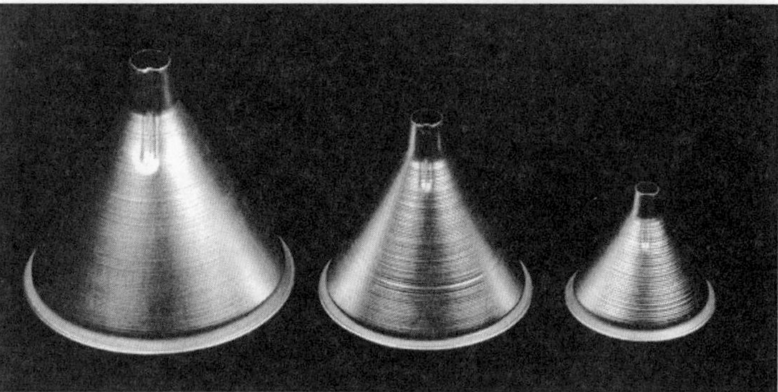

Precision Reloading Aluminum Funnels

Section 2: Shotshell Reloading

DILLON SL 900
Press Type: Progressive
Avg. Rounds Per Hour: NA
Weight: NA
Features: 12-ga. only; factory adjusted to load AA hulls; extra large 25-pound capacity shot hopper; fully-adjustable case-activated shotsystem; hardened steel starter crimp die; dual-action final crimp and taper die; tilt-out wad guide; auto prime; auto index; strong mount machine stand. From Dillon Precision Products.
Price: **$819.95**

HOLLYWOOD Automatic Shotshell Press
Press Type: Progressive
Avg. Rounds Per Hour: 1,800
Weight: 100 lbs.
Features: Ductile iron frame; fully automated press with shell pickup and ejector; comes completely set up for one gauge; one starter crimp; one finish crimp; wad guide for plastic wads; decap and powder dispenser unit; one wrench for inside die lock screw; one medium and one large spanner wrench for spanner nuts; one shellholder; powder and shot measures. Available for 10, 12, 20, 28 or .410. From Hollywood Engineering.
Price:...................................... **$3,600.00**

HOLLYWOOD Senior Turret Press
Press Type: Turret
Avg. Rounds Per Hour: 200
Weight: 50 lbs.
Features: Multi-stage press constructed of ductile iron comes completely equipped to reload one gauge; one starter crimp; one finish crimp; wad guide for plastic wads; decap and powder dispenser unit; one wrench for inside die lock screw; one medium and one large spanner wrench for spanner nuts; one shellholder; powder and shot measures. Available for 10, 12, 16, 20, 28 or .410. From Hollywood Engineering.
Price: **$700.00**

HOLLYWOOD Shotshell Die Sets
Complete 11/2 die set for one gauge to include: starter crimp; finish crimp; wad guide for plastic wads; decap and powder dispenser unit; wrench for inside die lock screw; medium and large spanner wrench for spanner nuts; shellholder. Available for 10, 12, 16, 20, 28 and .410. From Hollywood Engineering.
Price: **$195.00**

HORNADY 366 Auto
Press Type: Progressive
Avg. Rounds Per Hour: NA
Weight: 25 lbs.
Features: Heavy-duty die cast and machined steel body and components; auto primer feed system; large capacity shot and powder tubes; adjustable for right- or left-hand use; automatic charge bar with shutoff; swing-out wad guide; primer catcher at base of press; interchangeable shot and powder bushings; life-time warranty. Available for 12, 20, 28 2 3/4" and .410 2 1/2". From Hornady Mfg. Co.
Price: **$471.50**
Price: 366 Gas Assist option **$89.95**

LEE Load-All II
Press Type: Single stage
Avg. Rounds Per Hour: 100
Weight: 3 lbs., 3 oz.
Features: Loads steel or lead shot; built-in primer catcher at base with door in front for emptying; recesses at each station for shell positioning; optional primer feed. Comes with safety charge bar with 24 shot and powder bushings. Available for 12-, 16- or 20-gauge. From Lee Precision, Inc.
Price: **$49.98**

MEC 600 Jr. Mark V
Press Type: Single stage
Avg. Rounds Per Hour: 200
Weight: 10 lbs.
Features: Spindex crimp starter for shell alignment during crimping; a cam-action crimp die; Pro-Check to keep charge bar properly positioned; adjustable for three shells. Available in 10, 12, 16, 20, 28 gauges and .410 bore. Die set not included. From Mayville Engineering Company, Inc.
Price: **$107.00**
Price: Die set **$59.38**

HOLLYWOOD
Shotshell Die Parts

DIE/DIE PART	PRICE
Finish Crimp	$45.00
Crimp Start, w/lock ring, steel star	50.00
Steel Star, 6 & 8 point	15.00
Locking Screw, start crimp die	2.00
Decap/Powder Dispenser Unit	75.00
Decap Powder Pin	20.00
Locking Screw, decap powder pin	2.00
Lock Collar, wad guide spring finger	6.00
Lock Ring	5.00
Set Screw, lock ring	.40
Wad Guide Spring Finger	2.50
Wad Pressure Spring	3.00
Wad Ram	20.00
Wad Receiver, complete	70.00
Wad Receiver, stripped	45.00
Primer Rod Buffer Spring	2.00
Primer Rod Lock Ring, small	2.00
Primer Rod Lock Ring, large	2.50

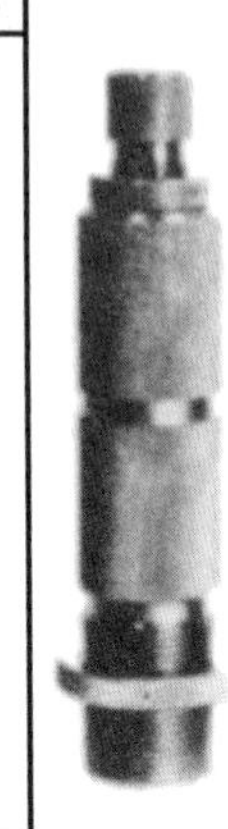

Hollywood Automatic Shotshell Press

Hornady 366 Auto

Lee Load-All II

MEC Grabber

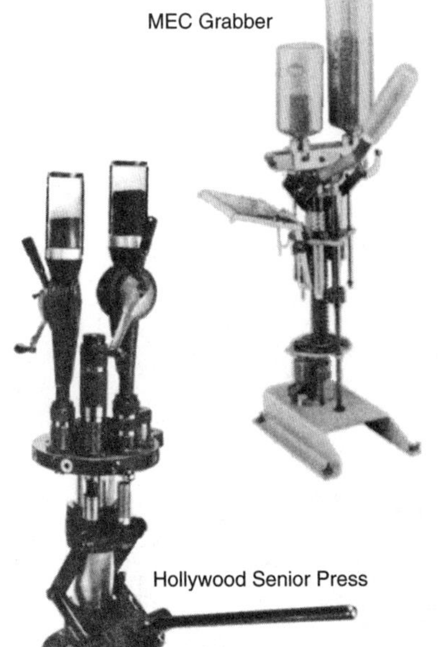

Hollywood Senior Press

MEC 600 Jr.

SHOTSHELL/ PRESSES

MEC Sizemaster
MEC Steelmaster
Ponsness/Warren L/S-1000
Ponsness/Warren Du-O-Matic 375C
MEC 9000G

MEC 650
Press Type: Progressive
Avg. Rounds Per Hour: 400
Weight: NA
Features: Six-station press; does not resize except as separate operation; auto primer feed standard; three crimping stations for starting, closing and tapering crimp. Die sets not available. Available in 12, 16, 20, 28 and .410. From Mayville Engineering Company, Inc.
Price: **$211.00**

MEC 8567 Grabber
Press Type: Progressive
Avg. Rounds Per Hour: 400
Weight: 15 lbs.
Features: Ten-station press; auto primer feed; auto-cycle charging; three-stage crimp; power ring resizer returns base to factory specs; resizes high and low base shells; optional kits to reload three shells and steel shot. Available in 12, 16, 20, 28 gauge and .410 bore. From Mayville Engineering Company, Inc.
Price: **$303.00**
Price: 3 kit, 12-ga. **$39.19**
Price: 3 kit, 20-ga. **$24.00**
Price: Steel shot kit **$23.22**

MEC 9000G
Press Type: Progressive
Avg. Rounds Per Hour: 400
Weight: 18 lbs.
Features: All same features as the MEC Grabber, but with auto-indexing and auto-eject. Finished shells automatically ejected from shell carrier to drop chute for boxing. Available in 12, 16, 20, 28 and .410. From Mayville Engineering Company, Inc.
Price: **$368.00**
Price: 3 kit, 12-ga. **$39.19**
Price: 3 kit, 20-ga. **$24.00**
Price: Steel shot kit **$23.22**

MEC 9000H
Press Type: Progressive
Avg. Rounds Per Hour: 400
Weight: 23 lbs.
Features: Same features as 9000G with addition of foot pedal-operated hydraulic system for complete automation. Operates on standard 110v household current. Comes with bushing-type charge bar and three bushings. Available in 12, 16, 20, 28 gauge and .410 bore. From Mayville Engineering Company, Inc.
Price: **$888.00**
Price: Steel shot kit **$22.54**

MEC Sizemaster
Press Type: Single stage
Avg. Rounds Per Hour: 150
Weight: 13 lbs.
Features: Power ring eight-fingered collet resizer returns base to factory specs; handles brass or steel, high or low base, heads; auto primer feed; adjustable for three shells. Available in 10, 12, 16, 20, 28 gauges and .410 bore. From Mayville Engineering Company, Inc.
Price: **$162.00**
Price: Die set, 12, 16, 20, 28, .410 .... **$88.67**
Price: Die set, 10-ga. **$104.06**
Price: Steel shot kit **$14.34**
Price: Steel shot kit, 12-ga. 3 1/2" **$70.27**

MEC Steelmaster
Press Type: Single stage
Avg. Rounds Per Hour: 150
Weight: 13 lbs.
Features: Same features as Sizemaster except can load steel shot. Press is available for 3 1/2" 10-ga. and 12-ga. 2 3/4, 3 or 3 1/2 inches. For loading lead shot, die sets available in 10, 12, 16, 20, 28 and .410. From Mayville Engineering Company, Inc.
Price: **$175.00**
Price: 31/2" **$196.00**

PONSNESS/WARREN Du-O-Matic 375C
Press Type: Progressive
Avg. Rounds Per Hour: NA
Weight: 31 lbs.
Features: Steel or lead shot reloader; large shot and powder reservoirs; bushing access plug for dropping in shot buffer or buckshot; positive lock charging ring to prevent accidental flow of powder; double-post construction for greater leverage; removable spent primer box; spring-loaded ball check for centering size die at each station; tip-out wad guide; two-gauge capacity tool head. Available in 10 (extra charge), 12, 16, 20, 28 and .410 with case lengths of 2 1/2, 2 3/4, 3 and 3 1/2 inches. From Ponsness/ Warren.
Price: **$383.95**
Price: 12-ga. 3 1/2"; 3" 12, 20, .410 .... **$305.00**
Price: 12, 20 2 3/4" **$383.95**
Price: 10-ga. press **$315.00**

PONSNESS/WARREN L/S-1000
Frame: Die cast aluminum
Avg. Rounds Per Hour: NA
Weight: 55 lbs.
Features: Fully progressive press to reload steel, bismuth or lead shot. Equipped with new Uni-Drop shot measuring and dispensing system which allows the use of all makes of shot in any size. Shells automatically resized and deprimed with new Auto-Size and De-Primer system. Loaded rounds drop out of shellholders when completed. Each shell pre-crimped and final crimped with Tru-Crimp system. Available in 10-gauge 3 1/2" or 12-gauge 2 3/4" and 3". 12-gauge 3 1/2" conversion kit also available. 20-gauge 2 3/4" and 3" special order only. From Ponsness/Warren.
Price: 12 ga. **$849.00**
Price: 10 ga. **$895.00**
Price: Tooling set **$189.00**

BILL FERGUSON

Lead Pot
High-quality 50-lb. capacity cast iron plumbers' pot with bale handle. Designed to fit Ferguson's Plumbers Furnace and adaptable for use with other heat sources. From Bill Ferguson.
Price: **$34.00**

Plumbers Furnace
Well-constructed lead melting furnace with over 43,000 BTUs of thermal capacity. High-pressure regulator and vapor hose required. From Bill Ferguson.
Price: **$165.00**

High Pressure Vapor Regulator
For use with Ferguson Plumbers Furnace using LP cylinder P.O.L. valve. Adjustable pressure from 0-45 psi with P.O.L. spud and nut, 1/4" NPT outlet for optional pressure gauge. From Bill Ferguson.
Price: **$48.00**

Plumbers Furnace Kit
Casting furnace that features 43,000 BTU thermal capacity, adjustable LP regulator with fittings, 6" long high-pressure hose, pressure gauge, cast iron plumbers' pot and heat shield. Melts a full pot of lead in 7 minutes. Comes complete with wide stand and bale handle. LP cylinder with standard P.O.L. valve required. From Bill Ferguson.
Price: **$245.00**
Price: Magnum Casting Furnace. . . . **$265.00**

LP Pressure Gauge
Fits in gauge port of Ferguson High Pressure Vapor Regulator for accurate LP vapor pressure control for Plumbers Furnace. Scale range 0-100 psi. From Bill Ferguson.
Price: **$12.50**

Heat Shield
Heavy gauge steel heat shield for use with Ferguson Plumbers Furnace and lead melting pot. Saves energy by keeping hot gases close to pot. Diameter: 75/8". From Bill Ferguson.
Price: 40 lb. **$9.00**
Price: 80 lb. **$45.00**

LP Vapor Hose
For use with Plumbers furnace. Comes complete with female 9/16-8 LH fittings for furnace and regulator. Rated 300-psi maximum vapor pressure. From Bill Ferguson.
Price: 6 ft. **$16.00**

LEE

Lead Pot
Drawn steel pot with capacity for 4 lbs. lead. Flat bottom for stability and good contact with heat supply. From Lee Precision, Inc.
Price: **$3.98**

Precision Melter
High-speed melter for ingot moulds with infinite heat control. Pot capacity of 4 lbs. 500 watts, AC only. From Lee Precision, Inc.
Price: 110-volt. **$39.98**
Price: 220-volt. **$43.98**

Pro 20
Large diameter, high-capacity 20-lb. melting pot. Features remote sensing thermostat; 700-watt tubular heating element; micro-adjustable flow control valve; front mounted replaceable valve spout. From Lee Precision, Inc.
Price: **$79.98**

Lee Pro 20

Lee Pro 4-20

Pro 4-20
Same features as the Pro 20 except an extra 4" of clearance under the spout to accept all brands of bullet moulds and most sinker moulds. Also includes an adjustable mould guide for quick, accurate positioning of mould. From Lee Precision, Inc.
Price: 110-volt. **$89.98**
Price: 220-volt. **$94.98**

Production Pot
Capacity for 10 lbs. lead. Melt time is less than 20 minutes using 500 watts power and less to maintain heat level. Large stable base with 2" clearance between up-front spout and base. Features infinite heat control thermostat mounted away from melt pot. Also available in 220-volt export model. From Lee Precision, Inc.
Price: 110-volt. **$62.98**
Price: 220-volt. **$66.98**

Production Pot IV
Has same features as Lee Production Pot except for 4" clearance between base and spout. From Lee Precision, Inc.
Price: 110-volt. **$66.98**
Price: 220-volt. **$70.98**

LYMAN

Lead Pot
Cast iron pot with 10-lb. capacity and flat bottom to prevent tipping. Weight: 1-lb. From Lyman Products Corporation.
Price: **$12.95**

Master Casting Kit
Includes Lyman Mini-Mag 8-lb. capacity furnace; Model 450 sizer/lubricator; long-handled casting dipper; ingot mould; and The Lyman Cast Bullet Handbook. Weight: 8 lbs., 4 oz. From Lyman Products Corporation.
Price: **$169.95**

Mag 20 Electric Furnace
Capacity for 20 lbs. lead. Features bottom pour valve system; adjustable mould guide for single or multiple cavity moulds; warming shelf for pre-heating blocks; industrial grade thermostat with indicator light; 800-watt heating system melts metal in 20 minutes. Weight: 15 lbs. 110- or 220-volt. From Lyman Products Corporation.
Price: **$283.25**

Ferguson Lead Pot

Magdipper Furnace
Designed for ladle caster with 4 3/8" diameter pot and 20-lb. capacity. Has same body construction, heating system and tip-resistant base of Lyman Mag 20. Weight: 10 lbs. 110-volt only. From Lyman Products Corporation.
Price: **$234.95**

Mini-Mag Furnace
Electric 8-lb. capacity casting furnace. Melts full load in 30 minutes. Weight: 4 lbs., 4 oz. 110- or 220-volt. From Lyman Products Corporation.
Price: 110 . . . . **$52.00**
Price: 220 . . . . **$55.00**

RCBS

Lead Pot
Heavy-duty cast iron pot holds up to 10 pounds of molten metal. Features a flat bottom, bail handle, pouring spout and tab lifter for gripping with tongs. From RCBS.
Price: **$16.95**

Pro-Melt Furnace
Features 22-lb. capacity melting pot with temperature range of 450° to 850° controlled by industrial-grade thermostat. Pot is made of steel with stainless steel liner and bottom pour valve. Fully adjustable mould guide. Can be set up for right- or left-hand use. 800 watts. From RCBS.
Price: 120 VAC **$330.95**
Price: 240 VAC **$347.95**

RAPINE

RSS20 Lead Pot
Stainless steel 20-lb. capacity thermostatically controlled lead pot. From Rapine Bullet Mould Mfg. Co.
Price: **$260.00**

BROWNELLS

Marvelux

Lead alloy fluxing agent non-corrosive to iron and steel. Reduces dross formation and increases fluidity of bullet alloys. Non-smoking, flameless and odorless. From Brownells, Inc.

Price: 1/2-lb. **$4.80**
Price: 1-lb. **$8.98**
Price: 4 lbs. **$20.25**

Industrial Thermometer

Constructed of 304 stainless steel, all welded construction. 2″ dial, 8″ long stem for immersion in liquids. Guaranteed accurate to .5 of 1% 200° to 1000° in 10°-increments. From Brownells, Inc.

Price: **$31.10**

CF VENTURES

Soft Gas Checks

Soft wax blend with 125-degree Fahrenheit melting point for making gas checks for cast bullets. Come in 5-lb. boxes.

Price: **$50.00**

BILL FERGUSON

Casting Thermometer

Constructed of corrosion resistant type 304 stainless steel with 8″ stem. Temperature range of 200° to 1000° Fahrenheit. Accuracy to within +/-1% of total scale range. From Bill Ferguson.

Price: 1/2-lb. **$9.95**

Lets Alloyer's Flux

Heavy-duty flux developed and formulated to introduce pulverized pure antimony to lead solution at very low working temperatures, 750° to 800° F, in 3 minutes. One pound disipates 25 lbs. of pulverized antimony. Comes in 1-, 3-, 5- and 50-lb. containers. From Bill Ferguson.

Price: 1-lb. **$6.00**
Price: 3 lbs. **$12.00**
Price: 5 lbs. **$22.50**
Price: 50 lbs. **$190.00**

Lets Flux

Low fuming, minimal odor, non-toxic, crystalline general purpose flux designed for bullet casting. Working temperatures of 550° to 850° F. Non-corrosive and contains no chlorides. Will not disipate pulverized antimony. Comes in 1-, 2-, 4- and 50-lb. containers. From Bill Ferguson.

Price: 1-lb. **$3.95**
Price: 2 lbs. **$6.50**
Price: 4 lbs. **$10.95**
Price: 50 lbs. **$129.00**

Clip and Debris Skimmer

Long handled skimmer for removing debris safely from molten lead. Comes in four diameters, 3″, 4″, 5″ and 6″. From Bill Ferguson.

Price: 3" **$14.00**
Price: 4" **$15.95**
Price: 5" **$18.50**
Price: 6" **$23.50**

Lets Pure Virgin Bar Tin

Come in 12″ 1-lb. bars. Assay 99.85%+. Calculate the number of inches of tin needed for the casting mix, mark the 12″ bar and dip into molten lead until exact amount melts off. From Bill Ferguson.

Price: **$7.50**

Lets Pure Pulverized Antimony

Designed for use with Lets Alloyers Flux to add antimony to molten lead at low working temperatures of 750° to 775°, 400° F. less than the melting point of antimony itself. Comes in 6-, 12.5- and 65-lb. containers. From Bill Ferguson.

Price: **$4.50**

Bill Ferguson Casting Thermometer

Bill Ferguson Clip & Debris Skimmer

Lyman Casting Thermometer

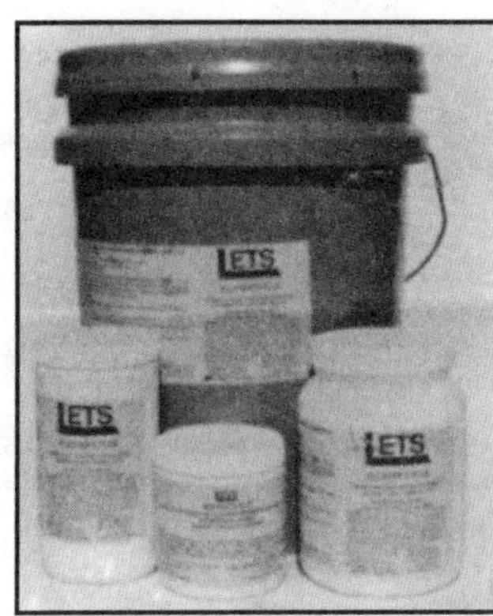

Bill Ferguson Lets Alloyer's Flux

BILL FERGUSON

Doe Run Primary Virgin Link Lead

For the Schuetzen blackpowder cartridge or muzzleloader caster. 99.98%+ pure. Each ingot approximately 5 lbs. From Bill Ferguson.

Price: Per pound **$1.00**

LBT

Hardness Tester

Rugged all-steel welded construction. Tests hardness of any cast bullet 1/2″ to 1″ long. Hardness scale runs from 6 BHN (pure lead) to 40 BHN (copper). Features direct scale readout and guaranteed accuracy to 1 BHN. From Lead Bullets Technology.

Price: **$69.00**

Mould Lube

Colloidial graphite in beeswax carrier extruded into 1/4″ diameter sticks for application to friction points on mould. Eliminates wear and keeps mould working smoothly. One stick supplied with each LBT mould. Comes in packages of four. From Lead Bullets Technology.

Price: **$4.00**

LEE

Ingot Mould

Lightweight aluminum body with wood handles and cavities for two 1/2-lb. and two 1-lb. ingots. From Lee Precision, Inc.

Price: **$13.98**

Lead Ladle

Convenient size ladle with wooden handle for bullet casting. Pour spout on either side for left- or right-hand use. From Lee Precision, Inc.

Price: **$2.98**

Casting Dipper

Features cast iron head, long stem and wooden handle. Weight: 6 oz. From Lyman Products Corporation.

Price: **$12.95**

LYMAN

Casting Thermometer

Stainless steel thermometer with measuring range from 200° Fahrenheit to 1000° F. Features 6″ stem and scale on face showing proper casting ranges for most popular alloys and pure lead. From Lyman Products Corporation.

Price: **$30.00**

Ingot Mould

Forms four ingots weighing 1-lb. each. Sides of mould have 30° draft for easy ingot ejection. Weight: 1-lb. From Lyman Products Corporation.

Price: **$15.75**

Mould Guide

For use with bottom pour furnaces. Provides precise set-screw adjustments to hold and align moulds. Compatible with Lyman moulds and those of similar design. Weight: 1-lb. From Lyman Products Corporation.

Price: **$16.50**

MAGMA

Master Lubricant

Protects moulds from rust. Comes in 4-oz., 8-oz. or 16-oz. containers. Smaller containers have spray nozzle. From Magma Engineering Co.

Price: 4-oz. **$16.50**
Price: 8-oz. **$22.00**
Price: 16-oz. **$40.00**

Flux

All synthetic flux. Small amount will flux 20 lbs. of metal. Comes in 1-lb. bricks. From Magma Engineering Company.

Price: **$14.25**

Section 3: Bullet Casting

MI-TE

Acculoy Bullet Metal

Premium bullet metal of tin-antimony-lead with 0.5% silver. Silver helps alloy flow, filling contours of mould cavity for sharp, filled-out bullets. Low operating temperature 600° to 625°. Comes in $8^1/_2$-lb. bars. From Mi-Te Bullets.

Price: 1-5, each **$9.50**
Price: 6-10, each **$9.00**
Price: 11+, each **$8.50**

MIDWAY

Drop Out Mould Release

Lubricant and rust prohibitor with Du Pont Teflon for bullet casters. Comes in 6-oz. aerosol can. From Midway Arms, Inc.

Price: **$6.99**

Rust Guard

Aerosol lubricant and rust preventative with Du Pont Teflon for protecting moulds. Comes in 6-oz. can. From Midway Arms, Inc.

Price: **$5.99**

Rust Inhibitor Chips

Impregnated 1″x 1″ rust inhibitor chips to protect moulds. Each chip protects up to 20 cubic inches of aluminum or steel. Come in packages of 50 or 200. From Midway Arms, Inc.

Price: 50 . . . . **$5.99**
Price: 200 . . . . **$16.99**

NEI

Flux

Flake-type fluxing agent for removing dross from molten lead. Comes in 4-oz. bag. From NEI Handtools, Inc.

Price: **$7.50**

Mould Prep

Liquid rust preventative for iron moulds. Contains isopropyl alcohol. Comes in 2-oz. plastic bottle. From NEI Handtools, Inc.

Price: **$4.95**

SP Lube

Sprue plate lube to prevent galling. Comes in 2-oz. bottle. From NEI Handtools, Inc.

Price: **$3.00**

RAPINE

Mould Prep

Micro-graphite, isopropyl alcohol suspension liquid designed to inhibit rust and corrosion. Comes in 2-oz. bottles. From Rapine Associates.

Price: **$3.99**

RCBS

Bullet Mould Handles

Solid steel frames with extra-long hardwood handles. One size fits all RCBS bullet moulds. From RCBS.

Price: **$26.38**

Ingot Mould

Heavy-duty iron mould to form four ingots. From RCBS.

Price: **$13.63**

Lead Dipper

Large-capacity bowl with tapered pouring spout and hardwood grip. Convertible for left-hand use. From RCBS.

Price: **$13.63**

Midway Drop Out Mould Release

RCBS Ingot Mould

NEI Flux and Mould Prep

ROWELL LADLES

Ladle No.	Capacity (lbs.)	Bowl Dia. (ins.)	Bowl Depth (ins.)	Handle (ins.)	Ladle (ins.)	Weight (lbs.)	Price
1	1	$2^1/_4$	1	9	16	$^3/_4$	$19.95
2	2	$2^1/_2$	$1^1/_2$	10	$17^1/_4$	1	20.25
3	4	3	$2^1/_4$	$12^1/_2$	$15^1/_2$	2	26.25
4	$4^1/_2$	4	2	16	20	4	31.25
5	9	5	$2^1/_2$	24	31	5	35.50
6	18	6	3	29	35	9	45.25
7	25	7	$4^1/_2$	29	36	10	51.50
8	40	8	$4^1/_2$	29	37	13	57.75
9	60	9	5	29	38	20	77.75
10	90	10	$5^1/_4$	29	39	25	88.50

No. 9 and No. 10 can be equipped with two handles for $19.75.

Rowell Bottom Pour Ladle

Lead Thermometer

A 1000° range and 1% accuracy thermometer. Features 6″ probe and $1^1/_2$″ glass-covered face. Comes with an adjustable 6″ handle. From RCBS.

Price: **$33.88**

REDDING

Ingot Mould

Cast iron ingot mould with capacity to cast four ingots. From Redding Reloading Equipment.

Price: **$16.50**

ROWELL

Bottom Pour Ladle

Clean pouring ladle eliminates skimming and wasted metal by delivering lead from the bottom of the ladle bowl. Internal trough inside bowl brings metal from the bottom to the side-pouring spout. Made of durable cast iron with flat base to prevent tipping when set down. Comes in ten sizes. Sizes 1 and 2 have steel bar handle with wood hand grip. Sliding iron sleeve on sizes 4 and up stays cool, protecting user from burns. From Advance Car Mover, Co.

Price: . . . . **See chart.**

SAECO

Lead Hardness Tester

Precision instrument to accurately determine hardness of bullet casting alloy. Measures hardness by determining depth of penetration of hardened steel indenter into bullet. Vernier scale calibrated in arbitrary units from 0 for pure lead to Saeco hardness of 10. From Redding Reloading Equipment.

Price: **$135.00**

SOURCES OF BULLET CASTING METAL

Action Bullets
1811 West 13th Ave.
Denver, CO 80204

Ames Metal Co.
4324 South Western Blvd.
Chicago, IL
312-523-3230

A Brigante & Co.
475 Rt. 32
Highland Mills, NY 10930

Buffalo Arms Co.
123 S. Third, Suite 6
Sandpoint, ID 83864
208-263-6953

Brownells, Inc.
200 S. Front St.
Montezuma, IA 50171
515-623-5401

C.J. Ballistics
P.O. Box 132
Acme, WA 98220
206-595-5001

Dillon Precision Products
8009 E. Dillon's Way
Scottsdale, AZ 85260

Essex Metals
1000 Brighton St.
Union, NJ 07083
800-282-8369

Fry Metals
4100 6th Ave.
Altoona, PA 16602
814-946-1611

Bill Ferguson, Metallurgist
P.O. Box 1238
Sierra Vista, AZ 85636
520-458-5321/FAX:520-458-9125

Art Green
485 South Robertson Blvd.
Beverly Hills, CA 90211
310-274-1283

Liberty Metals
2233 East 16th
Los Angeles, CA 90021
213-581-9171/FAX: 213-581-9351

Mi-Te Bullets
R.R. 1 Box 230
Ellsworth, KS 07439

Peerless Metals
1445 Osage St.
Denver, CO 80204
303-825-6394

RSR
720 South 7th Ave.
City of Industry, CA 91746-3124
818-330-2294

RSR Dallas
1111 West Mockingbird Lane
Dallas, TX 75247
214-631-6070

Signet Metal Corp.
551 Stewart Ave.
Brooklyn, NY 11222
718-384-5400/FAX: 718-388-7488

TCSR
3998 Hoffman Rd.
White Bear Lake, MN 55110-4626
800-328-5323

TR Metals
1 Pavillion Ave.
Riverside, NJ 08075
609-461-9000/
FAX:609-764-6340

KTS Mfg.
2611 Hwy. 40 East
Inglis, FL 34449
904-447-3571

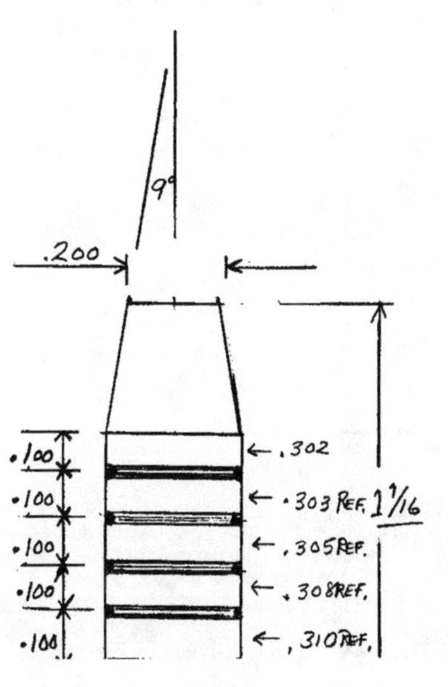

CORBIN

Core Moulds
Four-cavity and three-cavity moulds for standard and magnum cast cores. Mount to bench; requires no handles or mallets; eject fully-adjustable weight cores from precision honed cavities in tool steel dies. All calibers available. From Corbin Manufacturing & Supply, Inc.
Price: 4-cavity **$98.00**
Price: Insert, 4-cavity **$20.00**
Price: 3-cavity **$129.00**
Price: Insert, 3-cavity **$45.00**

HENSLEY & GIBBS

Bullet Moulds
Handcast moulds in 2-, 4- or 6-cavity designs. Standard moulds cut .001" to .002" over sizing diameter in alloy specified. Custom moulds closer to sizing diameter or over .002" larger than specified alloy. Standard matched moulds are cut consecutively with 1/2-grain maximum variance between the two. Custom matched moulds are same as standard match but will re-surface grind and re-cherry as needed. All custom moulds an additional $20.00. Moulds can be ordered complete with handles or without. From Ballisti-Cast Manufacturing.
Price: . . . . **See chart on page 355**.
Hand-Cast Molds
Blocks (2 cavity) with Sprue Plates & Screws $95.00
Blocks (4 cavity) with Sprue Plates & Screws $145.00
Blocks (6 cavity) with Sprue Plates & Screws $235.00
Handles (2, 4 & 6 cavity) . . . . $ 37.00
Wood For Handles (set) . . . . $ 5.00

DONALD EAGAN Bullet Moulds

Caliber	As Cast Diameter	As Cast Wgt. Grs	Type	Mould
22	.225	43	GC	MX-2-22
	.225	55	GC	MX-2-22Z
	.221-.227	55	Straight Tapered, GC	MX-3-22
6mm	.238-.246	65	Tapered, GC	MX-3-24X
	.244	80	GC	MX-2-243
	.250-.260	100	Straight Tapered, GC	MX-3-25X
7mm	.276-.287	145	Straight Tapered, GC	MX-3-28X
30	.300-.310	155	For short drive band bullets, GC	MX-2-30W
	.301-.310	160	Taper nose for all 30/30 and 30 WCF, GC	MX-2-30C
	.311	175	GC	MX-2-308
	.310	180	GC	MX-2-30
	.310	185	For 30-06 and 30-40, GC	MX-2-30H
	.304-.315	165	Straight tapered, GC	MX-3-30BR
	.3062-.312	165	Straight tapered, GC	MX-3-30KBR
	.302-.313	175	Straight tapered, GC	MX-3-30X
	.304-.312	155	Straight tapered, GC	MX-3-30J
	.304-.313	172	Straight tapered, GC	MX-3-30V
	.301-.313	190	Straight tapered, GC	MX-3-30G
	.299-.313	196	Straight tapered, GC	MX-3-30US
	.310	120	GC	MX-2-30CAR
	.304-.313	155	Straight tapered, GC	MX-3-30RJ
	.311	166	Tapered, GC	MX-3-30AR
	.313	188	Tapered	MX-3-30ARD
	.302-.312	190	Tapered, GC	MX-4-30A
	.302-.313	180	Tapered, plain base	MX-3-30S
	.304-.319	180	Tapered, plain base	MX-2-32C
32	.314-.324	190	Straight tapered, plain base	MX-3-32S
	.315-.325	210	GC	MX-4-32A
33	.329-.340	250	Straight tapered, GC	MX-3-338
35	.359-.364	220	Straight tapered, GC	MX-3-35M

BULLET CASTING/MOULDS

Section 3: Bullet Casting

LOWETH

Webley Mark II Mould

Moulds to produce Webley Mark II .455" 265-grain round-nose hollow base bullet and an exact copy of the naval bullet developed for the British Royal Navy Shooting Team; and 220-grain 455 Special Target bullet. Moulds made to original British government drawings of bullet. From Richard H. A. Loweth Firearms.

Price: . . . . **Contact manufacturer.**

LEE

Bullet Moulds

Aluminum 1- and 2-cavity mould blocks lathe-bored to roundness of .001" or less. Most bullets from Lee moulds can be used as cast without sizing. Lee single-cavity, double-cavity, hollow-point and hollow base single-cavity moulds come with sprue plate and wood handles. Hollowpoint and hollow base moulds have self-centering automatic core pins. From Lee Precision, Inc.

Price: 1-cavity **$19.98**
Price: 2-cavity **$24.98**
Price: Hollowpoint/hollow base **$25.98**
Price: Shotgun slug mould base. **$25.98**

HENSLEY & GIBBS Bullet Moulds

	Bullet			Mould	
Caliber	Dia.	Wgt. Grs.	Type	#	Comments
25 ACP	.252	50	PB	117	RGG
	.252	55	PB	306	RGG; SM
25-20	.257	58		32GC	SGG; OCG; MM; GC
	.257	65		32GC	SGG; OCG; MM; GC
7mm Nambu	.280	60	PB	134	RGG; OCG
8mm Nambu	.323, .321	100	PB	116	RGG
8mm Lebel Rev.	.323	125	PB	226	RGG; OCG; NDB; SM
30 Luger	.310	90	PB	93	SGG; MM
	.310	92	PB	113	RGG
30 M1 Carbine	.308	113			RGG; GC base
	.308	115	BB	254	RGG
32 Auto	.309	83	PB		RGG
32 Revolver	.312, .313	40	PB	354	RGG; LM
	.312, .313	90	PB	299	RGG; SM
	.312, .313	85	PB	26-4	RGG; OCG; 4DB
	.312, .313	98	PB	26-5	RGG; OCG; 5DB
	.312, .313	98	PB	65	RGG; OCG; BB; SWS; MM
	.312, .313	98	PB	252	RGG; OCG; BB
	.312, .313	90	PB	S216	RGG; OCG; MM; RSWS
	.312, .313	100	PB	216	RGG; OCG; MM; RSWS
	.312, .313	200	PB	220	RGG; OCG; MM; RSWS
	.312, .313	115	PB	361	RGG; OCG; SM
32 S&W Long	.312	100	PB	66	RGG; OCG; LM; SWS BB
	.312	100	BB	353	SGG; LEEF; LM
	.312	105			RGG; square corners, no bevels.
32-20	.312	105	PB	89	RGG; OCG; LM
	.312	115		89	RGG; OCG; LM
	.312	115	PB	67	RGG; MM
	.312	115	BB	388	RGG; OCG; MM
32 H&R Mag.	.313	106	PB		SGG; OCG; SWS; LM
380 Auto	.356	100	PB	S55	RGG; BB
9mm Luger	.356	98	BB	279	RGG; SM
	.356	115	PB	307	SGG
	.356	115	PB	308	RGG
	.356	125	PB	7	RGG
	.356	125	BB	115	RGG
	.356	125	BB	264	RGG; SWS; SM
	.356	125	BB	275	RGG; SWS; MM
	.356	125	PB	309	RGG; LM; BB
	.356	125	PB	310	RGG; BB
	.356	125	PB	318	RGG; RSWS; LM
	.356	125	BB	331	RGG
	.356	128	BB	317	RGG; LM
	.356	135	BB	286	RGG; MM
	.356	135	BB	314	RGG; German army Ogival.
	.356	140		313	RGG; OCG; also for revolver; SM
	.356	147	PB	378	RGG; SM
	.356	150	PB	363	SGG; LM
	.356	150	PB	377	RGG
9mm Makarov	.364	105	PB	375	RGG
38 Super	.356	115	BB	262	RGG; SWS; LM
	.356	130	PB	81	RGG; SWS; LM
	.356	130	PB	157	RGG; MM; RSWS
	.356	130	PB	583	RGG; OCG; SWS; MM
	.356	135	PB	55	BB
	.356	135	PB	161	RGG; MM; RSWS
	.356	145	PB	73	BB; SGG; OCG; SWS; SM
	.356	145	PB	123	RGG; SWS
	.356	150	PB	355	SGG; SWS; SM
	.356	152	BB	335	SGG; SWS; MM
	.356	155	BB	370	SGG; MM
	.356	158	BB	39BB	RGG; OCG
	.356	158	BB	316BB	SGG; OCG; MM
38 Special	.356	145	PB	219	RGG; LEEF; LM
	.356	145	BB	259	RGG; SWS
	.356	146	PB	244	BB; RGG; OCG; LM
	.356	150	PB	248	RGG; OCG; SWS; LM
38 Gold Cup	.356	148	BB		BB; RGG; OCG; SWS; LM
38 Spl./357 Mag.	.358	62	PB		RGG; LM
	.356	148	BB	251	RGG; LM
	.356	148	BB	334	SGG; LEEF; LM
	.358	100		234	GC base; RGG; OCG; SWS; MM
	.358	110	PB	41	BB; RGG; OCG; SWS; LM
	.358	130	PB	246	SGG; SWS; MM
	.358	135	PB	272	SGG; OCG

RGG = Round Grease Groove; SGG = Square Grease Groove; SM = Small Meplat; MM = Medium Meplat; LM = Large Meplat; OCG = One Crimp Groove; TCG = Two Crimp Grooves; PB = Plain Flat Base; BB = Bevel Base; GC = Gas Check; SWS = Semi- or Wadcutter Shoulder; 1DB = One Driving Band; 2DB = Two Driving Bands; 3DB = Three Driving Bands; 4DB = Four Driving Bands; 5DB = Five Driving Bands; RSWS = Rounded Semi-Wadcutter Shoulder; SBB = Short Bevel Base; LBB = Long Bevel Base; EB = Extended Base; OD = Oversize Diameter; NDB = No Driving Band in front of Crimp Groove; LEEF = Loaded Either End Forward; BRN = Bore Riding Nose. *Extra fee for special cross-venting for this design.

See page 175 for prices.

HENSLEY & GIBBS Bullet Moulds

	Bullet			Mould	
Caliber	Dia.	Wgt. Grs.	Type	#	Comments
38 Spl./357 Mag.	.358	140	BB	392	RGG; OCG; NDB
	.358	140	BB	313BB	RGG; OCG; also for rev. bullet; SM
	.358	125	PB	313PB	RGG; OCG; also for rev. bullet; SM
	.358	140		393	GC; RGG; OCG; LM
	.358	140	BB	511	SGG; OCG; MM
	.358	145	PB	63	BB; RGG; OCG
	.358	145	PB	73	BB; SGG; OCG; SM
	.358	146		159	RGG; OCG; SWS; tapered boattail; LM
	.358	148	PB	50	BB; RGG; OCG; SWS; LM
	.358	150	PB	9	BB; RGG; OCG; SWS; LM
	.358	130	PB	12C	GC; RGG; MM
	.358	140	PB	12B	GC; RGG; MM
	.358	150	PB	12A	GC; RGG; MM
	.358	150	PB	27	BB; RGG; OCG
	.358	150	PB	61	SGG; SWS; LM
	.358	150	PB	527	BB; RGG; SWS; LM
	.358	156		135	GC; RGG; TCG; SWS; LM
	.358	156	PB	218	RGG; OCG; SWS; LM
	.358	158	PB	28	BB; RGG; OCG
	.358	158	PB	36	RGG; OCG; SWS; LM
	.358	158	PB	39	BB and GC base; RGG; OCG
	.358	158	PB	48	BB; RGG; OCG; LM
	.358	158	PB	49	BB; RGG; OCG; MM
	.358	158	PB	52	RGG
	.358	158	PB	260	RGG; SM
	.358	158	PB	316	BB; SGG; OCG; MM
	.358	160	PB	51	BB and GC base; SGG; OCG; LM
	.358	160		236	GC; RGG; OCG; SWS; LM
	.358	160	PB	290	BB; SGG; OCG; SWS; LM
	.358	160	BB	801BB	SGG; OCG; SWS; LM
	.358	163*	PB	64	SGG; OCG; SWS; MM
	.358	165*	PB	37	BB; RGG; OCG; SWS; LM
	.358	165*	PB	56	RGG; OCG; TCG; SWS; LM
	.358	165*		268	RGG; OCG; SWS; LM
	.358	170*		30	GC; RGG
	.358	170*		394	GC; RGG; OCG; LM
	.358	173*	PB	43	SGG; OCG; SWS; LM
	.358	185*		376	RGG; OCG; LM
	.358	190*	PB	395	RGG; OCG; LM
	.358	125*		322-3	RGG; OCG; 3DB; SM
	.358	158*		322-4	RGG; OCG; 4DB; SM
	.358	190*		322-4GC	RGG; OCG; 3DB; SM; GC
	.358	175*	PB	57-3	RGG; OCG; 3DB; LM
	.358	200*	PB	57-4	RGG; OCG; 4DB; SM
	.358	200*	PB	138	RGG; OCG
	.358	215*	PB	257	
	.358	230*	BB	127	SGG; OCG; LM
357 Maximum	.357/.358	200*		319	SGG; OCG; SWS; LM
	.357/.358	200*		320	GC; OCG; MM
	.357/.358	200*		321	SGG; OCG; boattail bevel base; MM
375 Super Mag.	.376	165*		380-3	SGG; OCG; 3DB; MM
	.376	185*		380-3GC	SGG; OCG; 3DB; MM; GC
	.376	210*		380-4	SGG; OCG; 4DB; MM
	.376	235*		380-4GC	SGG; OCG; 4DB; MM; GC
	.376	270*		380-5	SGG; OCG; 5DB; MM
38-40	.401	180		6	BB; RGG; OCG
41 Long Colt	.401	185	PB	121	RGG
40 S&W/10mm	.401	125	PB	365	SGG
	.401	135	BB	374	RGG; SWS; SM
	.401	145	PB	360	SGG; revolvers/single shots only.
	.401	155	PB	373	RGG; SM
	.401	155	BB	S359BB	RGG; MM
	.401	175	PB	332	BB; RGG; SWS; MM
	.401	155	PB	S359PB	RGG; MM
	.401	180	BB	359BB	RGG; MM
	.401	190	BB	324	SGG; LM
	.401	200	PB	315	RGG; LM
	.401	200*	PB	396	RGG; OCG; LM
	.401	220*	PB	397	RGG; OCG; LM
41 AE	.410	180	BB	342BB	RGG; SWS; medium shoulder
41 Magnum	.410	79	PB	368	RGG; SWS; LM
	.410	175	PB	255	RGG; OCG; SWS; LM
	.410	175	PB	291	SGG; OCG
	.410	210	PB	253	RGG; LM
	.410	210	PB	256	BB and GC; RGG; OCG; SWS; LM
	.410	210*	PB	261	RGG; OCG; SWS; MM
	.410	210*	PB	263	RGG; OCG

RGG = Round Grease Groove; SGG = Square Grease Groove; SM = Small Meplat; MM = Medium Meplat; LM = Large Meplat; OCG = One Crimp Groove; TCG = Two Crimp Grooves; PB = Plain Flat Base; BB = Bevel Base; GC = Gas Check; SWS = Semi- or Wadcutter Shoulder; 1DB = One Driving Band; 2DB = Two Driving Bands; 3DB = Three Driving Bands; 4DB = Four Driving Bands; 5DB = Five Driving Bands; RSWS = Rounded Semi-Wadcutter Shoulder; SBB = Short Bevel Base; LBB = Long Bevel Base; EB = Extended Base; OD = Oversize Diameter; NDB = No Driving Band in front of Crimp Groove; LEEF = Loaded Either End Forward; BRN = Bore Riding Nose. *Extra fee for special cross-venting for this design.

See page 175 for prices.

#236 160gr

(3)(8)(9)(26)(73)

#290 160gr

(2)(4)(7)(9)(26)(73)

#801BB 160gr

(1)(7)(9)(26)(73)

#64 163gr*

(2)(7)(9)(26)(72)

#37 165gr*

(2)(4)(8)(9)(26)(73)

#56 165gr*

(2)(8)(9)(10)(26)(39)(73)

#268*

#15 240gr

(2)(6)(8)(9)

#35 240gr

(2)(8)(9)(26)(73)

#45 240gr

(2)(4)(6)(8)(9)(26
(73)

#235 240gr*

(3)(8)(9)(26)(73)

#107 *

245gr at 107A length, 185gr at 107B length, and 135gr at 107C length.

(2)(8)(9)(26)(73)

HENSLEY & GIBBS Bullet Moulds

Caliber	Bullet Dia.	Bullet Wgt. Grs.	Bullet Type	Mould #	Mould Comments
41 Magnum	.410	220*	PB	258	SGG; OCG; SWS; LM
44-40	.427	210	PB	44	RGG; OCG; NDB; LM
	.427	250	PB	44GC	RGG; OCG; NDB; LM
	.427	210	PB	44BB	RGG; OCG; NDB; LM
44	.429/.431	85	BB	443	RGG; LM
	.429/.431	87	PB	350	RGG; LM
	.429/.431	180	PB	180	RGG; LM; RSWS
	.429/.431	180	PB	273	SGG; OCG
	.429/.431	185	PB	245	RGG; SWS; MM
	.429/.431	185	BB	366	SGG; LEEF; LM
	.429/.431	195	PB	340	SGG; OCG; SM
	.429/.431	200		237	GC; RGG; OCG; SWS; LM
	.429/.431	200	PB	239	RGG; OCG; LM
	.429/.431	200		240	GC; RGG; OCG
	.429/.431	200	PB	241	RGG; OCG; SWS; LM
	.429/.431	205	PB	23	RGG; LM
	.429/.431	205	BB	330	RGG; OCG; SWS; LM
	.429/.431	210	BB	271	RGG; SWS
	.429/.431	220	PB	247	RGG; SWS
	.429/.431	225	BB	341	SGG; OCG; LM
	.429/.431	190	PB	142PB	RGG; SWS; LM
	.429/.431	230		142GC	RGG; SWS
	.429/.431	240	PB	15	GC; RGG; OCG
	.429/.431	240	PB	35	RGG; OCG; SWS; LM
	.429/.431	240	PB	45	BB and GC; RGG; OCG; SWS; LM
	.429/.431	240*		235	GC; RGG; SWS; LM
	.429/.431	135*	PB	107C	RGG; OCG; SWS; LM
	.429/.431	185*	PB	107B	RGG; OCG; SWS; LM
	.429/.431	245	PB	107A	RGG; OCG; SWS; LM
	.429/.431	225	PB	140PB	SGG; OCG; SWS; LM
	.429/.431	250		140GC	SGG; OCG; SWS; LM
	.429/.431	225*	PB	521PB	RGG; OCG; SWS; LM
	.429/.431	250*		521GC	RGG; OCG; SWS; LM
	.429/.431	270*	PB	326	SGG; OCG; SWS; LM
	.429/.431	280*	PB	367	RGG; OCG; LM
	.429/.431	280*	PB	503S	SGG; OCG; SWS; EB band; LM
	.429/.431	300*	BB	327	RGG; OCG; MM
	.429/.431	300*	PB	328	SGG; OCG; SWS; LM
	.429/.431	300*	BB	343	SGG; OCG; LM
	.429/.431	300*	BB	369	SGG; OCG; LM
	.429/.431	320*	PB	356	RGG; OCG; LM
	.429/.431	95*		352-2	SGG; 2DB; LM
	.429/.431	130*		352-2GC	SGG; 2DB; LM
	.429/.431	155*		352-3	SGG; 3DB; LM
	.429/.431	195*		352-3GC	SGG; 3DB; LM
	.429/.431	240*		352-4	SGG; 4DB; LM
	.429/.431	280*		352-4GC	SGG; 4DB; LM
	.429/.431	335*		352-5	SGG; 5DB; LM
	.429/.431	255*	BB	379-3GC	SGG; 3DB; OCG; LM
	.429/.431	300*	BB	379-4GC	SGG; 4DB; OCG; LM
	.429/.431	335*	BB	379-5	SGG; 5DB; OCG; LM
45 Auto	.452	155*	PB	358PB	RGG; SWS; SM
	.452	155*	BB	358BB	RGG; SWS; SM
	.452		PB	S242	RGG; SWS; MM
	.452	170	PB	938	SGG
	.452	172	PB	229	RGG; SWS
	.452	180	PB	293	RGG; SWS; LM
	.452	180	PB	337	RGG; SWS; MM
	.452	185	PB	130	BB; RGG; LM; RSWS
	.452	185	PB	163	2RGG; LM; RSWS
	.452	185	PB	242	RGG; SWS; MM
	.452	200	PB	68	BB; RGG; SWS; MM
	.452	200	PB	249	RGG
	.452	200	BB	265	SGG; SWS
	.452	200	BB	519	Available with PB; RGG
	.452	215	PB	78	BB; RGG; SWS; LM
	.452	215	PB	118	BB; RGG; SWS
	.452	215	BB	351	RGG; SWS; long tapered boattail; MM
	.452	220	BB	294	RGG; SWS; long tapered boattail; MM
	.452	230	PB	34	BB; RGG
	.452	230	PB	292	BB; SGG
	.452	240	PB	329	RGG; SWS; LM
	.452	219	BB	68BBA	SBB; 207-gr. lino; RGG; EB; SWS; MM
	.452	232	BB	68BBB	LBB; 219-gr. lino; RGG; EB; SWS; MM
	.452	231	PB	68S	218-gr. lino; RGG; EB; SWS; MM
	.452	239	BB	68BBS	LBB; 226-gr. lino; RGG; EB; SWS; MM

RGG = Round Grease Groove; SGG = Square Grease Groove; SM = Small Meplat; MM = Medium Meplat; LM = Large Meplat; OCG = One Crimp Groove; TCG = Two Crimp Grooves; PB = Plain Flat Base; BB = Bevel Base; GC = Gas Check; SWS = Semi- or Wadcutter Shoulder; 1DB = One Driving Band; 2DB = Two Driving Bands; 3DB = Three Driving Bands; 4DB = Four Driving Bands; 5DB = Five Driving Bands; RSWS = Rounded Semi-Wadcutter Shoulder; SBB = Short Bevel Base; LBB = Long Bevel Base; EB = Extended Base; OD = Oversize Diameter; NDB = No Driving Band in front of Crimp Groove; LEEF = Loaded Either End Forward; BRN = Bore Riding Nose. *Extra fee for special cross-venting for this design.

See page 175 for prices.

HENSLEY & GIBBS Bullet Moulds

Caliber	Bullet Dia.	Bullet Wgt. Grs.	Bullet Type	Mould #	Mould Comments
45 L.C./45 A.R.	.454/.452	160	PB	193	RGG; OCG; LM
	.454/.452	195	PB	312	SGG; OCG
	.454/.452	200	PB	21	RGG; OCG; MM
	.454/.452	200	PB	155	RGG; OCG; SWS; LM
	.454/.452	215	BB	529	RGG; OCG; SWS; LM
	.454/.452	230	PB	16	RGG; OCG
	.454/.452	230	PB	371	RGG; OCG; SWS
	.454/.452	240	PB	46	BB and GC; RGG; OCG; SWS; LM
	.454/.452	240	PB	502	SGG; OCG; SWS; LM
	.454/.452	250*	PB	22	RGG; MM
	.454/.452	255*	BB	387	RGG; OCG; LM
	.454/.452	260*	PB	501	SGG; OCG; SWS; LM
	.454/.452	265*	BB	339	RGG; OCG; LM
454 Casull	.4515	300*	PB	338	SGG; OCG; SWS; LM
	.4515	219*	PB	372-2GC	SGG; 2DB; LM
	.4515	257*	PB	372-3	SGG; 3DB; LM
	.4515	290*	PB	372-3GC	SGG; 3DB; LM
	.4515	340*	PB	372-4	SGG; 4DB; LM
45-70	.458	350*	PB	389	RGG; MM
	.458	355*	PB	348GC	RGG; OCG; SM
	.458	280*	PB	348	RGG; OCG; SM
	.458	300*	BB	348BB	RGG; OCG; SM
	.458	355*	PB	348GC	RGG; OCG; SM
	.458	275*	PB	345-3	SGG; 3DB; MM
	.458	325*	PB	345-4	SGG; 4DB; MM
	.458	395*	PB	345-5	SGG; 5DB; MM
	.458	285*	PB	344-3	SGG; 3DB; MM
	.458	340*	PB	344-4	SGG; 4DB; MM
	.458	405*	PB	344-5	SGG; 5DB; MM
	.458	360*	PB	346	RGG; TCG
	.458	380*	BB	346	RGG; TCG
	.458	405*		346GC	RGG; TCG
	.458	250*	PB	349-2	SGG; 2DB; OD; MM
	.458	300*	PB	349-3	SGG; 3DB; OD; MM
	.458	355*	PB	349-4	SGG; 4DB; OD; MM
	.458	405*	PB	349-5	SGG; 5DB; OD; MM
	.458	350*	PB	390-4	RGG; 4DB; BRN; SM
	.458	410*	PB	390-5	RGG; 5DB; BRN; SM
	.458	320*	PB	364-3GC	SGG; 3DB; MM
	.458	345*	PB	364-4	SGG; 4DB; MM
	.458	375*	PB	364-4GC	SGG; 4DB; MM
	.458	410*	PB	364-5	SGG; 5DB; MM
	.458	195*	PB	347-2	RGG; 2DB; MM
	.458	260*	PB	347-3	RGG; 3DB; MM
	.458	335*	PB	347-4	RGG; 4DB; MM
	.458	400*	PB	347-5	RGG; 5DB; MM
	.458	415*	PB	X347-5	RGG; 5DB; MM
	.458	400*	PB	391-5	RGG; 5DB; MM
	.458	425*	PB	X391-5	RGG; 5DB; MM

RGG = Round Grease Groove; SGG = Square Grease Groove; SM = Small Meplat; MM = Medium Meplat; LM = Large Meplat; OCG = One Crimp Groove; TCG = Two Crimp Grooves; PB = Plain Flat Base; BB = Bevel Base; GC = Gas Check; SWS = Semi- or Wadcutter Shoulder; 1DB = One Driving Band; 2DB = Two Driving Bands; 3DB = Three Driving Bands; 4DB = Four Driving Bands; 5DB = Five Driving Bands; RSWS = Rounded Semi-Wadcutter Shoulder; SBB = Short Bevel Base; LBB = Long Bevel Base; EB = Extended Base; OD = Oversize Diameter; NDB = No Driving Band in front of Crimp Groove; LEEF = Loaded Either End Forward; BRN = Bore Riding Nose. *Extra fee for special cross-venting for this design.

HENSLEY & GIBBS *Price Structure*

Mould/Mould Part	2	4	6
Complete, light/short bullets	$101.00	$135.00	$175.00
Complete, heavy/long bullets	111.00	145.00	190.00
Mould, no handles	85.00	122.00	148.00
Sprue cutter w/screws, trough-style	18.00	30.00	31.00
Sprue cutter w/screws, individual hole		40.00	
Handles	34.00	34.00	52.00
Blocks, only	68.00	93.00	118.00
Sprue cutter hinge or stop screw	2.00	2.00	2.00
Front/rear lock screws (2)	1.50	1.50	1.50
Handle retainer screws (2)	4.00	4.00	4.00
Handle pivot bolt/nut	1.50	1.50	2.00
Complete set of screws	9.50	9.50	10.50
Complete set of screws plus handle pivot bolt/nut	10.50	10.50	11.50
Wood Grips	5.00	5.00	6.00

Mould Handles

Precision steel mould handles fit all Lee moulds as well as most other brands of one- and two-cavity moulds. From Lee Precision, Inc.

Price: **$17.98**

LEE

Six-Cavity Commercial Moulds

Designed for heavy-duty volume production. Mould and blocks have steel bushing and alignment pins. Cam-operated sprue plate is hard-anodized and held with wave washers at each end. Handles not included. From Lee Precision, Inc.

Price: **$50.00**

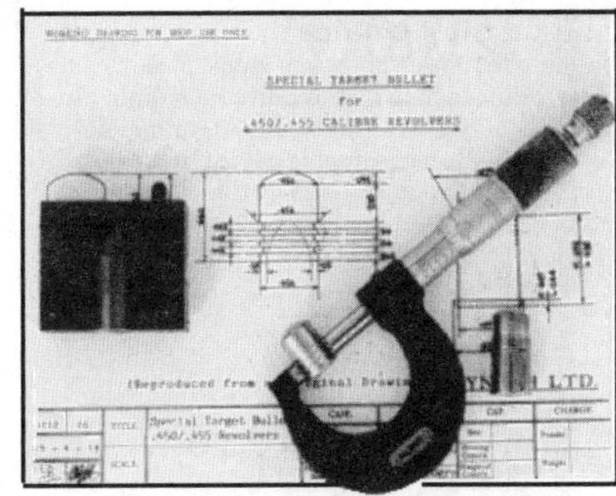

Loweth 455 Special Target Mould Design

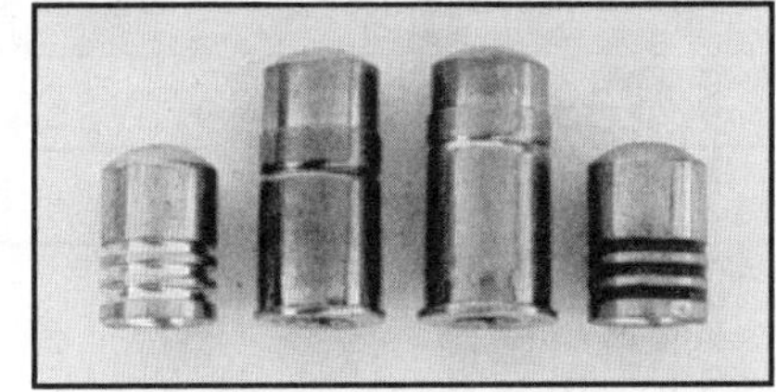

Loweth Special Target Bullets

Hensley & Gibbs 6-Cavity Mould

Section 3: Bullet Casting

Shotgun Slug Mould

The Lee 12-gauge Slug Mould features an exclusive "drive key" divider in the hollow base which serves to keep the wad from penetrating into the hollow base and ensures rotation of both wad and slug in a rifled barrel. Available for 1- or 7/8-oz. slug weights. Designed to be loaded in conventional trap hulls with standard trap wads. Comes complete with handles. From Lee Precision, Inc.

Price: **$25.98**

LYMAN

Ideal Moulds

Machined from high-grade steel; blocks are hand fit for precision alignment. Pistol bullet moulds available for all popular bullet designs and come in 2- or 4-cavity blocks. Rifle moulds available in 2-cavity only except where bullet size necessitates single cavity. From Lyman Products Corporation.

Price: Pistol, 2-cavity **$59.95**
Price: Pistol, 4-cavity **$85.95**
Price: Rifle **$59.95**

Shotgun Slug Moulds

Available for 12- or 20-gauge slugs. Mould casts hollow-base slugs, which require no rifling. Single-cavity only and cut into the larger double-cavity block. Require double cavity handles. From Lyman Products Corporation.

Price: **$59.95**

LBT Single Cavity Mould

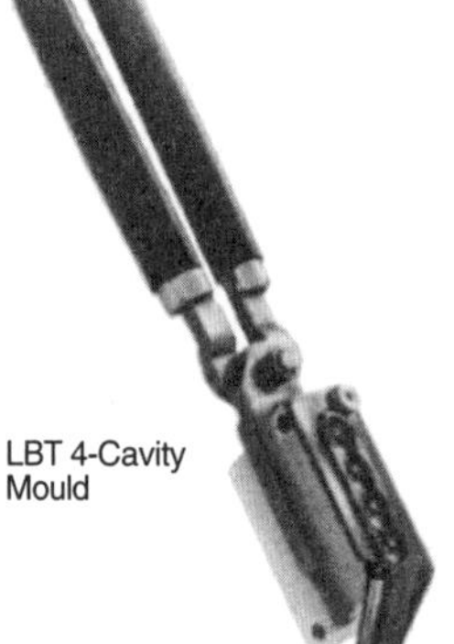

LBT 4-Cavity Mould

LEE Rifle Bullet Moulds

Dia.	Wgt. Grs.	Type	Ogive	Gas Check (C) / Micro Bands (M)	Mould
270-CALIBER					
.277	125	R	1	C	1-cavity
7MM CALIBER					
.285	130	R	1	C	1-cavity
30-CALIBER					
.309	113	F		C	2-cavity
.309	120	R	1	C	2-cavity
.309	130	R	1	C	1-cavity
.309	150	F		C	1-cavity
.309	160	R	1	C	1-cavity
.309	170	F		C	1-cavity
.309	180	R	1	C	1-cavity
.309	200	R	1	C	1-cavity
7.62x39 CALIBER					
.312	155	R	2		1-cavity
.312	160	R	2	M	1-cavity
7.65MM, 7.7MM, 303 BRITISH CALIBERS					
.312	185	R	1		1-cavity
338-CALIBER					
.338	220	R	1	C	1-cavity
45-70 CALIBER					
.457	340	F			1-cavity
.457	405	F			1-cavity*
.457	405	HB			1-cavity
.457	450	F			1-cavity
.457	500	F			1-cavity
50-70 CALIBER					
.515	450	F			1-cavity
.515	500	F			1-cavity

R = Round Nose; F = Flat. *Hollow Point

LEE Pistol Bullet Moulds

Dia.	Wgt. Grs.	Type	Ogive	Micro Bands (M) Gas Check(C)	Mould
32-20, 32 S&W LONG, 32 COLT NEW POLICE					
.311	93	R	1		2-, 6-cavity
.311	100	R	2		2-cavity
.314	85	WC		M	2-, 6-cavity
.314	90	SWC		M	2-, 6-cavity
38 SPECIAL, 38 S&W, 38 COLT NEW POLICE					
.358	148	WC			2-, 6-cavity
.358	105	SWC			2-, 6-cavity
.358	140	SWC			2-, 6-cavity
.358	166	SWC			2-, 6-cavity
.358	148	WC		M	2-, 6-cavity
.358	158	SWC		M	2-, 6-cavity
.358	158	SWC		C	2-, 6-cavity*
.358	158	R	2	M	2-, 6-cavity
.358	150	R	1		2-, 6-cavity
.358	150	WC	1		2-, 6-cavity
9MM LUGER, 38 SUPER AUTO, 380 AUTO					
.356	102	R	1		2-, 6-cavity
.356	111	R	1		2-, 6-cavity
.356	124	R	2	M	2-, 6-cavity
.356	124	TC		M	2-, 6-cavity
.356	120	TC			2-, 6-cavity
.356	125	R	2		2-, 6-cavity
.356	153	R	2		2-, 6-cavity
9MM MAKAROV					
.365	95	R	1		2-cavity
10MM AUTO					
.401	145	SWC			2-cavity
.401	175	SWC		M	2-, 6-cavity
.401	175	TC			
41 MAGNUM, 41 ACTION EXPRESS					
.410	195	SWC		M	2-, 6-cavity
.410	240	SWC			2-, 6-cavity
.410	210	SWC		M	2-, 6-cavity
.410	175	SWC		M	2-, 6-cavity
45 ACP, 45 AUTO RIM					
.452	200	SWC			2-, 6-cavity
44 SPECIAL, 44 MAGNUM, 44-40 (.427)					
.429	200	RF			
.429	208	WC			2-, 6-cavity
.429	214	SWC			2-, 6-cavity*
.429	240	SWC		C	2-, 6-cavity*
.429	255	SWC			2-, 6-cavity
.429	214	R	1		2-, 6-cavity
.429	240	R	2		2-, 6-cavity
.429	240	SWC		M	2-, 6-cavity
.430	310	RF			2-, 6-cavity
45 ACP, 45 AUTO RIM					
.452	155	SWC			2-, 6-cavity
.452	190	SWC			2-, 6-cavity
.452	200	SWC		M	2-, 6-cavity
.452	228	R	1		2-, 6-cavity*
.452	230	R	2		2-, 6-cavity
.452	230	TC			2-, 6-cavity
.452	230	TC			2-, 6-cavity
.452	252	SWC			2-, 6-cavity
.452	255	RF			2-, 6-cavity
45 COLT REVOLVER, 45 AUTO RIM					
.452	252	SWC			2-, 6-cavity
.452	255	RF			2-, 6-cavity

WC = Wadcutter; SWC = Semi-wadcutter; RF = Round with flat; RN = Round Nose; TC = Truncated Cone; M = Micro Bands Radius; C = Gas Check. *Hollow Point.

Mould Rebuild Kit

Includes sprue cutter, washer, all screws for mould block and handle. From Lyman Products Corporation.

Price: 1- and 2-cavity **$6.50**
Price: 4-cavity **$7.50**

LBT Bullet Moulds

Caliber	Wgt. Grs.	Type	Ogive*	Meplat	Length
HANDGUN / AUTO PISTOL					
25 Auto	50	FN	SA	.200	
32 ACP	75	FN	SA	.200	
380 Auto	100	FN	SA	.200	
	100	RN	SA	.200	
	110	FN	SA	.200	
	120	FN	SA	.200	
9MM	90	FN	SA	.200	
	95	TC	SA	.200	
	110	TC	SA	.200	
	125	TC	SA	.200	
	140	BR	SA	.200	
	120	FNBR	SA	.200	
10mm Auto	180	TC	SA	.200	
	185	FNB	SA	.200	
	165	SWC	SA	.200	
45 Auto	200	SWC	SA	.200	
	190	FNB	SA	.200	
	220	FNB	SA	.200	
	230	B	SA	.200	
HANDGUN / REVOLVER / WADCUTTERS					
32	100	WC	NA	NA	
38	150	WC	NA	NA	
375	170	WC	NA	NA	
41	200	WC	NA	NA	
44	230	WC	NA	NA	
45	260	WC	NA	NA	
HANDGUN / REVOLVER / SFN SERIES					
32	90	SFN	.160	.080	
	90	FN	.250	.090	
	100	SFN	.160	.080	
	115	FN	.250	.090	
	140	FN	.250	.090	
38	140	FN	.250	.090	
	160	FN	.250	.090	
	180	FN	.250	.090	
	200	FN	.250	.090	Crimp to nose .350 & .400
375	240	WFN	.250	.090	
41	200	WFN	.250	.090	
	220	WFN	.250	.090	
	250	WFN	.250	.090	
	300	WFN	.250	.090	
44	230	WFN	.250	.090	
	260	WFN	.250	.090	
	280	WFN	.250	.090	
	300	WFN	.250	.090	
45	250	WFN	.250	.090	
	280	WFN	.250	.090	
	325	WFN	.250	.090	
475	400	WFN	.250	.090	
500	400	WFN	.250	.090	
HANDGUN / REVOLVER / WLN SERIES					
38	180	WLN	.400	.090	
41	230	WLN	.400	.090	
44	300	WLN	.400	.090	
45	320	WLN	.400	.090	
HANDGUN / REVOLVER / LFN SERIES					
358	180	LFN	.130	.340	.725
	210	LFN	.130	.340	.840
375	210	LFN	.130	.340	.770
	225	LFN	.130	.340	.818
	240	LFN	.130	.340	.240
41	210	LFN	.130	.340	.660
	230	LFN	.130	.340	.715
	250	LFN	.130	.340	.774
44	250	LFN	.130	.340	.675
	280	LFN	.130	.340	.775
	300	LFN	.130	.340	.820
	320	LFN	.130	.340	.860
	350	LFN	.130	.340	.920
45	260	LFN	.130	.340	.675
	300	LFN	.130	.340	.775
	320	LFN	.130	.340	.820
	340	LFN	.130	.340	.870
475	380	LFN	.130	.340	.855
	400	LFN	.130	.340	.940
	420	LFN	.130	.340	.955
	440	LFN	.130	.340	.970
500	400	LFN	.130	.340	.820
	420	LFN	.130	.340	.820
	450	LFN	.130	.340	.855
HANDGUN / REVOLVER / K SERIES					
44	250	K		.340	
45	260	K		.340	
	315	K		.340	

Caliber	Wgt. Grs.	Type	Ogive*	Meplat	Length
RIFLE & SINGLE SHOT HANDGUN / LFN SERIES					
257	90	LFN	.130	.340	.745
	100	LFN	.130	.340	.820
	117	LFN	.130	.340	.950
270	120	LFN	.130	.340	.840
	140	LFN	.130	.340	.950
	150	LFN	.130	.340	1.010
7mm	130	LFN	.130	.340	.835
	150	LFN	.130	.340	.955
	170	LFN	.130	.340	1.070
310	150	LFN	.130	.340	.820
	170	LFN	.130	.340	.940
	180	LFN	.130	.340	.955
	200	LFN	.130	.340	1.010
323	150	LFN	.130	.340	.754
	170	LFN	.130	.340	.840
	200	LFN	.130	.340	.971
338	200	LFN	.130	.340	.990
	225	LFN	.130	.340	.880
	250	LFN	.130	.340	1.090
348	200	LFN	.130	.340	.850
	250	LFN	.130	.340	1.035
358	210	LFN	.130	.340	.840
	225	LFN	.130	.340	.880
	250	LFN	.130	.340	.965
375	225	LFN	.130	.340	.880
	240	LFN	.130	.340	.865
	275	LFN	.130	.340	.978
	300	LFN	.130	.340	1.057
40/416	350	LFN	.130	.340	1.025
	375	LFN	.130	.340	1.070
	400	LFN	.130	.340	1.155
458	300	LFN	.130	.340	.775
	340	LFN	.130	.340	.870
	450	LFN	.130	.340	1.072
	500	LFN	.130	.340	1.192
RIFLE & SINGLE SHOT / SPITZER					
223	50	SP	.264		.300
	55	SP	.264		.350
	60	SP	.264		.400
	66	SP	.264		.450
227	65	SP	.275		.410
	75	SP	.275		.410
243	75	SP	.295		.420
	90	SP	.295		.530
	100	SP	.295		.610
257	80	SP	.303		.370
	90	SP	.303		.440
	100	SP	.303		.510
	120	SP	.303		.650
264	100	SP	.310		.500
	120	SP	.310		.620
	130	SP	.310		.680
	150	SP	.310		.800
270	90	SP	.317		.380
	100	SP	.317		.440
	110	SP	.317		.500
	130	SP	.317		.600
7mm	110	SP	.322		.435
	120	SP	.322		.500
	140	SP	.322		.550
	150	SP	.322		.670
7.35/302	150	SP	.335		.565
	170	SP	.335		.670
	194	SP	.335		.800
310	140	SP	.341		.620
	160	SP	.341		.675
	180	SP	.341		.730
	206	SP	.341		.800
323	150	SP	.350		.480
	150	SP	.350		.480
	175	SP	.350		.590
	200	SP	.350		.700
	220	SP	.350		.800
338	200	SP	.360		.610
	225	SP	.360		.710
	246	SP	.360		.800
358	200	SP	.375		.500
	250	SP	.375		.730
375	275	SP	.385		.700
	310	SP	.385		.800
405-410		SP	.400		.500
	300	SP	.400		.600
	370	SP	.400		.800
458	350	SP	.425		.535
	400	SP	.425		.640
	500	SP	.425		.850
475	400	SP	.430		.550
	510	SP	.430		.800
512	500	SP	.450		.600
	600	SP	.450		.800

SA = Small Auto; FN = Flat Nose; RN = Round Nose; LFN = Long Flat Base; WFN = Wide Flat Nose; FNB = Flat Nose Ball; SP = Spitzer; K = Keith-style

Section 3: Bullet Casting

Mould Box
Made of tough plastic with snap-lock cover. Impervious to moisture, bore cleaner or oil. Fits single- and double-cavity moulds only. From Lyman Products Corporation.
Price: **$2.00**
Price: 10 .... **$12.50**

LYMAN
Mould Handles
Lyman no longer manufactures small single-cavity mould blocks. All current Lyman single- and double-cavity moulds are now made using standard large mould blocks and require large mould handles. Solid metal frame with hardwood handles designed to provide uniform grip. Three sizes available: small, for older single cavity moulds; large, for current manufacture large block single-cavity and double-cavity moulds; and four-cavity for Lyman four-cavity moulds. From Lyman Products Corporation.
Price: 1- and 2-cavity **$33.50**
Price: 4-cavity.................... **$31.95**

Sabot Slug Mould
A 20-gauge 350-grain slug designed to fit standard Winchester wads and be star-crimped. Comes complete with load data. From Lyman Products Corporation.
Price: **$59.95**

LYMAN Rifle Bullet Moulds

Bullet #	Caliber	Dia.	Wgt. Grs.	Top Punch #	Gas Check #	# Cavity Mould
225438	22	.225	44	438	GC	2
225415		.225	55	415	GC	2
225646		.225	55	415	GC	2
245496	6mm	.245	84	203	GC	2
257420	25	.257	65	420	GC	2
266469	6.5mm	.266	140	463	GC	2
268645		.268	150	463	GC	2
280642	270 Win.	.280	150	359		2
287346	7mm	.287	135	346	GC	2
287641		.287	160	359	GC	2
311359	30 M1/7.62x39mm	.311	115	359	GC	2
311410		.311	130	467		2
311466	30	.311	152	467	GC	2
311291		.311	170	465	GC	2
311041		.311	173	8	GC	2
311332		.311	180	413	GC	2
311644		.311	190	359	GC	2
311284		.311	210	467	GC	2
311316	32-20	.311	112	8	GC	2
311008		.311	115	8		2
314299	314	.314	200	467	GC	2
323470	8mm	.323	165	470	GC	2
358315	35	.358	204	311	GC	2
358009		.358	280	430	GC	2
375248	375/38-55	.375	249	449		2
375449		.375	264	449	GC	2
403169		.403	240	43		2
410660		.410	385	658		2
410655	40	.410	400	449		2
429434	44-40	.429	215	43	GC	2
439186	43 Spanish	.439	370	251	2	
457191	45	.457	292	191		2
457122	45 HP	.457	330	191		2
457124		.457	385	374		2
457643		.457	400	191		2
457193		.457	405	191		2
457406		.457	475	374	GC	2
457658		.457	480	658		2
457125		.457	500	374		2
457132	45 Postell	.457	535	132		2
515141	50	.515	425	141		2

LYMAN Pistol Bullet Moulds

Mould #	Caliber	Dia.	Wgt. Grs.	Top Punch #	Gas Check	# Cavity Mould
25235	25	.252	50	203		2
311252	30	.311	75	465		2
313249	32	.313	85	226		2
313631		.313	100	8	GC	2
35642	9mm	.356	90	311		2
356632		.356	100	402		2, 4
356402		.356	120	402		2, 4
356242		.356	120	311		2, 4
356634		.356	130	402		2, 4
356637		.356	147	429		2, 4
358345	38/357	.358	115	429		2
358093		.358	125	93		2
358495		.358	140	495		2, 4
358212		.358	145	311		2
358091		.358	150	495		2, 4
358477		.358	150	429		2, 4
358156		.358	155	429	GC	2, 4
358665		.358	158	495		2
358311		.358	160	311		2, 4
357446		.357	165	429		2, 4
358429		.358	170	429		2, 4
358430		.358	195	430		2
358627	357 Max.	.358	215	429	GC	2
364653	9mm Mak.	.364	95	226		2
401654	40 S&W/10mm	.401	150	43		2
401638		.401	175	43		2, 4
401043		.401	175	43		2
401633		.401	200	43		2
410610	41	.410	215	43	GC	2
427098	44-40	.427	205	43		2
427666		.427	200	649		2
429348	44/44 Mag.	.429	180	348		2
429303		.429	200	303	GC	2
429215		.429	210	421	GC	2, 4
429360		.429	235	360		2
429667		.429	240	649		2
429421		.429	245	421		2, 4
429383		.429	245	251		2
429244		.429	255	421	GC	2, 4
429640		.429	275	421	GC	2
429650		.429	300	421	GC	2
429649		.429	325	360	GC	2
452460	45	.452	200	460		2, 4
452630		.452	200	460		2, 4
452374		.452	225	374		2, 4
452424		.452	255	424		2
452490		.452	255	424	GC	2
452651		.452	325	424	GC	2
452664	45 LC	.452	250	649		2
454190	45 Colt	.454	250	190		2
		Hollowpoint Bullets				
356637	9mm	.356	125	429		
401638	10mm	.401	155	43		
429640	44	.429	250	421	GC	
452374	45	.452	180	374		

Bullet Moulds
For use with the Magma Master Caster automatic casting machine and manual Bullet Master. Over 40 bullet styles available. From Magma Engineering Co.
Price: **$67.50**

Lyman Pistol Bullet Moulds

Pistol	.25	.30	.32		9mm						.38/.357		
Bullet Number	252435	311252	313249	313631	356242	356632	356402	356242	356634	356637	358345	358093	358495
Weight (#2 Alloy)	50 gr.	75 gr.	85 gr.	100 gr.	90 gr.	100 gr.	120 gr.	120 gr.	130 gr.	147 gr.	115 gr.	125 gr.	140 gr.
Double Cavity Part #	2660435	2660252	2660249	2660631	2661242	2660632	2660402	2660242	2660634	2660637	2660345	2660093	2660495
Top Punch Number	203	465	226	8	311	402	402	311	402	429	429	93	495
Top Punch Part #	2786748	2786742	2786703	2786690	2786710	2786723	2786723	2786710	2786723	2786731	2786731	2786754	2786769
Four Cavity Part #	—	—	—	—	—	2670632	2670402	—	2670634	2670637	—	—	2670495

Pistol (cont'd)	.38/.357								.357 max	9mm mak.	40 S&W/10mm			
Bullet Number	358212	358091	358477	358156	358311	357446	358429	358430	358627	364653	401654	401638	401642	401633
Weight (#2 Alloy)	145 gr.	150 gr.	150 gr.	155 gr.	160 gr.	165 gr.	170 gr.	195 gr.	215 gr.	95 gr.	150 gr.	175 gr.	175 gr.	200 gr.
Double Cavity Part #	2660212	2660091	2660477	2660156	2660311	2660446	2660429	2660430	2660627	2660653	2660654	2660638	2660642	2660633
Top Punch Number	311	495	429	429	311	429	429	430	429	226	43	43	43	43
Top Punch Part #	2786710	2786769	2786731	2786731	2786710	2786731	2786731	2786732	2786731	2786703	2786691	2786691	2786691	2786691
Four Cavity Part #	—	2670091	2670477	2670156	2670311	2670446	2670429	—	—	—	—	2670638	—	—

Pistol (cont'd)	.41	.44/40	.44 & .44 mag										.45	
Bullet Number	410610	427098	429348	429303	429215	429360	429421	429383	429244	429640	429650	429649	452460	452630
Weight (#2 Alloy)	215 gr.	205 gr.	180 gr.	200 gr.	210 gr.	235 gr.	245 gr.	245 gr.	255 gr.	275 gr.	300 gr.	325 gr.	200 gr.	200 gr.
Double Cavity Part #	2660610	2660098	2660348	2660303	2660215	2660360	2660421	2660383	2660244	2660640	2660650	2660649	2660460	2660630
Top Punch Number	43	43	348	303	421	360	421	251	421	421	421	649	460	460
Top Punch Part #	2786691	2786691	2786716	2786709	2786729	2786717	2786729	2786704	2786729	2786729	2786729	2786778	2786740	2786740
Four Cavity Part #	—	—	—	—	2670215	—	2670421	—	2670244	—	—	—	2670460	2670630

Pistol (cont'd)	.45	.45 Colt .454 dia.	.45 Colt .452 dia.	.45 Colt .452 dia.	.45
Bullet Number	452374	454190	452424	452490	452651
Weight (#2 Alloy)	225 gr.	250 gr.	255 gr.	255 gr.	325 gr.
Double Cavity Part #	2660374	2660190	2660422	2660490	2660651
Top Punch Number	374	190	424	424	424
Top Punch Part #	2786719	2786700	2786730	2786730	2786730
Four Cavity Part #	2670374	—	—	—	—

Hollow Point Bullets	9mm	.10mm	.44	.45
Bullet Number	356637	401638	429640	452374
Weight (#2 Alloy)	125 gr.	155 gr.	250 gr.	180 gr.
Mould #	2658637	2650638	2650640	2658374
Top Punch Number	429	43	421	374
Top Punch Part #	2786731	2786691	2786729	2786719

DEVASTATOR H.P. BULLETS
"Big Mouth" hollow point bullets were designed for maximum expansion at handgun velocities when cast from softer alloys like wheelweight metal.

Lyman Rifle Bullet Moulds

Rifle	.22			6mm	.25	6.5mm		.270 Win.	7mm		.30 M1/ 7.62x39mm		.30	
Bullet Number	225438	225415	225646	245496	257420	266469	266645	280642	287346	287641	311359	311410	311466	311291
Weight (#2 Alloy)	44 gr.	55 gr.	55 gr.	84 gr.	65 gr.	140 gr.	150 gr.	150 gr.	135 gr.	160 gr.	115 gr.	130 gr.	152 gr.	170 gr.
Mould #	2660438	2660415	2660646	2660496	2660420	2660469	2660645	2660642	2660346	2660641	2660359	2660410	2660466	2660291
Top Punch Number	438	415	415	203	420	463	463	359	346	359	359	467	467	465
Top Punch Part #	2786733	2786726	2786726	2786748	2786728	2786741	2786741	2786772	2786715	2786772	2786772	2786743	2786743	2786742

Rifle cont'd.	.30				32/20		.314 dia.	8mm	.35		.375/ .38-55		.40 Cal. .406 dia.	.40 Cal. .410 dia. ★
Bullet Number	311041	311332	311644	311284	311316	311008	314299	323470	358315	358009	375248	375449	403169	410655
Weight (#2 Alloy)	173 gr.	180 gr.	190 gr.	210 gr.	112 gr.	115 gr.	200 gr.	165 gr.	204 gr.	280 gr.	249 gr.	264 gr.	240 gr.	400 gr.
Mould #	2660041	2660332	2660644	2660284	2660316	2660008	2660299	2660470	2660315	2660009	2660248	2660449	2660169	2640655
Top Punch Number	8	413	359	467	8	8	467	470	311	430	449	449	43	449
Top Punch Part #	2786690	2786725	2786772	2786743	2786690	2786690	2786743	2786745	2786710	2786732	2786736	2786736	2786691	2786736

Rifle cont'd.	.44/ 40	.43 Span. ★	.45 ★	H.P. ★	★	★	★	★	★ NEW	★	.50 ★	Shotgun Slugs		NEW Sabot Slug
Bullet Number	429434	439186	457191	457122	457124	457643	457193	457406	457658	457125	515141	20 ga.	12 ga.	12 ga.
Weight (#2 Alloy)	215 gr.	370 gr.	292 gr.	330 gr.	385 gr.	400 gr.	405 gr.	475 gr.	480 gr.	500 gr.	425 gr.	345 gr.	475 gr.	525 gr.
Mould #	2660434	2640186	2640191	2650122	2640124	2640643	2640193	2640406	2640658	2640125	2640141	2654020	2654012	2654112
Top Punch Number	43	251	191	191	374	191	191	374	658	374	141	—	—	Use with
Top Punch Part #	2786691	2786704	2786701	2786701	2786719	2786701	2786701	2786719	2786755	2786719	2786696	—	—	Win. Wads

MAGMA Bullet Moulds

Caliber	Wgt. Grs.	Type	Caliber	Wgt. Grs.	Type
30	115	RNBB		155	RN SWC
32	78	RN BB	BB		
	100	SGG BB	10mm	155	SWC BB
	98	WC BB		170	SWC BB
32-20	115	FP BB		175	SWC BB
380	95	RN BB		180	FP BB
9mm Mak.	93	RN		200	FP BB
9mm	115	RN BB	41	215	SWC BB
	122	FP BB	44	180	FP BB
	125	CN BB		215	SWC BB
	125	RN BB		240	SWC BB
	135	RN BB		240	RN BB
	147	FP BB		240	FP BB
38 Spl.	145	RN FB		300	FP BB
	150	RN FB	44-40	200	RN FP
	160	RN BB	45	150	SWC BB
	150	SWC BB		155	SWC
	160	SWC BB	BB&FB		
38	105	WCD BB		160	SWC FB
	125	FP BB		175	SWC BB
	148	WC DBB		180	SWC BB
SSG				185	SWC BB
	148	WC DBB		200	SWC BB
	148	WC BB		225	FP BB
	150	SWC BB		230	RN BB
	158	SWC BB	45 LC	250	RN FP BB
	158	RN BB		255	SWC BB
	180	FP BB		300	FP BB
38-40	180	RN FP BB	45-70	350	FP BB
10mm	140	RN FP BB		405	FP BB

RN = Round Nose; BB = Bevel Base; WC = Wadcutter: FP = Flat Point: SWC = Semi-Wadcutter; FB = Flat Base.

Magma 38-40, 44-40 and 4566.

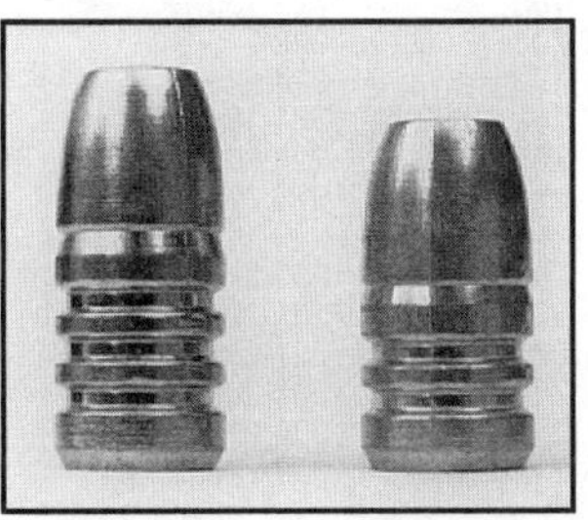

Magma 45-70 350-gr. and 405-gr. Bullets for Cowboy Action Shooting

Magma 30 Carbine, 9x21, 38 Special

Section 3: Bullet Casting

NEI

Bullet Moulds

Aluminum alloy single- and double-cavity bottom pour, four-cavity, single- and double-cavity nose pour, and customer design moulds with steel alignment pins, steel sockets, and steel sprue plates (1-, 2- and select 4-cavity only).

Price: 1-cavity **$70.00**
Price: 2-cavity.................... **$75.00**
Price: Large caliber double cavity ... **$80.00**
Price: Large caliber triple cavity..... **$95.00**
Price: Hollow base nose pour....... **$110.00**
Price: 4-cavity.................. **$100.00**
Price: 1-cavity nose pour **$95.00**
Price: Extra for 2 different cuts...... **$15.00**
Price: Extra for 2 different weights.... **$8.00**
Price: Extra tall mould block........ **$15.00**
Price: Custom, cherry NEI property . **$200.00**
Price: Custom, cherry customer property **$300.00**

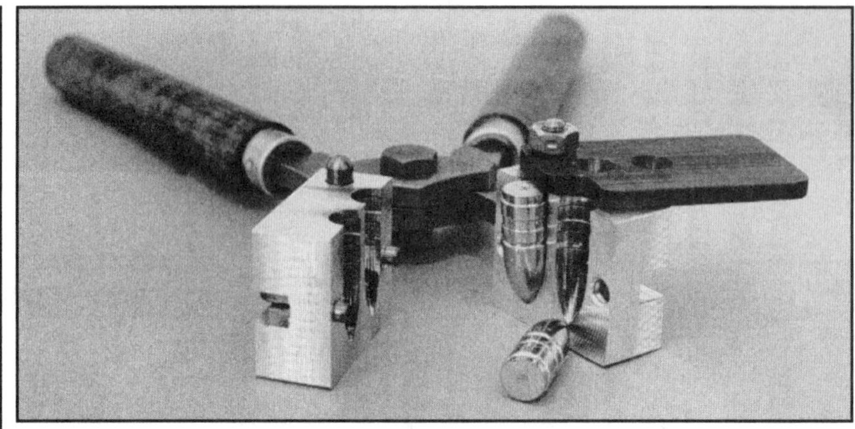

NEI Bullet Mould

NEI Bullet Moulds

Caliber	Dia.	Wgt.Grs.	Mould #
22 Hornet	.224	39	224-39-GC
22	.224	45	224-45-GC
22 CF	.224	54	224-54-GC
	.224	62	224-62-GC-DD
	.224	72	224-72-GC-DD
223	.224	55	224-55-GC
22 High Power	.228	60	228-60-GC
	.231	65	231-65-GC
6mm	.244	63	244-63-GC
	.244	65	244-65-GC
	.244	75	244-75-GC
	.244	92	244-92-GC
	.244	95	244-95-GC
	.244	100	244-100-GC
25 ACP	.251	51	251-51-PB
257 Bores	.257	70	257-70-GC
25 Cal.	.257	75	257-75-GC
25-20 Win.	.257	89	257-89-GC
257 Bolt	.257	100	257-100-GC
25-35 Win.	.257	114	257-114-GC
257 Bolt	.257	115	257-115-GC-DD
25 Cal.	.257	115	257-115-GC
6.5mm	.264	125	264-125-GC-DD
265 Cal.	.264	130	264-130-GC
264 Cal.	.264	160	264-160-GC
6.5x55mm	.270	130	270-130-GC
270	.277	130	277-130-GC
270 Win.	.277	100	277-100-GC-DD
	.277	125	277-185-GC-DD
284/7mm	.277	145	277-145-PP
7mm Nambu	.280	62	280-62-PB
284/7mm	.284	130	284-130-GC-DD
	.284	140	284-140-GC
7mm	.284	150	284-150-GC
	.284	150	284-150-GC-DD
	.284	154	284-154-GC
7.35 Carcano	.299	135	299-135-GC
	.300	140	300-140-GC
308	.301	162	301-162-PP
30 Cal.	.301	167	301-167-PP
	.301	175	301-175-PP
	.304	209	304-209-PP
	.308	80	308-80-GC
	.308	102	308-102-GC
	.308	108	308-108-GC
	.308	110	308-110-GC
	.308	121	308-121-GC
	.308	125	308-125-GC
	.308	135	308-135-GC
	.308	142	308-142-GC
	.308	150	308-150-GC
	.308	152	308-152-GC
	.308	155	308-155-GC
	.308	160	308-160-GC
	.308	161	308-161-GC
	.308	162	308-162-GC
	.308	173	308-173-GC
	.308	176	308-176-GC
	.308	178	308-178-GC
	.308	180	308-180-GC
	.308	180	308-180-GC-Hornet
Most 30s	.308	182	308-182-GC
All 30s	.308	186	308-186-GC
	.308	188	308-188-GC-DD
Most 30s	.308	189	308-189-GC
	.308	190	308-190-GC
	.308	191	308-191-GC
All 30s	.308	210	308-210-GC
Fast Twist 30s	.308	210	308-210-GC
30s	.309	100	309-100-BB
30 Carbine	.309	115	309-115-GC
30s	.310	78	310-78-GC
7.62x39	.311	145	311-145-GC
Some 30s	.311	154	311-154-GC
7.62x39	.311	155	311-155-GC
303 British	.311	190	311-190-GC
7.62 Mauser	.312	108	312-108-GC
32-20	.312	115	312-115-GC
32 LC	.313	95	313-95-HEEL
32 Pistol	.312	115	312-115-BB
32s	.312	125	312-125-GC
7.7 Jap	.312	145	312-145-GC
32s	.313	90	313-90-GC
32 Cal.	.313	95	313-95-BBWC
32 Pistol	.313	100	313-100-BB
32-20	.313	114	313-114-GC
	.313	115	313-115-GC
	.313	122	313-122-GC
7.7 Jap	.313	165	313-165-GC
7.62 Mauser	.313	180	313-180-GC
32 Colt	.315	95	315-95-BB
32	.315	110	315-110-BB
8mm	.316	160	316-160-GC
303 British	.316	200	316-200-GC
8mm	.318	175	318-175-GC
32-40 32 SP	.321	175	321-175-GC
32 SPL	.322	160	322-160-GC
	.322	165	322-165-GC-DD
8mm	.322	180	322-180-GC
32 Win. SP	.322	185	322-185-GC
	.322	205	322-205-GC
7.92 Kurtz	.324	125	324-125-GC
8mm	.324	167	324-167-GC
	.324	205	324-205-GC
8mm Kropechec	.326	220	326-220-GC
Roth-Steyr	.330	116	330-116-BB
318 Rimless	.330	245	330-245-GC
Large 8mm	.331	200	331-200-GC-DD
	.331	220	331-220-GC
	.338	200	338-200-GC
	.338	215	338-215-GC-DD
338	.338	245	338-245-GC

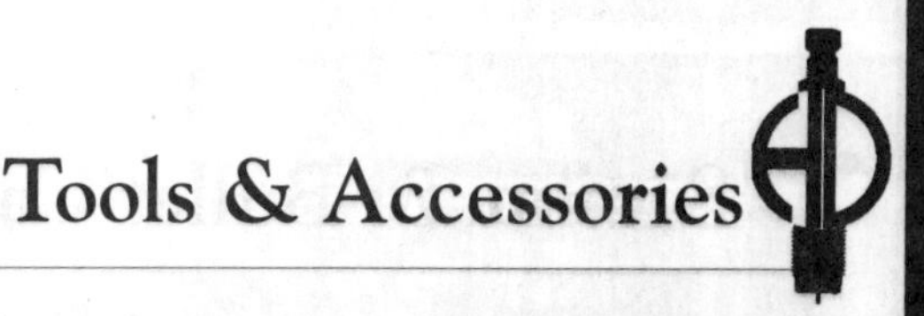

NEI Bullet Moulds

Caliber	Dia.	Wgt.Grs.	Mould #	Caliber	Dia.	Wgt.Grs.	Mould #
	.338	283	338-283-GC		.375	280	375-280-GC
Ballard	.344	210	344-210-PB		.375	290	375-290-GC-DD
	.348	220	348-220-GC-DD		.375	290	375-290-PP
348 Win.	.348	225	348-225-GC		.375	304	375-304-GC
	.348	240	348-240-GC		.375	310	375-310-GC
	.348	250	348-250-GC		.375	316	375-316-PB
35 Win. SL	.351	172	351-172-GC		.375	320	375-320-GC
Rossi 357	.354	160	354-160-BB	Old 38-55	.378	245	378-245-GC
	.354	171	354-171-GC	38-55	.379	245	379-245-GC
9mm	.355	69	355-69-PB		.380	236	380-236-BB
	.356	92	356-92-GC		.380	240	380-240-BB
	.356	116	356-116-T	41 Long Colt	.386	165	386-165-BB
	.356	120	356-120-GC		.388	198	388-198-PB
	.356	120	356-120-BB	40 Cal. Paper Patch	.395	320	395-320-PP
	.356	122	356-122-BB		.396	240	396-240-GC
	.356	124	356-124-GC	40 Sharps	.400	330	400-330-PP
	.356	125	356-125-BB		.400	370	400-370-PP
Long Bearing	.356	125	356-125-BB	40 S&W 10mm	.401	160	401-160-BB
9mm	.356	129	356-129-BB		.401	180	401-180-GC
9mm/38 Sup.	.356	140	356-140-BB		.401	200	401-200-BB
9mm	.356	142	356-142-BB		.403	300	403-300-GC
	.356	144	356-144-TRN	40-60 Win.	.404	210	404-210-GC
9mm/38 Sup.	.356	147	356-147-BB	40 Cal. Win.	.404	211	404-211-GC
	.356	155	356-155-BB	40 Win.	.404	250	404-250-GC
	.356	175	356-175-BB	40-XX Win. & Rem.	.405	300	405-300-GC
	.357	120	357-120-BB	40-XX Win.	.405	365	405-365-GC
38/357	.357	142	357-142-GC		.406	260	406-260-GC
38 Special	.357	185	357-185-GC		.406	325	406-325-PB
38/357	.358	77	358-77-BB		.408	215	408-215-GC
	.358	115	358-115-BB	40-82	.408	260	408-260-GC
38/357-9mm	.358	124	358-124-BB	408s	.408	285	408-285-BB
38/357	.358	125	358-125-GC		.408	330	408-330-PB
38/9mm	.358	125	358-125-BB		.408	360	408-360-GC-DD
	.358	128	358-128-BB	40-65	.408	400	408-400-PB
38/357	.358	135	358-135-BB	41 Long Colt	.410	200	410-200-LC
38/9mm	.358	140	358-140-PB		.41	200	41-200-LC
38/357	.358	148	358-148-GC	41 Colt	.41	205	41-205-LC
	.358	148	358-148-DEB	405 Win.	.410	410	410-410-GC
	.358	148	358-148-BB	Modern 40 cal.	.410	385	410-385-PB
	.358	150	358-150-BB	41 Mag.	.411	190	411-190-WC
	.358	151	358-151-BB		.411	195	411-195-GC
	.358	154	358-154-GC		.411	205	411-205-GC
	.358	154	358-154-BB		.411	210	411-210-GC
	.358	155	358-155-GC	41 S&W Mag.	.411	220	411-220-PB
	.358	158	358-158-BB		.411	225	411-225-GC
	.358	158	358-158-GC		.411	230	411-230-PB
	.358	160	358-160-PB		.411	238	411-238-PB
	.358	166	358-166-PB		.411	240	411-240-GC
	.358	167	358-167-BB	405 Win.	.411	350	411-350-GC
	.358	170	358-170-GC	405 Win. STD	.412	300	412-300-GC
	.358	170	358-170-PB	405 Win.	.412	325	412-325-GC-DD
	.358	171	358-171-GC		.415	330	415-330-GC
	.358	175	358-175-GC-152		.415	350	415-350-PB
	.358	175	358-175-GC-153	416s	.416	290	416-290-GC
	.358	175	358-175-RNGC		.416	320	416-320-PP
38 S&W	.358	180	358-180-PB		.416	375	416-375-GC-DD
	.358	180	358-180-BB	416 Rem.	.416	380	416-380-GC
38/357	.358	180	358-180-GC	404 Jeffery	.421	390	421-390-GC
	.358	180	358-180-PB		.422	370	422-370-BT
	.358	186	358-186-BT	10.3mm	.423	375	423-375-GC-DD
	.358	188	358-188-GC	10.75mm	.423	455	423-455-PP
	.358	191	358-191-GC	10.75x57	.424	350	424-350-GC
358 Rifle	.358	190	358-190-PB	44-40 WCF	.427	190	427-190-BB
35 Rifle	.358	208	358-208-GC	44-40	.427	205	427-205-GC
	.358	210	358-210-PB	44-40 WCF	.427	245	427-245-GC
35 Cal. Rifles	.358	220	358-220-GC		.427	250	427-250-PB
35 Rifle	.358	232	358-232-GC		.429	80	429-80-STACK
	.358	268	358-268-GC-DD		.429	185	429-185-WC
	.358	282	358-282-GC		.429	185	429-185-DEWC
	.358	300	358-300-GC		.429	196	429-196-GC
9mm Makarov	.363	115	363-115-PB		.429	198	429-198-BB
	.363	130	363-130-PB		.429	220	429-220-BB
Stevens	.363	210	363-210-PB	Hi Vel. 44s	.429	220	429-220-GC
35	.363	300	363-300-GC	44-40	.429	222	429-220-HB
9.3mm Rifle	.366	260	366-260-GC-DD		.429	225	429-225-GC
9.3mm	.366	304	366-304-GC		.429	230	429-230-GC
38 LC/38 Rook	.375	171	375-171-PB		.429	235	429-235-GC
375s	.375	200	375-200-GC		.429	235	429-235-PB
	.375	210	375-210-GC	STD 44	.429	240	429-240-BB
	.375	255	375-255-GC		.429	240	429-240-GC
	.375	277	375-277-PB	Ash Can	.429	245	429-245-WC

Section 3: Bullet Casting

NEI Bullet Moulds

Caliber	Dia.	Wgt.Grs.	Mould #
	.429	248	429-248-WC
	.429	250	429-250-GC
	.429	260	429-260-GC
	.429	270	429-270-PB
	.429	270	429-270-GC
44 Russian	.429	278	429-278-GC
	.429	280	429-280-GC
	.429	290	429-290-PB
	.429	295	429-295-GC
	.429	320	429-320-PB-SSK
	.429	330	429-330-GC
	.429	335	429-335-GC-DD
444 Marlin	.429	362	429-362-GC
44 Mag.	.429	325	429-325-BBJDJ
	.438	540	438-540-PP
43 Spanish	.439	375	439-375-GC-DD
	.439	375	439-375-GC
44 Long Colt	.44	220	44-220-LC
	.44	225	44-225-LC-HEEL
44 Sharps	.440	480	440-480-PP
	.440	492	440-492-PP
44 Long Colt	.445	208	445-208-LC
44-77 Sharps	.446	485	446-485-PB
44-60 ETC	.447	380	447-380-GC-DD
45-70 ETC	.45	410	45-410-PP
45-90 ETC	.45	500	45-500-PP
	.45	520	45-520-PP
	.45	599	45-599-PP
45 ACP	.451	160	451-160-BB
	.451	170	451-170-GC
	.451	175	451-175-BB
	.451	180	451-180-BB
	.451	190	451-190-BB
	.451	192	451-192-PB
	.451	200	451-200-BB
.725 OAL	.451	200	451-200-SP
	.451	202	451-202-BB
	.451	205	451-205-N
	.451	208	451-208-BB
	.451	210	451-210-BB
	.451	215	451-215-BB
Ash Can	.451	220	451-220-BBWC
	.451	225	451-225-BB
	.451	225	451-225-BBWC
	.451	225	451-225-PB
	.451	226	451-226-BB
	.451	229	451-229-BB
	.451	230	451-230-BB
	.451	230	451-230-GI
	.451	231	451-231-BB
	.451	236	451-236-GC
	.451	240	451-240-PB
	.451	245	451-245-BB
	.451	250	451-250-PB
	.451	255	451-255-GC
	.451	255	451-255-BB
	.451	260	451-260-PB
	.451	263	451-263-GC
	.451	272	451-272-BB
	.451	275	451-275-PB
	.451	275	451-275-GC
	.451	300	431-300-BB
	.451	305	451-305-GC
	.451	310	451-310-PB
	.451	325	451-325-PB
	.451	345	451-345-PB
Hand Cannon	.451	370	451-370-GC
	.451	380	451-380-GC
	.452	520	452-520-PB
1860 Army	.454	220	454-220-C&B
45 Long Colt	.454	230	454-230-HB
Old 45 Colt	.454	255	454-255-PB
	.454	270	454-270-PBK
	.454	315	454-315-PB
Keith Style	.454	325	454-325-PB
	.454	368	454-368-PB
577/450	.454	475	454-475-PB
455 Webley	.455	350	455-350-GC
	.456	170	456-170-PB
	.456	250	456-250-PB
	.458	300	458-300-GC
458 Win.	.458	300	458-300-GC
	.458	333	458-333-GC

Caliber	Dia.	Wgt.Grs.	Mould #
Light 45-70	.458	350	458-350-GC-DD
	.458	355	458-355-GC
	.458	360	458-360-GC-DD
	.458	385	458-385-BB
Also 405 GR PB	.458	405	458-405-GC
	.458	405	458-405-RNGC
	.458	405	458-405-PP
45-70	.458	405	458-405-HB
Gonic Arms	.458	405	458-405-PB
	.458	425	458-425-BT
	.458	440	458-440-GC
	.458	440	458-440-GC-DD
Orig. 45-70	.458	500	458-500-PB
458 Win.	458	500	458-500-GC-Hornet
	.458	510	458-510-GC
	.458	525	458-525-GC-DD
	.458	560	458-560-PB
458 SS	.458	600	458-600-PB
460 Weatherby	.458	645	458-645-GC
45-70	.460	480	460-480-GC
460 Weatherby	.460	505	460-505-GC
Old 45-70	.462	455	462-455-GC
500/465 Nitro	.466	475	466-475-GC
475 Revolver	.475	420	475-420-PB
475 Pistol	.475	435	475-435-PB
470 Nitro	.475	480	475-480-PB
	.475	435	475-435-PB
50 Action Exp.	.500	320	500-320-GC
	.500	325	500-325-BB
50 Sharps Ring	.500	410	500-410-SH
505 Gibbs	.505	540	505-540-GC
	.508	856	508-856-GC
50 Webley	.510	300	510-300-PB
	.510	430	510-430-GC
	.510	490	510-490-GC
50 Paper Patch	.510	500	510-500-PP
	.510	550	510-550-GC
	.510	625	510-625-GC-DD
	.510	625	510-625-PP
	.510	775	510-775-GC-DD
50 MG	.510	860	510-860-GC
	.511	300	511-300-GC
50 Hand Cannon	.511	450	511-450-PB
	.511	680	511-680-GC
	.512	420	512-420-PB
50-110 Win.	.512	435	512-435-GC
500 Nitro	.512	600	512-600-GC
	.512	640	512-640-PB
50-140 Sharps	.515	620	515-620-PB
50 Maynard	.540	524	524-524-BB
54 Sharps	.54	440	54-440-SH
	.540	475	540-475-SH
	.54	490	54-490-NS
	.54	490	54-490-OS
	.54	515	54-515-RT
	.543	490	543-490-SH
	.543	670	543-670-SH
534, 545, 552	.544	525	544-525-SH
56-50 Spencer	.556	420	556-420-PB
56 Orig. Sharps	.56	500	56-500-OS
58 Muzzle Load	.575	500	575-500-PB
58 Cal.	.575	595	575-595-PB
58 Cal.	.577	450	577-450-HB
577 Nitro	.577	900	577-900-PB
	.584	850	584-850-DD
58 Berdan	.586	725	586-725-PB
577 Nitro	.586	780	586-780-PB
	.587	1150	587-1150-PB
600 Nitro	.622	900	622-900-PB
12 Bore Paradox	.732	835	732-835-PB
12 Ga. Shot Gun	.734	570	734-570-PB
12 Bore	.740	725	740-725-PB
12 Bore Paradox	.746	840	746-840-PB
10 Bore	.774	1080	774-1080-PB
	.774	900	774-900-PB
10 Bore Paradox	.804	945	804-945-PB
	.820	1350	820-1350-PB
8 Bore	.835	1186	835-1186-PB
	.843	2800	843-2800-PB
	.875	1540	875-1540-PB
	.943	2250	943-2250-PB
4 Bore	.970	2000	970-2000-PB
	.999	3000	999-3000

RAPINE

Bullet Moulds

Single- and double-cavity moulds machined from high-strength aluminum alloy to precise caliber with highly-polished finish. Come with long wooden handles placed close together to reduce fatigue. From Rapine Bullet Mould Mfg. Co.

Price: Plain Base **$79.95**
Price: Hollow Base **$89.95**

RCBS

Bullet Moulds

Hand-machined from blocks of precision-cast, malleable iron. Hardened pins ensure permanent alignment. The sprue cutter is solid carbon steel, locked in place with Allen setscrew. Bullet roundness tolerance to .001". 200 different moulds available. From RCBS.

Price: Pistol or round ball **$61.95**
Price: Rifle or silhouette............ **$63.95**

Mould Handles

Solid steel frames with extra long wood handles. One size fits all RCBS moulds. From RCBS.

Price:.......................... **$31.95**

SAECO

Bullet Moulds

Two- and 4-cavity moulds machined from blocks of copper alloyed pearlitic cast iron for dimensional stability. Cavities cut using same cherry0 on digital equipment for uniformity. Steel sprue plate held against mould blocks by high-temperature Inconel spring washers. Mould handles are ductile iron castings with oak grips. Handles ordered separately. From Redding Reloading Equipment.

Price: 2-cavity.................... **$82.50**
Price: 4-cavity.................. **$150.00**
Price: Mould handles **$37.50**

OLD WEST Bullet Moulds

Caliber	Cast Size	Wgt. Grs.	Type	OAL	Caliber	Cast Size	Wgt. Grs.	Type	OAL
25	.253	56	PB	0.460	375	.377	260	PB	0.970
	.259	95	PB	0.770		.377	294	GC	1.072
	.259	106	GC	0.860	38-55	.381	255	PB	0.925
25-20	.259	75	PB	0.590		.381	286	GC	1.025
	.259	82	GC	0.680	40	.402	170	PB	0.570
6.5mm	.266	130	PB	1.00		.402	205	GC	0.680
	.266	145	GC	1.10	41	.407	250	PB	0.810
270	.279	140	PB	1.00		.407	280	GC	0.930
	.279	155	GC	1.10	40/41	.405	160		0.530
7mm	.286	145	PB	0.940		.411	210	PB	0.680
	.286	160	GC	1.04		.411	240	GC	0.760
	.287	160	PB	1.00		.411	275	PB	0.950
	.287	176	GC	1.10		.411	310	GC	0.950
30	.310	180	PB	1.00		.413	240	PB	0.750
	.310	198	GC	1.10		.413	280	PB	0.860
30 Carbine	.311	114	PB	0.665		.413	310	GC	0.980
	.311	130	GC	0.765	416	.419	360	PB	1.190
30-30	.311	170	PB	0.920		.419	400	GC	1.190
	.311	190	GC	1.015	44	.429	215	PB	0.670
32-20	.313	100	PB	0.545		.429	270	PB	0.810
	.313	118	GC	0.645		.430	240	PB	0.700
	.314	85	PB	0.490		.430	275	GC	0.810
	.314	100	GC	0.570		.430	315	GC	0.830
303	.316	195	PB	1.00		.431	220	PB	0.680
	.316	210	GC	1.10		.431	280	PB	0.820
32-40	.323	172	PB	0.865		.431	320	GC	0.910
	.323	189	GC	0.950		.432	215	PB	0.650
8mm	.326	190	PB	1.00		.432	255	GC	0.740
	.326	215	GC	1.10	45	.454	281	GC	
33	.340	215	PB	0.950		.454	310	PB	0.770
	.340	230	GC	1.04		.454	390	PB	0.970
348	.350	220	PB	0.960		.454	490	PB	1.20
	.350	245	GC	1.020	45-70	.462	255	PB	0.650
	.360	150	PB	0.660		.462	320	PB	0.850
	.360	170	GC	0.760		.462	360	GC	0.950
35	.350	220	GC	0.890	50	.515	385	PB	0.830
	.360	240	PB	1.00		.515	470	PB	1.070
	.360	270	GC	1.10		.515	525	PB	1.180

PB = Plain Base; GC = Gas Check.

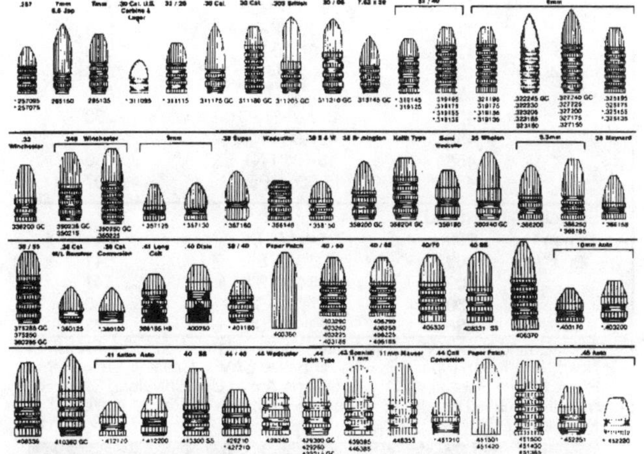

Rapine Bullet Moulds

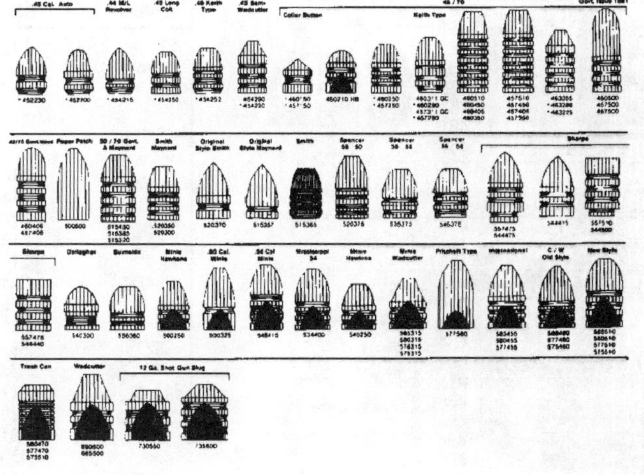

Special Order Moulds
Three- and 8-cavity and "magnum" moulds made on special order basis. From Redding Reloading Equipment.
Price: 1-cavity magnum **$82.50**
Price: 2-cavity magnum **$105.00**
Price: 3-cavity **$120.00**
Price: 8-cavity **$344.00**

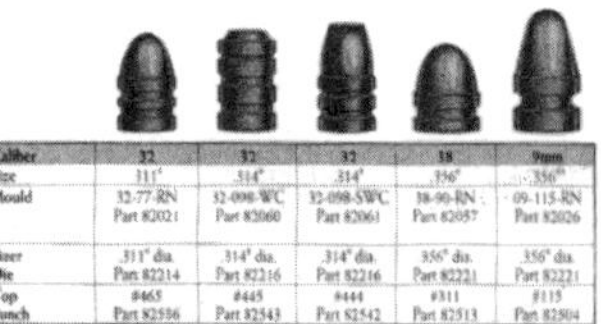

Caliber	32	32	32	38	9mm
Size	.311"	.314"	.314"	.356"	.356"
Mould	32-77-RN Part #2021	32-098-WC Part #2060	32-098-SWC Part #2061	38-90-RN Part #2057	09-115-RN Part #2026
Sizer Die	.311" dia. Part #2214	.314" dia. Part #2216	.314" dia. Part #2216	.356" dia. Part #2221	.356" dia. Part #2221
Top Punch	#465 Part #2556	#445 Part #2543	#444 Part #2542	#311 Part #2513	#115 Part #2504

38/357	38/357	38/357	40/10mm	10mm	10mm	41	44	44	44	44	44	44	45 Auto
.358"	.358	.358"	.401"	.400"	.400"	.410"	.430"	.430"	.430"	.430"	.430"	.430"	.452"
38-150-SWC Part #2032	38-158-RN Part #2064	38-158-SWC Part #2065	40-180-FN Part #2066	10mm-170-SWC Part #2067	10mm-200-SWC Part #2068	41-210-SWC Part #2039	44-225-SWC Part #2041	44-240-SWC Part #2042	44-245-SWC Part #2043	44-250-K Part #2080	44-250-SWC Part #2044	44-300-SWC Part #2079	45-185-BB-SWC Part #2052
.358" dia. Part #2223	.358" dia. Part #2223	.358" dia. Part #2223	.401" dia. Part #2245	.400" dia. Part #2243	.400" dia. Part #2243	.410" dia. Part #2226	.430" dia. Part #2229	.430" dia. Part #2229	.430" dia. Part #2229	.430" dia. Part #2229	.430" dia. Part #2229	.430" dia. Part #2229	.452" dia. Part #2233
#429 Part #2529	#311 Part #2513	#429 Part #2529	#558 Part #5558	#518 Part #5518	#518 Part #5518	#420 Part #2541	#421 Part #2527	#421 Part #2527	#421 Part #2527	#421 Part #2527	#421 Part #2527	#421 Part #2527	#680 Part #2545

9mm	9mm	9mm	9mm	9mm Makarov	38/357	38/357
.356"	.356"	.356"	.356"	.365"	.358"	.358"
9mm-124-RN Part #2062	09-124-RN-TG Part #2063	09-124-CN Part #2027	9mm-147-FN Part #2077	9mm-100-RN Part #2084	38-148-WC DE Part #2030	38-148-WC Part #2031
.356" dia. Part #2221	.356" dia. Part #2221	.356" dia. Part #2221	.356" dia. Part #2221	.365" dia. Part #2248	.358" dia. Part #2223	.358" dia. Part #2223
#401 Part #2521	#115 Part #2504	#402 Part #2522	#556 Part #5556	#551 Part #2551	#344 Part #2515	#429 Part #2529

45 Auto	45 Auto	45	45 Auto	45 Colt	45 Colt	45
.452"	.452"	.454"	.452"	.454"	.454"	.452"
45-200-SWC Part #2046	45-201-SWC Part #2047	44-225-CAV Part #2081	45-230-RN Part #2048	45-250-FN Part #2049	45-255-SWC Part #2050	45-300-SWC Part #2083
.452" dia. Part #2233	.452" dia. Part #2233	.454" dia. Part #2234	.452" dia. Part #2233	.454" dia. Part #2234	.454" dia. Part #2234	.452" dia. Part #2233
#460 Part #2534	#680 Part #2545	#552 Part #5552	#374 Part #2519	#190 Part #2506	#424 Part #2528	#424 Part #2528

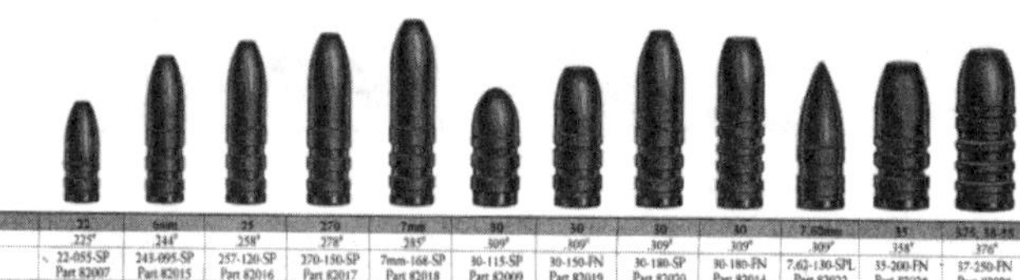

Caliber	22	6mm	25	270	7mm	30	30	30	30	7.62mm	35	375, 38-55
Size	.225"	.244"	.258"	.278"	.285"	.309"	.309"	.309"	.309"	.309"	.358"	.376"
Mould	22-055-SP Part #2007	243-095-SP Part #2015	257-120-SP Part #2016	270-150-SP Part #2017	7mm-168-SP Part #2018	30-115-SP Part #2009	30-150-FN Part #2019	30-180-SP Part #2020	30-180-FN Part #2014	7.62-130-SPL Part #2022	35-200-FN Part #2028	37-250-FN Part #2029
Sizer Die	.225" dia. Part #2240	.244" dia. Part #2202	.258" dia. Part #2204	.278" dia. Part #2206	.285" dia. Part #2209	.309" dia. Part #2212	.309" dia. Part #2212	.309" dia. Part #2212	.309" dia. Part #2212	.309" dia. Part #2212	.358" dia. Part #2223	.376" dia. Part #2225
Top Punch	#506 Part #5506	#509 Part #5509	#515 Part #5515	#529 Part #5529	#531 Part #5531	#535 Part #5535	#546 Part #5546	#541 Part #5541	#546 Part #5546	#554 Part #5554	#565 Part #5565	#570 Part #5570

40	40	40	416	44-40	45	45	45	45
.410"	.410"	.410"	.417"	.428"	.458"	.458"	.458"	.458"
40-300-SP-CSA Part #2070	40-350-SP-CSA Part #2072	40-400-SP-CSA Part #2074	416-350-FN Part #2075	44-200-FN Part #2036	45-300-FN Part #2051	45-325-FN-U Part #2045	45-405-FN+ Part #2053	45-500-FN+ Part #2054
.410" dia. Part #2226	.410" dia. Part #2226	.410" dia. Part #2226	.417" Part #2246	.428" dia. Part #2244	.458" dia. Part #2236	.458" dia. Part #2236	.458" dia. Part #2236	.458" dia. Part #2236
#378 Part #2520	#378 Part #2520	#378 Part #2520	#562 Part #5562	#595 Part #5595	#600 Part #5600	#383 Part #5583	#600 Part #5600	#600 Part #5600

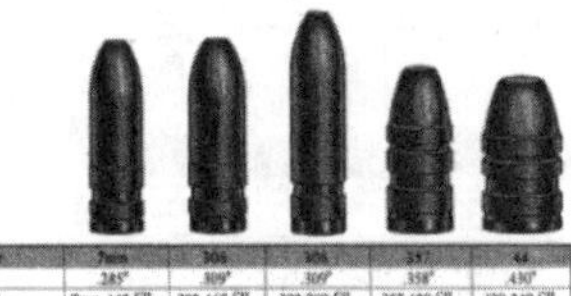

Caliber	7mm	308	308	357	44
Size	.285"	.309"	.309"	.358"	.430"
Mould	7mm-145-SIL Part #2150	308-165-SIL Part #2152	308-200-SIL Part #2153	357-180-SIL Part #2154	429-240-SIL Part #2156
Sizer Die	.285" dia. Part #2209	.309" dia. Part #2212	.309" dia. Part #2212	.358" dia. Part #2223	.430" dia. Part #2229
Top Punch	#531 Part #5531	#541 Part #5541	#541 Part #5541	#430 Part #2530	#422 Part #2526
Seater Plug	7mm SIL Part 09696	308 SIL Part 09697	308 SIL Part 09697	357 SIL Part 09698	44 SIL Part 09699

RCBS Cast Bullets
Alternate Sizes

Caliber	Size
22	.244
6mm	.243
25	.257
270	.277
7mm	.284
30	.308
	.310
	.311
32	.312
	.313
	.314
38/357	.354
	.355
38	.356
357	.357
375/38-55	.375
44-40	.427
44	.429
	.431
45	.450
	.451
45 Colt	.454
45	.457

RCBS Bullet Moulds

Caliber	Size	Mould #/Grs./Bullet Type	Top Punch #
PISTOL MOULDS			
32	.311	32-077-RN	465
	.314	32-098-WC	445
	.314	32-098-SWC	444
38	.356	38-090-RN	311
9mm	.356	09-115-RN	115
	.356	9mm-124-RN	401
	.356	09-124-RN-TG	115
	.356	09-124-CN	402
	.356	9mm-147-FN	556
9mm Mak.	.365	9mm-100-RN	551
38/357	.358	38-148-WC	429
	.358	38-148-WC-DE	344
	.358	38-150-SWC	429
	.358	38-158-RN	311
	.358	38-158-SWC	429
40/10mm	.401	40-180-FN	558
10mm	.400	10mm-170-SWC	518
	.400	10mm-200-SWC	518
41	.410	41-210-SWC	420
44	.430	44-225-SWC	421
	.430	44-240-SWC	421
	.430	44-245-SWC	421
	.430	44-250-K	421
	.430	44-250-SWC	421
	.430	44-300-SWC	421
45 Auto	.452	45-185-BB-SWC	680
	.452	45-200-SWC	460
	.452	45-201-SWC	680
45	.454	45-225-CAV	552
45 Auto	.452	45-230-RN	374
45 Colt	.454	45-250-FN	190
	.454	45-255-SWC	424
45	.452	45-300-SWC	424
RIFLE MOULDS			
22	.225	22-055-SP	506
6mm	.244	243-095-SP	509
25	.258	257-120-SP	515
270	.278	270-150-SP	529
7mm	.285	7mm-168-SP	531
30	.309	30-115-SP	535
	.309	30-150-FN	546
	.309	30-180-SP	541
	.309	30-180-FN	546
7.62mm	.309	7.62-130-SPL	554
35	.358	35-200-FN	565
375,38-55	.376	37-250-FN	570
40	.410	40-300-SP-CSA	378
	.410	40-350-SP-CSA	378
	.410	40-400-SP-CSA	378
416	.417	416-350-FN	562
44-40	.428	44-200-FN	595
45	.458	45-300-FN	600
	.458	45-325-FN-U	383
	.458	45-405-FN+	600
	.458	45-500-FN+	600
	.458	45-500-BPS+	607
SILHOUETTE MOULDS			
7mm	.285	7mm-145-SIL	531
308	.309	308-165-SIL	541
	.309	308-200-SIL	541
357	.358	357-180-SIL	430
44	.430	429-240-SIL	422

RN = Round Nose; WC = Wadcutter; SWC = Semi-Wadcutter; FN = Flat Nose; K = Keith Type; BB = Bevel Base; CAV = Cavalry; SP = Semi-Point; SPL = Special; CSA = C Sharps Arms; U = Universal; SIL = Silhouette; TG = Target; DE = Double End; CN = Conical Nose; PT = Pointed.

Bullet Moulds for Obsolete Cal.
Special order moulds available in single cavity magnum only. Six different bullet styles.
Style A: Cylindrical bullet similar to original factory bullets for most blackpowder cartridges. Diameter at front band is same diameter at base band. Rounded grease grooves.
Style B: Cylindrical bullet with front wiper band deleted. Rounded grease grooves.
Style C: Two-diameter bullet with front three bands slightly larger than bore diameter and rear three at groove diameter. Rounded grease grooves.
Style D: Two-diameter bullet same as Style C but without front wiper band. Rounded grease grooves.
Style E: Tapered bullet with front band near bore diameter tapering to slightly larger than groove diameter. Rounded grease grooves.
Style F: Hudson bullet. Two-diameter with front bands near bore diameter with two rear bands slightly larger than groove diameter. From Redding Reloading Equipment.
Price: .... **Contact manufacturer.**

Magnum Mould Blocks
Single- and double-cavity moulds made from SAECO double- and triple-cavity blocks with wider spacing for blackpowder silhouette bullets. Available in two calibers: 40 cal., 370- and 410-gr.; 45-cal. 480- and 525-gr. Special order moulds in any combination of caliber and/or weight. From Redding Reloading Equipment.
Price: Single-cavity................ **$82.50**
Price: Double-cavity.............. **$105.00**
Price: Special order, add **$24.00**

No.	221	243	257	284	270	281	078	071	073	302	264	316	311
Designation	60gr. SPGC	85gr. TCGC	100gr. TCGC	140 gr. SPGC	140gr. TCGC	145gr. FPGC	145gr. TCGC	180gr. TCGC	165gr. SPGC	120gr. RNGC	115gr. RNBB	150gr. FPGC	165gr. TCGC
Sizing Die	.225	.244	.258	.285	.278	.285	.285	.285	.285	.309	.309	.309	.309
Top Punch	22498	24243	25258	28264	27270	28311	28520	28520	28520	30467	30467	30530	30301
Description	Works Well in .223 Semi Autos	For all .243 & .244 Cal.	.25 Cal. Silhouette		Two perfect 60's shot at Reg. 6 IHMSA	Standard for 7mm	Silhouette	200 meters Silhouette	Heavy 7mm Bullet	For 30 MI, GC	For 30 MI	For 30-30	

	30 CAL. (cont.)			31 CAL.	32 CAL.						8 mm	9 mm/38 SUPER	
No.	307	315	301	305	327	323	325	326	321	322A	081	380	922
Designation	180gr. FPGC	175gr. TCGC	196gr. TCGC	180gr. FPGC	75gr. RN	95 gr. WC	95 gr. SWC	100gr. SWCBB	95gr. RN	118gr. FP	190gr. RNGC	95gr. RNBB	115gr. RNBB
Sizing Die	.309	.309	.309	.311	.313	.313	.313	.313	.313	.313	.323/.324	.356	.356
Top Punch	30301	30329	30301	30301	32465	32323	32467	32467	32465	30254	30530	35465	35311
Description		Bench Rest Style "E" Taper	Duplicates Original RG4	303 British	.32 ACP	Good .32 Long Target Bullet			.32 S&W Long	.32-20 Bullet	8 mm Rifle	Good .380 bullet	

	9 mm/38 SUPER (cont.)										9.2 mm	38/357-35 CAL.	
No.	925	377	384	115	924	383	928	929	910	930	940	952	953
Designation	115gr. SWBB	122gr. TCBB	122gr. RN	122 gr. RNBB	124gr. SWCGC	140gr. SWC	145gr. RNBB	145gr. SWCBB	150gr. RN	154gr. SWCBB	100gr. RNBB	148gr. WCBB	148gr. WC
Sizing Die	.356	.356	.356	.356	.356	.356/.357	.356/.357	.356/.357	.356	.356/.357	.365	.358	.358
Top Punch	35925	35375	35311	35311	35925	35429	35311	35925	35311	35925	35465	35550	35381
Description		Good Ballistics for 9mm	Good Feeding 9mm		Good Feeding SWC		38 Super	38 Super		38 Super Wilson Design	9mm Makarov	Target Bullet	GAR Design

No.	387	348	382	386	383	390	391	398	353	354	396	399	351
Designation	148gr. WCDBB	148gr. DBBWC	158gr. SWC	158gr. SWCBB	162gr. SWCGC	158gr. RN	158gr. RNBB	158gr. TC	180gr. FP	180gr. FPGC	180gr. TC	180gr. TCGC	200 gr. FP
Sizing Die	.358	.358	.358	.358	.358	.358	.358	.358	.358	.358	.358	.358	.358
Top Punch	35344	35344	35429	35429	35429	35311	35311	35399	35353	35353	35399	35399	35311
Description	148gr. Double Bevel Base WC	Single Groove DBB	Keith Design	Most Popular		Standard .38 Bullet			Super Long Range Bullet	GC Version of Popular 353			Heavy .357 Bullet

	41 CAL. (cont.)							416 CAL.	44 CAL.			
No.	412	417	408	413	415	410	418	*916	944	420	444	446-A
Designation	185gr. SWC	210gr. SWC	190gr. TC	210gr. TCBB	220gr. TCGC	220gr. FP	220gr. SWCBB	365gr. RNGC	200gr. WC	200 gr. TC	200gr. FPSWC	200gr. SWC
Sizing Die	.411	.411	.411	.411	.411	.411	.411	.417	.430	.430	.428	.430
Top Punch	41610	41610	41415	41415	41415	41415	41610	41916	44944	44428	44191	44191
Description						Pistol Silhouette	Bevel Base Keith Style	416 Rifles	GAR Design	Jim Hubert Design	44-40	

	45 CAL.												
No.	062-8	062	065	130	131	066	068	069	050	285	067	456	457
Designation	160gr. SPL	170gr. SPLBB	180gr. SWCBB	185gr. SWC	185gr. SWCBB	180gr. SWC	200gr. SWCBB	200gr. SWC	215gr. SWCBB	210gr. RNWC	225gr. TCBB	225gr. RN	225gr. RNBB
Sizing Die	.452	.452	.452	.452	.452	.452	.452	.452	.452	.452	.452	.452	.452
Top Punch	45452	45452	45429	45421	45421	45429	45429	45429	45424	45265	45375	45701	45701
Description	Behn Design	-V-MAXX .45 Behn Design	Lt. Wt. IPSC	Most Popular Lt. Target			Most Popular Combat Bullet		Bowling Pin Bullet	Best Feeding .45 ACP		Standard Round Nose	

				375 CAL.	40 CAL./10 mm						41 CAL.	
No.	358	395	352	373	040	043	045	047	048	401	416	419
Designation	200 gr. FPGC	200gr. TCGC	245gr. FPGC	265gr. FPGC	155gr. SWCBB	170gr. TCBB	170gr. SWCBB	200gr. TCBB	200gr. SWCBB	190gr.	170gr. SWCBB	200gr.SWCBB
Sizing Die	.358	.358	.358	.376	.401	.401	.401	.401	.401	.401	.411	.411
Top Punch	35311	35399	35311	37570	40048	40047	40048	40047	40048	40101	41447	41447
Description	Handgun Silhouette	Silhouette		Rifle	10mm Auto	10mm Auto	10mm Auto	10mm Auto	10mm Auto	.38-40	41 Auto Petty Design	41 Auto Petty Design

No.	445	442	441	440	439	429	424	428	431	430	432	433
Designation	220gr. SWCBB	246gr. RN	240gr. SWC	240gr. SWCBB	240gr. SWCGC	240gr. FP	240gr. TCGC	240gr. TC	250gr. FPGC	265gr. FP	265gr. FPGC	300gr. FPGC
Sizing Die	.430	.430	.430	.430	.430	.430	.430	.430	.430	.430	.430	.430
Top Punch	44191	44374	44421	44421	44421	44191	44428	44428	44191	44191	44191	44191
Description		Standard 44 Spec. Bullet	Standard Wt.44 Mag Keith Style			Superb Long Range Bullet	GC Version of Popular 428	Most Popular Silhouette	444 Marlin	Superb Long Range Bullet		Silhouette

						45 CAL. RIFLE							
No.	453	945	458	452	454	015	*017	*018	*019	*023	*021A	*022	*020
Designation	225gr. WC	255gr. SWCGC	255gr. SWC	255gr. SWC	300gr. SWCGC	300gr. FP	350gr. FPGC	405gr. FP	450gr. FPGC	375gr. SP	405gr. SPGC	500gr. FP	540gr. FPGC
Sizing Die	.452	.452	.452	.455	.452	.458	.458	.458	.458	.458	.458	.458	.458
Top Punch	45424	45424	45424	45452	45424	45015	45015	45015	45015	45702	45702	45610	45610
Description	Jan Libourel Design	For 45 Colt	For .45 Colt w/.452 Bore	For .45 Colt w/.454 Bore	Heavy .45 Colt & .454 Casull								

SAECO Bullet Moulds

Caliber	Bullet Grs. Wgt.	Bullet Type	Gas Check	Sizing Die	Top Punch
22	60	SP	GC	.225	22498
243	85	TC	GC	.244	24243
25	100	TC	GC	.258	25258
6.5mm	140	SP	GC	.265	26264
270	140	TC	GC	.278	27270
7mm	145	FP	GC	.285	28311
	145	TC	GC	.285	28520
	160	TC	GC	.285	28520
	165	SP	GC	.285	28520
30	120	RN	GC	.309	30467
	115	RNBB		.309	30467
	150	FP	GC	.309	30530
	165	TC	GC	.309	30301
	180	FP	GC	.309	30530
	175	TC	GC	N.R.	30329
	196	TC	GC	.309	30530
31	180	FP	GC	.311	30301
32	75	RN		.313	32465
	95	WC		.313	32323
	95	SWC		.313	32467
	100	SWCBB		.313	32467
	95	RN		.313	32465
	118	FP		.313	30254
8mm	190	RN	GC	.323/.324	30530
9mm/38 Super	95	RNBB		.356	35465
	115	RNBB		.356	35311
	115	SWBB		.356	35925
	122	TCBB		.356	35375
	122	RN		.356	35311
	122	RNBB		.356	35311
	124	SWC	GC	.356	35925
	140	SWC		.356/.357	35429
	145	RNBB		.356/.357	35311
	145	SWCBB		.356/.357	35925
	150	RN		.356	35311
	154	SWCBB		.356/.357	35925
9.2mm	100	RNBB		.365	35465
38/357-35	148	WCBB		.358	35550
	148	WC		.358	35381
	148	WCDBB		.358	35344
	148	DBBWC		.358	35344
	158	SWC		.358	35429
	158	SWCBB		.358	35429
	162	SWC	GC	.358	35429
	158	RN		.358	35311
	158	RNBB		.358	35311
	158	TC		.358	35399
	180	FP		.358	35353
	180	FP	GC	.358	35353
	180	TC		.358	35399
	180	TC	GC	.358	35399
	200	FP		.358	35311
	200	FP	GC	.358	35311
	200	TC	GC	.358	35399
	245	FP	GC	.358	35311
375	265	FP	GC	.376	37570
40/10mm	155	SWCBB		.401	40048

Caliber	Bullet Grs. Wgt.	Bullet Type	Gas Check	Sizing Die	Top Punch
	170	TCBB		.401	40047
	170	SWCBB		.401	40048
	200	TCBB		.401	40047
	200	SWCBB		.401	40048
	190			.401	40101
41	170	SWCBB		.411	41447
	200	SWCBB		.411	41447
	185	SWC		.411	41610
	210	SWC		.411	41610
	190	TC		.411	41415
	210	TCBB		.411	41415
	220	TC	GC	.411	41415
	220	FP		.411	41415
	220	SWCBB		.411	41610
416	365	RN	GC	.417	41916
44	200	WC		.430	44944
	200	TC		.430	44428
	200	FPSWC		.428	44191
	200	SWC		.430	44191
	220	SWCBB		.430	44191
	246	RN		.430	44374
	240	SWC		.430	44421
	240	SWCBB		.430	44421
	240	SWCGC		.430	44421
	240	FP		.430	44191
	240	TC	GC	.430	44428
	240	TC		.430	44428
	250	FP	GC	.430	44191
	265	FP		.430	44191
	265	FP	GC	.430	44191
	300	FP	GC	.430	44191
45	160	SPL		.452	45452
	170	SPLBB		.452	45452
	180	SWCBB		.452	45429
	185	SWC		.452	45421
	185	SWCBB		.452	45421
	180	SWC		.452	45429
	200	SWCBB		.452	45429
	200	SWC		.452	45429
	215	SWCBB		.452	45424
	210	RNWC		.452	45265
	225	TCBB		.452	45375
	225	RN		.452	45701
	225	RNBB		.452	45701
	225	WC		.452	45424
	255	SWC	GC	.452	45424
	255	SWC		.452	45424
	255	SWC		.455	45452
	300	SWC	GC	.452	54524
45 Rifle	300	FP		.458	45424
	350	FP	GC	.458	45015
	405	FP		.458	45015
	465	FP	GC	.458	45015
	375	SP		.458	45702
	405	SP	GC	.458	45702
	500	FP		.458	45525
	540	FP	GC	.458	45525

BB = Bevel Base; DBB = Double End Bevel Base; FB = Flat Base; FP = Flat Point; GC = Gas Check; NR = Not Required; RN = Round Nose; SP = Spitzer Point; SWC = Semi-Wadcutter; TC = Truncated Cone; WC = Wadcutter.

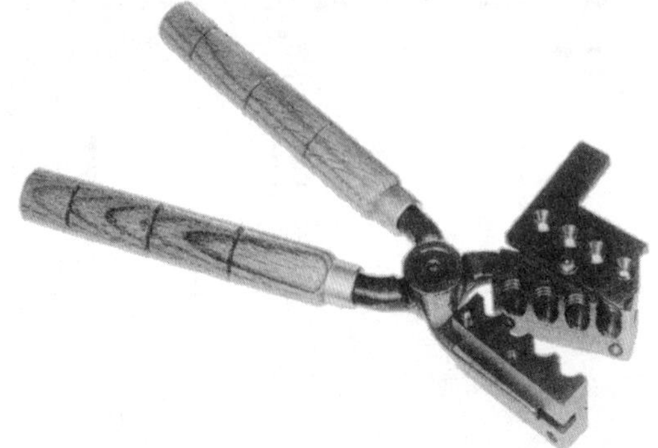

SAECO 4-Cavity Mould

HANNED LINE

NozeFirst Top Punch
Features a flat face to eliminate lubrisizer misalignment. Available in two formats to fit popular Saeco-type or Lyman/RCBS-type sizers. From The Hanned Line.
Price:RCBS/Lyman. **$29.95**
Price: Saeco **$32.95**

JAVELINA

Super Lube
NRA developed formula of 50% Alox 2138F and 50% pure yellow beeswax. Comes in 1.5 oz. hollow tube to fit most lubrisizers. From Midway.
Price: Each **$3.14**

LEE

Lube and Sizing Kit
Standard threaded size die with integral container. Bullets pushed through sizing die nose first. Gas checks automatically seated and crimped. Sized bullets are captured in special container. Comes complete with lube for single bullet size. From Lee Precision, Inc.
Price: **$16.98**

Liquid Alox
Liquid lube coats entire bullet and dries to varnish-like finish. Eliminates need for sizing of most cast bullets. Comes in 4-oz. bottle—enough to lube 1,000 bullets. From Lee Precision, Inc.
Price: **$2.75**

NRA Formula Alox
Contains 50% Alox 2138F and 50% commercial A-1 beeswax. Hollow stick fits most lubricators. Packed in tubes. From Lee Precision, Inc.
Price: **$3.98**
Price: 12 sticks **$42.00**

LYMAN

#450 Bullet Sizer/Lubricator
Short stroke, power link leverage system sizes, lubes and seats gas checks. C-type iron-steel cast frame is line bored for die alignment. Comes with gas check seater and Alox lubricant. Adaptable to all bullets by change of size die. Weight: 73/4 lbs. From Lyman Products Corporation.
Price: **$139.95**

Alox Lube
Comes in tubular form and fits all standard lube sizers. Best for rifle bullets. Weight: 1-oz. From Lyman Products Corporation.
Price: **$3.60**

Ideal Lubricant
Designed to increase accuracy and eliminate barrel leading. Available in solid or hollow sticks and will fit Lyman 40 sizer/lubricator and other similar tools. From Lyman Products Corporation.
Price: **$3.60**

Lube/Sizer Heater
Aluminum mounting plate/heating block drilled to accept Lyman, RCBS, Saeco and Star lubrisizers. 110-volt. From Lyman Products Corporation.
Price: 110v **$44.95**
Price: 220v **$46.00**

Orange Magic Bullet Lube
High temperature lube designed to allow higher cast bullet velocities without leading. From Lyman Products Corporation.
Price: **$3.95**

Lube/Size Dies and Top Punch
Now features 90° hole spacing for lubing bullets with hard lubricants. Precisely machined top punch fits bullet nose shape exactly (refer to chart in bullet mould section for correct bullet top punch). Tapered mouth and hardened interior of size die forms and lubes bullets. Interior dimension of size die corresponds to suggested diameters for all popular rifle and pistol calibers. From Lyman Products Corporation.
Price: Top Punch $7.50
Price: Sizing die $19.50

MAGMA

Star Lube-Sizer
Accessories for the Star Auto Lubricator/Sizer. Heated base for new hard wax bullet lubes; bullet feeder to automatically feed bullets from plastic tube; hard wax bullet lube. Bullet feeder includes setup for one caliber: small, 38-9mm; large, 10mm, 41, 44, 45. Special transfer bars and feed tubes required for short bullets, *e.g.* 25, 32, 380. From Magma Engineering Company.
Price: **$175.00**
Price: Heated base **$85.00**
Price: Bullet feeder. **$95.00**
Price: Star lube, per pound **$10.00**

NECO

Taurak Bullet Lube
Thick water soluble, high melting point, block grease lube for cast lead bullets to prevent leading at velocities in excess of 2200 fps. Available in 1" diameter sticks with or without a center hole. From NECO.
Price: **$3.50**

NEI

SP Lube
Sprue plate lube eliminates galling. Comes in 2-oz. container. From NEI Handtools, Inc.
Price: **$3.00**

RAPINE

Bullet Press Sizer
Designed specifically for large Civil War bullets, hollow base and solid base carbine bullets but can be used with other calibers. Sizes bullets to .001" increments using a series of size dies. Comes with one pusher for flat-base or hollow-base bullets. From Rapine Associates.
Price: **$41.95**
Price: Sizing die **$11.49**

Bullet lubricant for both blackpowder and modern bullets. Comes in 4-oz. bottle. From Rapine Associates.
Price: **$4.50**

REDDING

Double "C" Clamps
Designed for clamping the Saeco lubri-sizer to benchtop. Will accommodate bench thickness of up to 2 1/4". From Redding Reloading Equipment.
Price: **$22.50**

LBT Blue Lube

Hanned Top Punch

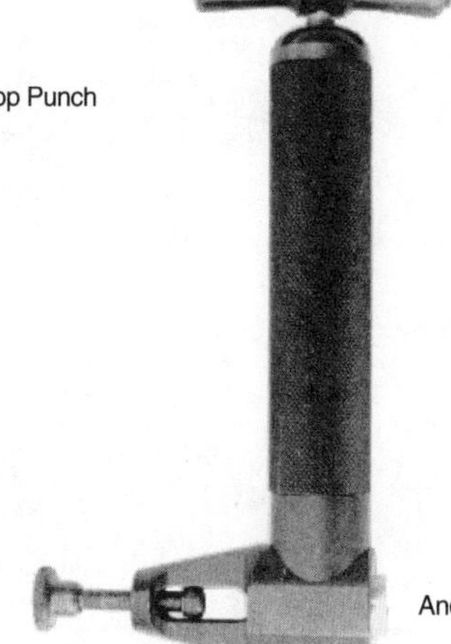
Andela Bullet Lubricator

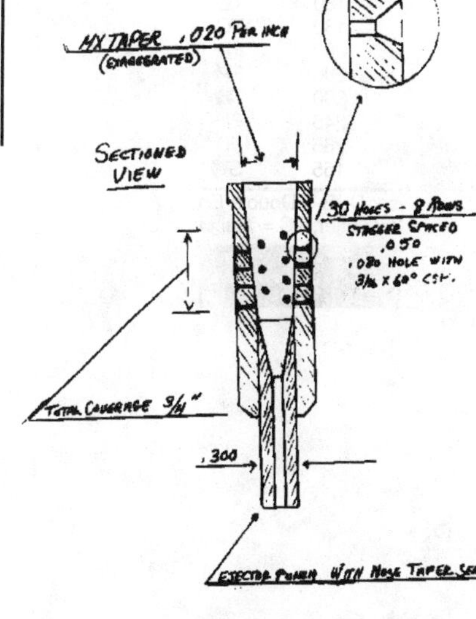

Donald Eagan Lube Die

Section 4: Bullet Casting

RCBS

Bullet Lube

Designed for RCBS Lube-A-Matic and other lube-sizers that use hollow-stick lubricant. Non-toxic, temperature-resistant blend of Alox and beeswax to NRA specifications. From RCBS.

Price: $3.95

Lube-A-Matic-2

Auto pressure control with finger tip adjustments for depth of sizing. Uses either Lube-A-Matic or Lyman dies. Will also seat gas checks. Sizer die and top punch not included. From RCBS.

Price: $157.95
Price: Bullet sizer die $20.95
Price: Top punch $7.95
Price: Accessory Base Plate-2 . . . . $26.95

ROOSTER

Bullet Film Lube

Emulsified liquid lube bonds tightly to cast or swaged bullets. Designed for low velocity pistol loads. Apply by dipping, tumbling or flood-coating. Lubes 100,000 bullets. Available in 16-oz., 1/2-gal. or 1-gallon quantities. From Rooster Laboratories.

Price: 16-oz.. . . . . $7.50
Price: 1/2-gal. $18.50
Price: 1-gal. $30.00

Bullet Lubes

Lubri-sizer high-melt cannelure lubes in choice of hardnesses. Zambini is hard tough lube intended for pistol bullets; melting point of 220° Fahrenheit. Comes in 2"x 6" commercial-size sticks and 1"x 4" hollow or solid sticks. HVR is soft but firm and designed for high-velocity rifle bullets; melting point of 220° Fahrenheit. Available in 1"x 4" sticks only. From Rooster Laboratories.

Price: Zambini 2x6, each $5.00
Price: Zambini 1x4, each $3.00
Price: HVR, each. $3.00
Price: BP-7, each. $3.00

Lee Lube and Sizing Kit

Lee Liquid Alox

Lyman Lube/Sizer Heater

Lyman Orange Magic Bullet Lube

Lyman Liquid Alox

Lithi Bee Bullet Lube

Lyman #450 Bullet Sizer/Lubricator

LYMAN Lube Size Dies

PISTOL		RIFLE	
CALIBER	DIAMETER	CALIBER	DIAMETER
22 Jet	.224, .225	244	.243, .244
221 Fireball	.224, .225	6mm	.243, .244
25 ACP	.251	25	.257, .258
30 Luger	.310	264 Win. Mag.	.264, .266
30 Herrett	.310	6.5mm	.264, .266
30 Mauser	.310	270 Win.	.277, .278
32 ACP	.311, .312, .313, .314	7mm	.284, .285
32-20	.311, .312, .313, .314	280 Rem.	.284, .285
32 S&W	.311, .312, .313, .314	284 Win.	.284, .285
32 H&R Mag.	.311, .312, .313, .314	30	.308, .309, .310
9mm Luger	.354, .355, .356	7.62 Russian	.310
38	.354, .355, .356	32-20 Win.	.310
38 Super Auto	.354, .355, .356	7.65mm Mauser	.311
380 Auto	.354, .355, .356	303 British	.313, .314
38 S&W	.357, .358, .359, .360	32 Win. Spl.	.321
38 Spl.	.357, .358, .359, .360	32 Win. SL	.321
357 Mag.	.357, .358, .359, .360	32 Rem.	.321
357 Max.	.357, .358, .359, .360	8mm Mauser	.323, .325
38-40	.400, .401	338 Win.	.338
10mm Auto	.400, .401	9mmx56	.354, .355, .356
40 S&W	.400, .401	9mmx57	.354, .355, .356
41 S&W Mag.	.410	35	.357, .358, .359
41 AE	.410	375 H&H Mag.	.375, .377, .378
44 S&W Spl.	.429, .430, .431	375 Win.	.375, .377, .378
44 Mag.	.429, .430, .431	38-55	.379
45 ACP	.450, .451, .452	38-40	.400, .401
45 Auto Rim	.450, .451, .452	44-40	.427, .428
45 Colt	.450, .451, .452	44 Spl.	.429, .430
45 Win. Mag.	.450, .451, .452	44 Mag.	.429, .430
45 Colt	.454	444 Marlin	.430, .431
445 Webley	.454	45-70	.457, .458, .459
22	.224, .225	458 Winchester	.457, .458, .459
243	.243, .244	50	.509, .512

Lyman Size Die and Top Punch

Midway Lubricator Heater

SAECO

Bullet Lubes

Saeco Gold is Alox-free formula to reduce leading to a minimum. Saeco Traditional rifle lube is NRA formula with Alox and natural beeswax mixture. Saeco Green for both pistol and rifle bullets contains no Alox and is slightly harder than the other two lubes. All available in solid or hollow sticks. From Redding Reloading Equipment.

Price: Each **$4.50**

Lubri-Sizer

Features solid cast iron body; swing-out gas-check seater for seating gas checks without sizing; adjustable pressure lubricant; two guide rods for alignment of top punch and sizing die; compound leverage; use with hollow- or solid-stick lube. Top punches and sizing dies not included. From Redding Reloading Equipment.

Price: **$195.00**

Sizing Dies

Made with unique pre-lead that fits "as cast" bullet diameter for depth of approximately .3-inch to ensure straight bullet feed alignment in die. Gentle taper constriction between the two diameters eliminates lead shearing. Dies are internally micro-honed. From Redding Reloading Equipment.

Price: **$36.00**

Top Punches

Tapered shoulder punch assures positive alignment with die body. Straight shank-type punches designed for Lyman and RCBS lubrisizers also available. From Redding Reloading Equipment.

Price: **$13.80**

SPG

Bullet Lube

Developed specifically for blackpowder cartridge shooting but can be used for smokeless loads. Helps keep fouling soft. From SPG Lubricants.

Price: Each Stick **$3.85**
1/4 lb. **$22.00**
3/4 lb. **$40.00**
3 lb. **$75.00**

ROBERT STILLWELL

Lube/Size Dies

Custom-made 257 through 530 dies for Star lubricator/sizer. Heat-treated to 60-62 C. From Robert Stillwell.

Price: $32.00
Price: Top punch (flat) $10.00
Price: Top punch (to fit) $16.00

Magma Star Helper

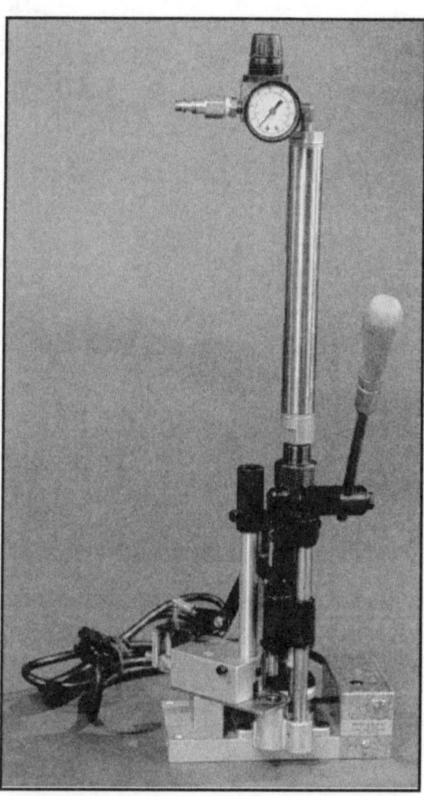

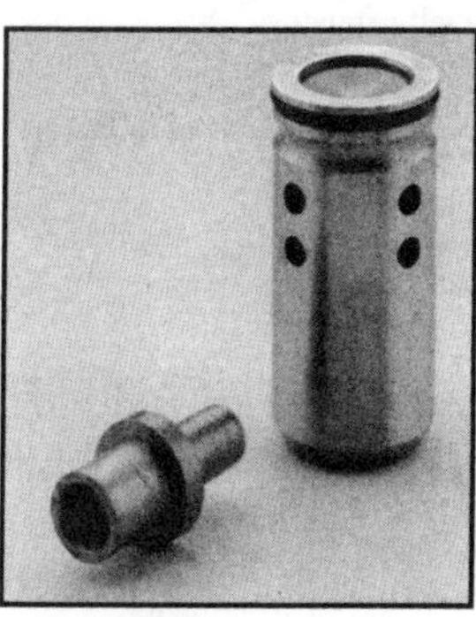

Lyman Lube/Size Die and Top Punch

NECO Taurak Bullet Lube

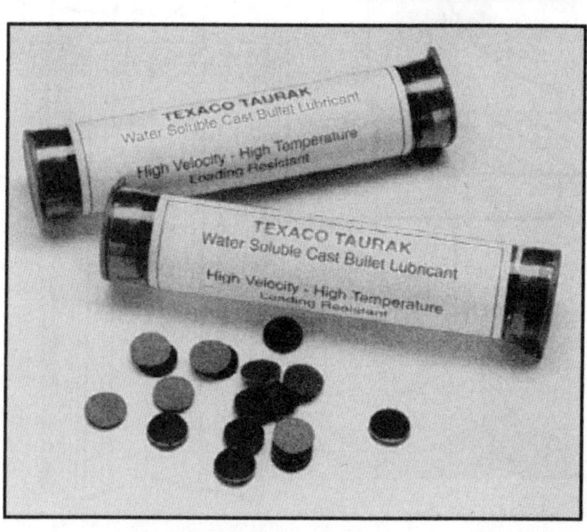

Section 3: Bullet Casting

THOMPSON

Bullet Lubes

Five wax-based lube offerings. Bear Lube Cold soft, non-sticky and requires 90° to flow; Bear Lube Heat is medium hard lube flows at 110°; Lazy Lube same as Bear Lube Heat but designed to flow through automated Star Luber; dry, non-sticky Blue Angel for the commercial caster and requires 125° to 140° flow temperature with melt point of 165°; Red Angel melts at 240° and will flow at 180° or lower; PS blackpowder cartridge lube. Available in 1"x 4", 1"x 8" or 2"x 6" sticks. For case and partial case prices contact manufacturer. From Thompson Bullet Lube Co.

Price: Bear, Blue Angel, each **$3.20**
Price: Red Angel, each **$3.50**
Price: PS **$3.50**

WTA

Cast Bullet Sizing Tool

Consists of a die, flat base and interchangeable bushings for use on any reloading press to size or expand the size of cast bullets. Bushings available in .001" increments. From WTA.

Price: .... **Contact manufacturer.**

Tamarack Bullet Lube

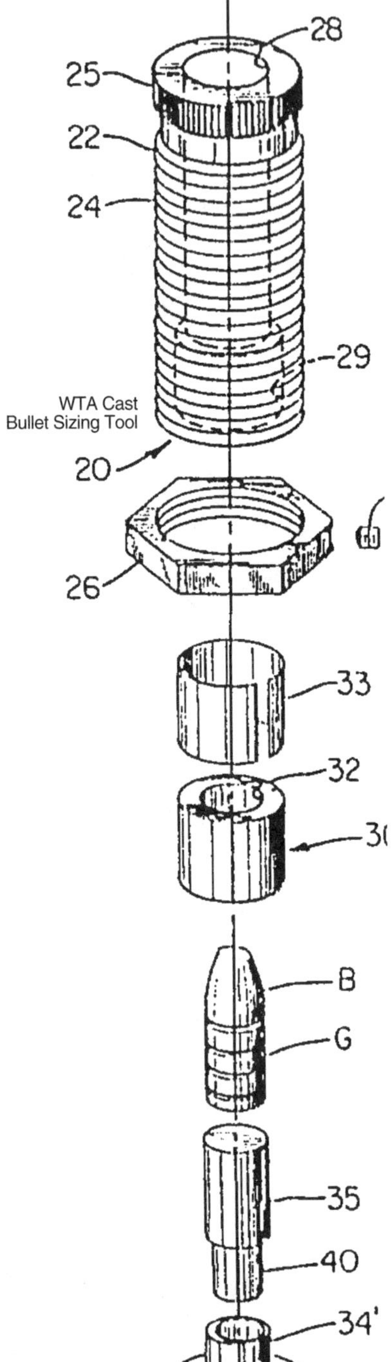

WTA Cast Bullet Sizing Tool

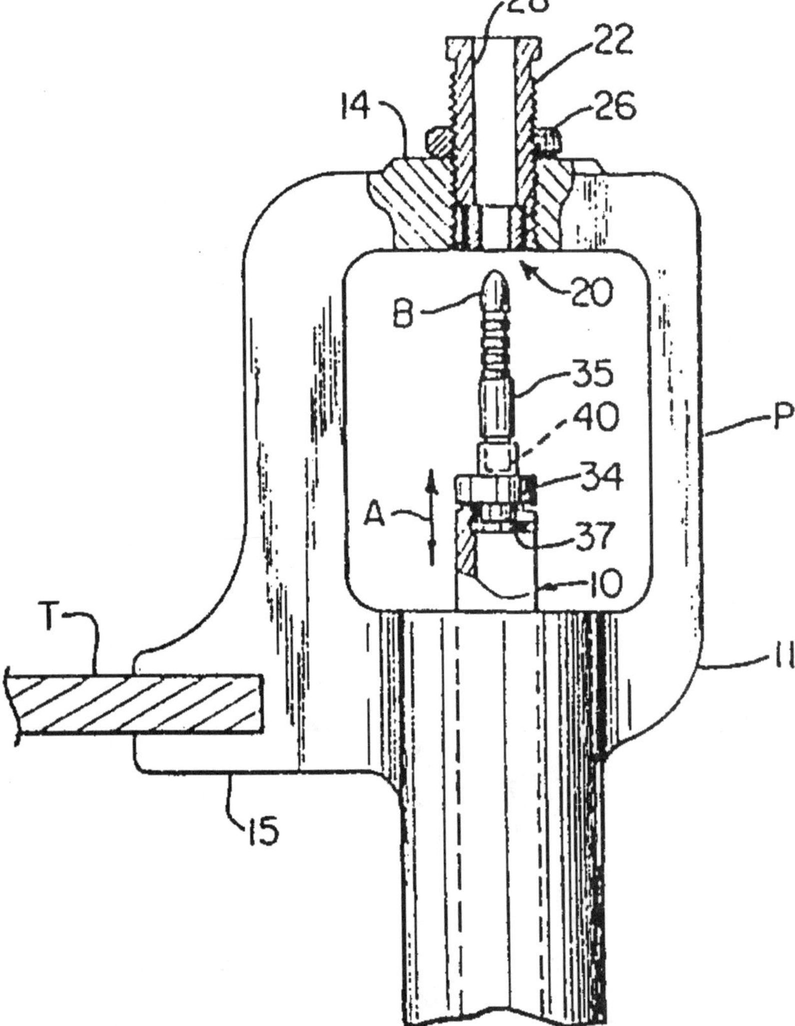

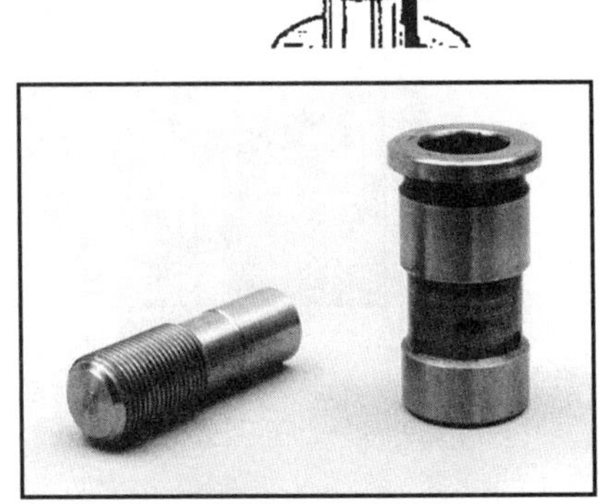

Robert Stillwell Lube/Size Die

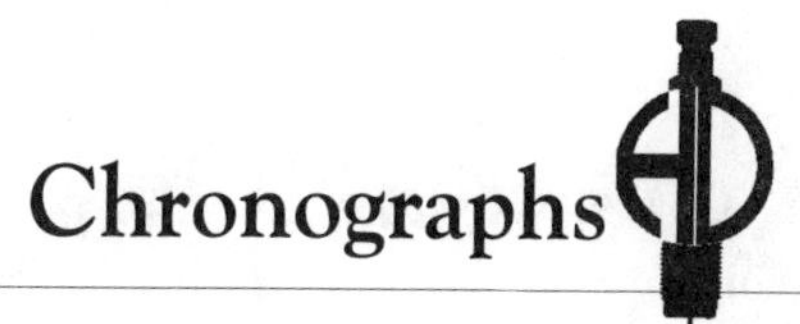

COMPETITION ELECTRONICS ProChrono
Velocity range from 56 to 9999 fps. Features LCD display, diffuser hoods, optional indoor lighting setup, remote control, infrared thermal printer and printer holder. Records and displays velocity, number of shots and average velocity. Operating temperature range from 32 to 100 degrees Fahrenheit. Mounting hold thread for tripod 1/4x20. Size: 16x4x3 1/4. Guide wire size: 3/16x16". Powered by one 9-volt alkaline battery. Battery not included. From Competition Electronics, Inc.
Price: **$114.95**
Price: Indoor lighting setup **$30.95**
Price: Remote control **$19.95**
Price: Infrared thermal printer **$125.00**
Price: Printer holder **$7.50**
Price: Extra diffusers **$4.00**
Price: Plastic Diffuser Hoods **$5.00**

OEHLER 35P Carrying Case
Hard plastic case holds Model 35P, three skyscreens, 4-foot rail, pair of folding stands, and spare paper and batteries. From Oehler Research.
Price: **$30.00**

OEHLER BNC/BNC Signal Cable
30-foot signal cables to connect Model 55 screens to chronograph. From Oehler Research.
Price:. . . . . **Call for price**

OEHLER Diffuser Assembly
Assembly includes rigid plastic diffuser with two side-rails for one Skyscreen III. From Oehler Research.
Price: **$30.00**

OEHLER Diffuser Assembly, Lighted
Clamps to hold tubular 120-volt incandescent bulb to add to diffuser assembly. Includes bulb, socket and cord. From Oehler Research.
Price: **$30.00**

OEHLER Model 35 Chronograph
Available with either two or three Skyscreen IIIs. Same features as 35P without printer and, in two skyscreen configuration, without proof channel. Comes with 2-foot mounting rail and battery. From Oehler Research.
Price: With 3 Skyscreen III **$225.00**

OEHLER Model 35BNC Chronograph
Same unit as Model 35P retaining built-in printer and proof channel but requires Model 55 photoelectric screens and uses 120v ac power instead of battery. From Oehler Research.
Price: **$400.00**

OEHLER Model 35P Chronograph
Model 35P uses three Skyscreen III detectors to proof velocity readouts by taking two readings per shot and comparing the two for extreme differences. Includes built-in printer with plain paper printout to record each round as fired. At end of shot string a statistical summary of valid shots with high, low, extreme spread, mean and standard deviation with asterisk denoting possible shot error. Uses 4MHz clock for higher accuracy at short screen spacings. Comes with 2-foot mounting rail and battery. From Oehler Research.
Price: **$345.00**

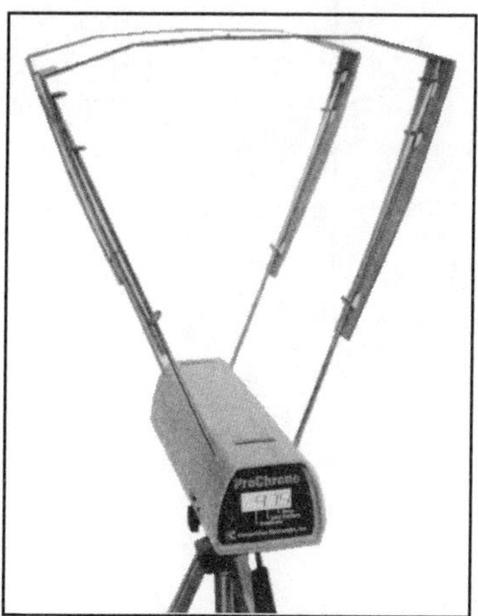

Competition Electronics

OEHLER Model 43 Personal Ballistics Laboratory
IBM-compatible host computer Model 43 measures firearm pressure curves, muzzle velocity, time-of-flight and downrange velocity using integrated multi-channel electronics; graphically shows point of impact on target with use of Acoustic Target, measures it and makes permanent record. Consists of 9x11x1.4" metal case connecting to computer via serial port and powered by internal rechargeable battery. Uses one set of three Skyscreens near muzzle and second set downrange. Both sets include proof channel. Host computer must be MS-DOS compatible and have CGA, EGA, VGA or Hercules graphics; a serial port; and minimum of 384K of free RAM. Optional equipment includes: Pressure strain gauge starter kit with five gauges, cables and connectors, cleaners and adhesives, soldering iron and other incidentals; Acoustic target with three acoustic sensors; downrange amplifier with 110-yard cable; Skyscreen mounting kit with 4-foot rail and two adjustable stands; set of three downrange Skyscreens. Comes with three Skyscreen IIIs, cables, an AC adapter/charger and all software including Ballistic Explorer. From Oehler Research.
Price: Model 43 . . . . **$800.00**
Price: Pressure strain gauge. **$170.00**
Price: Acoustic Target. **$600.00**
Price: Downrange amplifier **$150.00**
Price: Skyscreen mounting kit **$50.00**
Price: Extra strain gauges, 5 . . . . **$35.00**

OEHLER Printer Upgrade
To upgrade Model 35 to 35P by adding plain paper printer. From Oehler Research.
Price: **$145.00**

OEHLER Skyscreen III
For use with Oehler Model 12, 33 and 35 chronographs as replacement or spare. Complete with cable and moulded plastic diffuser assembly. From Oehler Research.
Price: **$35.00**

OEHLER Skyscreen III Plastic Shells
Four black outside pieces to repair damaged skyscreens. From Oehler Research.
Price: **$15.00**

OEHLER Skyscreen III Plastic Shell with Lenses
Kit includes both lenses and two black outside pieces to repair one skyscreen. From Oehler Research.
Price: **$15.00**

Section 4: Miscellaneous

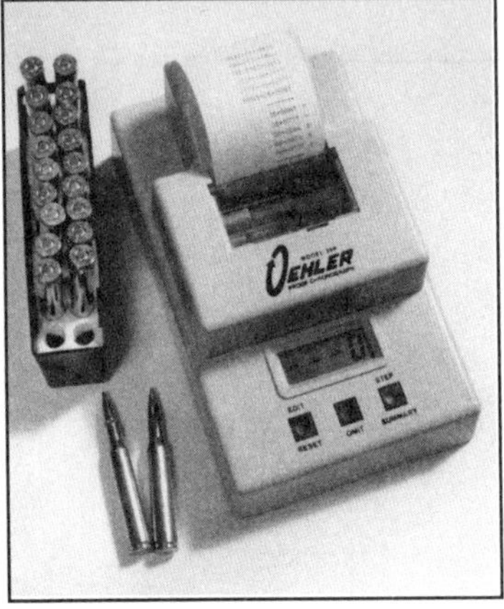

Oehler Model 35P

PACT Model 1

Shot number and velocity alternate on four-digit display. Provides statistical summary of average velocity, high and low velocities as well as standard deviation and average deviation. Holds up to 24 shots and recalls any one from memory. Optional infrared print driver allows communication with HP infrared printer. Comes with M5 skyscreens. From PACT.

Price: **$129.95**
Price: Infrared print driver.......... **$25.00**
Price: Infrared HP printer **$125.00**
Price: Skyscreen mounting bracket **$27.99**
Price: Light kit **$39.95**
Price: Carrying case **$16.95**

PACT PC2

Smaller version of PACT Professional chronograph. Maintains all basic features but with less memory, less powerful software and no printout capability. Optional serial port allows dumping of data to host computer; compatible with RCBS PC Bullet. Optional infrared print driver allows communication with HP battery powered printer. Comes with M5 skyscreens. From PACT.

Price: **$179.95**
Price: Infrared print driver.......... **$25.00**
Price: Infrared HP printer **$125.00**
Price: Skyscreen mounting bracket **$27.99**
Price: Light kit **$39.95**
Price: Carrying case **$16.95**

PACT Professional Chronograph

Chronograph with ballistics computer built in. Records in memory and displays each shot, shot number and velocity to tenth of a foot per second at top of 32-character display and current average velocity on lower half of display. Recalculates current string statistics: extreme spread, standard deviation and average deviation. Features "hot key" control to allow user interface with stored data to review any aspect of shot string. Holds up to 300 shots in memory. Ballistics computer features trajectory function to calculate optimal 100-yard zero to tenth of an inch, correcting for altitude and temperature or cross wind; drop tables based on entered data; calculates recoil, ballistic co-efficient; and includes terminal ballistics functions such as kinetic energy, momentum, IPSC power factor, Taylor knock-out and Wootters lethality index. Plain paper dot-matrix printer. Comes with M5 14"x12" skyscreens. Skyscreen mounting bracket and carrying case optional. From PACT.

Price: **$229.95**
Price: Skyscreen mounting bracket **$27.99**
Price: Light kit **$39.95**
Price: Carrying case **$17.99**
Price: Extra printing paper, 6 rolls **$12.00**

SHOOTING CHRONY MASTER CHRONY

Include Alpha, Beta, Delta or Gamma chronograph plus remote LCD unit with 16-foot cord. From Shooting Chrony, Inc.

Price: F-1 Master.......... **$104.95**
Price: Delta Master.......... **$109.95**
Price: Alpha Master **$119.95**
Price: Beta Master **$134.95**
Price: Gamma Master.......... **$199.95**

SHOOTING CHRONY ALPHA CHRONY

Made of 20-gauge steel, measures 2 3/4x4 1/4x7 1/2 and weighs only 2.5 lbs. Set up on tabletop or tripod. Features velocity range from 30 fps to 5000 fps; accuracy to +99.5%; measures high, low and average velocities, extreme spread and standard deviations; large LCD readout; individually calibrated. Readouts in fps or metric m/s. 1-string, 32-shot memory. Indoor shooting light fixture, stereo jack for optional remote control available. From Shooting Chrony, Inc.

Price: **$99.95**

SHOOTING CHRONY BETA CHRONY

In addition to all the standard features of the Alpha chronograph, the Beta offers memory for 60 numbered shots; data storage/information retrieval; computer interface. From Shooting Chrony, Inc.

Price: **$109.95**

SHOOTING CHRONY DELTA CHRONY

The low-priced starter for the Shooting Chrony line of chronographs. Features include LED readout of numbered shot velocities; delivery of high, low and average velocities of string; ability to switch from fps and mps; ability to upgrade to the Alpha Chrony. From Shooting Chrony.

Price: **$89.95**
Price: Upgrade.......... **$25.00**

SHOOTING CHRONY GAMMA CHRONY

All the features of the Beta plus 1000-shot memory with optimal 4000-8000-shot available; string size change capability; rapid-fire mode to measure up to 1800 rounds per minute; IBM interface; remote control.

Price: **$189.95**

PACT PC2

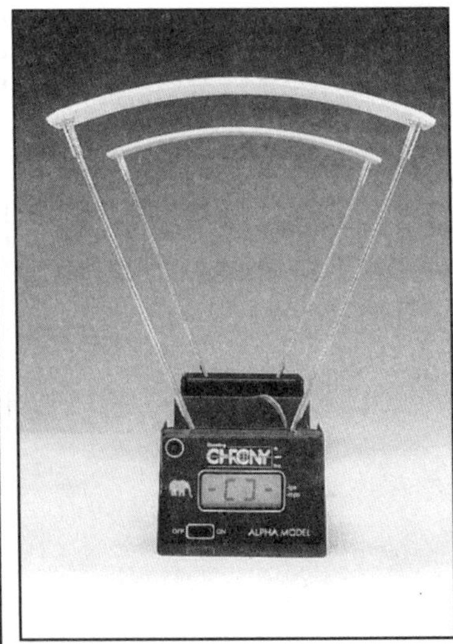

Shooting Chrony Alpha Chrony

HANDLOADER'S DIGEST REFERENCE

SMOKELESS POWDER—COMPOSITION AND BURN RATE
From Fastest Burning to Slowest

Manuf.	Powder	Granule Shape	Nitroglyc. %	Bulk Density	Suggested Primers	Primary Uses
Hodg.	Clays	Flake	P	0.475	Standard Pistol	Shotgun/Targ. Pistol
Norma	R-1	—	2	—	Standard Pistol	Targ. Pistol
Scott	Red Diam.	Diamond	22	—	Standard Pistol	Shotgun/Light Pistol
Vihta.	N310	Porous base cylin.	0	0.45	Standard Pistol	Targ. Pistol
Herc.	Red Dot	Flake	20	0.480	Standard Pistol	Shotgun/Light Pistol
Herc.	Bullseye	Flake	40	0.620	Standard Pistol	Light to Med. Pistol
Vihta.	N312	Porous base	0	0.435	Standard Pistol	Special Blank Powder
Win.	230*	Sphere	UN	0.715	Standard Pistol	Light Pistol
Scott	1000	Flake	0	—	Standard Pistol	Light to Med. Pistol/Shotgun
Vihta.	N318	Porous base flake	0	0.430	—	Shotgun
Scott	Nitro-100	Flake	27	0.510	Standard Pistol	Shotgun/Light Pistol
IMR	700X	Flake	29	0.500	Standard Pistol	Shotgun/Light Pistol
Win.	452AA*	Sphere	13	0.555	Standard Pistol	Shotgun/Light Pistol
Scott	453	Sphere	13	0.555	Standard Pistol	Shotgun/Light Pistol
Vihta.	N319	Porous base flake	0	0.430	—	Shotgun
Accur.	AA2	Sphere	24	0.750	Standard Pistol	Light to Mod. Pistol
Vihta.	N320	Porous base cylin.	0	0.500	Standard Pistol	Shotgun/Light to Mod. Pistol
Scott	Royal D	—	0	—	Standard Pistol	Shotgun/Light to Mod. Pistol
Vihta.	N321	Porous base flake	0	0.450	—	Shotgun
Win.	231	Sphere	22.5	0.700	Standard Pistol	Light to Mod. Pistol
Vihta.	N322	Porous base flake	0	0.430	—	Shotgun
Hodg.	HP-38	Sphere	P	0.635	Standard Pistol	Light to Mod. Pistol
Vihta.	N324	Porous base flake	0	0.470	—	Shotgun
Vihta.	N325	Porous base flake	0	0.520	—	Shotgun
Win.	WST	Sphere	20	0.535	Standard Pistol	Shotgun/Targ. Pistol
Vihta.	N326	Porous base flake	0	0.520	—	Shotgun
Hodg.	Int'l clays	Flake	P	0.525	—	Shotgun
Vihta.	N328	Porous base flake	0	0.500	—	Shotgun
Herc.	Green Dot	Flake	20	0.515	—	Shotgun
Vihta.	N330	Porous base cylin.	0	0.600	Standard Pistol	Light to Mod. Pistol
IMR	7625	Flake	0	0.640	Standard Pistol	Shotgun/Pistol
IMR	PB	Porous base	0	0.555	Standard Pistol	Shotgun/Light Pistol
Vihta.	N331	Porous base cylin.	0	0.680	Standard Pistol	9mm Luger/Light to Mod. Pistol
Scott	Pearl	—	0	—	Standard Pistol	Shotgun/Mod. Pistol
Win.	WSL	Sphere	34	0.765	Standard Pistol	Shotgun/Targ. Pistol
Hodg.	Univ. clays	Flake	P	0.650	Standard Pistol	Shotgun/Pistol
Win.	473AA*	Sphere	UN	0.665	—	Shotgun
Herc.	Unique	Flake	20	0.610	Standard Pistol	Mod.-Heavy Pistol/Light Cast-Bullet Rifle
Win.	WAP	Sphere	15	—	Standard Pistol	Pistol
Vihta.	N338	Porous base cylin.	0	0.540	—	Blanks/Shotgun
Accur.	AA5	Sphere	17	0.950	Standard Pistol	Sub-Sonic 9mm Luger/Mod. Pistol
Win.	WSF	Sphere	34	0.770	Standard Pistol	Shotgun/Mod. Pistol
Vihta.	N340	Porous base cylin.	0	0.560	Standard Pistol	Mod. to Heavy Pistol
Win.	540	Sphere	21	0.950	Standard Pistol	Shotgun/Pistol
Vihta.	N342	Porous base cylin.	0	0.560	Standard Pistol	Shotgun/Pistol
Herc.	HERCO	Flake	20	0.570	Standard Pistol	Shotgun/Mod. Pistol
Hodg.	HS6	Sphere	P	0.945	Standard Pistol	Mod. to Heavy Pistol/Shotgun
Vihta.	N344	Porous base flake	0	0.520	—	Shotgun
IMR	4756	Flake	0	0.610	Standard Pistol	Shotgun/Pistol
Vihta.	N347	Porous base flake	0	0.540	—	Shotgun
Scott	1250	Flake	0	—	Standard Pistol	Shotgun/Mod. Pistol

SMOKELESS POWDER—COMPOSITION AND BURN RATE
From Fastest Burning to Slowest

Manuf.	Powder	Granule Shape	Nitroglyc. %	Bulk Density	Suggested Primers	Primary Uses
Vihta.	3N37	Porous base cylin.	0	0.640	Standard Pistol	High Vel. 22 RF/Pistol/Shotgun
Vihta.	3N17	Porous base cylin.	0	0.520	Standard Pistol	22 Rimfire
Vihta.	3N36	Porous base cylin.	0	0.500	Standard Pistol	22 Rimfire
IMR	800X	Flake	29	—	—	Shotgun
Scott	1500	Flake	0	—	Standard or Mag. Pistol	Mod. to Heavy Pistol
Vihta.	N350	Porous base cylin.	0	0.570	Standard Pistol	Mod. to Heavy Pistol/Shotgun
Hodg.	HS7	Sphere	P	0.990	Standard Pistol	Shotgun/Heavy Pistol
Herc.	Blue Dot	Flake	20	0.780	Standard or Mag. Pistol	Mod. to Heavy Pistol/Shotgun
Accur.	AA7	Sphere	10.5	0.985	Standard or Mag. Pistol	9mm Luger/10mm/Mod. to Heavy Pistol
Win.	571	Sphere	21	0.955	—	Shotgun
Win.	630*	Sphere	UN	0.965	Mag. Pistol	Heavy Pistol
Herc.	2400	Tubular	15	0.870	Standard or Mag. Pistol	Heavy and Mag. Pistol
Vihta.	N110	Tubular	0	0.760	Standard or Mag. Pistol	Heavy and Mag. Pistol
Norma	R-123	—	0	—	Standard or Mag. Pistol	Heavy and Mag. Pistol
Accur.	AA9	Sphere	10	0.975	Mag. Pistol	Mag. Pistol/30 Carb/410
Hodg.	110	Sphere	P	0.975	Mag. Pistol	Mag. Pistol/30 Carb/410
Win.	296	Sphere	11	0.975	Mag. Pistol	Mag. Pistol/30 Carb/410
IMR	4759	Tubular	0	0.675	Standard/BR Only	Heavy Pistol and Light Cast-Bullet Rifle
Vihta.	N120	Tubular	0	0.820	Standard Rifle	Light Bullets in 22 Varmint Loads
IMR	4227	Tubular	0	0.870	Standard/BR Only	Heavy Pistol/Light Cast-Bullet Rifle
Vihta.	N125	Tubular	0	0.850	Standard Rifle	7.62X39
Hodg.	4227	Tubular	0	0.870	Standard/BR Only	Heavy Pistol/Light Cast-Bullet Rifle
Vihta.	N130	Tubular	0	0.850	Standard Rifle	Factory 22 & 6mm PPC
Win.	680*	Sphere	10	0.950	Mag. Only	454 Casull/Small Rifle Cases
Accur.	1680	Sphere	10	0.950	Mag. Only	454 Casull/Small Rifle Cases
T-Bird	680	Sphere	10	0.950	Mag. Only	454 Casull/Small Rifle Cases
Vihta.	N132	Tubular	0	0.860	Standard Rifle	5.56 Tracer/Limited Application
Norma	200	Tubular	0	—	Standard Rifle	Small Capacity Rifle
Vihta.	N133	Tubular	0	0.860	Standard Rifle	222, 223 & 45-70
IMR	4198	Tubular	0	0.850	Standard Rifle	Excellent Cast-Bullet Rifle
Scott**	4197	Tubular	0	0.850	Standard Rifle	Excellent Cast-Bullet Rifle
Hodg.	4198	Tubular	0	0.850	Standard Rifle	Excellent Cast-Bullet Rifle
Hodg.	4198SC	Tubular	0	0.880†	Standard Rifle	Excellent Cast-Bullet Rifle
B-West	BW-36	Tubular	0	—	Standard Rifle	Mod. Capacity Rifle
Herc.	RL7	Tubular	7	0.890	Standard Rifle	Mod. Capacity Rifle
Vihta.	N134	Tubular	0	0.860	Standard Rifle	7.62mm NATO Tracer
Accur.	2015BR	Tubular	0	0.900	Std./BR/Mag. Rifle	Mod. Capacity Rifle
Scott**	3032	Tubular	0	0.880	Standard Rifle	Mod. Capacity Rifle
IMR	3031	Tubular	0	0.880	Standard Rifle	Mod. Capacity Rifle
Norma	201	Tubular	0	—	Standard Rifle	Mod. Capacity Rifle
Hodg.	322	Tubular	0	0.920†	Standard Rifle	Mod. Capacity Rifle
Scott**	322	Tubular	0	0.920†	Standard Rifle	Mod. Capacity Rifle
B-West	IMR-8208	Tubular	—	—	Standard Rifle	Mod. Capacity Rifle
Accur.	2230	Sphere	10	—	Std./BR/Mag. Rifle	.223/Mod. Capacity Rifle
Win.	748	Sphere	10	0.995	Std./BR/Mag. Rifle	Mod. to Large Rifle
Hodg.	335	Sphere	P	1.035	Mag. Rifle	Mod. to Large Rifle
Hodg.	BL-C(2)	Sphere	P	1.035	Mag. Rifle	Mod. to Large Rifle
Accur.	2460	Sphere	10	0.975	Std./BR/Mag. Rifle	Mod. Capacity Rifle
IMR	4895	Tubular	0	0.920	Standard Rifle	Versatile/Gd. Cast Bullet & Reduced Lds.
Hodg.	4895	Tubular	0	0.920	Standard Rifle	Versatile/Gd. Cast Bullet & Reduced Lds.
Herc.	RL12	Tubular	7	1.000	Standard Rifle	Mod. Capacity Rifle

SMOKELESS POWDER—COMPOSITION AND BURN RATE
From Fastest Burning to Slowest

Manuf.	Powder	Granule Shape	Nitroglyc. %	Bulk Density	Suggested Primers	Primary Uses
Vihta.	N135	Tubular	0	0.860	Standard Rifle	7.62 Ball/Mod. Capacity Rifle
IMR	4064	Tubular	0	0.905	Standard Rifle	Mod. Capacity Rifle
Scott**	4065	Tubular	0	0.905	Standard Rifle	Mod. Capacity Rifle
Accur.	2520	Sphere	10	0.970	Std./BR/Mag. Rifle	Mod. Capacity Rifle
IMR	4320	Tubular	0	0.935	Standard Rifle	Mod. to Large Rifle
Norma	202	Tubular	0	—	Standard Rifle	Mod. to Large Rifle
Vihta.	N140	Tubular	0	0.860	Standard Rifle	Mod. to Large Rifle
Vihta.	N540	Tubular	P	0.860	Standard Rifle	Mod. to Large Rifle
Accur.	2700	Sphere	10	0.960	Std./BR/Mag. Rifle	Mod. to Large Rifle
Herc.	RL15	Tubular	7.5	0.920	Standard Rifle	Mod. Capacity Rifle
Hodg.	380	Sphere	P	0.967	Mag. Rifle	Mod. to Large Rifle
Scott**	4351	Tubular	0	0.910	Std./BR/Mag. Rifle	Large Rifle
Win.	760	Sphere	10	1.000	Std./BR/Mag. Rifle	Large Rifle
Hodg.	414	Sphere	P	0.995	Mag. Rifle	Large Rifle
Vihta.	N150	Tubular	0	0.850	Std./BR/Mag. Rifle	Large Rifle
Vihta.	N550	Tubular	P	0.850	Std./BR/Mag. Rifle	Large Rifle
Accur.	4350	Tubular	0	0.910	Std./BR/Mag. Rifle	Large & Mag. Rifle
IMR	4350	Tubular	0	0.910	Std./BR/Mag. Rifle	Large & Mag. Rifle
Hodg.	4350	Tubular	0	0.910	Std./BR/Mag. Rifle	Large & Mag. Rifle
Hodg.	4350SC	Tubular	0	0.945†	Std./BR/Mag. Rifle	Large & Mag. Rifle
Vihta.	24N64	Tubular	0	—	Mag. Rifle	Large & Mag. Rifle
Norma	204	Tubular	0	0.990	Std./BR/Mag. Rifle	Large & Mag. Rifle
Herc.	RL19	Tubular	11.5	0.890	Std./BR/Mag. Rifle	Large & Mag. Rifle
Vihta.	N160	Tubular	0	0.900	Mag. Rifle	Large & Mag. Rifle
Vihta.	N560	Tubular	P	0.900	Mag. Rifle	Large & Mag. Rifle
IMR	4831	Tubular	0	0.930†	Std./BR/Mag. Lg. Rifle	Large & Mag. Rifle
Hodg.	450	Tubular	P	0.990	Mag. Lg. Rifle	Large & Mag. Rifle
Hodg.	4831	Tubular	0	0.930	Std./BR/Mag. Lg. Rifle	Large & Mag. Rifle
Hodg.	4831SC	Tubular	0	0.960	Std./BR/Mag. Lg. Rifle	Large & Mag. Rifle
Scott**	4831	Tubular	0	0.930	Std./BR/Mag. Lg. Rifle	Large & Mag. Rifle
IMR	7828	Tubular	0	0.910†	Mag. Lg. Rifle/Fed. 215	Large & Mag. Rifle
Accur.	3100	Tubular	0	0.945***	Std./BR/Mag. Lg. Rifle	Large & Mag. Rifle
Win.	785*	Sphere	—	1.015	Mag. Lg. Rifle	Large & Mag. Rifle
Norma	MRP	Tubular	0	1.000†	Std./BR/Mag. Lg. Rifle	Large & Mag. Rifle
Norma	205*	Tubular	0	1.000	Std./BR/Mag. Lg. Rifle	Large & Mag. Rifle
Vihta.	N165	Tubular	0	0.900	Mag. Lg. Rifle	Large & Mag. Rifle
Herc.	RL22	Tubular	11.5	0.890	Std./BR/Mag. Lg. Rifle	Large & Mag. Rifle
Win.	WMR	Sphere	13.5	1.000	Mag. Lg. Rifle	Large & Mag. Rifle
Hodg.	1000	Tubular	0	—	Fed-215/Mag. Lg. Rifle	Mag. Rifle
Vihta.	170	Tubular	0	0.900†	Fed-215	Mag. Rifle/50 BMG
T-Bird	5020	Sphere	—	0.965	Fed-215	Mag. Rifle/50 BMG
Hodg.	570*	Tubular	0	0.945	Mag. Lg. Rifle/Fed-215	Mag. Rifle/50 BMG
Hodg.	870	Sphere	P	0.965	Fed-215	Mag. Rifle/50 BMG
Accur.	8700	Sphere	10	0.960	Fed-215	Mag. Rifle/50 BMG
T-Bird	870	Sphere	10	0.965	Fed-215	Mag. Rifle/50 BMG
Hodg.	5010*	Tubular	0	0.910	Fed-215	Mag. Rifle/50 BMG
T-Bird	5070	Sphere	—	0.965	Fed-215	Mag. Rifle/50 BMG

UN = % unavailable; P = % proprietary; * = Obsolete; ** = Recently Discontinued; *** = Conflicting density data from various sources; † = Estimated
VihtaVuori Oy data was included for completeness but VihtaVuori Oy rankings were based solely on information from their catalogue. Evidently VihtaVuori Oy uses shotgun pressures to compare *all* powders that are intended primarily for use in shotshell loading. Because of the lower pressures involved—compared to the pistol pressures all other powders in this table are compared at—VihtaVuori Oy's rankings for shotgun/pistol type powders differ considerably from those shown here.

MEASURED POWDER DENSITY
1″ High Circular Column

—Powder— Name	Type	Listed Bulk Density	Container Dia. (ins.)	Standard Funnel	6″ Drop Tube	Max.	—Reduction in Volume— 830 psi During	After	3320 psi During	After
Accurate/Scott—										
N-100	F	—	.357	0.445	0.497	0.550	54.3	53	—	—
			.410	0.477	0.509	0.543				
			.452	0.493	0.521	0.533				
#2 Imp.	B	—	.357	0.650	0.658	0.695	13.1	8	33.7	28
			.410	0.663	0.676	0.707				
			.452	0.677	0.691	0.715				
S1000	F	—	.357	0.450	0.486	0.497	34.3	23	52.3	45
			.410	0.469	0.489	0.497				
			.452	0.465	0.483	0.488				
Scot D	F	—	.357	0.460	0.470	0.501	29.4	15	48.1	40
			.410	0.483	0.509	0.531				
			.452	0.472	0.517	0.528				
453	B	0.555	.357	0.624	0.656	0.658	14.8	8	37.8	33
			.410	0.631	0.656	0.690				
			.452	0.634	0.660	0.686				
#5	B	0.950	.357	0.893	0.897	0.920	19.6	10	34.3	28
			.410	0.861	0.943	0.955				
			.452	0.875	0.943	0.974				
#7	B	0.985	.357	0.457	1.006	1.047	7.7	2	17.3	8
			.410	0.969	1.037	1.063				
			.452	0.965	1.019	1.064				
#9	B	0.975	.357	0.931	0.950	0.987	8.5	2	18.6	10
			.410	0.937	0.963	0.986				
			.452	0.946	0.967	0.988				
1680	B	0.950	.357	0.976	1.009	1.047	7.5	2	17.7	10
			.410	0.972	1.026	1.060				
			.452	0.979	1.038	1.061				
Hercules—										
Bullseye	F	0.620	.357	0.607	0.609	0.658	44.9	43	—	—
			.410	0.605	0.656	0.707				
			.452	0.608	0.667	0.689				
Red Dot	F	0.480	.357	0.400	0.447	0.467	54.9	50	—	—
			.410	0.409	0.455	0.477				
			.452	0.417	0.474	0.485				
Green Dot	F	0.515	.357	0.434	0.486	0.520	50.6	46	—	—
			.410	0.469	0.517	0.528				
			.452	0.488	0.514	0.533				
Unique	F	0.610	.357	0.497	0.542	0.568	43.4	43	—	—
			.410	0.514	0.554	0.565				
			.452	0.542	0.578	0.587				
Herco	F	0.570	.357	0.482	0.538	0.550	41.9	35	—	—
			.410	0.503	0.545	0.562				
			.452	0.505	0.564	0.571				
Bluedot	F	0.780	.357	0.665	0.755	0.759	25.4	15	44.0	40
			.410	0.707	0.744	0.766				
			.452	0.708	0.764	0.783				
2400	F	0.870	.357	0.837	0.871	0.901	17.1	13	34.1	30
			.410	0.844	0.898	0.909				
			.452	0.842	0.901	0.910				
Hodgdon—										
Clays	F	0.475	.357	0.407	0.464	0.475	39.0	35	—	—
			.410	0.449	0.486	0.494				
			.452	0.451	0.498	0.503				
HP-38	B	0.635	.357	0.639	0.725	0.748	27.4	20	45.3	40
			.410	0.687	0.724	0.735				
			.452	0.693	0.731	0.757				
Inter	F	0.525	.357	0.479	0.538	0.557	36.4	30	—	—
			.410	0.506	0.548	0.554				
			.452	0.509	0.554	0.559				

MEASURED POWDER DENSITY

1″ High Circular Column

—Powder— Name	Type	Listed Bulk Density	Container Dia. (ins.)	Standard Funnel	6″ Drop Tube	Max.	—Reduction in Volume— 830 psi During	830 psi After	3320 psi During	3320 psi After
Hodgdon—										
Univ	F	0.650	.357	0.591	0.624	0.658	23.6	15	41.9	36
			.410	0.608	0.670	0.682				
			.452	0.618	0.672	0.684				
HS6	F	0.945	.357	0.893	0.957	1.002	12.3	5	27.0	18
			.410	0.901	0.952	0.997				
			.452	0.903	0.974	1.004				
HS7	B	0.990	.357	0.897	0.972	1.021	12.3	5	24.4	20
			.410	0.937	0.947	1.031				
			.452	0.915	1.000	1.040				
H4227	B	0.870	.357	0.811	0.879	0.897	11.8	6	24.0	15
			.410	0.827	0.889	0.898				
			.452	0.837	.0899	0.908				
H110	B	0.975	.357	0.987	1.034	1.084	6.8	1	17.7	5
			.410	0.994	1.054	1.088				
			.452	0.995	1.057	1.090				
IMR—										
PB	F	0.555	.357	0.512	0.583	0.607	20.1	13	41.5	33
			.410	0.537	0.594	0.611				
			.452	0.535	0.594	0.614				
700X	F	0.500	.357	0.471	0.523	0.583	56.0	48	—	—
			.410	0.483	0.528	0.585				
			.452	0.488	0.554	0.583				
800X	F	—	.357	0.572	0.647	0.692	49.8	45	—	—
			.410	0.594	0.653	0.705				
			.452	0.587	0.660	0.712				
SR4756	F	0.610	.357	0.587	0.665	0.684	18.6	8	38.1	25
			.410	0.611	0.670	0.682				
			.452	0.606	0.670	0.679				
IMR4227	T[1]	0.870	.357	0.852	0.879	0.931	10.6	4	21.5	10
			.410	0.869	0.946	0.955				
			.452	0.875	0.934	0.946				
Winchester—										
WST	B	0.535	.357	0.516	0.564	0.602	26.4	18	47.1	40
			.410	0.545	0.574	0.619				
			.452	0.542	0.580	0.620				
WSL	B	0.765	.357	0.680	0.781	0.826	36.0	34	—	—
			.410	0.722	0.770	0.815				
			.452	0.712	0.776	0.815				
231	B	0.700	.357	0.645	0.714	0.748	28.4	20	45.5	40
			.410	0.690	0.724	0.756				
			.452	0.691	0.733	0.750				
WSF	B	0.770	.357	0.707	0.781	0.821	32.3	30	46.6	40
			.410	0.736	0.770	0.824				
			.452	0.731	0.792	0.833				
WAP	B	—	.357	0.800	0.841	0.875	12.8	2	28.0	15
			.410	0.815	0.855	0.889				
			.452	0.811	0.856	0.882				
540	B	0.950	.357	0.893	0.961	0.998	14.5	4	29.2	20
			.410	0.920	0.972	1.009				
			.452	0.920	0.995	1.017				
571	B	0.955	.357	0.905	0.968	1.021	14.1	4	28.4	19
			.410	0.929	0.991	1.020				
			.452	0.941	1.007	1.031				
296	B	0.975	.357	0.964	1.024	1.054	8.2	1	18.3	5
			.410	0.983	1.045	1.068				
			.452	0.982	1.054	1.073				

MEASURED POWDER DENSITY
Specified Case, Level Full

—Powder— Name	Type	Listed Bulk Density	Container Dia. (ins.)	Standard Funnel	6″ Drop Tube	Max.	—Reduction in Volume— 830 psi During	After	3320 psi During	After
Accurate/Scott—										
1680	B	0.950	222 Rem.	0.998	1.030	1.058	6.4	1.5	17.0	7.5
			308 Win.	0.984	1.026	1.054	6.4	1.5	17.0	7.5
			7mm Rem.Mag.	0.986	1.041	1.053	6.4	1.5	17.0	7.5
2230	B	—	222 Rem.	0.998	1.041	1.062	8.1	2.0	20.7	8.5
			308 Win.	1.011	1.047	1.065	8.1	2.0	20.7	8.5
			7mm Rem.Mag.	1.022	1.058	1.071	8.1	2.0	20.7	8.5
2460	B	0.975	222 Rem.	0.928	0.965	0.991	8.3	3.0	21.2	12.0
			308 Win.	0.928	0.965	0.977	8.3	3.0	21.2	12.0
			7mm Rem.Mag.	0.943	0.978	0.993	8.3	3.0	21.2	12.0
2495BR	T[1]	—	222 Rem.	0.839	0.871	0.885	9.4	2.0	20.9	10.5
			308 Win.	0.876	0.910	0.913	9.4	2.0	20.9	10.5
			7mm Rem.Mag.	0.887	0.918	0.929	9.4	2.0	20.9	10.5
2520	B	0.970	222 Rem.	0.945	0.988	1.012	7.7	1.5	20.0	12.0
			308 Win.	0.963	1.009	1.023	7.7	1.5	20.0	12.0
			7mm Rem.Mag.	0.968	1.025	1.029	7.7	1.5	20.0	12.0
2700	B	0.960	222 Rem.	0.938	0.963	0.988	8.2	1.5	20.2	10.0
			308 Win.	0.954	0.982	1.002	8.2	1.5	20.2	10.0
			7mm Rem.Mag.	0.956	1.004	1.018	8.2	1.5	20.2	10.0
4350	T[2]	0.950	222 Rem.	0.850	0.878	0.896	10.4	4.0	22.9	12.0
			308 Win.	0.888	0.916	0.929	10.4	4.0	22.9	12.0
			7mm Rem.Mag.	0.905	0.925	0.938	10.4	4.0	22.9	12.0
3100	T[2]	0.945	222 Rem.	0.853	0.896	0.903	8.8	2.5	20.2	9.0
			308 Win.	0.893	0.921	0.930	8.8	2.5	20.2	9.0
			7mm Rem.Mag.	0.915	0.935	0.942	8.8	2.5	20.2	9.0
8700	B	0.960	222 Rem.	0.924	0.977	1.019	7.8	2.0	20.4	10.0
			308 Win.	0.942	1.002	1.035	7.8	2.0	20.4	10.0
			7mm Rem.Mag.	0.958	1.006	1.041	7.8	2.0	20.4	10.0
Hercules—										
2400	F	0.870	222 Rem.	0.846	0.878	0.910	16.3	9.0	32.5	26.0
			308 Win.	0.846	0.890	0.933	16.3	9.0	32.5	26.0
			7mm Rem.Mag.	0.854	0.909	0.936	16.3	9.0	32.5	26.0
RX7	T[3]	0.890	222 Rem.	0.843	0.899	0.917	10.5	3.0	22.9	14.0
			308 Win.	0.879	0.923	0.937	10.5	3.0	22.9	14.0
			7mm Rem.Mag.	0.889	0.935	0.950	10.5	3.0	22.9	14.0
RX12	T[3]	1.000	222 Rem.	0.889	0.928	0.956	9.5	2.0	21.2	10.5
			308 Win.	0.916	0.960	0.977	9.5	2.0	21.2	10.5
			7mm Rem.Mag.	0.940	0.979	0.991	9.5	2.0	21.2	10.5
RX15	T[3]	0.920	222 Rem.	0.867	0.913	0.935	10.6	5.0	22.3	12.0
			308 Win.	0.911	0.951	0.956	10.6	5.0	22.3	12.0
			7mm Rem.Mag.	0.920	0.949	0.959	10.6	5.0	22.3	12.0
RX19	T[2]	0.890	222 Rem.	0.864	0.903	0.917	13.3	7.0	26.5	17.5
			308 Win.	0.895	0.940	0.951	13.3	7.0	26.5	17.5
			7mm Rem.Mag.	0.920	0.945	0.957	13.3	7.0	26.5	17.5
RX22	T[2]	0.890	222 Rem.	0.871	0.896	0.928	13.0	7.5	25.9	18.0
			308 Win.	0.907	0.940	0.947	13.0	7.5	25.9	18.0
			7mm Rem.Mag.	0.923	0.946	0.959	13.0	7.5	25.9	18.0
Hodgdon—										
H4227	T[3]	0.870	222 Rem.	0.818	0.871	0.882	11.8	6.0	24.0	15.0
			308 Win.	0.837	0.876	0.890	11.8	6.0	24.0	15.0
			7mm Rem.Mag.	0.843	0.887	0.898	11.8	6.0	24.0	15.0
H110	B	0.975	222 Rem.	0.995	1.027	1.069	6.8	1.0	17.7	5.0
			308 Win.	1.009	1.046	1.084	6.8	1.0	17.7	5.0
			7mm Rem.Mag.	1.006	1.058	1.090	6.8	1.0	17.7	5.0
H4198	T[1]	0.880	222 Rem.	0.776	0.814	0.822	10.8	2.5	24.1	10.0
			308 Win.	0.807	0.844	0.849	10.8	2.5	24.1	10.0
			7mm Rem.Mag.	0.820	0.847	0.854	10.8	2.5	24.1	10.0
H4198SC	T[2]	—	222 Rem.	0.850	0.896	0.906	9.5	2.5	20.3	10.0
			308 Win.	0.890	0.923	0.930	9.5	2.5	20.3	10.0
			7mm Rem.Mag.	0.892	0.933	0.946	9.5	2.5	20.3	10.0

MEASURED POWDER DENSITY

Specified Case, Level Full

—Powder— Name	Type	Listed Bulk Density	Container Dia. (ins.)	Standard Funnel	6″ Drop Tube	Max.	—Reduction in Volume— 830 psi During	After	3320 psi During	After
Hodgdon—										
H322	T[3]	—	222 Rem.	0.885	0.917	0.931	9.4	3.0	18.6	8.0
			308 Win.	0.897	0.942	0.953	9.4	3.0	18.6	8.0
			7mm Rem.Mag.	0.906	0.959	0.968	9.4	3.0	18.6	8.0
BL-C2	B	1.035	222 Rem.	0.991	1.041	1.065	6.5	1.5	16.3	6.0
			308 Win.	1.016	1.056	1.081	6.5	1.5	16.3	6.0
			7mm Rem.Mag.	1.020	1.064	1.084	6.5	1.5	16.3	6.0
H335	B	1.035	222 Rem.	0.991	1.037	1.058	6.3	1.5	15.7	5.5
			308 Win.	1.005	1.035	1.070	6.3	1.5	15.7	5.5
			7mm Rem.Mag.	1.011	1.055	1.076	6.3	1.5	15.7	5.5
H4895	T[2]	0.920	222 Rem.	0.878	0.913	0.924	9.5	3.5	19.1	10.5
			308 Win.	0.898	0.942	0.947	9.5	3.5	19.1	10.5
			7mm Rem.Mag.	0.913	0.949	0.959	9.5	3.5	19.1	10.5
H380	B	0.967	222 Rem.	0.917	0.952	0.981	6.9	1.5	17.4	5.5
			308 Win.	0.944	0.974	1.007	6.9	1.5	17.4	5.5
			7mm Rem.Mag.	0.951	0.981	1.008	6.9	1.5	17.4	5.5
H414	B	0.995	222 Rem.	0.935	0.988	1.027	6.8	1.5	17.0	7.0
			308 Win.	0.951	1.004	1.040	6.8	1.5	17.0	7.0
			7mm Rem.Mag.	0.957	1.018	1.049	6.8	1.5	17.0	7.0
H4350SC	T[3]	—	222 Rem.	0.899	0.935	0.945	8.9	3.0	20.2	10.0
			308 Win.	0.926	0.963	0.969	8.9	3.0	20.2	10.0
			7mm Rem.Mag.	0.940	0.982	0.988	8.9	3.0	20.2	10.0
H450	B	0.990	222 Rem.	0.928	0.963	0.981	7.9	1.5	19.0	8.5
			308 Win.	0.944	0.981	1.002	7.9	1.5	19.0	8.5
			7mm Rem.Mag.	0.947	1.001	1.014	7.9	1.5	19.0	8.5
H4831	T[2]	0.930	222 Rem.	0.892	0.913	0.928	8.6	2.0	20.0	9.0
			308 Win.	0.930	0.953	0.964	8.6	2.0	20.0	9.0
			7mm Rem.Mag.	0.945	0.964	0.974	8.6	2.0	20.0	9.0
H4831SC	T[3]	—	222 Rem.	0.906	0.928	0.945	9.0	2.5	19.7	9.5
			308 Win.	0.940	0.958	0.976	9.0	2.5	19.7	9.5
			7mm Rem.Mag.	0.952	0.982	0.992	9.0	2.5	19.7	9.5
H1000	T[3]	—	222 Rem.	0.889	0.942	0.952	8.8	3.0	19.2	10.0
			308 Win.	0.937	0.965	0.981	8.8	3.0	19.2	10.0
			7mm Rem.Mag.	0.947	0.985	0.992	8.8	3.0	19.2	10.0
H570	T[3]	—	222 Rem.	0.857	0.899	0.917	8.2	1.5	19.5	7.5
			308 Win.	0.912	0.939	0.947	8.2	1.5	19.5	7.5
			7mm Rem.Mag.	0.927	0.959	0.972	8.2	1.5	19.5	7.5
H870	B	0.965	222 Rem.	0.942	0.984	0.998	9.8	2.0	18.6	6.5
			308 Win.	0.958	1.005	1.023	9.8	2.0	18.6	6.5
			7mm Rem.Mag.	0.964	1.020	1.030	9.8	2.0	18.6	6.5
IMR—										
IMR4227	T[3]	0.870	222 Rem.	0.860	0.910	0.928	10.6	4.0	21.5	10.0
			308 Win.	0.883	0.940	0.942	10.6	4.0	21.5	10.0
			7mm Rem.Mag.	0.884	0.946	0.961	10.6	4.0	21.5	10.0
IMR4198	T[1]	0.850	222 Rem.	0.793	0.832	0.850	10.6	2.5	23.6	11.5
			308 Win.	0.833	0.874	0.884	10.6	2.5	23.6	11.5
			7mm Rem.Mag.	0.844	0.884	0.891	10.6	2.5	23.6	11.5
IMR3031	T[2]	0.880	222 Rem.	0.814	0.860	0.885	10.2	2.5	23.9	12.5
			308 Win.	0.853	0.893	0.902	10.2	2.5	23.9	12.5
			7mm Rem.Mag.	0.858	0.894	0.904	10.2	2.5	23.9	12.5
IMR4895	T[2]	0.920	222 Rem.	0.882	0.924	0.942	8.8	2.5	19.6	9.0
			308 Win.	0.907	0.949	0.961	8.8	2.5	19.6	9.0
			7mm Rem.Mag.	0.929	0.965	0.972	8.8	2.5	19.6	9.0
IMR4064	T[1]	0.905	222 Rem.	0.829	0.871	0.885	9.9	3.0	22.3	10.5
			308 Win.	0.872	0.905	0.920	9.9	3.0	22.3	10.5
			7mm Rem.Mag.	0.885	0.923	0.930	9.9	3.0	22.3	10.5
IMR4320	T[3]	0.935	222 Rem.	0.903	0.942	0.952	8.3	2.0	18.5	8.0
			308 Win.	0.923	0.974	0.981	8.3	2.0	18.5	8.0
			7mm Rem.Mag.	0.942	0.979	0.992	8.3	2.0	18.5	8.0

MEASURED POWDER DENSITY

Specified Case, Level Full

Powder Name	Powder Type	Listed Bulk Density	Container Dia. (ins.)	Standard Funnel	6″ Drop Tube	Max.	Reduction in Volume 830 psi During	830 psi After	3320 psi During	3320 psi After
IMR—										
IMR4350	T^2	0.910	222 Rem.	0.853	0.885	0.899	9.3	2.5	21.1	13.0
			308 Win.	0.890	0.930	0.942	9.3	2.5	21.1	13.0
			7mm Rem.Mag.	0.910	0.932	0.949	9.3	2.5	21.1	13.0
IMR4831	T^2	0.930	222 Rem.	0.864	0.889	0.910	8.8	2.5	20.0	8.0
			308 Win.	0.898	0.926	0.939	8.8	2.5	20.0	8.0
			7mm Rem.Mag.	0.917	0.946	0.958	8.8	2.5	20.0	8.0
IMR7828	T^2	—	222 Rem.	0.857	0.896	0.913	9.8	4.0	20.8	10.0
			308 Win.	0.900	0.937	0.953	9.8	4.0	20.8	10.0
			7mm Rem.Mag.	0.913	0.953	0.964	9.8	4.0	20.8	10.0
Norma—										
N-205	T^2	—	222 Rem.	0.928	0.975	0.995	9.3	3.0	20.2	8.0
			308 Win.	0.975	1.012	1.018	9.3	3.0	20.2	8.0
			7mm Rem.Mag.	0.981	1.025	1.034	9.3	3.0	20.2	8.0
Vihtavuori—										
N133	T^3	0.88	222 Rem.	0.853	0.896	0.927	9.1	2.0	18.8	8.0
			308 Win.	0.883	0.923	0.944	9.1	2.0	18.8	8.0
			7mm Rem.Mag.	0.887	0.930	0.950	9.1	2.0	18.8	8.0
N140	T^3	0.92	222 Rem.	0.867	0.919	0.935	9.3	2.0	19.2	8.0
			308 Win.	0.902	0.951	0.972	9.3	2.0	19.2	8.0
			7mm Rem.Mag.	0.924	0.961	0.975	9.3	2.0	19.2	8.0
N150	T^3	0.91	222 Rem.	0.860	0.882	0.920	8.6	2.0	18.5	6.0
			308 Win.	0.902	0.940	0.956	8.6	2.0	18.5	6.0
			7mm Rem.Mag.	0.915	0.943	0.954	8.6	2.0	18.5	6.0
N160	T^3	0.94	222 Rem.	0.885	0.935	0.952	8.8	2.0	19.0	7.0
			308 Win.	0.919	0.961	0.972	8.8	2.0	19.0	7.0
			7mm Rem.Mag.	0.939	0.971	0.984	8.8	2.0	19.0	7.0
N170	T^3	—	222 Rem.	0.896	0.935	0.953	8.6	2.0	19.0	7.0
			308 Win.	0.939	0.977	0.991	8.6	2.0	19.0	7.0
			7mm Rem.Mag.	0.961	0.985	0.995	8.6	2.0	19.0	7.0
24N64	T^3	0.84	222 Rem.	0.818	0.867	0.889	9.0	2.0	20.1	7.0
			308 Win.	0.882	0.905	0.918	9.0	2.0	20.1	7.0
			7mm Rem.Mag.	0.895	0.905	0.924	9.0	2.0	20.1	7.0
Winchester—										
296	B	0.975	222 Rem.	0.963	0.991	1.062	8.2	1.0	18.3	5.0
			308 Win.	0.984	1.026	1.068	8.2	1.0	18.3	5.0
			7mm Rem.Mag.	0.985	1.023	1.069	8.2	1.0	18.3	5.0
748	B	0.995	222 Rem.	0.956	0.984	1.051	7.1	1.5	17.2	8.0
			308 Win.	0.975	1.019	1.067	7.1	1.5	17.2	8.0
			7mm Rem.Mag.	0.972	1.044	1.074	7.1	1.5	17.2	8.0
760	B	1.000	222 Rem.	0.931	0.984	1.035	7.3	1.5	17.8	7.5
			308 Win.	0.944	0.995	1.044	7.3	1.5	17.8	7.5
			7mm Rem.Mag.	0.963	1.000	1.044	7.3	1.5	17.8	7.5
WMR	B	—	222 Rem.	0.889	0.942	0.988	7.6	2.0	18.7	9.5
			308 Win.	0.921	0.965	0.998	7.6	2.0	18.7	9.5
			7mm Rem.Mag.	0.926	0.970	1.011	7.6	2.0	18.7	9.5

Listed Bulk Density: As advertised or otherwise estimated, in grams per cubic centimeter (water is 1.00); Reduction in Volume: Percent Reduction in total column volume after listed pressure was applied long enough so that further change was minimal. Pressure was applied to the open top of a cylindrical column of presettled powder; During: Volume loss while pressure applied; After: Stable loss of volume after pressure removed; Experimental Density (measured in listed case or in circular column about 1″ high and of specified diameter): Standard Funnel = Powder dumped through standard handloader's funnel, excess struck off even with top of case; 6″ Drop Tube = Powder dumped through 6″ drop tube, excess struck off even with top of case; Maximum = Powder settled via vibrations as much as possible, excess struck off even with top of case

B = Ball Type (may include any combination of spheres and flattened spheres and may also be porous); PB = Porous Base (porous disks); F = Flake or very short disks (disks: may have one central perforation, may be porous and may be non-flat); T^1 = Short tubular granules (Diameter similar to length); T^2 = Medium tubular granules (Diameter about one-half length); T^3 = Long tubular granules (Diameter less than one-half length)

MAXIMUM SAAMI CARTRIDGE SPECIFICATIONS

Cartridge	Case Type	Dia. (ins.) Bullet					Shoulder Angle	Length (ins.) Head to Shoulder				Twist		Primer
		Bullet	Neck	Shoulder	Base	Rim		Head to Shoulder	Case	Min. OAL	Max. OAL	STD	OPT	
Rifle Cartridges														
17 Rem	C	.172	.199	.3558	.3759	.378	23°	1.3511	1.796	2.09	2.15	9	—	S
22 Hornet	A	.224	.2425	.2773	.2952	.350	5°38´	.8527	1.403	1.66	1.723	16	—	S
218 Bee	A	.224	.242	.3324	.3491	.408	15°	.9233	1.345	1.645	1.68	16	—	S
222 Rem	C	.224	.253	.3573	.3759	.378	23°	1.2645	1.7	2.04	2.13	14	—	S
223 Rem	C	.224	.253	.3542	.3759	.378	23°	1.4381	1.76	2.165	2.26	12	9	S
222 Rem Mag	C	.224	.253	.3571	.3754	.378	23°	1.4636	1.85	2.22	2.28	14	—	S
225 Win	A	.224	.260	.406	.422	.473	25°	1.53	1.93	2.42	2.5	14	—	L
22-250	C	.224	.254	.4142	.4668	.473	28°	1.5148	1.912	2.29	2.35	14	—	L
220 Swift	G	.224	.260	.402	.4449	.473	21°	1.7227	2.205	2.65	2.68	14	—	L
243 Win	C	.243	.276	.454	.4703	.473	20°	1.5598	2.045	2.54	2.71	10	—	L
6mm Rem/244 Rem	C	.243	.276	.4294	.4711	.473	26°	1.7249	2.233	2.73	2.825	9	12	L
25-20 Win	A	.257	.2738	.3332	.3492	.408	16°34´	.8573	1.33	1.53	1.592	13	14	S
256 Win Mag	A	.257	.285	.368	.379	.440	25°	.9838	1.281	1.54	1.59	14	—	S
25-35 Win	A	.257	.2816	.3642	.4224	.506	11°34´	1.3799	2.043	2.505	2.55	8	—	L
250 Sav	C	.257	.2856	.4142	.4668	.473	26°30´	1.5118	1.912	2.32	2.515	14	—	L
257 Rob/257 Rob +P	C	.257	.290	.4294	.4711	.473	20°45´	1.7277	2.233	2.62	2.78	10	12	L
25-06 Rem	C	.257	.290	.441	.4698	.473	17°30´	1.948	2.494	3.01	3.25	10	12	L
6.5x55 Swed Mauser	C	.2638	.2972	.4350	.4770	.479	25°	1.7043	2.165	3.025	3.15	7.9	—	L
6.5mm Rem Mag	E	.2645	.2980	.4952	.5126	.532	25°	1.7001	2.170	2.74	2.80	9	—	L
264 Win Mag	E	.264	.298	.491	.5127	.532	25°	2.0401	2.52	3.16	3.34	9	—	L
270 Win	C	.277	.308	.441	.4698	.473	17°30´	1.948	2.54	3.065	3.34	10	—	L
7-30 Waters	A	.284	.3062	.3991	.4215	.506	17°12´	1.5864	2.04	2.48	2.55	9.5	—	L
7mm-08	C	.284	.315	.454	.4703	.473	20°	1.5598	2.035	2.53	2.8	9	—	L
7mm Mauser	C	.284	.3207	.4294	.4711	.473	20°45´	1.7277	2.235	2.94	3.065	8	10	L
284 Win	I	.284	.320	.4748	.500	.473	35°	1.7749	2.17	2.765	2.8	10	—	L
280 Rem	C	.284	.315	.4412	.4700	.473	17°30´	1.9992	2.54	3.15	3.33	10.5	—	L
7mm Wby Mag	E	.284	.314	.492	.5117	.5315	N/A	2.012	2.549	3.1	3.38	12	10	L
7mm Rem Mag	E	.284	.3150	.4909	.5127	.532	25°	2.04	2.5	3.15	3.29	9.5	—	L
30 Carb	D	.308	.336	.336	.3548	.360	—	.9824	1.29	1.625	1.68	16	—	S
30-30 Win	A	.308	.3301	.4013	.4215	.506	15°39´	1.4405	2.0395	2.45	2.55	12	—	L
30 Rem	C	.307	.3318	.401	.4207	.422	23°	1.498	2.05	2.465	2.525	12	—	L
300 Sav	C	.308	.339	.4466	.4706	.473	30°	1.5586	1.871	2.495	2.6	12	—	L
307 Win	G	.308	.3435	.454	.4703	.506	20°	1.5598	2.015	2.53	2.56	12	—	L
308 Win	C	.308	.3435	.454	.4703	.473	20°	1.5598	2.015	2.49	2.81	12	—	L
30-40 Krag	A	.308	.338	.419	.4577	.545	21°6´	1.7251	2.314	2.965	3.089	10	—	L
30-06 Sprg	C	.308	.3397	.441	.4698	.473	17°30´	1.948	2.494	2.94	3.34	10	—	L
300 H&H Mag	E	.308	.338	.4498	.512	.532	8°30´	2.1046	2.85	3.42	3.6	10	—	L
308 Norma Mag	E	.308	.340	.489	.511	.530	25.76°	2.085	2.56	3.30	3.34	10	12	L
300 Win Mag	E	.308	.3397	.4891	.5126	.532	25°	2.1959	2.62	3.28	3.34	10	—	L
300 Wby Mag	E	.308	.337	.492	.5117	.5315	N/A	2.298	2.825	3.39	3.56	12	—	L
7.62x39	C	.311	.337	.396	.443	.447	17°30´	1.1984	1.528	2.17	2.2	9.4	—	S
303 Sav	A	.311	.3322	.4135	.439	.505	16°	1.3509	2.015	2.5	2.52	12	—	L
32-20 Win	A	.312	.3266	.3424	.3535	.408	5°42´	.8812	1.315	1.54	1.592	20	—	S
303 Brit	A	.312	.338	.401	.4601	.540	16°58´	1.7901	2.222	2.915	3.075	10	—	L
32-40 Win	A	.321	.3388	.3455	.424	.506	—	1.708	2.13	2.46	2.5	16	—	L
32 Rem	C	.321	.3437	.401	.4207	.422	23°	1.498	2.05	2.485	2.525	14	—	L
32 Win Spl	A	.321	.343	.4014	.4219	.506	14°31´	1.4461	2.04	2.48	2.565	16	—	L
8mm	C	.323	.3493	.431	.4698	.473	20°48´	1.8273	2.24	2.815	3.25	9	10	L
8mm Rem Mag	E	.323	.3541	.4868	.5126	.532	25°	2.389	2.85	3.45	3.6	9	—	L
338 Win Mag	E	.338	.369	.491	.5127	.532	25°	2.04	2.5	3.28	3.34	10	—	L
340 Wby Mag	E	.338	.367	.492	.5117	.5315	N/A	2.298	2.825	3.39	3.56	12	—	L
348 Win	A	.348	.3757	.4851	.553	.610	19°4´	1.6499	2.255	2.77	2.795	12	—	L
351 Win SL	H	.351	.377	.3775	.3805	.410	—	1.2	1.38	1.875	1.9	16	—	S
35 Rem	C	.358	.3838	.4259	.4574	.460	23°25´	1.5393	1.92	2.46	2.525	16	—	L
356 Win	G	.358	.388	.454	.4703	.506	20°	1.5598	2.015	2.53	2.56	12	—	L
358 Win	C	.358	.388	.454	.4703	.473	20°	1.5598	2.015	2.73	2.78	12	—	L
350 Rem Mag	E	.358	.388	.4952	.5126	.532	25°	1.7001	2.17	2.73	2.8	16	—	L
35 Whelen	C	.358	.388	.441	.4698	.473	17°30´	1.948	2.494	2.97	3.34	12	14	L
375 Win	B	.375	.400	.400	.4198	.506	—	1.8	2.02	2.53	2.56	12	—	L

MAXIMUM SAAMI CARTRIDGE SPECIFICATIONS

Cartridge	Case Type	Dia. (ins.) Bullet	Neck	Shoulder	Base	Rim	Shoulder Angle	Length (ins.) Head to Shoulder	Case	Min. OAL	Max. OAL	Twist STD	OPT	Primer
375 H&H Mag	E	.375	.402	.4478	.5121	.532	15°	2.4122	2.85	3.54	3.6	12	—	L
38-55 Win	B	.379	.3922	.3938	.421	.506	—	2.013	2.085	2.47	2.51	18	—	L
38-40 Win	A	.401	.4167	.4543	.4695	.525	6°48′	.9224	1.305	1.56	1.592	36	—	L
416 Rem Mag	E	.416	.447	.4868	.5126	.532	25°	2.389	2.85	3.35	3.36	14	—	L
416 Rigby	C	.416	.4461	.5402	.589	.590	45°	2.3557	2.9	3.63	3.75	16.5	—	L
44-40 Win	A	.427	.443	.4568	.4711	.525	4°	.9275	1.305	1.54	1.592	20	36	L
44 Rem Mag	B	.429	.456	.4561	.4569	.514	—	1.2	1.285	1.535	1.61	20	—	L
444 Mar	B	.429	.453	.4549	.4698	.514	—	2.0	2.225	2.5	2.57	38	—	L
45-70 Govt	B	.458	.480	.4813	.5055	.608	—	2.0	2.105	2.49	2.55	18	22	L
458 Win Mag	F	.458	.4811	.4825	.5126	.523	—	2.4	2.5	3.28	3.34	14	16	L
470 NE	A	.475	.5039	.5322	.5728	.6551	7°24′	2.3849	3.25	3.85	3.98	20	—	L
50 BMG[1]	C	.510	.560	.714	.804	.804	15°44′	3.006	3.91	5.40	5.45	16.5	—	CCI-35
Pistol and Revolver Cartridges														
22 Rem Jet Mag	C	.223	.251	.3657	.3759	.440	6°40′30″	.5984	1.288	1.61	1.659	10	—	S
221 Rem Fireball	C	.224	.253	.3607	.3759	.378	23°	1.0707	1.4	1.78	1.83	14	—	S
6mm BR-Rem	C	.243	.2705	.4598	.4703	.473	30°	1.0749	1.56	2.08	2.2	9	—	S
25 Auto	D	.251	.278	—	.278	.302	—	—	.615	.86	.91	16	—	S
256 Win Mag	A	.257	.285	.368	.379	.440	25°	.9838	1.281	1.54	1.59	14	—	S
7mm BR-Rem	C	.284	.3085	.4598	.4703	.473	30°	1.0749	1.52	Bullet Dependent		9.5	—	S
30 Luger	C	.308	.332	.3785	.3897	.394	18°	.6257	.85	1.13	1.175	9.8	—	S
32 Auto	H	.309	.3365	—	.3373	.358	—	—	.68	.94	.984	16	—	S
32 S&W	B	.312	.339	—	.339	.378	—	—	.605	.88	.93	16	18	S
32 CNP	B	.312	.337	—	.337	.375	—	—	.92	1.21	1.28	16	—	—
32 S&WL	B	.312	.337	—	.337	.375	—	—	.92	1.23	1.28	16	18	S
32 H&R Mag	B	.312	.337	—	.337	.375	—	—	1.075	1.3	1.35	16	—	S
32 SC	B	.313	.318	—	.318	.375	—	—	.65	.965	1.015	16	—	S
32 LC	B	.313	.318	—	.318	.381	—	—	.916	1.165	1.216	16	—	S
9mm Luger (+P)	D	.355	.380	—	.391	.394	—	—	.754	1	1.169	9.8	—	S
38 Auto, 38 Super Auto +P	H	.355	.384	—	.384	.406	—	—	.9	1.23	1.28	16	—	S
9mm Win Mag	D	.355	.379	—	.391	.394	—	—	1.16	1.545	1.575	10	—	S
380 Auto	D	.356	.373	—	.3739	.374	—	—	.68	.94	.984	12	16	S
38 SC	B	.375[2]	.379	—	.379	.440	—	—	.765	1.085	1.2	16	18	S
38 LC	B	.357	.378	—	.3789	.440	—	—	1.035	1.305	1.36	16	—	S
38 Spc (+P/Match)	B	.357	.379	—	.379	.440	—	—	1.155	1.4	1.55	16	18	S
357 Mag	B	.357	.379	—	.379	.440	—	—	1.29	1.54	1.59	16	18	S
357 Rem Max	B	.357	.379	—	.379	.440	—	—	1.605	1.94	1.99	14	—	S
38 CNP/38 S&W	B	.361	.3855	—	.3863	.440	—	—	.775	1.16	1.24	16	18	S
40 S&W	D	.400	.423	—	.424	.424	—	—	.85	1.085	1.135	16	—	S
10mm Auto	D	.400	.423	—	.425	.425	—	—	.992	1.24	1.26	16	—	L
41 Rem Mag	B	.410	.434	—	.4349	.492	—	—	1.29	1.54	1.59	18 3/4	—	L
41 AE	D	.411	.434	—	.435	.392	—	—	.866	1.1	1.152	18 3/4	—	L
44 S&W Spc	B	.429	.4565	—	.4569	.514	—	—	1.16	1.56	1.615	20	—	L
44 Rem Mag	B	.429	.456	—	.4569	.514	—	—	1.285	1.535	1.61	20	—	L
45 Auto (+P/Match)	D	.452 (J) .453 (L)	.473	—	.476	.480	—	—	.898	1.19	1.275	16	—	L
45 Auto Rim	B	.452	.472	—	.4755	.516	—	—	.898	1.225	1.275	15	16	L
45 Colt	B	.454 (L)	.480	—	.480	.512	—	—	1.285	1.55	1.6	16	—	L
45 Colt[1]	B	.452 (J)	.480	—	.480	.512	—	—	1.285	1.55	1.6	16	—	L
45 Win Mag	D	.452	.473	—	.476	.480	—	—	1.198	1.545	1.575	16	—	L
454 Casull[1]	B	.452	.480	—	.480	.512	—	—	1.385	1.7	1.725	16	—	L
50 AE	J	.510	.529	.5301	.543	.515	—	1.2	1.285	1.555	1.595	20	—	L

[1]Not SAAMI specifications
[2]Evidently a misprint in the SAAMI specifications

A = Rim, bottleneck; B = Rim, straight; C = Rimless, bottleneck; D = Rimless, straight; E = Belted, bottleneck; F = Belted, straight; G = Semi-rimmed, bottleneck; H = Semi-rimmed, straight; I = Rebated, bottleneck; J = Rebated, straight; S = Small; L = Large

All bullet diameters nominal

CASE CAPACITY FOR CARTRIDGES FIRED IN SPORTING CHAMBERS

Case Capacity							
Max. CC Grs.Water	Make	Bullet Wgt.Grs.	Type	Cart. OAL	Usable CC Grs.Water	Primer+Case Wgt.Grs.	Cartridge
Rifle Cartridges							
28.4	H	25	SP	2.15	26.5	92.1	17 Rem.
14.9	Si	45	S	1.72+	12.2	54.9	22 Hornet
17.9	Si	45	S	1.68	15.5	78.6	218 Bee
28.6	Si	52	HP	2.13	26.0	95.1	222 Rem.
31.1	Si	52	HP	2.26	28.8	100.5	223 Rem.
31.8	Si	52	HP	2.28	29.2	98.7	222 Rem. Mag.
42.0	Si	52	HP	2.50	40.6	148.8	225 Win.
44.9	Si	52	HP	2.35	42.5	169.4	22-250
51.1	Si	52	HP	2.68	49.0	163.5	220 Swift
56.7	Si	100	S	2.71	52.8	162.2	243 Win.
58.4	Si	100	S	2.82+	53.7	173.9	6mm Rem/244 Rem
23.0	Sp	60	S	1.59	18.1	83.6	256 Win Mag
39.0	R	117	FP	2.55	33.0	133.3	25-35 Win
48.2	Si	100	S	2.51+	43.2	156.3	250 Sav
58.1	Si	100	S	2.78	53.2	180.6	257 Rob/257 Rob+P
69.1	R	120	S	3.25	64.0	197.3	25-06 Rem
58.8	Si	100	S	2.90	56.8	188.2	6.5x55 Swed. Mauser
72.0	R	120	S	2.80	66.0	218.5	6.5mm Rem Mag
85.8	W	120	S	3.34	81.7	242.1	264 Win Mag
69.2	Si	130	SBT	3.34	65.4	195.2	270 Win
57.3	Sp	145	SBT	2.80	51.2	165.5	7mm-08
61.5	Sp	145	SBT	3.06+	56.8	182.9	7mm Mauser
69.6	Sp	145	SBT	2.80	61.3	200.3	284 Win
73.2	Sp	145	SBT	3.33	67.7	191.0	280 Rem
85.9	Sp	145	SBT	3.28	80.8	223.6	7mm Wby Mag
86.7	Sp	145	SBT	3.29	81.3	239.7	7mm Rem Mag
20.9	H	110	FMJ	1.68	15.5	75.5	30 Carb
46.7	Sp	170	FSP	2.55	37.8	137.8	30-30 Win
47.0	Sp	170	FSP	2.52+	37.4	131.2	30 Rem
55.7	H	150	SPBT	2.60	49.1	155.3	300 Sav
57.6	Sp	170	FSP	2.56	49.2	188.6	307 Win
58.0	H	150	SPBT	2.81	52.9	167.4	308 Win
57.1	H	150	SPBT	2.81	52.0	181.9	308 Win (Mil)
59.6	H	150	SPBT	3.09-	53.8	195.2	30-40 Krag
70.6	H	150	SPBT	3.34	67.6	190.4	30-06 Sprg
88.0	H	150	SPBT	3.60	82.2	255.4	300 H&H Mag
90.9	H	165	SPBT	3.30	80.0	249.6	308 Norma Mag
93.4	H	150	SPBT	3.34	86.8	242.8	300 Win Mag
105.7	H	150	SPBT	3.56	98.8	229.3	300 Wby Mag
35.9	H	130	SP	2.20	31.4	108[1]	7.62x39
50	Sp	170	FSP	2.52	40.4	142.6	303 Sav
21.4	W	86	LRN	1.59+	17.1	74.1	32-20 Win
58.8	H	150	SP	2.99	50.6	164.4	303 Brit
47.2	Sp	170	FP	2.50	38.1	131.0	32 Rem
48.3	Sp	170	FSP	2.56+	39.2	137.3	32 Win Spl
64.4	H	170	RN	2.81	56.9	179.7	8mm
99.3	H	150	SP	3.6	93.9	259.7	8mm Rem Mag
88.3	H	225	SP	3.34	78.3	237.9	338 Win Mag
101.9	H	225	SP	3.69	91.0	251.8	340 Wby Mag[2]
106.4	H	225	SP	3.69	95.4	224.8	340 Wby Mag
78.2	W	200	RN	2.78	66.7	257.6	348 Win
25.0	W	180	RN	1.90	20.2	89.4	351 Win SL
52.0	R	200	RN	2.52	44.0	156.6	35 Rem
58.1	W	250	FP	2.56	44.9	187.1	356 Win
59.2	Sp	250	S	2.78	47.4	175.6	358 Win

CASE CAPACITY FOR CARTRIDGES FIRED IN SPORTING CHAMBERS

Case Capacity							
Max. CC Grs.Water	Make	Bullet Wgt.Grs.	Type	Cart. OAL	Usable CC Grs.Water	Primer+Case Wgt.Grs.	Cartridge
72.7	—	—	—	—	—	223.6	350 Rem Mag
73.3	Sp	250	S	3.34	63.6	189.1	35 Whelen
51.1	H	220	FSP	2.56	40.5	150.8	375 Win
95.3	Sp	235	SS	3.60	86.5	258.2	375 H&H Mag
51.9	H	220	FSP	2.51	40.2	137.9	38-55 Win
41.0	CAST	180	FP	1.59+	32.9	97.7	38-40 Win
107.4	—	—	—	—	—	261.2	416 Rem Mag
130.5	—	—	—	—	—	337.2	416 Rigby
42.8	CAST	200	FP	1.59+	32	96.4	44-40 Win
40.2		240	JHP	1.61	25.2	113.3	44 Rem Mag
69.3	R	240	JSP	2.57	51.2	199.0	444 Mar
76.5	H	300	JHP	2.55	62.7	201.0	45-70 Govt
95.5	H	500	RN	3.34	74.7	229.9	458 Win Mag
149.3	—	—	—	—	—	321.6	470 NE
260	—	—	—	—	—	829	50 BMG
Pistol and Revolver Cartridges							
18.9	H	45	SP	1.65	16.2	75.3	22 Rem Jet Mag
23.7	Si	45	S	1.83	22.0	85.0	221 Rem Fireball
5.8	FAC	50	FMJ	0.91	4.4	28.4	25 Auto
23.0	Sp?	60	S	1.59	18.1	83.6	256 Win Mag
38.9	Si	120	S	2.18	33.7	136.8	7mm BR-Rem
9.8	H	71	FMJ	0.98+	7.0	39.3	32 Auto
9.3	W	86	LRN	0.93	6.2	B-29.1	32 S&W
12.1	H	71	FMJ	1.23	12.1	48.0	32 CNP/32 S&WL
13.8	W	86	LRN	1.35	14.8	58.0	32 H&R Mag
13.7	FAC	100	JSP	1.17-	11.4	62.6	9mm Luger/+P
18.7	FAC	100	JSP	1.28	15.5	60.1	38 Auto/+P
22.4	FAC	100	JSP	1.57	20.4	81.0	9mm Win Mag
11.1 +P	FAC	100	FMJ	0.98+	7.5	52.4	380 Auto/Super Auto
21.5	CAST	148	WC	1.36	14.8	64.3	38 LC
24.5	CAST	148	WC	1.55	20	67.6	38 Spc Match
24.5	H	158	JHP	1.55	18.2	67.6	38 Spc/+P
26.7	H	158	JHP	1.59	17.8	84.0	357 Mag
34.5	H	158	JHP	1.99	27.7	96.9	357 Rem Max
15.1	CAST	148	WC	1.24	9.5	58.5	38 CNP/38 S&W
20.2	CAST	180	RNFP	1.13+	10.6	68.3	40 S&W
24.7	CAST	180	RNFP	1.26	14.6	74.0	10mm Auto
35.6	Si	210	JHP	1.59	20.8	105.9	41 Rem Mag
21.6	Cast	180	RNFP	1.15+	12.3	76.3	41 AE
35.9	—	240	JHP	1.61+	25.9	95.5	44 S&W Spc
40.2	—	240	JHP	1.61	25.2	113.3	44 Rem Mag
27.1	W	230	FMJ	1.27+	17.6	84.8	45 Auto (+P/Match)
31.0	W	230	FMJ	1.27+	21.5	72.4*	45 Auto Rim
42.0	H	250	JHP	1.60	29.8	117.4	45 Colt
47.4	H	250	JHP	1.60	35.2	87.2*	45 Colt*
38.8	H	250	JHP	1.57+	29.3	109.1	45 Win Mag
46.8	H	250	JHP	1.72+	33.8	132.8	454 Casull*
50.0	IMI	300	JHP	1.59	35.4	168.7	50 AE

* = Semi-Balloon Head case
[1] 340 Wby. Mag. made from Win. 375 H&H case.
[2] Steel Berdan primed case.

H = Hornady; Si = Sierra; Sp = Speer; R = Remington; W = Winchester; FAC = Unknown factory bullet; SP = Spire Point; S = Spitzer; HP = Hollowpoint; FP = Flatpoint; SBT = Spitzer Boattail; FMJ = Full Metal Jacket; FSP = Flat- Softpoint; SPBT = Softpoint Boattail; LRN = Lead Round-nose; RN = Jacketed Round-nose; JHP = Jacketed Hollowpoint; JSP = Jacketed Softpoint; WC = Wadcutter; RNFP = Round-nose Flatpoint

Maximum Case Capacity is the volume of entire case interior in grains of water

Usable Case Capacity is the volume of entire case interior minus volume occupied by seated bullet

Handloader's Digest Periodical Publications

AAFTA News (M)
5911 Cherokee Ave., Tampa, FL 33604. Official newsletter of the American Airgun Field Target Assn.

Action Pursuit Games Magazine (M)
CFW Enterprises, Inc., 4201 W. Vanowen Pl., Burbank, CA 91505 818-845-2656. $4.99 single copy U.S., $5.50 Canada. Editor: Dan Reeves. World's leading magazine of paintball sports.

Air Gunner Magazine
4 The Courtyard, Denmark St., Wokingham, Berkshire RG11 2AZ, England/011-44-734-771677. $U.S. $44 for 1 yr. Leading monthly airgun magazine in U.K.

Airgun Ads
Box 33, Hamilton, MT 59840/406-363-3805; Fax: 406-363-4117. $35 1 yr. (for first mailing; $20 for second mailing; $35 for Canada and foreign orders.) Monthly tabloid with extensive For Sale and Wanted airgun listings.

The Airgun Letter
Gapp, Inc., 4614 Woodland Rd., Ellicott City, MD 21042-6329/410-730-5496; Fax: 410-730-9544; e-mail: staff@airgnltr.net; http://www.airgunletter.com. $21 U.S., $24 Canada, $27 Mexico and $33 other foreign orders, 1 yr. Monthly newsletter for airgun users and collectors.

Airgun World
4 The Courtyard, Denmark St., Wokingham, Berkshire RG40 2AZ, England/011-44-734-771677. Call for subscription rates. Oldest monthly airgun magazine in the U.K., now a sister publication to Air Gunner.

Alaska Magazine
Morris Communications, 735 Broad Street, Augusta, GA 30901/706-722-6060. Hunting, Fishing and Life on the Last Frontier articles of Alaska and western Canada.

American Firearms Industry
Nat'l. Assn. of Federally Licensed Firearms Dealers, 2455 E. Sunrise Blvd., Suite 916, Ft. Lauderdale, FL 33304. $35.00 yr. For firearms retailers, distributors and manufacturers.

American Guardian
NRA, 11250 Waples Mill Rd., Fairfax, VA 22030. Publications division. $15.00 1 yr. Magazine features personal protection; home-self-defense; family recreation shooting; women's issues; etc.

American Gunsmith
Belvoir Publications, Inc., 75 Holly Hill Lane, Greenwich, CT 06836-2626/203-661-6111. $49.00 *(12 issues)*. Technical journal of firearms repair and maintenance.

American Handgunner*
Publisher's Development Corp., 591 Camino de la Reina, Suite 200, San Diego, CA 92108/800-537-3006 $16.95 yr. Articles for handgun enthusiasts, competitors, police and hunters.

American Hunter *(M)*
National Rifle Assn., 11250 Waples Mill Rd., Fairfax, VA 22030 (Same address for both.) Publications Div. $35.00 yr. Wide scope of hunting articles.

American Rifleman *(M)*
National Rifle Assn., 11250 Waples Mill Rd., Fairfax, VA 22030 (Same address for both). Publications Div. $35.00 yr. Firearms articles of all kinds.

American Survival Guide
McMullen Angus Publishing, Inc., 774 S. Placentia Ave., Placentia, CA 92670-6846. 12 issues $19.95/714-572-2255; FAX: 714-572-1864.

Armes & Tir*
c/o FABECO, 38, rue de Trévise 75009 Paris, France. Articles for hunters, collectors, and shooters. French text.

Arms Collecting *(Q)*
Museum Restoration Service, P.O. Box 70, Alexandria Bay, NY 13607-0070. $22.00 yr.; $62.00 3 yrs.; $112.00 5 yrs.

Australian Shooter (formerly Australian Shooters Jour-nal)
Sporting Shooters' Assn. of Australia, Inc., P.O. Box 2066, Kent Town SA 5071, Australia. $60.00 yr. locally; $65.00 yr. overseas surface mail. Hunting and shooting articles.

The Backwoodsman Magazine
P.O. Box 627, Westcliffe, CO 81252. $16.00 for 6 issues per yr.; $30.00 for 2 yrs.; sample copy $2.75. Subjects include muzzle-loading, woodslore, primitive survival, trapping, homesteading, blackpowder cartridge guns, 19th century how-to.

Black Powder Cartridge News *(Q)*
SPG, Inc., P.O. Box 761, Livingston, MT 59047/Phone/Fax: 406-222-8416. $17 yr. (4 issues) ($6 extra 1st class mailing). For the blackpowder cartridge enthusiast.

Blackpowder Hunting *(M)*
Intl. Blackpowder Hunting Assn., P.O. Box 1180Z, Glenrock, WY 82637/307-436-9817. $20.00 1 yr., $36.00 2 yrs. How-to and where-to features by experts on hunting; shooting; ballistics; traditional and modern blackpowder rifles, shotguns, pistols and cartridges.

Black Powder Times
P.O. Box 234, Lake Stevens, WA 98258. $20.00 yr.; add $5 per year for Canada, $10 per year other foreign. Tabloid newspaper for blackpowder activities; test reports.

Blade Magazine
Krause Publications, 700 East State St., Iola, WI 54990-0001. $25.98 for 12 issues. Foreign price *(including Canada-Mexico)* $50.00. A magazine for all enthusiasts of handmade, factory and antique knives.

Caliber
GFI-Verlag, Theodor-Heuss Ring 62, 50668 K"ln, Germany. For hunters, target shooters and reloaders.

The Caller *(Q) (M)*
National Wild Turkey Federation, P.O. Box 530, Edgefield, SC 29824. Tabloid newspaper for members; 4 issues per yr. (membership fee $25.00)

Cartridge Journal *(M)*
Robert Mellichamp, 907 Shirkmere, Houston, TX 77008/713-869-0558. Dues $12 for U.S. and Canadian members (includes the newsletter); 6 issues.

The Cast Bullet*(M)*
Official journal of The Cast Bullet Assn. Director of Membership, 203 E. 2nd St., Muscatine, IA 52761. Annual membership dues $14, includes 6 issues.

COLTELLI, che Passione *(Q)*
Casella postale N.519, 20101 Milano, Italy/Fax:02-48402857. $15 1 yr., $27 2 yrs. Covers all types of knives—collecting, combat, historical. Italian text.

Combat Handguns*
Harris Publications, Inc., 1115 Broadway, New York, NY 10010.

Deer & Deer Hunting Magazine
Krause Publications, 700 E. State St., Iola, WI 54990-0001. $19.95 yr. (9 issues). For the serious deer hunter. Website: www.krause.com

The Derringer Peanut *(M)*
The National Association of Derringer Collectors, P.O. Box 20572, San Jose, CA 95160. A newsletter dedicated to developing the best derringer information. Write for details.

Deutsches Waffen Journal
Journal-Verlag Schwend GmbH, Postfach 100340, D-74503 Schwäbisch Hall, Germany/0791-404-500; FAX:0791-404-505 and 404-424. DM102 p. yr. *(interior)*; DM125.30 (abroad), postage included. Antique and modern arms and equipment. German text.

Double Gun Journal
P.O. Box 550, East Jordan, MI 49727/800-447-1658. $35 for 4 issues.

Ducks Unlimited, Inc. *(M)*
1 Waterfowl Way, Memphis, TN 38120

The Engraver *(M) (Q)*
P.O. Box 4365, Estes Park, CO 80517/970-586-2388; Fax: 970-586-0394. Mike Dubber, editor. The journal of firearms engraving.

The Field
King's Reach Tower, Stamford St., London SE1 9LS England. £36.40 U.K. 1 yr.; 49.90 *(overseas, surface mail)* yr.; £82.00 *(overseas, air mail)* yr. Hunting and shooting articles, and all country sports.

Field & Stream
Time4 Media, Two Park Ave., New York, NY 10016/212-779-5000. Monthly shooting column. Articles on hunting and fishing.

---

*Published bi-monthly
† Published weekly
‡Published three times per month. All others are published monthly.
M=Membership requirements; write for details.
Q=Published Quarterly.

Periodical Publications

Periodical Publications

Field Tests
Belvoir Publications, Inc., 75 Holly Hill Lane; P.O. Box 2626, Greenwich, CT 06836-2626/203-661-6111; 800-829-3361 *(subscription line)*. U.S. & Canada $29 1 yr., $58 2 yrs.; all other countries $45 1 yr., $90 2 yrs. *(air)*.

Fur-Fish-Game
A.R. Harding Pub. Co., 2878 E. Main St., Columbus, OH 43209. $15.95 yr. Practical guidance regarding trapping, fishing and hunting.

The Gottlieb-Tartaro Report
Second Amendment Foundation, James Madison Bldg., 12500 NE 10th Pl., Bellevue, WA 98005/206-454-7012;Fax:206-451-3959. $30 for 12 issues. An insiders guide for gun owners.

Gray's Sporting Journal
Gray's Sporting Journal, P.O. Box 1207, Augusta, GA 30903. $36.95 per yr. for 6 issues. Hunting and fishing journals. Expeditions and Guides Book *(Annual Travel Guide)*.

Gun List†
700 E. State St., Iola, WI 54990. $36.98 yr. *(26 issues)*; $65.98 2 yrs. *(52 issues)*. Indexed market publication for firearms collectors and active shooters; guns, supplies and services. Website: www.krause.com

Gun News Digest *(Q)*
Second Amendment Fdn., P.O. Box 488, Station C, Buffalo, NY 14209/716-885-6408;Fax:716-884-4471. $10 U.S.; $20 foreign.

The Gun Report
World Wide Gun Report, Inc., Box 38, Aledo, IL 61231-0038. $33.00 yr. For the antique and collectable gun dealer and collector.

Gunmaker *(M) (Q)*
ACGG, P.O. Box 812, Burlington, IA 52601-0812. The journal of custom gunmaking.

The Gunrunner
Div. of Kexco Publ. Co. Ltd., Box 565G, Lethbridge, Alb., Canada T1J 3Z4. $23.00 yr., sample $2.00. Monthly newspaper, listing everything from antiques to artillery.

Gun Show Calendar *(Q)*
700 E. State St., Iola, WI 54990. $14.95 yr. *(4 issues)*. Gun shows listed; chronologically and by state. Website: www.krause.com

Gun Tests
11 Commerce Blvd., Palm Coast, FL 32142. The consumer resource for the serious shooter. Write for information.

Gun Trade News
Bruce Publishing Ltd., P.O. Box 82, Wantage, Ozon OX12 7A8, England/44-1-235-771770; Fax: 44-1-235-771848. Britain's only "trade only" magazine exclusive to the gun trade.

Gun Week†
Second Amendment Foundation, P.O. Box 488, Station C, Buffalo, NY 14209. $35.00 yr. U.S. and possessions; $45.00 yr. other countries. Tabloid paper on guns, hunting, shooting and collecting *(36 issues)*.

Gun World
Y-Visionary Publishing, LP 265 South Anita Drive, Ste. 120, Orange, CA 92868. $21.97 yr.; $34.97 2 yrs. For the hunting, reloading and shooting enthusiast.

Guns & Ammo
Primedia, 6420 Wilshire Blvd., Los Angeles, CA 90048/213-782-2780. $23.94 yr. Guns, shooting, and technical articles.

Guns
Publishers Development Corporation, P.O. Box 85201, San Diego, CA 92138/800-537-3006. $19.95 yr. In-depth articles on a wide range of guns, shooting equipment and related accessories for gun collectors, hunters and shooters.

Guns Review
Ravenhill Publishing Co. Ltd., Box 35, Standard House, Bonhill St., London EC 2A 4DA, England. £20.00 sterling *(approx. U.S. $38 USA & Canada)* yr. For collectors and shooters.

H.A.C.S. Newsletter *(M)*
Harry Moon, Pres., P.O. Box 50117, South Slope RPO, Burnaby BC, V5J 5G3, Canada/604-438-0950; Fax:604-277-3646. $25 p. yr. U.S. and Canada. Official newsletter of The Historical Arms Collectors of B.C. *(Canada)*.

Handgunner*
Richard A.J. Munday, Seychelles house, Brightlingsen, Essex CO7 ONN, England/012063-305201. £18.00 *(sterling)*.

Handguns
Primedia, 6420 Wilshire Blvd., Los Angeles, CA 90048/323-782-2868. $23/94 yr. For the handgunning and shooting enthusiast.

Handloader*
Wolfe Publishing Co., 2626 Stearman Road, Ste. A, Prescott, AZ 86301/520-445-7810;Fax:520-778-5124. $22.00 yr. The journal of ammunition reloading.

INSIGHTS*
NRA, 11250 Waples Mill Rd., Fairfax, VA 22030. Editor, John E. Robbins. $15.00 yr., which includes NRA junior membership; $10.00 for adult subscriptions *(12 issues)*. Plenty of details for the young hunter and target shooter; emphasizes gun safety, marksmanship training, hunting skills

International Arms & Militaria Collector *(Q)*
Arms & Militaria Press, P.O. Box 80, Labrador, Qld. 4215, Australia. A$39.50 yr. *(U.S. & Canada)*, 2 yrs. A$77.50; A$37.50 *(others)*, 1 yr., 2 yrs. $73.50 all air express mail; surface mail is less. Editor: Ian D. Skennerton.

International Shooting Sport*/UIT Journal
International Shooting Union *(UIT)*, Bavariaring 21, D-80336 Munich, Germany. Europe: *(Deutsche Mark)* DM44.00 yr., 2 yrs. DM83.00; outside Europe: DM50.00 yr., 2 yrs. DM95.00 *(air mail postage included.)* For international sport shooting.

Internationales Waffen-Magazin
Habegger-Verlag Zürich, Postfach 9230, CH-8036 Zürich, Switzerland. SF 105.00 *(approx. U.S. $73.00)* surface mail for 10 issues. Modern and antique arms, self-defense. German text; English summary of contents.

The Journal of the Arms & Armour Society *(M)*
A. Dove, P.O. Box 10232, London, SW19 2ZD England. £15.00 surface mail; £20.00 airmail sterling only yr. Articles for the historian and collector.

Journal of the Historical Breechloading Smallarms Assn.
Published annually. P.O. Box 12778, London, SE1 6XB, England. $21.00 yr. Articles for the collector plus mailings of short articles on specific arms, reprints, newsletters, etc.

Knife World
Knife World Publications, P.O. Box 3395, Knoxville, TN 37927. $15.00 yr.; $25.00 2 yrs. Published monthly for knife enthusiasts and collectors. Articles on custom and factory knives; other knife-related interests, monthly column on knife identification, military knives.

Man At Arms*
P.O. Box 460, Lincoln, RI 02865. $27.00 yr., $52.00 2 yrs. plus $8.00 for foreign subscribers. The N.R.A. magazine of arms collecting-investing, with excellent articles for the collector of antique arms and militaria.

The Mannlicher Collector *(Q)(M)*
Mannlicher Collectors Assn., Inc., P.O. Box 7144, Salem Oregon 97303. $20/ yr. subscription included in membership.

MAN/MAGNUM
S.A. Man (Pty) Ltd., P.O. Box 35204, Northway, Durban 4065, Republic of South Africa. SA Rand 200.00 for 12 issues. Africa's only publication on hunting, shooting, firearms, bushcraft, knives, etc.

The Marlin Collector *(M)*
R.W. Paterson, 407 Lincoln Bldg., 44 Main St., Champaign, IL 61820.

Muzzle Blasts *(M)*
National Muzzle Loading Rifle Assn., P.O. Box 67, Friendship, IN 47021/812-667-5131. $35.00 yr. annual membership. For the blackpowder shooter.

Muzzleloader Magazine*
Scurlock Publishing Co., Inc., Dept. Gun, Route 5, Box 347-M, Texarkana, TX 75501. $18.00 U.S.; $22.50 U.S./yr. for foreign subscribers. The publication for blackpowder shooters.

National Defense *(M)**
American Defense Preparedness Assn., Two Colonial Place, Suite 400, 2101 Wilson Blvd., Arlington, VA 22201-3061/703-522-1820; FAX: 703-522-1885. $35.00 yr. Articles on both military and civil defense field, including weapons, materials technology, management.

National Knife Magazine *(M)*
Natl. Knife Coll. Assn., 7201 Shallowford Rd., P.O. Box 21070, Chattanooga, TN 37424-0070. Membership $35 yr.; $65.00 International yr.

National Rifle Assn. Journal *(British) (Q)*
Natl. Rifle Assn. *(BR.)*, Bisley Camp, Brookwood, Woking, Surrey, England. GU24, OPB. £24.00 Sterling including postage.

National Wildlife*
Natl. Wildlife Fed., 1400 16th St. NW, Washington, DC 20036, $16.00 yr. *(6 issues)*; International Wildlife, 6 issues, $16.00 yr. Both, $22.00 yr., includes all membership benefits. Write attn.: Membership Services Dept., for more information.

New Zealand GUNS*
Waitekauri Publishing, P.O. 45, Waikino 3060, New Zealand. $NZ90.00 *(6 issues)* yr. Covers the hunting and firearms scene in New Zealand.

New Zealand Wildlife *(Q)*
New Zealand Deerstalkers Assoc., Inc., P.O. Box 6514, Wellington, N.Z. $30.00 *(N.Z.)*. Hunting, shooting and firearms/game research articles.

North American Hunter* *(M)*
P.O. Box 3401, Minnetonka, MN 55343/612-936-9333; e-mail: huntingclub@pclink.com. $18.00 yr. *(7 issues)*. Articles on all types of North American hunting.

Outdoor Life
Time4 Media, Two Park Ave., New York, NY 10016. $16.95/yr. Extensive coverage of hunting and shooting. Shooting column by Jim Carmichel.

La Passion des Courteaux *(Q)*
Phenix Editions, 25 rue Mademoiselle, 75015 Paris, France. French text.

Paintball Games International Magazine
Aceville Publications, Castle House, 97 High St., Colchester, Essex, England CO1 1TH/011-44-206-564840. Write for subscription rates. Leading magazine in the U.K. covering competitive paintball activities.

Paintball News
PBN Publishing, P.O. Box 1608, 24 Henniker St., Hillsboro, NH 03244/603-464-6080. $35 U.S. 1 yr. Bi-weekly. Newspaper covering the sport of paintball, new product reviews and industry features.

Paintball Sports *(Q)*
Paintball Publications, Inc., 540 Main St., Mount Kisco, NY 10549/941-241-7400. $24.75 U.S. 1 yr., $32.75 foreign. Covering the competitive paintball scene.

Performance Shooter
Belvoir Publications, Inc., 75 Holly Hill Lane, Greenwich, CT 06836-2626/203-661-6111. $45.00 yr. *(12 issues)*. Techniques and technology for improved rifle and pistol accuracy.

Petersen's HUNTING Magazine
Primedia, 6420 Wilshire Blvd., Los Angeles, CA 90048. $19.94 yr.; Canada $29.34 yr.; foreign countries $29.94 yr. Hunting articles for all game; test reports.

P.I. Magazine
America's Private Investigation Journal, 755 Bronx Dr., Toledo, OH 43609. Chuck Klein, firearms editor with column about handguns.

Pirsch
BLV Verlagsgesellschaft mbH, Postfach 400320, 80703 Munich, Germany/089-12704-0;Fax:089-12705-354. German text.

---

*Published bi-monthly
† Published weekly
‡Published three times per month. All others are published monthly.
M=Membership requirements; write for details.
Q=Published Quarterly.

Periodical Publications

Point Blank
Citizens Committee for the Right to Keep and Bear Arms *(sent to contributors)*, Liberty Park, 12500 NE 10th Pl., Bellevue, WA 98005

POINTBLANK *(M)*
Natl. Firearms Assn., Box 4384 Stn. C, Calgary, AB T2T 5N2, Canada. Official publication of the NFA.

The Police Marksman*
6000 E. Shirley Lane, Montgomery, AL 36117. $17.95 yr. For law enforcement personnel.

Police Times *(M)*
3801 Biscayne Blvd., Miami, FL 33137/305-573-0070.

Popular Mechanics
Hearst Corp., 224 W. 57th St., New York, NY 10019. Firearms, camping, outdoor oriented articles.

Precision Shooting
Precision Shooting, Inc., 222 McKee St., Manchester, CT 06040. $37.00 yr. U.S. Journal of the International Benchrest Shooters, and target shooting in general. Also considerable coverage of varmint shooting, as well as big bore, small bore, schuetzen, lead bullet, wildcats and precision reloading.

Rifle*
Wolfe Publishing Co., 2626 Stearman Road, Ste. A, Prescott, AZ 86301/520-445-7810; Fax: 520-778-5124. $19.00 yr. The sporting firearms journal.

Rifle's Hunting Annual
Wolfe Publishing Co., 2626 Stearman Road, Ste. A, Prescott, AZ 86301/520-445-7810; Fax: 520-778-5124. $4.99 Annual. Dedicated to the finest pursuit of the hunt.

Rod & Rifle Magazine
Lithographic Serv. Ltd., P.O. Box 38-138, Wellington, New Zealand. $50.00 yr. *(6 issues)*. Hunting, shooting and fishing articles.

Safari* *(M)*
Safari Magazine, 4800 W. Gates Pass Rd., Tucson, AZ 85745/602-620-1220. $55.00 *(6 times)*. The journal of big game hunting, published by Safari Club International. Also publish Safari Times, a monthly newspaper, included in price of $55.00 national membership.

Second Amendment Reporter
Second Amendment Foundation, James Madison Bldg., 12500 NE 10th Pl., Bellevue, WA 98005. $15.00 yr. *(non-contributors)*.

Shoot! Magazine*
Shoot! Magazine Corp., 1770 West State Stret PMB 340, Boise ID 83702/208-368-9920; Fax: 208-338-8428. Website: www.shootmagazine.com $32.95 *(6 times/yr.)*. Articles of interest to the cowboy action shooter, or others interested the Western-era firearms and ammunition.

Shooter's News
23146 Lorain Rd., Box 349, North Olmsted, OH 44070/216-979-5258;Fax:216-979-5259. $29 U.S. 1 yr., $54 2 yrs.; $52 foreign surface. A journal dedicated to precision riflery.

Shooting Industry
Publisher's Dev. Corp., 591 Camino de la Reina, Suite 200, San Diego, CA 92108. $50.00 yr. To the trade. $25.00.

Shooting Sports USA
National Rifle Assn. of America, 11250 Waples Mill Road, Fairfax, VA 22030. Annual subscriptions for NRA members are $5 for classified shooters and $10 for non-classified shooters. Non-NRA member subscriptions are $15. Covering events, techniques and personalities in competitive shooting.

Shooting Sportsman*
P.O. Box 11282, Des Moines, IA 50340/800-666-4955 *(for subscriptions)*. Editorial: P.O. Box 1357, Camden, ME 04843. $19.95 for six issues. The magazine of wingshooting and fine guns.

The Shooting Times & Country Magazine *(England)*†
IPC Magazines Ltd., King's Reach Tower, Stamford St, 1 London SE1 9LS, England/0171-261-6180;Fax:0171-261-7179. £65 *(approx. $98.00)* yr.; £79 yr. overseas *(52 issues)*. Game shooting, wild fowling, hunting, game fishing and firearms articles. Britain's best selling field sports magazine.

Shooting Times
Primedia, 2 News Plaza, P.O. Box 1790, Peoria, IL 61656/309-682-6626. $16.97 yr. Guns, shooting, reloading; articles on every gun activity.

The Shotgun News‡
Primedia, 2 News Plaza, P.O. Box 1790, Peoria, IL 61656/800-495-8362. $28.95 yr.; foreign subscription call for rates. Sample copy $4.00. Gun ads of all kinds.

SHOT Business
National Shooting Sports Foundation, Flintlock Ridge Office Center, 11 Mile Hill Rd., Newtown, CT 06470-2359/203-426-1320; FAX: 203-426-1087. For the shooting, hunting and outdoor trade retailer.

Shotgun Sports
P.O. Box 6810, Auburn, CA 95604/916-889-2220; FAX:916-889-9106. $31.00 yr. Trapshooting how-to's, shotshell reloading, shotgun patterning, shotgun tests and evaluations, Sporting Clays action, waterfowl/upland hunting. Call 1-800-676-8920 for a free sample copy.

The Single Shot Exchange Magazine
PO box 1055, York SC 29745/803-628-5326 phone/fax. $31.50/yr., monthly. Articles of interest to the blackpowder cartridge shooter and antique arms collector.

Single Shot Rifle Journal* *(M)*
Editor John Campbell, PO Box 595, Bloomfield Hills, MI 48303/248-458-8415. Email: jcampbel@dmbb.com Annual dues $35 for 6 issues. Journal of the American Single Shot Rifle Assn.

The Sixgunner *(M)*
Handgun Hunters International, P.O. Box 357, MAG, Bloomingdale, OH 43910

The Skeet Shooting Review
National Skeet Shooting Assn., 5931 Roft Rd., San Antonio, TX 78253. $20.00 yr. *(Assn. membership includes mag.)* Competition results, personality profiles of top Skeet shooters, how-to articles, technical, reloading information.

Soldier of Fortune
Subscription Dept., P.O. Box 348, Mt. Morris, IL 61054. $29.95 yr.; $39.95 Canada; $50.95 foreign.

Sporting Clays Magazine
Patch Communications, 5211 South Washington Ave., Titusville, FL 32780/407-268-5010; FAX: 407-267-7216. $29.95 yr. *(12 issues)*. Official publication of the National Sporting Clays Association.

Sporting Goods Business
Miller Freeman, Inc., One Penn Plaza, 10th Fl., New York, NY 10119-0004. Trade journal.

Sporting Goods Dealer
Two Park Ave., New York, NY 10016. $100.00 yr. Sporting goods trade journal.

Sporting Gun
Bretton Court, Bretton, Peterborough PE3 8DZ, England. £27.00 *(approx. U.S. $36.00)*, airmail £35.50 yr. For the game and clay enthusiasts.

The Squirrel Hunter
P.O. Box 368, Chireno, TX 75937. $14.00 yr. Articles about squirrel hunting.

Stott's Creek Calendar
Stott's Creek Printers, 2526 S 475 W, Morgantown, IN 46160/317-878-5489. 1 yr (3 issues) $11.50; 2 yrs. (6 issues) $20.00. Lists all gun shows everywhere in convenient calendar form; call for information.

Super Outdoors
2695 Aiken Road, Shelbyville, KY 40065/502-722-9463; 800-404-6064; Fax: 502-722-8093. Mark Edwards, publisher. Contact for details.

TACARMI
Via E. De Amicis, 25; 20123 Milano, Italy. $100.00 yr. approx. Antique and modern guns. *(Italian text.)*

Territorial Dispatch—1800s Historical Publication *(M)*
National Assn. of Buckskinners, 4701 Marion St., Suite 324, Livestock Exchange Bldg., Denver, CO 80216. Michael A. Nester & Barbara Wyckoff, editors. 303-297-9671.

Trap & Field
1000 Waterway Blvd., Indianapolis, IN 46202. $25.00 yr. Official publ. Amateur Trapshooting Assn. Scores, averages, trapshooting articles.

Turkey Call* *(M)*
Natl. Wild Turkey Federation, Inc., P.O. Box 530, Edgefield, SC 29824. $25.00 with membership *(6 issues per yr.)*

Turkey & Turkey Hunting*
Krause Publications, 700 E. State St., Iola, WI 54990-0001. $13.95 *(6 issue p. yr.)*. Magazine with leading-edge articles on all aspects of wild turkey behavior, biology and the successful ways to hunt better with that info. Learn the proper techniques to calling, the right equipment, and more.

The Accurate Rifle
Precisions Shooting, Inc., 222 Mckee Street, Manchester CT 06040. $37 yr. Dedicated to the rifle accuracy enthusiast.

The U.S. Handgunner* *(M)*
U.S. Revolver Assn., 40 Larchmont Ave., Taunton, MA 02780. $10.00 yr. General handgun and competition articles. Bi-monthly sent to members.

U.S. Airgun Magazine
P.O. Box 2021, Benton, AR 72018/800-247-4867; Fax: 501-316-8549. 10 issues a yr. Cover the sport from hunting, 10-meter, field target and collecting. Write for details.

The Varmint Hunter Magazine *(Q)*
The Varmint Hunters Assn., Box 759, Pierre, SD 57501/800-528-4868. $24.00 yr.

Waffenmarkt-Intern
GFI-Verlag, Theodor-Heuss Ring 62, 50668 K"ln, Germany. Only for gunsmiths, licensed firearms dealers and their suppliers in Germany, Austria and Switzerland.

Wild Sheep *(M)* *(Q)*
Foundation for North American Wild Sheep, 720 Allen Ave., Cody, WY 82414. Website: http://iigi.com/os/non/fnaws/fnaws.htm; e-mail: fnaws@wyoming.com. Official journal of the foundation.

Wisconsin Outdoor Journal
Krause Publications, 700 E. State St., Iola, WI 54990-0001. $17.97 yr. *(8 issues)*. For Wisconsin's avid hunters and fishermen, with features from all over that state with regional reports, legislative updates, etc. Website: www.krause.com

Women & Guns
P.O. Box 488, Sta. C, Buffalo, NY 14209. $24.00 yr. U.S.; $72.00 foreign *(12 issues)*. Only magazine edited by and for women gun owners.

World War II*
Cowles History Group, 741 Miller Dr. SE, Suite D-2, Leesburg, VA 20175-8920. Annual subscriptions $19.95 U.S.; $25.95 Canada; 43.95 foreign. The title says it—WWII; good articles, ads, etc.

---

*Published bi-monthly
† Published weekly
‡Published three times per month. All others are published monthly.
M=Membership requirements; write for details.
Q=Published Quarterly.

HANDLOADER'S DIGEST HANDLOADER'S LIBRARY

FOR COLLECTOR ✳ HUNTER ✳ SHOOTER ✳ OUTDOORSMAN

IMPORTANT NOTICE TO BOOK BUYERS

Books listed here may be bought from Ray Riling Arms Books Co., 6844 Gorsten St., P.O. Box 18925, Philadelphia, PA 19119, Phone 215/438-2456; FAX: 215-438-5395. E-Mail: sales@rayrilingarms-books.com. Joe Riling is the researcher and compiler of "The Arms Library" and a seller of gun books for over 32 years. The Riling stock includes books classic and modern, many hard-to-find items, and many not obtainable elsewhere. These pages list a portion of the current stock. They offer prompt, complete service, with delayed shipments occurring only on out-of-print or out-of-stock books.

Visit our web site at **www.rayrilingarmsbooks.com** and order all of your favorite titles on line from our secure site.

NOTICE FOR ALL CUSTOMERS: Remittance in U.S. funds must accompany all orders. For your convenience we now accept VISA, MasterCard & American Express. For shipments in the U.S. add $7.00 for the 1st book and $2.00 for each additional book for postage and insurance. Minimum order $10.00. International Orders add $13.00 for the 1st book and $5.00 for each additional book. All International orders are shipped at the buyer's risk unless an additional $5 for insurance is included. USPS does not offer insurance to all countries unless shipped Air-Mail please e-mail or call for pricing.

Payments in excess of order or for "Backorders" are credited or fully refunded at request. Books "As-Ordered" are not returnable except by permission and a handling charge on these of 10% or $2.00 per book which ever is greater is deducted from refund or credit. Only Pennsylvania customers must include current sales tax.

A full variety of arms books also available from Rutgers Book Center, 127 Raritan Ave., Highland Park, NJ 08904/908-545-4344; FAX: 908-545-6686 or I.D.S.A. Books, 1324 Stratford Drive, Piqua, OH 45356/937-773-4203; FAX: 937-778-1922.

BALLISTICS AND HANDLOADING

ABC's of Reloading, 6th Edition, by C. Rodney James and the editors of Handloader's Digest, DBI Books, a division of Krause Publications, Iola, WI, 1997. 288 pp., illus. Paper covers. $21.95

The definitive guide to every facet of cartridge and shotshell reloading.

Accurate Arms Loading Guide Number 2, by Accurate Arms. McEwen, TN: Accurate Arms Company, Inc., 2000. Paper Covers. $18.95

Includes new data on smokeless powders XMR4064 and XMP5744 as well as a special section on Cowboy Action Shooting. The new manual includes 50 new pages of data. An appendix includes nominal rotor charge weights, bullet diameters.

The American Cartridge, by Charles Suydam, Borden Publishing Co. Alhambra, CA, 1986. 184 pp., illus. $24.95

An illustrated study of the rimfire cartridge in the United States.

Ammo and Ballistics, by Robert W. Forker, Safari Press, Inc., Huntington Beach, CA., 1999. 252 pp., illustrated. Paper covers. $18.95

Ballistic data on 125 calibers and 1,400 loads out to 500 yards.

Ammunition: Grenades and Projectile Munitions, by Ian V. Hogg, Stackpole Books, Mechanicsburg, PA, 1998. 144 pp., illus. $22.95

Concise guide to modern ammunition. International coverage with detailed specifications and illustrations.

Barnes Reloading Manual #2, Barnes Bullets, American Fork, UT, 1999. 668 pp., illus. $24.95

Features data and trajectories on the new weight X, XBT and Solids in calibers from .22 to .50 BMG.

Big Bore Rifles And Cartridges, Wolfe Publishing Co., Prescott, AZ, 1991. Paper covers. $26.00

This book covers cartridges from 8mm to .600 Nitro with loading tables.

Black Powder Guide, 2nd Edition, by George C. Nonte, Jr., Stoeger Publishing Co., So. Hackensack, NJ, 1991. 288 pp., illus. Paper covers. $14.95

How-to instructions for selection, repair and maintenance of muzzleloaders, making your own bullets, restoring and refinishing, shooting techniques.

Blackpowder Loading Manual, 3rd Edition, by Sam Fadala, DBI Books, a division of Krause Publications, Iola, WI, 1995. 368 pp., illus. Paper covers. $20.95

Revised and expanded edition of this landmark blackpowder loading book. Covers hundreds of loads for most of the popular blackpowder rifles, handguns and shotguns.

Cartridges of the World, 9th Edition, by Frank Barnes, Krause Publications, Iola, WI, 2000. 512 pp., illus. Paper covers. $27.95

Completely revised edition of the general purpose reference work for which collectors, police, scientists and laymen reach first for answers to cartridge identification questions.

Cartridge Reloading Tools of the Past, by R.H. Chamberlain and Tom Quigley, Tom Quigley, Castle Rock, WA, 1998. 167 pp., illustrated. Paper covers. $25.00

A detailed treatment of the extensive Winchester and Ideal line of handloading tools and bullet molds, plus Remington, Marlin, Ballard, Browning, Maynard, and many others.

Cast Bullets for the Black Powder Rifle, by Paul A. Matthews, Wolfe Publishing Co., Prescott, AZ, 1996. 133 pp., illus. Paper covers. $22.50

The tools and techniques used to make your cast bullet shooting a success.

Complete Blackpowder Handbook, 3rd Edition, by Sam Fadala, DBI Books, a division of Krause Publications, Iola, WI, 1997. 400 pp., illus. Paper covers. $21.95

Expanded and completely rewritten edition of the definitive book on the subject of blackpowder.

Complete Reloading Guide, by Robert & John Traister, Stoeger Publishing Co., Wayne, NJ, 1997. 608 pp., illus. Paper covers. $34.95

Perhaps the finest, most comprehensive work ever published on the subject of reloading.

Complete Reloading Manual, One Book / One Caliber. California: Load Books USA, 2000. $7.95 Each

Containing unabridged information from U. S. Bullet and Powder Makers. With thousands of proven and tested loads, plus dozens of various bullet designs and different powders. Spiral bound. Available in all Calibers.

Early Loading Tools & Bullet Molds, Pioneer Press, 1988. 88 pages, illustrated. Softcover. $7.50

European Sporting Cartridges: Volume 1, by Brad Dixon, Seattle, WA: Armory Publications, 1997. 1st edition. 250 pp., Illus. $60.00

Photographs and drawings of over 550 centerfire cartridge case types in 1,300 illustrations produced in Germany and Austria from 1875-1995.

European Sporting Cartridges: Volume 2, by Brad Dixon, Seattle, WA: Armory Publications, 2000. 1st edition. 240 pages. $60.00

An illustrated history of centerfire hunting and target cartridges produced in Czechoslovakia, Switzerland, Norway, Sweden, Finland, Russia, Italy, Denmark, Belguim from 1875 to 1998. Adds 50 specimens to volume 1, Germany-Austria. Also, illustrates 40 small arms magazine experiments during the late 19th Century, and includes the English-Language export ammunition catalogue of Kovo (Povaszke Strojarne), Prague, Czeck. from the 1930's.

Game Loads and Practical Ballistics for the American Hunter, by Bob Hagel, Wolfe Publishing Co., Prescott, AZ, 1992. 310 pp., illus. $27.90

Hagel's knowledge gained as a hunter, guide and gun enthusiast is gathered in this informative text.

German 7.9MM Military Ammunition 1888-1945, by Daniel Kent, Ann Arbor, MI: Kent, 1990. 153 pp., plus appendix. illus., b&w photos. $35.00

Handbook for Shooters and Reloaders, by P.O. Ackley, Salt Lake City, UT, 1998, (Vol. I), 567 pp., illus. Includes a separate exterior ballistics chart. $21.95 (Vol. II), a new printing with specific new material. 495 pp., illus. $20.95

Handgun Muzzle Flash Tests: How Police Cartridges Compare, by Robert Olsen, Paladin Press, Boulder, CO.Fully illustrated. 133 pages. Softcover. $20.00

Tests dozens of pistols and revolvers for the brightness of muzzle flash, a critical factor in the safety of law enforcement personnel.

Handgun Stopping Power; The Definitive Study, by Marshall & Sandow. Boulder, CO: Paladin Press, 1992. 240 pages. $45.00

Offers accurate predictions of the stopping power of specific loads in calibers from .380 Auto to .45 ACP, as well as such specialty rounds as the Glaser Safety Slug, Federal Hydra-Shok, MagSafe, etc. This is the definitive methodology for predicting the stopping power of handgun loads, the first to take into account what really happens when a bullet meets a man.

Handloader's Digest, 17th Edition, edited by Bob Bell. DBI Books, a division of Krause Publications, Iola, WI, 1997. 480 pp., illustrated. Paper covers. $27.95

Top writers in the field contribute helpful information on techniques and components. Greatly expanded and fully indexed catalog of all currently available tools, accessories and components for metallic, blackpowder cartridge, shotgun reloading and swaging.

Handloader's Manual of Cartridge Conversions, by John J. Donnelly, Stoeger Publishing Co., So. Hackensack, NJ, 1986. Unpaginated. $39.95

From 14 Jones to 70-150 Winchester in English and American cartridges, and from 4.85 U.K. to 15.2x28R Gevelot in metric cartridges. Over 900 cartridges described in detail.

Hatcher's Notebook, by S. Julian Hatcher, Stackpole Books, Harrisburg, PA, 1992. 488 pp., illus. $39.95

A reference work for shooters, gunsmiths, ballisticians, historians, hunters and collectors.

History and Development of Small Arms Ammunition; Volume 2 Centerfire: Primitive, and Martial Long Arms. by George A. Hoyem. Oceanside, CA: Armory Publications, 1991. 303 pages, illustrated. $60.00

Covers the blackpowder military centerfire rifle, carbine, machine gun and volley gun ammunition used in 28 nations and dominions, together with the firearms that chambered them.

History and Development of Small Arms Ammunition; Volume 4, American Military Rifle Cartridges. Oceanside, CA: Armory Publications, 1998. 244pp., illus. $60.00

Carries on what Vol. 2 began with American military rifle cartridges. Now the sporting rifle cartridges are at last organized by their originators-235 individual case types designed by eight makers of single shot rifles and four of magazine rifles from .50-140 Winchester Express to .22-15-60 Stevens. plus experimentals from .70-150 to .32-80. American Civil War enthusiasts and European collectors will find over 150 primitives in Appendix A to add to those in Volumes One and Two. There are 16 pages in full color of 54 box labels for Sharps, Remington and Ballard cartridges. There are large photographs with descriptions of 15 Maynard, Sharps, Winchester, Browning, Freund, Remington-Hepburn, Farrow and other single shot rifles, some of them rare one of a kind specimens.

Hodgdon Powder Data Manual #27, Hodgdon Powder Co., Shawnee Mission, KS, 1999. 800 pp. $27.95

Reloading data for rifle and pistol loads.

Hodgdon Shotshell Data Manual, Hodgdon Powder Co., Shawnee Mission, KS, 1999. 208 pp. $19.95

Contains hundreds of loads for lead shot, buck shot, slugs, bismuth shot and steel shot plus articles on ballistics, patterning, special reloads and much more.

Home Guide to Cartridge Conversions, by Maj. George C. Nonte Jr., The Gun Room Press, Highland Park, NJ, 1976. 404 pp., illus. $24.95

Revised and updated version of Nonte's definitive work on the alteration of cartridge cases for use in guns for which they were not intended.

Hornady Handbook of Cartridge Reloading, 5th Edition, Vol. I and II, Edited by Larry Steadman, Hornady Mfg. Co., Grand Island, NE, 2000., illus. $49.95

2 Volumes; Volume 1, 773 pp.; Volume 2, 717 pp. New edition of this famous reloading handbook covers rifle and handgun reloading data and ballistic tables.

Latest loads, ballistic information, etc.

How-To's for the Black Powder Cartridge Rifle Shooter, by Paul A. Matthews, Wolfe Publishing Co., Prescott, AZ, 1995. 45 pp. Paper covers. $22.50

Covers lube recipes, good bore cleaners and over-powder wads. Tips include compressing powder charges, combating wind resistance, improving ignition and much more.

The Illustrated Reference of Cartridge Dimensions, edited by Dave Scovill, Wolfe Publishing Co., Prescott, AZ, 1994. 343 pp., illus. Paper covers. $19.00

A comprehensive volume with over 300 cartridges. Standard and metric dimensions have been taken from SAAMI drawings and/or fired cartridges.

Kynock, by Dale J. Hedlund, Armory Publications, Seattle, WA, 2000. 130 pages, illus. 9" x 12" with four color dust jacket. $59.95

A comprehensive review of Kynoch shotgun cartridges covering over 50 brand names and case types, and over 250 Kynoch shotgun cartridge headstamps. Additional information on Kynoch metallic ammunition including the identity of the mysterious .434 Seelun.

Lee Modern Reloading, by Richard Lee, 350 pp. of charts and data and 85 illustrations. 512 pp. $24.95

Bullet casting, lubricating and author's formula for calculating proper charges for cast bullets. Includes virtually all current load data published by the powder suppliers. Exclusive source of volume measured loads.

Loading the Black Powder Rifle Cartridge, by Paul A Matthews, Wolfe Publishing Co., Prescott, AZ, 1993. 121 pp., illus. Paper covers. $22.50

Author Matthews brings the blackpowder cartridge shooter valuable information on the basics, including cartridge care, lubes and moulds, powder charges and developing and testing loads in his usual authoritative style.

HANDLOADER'S LIBRARY

Loading the Peacemaker—Colt's Model P, by Dave Scovill, Wolfe Publishing Co., Prescott, AZ, 1996. 227 pp., illus. $24.95
A comprehensive work about the history, maintenance and repair of the most famous revolver ever made, including the most extensive load data ever published.

Lyman Cast Bullet Handbook, 3rd Edition, edited by C. Kenneth Ramage, Lyman Publications, Middlefield, CT, 1980. 416 pp., illus. Paper covers. $19.95
Information on more than 5000 tested cast bullet loads and 19 pages of trajectory and wind drift tables for cast bullets.

Lyman Black Powder Handbook, edited by C. Kenneth Ramage, Lyman Products for Shooters, Middlefield, CT, 1975. 239 pp., illus. Paper covers. $14.95
Comprehensive load information for the modern blackpowder shooter.

Lyman Pistol & Revolver Handbook, 2nd Edition, edited by Thomas J. Griffin, Lyman Products Co., Middlefield, CT, 1996. 287 pp., illus. Paper covers. $18.95
The most up-to-date loading data available including the hottest new calibers, like 40 S&W, 9x21, 9mm Makarov, 9x25 Dillon and 454 Casull.

Lyman Reloading Handbook No. 48, edited by Thomas J. Griffen, Lyman Publications, Middlefield, CT, 1992. 480 pp., illus. Paper covers. $24.95
A comprehensive reloading manual complete with "How to Reload" information. Expanded data section with all the newest rifle and pistol calibers.

Lyman Shotshell Handbook, 4th Edition, edited by Edward A. Matunas, Lyman Products Co., Middlefield, CT, 1996. 330 pp., illus. Paper covers. $24.95
Has 9000 loads, including slugs and buckshot, plus feature articles and a full color I.D. section.

Lyman's Guide to Big Game Cartridges & Rifles, by Edward Matunas, Lyman Publishing Corporation, Middlefield, CT, 1994. 287 pp., illus. Paper covers. $17.95
A selection guide to cartridges and rifles for big game—antelope to elephant.

Making Loading Dies and Bullet Molds, by Harold Hoffman, H & P Publishing, San Angelo, TX, 1993. 230 pp., illus. Paper covers. $24.95
A good book for learning tool and die making.

Metallic Cartridge Reloading, 3rd Edition, by M.L. McPherson, DBI Books, a division of Krause Publications, Iola, WI., 1996. 352 pp., illus. Paper covers. $21.95
A true reloading manual with over 10,000 loads for all popular metallic cartridges and a wealth of invaluable technical data provided by a recognized expert.

Military Rifle and Machine Gun Cartridges, by Jean Huon, Alexandria, VA: Ironside International, 1995. 1st edition. 378 pages, over 1,000 photos. $34.95
Superb reference text.

Modern Combat Ammunition, by Duncan Long, Paladin Press, Boulder, CO, 1997, soft cover, photos, illus., 216 pp. $34.00
Now, Paladin's leading weapons author presents his exhaustive evaluation of the stopping power of modern rifle, pistol, shotgun and machine gun rounds based on actual case studies of shooting incidents. He looks at the hot new cartridges that promise to dominate well into the next century .40 S&W, 10mm auto, sub-sonic 9mm's - as well as the trusted standbys. Find out how to make your own exotic tracers, fléchette and sabot rounds, caseless ammo and fragmenting bullets.

Modern Exterior Ballistics, by Robert L. McCoy, Schiffer Publishing Co., Atglen, PA, 1999. 128 pp. $95.00
Advanced students of exterior ballistics and flight dynamics will find this comprehensive textbook on the subject a useful addition to their libraries.

Modern Handloading, by Maj. Geo. C. Nonte, Winchester Press, Piscataway, NJ, 1972. 416 pp., illus. $15.00
Covers all aspects of metallic and shotshell ammunition loading, plus more loads than any book in print.

Modern Reloading, by Richard Lee, Inland Press, 1996. 510 pp., illus. $24.98
The how-to's of rifle, pistol and shotgun reloading plus load data for rifle and pistol calibers.

Modern Sporting Rifle Cartridges, by Wayne van Zwoll, Stoeger Publishing Co., Wayne, NJ, 1998. 310 pp., illustrated. Paper covers. $21.95
Illustrated with hundreds of photos and backed up by dozens of tables and schematic drawings, this four-part book tells the story of how rifle bullets and cartridges were developed and, in some cases, discarded.

Modern Practical Ballistics, by Art Pejsa, Pejsa Ballistics, Minneapolis, MN, 1990. 150 pp., illus. $29.95
Covers all aspects of ballistics and new, simplified methods. Clear examples illustrate new, easy but very accurate formulas.

Mr. Single Shot's Cartridge Handbook, by Frank de Haas, Mark de Haas, Orange City, IA, 1996. 116 pp., illus. Paper covers. $21.50
This book covers most of the cartridges, both commercial and wildcat, that the author has known and used.

Nick Harvey's Practical Reloading Manual, by Nick Harvey, Australian Print Group, Maryborough, Victoria, Australia, 1995. 235 pp., illus. Paper covers. $24.95
Contains data for rifle and handgun including many popular wildcat and improved cartridges. Tools, powders, components and techniques for assembling optimum reloads with particular application to North America.

Nosler Reloading Manual #4, edited by Gail Root, Nosler Bullets, Inc., Bend, OR, 1996. 516 pp., illus. $26.99
Combines information on their Ballistic Tip, Partition and Handgun bullets with traditional powders and new powders never before used, plus trajectory information from 100 to 500 yards.

The Paper Jacket, by Paul Matthews, Wolfe Publishing Co., Prescott, AZ, 1991. Paper covers. $13.50
Up-to-date and accurate information about paper-patched bullets.

Reloading Tools, Sights and Telescopes for S/S Rifles, by Gerald O. Kelver, Brighton, CO, 1982. 163 pp., illus. Softcover. $15.00A listing of most of the famous makers of reloading tools, sights and telescopes with a brief description of the products they manufactured.

Reloading for Shotgunners, 4th Edition, by Kurt D. Fackler and M.L. McPherson, DBI Books, a division of Krause Publications, Iola, WI, 1997. 320 pp., illus. Paper covers. $19.95
Expanded reloading tables with over 11,000 loads. Bushing charts for every major press and component maker. All new presentation on all aspects of shotshell reloading by two of the top experts in the field.

The Rimfire Cartridge in the United States and Canada, Illustrated history of rimfire cartridges, manufacturers, and the products made from 1857-1984. by John L. Barber, Thomas Publications, Gettysburg, PA 2000. 1st edition. Profusely illustrated. 221 pages. $50.00
The author has written an encyclopedia of rimfire cartridges from the .22 to the massive 1.00 in. Gatling. Fourteen chapters, six appendices and an excellent bibliography make up a reference volume that all cartridge collectors should aquire.

Sierra 50th Anniversary, 4th Edition Rifle Manual,
Sierra Bullets, Santa Fe Springs, CA, 1997. 800 pp., illus. $26.99
New cartridge introductions, etc.

Sierra 50th Anniversary, 4th Edition Handgun Manual,
Sierra Bullets, Santa Fe, CA, 1997. 700 pp., illus. $21.99
Histories, reloading recommendations, bullets, powders and sections on the reloading process, etc.

Sixgun Cartridges and Loads, by Elmer Keith, The Gun Room Press, Highland Park, NJ, 1986. 151 pp., illus. $24.95
A manual covering the selection, uses and loading of the most suitable and popular revolver cartridges. Originally published in 1936. Reprint.

Speer Reloading Manual No. 13, edited by members of the Speer research staff, Omark Industries, Lewiston, ID, 1999. 621 pp., illustrated. $24.95
With thirteen new sections containing the latest technical information and reloading trends for both novice and expert in this latest edition. More than 9,300 loads are listed, including new propellant powders from Accurate Arms, Alliant, Hodgdon and Vihtavuori.

Street Stoppers, The Latest Handgun Stopping Power Street Results, by Marshall & Lanow. Boulder, CO, Paladin Press, 1996. 374 pages, illus. Softcover. $42.95
Street Stoppers is the long-awaited sequel to Handgun Stopping Power. It provides the latest results of real-life shootings in all of the major handgun calibers, plus more than 25 thought-provoking chapters that are vital to anyone interested in firearms, would ballistics, and combat shooting. This book also covers the street results of the hottest new caliber to hit the shooting world in years, the .40 Smith & Wesson. Updated street results of the latest exotic ammunition including Remington Golden Saber and CCI-Speer Gold Dot, plus the venerable offerings from MagSafe, Glaser, Cor-Bon and others. A fascinating look at the development of Hydra-Shok ammunition is included.

Understanding Ballistics, Revised 2nd Edition by Robert A. Rinker, Mulberry House Publishing Co., Corydon, IN, 2000. 430 pp., illus Paper covers. New, Revised and Expanded. 2nd Edition. $24.95
Explains basic to advanced firearm ballistics in understandable terms.

Why Not Load Your Own?, by Col. T. Whelen, Gun Room Press, Highland Park, NJ 1996, 4th ed., rev. 237 pp., illus. $20.00
A basic reference on handloading, describing each step, materials and equipment. Includes loads for popular cartridges.

Wildcat Cartridges Volumes 1 & 2 Combination, by the editors of Handloaders magazine, Wolfe Publishing Co., Prescott, AZ, 1997. 350 pp., illus. Paper covers. $39.95
A profile of the most popular information on wildcat cartridges that appeared in the Handloader magazine.

Handloader's Digest Shellholder Interchangeability Tables

by Robert G. Rowe

Introduction

When working on firearms, performing such tasks as testing firing pins and actions, you may want to make a dummy round or install a new primer into an empty case. Depending on the tools that are available, the process of pulling and installing the bullet and primer will probably involve the use of a reloading tool shellholder.

The following table enumerates over 1,500 cartridges that can be handled with the 39 holders from the RCBS standard list. Also, using l4 of their special-order listings, an additional 221, mostly the larger-caliber cases, can be worked. Do not misunderstand; this is not an attempt to out-engineer RCBS and the other shellholder manufacturers. The holders in this table do not fit all of the listed cartridges well enough for quantity reloading, but will work well enough for the occasional job.

WARNING: *Working with rimfire cartridges can be extremely dangerous. For the most part, shellholders are not shown for rimfire cartridges. There are some wildcats using rimfire cases, and a shellholder may be shown. This does not mean that their use is recommended; do so at your own risk. Pressure on the forward face of the rim as well as the rear can detonate the cartridge.*

RCBS shellholders are used because they have by far the largest selection of holders available. I also use their Ammo Master single-stage press (RCBS item #88701), as it has the capacity to handle up to 50 BMG-size cartridges and their 50 BMG and 700 N.E. shellholders. The RCBS Universal Decapping die (item # 87580) works well and handles cases up to .692-inch in diameter.

For cases larger than this, the rod can be removed from the die and used manually. For pulling bullets and making dummy rounds, I use their bullet-puller die (item # 09440) and collets (items #9419 through #09434). For seating the bullet in the brass, hopefully either you or your customer will have unfired or reformed brass. Incidentally, I have been unable to find the bullet puller and collets in the current RCBS catalog, but they were still shown in the 1998 Huntington catalog. As of the fall of 1998, RCBS does not sell a 12-caliber collet, but they will sell you a formed and threaded collet with no hole that you can complete. The 17-caliber will work with the 19-calibers.

Forster also sells a bullet puller (FBP 1010) and collets, but I haven't used them.

For pulling bullets from extremely long cartridges, you can modify the Lyman Acupress (item # 7730000) by removing some of the bottom portion of the threaded area with a hacksaw. This lengthens the usable area. I doubt that many of you will need this capacity, but it does work rather well.

The Lee primer holders are listed because I find that for priming, the Lee Improved Priming Tool (Lee item # 90231) is the quickest and handiest to use. I am not referring to the Lee Auto-Prime tool. Lee Precision has definite instructions for the use of their Auto-Prime, and these do not include use with a loose-fitting or modified shell holder. Always use proper safety procedures when priming. If the case is properly aligned in the holder, no unusual force is required to seat the primer. If you feel resistance, shift the case position. The 21 Lee primer shellholders will work with 1661 cartridges. The Lee catalog lists their #2 shellholder for 7x57 Mauser cases, but I have found that not all 7x57s will fit into a #2, so I suggest a #9 for use with the 7x57.

As for the modifications to the holders mentioned later, if you have to work with a Berdan primer, these are available from The Old Western Scrounger in California, and the primer hole in a shellholder can be enlarged with a carbide drill bit. For use with some of the foreign and antique cases with the Type A head (convex in shape) grind a trough in the floor of the shellholder, from the primer hole to the front. Do this–preferably–on a drill press. If you do not damage the top surface of the metal under the lips, the holder can still be used for its original intent.

To save the time having to shuffle through the list, I have listed different cartridges using the same case, i.e. 30/348 Ackley Imp. and 35/348 separately. Of course, there are many more cartridges that have not been listed, but perhaps the shellholder capacity chart at the end of the list will help with those. In this list, the zeros in front of some of the numbers in the RCBS list are for computer indexing purposes and should be ignored. The list is indexed by plain name (22 Williams) then named with a hyphen (22-250), then caliber-based on another case (22/06). Some of the cartridges listed here are so valuable as collectors items, you will probably not disassemble them unless possibly to make them inert.

The item numbers are mainly for reference purposes. However, you may find they have other uses. Also, you probably won't want to purchase all of the shellholders at one time. So for information purposes: the RCBS #3 is used 16 percent of the time, the #4 13 percent, the #14 5 percent, the #2 5 percent, the #10 6 percent, etc.

Abbreviations

0 – A shell holder is not available for this cartridge from this source
8 Lebel – Shellholder for 8mm French Lebel rifle
10 Ga.– Shellholder for 10-gauge shotshell
12 Ga – Shellholder for 10-gauge shotshell
16 Ga.– Shellholder for 16-gauge shotshell
20 Ga.– Shellholder for 20-gauge shotshell
450#2 NE – Shellholder for 450 #2 Nitro Express
470 NE – Shellholder for 470 Nitro Express
505 Gibbs – Shellholder for 505 Gibbs rifle
524 Cal.–32 Ga. Lancaster Ball
575 Cal.– 24 Ga. Lancaster Ball
577 NE – Shellholder for 577 Nitro Express
577 Ty or Tyran.– Shellholder for 577 A Square Tyrannosaur
577/450 MH – Shellholder for 577/450 Martini Henry
600 NE – Shellholder for 600 Nitro Express
610 Cal.– 28 Ga. Lancaster Ball
615 Cal.– 20 Bore Rifle
649 Cal.– 18 Ga.Lancaster Ball.
666 Cal.–16 Bore Rifle
693 Cal.– 14 Bore Rifle
700 NE – Shellholder for 700 Nitro Express
729 Cal.– 12 Bore Rifle
775 Cal.– 10 Bore Rifle
835 Cal.– 8 Bore Rifle
935 Cal.– 4 Bore Rifle
1200 Cal.– 3 Bore Rifle
Aus. Rewa – Australian current manufacture Smokeless Powder cartridge
B – Brenneke as in shellholder for 9.3x64 Brenneke
BR – Benchrest
B.S.A. – Birmingham Small Arms Co.
BMG – Browning Machinegun
BN – Bottleneck-shape cartridge design
BPE – Black Powder Express
C – Custom shellholder has to be special ordered
CF – Centerfire
Dixon designators – Letters and numbers after some metric cartridges (i.e. MB 111) refer to "European Sporting Cartridges" by Dixon designations
Exp. – Express
Fl.– Flanged Cartridge (Rimmed base)
G&H – Griffen & Howe
G. – Indicates that you must carefully grind a trough on a drill press from the primer hole to the front and possibly slightly behind the primer hole of the shell holder so that the holder will accept type A-type (or Mauser base) bases (convex in shape). Do not grind under the top lips of the holder so that it will still work with the modern cartridges.
Ga.– Gauge name of shotshell
H&H – Holland & Holland
ICL – Imperial Chemicals Limited
I.P. – Inside Primed

IHMSA – International Handgun Metallic Silhouette Assn.
Imp. – Improved Design
L – At head of column, Lee Precision
LMR – Lightning Magazine Rifle
Laz. – Lazzeroni
MH – Martini Henry (577-450 MH)
MS – Mannlicher Schoenauer
NE – Nitro Express
R – As part of name of cartridge, a rimmed or flanged case
R – At head of column, R. C. B. S.
R.W.A. – Rifle Works Armory – Gain Twist Barrel Co.
Rem.– Remington
R – Rimmed cartridge (flanged)
RTT – Cartridge rim is too thick for available shell holders from this source.
S&W – Smith & Wesson
SLR – Self-loading Rifle
S.S. –Shotshell shape)
Silhouette – See IHMSA
STA – Shooting Times Alaskan
Std. – Standard
Str. – Straight-case design
STW – Shooting Times Westerner
Type A Base – Those with a convex-shaped base, similar to Mauser base.
W.R. – Westley Richards
Win. – Winchester

Non-standard numbers such as 06 for 6mm and 729 caliber instead of 12 gauge are used for indexing purposes with the computer. I hope that the table helps you as it has me.

– Robert G. Rowe

Handloader's Digest Shellholder Capacities

by Rim Dia

(Dimensions are in thousands of an inch)

RCBS	Lee	Rim Dia.	Groove or	Rim Thickness
29	15	297	247	40
12	20	352	295	61
17	7	355	311	42
10	4	373	332	40
23	4	375	335	53
16	19	390	345	50
39	19	403	343	50
1	1	405	352	60
25	0	410	375	42
19	1	420	358	49
6	1	434	383	58
27	12	436	375	48
32	12	444	371	59
9	2	457	398	50
15	10	468	420	48
11	10	473	410	48
36	2A	474	408	53
3	2	480	413	50
30	9	485	430	55
18	11	499	440	57
2	3	503	420	60
21	11	508	450	57
28	11	510	446	60
8	13	513	468	86
20	13	513	482	60
34	9	513	446	55
35	14	523	475	60
33	11	525	465	60
38	5	527	476	58
4	5	534	475	56
7	5	537	454	60
24	16	545	458	73
26	5	562	482	58
13	16	570	490	58
37	18	588	494	73
14	8	596	505	70
5	8	602	545	70
22	17	632	525	85
8 Lebel	17	634	548	70
450 #2 NE	0	647	563	83
470 NE	0	652	575	45
31	0	658	557	65
505 Gibbs	0	661	572	68
450 #2 NE	0	664	575	77
577	0	693	605	60
577 NE	0	738	658	48
577/450	0	745	665	55
20 Ga. SS	0	760	708	54
600 NE	0	804	696	61
50 Cal BMG	0	810	680	85
16 Ga. SS	0	818	751	60
700 NE	0	879	780	78
12 Ga. SS	0	880	814	60
10 Ga. SS	0	916	860	69

Cartridges and Shell Holders

Cartridge	Metric/Inch	RCBS #	LEE#	Item #
12 Cooper CM	Inch	C	0	1
12 Dart	Inch	29	15	2
14 Bee	Inch	1	1	3
14 Carbine	Inch	17	7	4
14 Cooper C M	Inch	C	0	5
14 Dart	Inch	29	15	6
14 Flea	Inch	17	7	7
14 H & R Mag	Inch	23	4	8
14 Hornet	Inch	12	20	9
14 Jones CF	Inch	12	20	10
14/221 (14-224 Walker)	Inch	10	4	11
14/222	Inch	10	4	12
14/222 Mag.	Inch	10	4	13
14/223	Inch	10	4	14
17 Ackley Bee	Inch	1	1	15
17 Alton Jones	Inch	12	20	16
17 Bumble Bee	Inch	1	1	17
17 CCM (Cooper C.F. Mag)	Inch	12	20	18
17 Danne	Inch	10	4	19
17 Dart	Inch	29	15	20
17 Eichelberger Bee	Inch	1	1	21
17 Flea	Inch	17	7	22
17 Flintstone S E	Inch	3	2	23
17 HE Bee	Inch	1	1	24
17 Hornet Ackley Imp.	Inch	12	20	25
17 Javalina	Inch	10	4	26
17 K Hornet (Kilbourn)	Inch	12	20	27
17 Keno	Inch	17	7	28
17 Kimber Hornet	Inch	12	20	29
17 Landis Woodsman	Inch	10	4	30
17 Mach III	Inch	10	4	31
17 Mach IV	Inch	10	4	32
17 Magnum (222 Mag.)	Inch	10	4	33
17 Pee Wee	Inch	17	7	34
17 Remington	Inch	10	4	35
17 Saunders Super Jet (17-31*)	Inch	6	1	36
17 Super Pee Wee Rimless	Inch	19	1	37
17 Super Pee Wee Rimmed	Inch	2	3	38
17 V L R	Inch	10	4	39
17 Vixen	Inch	29	15	40
17/22 Sav. HP Imp.	Inch	2	3	41
17/222	Inch	10	4	42
17/222 Rimmed	Inch	32	12	43
17/223	Inch	10	4	44
17/224 Weatherby	Inch	27	12	45
17/225 Win.	Inch	11	10	46
17/30 Carbine Pee Wee	Inch	17	7	47
170 Landis Super Eyebunger	Inch	19	1	48
170-250-4000 Landis	Inch	3	2	49
170-4000 Landis Express	Inch	3	2	50
19 Calhoun (4.85mm)	Inch	12	20	51
19/223 Calhoun (4.85mm)	Inch	10	4	52
2 R Lovell (Imp 22-3000)	Inch	16	19	53
20 Dart	Inch	29	15	54
20 Eichelberger Bee	Inch	1	1	55
20 PPC	Inch	32	12	56
20 TNT (20 Remington)	Inch	10	4	57
20 Vartarg (20 VT)	Inch	10	4	58
20 Vartarg Turbo (20VTT)	Inch	10	4	59
20/222 Magnum	Inch	10	4	60
20/222 T. Holmes	Inch	2	3	61
20/223 (5mm/223)	Inch	10	4	62
200 Asp	Inch	3	2	63
217 Elliot Express	Inch	24	16	64
218 Bee	Inch	1	1	65
218 Bee Ackley Imp.	Inch	1	1	66
218 ICL Bobcat	Inch	1	1	67
218 Mashburn Bee	Inch	1	1	68
219 Donaldson Wasp Rimmed	Inch	2	3	69
219 ICL Wolverine	Inch	2	3	70
219 Stingray	Inch	2	3	71
219 Zipper	Inch	2	3	72
219 Zipper Imp.	Inch	2	3	73
22 Short Krag	Inch	7	5	74
22 Adolph Long Range Pistol	Inch	32	12	75
22 Arg. (22/7.65 Arg.)	Inch	3	2	76
22 Baby Niedner	Inch	1	1	77
22 Belted Exp. Ackley	Inch	3	2	78
22 BR Remington	Inch	3	2	79
22 Brat	Inch	3	2	80
22 Carbine B. Schuetz	Inch	17	7	81
22 CCM (Cooper)	Inch	C	0	82
22 CHeeta Mark I Large Primer	Inch	3	2	83
22 CHeeta Mark I Small Primer	Inch	3	2	84
22 Cotterman	Inch	6	1	85
22 Dart	Inch	29	15	86
22 Donaldson Wasp Rimmed	Inch	2	3	87
22 Donaldson Wasp Rimless	Inch	19	1	88
22 Eager	Inch	23	4	89
22 Extra Long Maynard	Inch	12	20	90
22 Gebby Std. Varminter	Inch	3	2	91
22 Gebby Varminter Junior	Inch	2	3	92
22 Gebby Varminter Senior	Inch	3	2	93
22 Harvey K Chuck	Inch	12	20	94
22 Hornet	Inch	12	20	95
22 ICL Gopher	Inch	12	20	96
22 J G R rimless JGR Gunsport	Inch	C	0	97
22 Jay Bird	Inch	3	2	98
22 K Chuck	Inch	12	20	99
22 K Hornet	Inch	12	20	100
22 K S S (Krag Super Short)	Inch	3	2	101
22 Lindahl Rimless Chucker	Inch	19	1	102
22 Lindahl Rimmed Chucker	Inch	2	3	103
22 Long Snapper	Inch	12	20	104
22 Lovell Max (22/3000)	Inch	16	19	105
22 Marciante Blue Streak	Inch	2	3	106
22 Miller Krag	Inch	7	5	107
22 MS (22/6.5x54MS)	Inch	3	2	108
22 Newton 2nd model (06)	Inch	3	2	109
22 Newton-Krag (22 Special)	Inch	7	5	110
22 Niedner Mag. # 1	Inch	2	3	111
22 Niedner Mag. Rimless Mag.	Inch	19	1	112

Cartridges and Shell Holders, *continued*

Cartridge	Metric/Inch	RCBS #	LEE#	Item #
22 Niedner Rimmed Mag. #2	Inch	2	3	113
22 Orphan	Inch	3	2	114
22 Patrick	Inch	3	2	115
22 PPC	Inch	32	12	116
22 PPC Rimmed	Inch	18	11	117
22 Rem. Jet (22 CF Magnum)	Inch	6	1	118
22 Rem. Jet Imp (22 Sabre etc	Inch	6	1	119
22 Rush #1	Inch	17	7	120
22 Rush #2	Inch	29	15	121
22 Savage HP (5.6x52R) & Imp	Inch	2	3	122
22 Short Krag Ack. Imp.	Inch	7	5	123
22 Spitfire #1	Inch	17	7	124
22 Spitfire #2 (5.57 Json)	Inch	17	7	125
22 Squirrel	Inch	12	20	126
22 Super Bower	Inch	2	3	127
22 Super Jet	Inch	6	1	128
22 Super Jet Ackley	Inch	6	1	129
22 Super P D C	Inch	3	2	130
22 Talbot	Inch	3	2	131
22 Varmint R	Inch	7	5	132
22 Varminteer (22-250)	Inch	3	2	133
22 Vartarg (22VT)	Inch	10	4	134
22 Vartarg Turbo (VTT)	Inch	10	4	135
22 Waldog	Inch	32	12	136
22 Wesson (22/30-30)	Inch	2	3	137
22 Williams	Inch	12	20	138
22 Win. C F (5.6 x 35R)	Inch	12	20	139
22-10-45 Maynard 1882	Inch	12	20	140
22-15-60 Stevens	Inch	12	20	141
22-240 Johnson Special	Inch	3	2	142
22-250 Ackley IMP.	Inch	3	2	143
22-250 Remington	Inch	3	2	144
22-250 Shannon Imp.	Inch	3	2	145
22-30 Barr-Nix	Inch	11	10	146
22-3000 G&H	Inch	16	19	147
22-348 Miller	Inch	5	8	148
22-3500 Dalrymple	Inch	19	1	149
22-4000 Sedgley Schnerring	Inch	3	2	150
22-4000 Senior Varminter	Inch	2	3	151
22-6-40 Contender	Inch	12	20	152
22/06 Ashurst	Inch	3	2	153
22/06 Easling	Inch	3	2	154
22/06 Niedner	Inch	3	2	155
22/06 Triplex Long Neck	Inch	3	2	156
22/06.5 MS	Inch	3	2	157
22/243 Middlestead	Inch	3	2	158
22/275 Mag.	Inch	4	5	159
22/284 Win. (Hutton)	Inch	3	2	160
22/30 Luger	Inch	16	19	161
22/30 US Carb (5.6x33 Johnson)	Inch	17	7	162
22/30-30 Imp.	Inch	2	3	163
22/303 Sprinter,Rocket&Var. R	Inch	7	5	164
22/32-20	Inch	1	1	165
22/350 Rem.	Inch	4	5	166
22/378 Eargesplitten LB	Inch	14	8	167
22/6/40	Inch	12	20	168

Cartridge	Metric/Inch	RCBS #	LEE#	Item #
22/6mm CJ	Inch	3	2	169
220 Jaybird	Inch	3	2	170
220 Rook Rifle CF Long	Inch	29	15	171
220 Russian	Inch	32	12	172
220 Shannon Swift	Inch	11	10	173
220 Swift	Inch	11	10	174
220 Swift PMVF	Inch	11	10	175
220 T K Lee	Inch	7	5	176
220 Weatherby Rocket	Inch	11	10	177
220 Wotkyns Wilson Arrow	Inch	11	10	178
220/303 Brit. Shannon	Inch	7	5	179
221 Rem. Fireball	Inch	10	4	180
222 Eichhorn Lynx (5.7x43)	Inch	10	4	181
222 K Rem.	Inch	10	4	182
222 Rem. Mag.	Inch	10	4	183
222 Rem. Mag. Imp.	Inch	10	4	184
222 Rem. PPC Rimmed	Inch	6	1	185
222 Remington	Inch	10	4	186
222 Rimmed (222 Super)	Inch	32	12	187
223 Rem. (5.56x45)	Inch	10	4	188
224 Clark	Inch	3	2	189
224 Critzer Comet	Inch	1	1	190
224 Donaldson Ace	Inch	11	10	191
224 Durham Jet	Inch	3	2	192
224 Eden	Inch	3	2	193
224 Eichelberger Bee	Inch	1	1	194
224 Harvey Kay-Chuk	Inch	12	20	195
224 ICL Marmot	Inch	11	10	196
224 Lightning	Inch	7	5	197
224 Pfeifer Magnum	Inch	7	5	198
224 R-C Maxi	Inch	6	1	199
224 Stark JDJ	Inch	18	11	200
224 Weatherby	Inch	27	12	201
225 M R	Inch	2	3	202
225 Wasp	Inch	17	7	203
225 Winchester	Inch	11	10	204
226 Barnes QT (quick twist)	Inch	3	2	205
226 Exp. J B Smith	Inch	3	2	206
226 JDJ	Inch	7	5	207
228 Ackley Mag. Belted	Inch	3	2	208
228 Ackley unbelted Med length	Inch	3	2	209
228 Hawk	Inch	3	2	210
228 Krag Ackley	Inch	7	5	211
228 Miller PMVF	Inch	4	5	212
228 Weatherby	Inch	4	5	213
228/22-250 R & M	Inch	3	2	214
228/270 R & M	Inch	3	2	215
228/284 R & M	Inch	3	2	216
23 Thunderbolt (23 Lovell Mag.	Inch	4	5	217
230 Ackley (Long)	Inch	3	2	218
230 Ackley Short	Inch	3	2	219
230 Barnes	Inch	3	2	220
230 C. F. Revolver	Inch	C	0	221
236 Gipson	Inch	3	2	222
236 Super	Inch	3	2	223
236/220 Gipson (6m Swift)	Inch	11	10	224

Cartridges and Shell Holders, *continued*

Cartridge	Metric/Inch	RCBS #	LEE#	Item
240 Beltd Rless NE (Apex) H&H	Inch	3	2	225
240 Cobra	Inch	11	10	226
240 Elliot Cobra	Inch	11	10	227
240 Flanged NE H & H	Inch	18	11	228
240 Gebby Sup. Varminteer	Inch	3	2	229
240 Gebby Super Mag.	Inch	4	5	230
240 Gibbs (24 Gibs)	Inch	3	2	231
240 Madame	Inch	19	1	232
240 Mashburn Falcon	Inch	3	2	233
240 Olsen	Inch	2	3	234
240 Page Pooper	Inch	3	2	235
240 Page Super Pooper	Inch	3	2	236
240 SGW	Inch	3	2	237
240 Super Varminter	Inch	3	2	238
240 Weatherby Mag.	Inch	3	2	239
242 Rimless NE Vickers	Inch	3	2	240
243 (6x48m) US Mil Exp	Inch	3	2	241
243 Ackley Imp.	Inch	3	2	242
243 Epps Imp.	Inch	3	2	243
243 J S Shannon	Inch	3	2	244
243 Mashburn Imp.	Inch	3	2	245
243 Myra	Inch	10	4	246
243 RCBS	Inch	3	2	247
243 Reynolds Special	Inch	3	2	248
243 RKB	Inch	7	5	249
243 Rock Chucker	Inch	3	2	250
243 Super Rock Chucker	Inch	3	2	251
243 Winchester	Inch	3	2	252
243/30-06	Inch	3	2	253
243/303 Brit.	Inch	7	5	254
244 Belted Rless Mag H&H	Inch	4	5	255
244 Durham Mag.	Inch	4	5	256
244 Gipson	Inch	11	10	257
244 Halger Mag Rimless	Inch	3	2	258
244 Rem.	Inch	3	2	259
244 Rem. Ackley Imp.	Inch	3	2	260
244 Rem. Mashburn Imp.	Inch	3	2	261
246 Purdey	Inch	13	16	262
25 A.C.P. (6.35mm)	Inch	29	15	263
25 Ackley Mag.	Inch	4	5	264
25 Ackley Short Krag	Inch	7	5	265
25 Adolph Auto	Inch	3	2	266
25 Brader Sharp Shoulder	Inch	2	3	267
25 Bullberry T C	Inch	2	3	268
25 Burgess	Inch	3	2	269
25 Donaldson Wasp	Inch	2	3	270
25 G & A (Guns & Ammo)	Inch	13	16	271
25 Gibbs (not 256)	Inch	3	2	272
25 Hornet	Inch	12	20	273
25 Hornet Jr.	Inch	12	20	274
25 ICL Mag.	Inch	4	5	275
25 IHMSA	Inch	3	2	276
25 Krag Imp.	Inch	7	5	277
25 Lago	Inch	6	1	278
25 Neidner	Inch	3	2	279
25 Newton 1905	Inch	32	12	280

Cartridge	Metric/Inch	RCBS #	LEE#	Item
25 Newton 1908	Inch	2	3	281
25 Newton 1909	Inch	7	5	282
25 Newton Express	Inch	13	16	283
25 Newton Special 1910	Inch	24	16	284
25 Newton Special rimless	Inch	3	2	285
25 Remington	Inch	19	1	286
25 Roberts	Inch	3	2	287
25 Screwball	Inch	1	1	288
25 Souper	Inch	3	2	289
25 Souper Improved	Inch	3	2	290
25 Tomcat (25-35 Tomcat)	Inch	2	3	291
25 Ugalde TCU	Inch	10	4	292
25 Whelen	Inch	3	2	293
25 x47	Inch	10	4	294
25-06 Ackley Imp.	Inch	3	2	295
25-06 CRP	Inch	3	2	296
25-06 Mashburn	Inch	3	2	297
25-06 Remington	Inch	3	2	298
25-06 Vickery	Inch	3	2	299
25-06 Wilson	Inch	3	2	300
25-20 Winchester WCF	Inch	1	1	301
25-20-86 Stevens Rabbeth SS	Inch	16	19	302
25-21-86 Stevens	Inch	16	19	303
25-25-22 Longoria	Inch	16	19	304
25-25-86 Stevens	Inch	16	19	305
25-35 Ackley Imp.	Inch	2	3	306
25-35 ICL Coyote	Inch	2	3	307
25-35 Winchester (6.5x52R)	Inch	2	3	308
25-36 Marlin	Inch	2	3	309
25/222 Copperhead	Inch	10	4	310
25/222 Rem Mag	Inch	10	4	311
25/224 Weatherby	Inch	27	12	312
25/225 Win	Inch	11	10	313
25/264 Win.	Inch	4	5	314
25/270 ICL Ram (257 ICL)	Inch	3	2	315
25/284 Winchester	Inch	3	2	316
25/30-30	Inch	2	3	317
25/303 Epps	Inch	7	5	318
25/308 Wilson	Inch	3	2	319
25/350 Rem.	Inch	4	5	320
250 Ackley Mag.	Inch	4	5	321
250 Bennett Magnum	Inch	4	5	322
250 Don- Ace	Inch	3	2	323
250 Durham Mag.	Inch	4	5	324
250 Gipson Mag.	Inch	4	5	325
250 Helldiver	Inch	3	2	326
250 Myra	Inch	10	4	327
250-3000 Imp. (250 Ackley)	Inch	3	2	328
250-3000 Savage (250 Sav. HP)	Inch	3	2	329
250/06 Wilson	Inch	3	2	330
255 Dean	Inch	1	1	331
255 Rook Rifle Jeffery	Inch	1	1	332
256 Gipson	Inch	4	5	333
256 Magnum Gibbs rimless	Inch	11	10	334
256 R Mannlicher (6.5 x 53R M-S)	Inch	7	5	335
256 Newton	Inch	3	2	336

Cartridges and Shell Holders, *continued*

Cartridge	Metric or Inch	RCBS #	LEE#	Item #
256 Swift Rimless	Inch	9	2	337
256 Winchester Mag.	Inch	6	1	338
256/06	Inch	3	2	339
257 Arch	Inch	2	3	340
257 Arnold	Inch	4	5	341
257 Baker Mag.	Inch	4	5	342
257 Big Horn	Inch	3	2	343
257 Condor	Inch	13	16	344
257 Critser Mag.	Inch	4	5	345
257 Durham Jet	Inch	3	2	346
257 ICL Whitetail	Inch	11	10	347
257 J D J and #2	Inch	11	10	348
257 Jamison	Inch	13	16	349
257 Kimber	Inch	10	4	350
257 Mag. Revolver	Inch	12	20	351
257 Mashburn	Inch	11	10	352
257 Mashburn Imp.	Inch	3	2	353
257 Roberts	Inch	3	2	354
257 Roberts Ackley Imp.	Inch	3	2	355
257 S. T. Westerner	Inch	4	5	356
257 Sabre Cat	Inch	2	3	357
257 V J	Inch	10	4	358
257 Weatherby Mag.	Inch	4	5	359
258 Condor	Inch	4	5	360
26 Epps	Inch	3	2	361
26 G & A (Guns & Ammo)	Inch	13	16	362
26 Rimless NE BSA	Inch	4	5	363
260 A A R	Inch	3	2	364
260 Bobcat	Inch	3	2	365
260 Remington	Inch	3	2	366
263 Express (6.5/308)	Inch	3	2	367
263 Sabre (Shannon)	Inch	3	2	368
264 Durham Mag.	Inch	4	5	369
264 Hollis	Inch	3	2	370
264 Short Connell Mag.	Inch	4	5	371
264 Thor	Inch	4	5	372
264 Win Mag. Imp	Inch	4	5	373
264 Winchester Mag.	Inch	4	5	374
264 x61 Shannon	Inch	4	5	375
265 RCBS	Inch	3	2	376
270 Ackley Imp.	Inch	3	2	377
270 Ackley Mag.	Inch	4	5	378
270 Arnold	Inch	4	5	379
270 Brooks Short Mag.	Inch	4	5	380
270 Durham Mag.	Inch	3	2	381
270 Gibbs	Inch	3	2	382
270 Gipson Magnum	Inch	4	5	383
270 Helldiver Wallack&Hubbard	Inch	3	2	384
270 I C L Jaguar	Inch	3	2	385
270 ICL Magnum	Inch	4	5	386
270 IHMSA	Inch	3	2	387
270 J D J	Inch	11	10	388
270 Mashburn Mag. Long	Inch	4	5	389
270 Mashburn Mag. Short	Inch	4	5	390
270 Mashburn Super Mag.	Inch	4	5	391
270 Max	Inch	6	1	392

Cartridge	Metric or Inch	RCBS #	LEE#	Item #
270 Newton Ackley Imp. NB	Inch	4	5	393
270 Niedner Magnum	Inch	4	5	394
270 Redding	Inch	3	2	395
270 Ren (270/22 Hornet)	Inch	12	20	396
270 Rimmed	Inch	7	5	397
270 Savage Titus	Inch	3	2	398
270 Souper	Inch	3	2	399
270 TNT	Inch	3	2	400
270 V J	Inch	10	4	401
270 Weatherby Mag.	Inch	4	5	402
270 Winchester	Inch	3	2	403
270-4000 Gipson	Inch	4	5	404
270/223	Inch	10	4	405
270/257 Imp. Ackley (6.86EPRS)	Inch	3	2	406
270/284 Win.	Inch	3	2	407
270/300 Weatherby	Inch	4	5	408
270/303R Epps	Inch	7	5	409
270/308 Don-Ace	Inch	3	2	410
270/308 Imp.	Inch	3	2	411
270/338 Win.	Inch	4	5	412
270/6mm Rem.	Inch	3	2	413
270/7mm Rem Mag	Inch	4	5	414
275 #2 Rigby Mag. (7mmR)	Inch	4	5	415
275 Bennett	Inch	4	5	416
275 Bland Maxim	Inch	13	16	417
275 Bltd. Rless Mag NE H & H	Inch	4	5	418
275 Flanged Mag. H&H	Inch	22	17	419
275 Jeffery Rook Rifle	Inch	1	1	420
275 Rimless Rigby (7x57)	Inch	3	2	421
276 Ackley Mag.	Inch	4	5	422
276 B-J Express	Inch	4	5	423
276 Carlson	Inch	4	5	424
276 Dubiel Magnum	Inch	4	5	425
276 Enfield P-13 Exp.	Inch	4	5	426
276 Newton	Inch	4	5	427
276 Pedersen	Inch	3	2	428
277 Brooks Short Mag.	Inch	4	5	429
277 Smith	Inch	4	5	430
28 Ross (28 Roosevelt)	Inch	18	11	431
28-30-120 Stevens	Inch	32	12	432
280 Dubiel	Inch	4	5	433
280 Flanged N E (Lancaster)	Inch	5	8	434
280 Gipson Super Magnum	Inch	4	5	435
280 Halger Magnum	Inch	13	16	436
280 Rem.	Inch	3	2	437
280 Rem. Imp. Ackley	Inch	3	2	438
280 Rem. J R S	Inch	3	2	439
280 Rimless Jeffery (333-280)	Inch	4	5	440
280 Rimless Ross	Inch	37	18	441
280 W. R. Hi Velocity	Inch	3	2	442
280/06	Inch	3	2	443
280/30 British (4.85x49)	Inch	3	2	444
284 Jamison	Inch	13	16	445
284 Jet Durham Mag.	Inch	4	5	446
284 Williams	Inch	4	5	447
284 Winchester	Inch	3	2	448

Cartridges and Shell Holders, *continued*

Cartridge	Metric or Inch	RCBS #	LEE#	Item #
285 OKH	Inch	3	2	449
288 Barnes Supreme	Inch	4	5	450
297 C F Revolver	Inch	17	7	451
297/230 Lancaster Sporting	Inch	17	7	452
297/230 Morris Long	Inch	12	20	453
297/230 Morris Short	Inch	12	20	454
297/250 Express	inch	11	10	455
297/250 Rook	Inch	12	20	456
298 Minex	Inch	1	1	457
30 Adolph #1	Inch	3	2	458
30 Alaskan Bower	Inch	2	3	459
30 Alaskan Mag.	Inch	4	5	460
30 American	Inch	21	11	461
30 Apache (30/223)	Inch	10	4	462
30 Arch Imp.	Inch	2	3	463
30 B R Rem. (308 B R)	Inch	3	2	464
30 Blaser Rimmed (30R)	Inch	4	5	465
30 Borchardt (7.65mm)	Inch	10	4	466
30 CCBS	Inch	3	2	467
30 Cody Express	Inch	37	18	468
30 Donaldson Wasp	Inch	2	3	469
30 G & A (Guns & Ammo)	Inch	13	16	470
30 Gibbs	Inch	3	2	471
30 Herrett	Inch	2	3	472
30 Howell	Inch	5	8	473
30 ICL Mag.	Inch	4	5	474
30 IHMSA	Inch	3	2	475
30 Imp. Arch	Inch	2	3	476
30 Johnson	Inch	3	2	477
30 Kurz	Inch	3	2	478
30 Lever Power	Inch	15	10	479
30 Luger (7.65 Parabellum)	Inch	16	19	480
30 M1 Carbine	Inch	17	7	481
30 Mauser (7.63x25mm)	Inch	16	19	482
30 Merrill	Inch	11	10	483
30 Newton Belted (30/338 Win)	Inch	4	5	484
30 Newton non belted	Inch	4	5	485
30 NJM	Inch	3	2	486
30 Pedersen (US Pistol)	Inch	12	20	487
30 Purdey Flanged Nitro	Inch	7	5	488
30 Rem. Auto	Inch	19	1	489
30 Rimmed Mag.	Inch	24	16	490
30 Short Wolfe	Inch	14	8	491
30 Smith	Inch	4	5	492
30 Streaker Revolver	Inch	2	3	493
30 Super Mag. Flanged H & H	Inch	22	17	494
30 Viper	Inch	4	5	495
30-06 Accelerator	Inch	3	2	496
30-06 Ackley Imp.	Inch	3	2	497
30-06 ICL Caribou	Inch	3	2	498
30-06 Springfield (7.62x63mm)	Inch	3	2	499
30-06 Springfield Armor Pierc.	Inch	3	2	500
30-06 WCF	Inch	3	2	501
30-20 Hoffman	Inch	1	1	502
30-30 Ackley Imp. Win.	Inch	2	3	503
30-30 Rem. (30 Rem.)	Inch	19	1	504

Cartridge	Metric or Inch	RCBS #	LEE#	Item #
30-30 Wesson	Inch	32	12	505
30-30 Win. Accelerator	Inch	2	3	506
30-30 Win. (7.62x51R)	Inch	2	3	507
30-40 Krag Jorgensen	Inch	7	5	508
30-78 Single Shot	Inch	2	3	509
30/222 Rem French Sur Armes	Inch	10	4	510
30/222 Rem Mag.	Inch	10	4	511
30/224 Wthby.	Inch	27	12	512
30/284 Win. (Meyer or HB)	Inch	3	2	513
30/30 Carb. Kurz	Inch	3	2	514
30/338	Inch	4	5	515
30/348 Imp. Ackley (Hutton)	Inch	5	8	516
30/350 Rem	Inch	4	5	517
30/357 Hoskins	Inch	6	1	518
30/357 Paxton	Inch	6	1	519
30/378 Arch	Inch	14	8	520
30/378 Weatherby	Inch	14	8	521
30/416 Rigby Imp.	Inch	37	18	522
30/444 Marlin	Inch	28	11	523
30/505 Super Mag	Inch	470 NE	0	524
30/8mm Rem.	Inch	4	5	525
300 (295) Rook Rifle	Inch	16	19	526
300 Ackley Imp.	Inch	4	5	527
300 Adrian	Inch	7	5	528
300 Apex AAR	Inch	4	5	529
300 Arnold	Inch	4	5	530
300 Bennett Mag.	Inch	4	5	531
300 Bltd. Rless Mag. H & H	Inch	4	5	532
300 Canadian Mag.	Inch	4	5	533
300 Dakota	Inch	13	16	534
300 Durham Mag.	Inch	4	5	535
300 Gates Mag.	Inch	3	2	536
300 H & H Mag Imp.	Inch	4	5	537
300 Hammond	Inch	4	5	538
300 Helldiver	Inch	3	2	539
300 Hoffman	Inch	4	5	540
300 ICL Grizzly	Inch	4	5	541
300 ICL Grizzly Cub	Inch	4	5	542
300 ICL Magnum	Inch	4	5	543
300 ICL Tornado	Inch	3	2	544
300 Imperial Mag.	Inch	4	5	545
300 Jamison	Inch	13	16	546
300 Jarrett	Inch	4	5	547
300 Kong	Inch	14	8	548
300 Mashburn Short Mag.	Inch	4	5	549
300 Mashburn Super Mag.	Inch	4	5	550
300 MER	Inch	14	8	551
300 Pegasus	Inch	14	8	552
300 Phoenix	Inch	37	18	553
300 PMVF Powell & Miller	Inch	4	5	554
300 RCBS Kodiak Mag.	Inch	4	5	555
300 Rem Ultra Mag	Inch	4	5	556
300 Rook (300 Long CF)	Inch	10	4	557
300 Rook Rifle (295)	Inch	10	4	558
300 Savage	Inch	3	2	559
300 Sherwood (Long Kynoch)	Inch	16	19	560

Shellholder Interchangeability Tables

Cartridges and Shell Holders, *continued*

Cartridge	Metric or Inch	RCBS #	LEE#	Item #
300 Super Mag.Flanged H&H	Inch	37	18	561
300 TNT	Inch	3	2	562
300 Tooley Mag. Extreme	Inch	13	16	563
300 Wade Mag.	Inch	4	5	564
300 Weatherby Mag.	Inch	4	5	565
300 Whisper	Inch	10	4	566
300 Wilkenson	Inch	C	0	567
300 Winchester Mag.	Inch	4	5	568
303 Adder Midrange 1 1/2"	Inch	24	16	569
303 British	Inch	7	5	570
303 British Imp. Epps	Inch	7	5	571
303 Elliot Exp.	Inch	24	16	572
303 ICL Imp.	Inch	7	5	573
303 Magnum Rimless Jeffery	Inch	14	8	574
303 Mauser (7.65 Fraser)	Inch	3	2	575
303 Savage	Inch	21	11	576
303 Wilkensen Adapter	Inch	C	0	577
303-375 Axite (375-303)	Inch	8	13	578
303/270 Rimmed	Inch	24	16	579
305 Rook (310/300 Rook)	Inch	1	1	580
307 Winchester	Inch	2	3	581
308 Accelerator	Inch	3	2	582
308 B-J Express	Inch	4	5	583
308 Barnes Supreme	Inch	4	5	584
308 BR 1 3/4" TNT	Inch	3	2	585
308 Doggie	Inch	3	2	586
308 Hammond	Inch	4	5	587
308 Norma Mag.	Inch	4	5	588
308 Rem. B R	Inch	3	2	589
308 Whisper	Inch	10	4	590
308 Win. (7.62x51mm)	Inch	3	2	591
308 Winchester Short 1.778	Inch	3	2	592
308 x 1" JMP	Inch	3	2	593
308 x 1.5" Barnes	Inch	3	2	594
309 Hammond	Inch	14	8	595
309 JDJ	Inch	28	11	596
310 Cadet Martini 1 1/16"	Inch	1	1	597
310 Cattle Killer 7/8"	Inch	1	1	598
310 Rook (305 & 310/300 K)	Inch	1	1	599
311 Imperial Mag.	Inch	4	5	600
312 Express	Inch	4	5	601
318 Rimless N. E. W. Richards	Inch	3	2	602
32 ACP (7,65mm)	Inch	17	7	603
32 Bullard (32-40-150)	Inch	14	8	604
32 Colt LMR (32-20)	Inch	6	1	605
32 Ex-Short CF Protector	Inch	17	7	606
32 Extra Long Ballard (1.24")	Inch	16	19	607
32 H & R Mag.	Inch	23	4	608
32 Ideal (32-25-150)	Inch	1	1	609
32 Long CF (320 Long Rev.)	Inch	10	4	610
32 Long Colt (320 Rook) .78"	Inch	16	19	611
32 Long Rifle (320 Long Rev.)	Inch	10	4	612
32 Mervin Hulbert Short	Inch	23	4	613
32 New Police (32 S&W Long)	Inch	23	4	614
32 Rem. Rifle	Inch	19	1	615
32 S & W	Inch	23	4	616

Cartridge	Metric or Inch	RCBS #	LEE#	Item #
32 S & W Long	Inch	23	4	617
32 S&W Revolving Rifle	Inch	6	1	618
32 Short Colt	Inch	16	19	619
32 Webley (320 Rev.)	Inch	16	19	620
32 Win. S L R	Inch	16	19	621
32 Win. Special	Inch	2	3	622
32-20 Hoffman	Inch	10	4	623
32-20 Win. WCF & Pistol	Inch	1	1	624
32-30 Rem.	Inch	6	1	625
32-35-156 Stevens & Maynard	Inch	2	3	626
32-40 Ballard & Winchester	Inch	18	11	627
32-40-150 Rem. (Hepburn #3)	Inch	7	5	628
32-40-22 Niedner (22 Hi Power)	Inch	2	3	629
32-44 X Long (S&W) aka 30 S&W	Inch	6	1	630
32/505 Super Mag.	Inch	470 NE	0	631
320 Long Rook 25/32" .780"	Inch	10	4	632
320 Rev. Long (32 LCF) .905"	Inch	10	4	633
320 Short Rev. .660"	Inch	16	19	634
320/230 Rook	Inch	10	4	635
321 Greener (R 3 1/4")	Inch	8 Lebel	17	636
322 Rigby NE	Inch	24	16	637
322 Swift (Match)	Inch	4	5	638
323 Critiser	Inch	4	5	639
33 Belted Rless NE BSA (330)	Inch	4	5	640
33 G & A (Guns & Ammo)	Inch	13	16	641
33 Newton	Inch	4	5	642
33 Poachers Pet	Inch	4	5	643
33 Win. CF	Inch	5	8	644
33-50 O'Neil (33 Mauser)	Inch	3	2	645
33/308	Inch	3	2	646
33/308 Smith	Inch	3	2	647
330 Dakota	Inch	13	16	648
333 Ackley Imp. Mag.	Inch	4	5	649
333 Ackley Short Mag.	Inch	4	5	650
333 Barnes Supreme	Inch	4	5	651
333 Express B-J	Inch	4	5	652
333 Flanged NE Jeffery	Inch	37	18	653
333 Griffen & Howe	Inch	4	5	654
333 OKH non belted JDJ	Inch	3	2	655
333 Rimless N. E. Jeffery	Inch	35	14	656
333 x 61 Carlson Mag.	Inch	4	5	657
334 OKH Belted	Inch	4	5	658
338 A & H	Inch	13	16	659
338 A Square	Inch	14	8	660
338 ABE	Inch	13	16	661
338 Arnold	Inch	4	5	662
338 ASS	Inch	2	3	663
338 B G S	Inch	13	16	664
338 Black Mesa Exp.	Inch	4	5	665
338 Collins	Inch	14	8	666
338 Excalibur	Inch	14	8	667
338 Gibbs	Inch	3	2	668
338 IHMSA	Inch	3	2	669
338 Imperial Mag.	Inch	4	5	670
338 Jamison	Inch	13	16	671
338 JDJ Whisper	Inch	2	3	672

Cartridges and Shell Holders, *continued*

Cartridge	Metric/Inch	RCBS #	LEE#	Item
338 Lapua Mag. (8.58x71)	Inch	37	18	673
338 Scovill	Inch	3	2	674
338 Whisper JDJ	Inch	3	2	675
338 Winchester Mag.	Inch	4	5	676
338-06 (338/30-06)	Inch	3	2	677
338-74 Keith Rimmed	Inch	4	5	678
338/06 Improved	Inch	3	2	679
338/223 Straight 338-223 Long	Inch	10	4	680
338/270 H G T	Inch	3	2	681
338/284	Inch	3	2	682
338/30-30	Inch	2	3	683
338/300 H&H	Inch	4	5	684
338/300 Win.	Inch	4	5	685
338/303	Inch	7	5	686
338/308 Ackley Imp.	Inch	3	2	687
338/308 Baby Magnum	Inch	3	2	688
338/378 K T	Inch	14	8	689
338/378 Kubla Khan	Inch	14	8	690
338/378 Weatherby	Inch	14	8	691
338/404 Sniper	Inch	13	16	692
338/416 Brooks & Sniper	Inch	37	18	693
338/50 Talbot	Inch	50 BMG	0	694
338/8mm Rem.	Inch	4	5	695
339 Deja Vu	Inch	4	5	696
340 Gerbil	Inch	13	16	697
340 Gibbs	Inch	3	2	698
340 Rawson Mag.	Inch	14	8	699
340 Revolver	Inch	1	1	700
340 Weatherby	Inch	4	5	701
345 Machine Rifle	Inch	10	4	702
348 Win.	Inch	5	8	703
348 Win. Ackley Imp.	Inch	5	8	704
35 Ackley Mag. 40* Short	Inch	4	5	705
35 Ackley Mag. Imp. Long	Inch	4	5	706
35 Apex Mag.	Inch	4	5	707
35 Brown & Whelen	Inch	3	2	708
35 Burgess	Inch	3	2	709
35 G & H	inch	4	5	710
35 IHMSA	Inch	3	2	711
35 Lever Power	Inch	20	13	712
35 Newton	Inch	4	5	713
35 Remington Rifle	Inch	9	2	714
35 Rimmed Mag.	Inch	24	16	715
35 S&W Auto	Inch	10	4	716
35 Whelen	Inch	3	2	717
35 Whelen Ackley Imp.	Inch	3	2	718
35 Win. S L R	Inch	19	1	719
35 Winchester	Inch	7	5	720
35-30 Maynard 1882	Inch	28	11	721
35-40 Maynard 1882	Inch	18	11	722
35/284 Win. (Hutton)	Inch	3	2	723
35/30-30 (35-30)	Inch	2	3	724
35/318 NE Rimless WR	Inch	3	2	725
35/348 Win.	Inch	5	8	726
35/378 Wthby	Inch	14	8	727
35/444 Marlin	Inch	28	11	728

Cartridge	Metric/Inch	RCBS #	LEE#	Item
35/505 Super Mag	Inch	470 NE	0	729
350 G. & H. (350 H & H Mag)	Inch	4	5	730
350 Maine Guide	Inch	2	3	731
350 Mashburn Short Mag.	Inch	4	5	732
350 Mashburn Super Mag.	Inch	4	5	733
350 Rem. Mag.	Inch	4	5	734
350 Rigby #2 Rimmed (2 3/4")	Inch	4	5	735
350 Rigby Flanged (450-350)	Inch	4	5	736
350 Smith	Inch	4	5	737
350 Williams	Inch	4	5	738
350/7mm Rigby	Inch	4	5	739
351 Win. SLR	Inch	1	1	740
354 Ross	Inch	13	16	741
356 Federal Auto	Inch	1	1	742
356 TSW (Team S&W) Auto Pistol	Inch	1	1	743
356 Winchester	Inch	2	3	744
357 Auto Mag.	Inch	3	2	745
357 Elliot Exp.	Inch	24	16	746
357 Herrett	Inch	2	3	747
357 L & L	Inch	28	11	748
357 Magnum Pistol	Inch	6	1	749
357 Magnum Rifle	Inch	6	1	750
357 Peterbuilt	Inch	3	2	751
357 Rem. Max	Inch	6	1	752
357 Sig Auto	Inch	27	19	753
357 Super Mag. by E Gates	Inch	6	1	754
357/44 Bains Davis	Inch	8	13	755
357/44 Bobcat	Inch	18	11	756
357/45 L A R (G. W. M.)	Inch	3	2	757
357/45 Long Colt	Inch	20	11	758
358 B-J Express	Inch	4	5	759
358 Barnes Supreme	Inch	4	5	760
358 JDJ	Inch	28	11	761
358 Lee Mag.	Inch	11	10	762
358 Norma Mag.	Inch	4	5	763
358 S. T. Alaskan	Inch	4	5	764
358 SOB	Inch	4	5	765
358 Super Bower	Inch	28	11	766
358 Winchester	Inch	3	2	767
358 Yukoner	Inch	4	5	768
360 #5 Rook (1.05")	Inch	9	2	769
360 Alex Henry 2 7/16"	Inch	36	2A	770
360 B. P. Express 2 1/4"	Inch	34	9	771
360 Cane or Garden Gun	Inch	9	2	772
360 Gibbs #1	Inch	3	2	773
360 Gibbs #2	Inch	3	2	774
360 Gibbs #3	Inch	33	11	775
360 Imperial Mag.	Inch	4	5	776
360 NE 2 1/4"	Inch	34	9	777
360 NE #2 3"	Inch	31	0	778
360 Nitro for B P 2 1/4"	Inch	34	9	779
360 Rev. (38 Short)	Inch	3	2	780
360 W. R. #3	Inch	28	11	781
360/300 Fraser (300) .95"	Inch	30	9	782
369 NE Purdey	Inch	8 Lebel	17	783
37 Rimmed	Inch	7	5	784

Cartridges and Shell Holders, *continued*

Cartridge	Metric/Inch	RCBS #	LEE#	Item
373 Express	Inch	28	11	785
375 A-Square	Inch	14	8	786
375 Ackley Imp.	Inch	4	5	787
375 Alaskan	Inch	5	8	788
375 Barnes Supreme	Inch	4	5	789
375 Belted Rimless Mag. H&H	Inch	4	5	790
375 Black Mesa Exp.	Inch	4	5	791
375 Breeding	Inch	13	16	792
375 Dakota	Inch	13	16	793
375 Durham Short Magnum	Inch	4	5	794
375 Epstein Ballistek	Inch	4	5	795
375 Express	Inch	28	11	796
375 Flanged Mag. NE H&H	Inch	22	17	797
375 Flanged NE 2 1/2"	Inch	13	16	798
375 Gipson-Newton	Inch	3	2	799
375 Hawk/ Scovill	Inch	3	2	800
375 Hoffman	Inch	4	5	801
375 Howdah	Inch	470 NE	0	802
375 Howell	Inch	13	16	803
375 ICL Kodiak	Inch	4	5	804
375 ICL Mag.	inch	4	5	805
375 JDJ	Inch	28	11	806
375 JDJ Whisper	Inch	3	2	807
375 JRS (Jones Rhino Stomper)	Inch	4	5	808
375 Mashburn Long Mag.	Inch	4	5	809
375 Newton Belted (375-378 CT)	Inch	4	5	810
375 Payne Express	Inch	5	8	811
375 Rless NE 2 1/4" 9.5x57 MS	Inch	3	2	812
375 Scovill	Inch	3	2	813
375 Shannon	Inch	3	2	814
375 Super Mag.	Inch	2	3	815
375 Weatherby Mag.	Inch	4	5	816
375 Whelen	Inch	3	2	817
375 Whelen Ackley Imp.	Inch	3	2	818
375 Winchester	Inch	2	3	819
375 x 38-40 Rimless	Inch	3	2	820
375-303 Axite W. R.	Inch	28	11	821
375-370 Fl. 2 1/2" (370 NE) #2	Inch	4	5	822
375/06 (375 Whelen & JDJ	Inch	3	2	823
375/284	Inch	3	2	824
375/338 (Chatfield-Taylor)	Inch	4	5	825
375/348	Inch	5	8	826
375/405 Longo	Inch	24	16	827
377 Elliot	Inch	4	5	828
378 Weatherby	Inch	14	8	829
38 Ballard Ex Long & Wesson	Inch	6	1	830
38 Colt Auto	Inch	39	19	831
38 Colt Lightning Mag. Rifle	Inch	4	5	832
38 Colt New Police (38 S & W)	Inch	6	1	833
38 Colt Super Auto	Inch	39	19	834
38 Long Colt	Inch	6	1	835
38 Merwin- Hulbert Rev.	Inch	9	2	836
38 S & W Rev. (Colt New Police	Inch	6	1	837
38 Short Colt Long Case .762"	Inch	6	1	838
38 Short Colt Short Case	Inch	6	1	839
38 Webley Rev.	Inch	3	2	840

Cartridge	Metric/Inch	RCBS #	LEE#	Item
38-35-215 Stevens Everlasting	Inch	8	13	841
38-40 (38 Win. C. F.)	Inch	35	14	842
38-40-245 Rem. Hepburn (38-36	Inch	24	16	843
38-45-190 Bullard (38 Bullard)	Inch	4	5	844
38-45-256 Stevens	Inch	7	5	845
38-50 Ballard (Everlasting)	Inch	8	13	846
38-50 Maynard 1882	Inch	28	11	847
38-50-265 Rem. Hepburn	Inch	24	16	848
38-55 Win. & Ballard & Marlin	Inch	2	3	849
38-56 Ron Long	Inch	14	8	850
38-56 Shilo Sharps	Inch	14	8	851
38-56 Win. CF	Inch	14	8	852
38-56 Win. CF Imp.	Inch	14	8	853
38-70 Winchester	Inch	5	8	854
38-72 Winchester	Inch	7	5	855
38-90 Win. Express	Inch	13	16	856
38/45 Auto (45/38 Auto)	Inch	3	2	857
380 Auto (9mm Kurz 9x17)	Inch	10	4	858
380 Long Rook Rifle 31/32"	Inch	6	1	859
380 Revolver Short	Inch	6	1	860
380 Rigby 1 3/4"	Inch	18	11	861
380 Rigby 2 1/4"	Inch	18	11	862
40 BSA Rifle	Inch	3	2	863
40 S & W Auto (10mm Short)	Inch	27	19	864
40 x 1 7/8"	Inch	28	11	865
40 x 2" (10.6x51)	Inch	4	5	866
40- 40 Maynard 1865	Inch	50 BMG	0	867
40- 40 Maynard 1873	Inch	C	0	868
40- 40 Maynard 1882	Inch	24	16	869
40- 45-265 Rem. 1 7/8"	Inch	7	5	870
40- 50-265 Sharps B N 1 11/16"	Inch	5	8	871
40- 50-265 Sharps Str 1 7/8"	Inch	5	8	872
40- 60 Colt N.L. (Marlin)	Inch	5	8	873
40- 60 Marlin	Inch	5	8	874
40- 60 Maynard 1882	Inch	24	16	875
40- 60 Win. (40-60 Colt)	Inch	8 Lebel	17	876
40- 63 Ballard Everlasting	Inch	5	8	877
40- 65 Ballard Everlasting	Inch	14	8	878
40- 65 Ron Long 406	Inch	14	8	879
40- 65 Win. and Marlin	Inch	5	8	880
40- 70 Ballard	Inch	5	8	881
40- 70 Maynard 1865	Inch	C	RTT	882
40- 70 Maynard 1882	Inch	7	5	883
40- 70 Peabody What Cheer	Inch	577 Ty	0	884
40- 70 Winchester	Inch	14	8	885
40- 70-330 Sharps Str 2 1/2"	Inch	14	8	886
40- 70-330 Sharps & Rem BN	Inch	22	17	887
40- 70-330 Sharps BN 40 2 1/4"	Inch	14	8	888
40- 72-330 Winchester	Inch	4	5	889
40- 75-259 Bullard	Inch	8 Lebel	17	890
40- 82-260 Win. C F	Inch	14	8	891
40- 90-370 Sharps BN	Inch	14	8	892
40- 90-370 Sharps Str	Inch	13	16	893
40- 90-400 Bullard	Inch	505 Gibbs	0	894
40- 90-500 Peabody What Cheer	Inch	577 Ty	0	895

Cartridges and Shell Holders, *continued*

Cartridge	Metric/Inch	RCBS #	LEE#	Item
40-110 Winchester CF Express	Inch	450 #2 NE	0	896
40/348 Ackley Imp.	Inch	5	8	897
40/348 Win.	Inch	5	8	898
400 B S A	Inch	4	5	899
400 Corbon JDJ	Inch	3	2	900
400 Jeffery Cordite Exp Rimmed	Inch	31	0	901
400 N for B P 3" (Light Exp.)	Inch	4	5	902
400 Niedner	Inch	4	5	903
400 W. Richards 2 3/4"	Inch	37	18	904
400 Whelen	Inch	3	2	905
400 Whelen Magnum	Inch	4	5	906
400 Williams	Inch	4	5	907
400/350R NE 2 3/4"	Inch	4	5	908
400/360 NE 2 3/4" Purdey	Inch	4	5	909
400/360 NE 2 3/4" W.R. Rimmed	Inch	4	5	910
400/360 NE 2 3/4" W.R. Rless	Inch	11	10	911
400/360 Rigby by D. Frazier	Inch	4	5	912
400/375 Belted NE H&H	Inch	3	2	913
401 Herter Powermag	Inch	34	9	914
401 Winchester	Inch	3	2	915
401 Winchester S. L. R.	Inch	3	2	916
404 B-J Exp.	Inch	4	5	917
404 Barnes Supreme	Inch	4	5	918
404 Rless NE Jeffery (10.75x73	Inch	13	16	919
405 Winchester	Inch	24	16	920
408 Win. Magnum	Inch	4	5	921
408 Winchester Experimental	Inch	20	13	922
41 Action Express	Inch	16	19	923
41 Avenger Barnes)	Inch	3	2	924
41 CF Derringer	Inch	34	9	925
41 JDJ	Inch	28	11	926
41 JMP Jurras Mag P (Auto Mag	Inch	3	2	927
41 Long Colt	Inch	3	2	928
41 Mag. (S&W & Rem.)	Inch	30	9	929
41 Short Colt D A Long Case	Inch	3	2	930
41 Wheems SA Pistol	Inch	9	2	931
41 Wildey	Inch	16	19	932
41/505 Super Mag	Inch	470 NE	0	933
410 Revolver Long .684"	Inch	3	2	934
411 Bear Swamp	Inch	14	8	935
411 Hawk	Inch	3	2	936
411 JDJ	Inch	28	11	937
411 KDF	Inch	4	5	938
411 Mag. (338 Win.)	Inch	4	5	939
411 Whammy by JDJ	Inch	4	5	940
411/300 Win. Mag.	Inch	4	5	941
411/460 Wthby.	Inch	14	8	942
414 Gates	Inch	20	2A	943
416 Barnes Supreme	Inch	4	5	944
416 Chapuis	Inch	450#2 NE	0	945
416 Dakota	Inch	13	16	946
416 Express	Inch	4	5	947
416 H & C Mag.	Inch	14	8	948
416 Hoffmam	Inch	4	5	949
416 Howdah	Inch	470 NE	0	950
416 Howell	Inch	13	16	951

Cartridge	Metric/Inch	RCBS #	LEE#	Item
416 JDJ	Inch	28	11	952
416 Remington	Inch	4	5	953
416 Rigby	Inch	37	18	954
416 Taylor	Inch	4	5	955
416 Weatherby	Inch	5	8	956
416/338	Inch	4	5	957
416/348 Win.	Inch	5	8	958
42 Russian (10.75x58R) Rifle	Inch	C	0	959
423 Hoffman	Inch	21	11	960
423 Van Horn Nitro	Inch	14	8	961
424 OKH	Inch	4	5	962
425 Express	Inch	4	5	963
425 Lee Mag.	Inch	11	10	964
425 Wes. Richards Rebated R	Inch	11	10	965
425 Wes. Richards Semi Rimmed	Inch	33	11	966
43 Egyptian Guard (11.43 x50R)	Inch	577 Ty	0	967
43 Russian (43 Berdan)	Inch	450 #2 NE	0	968
43 Spanish Rem. (11&11.1x58R)	Inch	22	17	969
43 Werndl (11.15x58R)	Inch	577 Ty	0	970
430 Long Rook (Carbine 1.025")	Inch	28	11	971
44 Auto Mag	Inch	3	2	972
44 Bull Dog Webley	Inch	18	11	973
44 Colt Black Powder	Inch	18	11	974
44 Colt L. M. R. (44-40 Marlin	Inch	18	11	975
44 Evans Long (New Model)	Inch	8	13	976
44 Evans Short	Inch	8	13	977
44 Express	Inch	5	8	978
44 Extra Long Ballard (S. S.)	Inch	4	5	979
44 Game Getter Marble Rd Ball	Inch	24	16	980
44 Henry C. F.	Inch	4	5	981
44 Long Ballard (X Lng Howard	Inch	8	13	982
44 Magnum Rifle	Inch	18	11	983
44 Merwin & Hulbert Rev.	Inch	18	11	984
44 Rem. Mag.	Inch	18	11	985
44 S & W American	Inch	18	11	986
44 S & W Magnum	Inch	18	11	987
44 S & W Russian	Inch	7	5	988
44 S & W Special	Inch	18	11	989
44 SM	Inch	28	11	990
44 Van Houten Super	Inch	20	13	991
44 W. C. F. & others (44-40)	Inch	18	11	992
44 Webley Revolver (442 RIC)	Inch	18	11	993
44 Wesson Extra Long (44 Long)	Inch	20	13	994
44 Wildey	Inch	16	19	995
44- 40 Extra Long Winchester	Inch	18	11	996
44- 40 WCF (44 WCF)	Inch	18	11	997
44- 60 Maynard 1882	Inch	5	8	998
44- 60 Sharps BN 1 7/8"	Inch	22	17	999
44- 60 Winchester	Inch	22	17	1000
44- 60-395 Peabody Creedmoor	Inch	22	17	1001
44- 65 Stevens	Inch	24	16	1002
44- 70 Maynard 1882	Inch	5	8	1003
44- 75 Ballard Everlasting	Inch	14	8	1004
44- 77-380 Sharps & Rem BN	Inch	22	17	1005
44- 85 Wesson (42-85)	Inch	4	5	1006
44- 90 -405 Sharps BN	Inch	22	17	1007

Cartridges and Shell Holders, *continued*

Cartridge	Metric/Inch	RCBS #	LEE#	Item
44- 90 -500 Rem.Special BN	Inch	22	17	1008
44- 90 Rem. Straight	Inch	5	8	1009
44- 95-550 Peabody What Cheer	Inch	577 NE	0	1010
44-100 Ballard	Inch	22	17	1011
44-100 Maynard 1882	Inch	5	8	1012
44-100 Wesson (42)	Inch	8 Lebel	17	1013
44-100-500 Rem. Creedmore	Inch	5	8	1014
44/505 Super Mag	Inch	470 NE	0	1015
440 Short Revolver	Inch	28	11	1016
442 Carbine 1 1/4"	Inch	28	11	1017
442 Rev.CF RIC (44 Webley)	Inch	18	11	1018
444 Marlin	Inch	28	11	1019
445 Super Magnum (Gates)	Inch	18	11	1020
45 ACP	Inch	3	2	1021
45 ACP Short	Inch	3	2	1022
45 Auto Rim	Inch	13	16	1023
45 Colt Rev. (45 Long Colt)	Inch	20	13	1024
45 J Magnum	Inch	3	2	1025
45 Long Colt Benet Ins Primed	Inch	20	13	1026
45 S.& W. Schofield	Inch	4	5	1027
45 Silhouette IHMSA	Inch	14	8	1028
45 Super ACP	Inch	3	2	1029
45 Webley Rev.	Inch	4	5	1030
45 Wildey	Inch	16	19	1031
45 Win. Magnum	Inch	36	2A	1032
45- 50-290 Peabody SPORTING	Inch	505Gibbs	0	1033
45- 60 Wesson (Kittredge Rem.	Inch	13	16	1034
45- 60 Winchester	Inch	5	8	1035
45- 70 Maynard 1882	Inch	5	8	1036
45- 70 U S Govt.	Inch	14	8	1037
45- 70 Van Choate 2 1/4"	Inch	14	8	1038
45- 75 Winchester BN	Inch	31	0	1039
45- 75-400 Sharps Str (45-70)	Inch	14	8	1040
45- 80 Sharps 3 1/8"	Inch	14	8	1041
45- 80-420 Sharps 2 1/10"	Inch	14	8	1042
45- 82 Win.	Inch	14	8	1043
45- 85 Bullard	Inch	14	8	1044
45- 85 Win.	Inch	14	8	1045
45- 90 Win CF	Inch	14	8	1046
45- 90-550 Sharps Str. 2 3/4"	Inch	14	8	1047
45- 95 Peabody	Inch	577Ty	0	1048
45-100 Ballard Everlasting	Inch	22	17	1049
45-100 Sharps Str. 2.1"	Inch	14	8	1050
45-100-500 Sharps Str 2.4"	Inch	14	8	1051
45-100-500 Sharps Str 2.875"	Inch	14	8	1052
45-120-550 Sharps Str 3 1/4"	Inch	14	8	1053
45-125 Sharps Str. 3 1/4"	Inch	14	8	1054
45-125 Winchester Express	Inch	505Gibbs	0	1055
45/348 Win. Ackley Imp.	Inch	5	8	1056
450 Ackley	Inch	4	5	1057
450 Alaskan (450/348)	Inch	5	8	1058
450 Assegai	Inch	577Ty	0	1059
450 B-J Express	Inch	4	5	1060
450 B. P. Exp 3 1/4" (45 Eley	Inch	31	0	1061
450 Barnes Supreme	Inch	4	5	1062
450 Carbine W. R.#1 1 9/16"	Inch	450#2 NE	0	1063
450 Dakota	Inch	14	8	1064
450 Fuller	Inch	5	8	1065
450 G & A	Inch	13	16	1066
450 Howell	Inch	13	16	1067
450 Kangaroo Rifle #1 1 1/2"	Inch	37	18	1068
450 Long Rifle 1 19/64"	Inch	20	13	1069
450 Mag.Exp. Pistol	Inch	3	2	1070
450 Mashburn Mag.	Inch	4	5	1071
450 NE 3.25" Rigby	Inch	31	0	1072
450 NE 3.5" #2 Jeffery	Inch	450#2 NE	0	1073
450 Needham Front Loading	Inch	0	0	1074
450 Rev. (450 Adams)	Inch	20	13	1075
450 Rigby Match 2.4"	Inch	14	8	1076
450 Rigby Rimless Mag.	Inch	14	8	1077
450 Smith	Inch	4	5	1078
450 Soper 2 1/2" 1879	Inch	31	0	1079
450 Walker	Inch	505 Gibbs	0	1080
450 Watts Magnum	Inch	4	5	1081
450/348 Ackley Imp.	Inch	5	8	1082
450/400 B P Exp. 2 7/8"	Inch	31	0	1083
450/400 B P Exp. 2 3/8"	Inch	31	0	1084
450/400 BPE 3 1/4" (40 Eley)	Inch	31	0	1085
450/400 N E 2 3/8"	Inch	31	0	1086
450/400 N E 3" Jeffery (400S	Inch	31	0	1087
450/400 N E 3 1/4"	Inch	31	0	1088
450/400 Nitro for BP 2 3/8"	Inch	31	0	1089
450/400 Nitro for BP 3 1/4"	Inch	31	0	1090
450/400 T Turner #2 450 Turner	Inch	37	18	1091
451 Detonics	Inch	3	3	1092
455 Colt (455 Webley Mk I)	Inch	26	5	1093
455 Enfield Mk 1 Revolver	Inch	4	5	1094
455 Rev. Mk II Webley Cordite	Inch	38	5	1095
455 Webley Automatic Pistol	Inch	34	9	1096
458 Arnold	Inch	4	5	1097
458 Canadian Mag.	Inch	4	5	1098
458 Lott	Inch	4	5	1099
458 RCBS	Inch	14	8	1100
458 Whisper	Inch	4	5	1101
458 Win. Mag.	Inch	4	5	1102
458 x 1 1/2" Barnes (11.63x33)	Inch	4	5	1103
458 x 2" American	Inch	4	5	1104
460 A Square Short	Inch	14	8	1105
460 G & A (Guns & Ammo)	Inch	13	16	1106
460 Howdah	Inch	470 NE	0	1107
460 Van Horn	Inch	14	8	1108
460 Weatherby	Inch	14	8	1109
461 Gibbs #1	Inch	577 Ty	0	1110
461 Gibbs #2	Inch	577 Ty	0	1111
461 Turner # 8	Inch	577 Ty	0	1112
470 Capstick	Inch	4	5	1113
470 N E	Inch	470 NE	0	1114
475 Ackley/OKH Mag.	Inch	4	5	1115
475 A & M Magnum	Inch	5	8	1116
475 Barnes Supreme	Inch	4	5	1117
475 Howdah	Inch	470 NE	0	1118
475 J D J Pistol	Inch	14	8	1119

Shellholder Interchangeability Tables

Cartridges and Shell Holders, *continued*

Cartridge	Metric/Inch	RCBS #	LEE#	Item
475 JDJ Rifle (12.9x73.8)	Inch	14	8	1120
475 Linebaugh	Inch	14	8	1121
475 N E Str. Flg. 3 1/4"	Inch	31	0	1122
475 NE #2 3 1/2" & Jeffery	Inch	450 #2 NE	0	1123
475 Wildey Mag.	Inch	16	19	1124
476 Enfield Mk. III Rev.	Inch	4	5	1125
476 N E W. Richards 3"	Inch	470 NE	0	1126
495 A Square	Inch	14	8	1127
50 Action Express	Inch	28	11	1128
50 Alaskan JDJ	Inch	5	8	1129
50 Browning BMG (12.7x99)	Inch	50 BMG	0	1130
50 Longson (50BMG Improved)	Inch	50 BMG	0	1131
50 Rem M 71 Army Inside Primed	Inch	577 Ty	0	1132
50 Remington Navy	Inch	505Gibbs	0	1133
50 Talbot FCSA	Inch	50 BMG	0	1134
50 US Carbine	Inch	31	0	1135
50- 70 Govt. Ferington Primer	Inch	450#2 NE	0	1136
50- 70 Maynard 1882 Int. Prime	Inch	31	0	1137
50- 70 Musket 50 U S Govt.	Inch	31	0	1138
50- 90-450 Sharps 2 1/2" Str.	Inch	31	0	1139
50- 95 Winchester Express	Inch	31	0	1140
50-100 Maynard 1882	Inch	31	0	1141
50-100 Sharps 2 1/2" Straight	Inch	31	0	1142
50-100 Winchester	Inch	31	0	1143
50-105 Winchester	Inch	31	0	1144
50-110 Sharps 2 1/2" Str.	Inch	31	0	1145
50-110 Winchester (50 Express)	Inch	31	0	1146
50-115-300 Bullard	Inch	31	0	1147
50-140 Sharps 700 3 1/4"	Inch	31	0	1148
50-140 Winchester Exp.	Inch	31	0	1149
50-50 Maynard 1865	Inch	50 BMG	0	1150
50-50 Maynard 1882	Inch	31	0	1151
500 Jeffery & Schuler Rless	Inch	14	8	1152
500 #2 Exp. (577/500) 2 13/16"	Inch	20 Ga.	0	1153
500 A Square	Inch	14	8	1154
500 B.P. Exp 3 " (50 Eley)	Inch	470 NE	0	1155
500 B.P. Exp 3 1/4"	Inch	470 NE	0	1156
500 Eley Rev. (500 Tranter)	Inch	37	18	1157
500 Howdah by Jurras	Inch	470 NE	0	1158
500 Linebaugh 1 1/4"	Inch	5	8	1159
500 N E 3"	Inch	470 NE	0	1160
500 N E 3 1/4"	Inch	470 NE	0	1161
500 Nitro for BP 3 "	Inch	470 NE	0	1162
500 Nitro for BP 3 1/4"	Inch	470 NE	0	1163
500 Rafiki (Wes. Rich.)	Inch	700 NE	0	1164
500 Whisper 2 1/4" JDJ	Inch	14	8	1165
500 Whisper 2" JDJ	Inch	14	8	1166
500/416 Krieghoff	Inch	470 NE	0	1167
500/450 NE 3.25" Mag.	Inch	31	0	1168
500/450 #1 Exp. 2 3/4" B. P.	Inch	505Gibbs	0	1169
500/450 #1 Musket 2 1/4"	Inch	577 Ty	0	1170
500/450 #1 Nitro for BP 2.75"	Inch	505 Gibbs	0	1171
500/450 #2 Musket	Inch	577 Ty	0	1172
500/450 3.375" Mag. Exp.	Inch	577 Ty	0	1173
500/450 BPE 3.25" Mag.	Inch	31	0	1174
500/450 Nitro for BP 3.25"	Inch	470 NE	0	1175

Cartridge	Metric/Inch	RCBS #	LEE#	Item
500/450 Webley Carb. 1 11/16"	Inch	577 Ty	0	1176
500/465 NE	Inch	470 NE	0	1177
505 Barnes Supreme	Inch	14	8	1178
505 Rimless Mag. Gibbs	Inch	505Gibbs	0	1179
505 Super Mag.	Inch	470 NE	0	1180
510 N E	Inch	31	0	1181
510 Wells Exp. (JGS)	Inch	14	8	1182
524 Cal. 32 Ga. Lancaster Ball	Inch	470 NE	0	1183
55-100 Maynard 1882	Inch	577 NE	0	1184
550 Cal. 28 Ga. Lancaster Ball	Inch	20 Ga.	0	1185
550 Ivory Exp.	Inch	14	8	1186
57 Snider	Inch	577 NE	0	1187
577 A. Henry See 20/577 Misc	Inch	20 Ga.	0	1188
577 B. P. Exp. 2 3/4"	Inch	577-450	0	1189
577 B. P. Exp. 3 "	Inch	577-450	0	1190
577 Howdah	Inch	577-450	0	1191
577 N E 2 3/4"	Inch	577-450	0	1192
577 N E 3 "	Inch	577-450	0	1193
577 Nitro for B P 2 3/4"	Inch	577-450	0	1194
577 Nitro for B P 3"	Inch	577-450	0	1195
577 Rewa (600-577 Rewa)	Inch	600 NE	0	1196
577 Short 1.625"	Inch	577-450	0	1197
577 Snider paper case Step	Inch	577-450	0	1198
577 Tyrannosaur	Inch	577 Ty	0	1199
577 Webley Rev. Boxer Prim.	Inch	577-450	0	1200
577-28-450 Webley Rev. (58 Cal	Inch	577-450	0	1201
577/450 M Henry (450 Exp 58mm	Inch	577-450	0	1202
577/500 N E 3 1/8" Mag	Inch	600 NE	0	1203
577/500 #2 B P Exp. 2 13/16"	inch	20 Ga.	0	1204
577/500 Nitro for BP 2 13/16"	Inch	600 NE	0	1205
579 Cal (24 Bore) Paradox	Inch	50 BMG	0	1206
579 Cal. 24 Ga. Lancaster Ball	Inch	577-450	0	1207
58 Carbine Berdan (U S Carb)	Inch	600 NE	0	1208
58 U S Musket C F 1865 Short	Inch	600 NE	0	1209
585 Nyati	Inch	450 #2 NE	0	1210
585 Wells	Inch	450 #2 NE	0	1211
60 Cal. U S Machine Gun	Inch	C	0	1212
600 Nitro Express 3 "	Inch	600 NE	0	1213
600 Szecsei	Inch	50 BMG	0	1214
600-577 Rewa	Inch	600 NE	0	1215
615 Cal. (20 Bore) Paradox	Inch	20 Ga.	0	1216
649 Cal. 18 Ga. Lancaster Ball	Inch	C	0	1217
662 Cal (16 Bore) Paradox	Inch	16 Ga.	0	1218
70-150 Winchester	Inch	12 Ga.	0	1219
700 NE	Inch	700 NE	0	1220
700 Szecsei	Inch	50 BMG	0	1221
700-577 N. E. Westly Richards	Inch	700 NE	0	1222
705 Cal. 14 Ga. Lancaster Ball	Inch	12 Ga.	0	1223
729 Cal. (12 Bore) Paradox	Inch	12 Ga.	0	1224
775 Cal. (10 Bore) 2 7/8"	Inch	10 Ga.	0	1225
775 Cal. (10 Bore) 3 1/4"	Inch	10 Ga.	0	1226
835 Cal (8 Bore) Paradox	Inch	C	0	1227
985 Cal 4 Bore Australian Rewa	Inch	C	0	1228
02.7 Kolibri	Metric	C	0	1229
03 Kolibri	Metric	C	0	1230
04.25 Liliput (4.25 Erika)	Metric	C	0	1231

Cartridges and Shell Holders, *continued*

Cartridge	Metric/Inch	RCBS #	LEE#	Item
04.35 x45 German DAG	Metric	10	4	1232
04.6 x36 German H & K	Metric	17	7	1233
04.85 x49 British (19 cal.)	Metric	10	4	1234
05 Bergmann grooved	Metric	C	0	1235
05 CCM (Cooper)	Metric	C	0	1236
05 Clement	Metric	C	0	1237
05 Craig Center Fire	Metric	C	0	1238
05.0/223 (20 T N T)	Metric	10	4	1239
05.45 x18 Soviet	Metric	29	15	1240
05.45 x39 Soviet (aka RWS.215)	Metric	1	1	1241
05.5 Swiss Eiger	Metric	C	RTT	1242
05.5 Velo Dog	Metric	12	20	1243
05.56 x45 Nato (223 Rem.)	Metric	23	4	1244
05.6 x33 Johnson (22/30 US C)	Metric	17	7	1245
05.6 x33 Rook Rimless (5.7)	Metric	12	20	1246
05.6 x35R Vierling (22 WCF)	Metric	12	20	1247
05.6 x39 Lapua (Finn. & Rus.)	Metric	32	12	1248
05.6 x40 Russian	Metric	1	1	1249
05.6 x50 Magnum	Metric	3	2	1250
05.6 x50R Magnum	Metric	6	1	1251
05.6 x52R (22 Savage HP)	Metric	2	3	1252
05.6 x57 RWS	Metric	3	2	1253
05.6 x57R RWS	Metric	4	5	1254
05.6 x61 Vom Hofe Super Exp.	Metric	21	11	1255
05.6 x61R Vom Hofe Super Exp.	Metric	5	8	1256
05.7 mm Johnson (22 Spitfire)	Metric	17	7	1257
05.7 x28 FN P90	Metric	C	0	1258
05.7 x43 (222 Eichhorn Lynx)	Metric	10	4	1259
06 Ackley Belted Exp.	Metric	3	2	1260
06 Ackley Imp 6mm Rem	Metric	3	2	1261
06 Ackley Mag. (300)	Metric	4	5	1262
06 Arch	Metric	2	3	1263
06 Arnold	Metric	4	5	1264
06 Atlas	Metric	4	5	1265
06 B R Rem.	Metric	3	2	1266
06 Bullberry	Metric	2	3	1267
06 Carlson	Metric	4	5	1268
06 Donaldson Ace	Metric	11	10	1269
06 Donaldson Intl.	Metric	3	2	1270
06 Donaldson Wasp	Metric	2	3	1271
06 Durham Intl.	Metric	3	2	1272
06 Eichelberger Bee	Metric	1	1	1273
06 Ellis Target	Metric	3	2	1274
06 Express Junior	Metric	3	2	1275
06 Gipson	Metric	3	2	1276
06 H L S	Metric	3	2	1277
06 Hotdog	Metric	3	2	1278
06 Intl. Rem. Walker	Metric	3	2	1279
06 J D J #2	Metric	11	10	1280
06 J M R	Metric	3	2	1281
06 Jessica	Metric	3	2	1282
06 Krag Ackley Imp.	Metric	7	5	1283
06 Krag Ackley Imp. Short	Metric	7	5	1284
06 KSS Krag Super Short	Metric	3	2	1285
06 Lee Navy rimless	Metric	2	3	1286
06 Mach IV	Metric	4	5	1287

Cartridge	Metric/Inch	RCBS #	LEE#	Item
06 McLaren	Metric	3	2	1288
06 Micro-Flite	Metric	2	3	1289
06 mm ET	Metric	11	10	1290
06 Nicholson	Metric	4	5	1291
06 Niedner Magnum	Metric	19	1	1292
06 Nieomiller	Metric	3	2	1293
06 PPC	Metric	32	12	1294
06 Rem. (6x56.5)	Metric	3	2	1295
06 S A W Exp. Long 6x49)	Metric	1	1	1296
06 Sabre	Metric	4	5	1297
06 Shipley Pipsqueak	Metric	10	4	1298
06 SM Wasp	Metric	3	2	1299
06 Souper	Metric	3	2	1300
06 Stroup	Metric	3	2	1301
06 Super Bower	Metric	2	3	1302
06 Swift	Metric	11	10	1303
06 T. C .U. Ugalde	Metric	10	4	1304
06 VA Hornet	Metric	12	20	1305
06 Vartarg Turbo (6VTT)	Metric	10	4	1306
06 x29.5R Stahl	Metric	23	4	1307
06 x39	Metric	3	2	1308
06 x44 BR	Metric	3	2	1309
06 x45 (6-223Rem.)	Metric	10	4	1310
06 x47 (6-222 Rem.)	Metric	10	4	1311
06 x50 S & H	Metric	3	2	1312
06 x54 M. S.	Metric	11	10	1313
06 x55 Imp. Arch	Metric	2	3	1314
06 x57 Mauser	Metric	3	2	1315
06 x58 Forster	Metric	3	2	1316
06 x58R Forster (6.2x58R)	Metric	2	3	1317
06 x62 Freres	Metric	3	2	1318
06 x62R Freres (6mm Richard)	Metric	4	5	1319
06.0/06.5x54 MS	Metric	3	2	1320
06.0/22-250	Metric	3	2	1321
06.0/222 Rem Mag Imp.	Metric	10	4	1322
06.0/222Mag Shipley	Metric	10	4	1323
06.0/224 Weatherby	Metric	27	12	1324
06.0/225 Win.	Metric	11	10	1325
06.0/250 Savage Original	Metric	3	2	1326
06.0/250 Walker (6mm Intl.)	Metric	3	2	1327
06.0/257	Metric	3	2	1328
06.0/257 Ackley Imp.	Metric	3	2	1329
06.0/270	Metric	3	2	1330
06.0/284	Metric	16	19	1331
06.0/30-06 Imp.	Metric	3	2	1332
06.0/30-06 Talbot	Metric	3	2	1333
06.0/30-30	Metric	2	3	1334
06.0/30-30 Imp	Metric	2	3	1335
06.0/303 Epps	Metric	7	5	1336
06.0/303 Imp.	Metric	7	5	1337
06.0/308 (243 Win.)	Metric	3	2	1338
06.0/350	Metric	4	5	1339
06.17 Flash	Metric	4	5	1340
06.17 Spitfire	Metric	4	5	1341
06.35 ACP (25 ACP)	Metric	29	15	1342
06.35x19	Metric	23	4	1343

Cartridges and Shell Holders, *continued*

Cartridge	Metric/Inch	RCBS #	LEE#	Item
06.35x47 TC	Metric	10	4	1344
06.35x59	Metric	3	2	1345
06.5 AIM	Metric	4	5	1346
06.5 Apex Super	Metric	4	5	1347
06.5 Barnes QT	metric	4	5	1348
06.5 Bearcat	Metric	4	5	1349
06.5 Bergmann Grooved	Metric	1	19	1350
06.5 Brooks	Metric	4	5	1351
06.5 Bullberry	Metric	2	3	1352
06.5 Critser	Metric	4	5	1353
06.5 Express Junior	Metric	3	2	1354
06.5 Gibbs (M. S. Mod 1903)	Metric	3	2	1355
06.5 Gipson	Metric	4	5	1356
06.5 Hi Vel. Flang. (256 Rim)	Metric	4	5	1357
06.5 ICL Boar	Metric	3	2	1358
06.5 ICL Mag	Metric	4	5	1359
06.5 IHMSA	Metric	3	2	1360
06.5 Jaco	Metric	34	9	1361
06.5 JDJ #1	Metric	11	10	1362
06.5 JDJ #2	Metric	2	3	1363
06.5 Mach IV	Metric	4	5	1364
06.5 Mashburn Super Mag.	Metric	4	5	1365
06.5 Panther	Metric	3	2	1366
06.5 Redding	Metric	3	2	1367
06.5 Shaman	Metric	34	9	1368
06.5 Spence Special	Metric	3	2	1369
06.5 STW (Shooting Times)	Metric	4	5	1370
06.5 Super Bower	Metric	2	3	1371
06.5 Talbot	Metric	3	2	1372
06.5 TCU Ugalde	Metric	10	4	1373
06.5 Wasp	Metric	7	5	1374
06.5 Whisper JDJ	Metric	10	4	1375
06.5 x27R Ronezewski	Metric	6	1	1376
06.5 x40R Sauer & Roth	Metric	C	RTT	1377
06.5 x48R Sauer (6.6)	Metric	34	9	1378
06.5 x50 Arisaka (Rimed JDJ)	Metric	15	10	1379
06.5 x50 Jap Service (Semi R)	Metric	21	11	1380
06.5 x52 (51 American)	Metric	3	2	1381
06.5 x52 Carcano	Metric	9	2	1382
06.5 x52 Carcano Imp.	Metric	9	2	1383
06.5 x52R (25-35 WCF)	Metric	2	3	1384
06.5 x53 R M S Dutch (256 M	Metric	7	5	1385
06.5 x53.5R Daudeteau #12	Metric	4	5	1386
06.5 x54 M S Rimless Greek	Metric	9	2	1387
06.5 x54 Mauser Kurz	Metric	3	2	1388
06.5 x55 Ackley Imp.	Metric	2	3	1389
06.5 x55 Arch	Metric	2	3	1390
06.5 x55 Daniash Krag	Metric	2	3	1391
06.5 x55 Swedish	Metric	2	3	1392
06.5 x57 Mauser	Metric	3	2	1393
06.5 x57R Mauser	Metric	4	5	1394
06.5 x58 Portuguese Vergueiro	Metric	3	2	1395
06.5 x58R Krag	Metric	14	8	1396
06.5 x58R Sauer	Metric	34	9	1397
06.5 x61 Mauser (Sweden)	Metric	3	2	1398
06.5 x61R Mauser (Sweden)	Metric	4	5	1399
06.5 x64 Brenneke	Metric	3	2	1400
06.5 x64R Kepplinger	Metric	4	5	1401
06.5 x65 R W S	Metric	3	2	1402
06.5 x65R R W S	Metric	4	5	1403
06.5 x68 Schuler	Metric	28	11	1404
06.5 x68R Schuler	Metric	5	8	1405
06.5 x70R Sauer (6.6)	Metric	27	19	1406
06.5/06 A Square	Metric	3	2	1407
06.5/07x61 S & H	Metric	4	5	1408
06.5/08 A Square	Metric	3	2	1409
06.5/08mm Rem.	Metric	4	5	1410
06.5/221	Metric	10	4	1411
06.5/223	Metric	10	4	1412
06.5/250 Savage	Metric	3	2	1413
06.5/257 Roberts Jap	Metric	3	2	1414
06.5/257 Weatherby	Metric	4	5	1415
06.5/270 Imp. Van Arsdall	Metric	3	2	1416
06.5/280 Imp. RCBS	Metric	3	2	1417
06.5/284 Win. (6.5 Reindeer)	Metric	3	2	1418
06.5/30-06	Metric	3	2	1419
06.5/300 Win Mag	Metric	4	5	1420
06.5/300 Wthby. (W W H)	Metric	4	5	1421
06.5/303 Epps	Metric	7	5	1422
06.5/308 (260 Rem & 263 Exp)	Metric	3	2	1423
06.5/308 Imp. (260 Imp)	Metric	3	2	1424
06.5/350	Metric	4	5	1425
06.5/378 Wthby.	Metric	14	8	1426
06.5/405 Donaldson	Metric	24	16	1427
06.5/416 Talbot	Metric	37	18	1428
06.53 Scramjet (Laz.)	Metric	4	5	1429
06.6 x48R Sauer (6.5)	Metric	34	9	1430
06.7 x60 Eichhorn EGM	Metric	3	2	1431
06.71 Blackbird (Laz.)	Metric	13	16	1432
06.71 Phantom (Laz.)	Metric	4	5	1433
07 Ackley Mag.	Metric	4	5	1434
07 B. R. Rem.	Metric	3	2	1435
07 Bullberry	Metric	2	3	1436
07 Cowen Long Neck	Metric	4	5	1437
07 CUT Cast Ugalde Talbot	Metric	10	4	1438
07 D H	Metric	14	8	1439
07 Dakota	Metric	13	16	1440
07 Donaldson Wasp	Metric	2	3	1441
07 Express	Metric	5	8	1442
07 French Rev.	Metric	16	19	1443
07 Gibbs	Metric	3	2	1444
07 Gibbs Imp. by Talbot	Metric	3	2	1445
07 Gipson Super Mag.	Metric	4	5	1446
07 Gradle (Roy Gradle)	Metric	4	5	1447
07 Holmes Mag.	Metric	4	5	1448
07 ICL Magnum	Metric	4	5	1449
07 ICL Tortilla	Metric	3	2	1450
07 ICL Wapiti	Metric	4	5	1451
07 IHMSA Rimless	Metric	3	2	1452
07 IHMSA Rimmed (7mm Intl. R)	Metric	2	3	1453
07 Imp. Arch	Metric	2	3	1454
07 Imperial Mag	Metric	13	16	1455

Cartridges and Shell Holders, *continued*

Cartridge	Metric/Inch	RCBS #	LEE#	Item
07 International Rimmed	Metric	2	3	1456
07 JDJ #1	Metric	11	10	1457
07 JDJ #2	Metric	2	3	1458
07 JRS (John Sundra)	Metric	3	2	1459
07 L & L	Metric	28	11	1460
07 Mashburn Long Magnum	Metric	4	5	1461
07 Mashburn Super Mag.	Metric	4	5	1462
07 Merrill	Metric	11	10	1463
07 Micro-Flite	Metric	28	11	1464
07 Nambu (Baby)	Metric	17	7	1465
07 Newton	Metric	24	16	1466
07 Rawson Mag.	Metric	14	8	1467
07 Remington Magnum	Metric	4	5	1468
07 Reynolds Mag.	Metric	4	5	1469
07 Rigby Mag. (275 #2) Rimmed	Metric	4	5	1470
07 Rimd Mag. H&H (7 Flanged)	Metric	24	16	1471
07 Rocket	Metric	11	10	1472
07 S. T. Easterner	Metric	2	3	1473
07 S. T. Westerner	Metric	4	5	1474
07 Short Mag.	Metric	14	8	1475
07 Simpson GLC	Metric	3	2	1476
07 Smith Magnum	Metric	4	5	1477
07 Super Bower	Metric	2	3	1478
07 T&R (Taylor & Robbins	Metric	4	5	1479
07 Talbot	Metric	3	2	1480
07 TCU (Ugalde)	Metric	10	4	1481
07 Titus	Metric	3	2	1482
07 TNT	Metric	3	2	1483
07 Venturian	Metric	4	5	1484
07 Victoria Mag.	Metric	4	5	1485
07 Wade Super	Metric	13	16	1486
07 Walking Stick Dumonthier	Metric	16	19	1487
07 Weatherby Mag.	Metric	4	5	1488
07 Whisper	Metric	10	4	1489
07 x1.75"	Metric	3	2	1490
07 x33 Sako 7x33 Finnish)	Metric	16	19	1491
07 x49 Medium Mauser	Metric	3	2	1492
07 x54 Mauser	Metric	3	2	1493
07 x57 Mauser	Metric	3	9	1494
07 x57R Mauser	Metric	26	5	1495
07 x61 Norma Mag	Metric	4	5	1496
07 x61 Norma Super	Metric	4	5	1497
07 x61 Sharpe & Hart Super	Metric	4	5	1498
07 x64 Brenneke	Metric	3	2	1499
07 x65 R Brenneke (64R)	Metric	26	5	1500
07 x66 Randle	Metric	4	5	1501
07 x66 Vom Hofe Super Exp.	Metric	18	11	1502
07 x72 R Brenneke & Sauer	Metric	34	9	1503
07 x73 Vom Hofe Belted	Metric	4	5	1504
07 x75 R Vom Hofe Super Exp.	Metric	4	5	1505
07 -30 Waters	Metric	2	3	1506
07.0/06.5 Rem Mag	Metric	4	5	1507
07.0/08 Rem.	Metric	3	2	1508
07.0/222	Metric	10	4	1509
07.0/223	Metric	10	4	1510
07.0/30 JDJ Imp.	Metric	2	3	1511

Cartridge	Metric/Inch	RCBS #	LEE#	Item
07.0/30-120	Metric	2	3	1512
07.0/300 Win.	Metric	4	5	1513
07.0/300 Wthby.	Metric	4	5	1514
07.0/303 Epps	Metric	7	5	1515
07.0/303 Imp.	Metric	7	5	1516
07.0/308 Durham	Metric	3	2	1517
07.0/308 Imp.	Metric	3	2	1518
07.0/308 Rem	Metric	3	2	1519
07.0/320 Revolver	Metric	23	4	1520
07.0/338 Win.	Metric	4	5	1521
07.0/348 Win. Imp.	Metric	5	8	1522
07.0/350 Remington	Metric	4	5	1523
07.21 Firehawk (Laz.)	Metric	13	16	1524
07.21 Tomahawk	Metric	37	18	1525
07.35 Italian Carcano (7.5x51)	Metric	9	2	1526
07.35 Terni (Carcano)	Metric	9	2	1527
07.5 French Ord. Rifle	Metric	20	13	1528
07.5 Swiss,Swede,Norwegian Rev	Metric	1	1	1529
07.5 x54 French MAS MLE 1929C	Metric	36	2A	1530
07.5 x55 Schmidt-Rubin (x53)	Metric	21	11	1531
07.62 Nagant Rev. (Russian)	Metric	1	1	1532
07.62 x25 Tokarev	Metric	16	19	1533
07.62 x33	Metric	3	2	1534
07.62 x39 Soviet M 43	Metric	32	12	1535
07.62 x45 Czech M52	Metric	15	10	1536
07.62 x51 NATO (308)	Metric	3	2	1537
07.62 x51R (30-30 Win)	Metric	2	3	1538
07.62 x53R Russian (54R)	Metric	13	16	1539
07.63 Mannlicher (7.65) Str.	Metric	17	7	1540
07.65 ACP (32) (Mauser Pistol	Metric	17	7	1541
07.65 Mannlicher Pistol (7.63)	Metric	17	7	1542
07.65 MAS Long French	Metric	12	20	1543
07.65 Pickert (inside primed)	Metric	16	19	1544
07.65 Roth-Sauer Former	Metric	12	20	1545
07.65 x53 Mauser Kortnek	Metric	11	10	1546
07.7 x 54R Pollard	Metric	7	5	1547
07.7 x58 Jap Rifle (31 Jap)	Metric	2	2	1548
07.7 x58SR Jap machine gun	Metric	21	11	1549
07.7 x60R Hebler	Metric	5G	8G	1550
07.82 Patriot	Metric	14	8	1551
07.82 Warbird (Lazzeroni)	Metric	14	8	1552
07.9 x57 J or S Mauser (8mm)	Metric	2	3	1553
07.92 x33 Kurz	Metric	3	2	1554
07.92 x61 Norwegian Colt MG	Metric	3	2	1555
08 Arden & Warner Mag.	Metric	4	5	1556
08 Express	Metric	5	8	1557
08 Garden Rifle (8.15x40R)	Metric	C	0	1558
08 Gibbs	Metric	3	2	1559
08 IHMSA	Metric	3	2	1560
08 Lebel Revolver	Metric	1	1	1561
08 Mauser (7.92 or 8x57) S	Metric	3	2	1562
08 Nambu	Metric	25	0	1563
08 Payne Express	Metric	5	8	1564
08 Rast-Gasser	Metric	19	1	1565
08 Rem. Magnum	Metric	4	5	1566
08 Roth-Styer	Metric	17	7	1567

Cartridges and Shell Holders, *continued*

Cartridge	Metric/Inch	RCBS #	LEE#	Item
08 Stransky Magnum	Metric	4	5	1568
08 x42R (M88) MB	Metric	5G	8G	1569
08 x48R Sauer	Metric	34	9	1570
08 x50R Austrian Mannlicher S.	Metric	13	16	1571
08 x50R Lebel Rifle	Metric	8 Lebel	17	1572
08 x50R Siamese T 45 Mauser	Metric	5	8	1573
08 x51 Mauser	Metric	3	2	1574
08 x52R Siamese T 66	Metric	14	8	1575
08 x53R Murata (Meiji 20-8mm)	Metric	37	18	1576
08 x54 Krag-Jorgensen	Metric	36	2A	1577
08 x56 M. S.	Metric	3	2	1578
08 x56R Hungarian Mannlicher	Metric	13	16	1579
08 x56R Kropatschek	Metric	8 Lebel	17	1580
08 x56R Mann. Schoenaur	Metric	18	11	1581
08 x57 J Mauser (7.92)	Metric	3	2	1582
08 x57 JS Mauser (7.92)	Metric	3	2	1583
08 x57R 360 (8.15)	Metric	36	2A	1584
08 x58R Dannish Krag	Metric	14	8	1585
08 x58R Sauer	Metric	34	9	1586
08 x59 Breda	Metric	4	5	1587
08 x60 Mauser R	Metric	3	2	1588
08 x60 Mauser S	Metric	3	2	1589
08 x60R Mauser	Metric	4	5	1590
08 x60R Mauser Mag Bombe	Metric	4	5	1591
08 x60R Portugeuse Guedes	Metric	8 LebelG	17	1592
08 x63 Swedish	Metric	2	3	1593
08 x64 Brenneke S	Metric	2	3	1594
08 x65R Brenneke S	Metric	4	5	1595
08 x68 S Magnum (323 bullet)	Metric	34	9	1596
08 x71 Peterlongo	Metric	3	2	1597
08 x72R Sauer & Brenneke	Metric	34	9	1598
08 x75 Behr	Metric	2	3	1599
08 x75R	Metric	4	5	1600
08.0/284 Win	Metric	3	2	1601
08.0/30-06	Metric	3	2	1602
08.0/30-06 Imp.	Metric	3	2	1603
08.0/300 Gates Mag.	Metric	3	2	1604
08.0/300 Win	Metric	4	5	1605
08.0/308 Norma Mag.	Metric	4	5	1606
08.0/338 Win. (8mm PMM)	Metric	4	5	1607
08.0/350 Mag.	Metric	4	5	1608
08.0/378 Weathby	Metric	14	8	1609
08.15 x46R Frohn (46.5)	Metric	2	3	1610
08.2 x53R Sako	Metric	13	16	1611
08.5 x63 REB Meyer	Metric	3	2	1612
08.58 x71 (338 Lapua Mag.)	Metric	14	8	1613
08.59 Titan (Laz.)	Metric	14	8	1614
08.59 Galaxy	Metric	14	8	1615
09 Action Express	Metric	16	19	1616
09 Bayard Bergman Largo 9x24	Metric	16	19	1617
09 Browning Long	Metric	1	1	1618
09 Danish Rev.	Metric	15	10	1619
09 Federal	Metric	6	1	1620
09 Gasser Kroh Rev.	Metric	32	12	1621
09 Glisenti	Metric	16	19	1622
09 IHMSA	Metric	6	1	1623

Cartridge	Metric/Inch	RCBS #	LEE#	Item
09 Jap Rev.	Metric	9	2	1624
09 Luger (9x19)	Metric	16	19	1625
09 Machine Machine Pistol	Metric	16	19	1626
09 Mauser Export Model	Metric	16	19	1627
09 Nambu	Metric	6	1	1628
09 Russian Makarov	Metric	16	19	1629
09 Sporting Round	Metric	3	2	1630
09 Steyr Pistol (9x23) 1912	Metric	16	19	1631
09 Super Cooper	Metric	10	4	1632
09 Ultra (9x18)	Metric	16	19	1633
09 Winchester Mag.	Metric	16	19	1634
09 x17 Former	Metric	23	4	1635
09 x21 Italian Police	Metric	16	19	1636
09 x23 Steyr (9x24)	Metric	16	19	1637
09 x25 Dillon	Metric	27	19	1638
09 x30 Grom	Metric	16	19	1639
09 x30 R (38 X Long)	Metric	14	8	1640
09 x56 M. S.	Metric	3	2	1641
09 x57 Mauser	Metric	3	2	1642
09 x57R Mauser	Metric	4	5	1643
09 x64 B or K (358 Norma M.)	Metric	4	5	1644
09 x70R Maus. (400/360 W. R.)	Metric	4	5	1645
09 x71 Peterlongo	Metric	3	2	1646
09 x71R Peterlongo	Metric	3	2	1647
09.1 x40R Tesching	Metric	C	RTT	1648
09.3 JDJ	Metric	28	11	1649
09.3 North American Rimmed	Metric	5	8	1650
09.3 U.S.A.	Metric	4	5	1651
09.3 x48R (360 Wr. Exp. #3)	Metric	34	9	1652
09.3 x53 Swiss Spt. rimless	Metric	2	3	1653
09.3 x53R Swiss & Finnish	Metric	13	16	1654
09.3 x53R Swiss Sporting	Metric	14	8	1655
09.3 x57 Mauser (9.2)	Metric	3	2	1656
09.3 x57R Hunting (360 2 1/4"	Metric	26	5	1657
09.3 x62 Mauser	Metric	3	2	1658
09.3 x64 Brenneke	Metric	21	11	1659
09.3 x65R Collath	Metric	28	11	1660
09.3 x66 Eerkki Kauppi	Metric	2	3	1661
09.3 x70 Magnum (rimless)	Metric	13	16	1662
09.3 x70R (400/360 Exp)	Metric	34	9	1663
09.3 x72R Nimrod	Metric	34	9	1664
09.3 x72R Sauer	Metric	4	5	1665
09.3 x74R Forester	Metric	4	5	1666
09.3 x82R Nimrod	Metric	34	9	1667
09.4 Dannish Rev.	Metric	32	12	1668
09.5 x57 MS 56,56.7&375 2 1/4	Metric	3	2	1669
09.5 x60R Turkish Mauser	Metric	5G	8G	1670
09.5 x73 Miller-Greiss	Metric	13	16	1671
09.53 Saturn	Metric	14	8	1672
09.8 Auto Colt	Metric	1	1	1673
10 Dutch Rev.	Metric	34	9	1674
10 Dutch Soerabaja Rev.M	Metric	34	9	1675
10 German Nagant Rev.	Metric	34	9	1676
10 Short S & W Auto Pistol	Metric	27	19	1677
10 Wildey	Metric	3	2	1678
10.15 x61R Jarmann	Metric	C	0	1679

Cartridges and Shell Holders, *continued*

Cartridge	Metric/Inch	RCBS #	LEE#	Item
10.15 x63R Serbian Mauser 1878	Metric	5G	8G	1680
10.3 x60R Swiss (450-400 2.37"	Metric	5	8	1681
10.3 x65R Baenziger Swiss Targ	Metric	C	RTT	1682
10.4 Ital. Glisenti (10.35)	Metric	7	5	1683
10.4 Swiss Revolver (10.4x20R)	Metric	4	5	1684
10.4 x47R Italian Vetterli	Metric	C	RTT	1685
10.5 x47R	Metric	5G	8G	1686
10.57 Meteor (Laz.)	Metric	14	8	1687
10.6 x51 (416x2')	metric	4	5	1688
10.66 x57.5R Russian 1869	Metric	450 #2 NE	0	1689
10.75 Hoffman (x 68)	Metric	21	11	1690
10.75 x47R Schutzen	Metric	14G	8G	1691
10.75 x57 (Mannlicher)	Metric	3	2	1692
10.75 x58R Russian Berdan 43 R	Metric	450 #2 NE	0	1693
10.75 x63 Mauser	Metric	18	11	1694
10.75 x65R Collath	Metric	13	16	1695
10.75 x68 Mauser	Metric	18	11	1696
10.75 x70R Barella (Stahl)	Metric	5G	8G	1697
10.75 x73 (404 Jeffery)	Metric	13	16	1698
10.8 x47 Martini	Metric	C	RTT	1699
11 French Ordnance Rev.	Metric	7	5	1700
11 German Rev. (10.6 & 10.8)	Metric	8	13	1701
11 Wildey	Metric	3	2	1702
11 x50R Belgian Albini	Metric	577 Ty	0	1703
11 x52R Dutch Beaumont (43 Bea	Metric	31	0	1704
11 x53R Belgian Comblain M 71	Metric	577 TyG	0	1705
11 x59R (60R) Gras Vickers	Metric	577 TyG	0	1706
11 x60R Jap Murata	Metric	577 Ty	0	1707
11.15 x58R (11x58R & 43 Span)	Metric	22	17	1708
11.15 x58R Werndl 73 &7	Metric	450 #2 NE	RTT	1709
11.15 x60R (43) Mauser	Metric	8 LebelG	17	1710
11.15 x65R Schutzen (LK)	Metric	4	5	1711
11.2 Krieghoff	Metric	5G	8G	1712
11.2 x51R Kropatchek	Metric	5	8	1713
11.2 x60 Mauser & Schuler	Metric	3	2	1714
11.2 x72 Mauser & Schuler	Metric	3	2	1715
11.3 x50R Beaumont M 71	Metric	577 Ty	0	1716
11.4 x50R Brazilian Comblain	Metric	C	RTT	1717
11.4 x50R Werndl (11.3)	Metric	37G	18	1718
11.4 x51R Danish & 11.3&45	Metric	8 Lebel	17	1719
11.43 x50R Egyptian Rem.	Metric	577 Ty	0	1720
11.43 x50R Egyptian Rem. Guard	Metric	577 Ty	0	1721
11.43 x55R Turkish Pea-Martini	Metric	577 Ty	0	1722
11.5 x57R Sp. Reformado 2 1/4"	Metric	577 Ty	0	1723
11.7 x51R Dan. Rem.	Metric	5	8	1724
11.75R Montenegrin Rev.	Metric	22	17	1725
12 Devisme Revolver	Metric	4	5	1726
12 x44R Rem. M67 (12.17&12.7)	Metric	22	17	1727
12.5 x70 Schuler (500 Jeffery	Metric	14	8	1728
12.7 x57 ANTHIS French	Metric	14	8	1729
12.7 x70 Schuler (12.5)	Metric	14	8	1730
12.7 x99 (50 BMG)	Metric	50 BMG	0	1731
12.9 x73.8 JDJ Rifle (475)	Metric	14	8	1732
12.9x50.8 JDJ	Metric	14	8	1733

BIBLIOGRAPHY

Aagaard, Finn, Jan. 1999, *Rifle* magazine, "22 Long Rifle," Wolfe Publishing Co.

Ackley, P.O., 1962, *Handbook for Shooters & Reloaders*, Vol. I, Plaza Publishing Co.

Ackley, P.O., 1996, *Handbook for Shooters & Reloaders*, Vol. II, Plaza Publishing Co.

Adolph, Fred, 1915, *Modern Guns*, Adolph Genoa, N.Y.

Alpin, Art, et al, 1996, *Any Shot You Want*, A Square loading manual, On Target Press

Andersen P, Andresen V & Stromstad T., 1995, Cartridge Cases

Arnold Arms Co., 1998, Catalog, Proprietary Cartridges, Arnold Arms

Barlerin, J., January 1997, *Cartridge Researcher*, European Cartridge Assn.

Barnes, F.C., edited by Amber, J., 1972, *Cartridges of the World*, 3rd Edition, Digest Books

Barnes, F.C., edited by Bussard, Mike, 1993, *Cartridges of the World*, 7th Edition, DBI Books

Bell, Sherman, Autumn 1997, *Double Gun Journal*, "British Doubles A to Z," Double Gun J. Inc.

Benke, C., July 1997, *Rifle* magazine, "256 Newton," Wolfe Publishing Co.

Benke, C., Nov. 1990, *Handloader* magazine, "6.5 Gibbs," Wolfe Publishing Co.

Benke, C., 1997, *Handloaders Digest*, "The 264 Thor," Krause Publications Inc.

Benke, C., Aug. 1998, *Handloader* magazine, "6.5 Mach IV," Wolfe Publishing Co.

Brennan, Dave, Sept. 1998, *Precision Shooting* magazine, Letters to the Editor, 6.5 AIM, Precision Shooting Inc.

Briggs, P, July 1984, *Handloader* magazine, "7mm Intl. Rimmed," Wolfe Publishing Co.

Buttweiler, R.T., June 1997, *Collectors Ammunition Auction Catalog*, Vol. XI, #3, W&C Printing Co.

Buttweiler, R.T., Oct. 1997, *Collector Ammunition*, Vol. XII, #1, W&C Printing Co.

Cartridge Researcher, July 1997, #386-11, European Cartridge Assn.

C-H Tool & Die, 1997, C-H Tool & Die/4-D Custom Die Co., Reloading Equipment Catalog 1997-98,

Calhoon, James, Winter 1998, *Small Caliber News*, James Calhoon, Small Caliber News Inc.

Chicoine, D.R., Dec. 1997, *Bullet 'N Press* magazine, Vol. 2, #4, Pg. 8, Bullet 'N Press Publishers

Conrad, R., Sept. 1992, *Handloader* magazine, The 375/06 for Alaska, Wolfe Publishing Co.

Datig, Fred, 1956, *Cartridges for Collectors*, Vols. 1-4, Borden Publishing Co.

de Haas, Frank, 1994, *Mr. Single Shot's Cartridge Handbook*, F. de Haas, publisher

Dixon, Jim, 1996, *Gun Digest*, 50th Ed., "775 Rigby," DBI Inc., publishers

Dixon, W.B., 1997, *European Sporting Cartridges*, Vol. I, Armory Publications Inc.

Donnelly, J.J., 1987, *The Handloader's Manual of Cartridge Conversions*, Stoeger Publishing Co.

Dustin, John, Dec. 1997, *Precision Shooting* magazine, Vol. 45, #8, Pg. 67, Precision Shooting Inc.

Eager, Randall L., Fall 1998, *Small Caliber News*, Small Caliber News Inc.

Eichelberger, W.A., Fall 1998, *Small Caliber News*, Small Caliber News Inc.

Erlmeier & Brandt, 1980, *Manual of Pistol & Revolver Cartridges*, Vols. I, II &III, Schwend Gmbh

European Cartridge Research Assn., 1997, ECRA Cartridge Data Viewer, ECRA

Fadala, Sam, Sept. 1998, *Rifle* magazine, ".375 Breeding," Wolfe Publishing Co.

Fleming, Bill, 1993, *British Sporting Rifle Cartridges*, Armory Publications

Forker, Bob, April 1995, *Guns & Ammo* magazine, "Designing a Wildcat," Petersen Publishing Co.

Foral, Jim, Jan. 1998, *Rifle* Magazine, #175, "Early 25 Cal. Hi Powers," Wolfe Publishing Co.

Franzen, Fredrik, Autumn 1998, *Double Gun Journal*, Behr & Vertikalbloch Verschluss, DGJ Inc.

Fuller, S.L., Editor, 1983, *The Cartridge Collector's Notebook*, from the Library of C.H. Yurst Jr.

Gates, Elgin, 1968, *Metallic Silhouette Shooting*, DBI Books Inc.

Gottfredson, Jacob, Nov. 1998, etc., *Precision Shooting* magazine, "BEST Muzzle Brake," Precision Shooting Inc.

Gregson, J., Jan. 1999, *Shooting Sportsman* magazine, "Anything but Bland," Down East Enterprise Inc.

Gun Parts Corp., 1995, *World Guide To Gun Parts*, 19th Edition, Gun Parts Corp.

Gun Parts Corp., 1997, *World Guide to Gun Parts*, 21st Edition, Gun Parts Corp.

Henry, D.L., 1997, *Handloaders Digest*, 17th Edition, "Wildcatting the 9.3," Krause Publications Inc.

Hoffman, H., Nov. 1987, *Handloader* magazine, "30-20 Hoffman," Wolfe Publishing Co.

Huon, J., March 1998, *Cartridge Researcher*, "9x30 Grom," European Cartridge Research Assn.

Howell, Ken, 1995, *Designing and Forming Custom Cartridges for Rifles and Handguns*, Precision Shooting Inc.

Hoyem, George A., 1985, *British Sporting Guns & Rifles*, Vol. III, Armory Publications

Hoyem, George A., 1981, *British Sporting Guns & Rifles*, Vol. I, Armory Publications

Hoyem, George A., 1996, *Cartridge Catalogues*, Armory Publications

Huntington, 1997, *Huntington Catalog*, Huntington

International Ammunition Association, July-August 1997, Issue 396, International Ammunition Assn.

Jamison, R., June 1997, *Shooting Times* magazine, "284 & 338 Jamison," PJS Publishing Co.

Jamison, R., Sept. 1997, *Shooting Times* magazine, "300 Jamison," PJS Publishing Co.

Jamison, R., Feb. 1999, *Shooting Times* magazine, "Fascinating World of Rifle Bores," PJS Publishing Co.

Jarrett, K., April 1996, *Precision Shooting* magazine, Precision Shooting Inc.

Jeffery, W.J. & Co., 1912, *Jeffery's Guns*, Rifles & General Shooting Accessories, W J Jeffery & Co.

John & James, Nov. 1998, *Guns & Ammo* magazine, "224 Boz," Peterson Publishing Co.

Jones, J.D., 1995, SSK Industries, Sales Brochure, SSK Industries

Kettelkamp, D. & Malson, D., 1996, "Hunting Southern Africa With Muzzle Loading Rifles," Ventures International Publishing Co.

Kindler, Todd, 1995, *The Sensational Seventeens*, Woodchuck Den Publishers

Kindler, Todd, April 1998, *Small Caliber* News, "New Developments," Woodchuck Den Publishers

King, R D. & R.A., 1982, *The Cartridges of Edward Maynard*, Benton Printers & Lithographers

Kohlmann, Heinrich, Sept. 1998, *Cartridge Researcher*, European Cartridge Research Assn.

Labbett, P., 1980, *Military Small Arms Ammo*, 1945-1980, Arms & Armour Press

Landis, C. R., 1947, *Twenty-Two Caliber Varmint Rifles*, Small Arms Technical Publishing Co.

Landis, C. R., 1951, *Woodchucks & Woodchuck Rifles*, Wolfe Publishing Co.

Lee, Richard, 1997, *Lee Precision Reloading Catalog*, Lee Precision Inc.

BIBLIOGRAPHY, CONTINUED

Mack, A. J., 1989, "Cartridge Case Measurements," Amrex Enterprises

Malloy, John, 1998, *Gun Digest*, 52nd Edition, "Handguns Today," Krause Publications

Martin, Bradley, Jan. 1998, Correspondence re: 3 Bore rifle

Matthews, G., Feb. 1994, *Handloade*r magazine, "338-284 Canadian KCG," Wolfe Publishing Co.

Matthews, G., Nov. 1993, *Handloader* magazine, "375 Hawks-Scovill," Wolfe Publishing Co.

Nonte, George C., 1961, *Home Guide to Cartridge Conversions*, Gun Room Press

Old Western Scrounger, 1997 Catalog, Old Western Scrounger

Patric, J., May 1998, *Precision Shooting* magazine, "Shooting the 25 Souper Imp.," Precision Shooting Inc.

Petrov, Michael, Feb. 1998, *Precision Shooting* magazine, Hoffman Arms Co., Precision Shooting Inc.

Petrov, Michael, Mar. 1998, *Precision Shooting* magazine, Niedner Rifle Corp., Precision Shooting Inc.

Petty, Charles, April 1998, *Handloader magazine*, ".400 Corbon," Wolfe Publishing Co.

Putzke, Harley, 1998, *Very High Power* 1998, #1, "Loose Thoughts & Comments," FCSA

RCBS, 1996, RCBS *Special Order Catalog*, Blount Inc.

RCBS, 1996, RCBS, *CCI & Speer Catalog*, Blount Inc.

RCBS, 1997, RCBS *Special Order Catalog*, Blount Inc.

Richards, J., 1991, *British Cartridge* Guide, Z-Towne Images

Rush, Jack, Fall 1998, *Small Caliber News*, Small Caliber News Inc.

Scovill, Dave, Sept. 1998, *Rifle* magazine, ".375 Alaskan," Wolfe Publishing Co.

Scovill, Dave, 1993, *Illustrated Reference of Cartridge Dimensions*, Wolfe Publishing Co.

Scovill, Dave, Sept. 2001, *Rifle* magazine, "375 Hawk/Scovill" Wolfe Publishing Co.

Sengal, Gil, March 1998, *Rifle* magazine, "Mysterious 12.7x70," Wolfe Publishing Co.

Sengal, Gil, Feb. 1999, *Handloader* magazine, ".25-20 Single Shot," Wolfe Publishing Co.

Seyfried, R., July 1994, *Guns & Ammo* magazine, "404 Jeffery," Petersen Publishing Co.

Seyfried, R., June 1998, *Guns & Ammo* Magazine, "Ultra Yardage 22s," Petersen Publishing Co.

Seyfried, R., Dec. 1998, *Guns & Ammo* magazine, "We Rest Our Case," Petersen Publishing Co.

Sharpe, P., 1937, *Complete Guide to Handloading*, 3rd Edition, Wolfe Publishing Co.

Simmons, Richard F., 1947, *Wildcat Cartridges*, William Morrow & Co.

Simpson, Layne, Feb. 1998, *Shooting Times* magazine, "Dependable Dozen," PJS Publishing Co.

Simpson, Layne, Sept. 1998, *Shooting Times* magazine, "Questions & Answers," PJS Publishing Co.

Simpson, Layne, Dec. 1998, *Handloader* magazine, "Benchtopics," Wolfe Publishing Co.

Simpson, Layne, Dec. 1998, *Shooting Times* magazine, "Rem's New Ultra Mag," PJS Publishing Co.

Simpson, Layne, Dec. 1998, *Shooting Times* magazine, "Q&A" (338 BGS), PJS Publishing Co.

Solyntjes, G., Sept. 1990, *Handloader* magazine, 22 Cheeta, Wolfe Publishing Co.

Speck, A., Jan. 1997, *Handloader* magazine, "8mm Stansky," Wolfe Publishing Co.

Speegle, B.L., Mar. 1988, *Man At Arms* magazine, "Collecting English Rook Rifles," A. Mowbray, publisher

Talbot, Skip, 1998, Personal Correspondence, Unpublished

Timerson, Ed, Dec. 1998, *Precision Shooting* magazine, "A Varmint Hunters Wildcat," Precision Shooting Inc.

Trast, Ira, Various Years, *World Guide to Gun Parts*, Gun Parts Corp.

Tulp, Martin, Nov. 1998, *The Cartridge Researcher*, "All About Boring," European Cart. Research Assn.

van Zwoll, Wayne, June 1998, *Handloader* magazine, #193, Wolfe Publishing Co.

van Zwoll, Wayne, July 1992, *Rifle* magazine, "6.5 Redding," Wolfe Publishing Co.

Waters, K. Jan. 1974, *Rifle* magazine, "Pet Loads 7x61," Wolfe Publishing Co.

Waters, K., July 1975, *Handloader* magazine, "458 RCBS," Wolfe Publishing Co.

Waters, K. Nov. 1984, *Handloader* magazine, "35 Greevy," Wolfe Pub. Company

Waters, K., May 1985, *Handloader* magazine, "22 Niedner," Wolfe Publishing Co.

Waters, K., July 1997, *Handloader* magazine, "375 Express," Wolfe Publishing Co.

Waters, Ken, March 1998, *Rifle* magazine, "An Uncommon Westley Richards," Wolfe Publishing Co.

Westley Richards & Co., 1998, *Rifle Cartridges Catalog*, Printed in England

Wolf, Harald, 1998, *Hatari Times Intl.*, #2, "9.3x70 Mag.," Hatari Verlag

Wolf, Harald, 1998, *Hatari Times Intl.*, #3, "Present of Djunblad Bey," Hatari Verlag

Wolfe, Dave, 1980, *Yours Truly Harvey Donaldson*, Wolfe Publishing Co.

Wolfe Editors, 1992, *Wildcat Cartridges*, Vol. I, Wolfe Publishing Co.

Wolfe Editors, 1992, *Wildcat Cartridges*, Vol. II, Wolfe Publishing Co.

Wright, Dick, August 1998, *Precision Shooting*, "Home on the Range," Precision Shooting Inc.

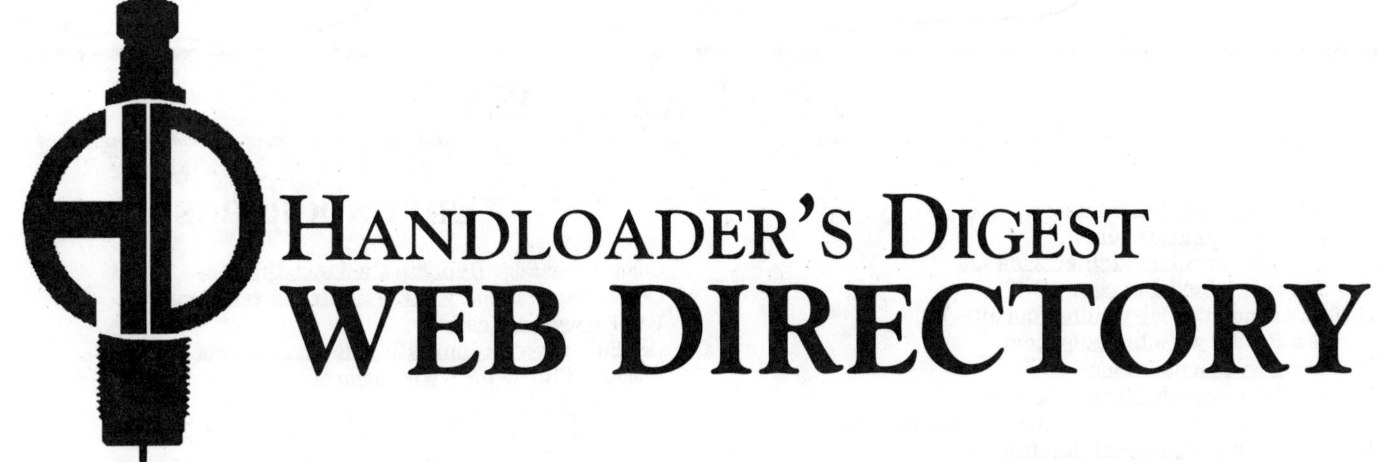

HANDLOADER'S DIGEST WEB DIRECTORY

by Holt Bodinson

WHILE THE "DOT-coms" may have hit the skids on Wall Street, the World Wide Web continues to branch out to become an increasingly essential source of information and e-commerce for the firearms community.

This year the U.S. Commerce Department reported that 143 million Americans, or 54% of the country, were regularly using the Internet--an increase of 26% over the previous year. It is estimated that each month 2 million more Americans hook-up to cruise the Web. The future looks even brighter with 90% of young Americans between the ages of five and 17 currently using computers.

The **Handloader's Digest** Web Directory is in its fourth year of publication. The trend is clear. More and more firearm-related businesses are striking out and creating their own discrete web pages, and it's never been easier with the inexpensive software programs now available.

The Internet is a dynamic environment and, since our last edition, there have been many changes. Companies have consolidated and adopted a new owner's website address. Many of the smaller, specialized collector forums are now grouped and thriving at www.gunandknife.com/ forums. New companies have appeared and old companies have disappeared. Search engines are now more powerful than ever and seem to root out even the most obscure reference to a product name or manufacturer.

The following index of current Web addresses is offered to our readers as a convenient jumping-off point. Half the fun is just exploring what's out there. Considering that most of the Web pages have hot links to other firearm-related Web pages, the Internet trail just goes on-and-on once you've taken the initial step to go online.

Here are a few pointers:

If the website you desire is not listed, try using the full name of the company or product, typed without spaces, between www.-and-.com, for example, www.krause.com. Probably 95% of current websites are based on this simple, self- explanatory format.
Try a variety of search engines like **Microsoft Internet Explorer, Metacrawler, GoTo.com, Yahoo, HotBot, AltaVista, Lycos, Excite, InfoSeek, Looksmart, Google, and WebCrawler** while using key words such as gun, firearm, rifle, pistol, blackpowder, shooting, hunting— frankly, any word that relates to the sport. Each search engine seems to comb through the World Wide Web in a different fashion and produces different results. We find **Metacrawler** to be among the best. Accessing the various search engines is simple. Just type www.metacrawler.com for example, and you're on your way.

Welcome to the digital world of the Web. Enjoy our Directory!

AMMUNITION AND COMPONENTS

3-D Ammunition **www.3dammo.com**
Accurate Arms Co. Inc **www.accuratepowder.com**
ADCO/Nobel Sport Powder **www.adcosales.com**
Aguila Ammunition **www.aguilaammo.com**
All Purpose Ammunition **www.dragonbreath.com**
Alliant Powder **www.alliantpowder.com**
Ammo Depot **www.ammodepot.com**
Arizona Ammunition, Inc. **www.arizonaammunition.com**
A-Zoom Ammo **www.a-zoom.com**
Ballard Rifle & Cartridge LLC **www.ballardrifles.com**
Ballistic Products, Inc. **www.ballisticproducts.com**
Barnes Bullets **www.barnesbullets.com**
Baschieri & Pellagri **www.baschieri-pellagri.com**
Beartooth Bullets **www.beartoothbullets.com**
Bell Brass **www.bellbrass.com**
Berger Bullets, Ltd. **www.bergerbullets.com**
Berry's Mfg., Inc. **www.berrysmfg.com**
Big Bore Bullets of Alaska **www.awloo.com/bbb/index.htm**
Big Bore Express **www.bigbore.com**
Bismuth Cartridge Co. **www.bismuth-notox.com**
Black Hills Ammunition, Inc. **www.black-hills.com**
Brenneke of America Ltd. **www.brennekeusa.com**
Buffalo Arms **www.buffaloarms.com**
Bull-X inc. **www.bull-x.com**
Calhoon, James, Bullets **www.jamescalhoon.com**
Cast Performance Bullet **www.castperformance.com**
CCI **www.cci-ammunition.com**
Century Arms **www.centuryarms.com**
Cheaper Than Dirt **www.cheaperthandirt.com**
Cheddite France **www.cheddite.com**
Claybuster Wads **www.claybuster.com**
Clean Shot Powder **www.cleanshot.com**
Cole Distributing **www.cole-distributing.com**
Cor-Bon **www.cor-bon.com**
Denver Bullet Co. **denbullets@aol.com**
Dillon Precision **www.dillonprecision.com**
DKT, Inc. **www.dktinc.com**
Dynamit Nobel RWS Inc. **www.dnrws.com**
Elephant/Swiss Black Powder **www.elephantblackpowder.com**
Eley Ammunition **www.remington.com**
Eley Hawk Ltd. **www.eleyhawk.com**
Eley Limited **www.eley.co.uk**
Federal Cartridge Co. **www.federalcartridge.com**
Fiocchi of America **www.fiocchiusa.com**
Fowler Bullets **www.benchrest.com/fowler**
Garrett Cartridges **www.garrettcartridges.com**
Glaser Safety Slug, Inc. **www.safetyslug.com**

WEB DIRECTORY

GOEX Inc. **www.goexpowder.com**
Graf & Sons **www.grafs.com**
Hawk Bullets **www.hawkbullets.com**
Hevi.Shot **www.hevishot.com**
Hi-Tech Ammunition **www.iidbs.com/hitech**
Hodgdon Powder **www.hodgdon.com**
Hornady **www.hornady.com**
Hull Cartridge **www.hullcartridge.com**
Huntington Reloading Products **www.huntingtons.com**
Impact Bullets **www.impactbullets.com**
IMR Smokeless Powders **www.imrpowder.com**
Kent Cartridge America **www.kentgamebore.com**
Kynoch Ammunition **www.kynochammunition.com**
Lapua **www.lapua.com**
Lawrence Brand Shot **www.metalico.com**
Lazzeroni Arms Co. **www.lazzeroni.com**
Lightfield Ammunition Corp **www.lightfield-ammo.com**
Lomont Precision Bullets **www.klomont.com/kent**
Lost River Ballistic Technologies, Inc. **www.lostriverballistic.com**
Lyman **www.lymanproducts.com**
Magnus Bullets **www.magnusbullets.com**
MagSafe Ammunition **www.realpages.com/magsafeammo**
Magtech **www.magtechammunition.com**
Mast Technology **www.bellammo.com**
Masterclass Bullet Co. **www.mastercast.com**
Meister Bullets **www.meisterbullets.com**
Midway USA **www.midwayusa.com**
Miltex,Inc. **www.miltexusa.com**
MK Ballistic Systems **www.mkballistics.com**
Mullins Ammunition **www.mullinsammunition.com**
National Bullet Co. **www.nationalbullet.com**
Nobel Sport **www.adcosales.com**
Nobel Sport **www.snpe.com**
Norma **www.norma.cc**
Nosler Bullets Inc **www.nosler.com**
Old Western Scrounger **www.ows-ammunition.com**
Oregon Trail/Trueshot **www.trueshotbullets.com**
(formerly Laser-Cast)
Pattern Control **www.patterncontrol.com**
PMC-Eldorado Cartridge **www.pmcammo.com**
Polywad **www.polywad.com**
Pro Load Ammunition **www.proload.com**
Rainier Ballistics **www.rainierballistics.com**
Ram Shot Powder **www.ramshot.com**
Reloading Specialties Inc. **www.reloadingspecialties.com**
Remington **www.remington.com**
Sauvestre Slug **kengsfirearms@mindspring.com**
Sellier & Bellot USA inc. **www.sb-usa.com**
Shilen **www.shilen.com**
Sierra **www.sierrabullets.com**
Speer Bullets **www.speer-bullets.com**
Sporting Supplies Int'l Inc. **www.ssiintl.com**
Starline **www.starlinebrass.com**
Triton Cartridge **www.triton-ammo.com**
Tru-Tracer **www.trutracer.com**
Vihtavuori Lapua **www.lapua.com**
West Coast Bullets **www.westcoastbullet.com**
Western Powders Inc. **www.westernpowders.com**
Widener's Reloading & Shooters Supply **www.wideners.com**
Winchester Ammunition **www.winchester.com**
Wolf Ammunition **www.wolfammo.com**
Woodleigh Bullets **www.woodleighbullets.com.au**
Zanders Sporting Goods **www.gzanders.com**

CHRONOGRAPHS

Competitive Edge **Dynamics www.cedhk.com**
Oehler Research Inc. **www.oehler-research.com**
PACT **www.pact.com**
ProChrony **www.competitionelectronics.com**
Shooting Chrony Inc **www.chrony.ca**

RELOADING TOOLS AND SUPPLIES

Ballisti-Cast Mfg. **www.powderandbow.com/ballist**
Bruno Shooters Supply **www.brunoshooters.com**
CH Tool & Die **www.cdhd.com**
Corbin Mfg & Supply Co. **www.corbins.com**
Dillon Precision **www.dillonprecision.com**
Forster Precision Products **www.forsterproducts.com**
Hanned Line **www.hanned.com**
Harrell's Precision **www.harrellsprec.com**
Hornady **www.hornady.com**
Huntington Reloading Products **www.huntingtons.com**
J & J Products Co. **www.jandjproducts.com**
Lee Precision,Inc. **www.leeprecision.com**
Littleton Shotmaker **www.leadshotmaker.com**
Lyman **www.lymanproducts.com**
Magma Engineering **www.magmaengr.com**
Mayville Engineering Co. *(MEC)* **www.mecreloaders.com**
Midway **www.midwayusa.com**
Moly-Bore **www.molybore.com**
MTM Case-Guard **www.mtmcase-guard.com**
NECO **www.neconos.com**
NEI Handtools Inc. **www.neihandtools.com**
Neil Jones Custom Products **www.neiljones.com**
Ponsness/Warren **www.reloaders.com**
Ranger Products
www.pages.prodigy.com/rangerproducts.home.htm
Rapine Bullet Mold Mfg Co. **www.bulletmolds.com**
RCBS **www.rcbs.com**
Redding Reloading Equipment **www.redding-reloading.com**
Russ Haydon's Shooting Supplies **www.shooters-supply.com**
Sinclair Int'l Inc. **www.sinclairintl.com**
Stoney Point Products Inc **www.stoneypoint.com**
Thompson Bullet Lube Co. **www.thompsonbulletlube.com**
Wilson *(L.E. Wilson)* **www.lewilson.com**

RESTS—BENCH, PORTABLE, ATTACHABLE

B-Square **www.b-square.com**
Bullshooter **www.bullshootersightingin.com**
Desert Mountain Mfg. **www.bench-master.com**
Harris Engineering Inc. **www.cyberteklabs.com/harris/main/htm**
Kramer Designs **www.snipepod.com**
L Thomas Rifle Support **www.ltsupport.com**
Level-Lok **www.levellok.com**
Midway **www.midwayusa.com**
Ransom International **www.ransom-intl.com**
R.W. Hart **www.rwhart.com**
Sinclair Intl, Inc. **www.sinclairintl.com**
Stoney Point Products **www.stoneypoint.com**
Target Shooting **www.targetshooting.com**
Varmint Masters **www.varmintmasters.com**
Versa-Pod **www.versa-pod.com**

Handloader's Digest Product & Service Directory

Ammunition Components, Shotshell
A.W. Peterson Gun Shop, Inc.
Ballistic Product, Inc.
Blount, Inc., Sporting Equipment Div.
CCI Ammunition
Cheddite France S.A.
Claybuster Wads & Harvester Bullets
Garcia National Gun Traders, Inc.
Peterson Gun Shop, Inc., A.W.
Precision Reloading, Inc.
Ravell Ltd.
Tar-Hunt Custom Rifles, Inc.
Tar-Hunt Custom Rifles, Inc.
The A.W. Peterson Gun Shop, Inc.
Vitt/Boos

Ammunition Components--Bullets, Powder, Primers, Cases
3-D Ammunition & Bullets
A.W. Peterson Gun Shop, Inc.
Acadian Ballistic Specialties
Accuracy Unlimited
Accurate Arms Co., Inc.
Action Bullets & Alloy Inc
ADCO Sales, Inc.
Alaska Bullet Works, Inc.
Alliant Techsystems Smokeless Powder Group
Allred Bullet Co.
Alpha LaFranck Enterprises
American Products, Inc.
Arizona Ammunition, Inc.
Armfield Custom Bullets
A-Square Company, Inc.
Atlantic Rose, Inc.
Baer's Hollows
Ballard Rifle & Cartridge Co., LLC
Barnes
Barnes Bullets, Inc.
Beartooth Bullets
Bell Reloading, Inc.
Berger Bullets Ltd.
Berry's Mfg., Inc.
Big Bore Bullets of Alaska
Big Bore Express
Bitterroot Bullet Co.
Black Belt Bullets *(See Big Bore Express)*
Black Hills Shooters Supply
Black Powder Products
Blount, Inc., Sporting Equipment Div.
Blue Mountain Bullets
Brenneke KG, Wilhelm
Briese Bullet Co., Inc.
Brown Co, E. Arthur
Brown Dog Ent.
BRP, Inc. High Performance Cast Bullets
Buck Stix--SOS Products Co.
Buckeye Custom Bullets
Buckskin Bullet Co.
Buffalo Arms Co.
Buffalo Bullet Co., Inc..
Buffalo Rock Shooters Supply
Bullseye Bullets
Bull-X, Inc.
Butler Enterprises
Cambos Outdoorsman
Canyon Cartridge Corp.
Cascade Bullet Co., Inc.
Cast Performance Bullet Company
Casull Arms Corp.
CCI Ammunition
Champion's Choice, Inc.
Cheddite France S.A.
CheVron Bullets
Chuck's Gun Shop
Clean Shot Technologies
Colorado Sutlers Arsenal *(See Cumberland States)*
Competitor Corp. Inc.
Cook Engineering Service
Cor-Bon Bullet & Ammo Co.
Cumberland States Arsenal
Cummings Bullets
Curtis Cast Bullets
Curtis Gun Shop *(See Curtis Cast Bullets)*
Custom Bullets by Hoffman
D&J Bullet Co. & Custom Gun Shop, Inc.
Dakota Arms, Inc.
Davide Pedersoli and Co.
DKT, Inc.
Dohring Bullets
Eichelberger Bullets, Wm.
Eldorado Cartridge Corp *(See PMC/Eldorado)*
Federal Cartridge Co.
Fiocchi of America Inc.
Fish Mfg. Gunsmith Sptg. Co., Marshall
Forkin, Ben *(See Belt MTN Arms)*
Forkin Arms
Fowler Bullets
Fowler, Bob *(See Black Powder Products)*
Foy Custom Bullets
Freedom Arms, Inc.
Garcia National Gun Traders, Inc.
Gehmann, Walter *(See Huntington Die Specialties)*
GOEX Inc.
Golden Bear Bullets
Gotz Bullets
Grayback Wildcats
Green Mountain Rifle Barrel Co., Inc.
Grier's Hard Cast Bullets
GTB
Gun City
Hammets VLD Bullets
Hardin Specialty Dist.
Harris Enterprises
Harrison Bullets
Hart & Son, Inc.
Hawk Laboratories, Inc. *(See Hawk, Inc.)*
Hawk, Inc.
Haydon Shooters Supply, Russ
Heidenstrom Bullets
Hercules, Inc. *(See Alliant Techsystems, Smokeless)*
Hi-Performance Ammunition Company
Hirtenberger Aktiengesellschaft
Hobson Precision Mfg. Co.
Hodgdon Powder Co.
Hornady Mfg. Co.
HT Bullets
Hunters Supply, Inc.
Impact Case Co.
Imperial Magnum Corp.
IMR Powder Co.
Intercontinental Distributors, Ltd.
J&D Components
J&L Superior Bullets *(See Huntington Die Special)*
J.R. Williams Bullet Co.
James Calhoon Mfg.
James Calhoon Varmint Bullets
Jensen Bullets
Jensen's Firearms Academy
Jericho Tool & Die Co., Inc.
Jester Bullets
JLK Bullets
JRP Custom Bullets
Ka Pu Kapili
Kaswer Custom, Inc.
Keith's Bullets
Keng's Firearms Specialty, Inc. / US Tactical Systems
Ken's Kustom Kartridges
Kent Cartridge Mfg. Co. Ltd.
KLA Enterprises
Knight Rifles
Knight Rifles *(See Modern Muzzle Loading, Inc.)*
Lapua Ltd.
Lawrence Brand Shot *(See Precision Reloading)*
Legend Products Corp.
Liberty Shooting Supplies
Lightning Performance Innovations, Inc.
Lindsley Arms Cartridge Co.
Littleton, J. F.
Lomont Precision Bullets
Loweth, Richard H.R.
Lyman Products Corp.
Magnus Bullets
Maine Custom Bullets
Maionchi-L.M.I.
Marchmon Bullets
Markesbery Muzzle Loaders, Inc.
MarMik, Inc.
MAST Technology
McMurdo, Lynn *(See Specialty Gunsmithing)*
Meister Bullets *(See Gander Mountain)*
Men-Metallwerk Elisenhuette GmbH
Merkuria Ltd.
Michael's Antiques
Mitchell Bullets, R.F.
MI-TE Bullets
Montana Precision Swaging
Mountain State Muzzleloading Supplies, Inc.
Mulhern, Rick
Murmur Corp.
Nagel's Custom Bullets
National Bullet Co.
Naval Ordnance Works
Necromancer Industries, Inc.
North American Shooting Systems
North Devon Firearms Services
Northern Precision Custom Swaged Bullets
Nosler, Inc.
OK Weber,Inc.
Oklahoma Ammunition Co.
Old Wagon Bullets

Old Western Scrounger,Inc.
Oregon Trail Bullet Company
Pacific Cartridge, Inc.
Pacific Rifle Co.
Page Custom Bullets
Pease Accuracy
Penn Bullets
Peterson Gun Shop, Inc., A.W.
Petro-Explo Inc.
Phillippi Custom Bullets, Justin
Pinetree Bullets
PMC / Eldorado Cartridge Corp.
Polywad, Inc.
Power Plus Enterprises, Inc.
Precision Delta Corp.
Precision Munitions, Inc.
Prescott Projectile Co.
Price Bullets, Patrick W.
PRL Bullets, c/o Blackburn Enterprises
Professional Hunter Supplies *(See Star Custom Bull)*
Proofmark Corp.
R.I.S. Co., Inc.
Rainier Ballistics Corp.
Ramon B. Gonzalez Guns
Ravell Ltd.
Redwood Bullet Works
Reloading Specialties, Inc.
Remington Arms Co., Inc.
Rhino
Robinson H.V. Bullets
Rubright Bullets
Russ Haydon Shooters' Supply
SAECO *(See Redding Reloading Equipment)*
Scharch Mfg., Inc.
Schneider Bullets
Schroeder Bullets
Schumakers Gun Shop
Scot Powder
Seebeck Assoc., R.E.
Shappy Bullets
Sharps Arms Co., Inc., C.
Shilen, Inc.
Sierra Bullets
SOS Products Co. *(See Buck Stix-SOS Products Co.)*
Southern Ammunition Co., Inc.
Specialty Gunsmithing
Speer Bullets
Spencer's Custom Guns
Stanley Bullets
Star Ammunition, Inc.
Star Custom Bullets
Starke Bullet Company
Starline, Inc.
Stewart's Gunsmithing
Swift Bullet Co.
T.F.C. S.p.A.
Taracorp Industries, Inc.
TCCI
TCSR
The A.W. Peterson Gun Shop, Inc.
The Ordnance Works
Thompson Bullet Lube Co.
Thompson Precision
TMI Products *(See Haselbauer Products, Jerry)*
Traditions Performance Firearms
Trico Plastics
True Flight Bullet Co.
Tucson Mold, Inc.
Unmussig Bullets, D. L.
USAC
Vann Custom Bullets
Vihtavuori Oy/Kaltron-Pettibone
Vincent's Shop
Viper Bullet and Brass Works
Vom Hoffe *(See Old Western Scrounger, Inc., The)*
Warren Muzzleloading Co., Inc.
Watson Trophy Match Bullets
Weatherby, Inc.
Western Nevada West Coast Bullets
Widener's Reloading & Shooting Supply, Inc.
Winchester Div. Olin Corp.
Winkle Bullets
Woodleigh *(See Huntington Die Specialties)*
Worthy Products, Inc.
Wyant Bullets
Wyoming Custom Bullets
Zero Ammunition Co., Inc.

Ammunition, Foreign
A.W. Peterson Gun Shop, Inc.
Ad Hominem
AFSCO Ammunition
Armscorp USA, Inc.
Atlantic Rose, Inc.
B & P America
Beeman Precision Airguns
Cape Outfitters
CBC
Cheddite France S.A.
Cubic Shot Shell Co., Inc.
Dead Eye's Sport Center
Diana *(See U.S. Importer -Dynamit Nobel-RWS, Inc.)*
DKT, Inc.
Dynamit Nobel-RWS, Inc.
E. Arthur Brown Co.
Fiocchi of America Inc.
First Inc., Jack
Gamebore Division, Polywad Inc
Gibbs Rifle Co., Inc.
GOEX Inc.
Goodwin's Gun Shop
Gunsmithing, Inc.
Hansen & Co. *(See Hansen Cartridge Co.)*
Heidenstrom Bullets
Hirtenberger Aktiengesellschaft
Hornady Mfg. Co.
IMX, LLC
Intrac Arms International
K.B.I. Inc
MagSafe Ammo Co.
Maionchi-L.M.I.
Mandall Shooting Supplies Inc.
Marksman Products
MAST Technology
Merkuria Ltd.
Mullins Ammunition
Navy Arms Company
Oklahoma Ammunition Co.
Old Western Scrounger,Inc.
P.S.M.G. Gun Co.
Paragon Sales & Services, Inc.
Peterson Gun Shop, Inc., A.W.
Petro-Explo Inc.
Precision Delta Corp.
R.E.T. Enterprises
Ramon B. Gonzalez Guns
RWS *(See US Importer-Dynamit Nobel-RWS, Inc.)*
Samco Global Arms, Inc.
Sentinel Arms
Southern Ammunition Co., Inc.
Speer Bullets
Stratco, Inc.
T.F.C. S.p.A.
The A.W. Peterson Gun Shop, Inc.
The BulletMakers Workshop
The Paul Co.
Victory Ammunition
Vihtavuori Oy/Kaltron-Pettibone
Vom Hoffe *(See Old Western Scrounger, Inc., The)*

Bullet Casting, Accessories
Ballisti-Cast, Inc.
Buffalo Arms Co.
Bullet Metals
Cast Performance Bullet Company
CFVentures
Cooper-Woodward
Davide Pedersoli and Co.
Ferguson, Bill
Lee Precision, Inc.
Lithi Bee Bullet Lube
Lyman Products Corp.
Magma Engineering Co.
Ox-Yoke Originals, Inc.
Rapine Bullet Mould Mfg. Co.
SPG LLC
The A.W. Peterson Gun Shop, Inc.
The Gun Works
The Hanned Line
United States Products Co.

Bullet Casting, Furnaces & Pots
Ballisti-Cast, Inc.
Buffalo Arms Co.
Bullet Metals
Ferguson, Bill
GAR
Lee Precision, Inc.
Lyman Products Corp.
Magma Engineering Co.
Rapine Bullet Mould Mfg. Co.
The A.W. Peterson Gun Shop, Inc.
The Gun Works
Thompson Bullet Lube Co.

Bullet Casting, Lead
Action Bullets & Alloy Inc
Ames Metal Products
Belltown Ltd.
Buckskin Bullet Co.
Buffalo Arms Co.
Bullet Metals
Bullseye Bullets
Hunters Supply, Inc.
Jericho Tool & Die Co., Inc.
Lee Precision, Inc.
Lithi Bee Bullet Lube
Magma Engineering Co.
Montana Precision Swaging
Ox-Yoke Originals, Inc.
Penn Bullets
Proofmark Corp.
SPG LLC
Splitfire Sporting Goods, L.L.C.
The A.W. Peterson Gun Shop, Inc.
The Gun Works
Walters Wads

Bullet Pullers
Battenfeld Technologies
Davide Pedersoli and Co.
Hollywood Engineering
Royal Arms Gunstocks
The A.W. Peterson Gun Shop, Inc.
The Gun Works

Bullet Tools
Brynin, Milton
Camdex, Inc.
Corbin Mfg. & Supply, Inc.
Cumberland Arms
Eagan, Donald V.
Holland's Gunsmithing
Hollywood Engineering
Lee Precision, Inc.
Necromancer Industries, Inc.
Niemi Engineering, W. B.
North Devon Firearms Services
Rorschach Precision Products
Sport Flite Manufacturing Co.
The A.W. Peterson Gun Shop, Inc.
The Hanned Line
WTA Manufacturing

Bullet, Case & Die Lubricants
Beartooth Bullets
Bonanza *(See Forster Products)*
Brown Co, E. Arthur
Buckskin Bullet Co.
Buffalo Arms Co.
Camp-Cap Products
CFVentures
Cooper-Woodward
CVA
E-Z-Way Systems
Ferguson, Bill
Forster Products
GAR
Guardsman Products
Heidenstrom Bullets
Hollywood Engineering
Hornady Mfg. Co.
Imperial *(See E-Z-Way Systems)*
Knoell, Doug
L.B.T.
Le Clear Industries *(See E-Z-Way Systems)*
Lee Precision, Inc.

Lithi Bee Bullet Lube
MI-TE Bullets
Paco's *(See Small Custom Mould & Bullet Co)*
RCBS Div. of Blount
Reardon Products
Rooster Laboratories
Shay's Gunsmithing
Small Custom Mould & Bullet Co.
Tamarack Products, Inc.
Uncle Mike's *(See Michaels of Oregon Co.)*
Warren Muzzleloading Co., Inc.
Widener's Reloading & Shooting Supply, Inc.
Young Country Arms

Cartridges for Collectors
"Gramps" Antiques
Ackerman & Co.
Ad Hominem
Armory Publications
British Antiques
Cameron's
Campbell, Dick
Cartridge Transfer Group, Pete de Coux
Cherry Creek State Park Shooting Center
Cole's Gun Works
Colonial Repair
Cubic Shot Shell Co., Inc.
de Coux, Pete *(See Cartridge Transfer Group)*
Duane's Gun Repair *(See DGR Custom Rifles)*
Ed's Gun House
Ed's Gun House
Enguix Import-Export
Epps, Ellwood/Isabella *(See Gramps)*
First Inc., Jack
Fitz Pistol Grip Co.
Forty Five Ranch Enterprises
Goergen's Gun Shop, Inc.
Goodwin's Gun Shop
Grayback Wildcats
Gun City
Gun Hunter Books *(See Gun Hunter Trading Co)*
Gun Hunter Trading Co.
Kelley's
Liberty Shooting Supplies
Mandall Shooting Supplies Inc.
MAST Technology
Michael's Antiques
Montana Outfitters, Lewis E. Yearout
Pasadena Gun Center
Samco Global Arms, Inc.
SOS Products Co. *(See Buck Stix-SOS Products Co.)*
Stone Enterprises Ltd.
The Country Armourer
The Gun Parts Corp.
The Gun Room Press
Vom Hoffe *(See Old Western Scrounger, Inc., The)*
Ward & Van Valkenburg
Winchester Consultants
Yearout, Lewis E. *(See Montana Outfitters)*
Case & Ammunition Processors,

Case Cleaners & Polishing Media
3-D Ammunition & Bullets
Battenfeld Technologies
Belltown Ltd.
Buffalo Arms Co.
Chem-Pak Inc.
G96 Products Co., Inc.
Lee Precision, Inc.
Penn Bullets
The A.W. Peterson Gun Shop, Inc.
The Gun Works
Tru-Square Metal Products Inc.
VibraShine, Inc.

Case Preparation Tools

Battenfeld Technologies
CONKKO
Dewey Mfg. Co., Inc., J.
High Precision
Hoehn Sales, Inc.
K&M Services
Lee Precision, Inc.
Match Prep--Doyle Gracey
Plum City Ballistic Range
RCBS Div. of Blount
Russ Haydon Shooters' Supply
Sinclair International, Inc.
Stoney Point Products, Inc.
The A.W. Peterson Gun Shop, Inc.

Case Trimmers, Trim Dies & Accessories
Buffalo Arms Co.
Fremont Tool Works
Goodwin's Gun Shop
Hollywood Engineering
K&M Services
Lyman Products Corp.
Match Prep--Doyle Gracey
OK Weber,Inc.
Ozark Gun Works
Redding Reloading Equipment
The A.W. Peterson Gun Shop, Inc.
Time Precision

Case Tumblers, Vibrators, Media & Accessories
4-D Custom Die Co.
Battenfeld Technologies
Berry's Mfg., Inc.
Dillon Precision Products, Inc.
Goodwin's Gun Shop
Penn Bullets
Raytech Div. of Lyman Products Corp.
The A.W. Peterson Gun Shop, Inc.
Tru-Square Metal Products Inc.
VibraShine, Inc.

Chronographs & Pressure Tools
Air Rifle Specialists
Brown Co, E. Arthur
C.W. Erickson's L.L.C.
Canons Delcour
Clearview Products
Competition Electronics, Inc.
Custom Chronograph, Inc.
D&H Precision Tooling
Hege Jagd-u. Sporthandels GmbH
Hutton Rifle Ranch
Kent Cartridge Mfg. Co. Ltd.
Mac-1 Airgun Distributors
Oehler Research,Inc.
P.A.C.T., Inc.
Romain's Custom Guns, Inc.
Savage Arms, Inc.
Shooting Chrony, Inc.
Spencer's Custom Guns
Stratco, Inc.
Tepeco

Cleaners & Degreasers
Belltown Ltd.
Camp-Cap Products
G96 Products Co., Inc.
Goodwin's Gun Shop
Hafner World Wide, Inc.
Half Moon Rifle Shop
Kleen-Bore,Inc.
LEM Gun Specialties Inc. The Lewis Lead Remover
Modern Muzzleloading, Inc
Northern Precision Custom Swaged Bullets
Parker & Sons Shooting Supply
Perazone-Gunsmith, Brian
PrOlixrÆ Lubricants
R&S Industries Corp.
Sheffield Knifemakers Supply, Inc.
Shooter's Choice Gun Care
Sierra Specialty Prod. Co.
The A.W. Peterson Gun Shop, Inc.
The Gun Works
United States Products Co.

Computer Software -Ballistics
Action Target, Inc.
AmBr Software Group Ltd.
Arms Software
Arms, Programming Solutions *(See Arms Software)*
Barnes Bullets, Inc.
Canons Delcour
Corbin Mfg. & Supply, Inc.
Data Tech Software Systems
Hodgdon Powder Co.
J.I.T. Ltd.
Jensen Bullets
Kent Cartridge Mfg. Co. Ltd.
Maionchi-L.M.I.
Oehler Research,Inc.
Outdoor Sports Headquarters, Inc.
P.A.C.T., Inc.
Pejsa Ballistics
Powley Computer *(See Hutton Rifle Ranch)*
RCBS Div. of Blount
Sierra Bullets
The Ballistic Program Co., Inc.
The Country Armourer
Tioga Engineering Co., Inc.
Vancini, Carl *(See Bestload, Inc.)*
W. Square Enterprises

Die Accessories, Metallic
High Precision
King & Co.
MarMik, Inc.
Rapine Bullet Mould Mfg. Co.
Redding Reloading Equipment
Sport Flite Manufacturing Co.
The A.W. Peterson Gun Shop, Inc.
Wolf's Western Traders

Dies, Metallic
4-D Custom Die Co.
Dakota Arms, Inc.
Dillon Precision Products, Inc.
Dixie Gun Works
Fremont Tool Works
Goodwin's Gun Shop
Gruning Precision Inc
Jones Custom Products, Neil A.
King & Co.
Lee Precision, Inc.
Montana Precision Swaging
Neil A. Jones Custom Products
Ozark Gun Works
Rapine Bullet Mould Mfg. Co.
RCBS Div. of Blount
Redding Reloading Equipment
Romain's Custom Guns, Inc.
Sport Flite Manufacturing Co.
The A.W. Peterson Gun Shop, Inc.
Vega Tool Co.
Wolf's Western Traders

Dies, Shotshell
Goodwin's Gun Shop
Lee Precision, Inc.
MEC, Inc.
The A.W. Peterson Gun Shop, Inc.

Dies, Swage
4-D Custom Die Co.
Bullet Swaging Supply Inc.
Goodwin's Gun Shop
Hollywood Engineering
Sport Flite Manufacturing Co.
The A.W. Peterson Gun Shop, Inc.

Gauges, Calipers & Micrometers
Blue Ridge Machinery & Tools, Inc.
Goodwin's Gun Shop
Gruning Precision Inc
K&M Services
King & Co.
Starrett Co., L. S.
Stoney Point Products, Inc.

Labels, Boxes & Cartridge Holders
Ballistic Product, Inc.
Berry's Mfg., Inc.
Brocock Ltd.
Brown Co, E. Arthur
Cabinet Mtn. Outfitters Scents & Lures
Cheyenne Pioneer Products
Del Rey Products
DeSantis Holster & Leather Goods, Inc.
Fitz Pistol Grip Co.
Flambeau Products Corp.
Goodwin's Gun Shop
Hafner World Wide, Inc.

J&J Products, Inc.
Kolpin Mfg., Inc.
Liberty Shooting Supplies
Midway Arms, Inc.
MTM Molded Products Co., Inc.
Pendleton Royal, c/o Swingler Buckland Ltd.
Ziegel Engineering

Lead Wires & Wire Cutters
3-D Ammunition & Bullets
Ames Metal Products
Big Bore Express
Bullet Swaging Supply Inc.
Goodwin's Gun Shop
Lightning Performance Innovations, Inc.
Montana Precision Swaging
Northern Precision Custom Swaged Bullets
Sport Flite Manufacturing Co.
Star Ammunition, Inc.
Unmussig Bullets, D. L.

Load Testing & Product Testing
Ballistic Research
Bitterroot Bullet Co.
Bridgeman Products
Briese Bullet Co., Inc.
Buckskin Bullet Co.
Bull Mountain Rifle Co.
CFVentures
Claybuster Wads & Harvester Bullets
Clearview Products
D&H Precision Tooling
Dead Eye's Sport Center
Defense Training International, Inc.
Duane's Gun Repair *(See DGR Custom Rifles)*
Gonzalez Guns, Ramon B
Gun Hunter Books *(See Gun Hunter Trading Co)*
Gun Hunter Trading Co.
H.P. White Laboratory, Inc.
Hank's Gun Shop
Henigson & Associates, Steve
Hoelscher, Virgil
Hutton Rifle Ranch
Jackalope Gun Shop
Jensen Bullets
L E Jurras & Assoc.
Liberty Shooting Supplies
Linebaugh Custom Sixguns
Lomont Precision Bullets
Maionchi-L.M.I.
MAST Technology
McMurdo, Lynn *(See Specialty Gunsmithing)*
Middlebrooks Custom Shop
Modern Gun Repair School
Multiplex International
Northwest Arms
Oil Rod and Gun Shop
Plum City Ballistic Range
R.A. Wells Custom Gunsmith
Ramon B. Gonzalez Guns
Rupert's Gun Shop
Small Custom Mould & Bullet Co.
SOS Products Co. *(See Buck Stix-SOS Products Co.)*
Spencer's Custom Guns
Trinidad St. Jr Col Gunsmith Dept.
Vancini, Carl *(See Bestload, Inc.)*
Vulpes Ventures, Inc. Fox Cartridge Division)
W. Square Enterprises
X-Spand Target Systems

Loading Blocks, Metallic & Shotshell
Battenfeld Technologies
Buffalo Arms Co.
Jericho Tool & Die Co., Inc.
Sinclair International, Inc.
The A.W. Peterson Gun Shop, Inc.

Lubrisizers, Dies & Accessories
Ballisti-Cast, Inc.
Ben's Machines
Buffalo Arms Co.
Cast Performance Bullet Company
Chem-Pak Inc.
Cooper-Woodward
GAR
Hart & Son, Inc.
Javelina Lube Products
Lee Precision, Inc.
Lithi Bee Bullet Lube
Lyman Products Corp.
Magma Engineering Co.
Redding Reloading Equipment
SPG LLC
The A.W. Peterson Gun Shop, Inc.
Thompson Bullet Lube Co.
United States Products Co.

Moulds & Mould Accessories
Ad Hominem
American Products, Inc.
Ballisti-Cast, Inc.
Buffalo Arms Co.
Cast Performance Bullet Company
GAR
Lee Precision, Inc.
Lyman Products Corp.
Magma Engineering Co.
NEI Handtools, Inc.
Old West Bullet Moulds
Penn Bullets
Rapine Bullet Mould Mfg. Co.
Redding Reloading Equipment
S&S Firearms
Small Custom Mould & Bullet Co.
The A.W. Peterson Gun Shop, Inc.
The Gun Works
Wolf's Western Traders

Powder Measures, Scales, Funnels & Accessories
4-D Custom Die Co.
Battenfeld Technologies
Buffalo Arms Co.
Dillon Precision Products, Inc.
Fremont Tool Works
Frontier
GAR
High Precision
Hoehn Sales, Inc.
Jones Custom Products, Neil A.
Modern Muzzleloading, Inc
Neil A. Jones Custom Products
Peter Dyson & Son Ltd.
Precision Reloading, Inc.
RCBS Div. of Blount
Redding Reloading Equipment
Sanders Gun and Machine Shop
The A.W. Peterson Gun Shop, Inc.
The Gun Works
Vega Tool Co.
VibraShine, Inc.

Press Accessories, Metallic
Buffalo Arms Co.
Efficient Machinery Co
Hollywood Engineering
R.E.I.
Redding Reloading Equipment
The A.W. Peterson Gun Shop, Inc.
Thompson Tool Mount
Vega Tool Co.

Press Accessories, Shotshell
Efficient Machinery Co
Hollywood Engineering
Lee Precision, Inc.
MEC, Inc.
Precision Reloading, Inc.
R.E.I.
The A.W. Peterson Gun Shop, Inc.

Presses, Arbor
Blue Ridge Machinery & Tools, Inc.
Goodwin's Gun Shop
K&M Services
The A.W. Peterson Gun Shop, Inc.

Presses, Metallic
4-D Custom Die Co.
Battenfeld Technologies
Dillon Precision Products, Inc.
Fremont Tool Works
Goodwin's Gun Shop
Hornady Mfg. Co.
Lee Precision, Inc.
RCBS Div. of Blount
Redding Reloading Equipment
The A.W. Peterson Gun Shop, Inc.

Presses, Shotshell
Ballistic Product, Inc.
Dillon Precision Products, Inc.
Goodwin's Gun Shop
Hornady Mfg. Co.
MEC, Inc.
Precision Reloading, Inc.
The A.W. Peterson Gun Shop, Inc.

Presses, Swage
Bullet Swaging Supply Inc.
MAST Technology
The A.W. Peterson Gun Shop, Inc.

Priming Tools & Accessories
Goodwin's Gun Shop
Hart & Son, Inc.
K&M Services
RCBS Div. of Blount
Simmons, Jerry
Sinclair International, Inc.
The A.W. Peterson Gun Shop, Inc.

Reloading Tools and Accessories
4-D Custom Die Co.
Advance Car Mover Co., Rowell Div.
American Products, Inc.
Ammo Load, Inc.
Armfield Custom Bullets
Armite Laboratories
Arms Corporation of the Philippines
Atlantic Rose, Inc.
Atsko/Sno-Seal, Inc.
Bald Eagle Precision Machine Co.
Ballistic Product, Inc.
Belltown Ltd.
Ben William's Gun Shop
Ben's Machines
Berger Bullets Ltd.
Berry's Mfg., Inc.
Blount, Inc., Sporting Equipment Div.
Blue Mountain Bullets
Blue Ridge Machinery & Tools, Inc.
Bonanza *(See Forster Products)*
Break-Free, Inc.
Brown Co, E. Arthur
BRP, Inc. High Performance Cast Bullets
Brynin, Milton
B-Square Company, Inc.
Buck Stix--SOS Products Co.
Buffalo Arms Co.
Bull Mountain Rifle Co.
Bullseye Bullets
C&D Special Products *(See Claybuster Wads & Harves Camdex, Inc.)*
Camp-Cap Products
Canyon Cartridge Corp.
Case Sorting System
CH Tool & Die Co *(See 4-D Custom Die Co)*
Chem-Pak Inc.
CheVron Bullets
Claybuster Wads & Harvester Bullets
CONKKO
Cook Engineering Service
Crouse's Country Cover
Cumberland Arms
Curtis Cast Bullets
Custom Products *(See Jones Custom Products)*
CVA
D.C.C. Enterprises
Davide Pedersoli and Co.
Davis, Don
Davis Products, Mike
Denver Instrument Co.
Dewey Mfg. Co., Inc., J.
Dillon Precision Products, Inc.
Dropkick
E&L Mfg., Inc.
Eagan, Donald V.
Eezox, Inc.
Eichelberger Bullets, Wm.
Enguix Import-Export

Directory of the Handloader's Trade

Euroarms of America, Inc.
E-Z-Way Systems
Federated-Fry *(See Fry Metals)*
Feken, Dennis
Ferguson, Bill
First Inc., Jack
Fisher Custom Firearms
Fitz Pistol Grip Co.
Flambeau Products Corp.
Flitz International Ltd.
Forster Products
Fremont Tool Works
Fry Metals
Gehmann, Walter *(See Huntington Die Specialties)*
Graf & Sons
Graphics Direct
Graves Co.
Green, Arthur S.
Greenwood Precision
GTB
Gun City
Hanned Precision *(See Hanned Line, The)*
Harrell's Precision
Harris Enterprises
Harrison Bullets
Haydon Shooters Supply, Russ
Heidenstrom Bullets
High Precision
Hirtenberger Aktiengesellschaft
Hoch Custom Bullet Moulds *(See Colorado Shooter's)*
Hodgdon Powder Co.
Hoehn Sales, Inc.
Hoelscher, Virgil
Holland's Gunsmithing
Hondo Ind.
Hornady Mfg. Co.
Howell Machine
Hunters Supply, Inc.
Hutton Rifle Ranch
Image Ind. Inc.
Imperial Magnum Corp.
INTEC International, Inc.
Iosso Products
J&L Superior Bullets *(See Huntington Die Special)*
Javelina Lube Products
JGS Precision Tool Mfg.
JLK Bullets
Jonad Corp.
Jones Custom Products, Neil A.
Jones Moulds, Paul
K&M Services
Kapro Mfg.Co. Inc. *(See R.E.I.)*
Knoell, Doug
Korzinek Riflesmith, J.
L.A.R. Mfg., Inc.
L.E. Wilson, Inc.
Lapua Ltd.
Le Clear Industries *(See E-Z-Way Systems)*
Lee Precision, Inc.
Legend Products Corp.
Liberty Metals
Liberty Shooting Supplies
Lightning Performance Innovations, Inc.
Lithi Bee Bullet Lube
Littleton, J. F.
Lock's Philadelphia Gun Exchange
Lortone Inc.
Loweth, Richard H.R.
Lyman Instant Targets, Inc. *(See Lyman Products)*
Lyman Products Corp.
MA Systems
Magma Engineering Co.
MarMik, Inc.
Marquart Precision Co.
MAST Technology
Match Prep--Doyle Gracey
Mayville Engineering Co. *(See MEC, Inc.)*
MCS, Inc.
MEC, Inc.
Midway Arms, Inc.
MI-TE Bullets
Montana Armory, Inc *(See C. Sharps Arms Co. Inc.)*
Mo's Competitor Supplies *(See MCS Inc)*
Mountain South
Mountain State Muzzleloading Supplies, Inc.
MTM Molded Products Co., Inc.
Multi-Scale Charge Ltd.
MWG Co.
Navy Arms Company
Necromancer Industries, Inc.
Newman Gunshop
North Devon Firearms Services
October Country Muzzleloading
Old West Bullet Moulds
Omark Industries,Div. of Blount,Inc.
Original Box, Inc.
Outdoor Sports Headquarters, Inc.
Paco's *(See Small Custom Mould & Bullet Co)*
Paragon Sales & Services, Inc.
Pease Accuracy
Pinetree Bullets
Ponsness/Warren
Prairie River Arms
Prime Reloading
Professional Hunter Supplies *(See Star Custom Bull)*
Pro-Shot Products, Inc.
R.A. Wells Custom Gunsmith
R.E.I.
R.I.S. Co., Inc.
Rapine Bullet Mould Mfg. Co.
Reloading Specialties, Inc.
Rice, Keith *(See White Rock Tool & Die)*
Rochester Lead Works
Rooster Laboratories
Rorschach Precision Products
SAECO *(See Redding Reloading Equipment)*
Sandia Die & Cartridge Co.
Saunders Gun & Machine Shop
Saville Iron Co. *(See Greenwood Precision)*
Scot Powder Co. of Ohio, Inc.
Seebeck Assoc., R.E.
Sharp Shooter Supply
Sharps Arms Co., Inc., C.
Shiloh Creek
Shiloh Rifle Mfg.
Sierra Specialty Prod. Co.
Silver Eagle Machining
Skip's Machine
Small Custom Mould & Bullet Co.
Sno-Seal, Inc. *(See Atsko/Sno-Seal)*
SOS Products Co. *(See Buck Stix-SOS Products Co.)*
Spencer's Custom Guns
SPG LLC
Sportsman Supply Co.
SSK Industries
Stalwart Corporation
Star Custom Bullets
Starr Trading Co., Jedediah
Stillwell, Robert
Stoney Point Products, Inc.
Stratco, Inc.
Tamarack Products, Inc.
Taracorp Industries, Inc.
TCCI
TCSR
TDP Industries, Inc.
Tetra Gun Lubricants *(See FTI, Inc.)*
The Hanned Line
The Protector Mfg. Co., Inc.
Thompson / Center Arms
Timber Heirloom Products
TMI Products *(See Haselbauer Products, Jerry)*
Vega Tool Co.
Venco Industries, Inc. *(See Shooter's Choice)*
VibraShine, Inc.
Vibra-Tek Co.
Vihtavuori Oy/Kaltron-Pettibone
Vitt/Boos
W.B. Niemi Engineering
W.J. Riebe Co.
Waechter
WD-40 Co.
Webster Scale Mfg. Co.
White Rock Tool & Die
Widener's Reloading & Shooting Supply, Inc.
Wise Custom Guns
Woodleigh *(See Huntington Die Specialties)*
Yesteryear Armory & Supply
Young Country Arms

Scopes, Mounts, Accessories, Optical Equipment

A.R.M.S., Inc.
ABO *(USA)* Inc
Accu-Tek
Ackerman, Bill *(See Optical Services Co)*
Action Direct, Inc.
ADCO Sales, Inc.
Adventurer's Outpost
Aimpoint c/o Springfield, Inc.
Aimtech Mount Systems
Air Rifle Specialists
Air Venture Airguns
All Rite Products, Inc.
Alley Supply Co.
Alpec Team, Inc.
Apel GmbH, Ernst
ArmaLite, Inc.
Arundel Arms & Ammunition, Inc., A.
B.A.C.
Baer Custom, Inc, Les
Bansner's Ultimate Rifles, LLC
Barrett Firearms Manufacturer, Inc.
Beaver Park Product, Inc.
BEC, Inc.
Beeman Precision Airguns
Ben William's Gun Shop
Benjamin/Sheridan Co., Crossman
BKL Technologies
Blount, Inc., Sporting Equipment Div.
Blount/Outers
Borden Rifles Inc
Brockman's Custom Gunsmithing
Brocock Ltd.
Brown Co, E. Arthur
Brownells, Inc.
Brunton U.S.A.
BSA Optics
B-Square Company, Inc.
Bull Mountain Rifle Co.
Burris Co., Inc.
Bushmaster Firearms
Bushnell Sports Optics Worldwide
Butler Creek Corp.
Cabela's
Carl Zeiss Inc.
Center Lock Scope Rings
Chuck's Gun Shop
Clark Custom Guns, Inc.
Clearview Mfg. Co., Inc.
Compass Industries, Inc.
Compasseco, Ltd.
Concept Development Corp.
Conetrol Scope Mounts
Creedmoor Sports, Inc.
Crimson Trace Lasers
Crosman Airguns
Custom Quality Products, Inc.
D&H Prods. Co., Inc.
D.C.C. Enterprises
Daisy Mfg. Co.
Del-Sports, Inc.
DHB Products
E. Arthur Brown Co.
Eclectic Technologies, Inc.
Ed Brown Products, Inc.
Edmund Scientific Co.
Ednar, Inc.
Eggleston, Jere D.
Emerging Technologies, Inc. *(See Laseraim Technology)*
Entre`prise Arms, Inc.
Euro-Imports
Evolution Gun Works Inc.
Excalibur Electro Optics Inc
Excel Industries Inc.
Faloon Industries, Inc.
Farr Studio, Inc.
Federal Arms Corp. of America
Freedom Arms, Inc.
Fujinon, Inc.
G.G. & G.
Galati International
Gentry Custom Gunmaker, David
Gil Hebard Guns Inc.
Gilmore Sports Concepts
Gonzalez Guns, Ramon B
Goodwin's Gun Shop
GSI, Inc.

Product & Service Directory

Gun South, Inc. *(See GSI, Inc.)*
Guns
Guns Div. of D.C. Engineering, Inc.
Gunsmithing, Inc.
Hakko Co. Ltd.
Hammerli USA
Harris Gunworks
Harvey, Frank
Hertel & Reuss
Hiptmayer, Armurier
Hiptmayer, Klaus
HiTek International
Holland's Gunsmithing
Impact Case Co.
Ironsighter Co.
Jeffredo Gunsight
Jena Eur
Jerry Phillips Optics
Jewell Triggers, Inc.
John Masen Co. Inc.
John's Custom Leather
Kahles A Swarovski Company
Kalispel Case Line
KDF, Inc.
Keng's Firearms Specialty, Inc. / US Tactical Systems
KenPatable Ent., Inc.
Kesselring Gun Shop
Kimber of America, Inc.
Kowa Optimed, Inc.
KVH Industries, Inc.
Kwik-Site Co.
L&S Technologies Inc *(See Aimtech Mount Systems)*
L.A.R. Mfg., Inc.
Laser Devices, Inc.
Laseraim Technologies, Inc.
LaserMax, Inc.
Leapers, Inc.
Lee Co., T. K.
Leica USA, Inc.
Leupold & Stevens, Inc.
Lightforce U.S.A. Inc.
List Precision Engineering
Lohman Mfg. Co., Inc.
Lomont Precision Bullets
London Guns Ltd.
Mac-1 Airgun Distributors
Mag-Na-Port International, Inc.
Mandall Shooting Supplies Inc.
Marksman Products
Maxi-Mount Inc.
McBros Rifle Co.
McCann's Machine & Gun Shop
McMillan Optical Gunsight Co.
MCS, Inc.
MDS
Merit Corp.
Military Armament Corp.
Millett Sights
Mirador Optical Corp.
Mitchell Optics, Inc.
MMC
Mo's Competitor Supplies *(See MCS Inc)*
MWG Co.
Navy Arms Company
New England Custom Gun Service
Nightforce (See Lightforce USA Inc)
Nikon, Inc.
Norincoptics *(See BEC, Inc.)*
Olympic Optical Co.
Optical Services Co.
Orchard Park Enterprise
Oregon Arms, Inc. *(See Rogue Rifle Co., Inc.)*
Ozark Gun Works
P.M. Enterprises, Inc. / Precise Metalsmithing
Parker & Sons Shooting Supply
Parsons Optical Mfg. Co.
PECAR Herbert Schwarz GmbH
PEM's Mfg. Co.
Pentax Corp.
PMC / Eldorado Cartridge Corp.
Precise Metalsmithing Enterprises / P.M. Enterprises
Precision Sport Optics
Premier Reticles
R.A. Wells Custom Gunsmith
Ram-Line Blount, Inc.
Ramon B. Gonzalez Guns
Ranch Products
Randolph Engineering Inc.
Rice, Keith *(See White Rock Tool & Die)*
Robinson Armament Co.
Rogue Rifle Co., Inc.
Romain's Custom Guns, Inc.
S&K Scope Mounts
Sanders Custom Gun Service
Sanders Gun and Machine Shop
Schmidt & Bender, Inc.
Schumakers Gun Shop
Scope Control, Inc.
ScopLevel
Score High Gunsmithing
Seecamp Co. Inc., L. W.
Segway Industries
Selsi Co., Inc.
Sharp Shooter Supply
Shepherd Enterprises, Inc.
Sightron, Inc.
Simmons Outdoor Corp.
Six Enterprises
Southern Bloomer Mfg. Co.
Splitfire Sporting Goods, L.L.C.
Sportsmatch U.K. Ltd.
Springfield, Inc.
SSK Industries
Stiles Custom Guns
Stoeger Industries
Stoney Point Products, Inc.
Sturm Ruger & Co. Inc.
Sunny Hill Enterprises, Inc.
Swarovski Optik North America Ltd.
Swift Instruments, Inc.
T.K. Lee Co.
TacStar
Talley, Dave
Tasco Sales, Inc.
Tele-Optics
The A.W. Peterson Gun Shop, Inc.
The Outdoor Connection,Inc.
Thompson / Center Arms
Thompson Target Technology
Traditions Performance Firearms
Trijicon, Inc.
Truglo, Inc
Ultra Dot Distribution
Uncle Mike's *(See Michaels of Oregon Co.)*
Unertl Optical Co., Inc.
United Binocular Co.
United States Optics Technologies, Inc.
Valor Corp.
Virgin Valley Custom Guns
Visible Impact Targets
Voere-KGH m.b.H.
Warne Manufacturing Co.
Warren Muzzleloading Co., Inc.
WASP Shooting Systems
Watson Trophy Match Bullets
Weaver Products
Weaver Scope Repair Service
Weigand Combat Handguns, Inc.
Wessinger Custom Guns & Engraving
Westley Richards & Co.
White Rock Tool & Die
White Shooting Systems, Inc. *(See White Muzzleload)*
Whitestone Lumber Corp.
Wideview Scope Mount Corp.
Wilcox Industries Corp
Wild West Guns
Williams Gun Sight Co.
York M-1 Conversions
Zanotti Armor, Inc.

Shellholders
Fremont Tool Works
Goodwin's Gun Shop
Hart & Son, Inc.
Hollywood Engineering
K&M Services
King & Co.
Protektor Model
The A.W. Peterson Gun Shop, Inc.
Vega Tool Co.

Shotshell Miscellany
American Products, Inc.
Ballistic Product, Inc.
Bridgeman Products
Goodwin's Gun Shop
Lee Precision, Inc.
MEC, Inc.
Precision Reloading, Inc.
R.E.I.
T&S Industries, Inc.
The A.W. Peterson Gun Shop, Inc.
The Gun Works
Vitt/Boos
Ziegel Engineering

Stuck Case Removers
Goodwin's Gun Shop
MarMik, Inc.
The A.W. Peterson Gun Shop, Inc.
Tom's Gun Repair, Thomas G. Ivanoff

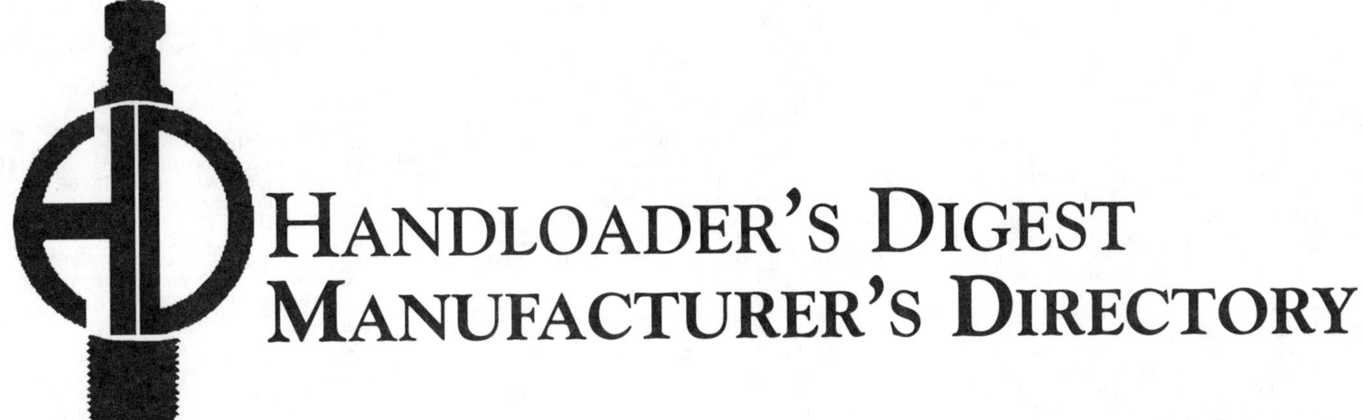

HANDLOADER'S DIGEST MANUFACTURER'S DIRECTORY

SYMBOLS

"Gramps" Antiques, Ellwood & Isabella Epps , Box 341, Washago, ON L0K 2B0 CANADA/ 705-689-5348

"Su-Press-On",Inc., PO Box 09161, Detroit, MI 48209 / 313-842-4222

NUMBERS

100 Straight Products, Inc., P.O. Box 6148, Omaha, NE 68106 402-556-1055; FAX: 402-556-1055

3-D Ammunition & Bullets, PO Box 433, Doniphan, NE 68832 / 402-845-2285; or 800-255-6712; FAX: 402-845-6546

3-Ten Corp., P.O. Box 269, Feeding Hills, MA 01030 / 413-789-2086; FAX: 413-789-1549

4-D Custom Die Co., 711 N. Sandusky St., PO Box 889, Mt. Vernon, OH 43050-0889 740-397-7214; FAX: 740-397-6600 info@ch4d.com ch4d.com

A

A.R.M.S., Inc., 230 W. Center St., West Bridgewater, MA 02379-1620 / 508-584-7816; FAX: 508-588-8045

A.W. Peterson Gun Shop, Inc., 4255 W. Old U.S. 441, Mt. Dora, FL 32757-3299 / 352-383-4258; FAX: 352-735-1001

ABO *(USA)* Inc, 615 SW 2nd Avenue, Miami, FL 33130 / 305-859-2010; FAX: 305-859-2099

Acadian Ballistic Specialties, P.O. Box 787, Folsom, LA 70437 / 504-796-0078 gunsmith@neasolft.com

Accuracy Unlimited, 7479 S. DePew St., Littleton, CO 80123

Accuracy Unlimited, 16036 N. 49 Ave., Glendale, AZ 85306 / 602-978-9089; FAX: 602-978-9089 frankglenn@earthlink.net

Accura-Site *(See All's, The Jim Tembelis Co., Inc.)*

Accurate Arms Co., Inc., 5891 Hwy. 230 West, McEwen, TN 37101 / 931-729-4207; FAX: 931-729-4211 email@accuratecompanies.com www.accuratepowder.com

Accu-Tek, 4510 Carter Ct, Chino, CA 91710

Ace Custom 45's, Inc., 1880 1/2 Upper Turtle Creek Rd., Kerrville, TX 78028 / 830-257-4290; FAX: 830-257-5724 www.acecustom45.com

Ackerman & Co., Box 133 US Highway Rt. 7, Pownal, VT 05261 / 802-823-9874 muskets@togsther.net

Ackerman, Bill *(See Optical Services Co)*

Acra-Bond Laminates, 134 Zimmerman Rd., Kalispell, MT 59901 / 406-257-9003; FAX: 406-257-9003 merlins@digisys.net www.acrabondlaminates.com

Action Bullets & Alloy Inc, RR 1, PO Box 189, Quinter, KS 67752 / 785-754-3609; FAX: 785-754-3629 bullets@ruraltel.net

Action Direct, Inc., PO Box 770400, Miami, FL 33177 / 305-969-0056; FAX: 530-734-3760 action-direct.com

Action Target, Inc., PO Box 636, Provo, UT 84603 / 801-377-8033; FAX: 801-377-8096

Actions by "T" Teddy Jacobson, 16315 Redwood Forest Ct., Sugar Land, TX 77478 / 281-277-4008; FAX: 281-277-9112 tjacobson@houston.rr.com www.actionsbyt.com

Ad Hominem, 3130 Gun Club Lane, RR #3, Orillia, ON L3V 6H3 CANADA / 705-689-5303; FAX: 705-689-5303

ADCO Sales, Inc., 4 Draper St. #A, Woburn, MA 01801 / 781-935-1799; FAX: 781-935-1011

Advance Car Mover Co., Rowell Div., P.O. Box 1, 240 N. Depot St., Juneau, WI 53039 / 414-386-4464; FAX: 414-386-4416

Adventure 16, Inc., 4620 Alvarado Canyon Rd., San Diego, CA 92120 / 619-283-6314

Adventurer's Outpost, P.O. Box 547, Cottonwood, AZ 86326-0547 / 800-762-7471; FAX: 602-634-8781

Aero Peltor, 90 Mechanic St, Southbridge, MA 01550 / 508-764-5500; FAX: 508-764-0188

AFSCO Ammunition, 731 W. Third St., P.O. Box L, Owen, WI 54460 / 715-229-2516

Ahlman Guns, 9525 W. 230th St., Morristown, MN 55052 / 507-685-4243; FAX: 507-685-4280 www.ahlmans.com

Aimpoint c/o Springfield, Inc., 420 W. Main St, Geneseo, IL 61254 / 309-944-1702

Aimtech Mount Systems, PO Box 223, Thomasville, GA 31799 / 229-226-4313; FAX: 229-227-0222 aimtech@surfsouth.com www.aimtech-mounts.com

Air Arms, Hailsham Industrial Park, Diplocks Way, Hailsham, E. Sussex, BN27 3JF ENGLAND / 011-0323-845853

Air Rifle Specialists, P.O. Box 138, 130 Holden Rd., Pine City, NY 14871-0138 / 607-734-7340; FAX: 607-733-3261 ars@stny.rr.com www.air-rifles.com

Air Venture Airguns, 9752 E. Flower St., Bellflower, CA 90706 / 310-867-6355

Airrow, 11 Monitor Hill Rd, Newtown, CT 06470 / 203-270-6343

Ajax Custom Grips, Inc., 9130 Viscount Row, Dallas, TX 75247 / 214-630-8893; FAX: 214-630-4942

Alaska Bullet Works, Inc., 9978 Crazy Horse Drive, Juneau, AK 99801 / 907-789-3834; FAX: 907-789-3433

All Rite Products, Inc., 9554 Wells Circle, Suite D, West Jordan, UT 84088-6226 / 800-771-8471; FAX: 801-280-8302 www.allriteproducts.com

Alley Supply Co., PO Box 848, Gardnerville, NV 89410 / 775-782-3800 FAX: 775-782-3827 jetalley@aol.com www.alleysupplyco.com

Alliant Techsystems Smokeless Powder Group, P.O. Box 6, Rt. 114, Bldg. 229, Radford, VA 24141-0096 www.alliantpowder.com

Allred Bullet Co., 932 Evergreen Drive, Logan, UT 84321 / 435-752-6983; FAX: 435-752-6983

All's, The Jim J. Tembelis Co., Inc., 216 Loper Ct., Neenah, WI 54956 / 920-725-5251; FAX: 920-725-5251

Alpec Team, Inc., 201 Ricken Backer Cir., Livermore, CA 94550 / 510-606-8245; FAX: 510-606-4279

Alpha 1 Drop Zone, 2121 N. Tyler, Wichita, KS 67212 / 316-729-0800

Alpha LaFranck Enterprises, P.O. Box 81072, Lincoln, NE 68501 / 402-466-3193

AmBr Software Group Ltd., P.O. Box 301, Reistertown, MD 21136-0301 / 800-888-1917; FAX: 410-526-7212

American Ammunition, 3545 NW 71st St., Miami, FL 33147 / 305-835-7400; FAX: 305-694-0037

American Derringer Corp., 127 N. Lacy Dr., Waco, TX 76705 / 800-642-7817; or 254-799-9111; FAX: 254-799-7935

American Handgunner Magazine, 591 Camino de la Reina, Ste 200, San Diego, CA 92108 / 619-297-5350; FAX: 619-297-5353

American Products, Inc., 14729 Spring Valley Road, Morrison, IL 61270 /815-772-3336; FAX: 815-772-8046

American Safe Arms, Inc., 1240 Riverview Dr., Garland, UT 84312 / 801-257-7472; FAX: 801-785-8156

American Target, 1328 S. Jason St., Denver, CO 80223 / 303-733-0433; FAX: 303-777-0311

Ames Metal Products, 4323 S. Western Blvd., Chicago, IL 60609 / 773-523-3230; or 800-255-6937; FAX: 773-523-3854

Ammo Load, Inc., 1560 E. Edinger, Suite G, Santa Ana, CA 92705 / 714-558-8858; FAX: 714-569-0319

Andela Tool & Machine, Inc., RD3, Box 246, Richfield Springs, NY 13439

AO Sight Systems, 2401 Ludelle St., Fort Worth, TX 76105 / 888-744-4880; or 817-536-0136 FAX: 817-536-3517

Apel GmbH, Ernst, Am Kirschberg 3, D-97218, Gerbrunn, GERMANY / 0 (931) 707192 info@eaw.de www.eaw.de

Arizona Ammunition, Inc., 21421 No. 14th Ave., Suite E, Phoenix, AZ 85027 / 623-516-9004; FAX: 623-516-9012 www.azammo.com

Manufacturer's Directory

ArmaLite, Inc., P.O. Box 299, Geneseo, IL 61254 / 800-336-0184; or 309-944-6939; FAX: 309-944-6949
Armfield Custom Bullets, 10584 County Road 100, Carthage, MO 64836 / 417-359-8480; FAX: 417-359-8497
Armite Laboratories, 1560 Superior Ave., Costa Mesa, CA 92627 / 213-587-7768; FAX: 213-587-5075
Armor Metal Products, PO Box 4609, Helena, MT 59604 / 406-442-5560; FAX: 406-442-5650
Armory Publications, 17171 Bothall Way NE, #276, Seattle, WA 98155 / 206-364-7653; FAX: 206-362-9413 armorypub@aol.com www.grocities.com/armorypub
Arms & Armour Press, Wellington House, 125 Strand, London, WC2R 0BB ENGLAND / 0171-420-5555; FAX: 0171-240-7265
Arms Corporation of the Philippines, Bo. Parang Marikina, Metro Manila, PHILIPPINES / 632-941-6243; or 632-941-6244; FAX: 632-942-0682
Arms Ingenuity Co., P.O. Box 1, 51 Canal St., Weatogue, CT 06089 / 203-658-5624
Arms Software, 4851 SW Madrona St., Lake Oswego, OR 97035 / 800-366-5559; or 503-697-0533; FAX: 503-697-3337
Arms, Programming Solutions *(See Arms Software)*
Armscorp USA , Inc., 4424 John Ave., Baltimore, MD 21227 / 410-247-6200; FAX: 410-247-6205 info@armscorpusa.com www.armscorpusa.com
Aro-Tek Ltd., 206 Frontage Rd. North, Suite C, Pacific, WA 98047 / 206-351-2984; FAX: 206-833-4483
Arundel Arms & Ammunition, Inc., A., 24A Defense St., Annapolis, MD 21401 / 410-224-8683
Ashley Outdoors, Inc., 2401 Ludelle St, Fort Worth, TX 76105 / 888-744-4880; FAX: 800-734-7939
Aspen Outfitting Co., Jon Hollinger , 9 Dean St, Aspen, CO 81611 / 970-925-3406
A-Square Company, Inc., 1230 S. Hurstbourne Parkway, Liberty Center II, Suite 220, Louisville, KY 40222 / 502-719-3006; FAX: 502-719-3030
ATK, 2299 Snake River Ave., PO Box 856, Lewiston, ID 83501 / 800-627-3640; or 208-746-2351; FAX: 208-799-3904
AKT/Outers, PO Box 39, Onalaska, WI 54650 / 608-781-5800; FAX: 608-781-0368
Atlantic Rose, Inc., P.O. Box 10717, Bradenton, FL 34282-0717
Atsko/Sno-Seal, Inc., 2664 Russell St., Orangeburg, SC 29115 / 803-531-1820; FAX: 803-531-2139
Autauga Arms, Inc., Pratt Plaza Mall No. 13, Prattville, AL 36067 / 800-262-9563; FAX: 334-361-2961
Axtell Rifle Co., 353 Mill Creek Road, Sheridan, MT 59749 / 406-842-5814

B

B & P America, 12321 Brittany Cir, Dallas, TX 75230 / 972-726-9069
B&D Trading Co., Inc., 3935 Fair Hill Rd., Fair Oaks, CA 95628 / 800-334-3790; or 916-967-9366; FAX: 916-967-4873
B.A.C., 17101 Los Modelos St., Fountain Valley, CA 92708 / 435-586-3286
Badger Shooters Supply, Inc., P.O. Box 397, Owen, WI 54460 / 800-424-9069; FAX: 715-229-2332
Baelder , Harry , Alte Goennebeker Strasse 5, 24635, Rickling, GERMANY / 04328-722732; FAX: 04328-722733
Baer Custom, Inc, Les, 29601 34th Ave, Hillsdale, IL 61257 / 309-658-2716; FAX: 309-658-2610
Baer's Hollows, P.O. Box 284, Eads, CO 81036 / 719-438-5718
Bald Eagle Precision Machine Co., 101-A Allison St., Lock Haven, PA 17745 / 570-748-6772; FAX: 570-748-4443
Balickie, Joe, 408 Trelawney Lane, Apex, NC 27502 / 919-362-5185
Ballard Rifle & Cartridge Co., LLC, 113 W Yellowstone Ave, Cody, WY 82414 / 307-587-4914; FAX: 307-527-6097 ballard@wyoming.com
Ballistic Product, Inc., 20015 75th Ave. North, Corcoran, MN 55340-9456 / 763-494-9237; FAX: 763-494-9236 info@ballisticproducts.com www.ballisticproducts.com
Ballistic Research, 1108 W. May Ave., McHenry, IL 60050 / 815-385-0037
Ballisti-Cast , Inc., 6347 49th St. NW, Plaza, ND 58771 / 701-497-3333; FAX: 701-497-3335
Bansner's Ultimate Rifles, LLC, P.O. Box 839, 261 E. Main St., Adamstown, PA 19501 / 717-484-2370; FAX: 717-484-0523 bansner@aol.com
Barnes, 4347 Tweed Dr., Eau Claire, WI 54703-6302
Barnes Bullets, Inc., P.O. Box 215, American Fork, UT 84003 / 801-756-4222; or 800-574-9200; FAX: 801-756-2465 email@barnesbullets.com barnesbullets.com
Barrett Firearms Manufacturer, Inc., P.O. Box 1077, Murfreesboro, TN 37133 / 615-896-2938; FAX: 615-896-7313
Bartlett Engineering, 40 South 200 East, Smithfield, UT 84335-1645 /801-563-5910
Battenfeld Technologies, 5875 W. Van Horn Tavern Rd., Columbia, MO 65203 / 573-445-9200; FAX: 573-447-4158 battenfeldtechnologies.com
Bauska Barrels, 105 9th Ave. W., Kalispell, MT 59901 / 406-752-7706
Bear Arms, 374-A Carson Road, St. Mathews, SC 29135
Beartooth Bullets, PO Box 491, Dept. HLD, Dover, ID 83825-0491 / 208-448-1865 bullets@beartoothbullets.com beartoothbullets.com
Beaver Park Product, Inc., 840 J St., Penrose, CO 81240 / 719-372-6744
BEC, Inc., 1227 W. Valley Blvd., Suite 204, Alhambra, CA 91803 / 626-281-5751; FAX: 626-293-7073
Beeks, Mike. *(See Grayback Wildcats)*
Beeman Precision Airguns, 5454 Argosy Dr., Huntington Beach, CA 92649 / 714-890-4800; FAX: 714-890-4808
Behlert Precision, Inc., P.O. Box 288, 7067 Easton Rd., Pipersville, PA 18947 / 215-766-8681; or 215-766-7301; FAX: 215-766-8681
Beitzinger , George , 116-20 Atlantic Ave, Richmond Hill, NY 11419 / 718-847-7661
Belding's Custom Gun Shop, 10691 Sayers Rd., Munith, MI 49259 / 517-596-2388
Bell & Carlson, Inc., Dodge City Industrial Park, 101 Allen Rd., Dodge City, KS 67801 / 800-634-8586; or 620-225-6688; FAX: 620-225-6688 email@bellandcarlson.com www.bellandcarlson.com
Bell Reloading, Inc., 1725 Harlin Lane Rd., Villa Rica, GA 30180
Belltown Ltd., 11 Camps Rd., Kent, CT 06757 / 860-354-5750; FAX: 860-354-6764
Ben William's Gun Shop, 1151 S. Cedar Ridge, Duncanville, TX 75137 / 214-780-1807
Benjamin/Sheridan Co., Crossman, Rts. 5 and 20, E. Bloomfield, NY 14443 / 716-657-6161; FAX: 716-657-5405 www.crosman.com
Ben's Machines, 1151 S. Cedar Ridge, Duncanville, TX 75137 / 214-780-1807; FAX: 214-780-0316
Beomat of America, Inc., 300 Railway Ave., Campbell, CA 95008 / 408-379-4829
Berger Bullets Ltd., 5443 W. Westwind Dr., Glendale, AZ 85310 / 602-842-4001; FAX: 602-934-9083
Berry's Mfg., Inc., 401 North 3050 East St., St. George, UT 84770 / 435-634-1682; FAX: 435-634-1683 sales@berrysmfg.com www.berrysmfg.com
Biesen , Al , 5021 Rosewood, Spokane, WA 99208 / 509-328-9340
Biesen , Roger , 5021 W. Rosewood, Spokane, WA 99208 / 509-328-9340
Big Bear Arms & Sporting Goods, Inc., 1112 Milam Way, Carrollton, TX 75006 / 972-416-8051; or 800-400-BEAR; FAX: 972-416-0771
Big Bore Bullets of Alaska, PO Box 521455, Big Lake, AK 99652 / 907-373-2673; FAX: 907-373-2673 doug@mtaonline.net ww.awloo.com/bbb/index.
Big Bore Express, 16345 Midway Rd., Nampa, ID 83651 / 208-466-9975; FAX: 208-466-6927 bigbore.com
Bilinski, Bryan. *(See: Fieldsport .Ltd.)*
Birchwood Casey, 7900 Fuller Rd., Eden Prairie, MN 55344 / 800-328-6156; or 612-937-7933; FAX: 612-937-7979
Bitterroot Bullet Co., PO Box 412, 2001 Cedar Ave., Lewiston, ID 83501-0412 / 208-743-5635; FAX: 208-743-5635 brootbil@lewiston.com
BKL Technologies, PO Box 5237, Brownsville, TX 78523
Black Belt Bullets *(See Big Bore Express)*
Black Hills Ammunition, Inc., P.O. Box 3090, Rapid City, SD 57709-3090 / 605-348-5150; FAX: 605-348-9827
Black Hills Shooters Supply, P.O. Box 4220, Rapid City, SD 57709 / 800-289-2506
Black Powder Products, 67 Township Rd. 1411, Chesapeake, OH 45619 / 614-867-8047
Blacksmith Corp., PO Box 280, North Hampton, OH 45349 / 800-531-2665; FAX: 937-969-8399 bcbooks@glasscity.net
BlackStar AccuMax Barrels, 11501 Brittmoore Park Drive, Houston, TX 77041 / 281-721-6040; FAX: 281-721-6041
BlackStar Barrel Accurizing *(See BlackStar AccuMax)*
Blacktail Mountain Books, 42 First Ave. W., Kalispell, MT 59901 / 406-257-5573
Blammo Ammo, P.O. Box 1677, Seneca, SC 29679 / 803-882-1768
Blue and Gray Products Inc *(See Ox-Yoke Originals)*
Blue Book Publications, Inc., 8009 34th Ave. S. Ste. 175, Minneapolis, MN 55425 / 800-877-4867; or 612-854-5229; FAX: 612-853-1486 bluebook@bluebookinc.com www.bluebookinc.com
Blue Mountain Bullets, HC 77, PO Box 231, John Day, OR 97845 / 541-820-4594
Blue Ridge Machinery & Tools, Inc., PO Box 536-GD, Hurricane, WV 25526 / 800-872-6500; FAX: 304-562-5311 blueridgemachine@worldnet.att.net blueridgemachiney.com
Bob's Gun Shop, P.O. Box 200, Royal, AR 71968 / 501-767-1970; FAX: 501-767-1970 gunparts@hsnp.com www.gun-parts.com
Bo-Mar Tool & Mfg. Co., 6136 State Hwy 300, Longview, TX 75604 / 903-759-4784; FAX: 903-759-9141 marykor@earthlink.net bo-mar.com
Bonanza **(See Forster Products)**, 310 E Lanark Ave, Lanark, IL 61046 / 815-493-6360; FAX: 815-493-2371
Bond Custom Firearms, 8954 N. Lewis Ln., Bloomington, IN 47408 / 812-332-4519
Boone's Custom Ivory Grips, Inc., 562 Coyote Rd., Brinnon, WA 98320 / 206-796-4330
Borden Ridges Rimrock Stocks, RR 1 Box 250 BC, Springville, PA 18844 / 570-965-2505; FAX: 570-965-2328
Borden Rifles Inc, RD 1, Box 250BC, Springville, PA 18844 / 717-965-2505; FAX: 717-965-2328
Border Barrels Ltd., Riccarton Farm, Newcastleton, SCOTLAND UK

DIRECTORY OF THE HANDLOADER'S TRADE

Bowen Classic Arms Corp., PO Box 67, Louisville, TN 37777 / 865-984-3583 www.bowenclassicarms.com
Bowerly , Kent , 710 Golden Pheasant Dr, Redmond, OR 97756 / 541-595-6028
Boyds' Gunstock Industries, Inc., 25376 403RD AVE, MITCHELL, SD 57301 / 605-996-5011; FAX: 605-996-9878
Bradley Gunsight Co., P.O. Box 340, Plymouth, VT 05056 / 860-589-0531; FAX: 860-582-6294
Break-Free, Inc., 1035 S Linwood Ave., Santa Ana, CA 92705 / 714-953-1900; FAX: 714-953-0402
Brenneke KG, Wilhelm, PO Box 1646, 30837 Langenhagen, GERMANY / 0511-97262-0; FAX: 0511-97262-62 info@brenneke.de www.brenneke.com
Bridgeman Products, Harry Jaffin , 153 B Cross Slope Court, Englishtown, NJ 07726 / 732-536-3604; FAX: 732-972-1004
Briese Bullet Co., Inc., RR1, Box 108, Tappen, ND 58487 / 701-327-4578; FAX: 701-327-4579
British Antiques, PO Box 35369, Tucson, AZ 85740 / 520-575-9063 britishantiques@hotmail.com
Brockman's Custom Gunsmithing, P.O. Box 357, Gooding, ID 83330 / 208-934-5050
Brocock Ltd., 43 River Street, Digbeth, Birmingham, B5 5SA ENGLAND / 011-021-773-1200; FAX: 011-021-773-1211 sales@brocock.co.un www.brocock.co.uk
Brooks Tactical Systems, 279-C Shorewood Ct., Fox Island, WA 98333 / 253-549-2866 FAX: 253-549-2703 brooks@brookstactical.com www.brookstactical.com
Brown Co, E. Arthur, 3404 Pawnee Dr, Alexandria, MN 56308 / 320-762-8847
Brown Dog Ent., 2200 Calle Camelia, 1000 Oaks, CA 91360 / 805-497-2318; FAX: 805-497-1618
Brown Precision, Inc., 7786 Molinos Ave., Los Molinos, CA 96055 / 530-384-2506; FAX: 916-384-1638 www.brownprecision.com
Brownells, Inc., 200 S. Front St., Montezuma, IA 50171 / 641-623-5401; FAX: 641-623-3896 orderdesk@brownells.com www.brownells.com
Browning Arms Co., One Browning Place, Morgan, UT 84050 / 801-876-2711; FAX: 801-876-3331
BRP, Inc. High Performance Cast Bullets, 1210 Alexander Rd., Colorado Springs, CO 80909 / 719-633-0658
Brunton U.S.A., 620 E. Monroe Ave., Riverton, WY 82501 / 307-856-6559; FAX: 307-856-1840
Brynin , Milton , P.O. Box 383, Yonkers, NY 10710 / 914-779-4333
BSA Optics, 3911 SW 47th Ave. Ste. 914, Ft Lauderdale, FL 33314 / 954-581-2144; FAX: 954-581-3165 4inforbasaoptics.com www.bsaoptics.com
B-Square Company, Inc., ; , P.O. Box 11281, 2708 St. Louis Ave., Ft. Worth, TX 76110 / 817-923-0964; or 800-433-2909; FAX: 817-926-7012
Buchsenmachermeister, P. Hofer Jagdwaffen , Buchsenmachermeister, Kirchgasse 24 A-9170, Ferlach, AUSTRIA / 43 4227 3683; FAX: 43 4227 368330 peterhofer@hoferwaffen.com www.hoferwaffen.com
Buck Stix--SOS Products Co., Box 3, Neenah, WI 54956
Buckeye Custom Bullets, 6490 Stewart Rd., Elida, OH 45807 / 419-641-4463
Buckhorn Gun Works, 8109 Woodland Dr., Black Hawk, SD 57718 / 605-787-6472
Buckskin Bullet Co., P.O. Box 1893, Cedar City, UT 84721 / 435-586-3286
Budin, Dave. See: DEL-SPORTS, INC.
Buffalo Arms Co., 99 Raven Ridge, Sandpoint, ID 83864 / 208-263-6953; FAX: 208-265-2096 www.buffaloarms.com
Buffalo Bullet Co., Inc.., 12637 Los Nietos Rd., Unit A, Santa Fe Springs, CA 90670 / 800-423-8069; FAX: 562-944-5054
Buffalo Rock Shooters Supply, R.R. 1, Ottawa, IL 61350 / 815-433-2471
Bull Mountain Rifle Co., 6327 Golden West Terrace, Billings, MT 59106 / 406-656-0778
Bullberry Barrel Works, Ltd., 2430 W. Bullberry Ln. 67-5, Hurricane, UT 84737 / 435-635-9866; FAX: 435-635-0348
Bullet Metals, PO Box 1238, Sierra Vista, AZ 85636 / 520-458-5321; FAX: 520-458-1421 info@theantimonyman.com bullet_metals.com
Bullet N Press, 1210 James St., Gastonia, NC 28052 / 704-853-0265 gnpress@nemaine.com www.nemaine.com/bnpress
Bullet Swaging Supply Inc., PO Box 1056, 303 McMillan Rd, West Monroe, LA 71291 / 318-387-3266; FAX: 318-387-7779 leblackmon@colla.com
Bullseye Bullets, 1808 Turkey Creek Rd. #9, Plant City, FL 33567 / 800-741-6343 bbullets8100@aol.com
Bull-X, Inc., 520 N. Main, Farmer City, IL 61842 / 309-928-2574; or 800-248-3845; FAX: 309-928-2130
Burris Co., Inc., PO Box 1747, 331 E. 8th St., Greeley, CO 80631 / 970-356-1670; FAX: 970-356-8702
Bushmaster Firearms, 999 Roosevelt Trail, Windham, ME 04062 / 800-998-7928; FAX: 207-892-8068 info@bushmaster.com www.bushmaster.com
Bushnell Sports Optics Worldwide, 9200 Cody, Overland Park, KS 66214 / 913-752-3400; or 800-423-3537; FAX: 913-752-3550
Butler Creek Corp., 290 Arden Dr., Belgrade, MT 59714 / 800-423-8327; or 406-388-1356; FAX: 406-388-7204
Butler Enterprises, 834 Oberting Rd., Lawrenceburg, IN 47025 / 812-537-3584

C

C&D Special Products *(See Claybuster Wads & Harves)*
C. Sharps Arms Co. Inc./Montana Armory, 100 Centennial Dr., PO Box 885, Big Timber, MT 59011 / 406-932-4353; FAX: 406-932-4443
C.W. Erickson's L.L.C., 530 Garrison Ave NE, PO Box 522, Buffalo, MN 55313 / 763-682-3665; FAX: 763-682-4328 www.archerhunter.com
Cabela's, One Cabela Drive, Sidney, NE 69160 / 308-254-5505; FAX: 308-254-8420
Cabinet Mtn. Outfitters Scents & Lures, P.O. Box 766, Plains, MT 59859 / 406-826-3970
Calibre Press, Inc., 666 Dundee Rd., Suite 1607, Northbrook, IL 60062 / 800-323-0037; FAX: 708-498-6869
Cali'co Hardwoods, Inc., 3580 Westwind Blvd., Santa Rosa, CA 95403 / 707-546-4045; FAX: 707-546-4027 calicohardwoods@msn.com
California Sights (See Fautheree, Andy)
Cambos Outdoorsman, 532 E. Idaho Ave., Ontario, OR 97914 / 541-889-3135; FAX: 541-889-2633
Camdex, Inc., 2330 Alger, Troy, ML 48083 / 810-528-2300; FAX: 810-528-0989
Cameron's, 16690 W. 11th Ave., Golden, CO 80401 / 303-279-7365; FAX: 303-628-5413
Campbell , Dick , 20000 Silver Ranch Rd., Conifer, CO 80433 / 303-697-0150; FAX: 303-697-0150
Camp-Cap Products, P.O. Box 3805, Chesterfield, MO 63006 / 314-532-4340; FAX: 314-532-4340
Canons Delcour, Rue J.B. Cools, B-4040, Herstal, BELGIUM / 32.(0)42.40.61.40; FAX: 32(0)42.40.22.88
Canyon Cartridge Corp., P.O. Box 152, Albertson, NY 11507 FAX: 516-294-8946
Cape Outfitters, 599 County Rd. 206, Cape Girardeau, MO 63701 / 573-335-4103; FAX: 573-335-1555
Carl Zeiss Inc., 13005 N Kingston Ave, Chester, VA 23836 / 800-441-3005; FAX: 804-530-8481
Carter's Gun Shop, 225 G St., Penrose, CO 81240 / 719-372-6240
Cartridge Transfer Group, Pete de Coux, HC 30 Box 932 G, Prescott, AZ 86305-7447 / 928-776-8285; FAX: 928-776-8276 pdbullets@commspeed.net
Cascade Bullet Co., Inc., 2355 South 6th St., Klamath Falls, OR 97601 / 503-884-9316
Case Sorting System, 12695 Cobblestone Creek Rd., Poway, CA 92064 / 619-486-9340
Cash Mfg. Co., Inc., P.O. Box 130, 201 S. Klein Dr., Waunakee, WI 53597-0130 / 608-849-5664; FAX: 608-849-5664
Cast Performance Bullet Company, PO Box 153, Riverton, WY 82501 / 307-857-2940; FAX: 307-857-3132 castperform@wyoming.com castperformance.com
Casull Arms Corp., P.O. Box 1629, Afton, WY 83110 / 307-886-0200
Caywood , Shane J. , P.O. Box 321, Minocqua, WI 54548 / 715-277-3866
CBC, Avenida Humberto de Campos 3220, 09400-000, Ribeirao Pires, SP, BRAZIL / 55-11-742-7500; FAX: 55-11-459-7385
CCI Ammunition, P.O. Box 856, Lewiston, ID 83501 / 208-746-2351 www.cci_ammunition.com
Center Lock Scope Rings, 9901 France Ct., Lakeville, MN 55044 / 612-461-2114
CFVentures, 509 Harvey Dr., Bloomington, IN 47403-1715
CH Tool & Die Co *(See 4-D Custom Die Co)*, 711 N Sandusky St, PO Box 889, Mt Vernon, OH 43050-0889 / 740-397-7214; FAX: 740-397-6600
Chambers Flintlocks Ltd., Jim, 116 Sams Branch Rd, Candler, NC 28715 / 828-667-8361; FAX: 828-665-0852
Champion Target Co., 232 Industrial Parkway, Richmond, IN 47374 / 800-441-4971
Champion's Choice, Inc., 201 International Blvd., LaVergne, TN 37086 / 615-793-4066; FAX: 615-793-4070
Chapman, J Ken.*(See Old WestBullet Moulds)*
Cheddite France S.A., 99 Route de Lyon, F-26501, Bourg-les-Valence, FRANCE / 33-75-56-4545; FAX: 33-75-56-3587 export@cheddite.com
Chem-Pak Inc., PO Box 2058, Winchester, VA 22604-1258 / 800-336-9828; or 540-667-1341; FAX: 540-722-3993 info@chem-pak.com www.chem-pak.com
Cherry Creek State Park Shooting Center, 12500 E. Belleview Ave., Englewood, CO 80111 / 303-693-1765
CheVron Bullets, RR1, Ottawa, IL 61350 / 815-433-2471
Cheyenne Pioneer Products, PO Box 28425, Kansas City, MO 64188 / 816-413-9196; FAX: 816-455-2859 cheyennepp@aol.com www.cartridgeboxes.com
Chicasaw Gun Works, 4 Mi. Mkr., Pluto Rd. Box 868, Shady Spring, WV 25918-0868 / 304-763-2848; FAX: 304-763-3725
Christensen Arms, 385 N. 3050 E., St. George, UT 84790 / 435-624-9535; FAX: 435-674-9293
Chuck's Gun Shop, P.O. Box 597, Waldo, FL 32694 / 904-468-2264
Chuilli , Stephen , 8895 N. Military Trl. Ste., Ste. 201E, Palm Beach Gardens, FL 33410
Cincinnati Swaging, 2605 Marlington Ave., Cincinnati, OH 45208
Clark Custom Guns, Inc., 336 Shootout Lane, Princeton, LA 71067 / 318-949-9884; FAX: 318-949-9829
Claro Walnut Gunstock Co., 1235 Stanley Ave., Chico, CA 95928 / 530-342-5188; FAX: 530-342-5199

MANUFACTURER'S DIRECTORY

Claybuster Wads & Harvester Bullets, 309 Sequoya Dr., Hopkinsville, KY 42240 / 800-922-6287; or 800-284-1746; FAX: 502-885-8088 50
Clean Shot Technologies, 21218 St. Andrews Blvd. Ste 504, Boca Raton, FL 33433 / 888-866-2532
Clearview Mfg. Co., Inc., 413 S. Oakley St., Fordyce, AR 71742 / 501-352-8557; FAX: 501-352-7120
Clearview Products, 3021 N. Portland, Oklahoma City, OK 73107
Clift Mfg., L. R., 3821 hammonton Rd, Marysville, CA 95901 / 916-755-3390; FAX: 916-755-3393
Clift Welding Supply & Cases, 1332-A Colusa Hwy., Yuba City, CA 95993 / 916-755-3390; FAX: 916-755-3393
Cloward's Gun Shop, 4023 Aurora Ave. N, Seattle, WA 98103 / 206-632-2072
C-More Systems, P.O. Box 1750, 7553 Gary Rd., Manassas, VA 20108 / 703-361-2663; FAX: 703-361-5881
Coffin , Charles H. , 3719 Scarlet Ave., Odessa, TX 79762 / 915-366-4729; FAX: 915-366-4729
Coffin , Jim *(See Working Guns)*
Cole's Gun Works, Old Bank Building, Rt. 4 Box 250, Moyock, NC 27958 / 919-435-2345
Colonial Repair, 47 NAVARRE ST, ROSLINDALE, MA 02131-4725 / 617-469-4951
Colorado Gunsmithing Academy, RR 3 Box 79B, El Campo, TX 77437 / 719-336-4099; or 800-754-2046; FAX: 719-336-9642
Colorado School of Trades, 1575 Hoyt St., Lakewood, CO 80215 / 800-234-4594; FAX: 303-233-4723
Colorado Sutlers Arsenal *(See Cumberland States)*
Compass Industries, Inc., 104 East 25th St., New York, NY 10010 / 212-473-2614; or 800-221-9904; FAX: 212-353-0826
Compasseco, Ltd., 151 Atkinson Hill Ave., Bardtown, KY 40004 / 502-349-0910
Competition Electronics, Inc., 3469 Precision Dr., Rockford, IL 61109 / 815-874-8001; FAX: 815-874-8181
Competitor Corp. Inc., Appleton Business Center, 30 Tricnit Road Unit 16, New Ipswich, NH 03071 / 603-878-3891; FAX: 603-878-3950
Concept Development Corp., 16610 E. Laser Drive, Suite 5, Fountain Hills, AZ 85268-6644
Conetrol Scope Mounts, 10225 Hwy. 123 S., Seguin, TX 78155 / 210-379-3030; or 800-CONETROL; FAX: 210-379-3030
CONKKO, P.O. Box 40, Broomall, PA 19008 / 215-356-0711
Conrad , C. A. , 3964 Ebert St., Winston-Salem, NC 27127 / 919-788-5469
Cook Engineering Service, 891 Highbury Rd., Vict, 3133 AUSTRALIA
Cooper-Woodward, 3800 Pelican Rd., Helena, MT 59602 / 406-458-3800 dolymama@msn.com
Corbin Mfg. & Supply, Inc., 600 Industrial Circle, P.O. Box 2659, White City, OR 97503 / 541-826-5211; FAX: 541-826-8669
Cor-Bon Bullet & Ammo Co., 1311 Industry Rd., Sturgis, SD 57785 / 800-626-7266; FAX: 800-923-2666
Creedmoor Sports, Inc., P.O. Box 1040, Oceanside, CA 92051 / 619-757-5529
Crimson Trace Lasers, 8090 SW Cirrus Dr., Beverton, OR 97008 / 800-442-2406; FAX: 503-627-0166 www.crimsontrace.com
Crosman Airguns, Rts. 5 and 20, E. Bloomfield, NY 14443 / 716-657-6161; FAX: 716-657-5405
Crouse's Country Cover, P.O. Box 160, Storrs, CT 06268 / 860-423-8736
CRR , Inc./Marble's Inc., 420 Industrial Park, P.O. Box 111, Gladstone, MI 49837 / 906-428-3710; FAX: 906-428-3711
Cryo-Accurizing, 2101 East Olive, Decatur, IL 62526 / 801-395-2796; FAX: 217-423-3075
Cubic Shot Shell Co., Inc., 98 Fatima Dr., Campbell, OH 44405 / 330-755-0349
Cumberland Arms, 514 Shafer Road, Manchester, TN 37355 / 800-797-8414
Cumberland States Arsenal, 1124 Palmyra Road, Clarksville, TN 37040
Cummings Bullets, 1417 Esperanza Way, Escondido, CA 92027
Curly Maple Stock Blanks *(See Tiger-Hunt)*
Curtis Cast Bullets, 527 W. Babcock St., Bozeman, MT 59715 / 406-587-8117; FAX: 406-587-8117
Curtis Gun Shop *(See Curtis Cast Bullets)*
Custom Bullets by Hoffman, 2604 Peconic Ave., Seaford, NY 11783
Custom Checkering Service, Kathy Forster, 2124 S.E. Yamhill St., Portland, OR 97214 / 503-236-5874
Custom Chronograph, Inc., 5305 Reese Hill Rd., Sumas, WA 98295 / 360-988-7801
Custom Gun Products, 5021 W. Rosewood, Spokane, WA 99208 / 509-328-9340
Custom Products *(See Jones Custom Products)*
Custom Quality Products, Inc., 345 W. Girard Ave., P.O. Box 71129, Madison Heights, MI 48071 / 810-585-1616; FAX: 810-585-0644
Custom Riflestocks, Inc., Michael M. Kokolus, 7005 Herber Rd., New Tripoli, PA 18066 / 610-298-3013; FAX: 610-298-2431 mkokolus@prodigy.net
Custom Tackle and Ammo, P.O. Box 1886, Farmington, NM 87499 / 505-632-3539
CVA, 5988 Peachtree Corners East, Norcross, GA 30071 / 800-251-9412; FAX: 404-242-8546

D

D&D Gunsmiths, Ltd., 363 E. Elmwood, Troy, MI 48083 / 810-583-1512; FAX: 810-583-1524
D&G Precision Duplicators *(See Greene Precision)*
D&H Precision Tooling, 7522 Barnard Mill Rd., Ringwood, IL 60072 / 815-653-4011
D&H Prods. Co., Inc., 465 Denny Rd., Valencia, PA 16059 / 412-898-2840; or 800-776-0281; FAX: 412-898-2013
D&J Bullet Co. & Custom Gun Shop, Inc., 426 Ferry St., Russell, KY 41169 / 606-836-2663; FAX: 606-836-2663
D.C.C. Enterprises, 259 Wynburn Ave., Athens, GA 30601
D.D. Custom Stocks, R.H. "Dick" Devereaux, 5240 Mule Deer Dr., Colorado Springs, CO 80919 / 719-548-8468
Daisy Mfg. Co., PO Box 220, Rogers, AR 72757 / 501-621-4210; FAX: 501-636-0573
Dakota Arms, Inc., 130 Industry Road, Sturgis, SD 57785 / 605-347-4686; FAX: 605-347-4459 info@dakotaarms.com dakotaarms.com
Data Tech Software Systems, 19312 East Eldorado Drive, Aurora, CO 80013
David Clark Co., Inc., PO Box 15054, Worcester, MA 01615-0054 / 508-756-6216; FAX: 508-753-5827 sales@davidclark.com davidclark.com
David W. Schwartz Custom Guns, 2505 Waller St, Eau Claire, WI 54703 / 715-832-1735
Davide Pedersoli and Co., Via Artigiani 57, Gardone VT, Brescia 25063, ITALY / 030-8912402; FAX: 030-8911019 www.davide_pedersol.com
Davis , Don , 1619 Heights, Katy, TX 77493 / 713-391-3090
Davis Products, Mike, 643 Loop Dr., Moses Lake, WA 98837 / 509-765-6178; or 509-766-7281
Dayton Traister, 4778 N. Monkey Hill Rd., P.O. Box 593, Oak Harbor, WA 98277 / 360-679-4657; FAX: 360-675-1114
DBI Books Division of Krause Publications, 700 E State St, Iola, WI 54990-0001 / 715-445-2214
de Coux, Pete *(See Cartridge Transfer Group)*
Dead Eye's Sport Center, 76 Baer Rd., Shickshinny, PA 18655 / 570-256-7432 deadeyeprizz@aol.com
Decker Shooting Products, 1729 Laguna Ave., Schofield, WI 54476 / 715-359-5873; FAX: 715-355-7319
Defense Training International, Inc., 749 S. Lemay, Ste. A3-337, Ft. Collins, CO 80524 / 303-482-2520; FAX: 303-482-0548
deHaas Barrels, RR 3, Box 77, Ridgeway, MO 64481 / 816-872-6308
Del Rey Products, P.O. Box 5134, Playa Del Rey, CA 90296-5134 / 213-823-0494
Del-Sports, Inc., Dave Budin , Box 685, 817 Main St., Margaretville, NY 12455 / 845-586-4103; FAX: 845-586-4105
Delta Arms Ltd., P.O. Box 1000, Delta, VT 84624-1000
Delta Frangible Ammunition LLC, PO Box 2350, Stafford, VA 22555-2350 / 540-720-5778; or 800-339-1933; FAX: 540-720-5667 dfa@dfanet.com www.dfanet.com
Denver Instrument Co., 6542 Fig St., Arvada, CO 80004 / 800-321-1135; or 303-431-7255; FAX: 303-423-4831
DeSantis Holster & Leather Goods, Inc., P.O. Box 2039, 149 Denton Ave., New Hyde Park, NY 11040-0701 / 516-354-8000; FAX: 516-354-7501
Desert Mountain Mfg., P.O. Box 130184, Coram, MT 59913 / 800-477-0762; or 406-387-5361; FAX: 406-387-5361
Detroit-Armor Corp., 720 Industrial Dr. No. 112, Cary, IL 60013 / 708-639-7666; FAX: 708-639-7694
Devereaux, R.H. "Dick" *(See D.D. Custom)*
Dewey Mfg. Co., Inc., J., PO Box 2014, Southbury, CT 06488 / 203-264-3064; FAX: 203-262-6907 deweyrods@worldnet.att.net www.deweyrods.com
DGR Custom Rifles, 4191 37th Ave SE, Tappen, ND 58487 / 701-327-8135
DHB Products, P.O. Box 3092, Alexandria, VA 22302 / 703-836-2648
Diamond Mfg. Co., P.O. Box 174, Wyoming, PA 18644 / 800-233-9601
Diana *(See U.S. Importer -Dynamit)* Nobel-RWS, Inc., 81 Ruckman Rd., Closter, NJ 07624 / 201-767-7971; FAX: 201-767-1589
Dilliott Gunsmithing, Inc., 657 Scarlett Rd., Dandridge, TN 37725 / 865-397-9204 gunsmithd@aol.com dilliottgunsmithing.com
Dillon, Ed, 1035 War Eagle Dr. N., Colorado Springs, CO 80919 / 719-598-4929; FAX: 719-598-4929
Dillon Precision Products, Inc., 8009 East Dillon's Way, Scottsdale, AZ 85260 / 480-948-8009; or 800-762-3845; FAX: 480-998-2786 sales@dillonprecision.com www.dillonprecision.com
Dixie Gun Works, P.O. Box 130, Union City, TN 38281 / 731-885-0700; FAX: 731-885-0440
Dixon Muzzleloading Shop, Inc., 9952 Kunkels Mill Rd., Kempton, PA 19529 / 610-756-6271 dixonmuzzleloading.com
DKT, Inc., 14623 Vera Drive, Union, MI 49130-9744 / 800-741-7083 orders; FAX: 616-641-2015
Dohring Bullets, 100 W. 8 Mile Rd., Ferndale, MI 48220
Donnelly , C. P. , 405 Kubli Rd., Grants Pass, OR 97527 / 541-846-6604
Douglas Barrels Inc., 5504 Big Tyler Rd., Charleston, WV 25313-1398 / 304-776-1341; FAX: 304-776-8560 www.benchrest.com/douglas
DPMS *(Defense Procurement Manufacturing Services, Inc.)*, 13983 Industry Avenue, Becker, MN 55308 / 800-578-DPMS; or 763-261-5600 FAX: 763-261-5599
Dropkick, 1460 Washington Blvd., Williamsport, PA 17701 / 717-326-6561; FAX: 717-326-4950
Duane's Gun Repair *(See DGR Custom Rifles)*

Directory of the Handloader's Trade

Duncan's Gun Works, Inc., 1619 Grand Ave., San Marcos, CA 92069 / 760-727-0515
Dynamit Nobel-RWS, Inc., 81 Ruckman Rd., Closter, NJ 07624 / 201-767-7971; FAX: 201-767-1589

E

E&L Mfg., Inc., 4177 Riddle By Pass Rd., Riddle, OR 97469 / 541-874-2137; FAX: 541-874-3107
E. Arthur Brown Co., 3404 Pawnee Dr., Alexandria, MN 56308 / 320-762-8847
Eagan, Donald V. , P.O. Box 196, Benton, PA 17814 / 717-925-6134
E-A-R, Inc., Div. of Cabot Safety Corp., 5457 W. 79th St., Indianapolis, IN 46268 / 800-327-3431; FAX: 800-488-8007
Eclectic Technologies, Inc., 45 Grandview Dr., Suite A, Farmington, CT 06034
Ed Brown Products, Inc., P.O. Box 492, Perry, MO 63462 / 573-565-3261; FAX: 573-565-2791 www.edbrown.com
Edmund Scientific Co., 101 E. Gloucester Pike, Barrington, NJ 08033 / 609-543-6250
Ednar, Inc., 2-4-8 Kayabacho, Nihonbashi Chuo-ku, Tokyo, JAPAN / 81*(Japan)*-3-3667-1651; FAX: 81-3-3661-8113
Ed's Gun House, Ed Kukowski , PO Box 62, Minnesota City, MN 55959 / 507-689-2925
Eezox, Inc., P.O. Box 772, Waterford, CT 06385-0772 / 800-462-3331; FAX: 860-447-3484
Effebi SNC-Dr. Franco Beretta, via Rossa, 4, 25062, ITALY / 030-2751955; FAX: 030-2180414
Efficient Machinery Co, 12878 N.E. 15th Pl., Bellevue, WA 98005 / 425-453-9318; or 800-375-8554; FAX: 425-453-9311 priemc@aol.com www.sturdybench.com
Eggleston , Jere D. , 400 Saluda Ave., Columbia, SC 29205 / 803-799-3402
Eichelberger Bullets, Wm., 158 Crossfield Rd., King Of Prussia, PA 19406
Eldorado Cartridge Corp *(See PMC/Eldorado)*
Electronic Shooters Protection, Inc., 11997 West 85th Place, Arvada, CO 80005 / 800-797-7791; FAX: 303-456-7179
Electronic Trigger Systems, Inc., PO Box 13, 230 Main St. S., Hector, MN 55342 / 320-848-2760; FAX: 320-848-2760
Eley Ltd., P.O. Box 705, Witton, Birmingham, B6 7UT ENGLAND / 021-356-8899; FAX: 021-331-4173
Elite Ammunition, P.O. Box 3251, Oakbrook, IL 60522 / 708-366-9006
Emerging Technologies, Inc. *(See Laseraim Technolo)*
Enguix Import-Export, Alpujarras 58, Alzira, Valencia, SPAIN / (96) 241 43 95; FAX: (96) (241 43 95
Entre`prise Arms, Inc., 15861 Business Center Dr., Irwindale, CA 91706
Epps , Ellwood/Isabella *(See Gramps)* , Box 341, Washago, ON L0K 2B0 CANADA / 705-689-5348
Epps, Ellwood & Isabella. *(See Gramps Antiques)*
Erhardt , Dennis , 4508 N. Montana Ave., Helena, MT 59602 / 406-442-4533
Estate Cartridge, Inc., 12161 FM 830, Willis, TX 77378 / 409-856-7277; FAX: 409-856-5486
Euroarms of America, Inc., PO Box 3277, Winchester, VA 22604 / 540-662-1863; FAX: 540-662-4464
Euro-Imports, 905 West Main Street, Suite E, El Cajon, CA 92020 / 619-442-7005; FAX: 619-442-7005
Eversull Co., Inc., 1 Tracemont, Boyce, LA 71409 / 318-793-8728; FAX: 318-793-5483 bestguns@aol.com
Evolution Gun Works Inc., 4050 B-8 Skyron Dr., Doylestown, PA 18901 / 215-348-9892; FAX: 215-348-1056
Excalibur Electro Optics Inc, P.O. Box 400, Fogelsville, PA 18051-0400 / 610-391-9105; FAX: 610-391-9220
Excel Industries Inc., 4510 Carter Ct., Chino, CA 91710 / 909-627-2404; FAX: 909-627-7817
Executive Protection Institute, PO Box 802, Berryville, VA 22611 / 540-554-2540 rwk@crosslink.com personalprotecion.com
E-Z-Way Systems, PO Box 4310, Newark, OH 43058-4310 / 614-345-6645; or ; FAX: 614-345-6600

F

Faloon Industries, Inc., PO Box 1060, Tijeras, NM 87059 / 505-281-3783
Farr Studio, Inc., 1231 Robinhood Rd., Greeneville, TN 37743 / 615-638-8825
Federal Arms Corp. of America, 7928 University Ave, Fridley, MN 55432 / 612-780-8780; FAX: 612-780-8780
Federal Cartridge Co., 900 Ehlen Dr., Anoka, MN 55303 / 612-323-2300; FAX: 612-323-2506
Federal Champion Target Co., 232 Industrial Parkway, Richmond, IN 47374 / 800-441-4971; FAX: 317-966-7747
Federated-Fry *(See Fry Metals)*
Feken , Dennis , Rt. 2, Box 124, Perry, OK 73077 / 405-336-5611
Ferguson , Bill , P.O. Box 1238, Sierra Vista, AZ 85636 / 520-458-5321; FAX: 520-458-9125
Fibron Products, Inc., P.O. Box 430, Buffalo, NY 14209-0430 / 716-886-2378; FAX: 716-886-2394
Fieldsport Ltd., Bryan Bilinski , 3313 W South Airport Rd, Traverse Vity, MI 49684 / 616-933-0767
Fiocchi of America Inc., 5030 Fremont Rd., Ozark, MO 65721 / 417-725-4118; or 800-721-2666; FAX: 417-725-1039
First Inc., Jack, 1201 Turbine Dr., Rapid City, SD 57701 / 605-343-9544; FAX: 605-343-9420
Fish Mfg. Gunsmith Sptg. Co., Marshall, Rd. Box 2439, Rt. 22 N, Westport, NY 12993 / 518-962-4897; FAX: 518-962-4897
Fisher , Jerry A. , 631 Crane Mt. Rd., Big Fork, MT 59911 / 406-837-2722
Fisher Custom Firearms, 2199 S. Kittredge Way, Aurora, CO 80013 / 303-755-3710
Fitz Pistol Grip Co., P.O. Box 744, Lewiston, CA 96052-0744 / 916-778-0240
Flambeau Products Corp., 15981 Valplast Rd., Middlefield, OH 44062 / 216-632-1631; FAX: 216-632-1581
Flitz International Ltd., 821 Mohr Ave., Waterford, WI 53185 / 414-534-5898; FAX: 414-534-2991
Flores Publications Inc, J *(See Action Direct Inc.)*, PO Box 830760, Miami, FL 33283 / 305-559-4652; FAX: 305-559-4652
Folks , Donald E. , 205 W. Lincoln St., Pontiac, IL 61764 / 815-844-7901
Forgett, Valmore. *(See Navy Arms Company)*
Forkin , Ben *(See Belt MTN Arms)*
Forkin Arms, 205 10th Avenue S.W., White Sulphur Spring, MT 59645 / 406-547-2344
Forster , Kathy *(See Custom Checkering)*
Forster Products, 310 E Lanark Ave, Lanark, IL 61046 / 815-493-6360; FAX: 815-493-2371
Forthofer's Gunsmithing & Knifemaking, 5535 U.S. Hwy 93S, Whitefish, MT 59937-8411 / 406-862-2674
Forty Five Ranch Enterprises, Box 1080, Miami, OK 74355-1080 / 918-542-5875
Fowler Bullets, 806 Dogwood Dr., Gastonia, NC 28054 / 704-867-3259
Fowler, Bob *(See Black Powder Products)*
Foy Custom Bullets, 104 Wells Ave., Daleville, AL 36322
Francotte & Cie S.A. Auguste, rue de Trois Juin 109, 4400 Herstal-Liege, BELGIUM / 32-4-248-13-18; FAX: 32-4-948-11-79
Fred F. Wells / Wells Sport Store, 110 N Summit St, Prescott, AZ 86301 / 520-445-3655
Freedom Arms, Inc., P.O. Box 150, Freedom, WY 83120 / 307-883-2468; FAX: 307-883-2005
Fremont Tool Works, 1214 Prairie, Ford, KS 67842 / 316-369-2327
Frontier, 2910 San Bernardo, Laredo, TX 78040 / 956-723-5409; FAX: 956-723-1774
Fry Metals, 4100 6th Ave., Altoona, PA 16602 / 814-946-1611
Fujinon, Inc., 10 High Point Dr., Wayne, NJ 07470 / 201-633-5600; FAX: 201-633-5216
FWB, Neckarstrasse 43, 78727, Oberndorf a. N., GERMANY / 07423-814-0; FAX: 07423-814-89

G

G.G. & G., 3602 E. 42nd Stravenue, Tucson, AZ 85713 / 520-748-7167; FAX: 520-748-7583
G.H. Enterprises Ltd., Bag 10, Okotoks, AB T0L 1T0 CANADA / 403-938-6070
G96 Products Co., Inc., 85 5th Ave, Bldg. #6, Paterson, NJ 07544 / 973-684-4050; FAX: 973-684-3848 g96prod@aol
Gaillard Barrels, P.O. Box 21, Pathlow, SK S0K 3B0 CANADA / 306-752-3769; FAX: 306-752-5969
Galati International, PO Box 10, 616 Burley Ridge Rd., Wesco, MO 65586 / 573-775-2308; FAX: 573-775-4308 support@galatiinteenation.com www.galatiinternational.com
Game Haven Gunstocks, 13750 Shire Rd., Wolverine, MI 49799 / 616-525-8257
Gamebore Division, Polywad Inc, PO Box 7916, Macon, GA 31209 / 912-477-0669
GAR, 590 McBride Avenue, West Paterson, NJ 07424 / 973-754-1114; FAX: 973-754-1114 garreloading@aol.com
Garcia National Gun Traders, Inc., 225 SW 22nd Ave., Miami, FL 33135 / 305-642-2355
Garrett Cartridges Inc., PO Box 178, Chehalis, WA 98532 / 360-736-0702 garrettcartridges.com
Garthwaite Pistolsmith, Inc., Jim, Rt 2 Box 310, Watsontown, PA 17777 / 570-538-1566; FAX: 570-538-2965
Gary Schneider Rifle Barrels Inc., 12202 N. 62nd Pl., Scottsdale, AZ 85254 / 602-948-2525
GDL Enterprises, 409 Le Gardeur, Slidell, LA 70460 / 504-649-0693
Gehmann, Walter *(See Huntington Die Specialties)*
Gentex Corp., 5 Tinkham Ave., Derry, NH 03038 / 603-434-0311; FAX: 603-434-3002 sales@derry.gentexcorp.com www.derry.gentexcorp.com
Gentry Custom Gunmaker, David, 314 N Hoffman, Belgrade, MT 59714 / 406-388-GUNS davidgent@mcn.net gentrycustom.com
Gerald Pettinger Books, see Pettinger Books, Rt. 2, Box 125, Russell, IA 50238 / 641-535-2239 gpettinger@lisco.com
Gervais, Mike, 3804 S. Cruise Dr., Salt Lake City, UT 84109 / 801-277-7729
Getz Barrel Co., P.O. Box 88, Beavertown, PA 17813 / 717-658-7263
Gibbs Rifle Co., Inc., 211 Lawn St, Martinsburg, WV 25401 / 304-262-1651; FAX: 304-262-1658
Gil Hebard Guns Inc., 125 Public Square, Knoxville, IL 61448 / 309-289-2700; FAX: 309-289-2233
Gillmann , Edwin , 33 Valley View Dr., Hanover, PA 17331 / 717-632-1662
Gilmore Sports Concepts, 5949 S. Garnett, Tulsa, OK 74146 /918-250-3810; FAX: 918-250-3845 gilmore@webzone.net www.gilmoresports.com
Giron , Robert E. , 12671 Cousins Rd.., Peosta, IA 52068 / 412-731-6041
Glaser Safety Slug, Inc., PO Box 8223, Foster City, CA 94404 / 800-221-3489; FAX: 510-785-6685 safetyslug.com
Goens , Dale W. , P.O. Box 224, Cedar Crest, NM 87008 / 505-281-5419

MANUFACTURER'S DIRECTORY

Goergen's Gun Shop, Inc., 17985 538th Ave, Austin, MN 55912 / 507-433-9280; FAX: 507-433-9280
GOEX Inc., PO Box 659, Doyline, LA 71023-0659 / 318-382-9300; FAX: 318-382-9303 mfahringer@goexpowder.com www.goexpowder.com
Golden Age Arms Co., 115 E. High St., Ashley, OH 43003 / 614-747-2488
Golden Bear Bullets, 3065 Fairfax Ave., San Jose, CA 95148 / 408-238-9515
Gonzalez Guns, Ramon B, PO Box 370, 93 St. Joseph's Hill Rd, Monticello, NY 12701 / 914-794-4515
Goodwin, Fred. *(See Goodwin's Gun Shop)*
Goodwin's Gun Shop, Fred Goodwin , Sherman Mills, ME 04776 / 207-365-4451
Gotz Bullets, 11426 Edgemere Ter., Roscoe, IL 61073-8232
Graf & Sons, 4050 S Clark St, Mexico, MO 65265 / 573-581-2266; FAX: 573-581-2875
Granite Mountain Arms, Inc, 3145 W Hidden Acres Trail, Prescott, AZ 86305 / 520-541-9758; FAX: 520-445-6826
Graphics Direct, P.O. Box 372421, Reseda, CA 91337-2421 / 818-344-9002
Graves Co., 1800 Andrews Ave., Pompano Beach, FL 33069 / 800-327-9103; FAX: 305-960-0301
Grayback Wildcats, Mike Beeks , 5306 Bryant Ave., Klamath Falls, OR 97603 / 541-884-1072
Great American Gunstock Co., 3420 Industrial Drive, Yuba City, CA 95993 / 530-671-4570; FAX: 530-671-3906
Green , Arthur S. , 485 S. Robertson Blvd., Beverly Hills, CA 90211 / 310-274-1283
Green , Roger M. , P.O. Box 984, 435 E. Birch, Glenrock, WY 82637 / 307-436-9804
Green Mountain Rifle Barrel Co., Inc., P.O. Box 2670, 153 West Main St., Conway, NH 03818 / 603-447-1095; FAX: 603-447-1099
Greenwood Precision, P.O. Box 407, Rogersville, MO 65742 / 417-725-2330
Grier's Hard Cast Bullets, 1107 11th St., LaGrande, OR 97850 / 503-963-8796
Griffin & Howe, Inc., 33 Claremont Rd., Bernardsville, NJ 07924 / 908-766-2287
Gruning Precision Inc, 7101 Jurupa Ave., No. 12, Riverside, CA 92504 / 909-689-6692; FAX: 909-689-7791 gruningprecision@earthlink.net www.gruningprecision.com
GSI, Inc., 7661 Commerce Ln., Trussville, AL 35173 / 205-655-8299
GTB, 482 Comerwood Court, San Francisco, CA 94080 / 650-583-1550
Guarasi, Robert. *(See Wilcox Industries Corp)*
Guardsman Products, 411 N. Darling, Fremont, MI 49412 / 616-924-3950
Gun Accessories *(See Glaser Safety Slug, Inc.)*, PO Box 8223, Foster City, CA 94404 / 800-221-3489; FAX: 510-785-6685
Gun City, 212 W. Main Ave., Bismarck, ND 58501 / 701-223-2304
Gun Hunter Books *(See Gun Hunter Trading Co)*, 5075 Heisig St, Beaumont, TX 77705 / 409-835-3006; FAX: 409-838-2266 gunhuntertrading@hotmail.com
Gun Hunter Trading Co., 5075 Heisig St., Beaumont, TX 77705 / 409-835-3006; FAX: 409-838-2266 gunhuntertrading@hotmail.com
Gun List (See Krause Publications), 700 E State St, Iola, WI 54945 / 715-445-2214; FAX: 715-445-4087
Gun South, Inc. *(See GSI, Inc.)*
Guncraft Books *(See Guncraft Sports Inc.)*, 10737 Dutchtown Rd, Knoxville, TN 37932 / 865-966-4545; FAX: 865-966-4500 findit@guncraft.com www.usit.net/guncraft
Guncraft Sports Inc., 10737 Dutchtown Rd., Knoxville, TN 37932 / 865-966-4545; FAX: 865-966-4500 findit@guncraft.com www.usit.net/guncraft
Gunnerman Books, PO Box 217, Owosso, MI 48867 / 989-729-7018
Guns, 81 E. Streetsboro St., Hudson, OH 44236 / 330-650-4563 jcpevear@aol.com
Guns Div. of D.C. Engineering, Inc., 8633 Southfield Fwy., Detroit, MI 48228 / 313-271-7111; or 800-886-7623; FAX: 313-271-7112 guns@rifletech.com www.rifletech.com
GUNS Magazine, 591 Camino de la Reina, Suite 200, San Diego, CA 92108 / 619-297-5350; FAX: 619-297-5353
Gunsmithing Ltd., 57 Unquowa Rd., Fairfield, CT 06430 / 203-254-0436; FAX: 203-254-1535
Gunsmithing, Inc., 30 West Buchanan St., Colorado Springs, CO 80907 / 719-632-3795; FAX: 719-632-3493

H

H&P Publishing, 7174 Hoffman Rd., San Angelo, TX 76905 / 915-655-5953
H.P. White Laboratory, Inc., 3114 Scarboro Rd., Street, MD 21154 / 410-838-6550; FAX: 410-838-2802
Hafner World Wide, Inc., PO Box 1987, Lake City, FL 32055 / 904-755-6481; FAX: 904-755-6595 hafner@isgroupe.net
Hakko Co. Ltd., 1-13-12, Narimasu, Itabashiku Tokyo, JAPAN / 03-5997-7870/2; FAX: 81-3-5997-7840
Half Moon Rifle Shop, 490 Halfmoon Rd., Columbia Falls, MT 59912 / 406-892-4409
Hammerli USA, 19296 Oak Grove Circle, Groveland, CA 95321 FAX: 209-962-5311
Hammets VLD Bullets, P.O. Box 479, Rayville, LA 71269 / 318-728-2019
Handgun Press, PO Box 406, Glenview, IL 60025 / 847-657-6500; FAX: 847-724-8831 jschroed@inter-access.com
Hank's Gun Shop, Box 370, 50 West 100 South, Monroe, UT 84754 / 801-527-4456
Hanned Precision *(See Hanned Line, The)*
Hansen & Co. *(See Hansen Cartridge Co.)*, 244-246 Old Post Rd, Southport, CT 06490 / 203-259-6222; FAX: 203-254-3832
Hanson's Gun Center, Dick, 233 Everett Dr, Colorado Springs, CO 80911
Hardin Specialty Dist., P.O. Box 338, Radcliff, KY 40159-0338 / 502-351-6649
Harper's Custom Stocks, 928 Lombrano St., San Antonio, TX 78207 / 210-732-5780
Harrell's Precision, 5756 Hickory Dr., Salem, VA 24133 / 703-380-2683
Harris Engineering Inc., Dept GD54, Barlow, KY 42024 / 502-334-3633; FAX: 502-334-3000
Harris Enterprises, P.O. Box 105, Bly, OR 97622 / 503-353-2625
Harris Gunworks, 11240 N. Cave Creek Rd., Ste. 104, Phoenix, AZ 85020 / 602-582-9627; FAX: 602-582-5178
Harris Publications, 1115 Broadway, New York, NY 10010 / 212-807-7100; FAX: 212-627-4678
Harrison Bullets, 6437 E. Hobart St., Mesa, AZ 85205
Harry Lawson Co., 3328 N. Richey Blvd., Tucson, AZ 85716 / 520-326-1117
Hart & Son, Inc., Robert W. , 401 Montgomery St, Nescopeck, PA 18635 / 717-752-3655; FAX: 717-752-1088
Hart Rifle Barrels,Inc., PO Box 182, 1690 Apulia Rd., Lafayette, NY 13084 / 315-677-9841; FAX: 315-677-9610 hartrb@aol.com hartbarrels.com
Harvey , Frank , 218 Nightfall, Terrace, NV 89015 / 702-558-6998
Harwood , Jack O. , 1191 S. Pendlebury Lane, Blackfoot, ID 83221 / 208-785-5368
Hastings Barrels, 320 Court St., Clay Center, KS 67432 / 913-632-3169; FAX: 913-632-6554
Hawk Laboratories, Inc. *(See Hawk, Inc.)*, 849 Hawks Bridge Rd, Salem, NJ 08079 / 609-299-2700; FAX: 609-299-2800
Hawk, Inc., 849 Hawks Bridge Rd., Salem, NJ 08079 / 609-299-2700; FAX: 609-299-2800
Hawken Shop, The *(See Dayton Traister)*
Haydon Shooters Supply, Russ, 15018 Goodrich Dr NW, Gig Harbor, WA 98329-9738 / 253-857-7557; FAX: 253-857-7884
Hecht, Hubert J, Waffen-Hecht, PO Box 2635, Fair Oaks, CA 95628 / 916-966-1020
Hege Jagd-u. Sporthandels GmbH, P.O. Box 101461, W-7770, Ueberlingen a. Boden, GERMANY
Heidenstrom Bullets, Urdngt 1, 3937 Heroya, NORWAY,
Heinie Specialty Products, 301 Oak St., Quincy, IL 62301-2500 / 217-228-9500; FAX: 217-228-9502 rheinie@heinie.com www.heinie.com
Henigson & Associates, Steve, PO Box 2726, Culver City, CA 90231 / 310-305-8288; FAX: 310-305-1905
Hensley, Gunmaker, Darwin, PO Box 329, Brightwood, OR 97011 / 503-622-5411
Heppler, Keith. *(See Keith's Custom Gunstocks)*
Hercules, Inc. *(See Alliant Techsystems, Smokeless)*
Heritage / VSP Gun Books, PO Box 887, McCall, ID 83638 / 208-634-4104; FAX: 208-634-3101
Hertel & Reuss, Werk fr Optik und Feinmechanik GmbH, Quellhofstrasse 67, 34 127, GERMANY / 0561-83006; FAX: 0561-893308
Hesco-Meprolight, 2139 Greenville Rd., LaGrange, GA 30241 / 706-884-7967; FAX: 706-882-4683
Hidalgo, Tony, 12701 SW 9th Pl., Davie, FL 33325 / 954-476-7645
High Precision, Bud Welsh , 80 New Road, E. Amherst, NY 14051 / 716-688-6344; FAX: 716-688-0425
High Tech Specialties, Inc., P.O. Box 839, 293 E Main St., Rear, Adamstown, PA 19501 / 717-484-0405; FAX: 717-484-0523 bansner@aol.com
Hi-Performance Ammunition Company, 484 State Route 366, Apollo, PA 15613 / 412-327-8100
Hiptmayer, Armurier, RR 112 750, P.O. Box 136, Eastman, PQ J0E 1P0 CANADA / 514-297-2492
Hiptmayer, Klau , RR 112 750, P.O. Box 136, Eastman, PQ J0E 1P0 CANADA / 514-297-2492
Hirtenberger Aktiengesellschaft, Leobersdorferstrasse 31, A-2552, Hirtenberg, / 43(0)2256 81184; FAX: 43(0)2256 81807
HiTek International, 484 El Camino Real, Redwood City, CA 94063 / 415-363-1404; or 800-54-NIGHT; FAX: 415-363-1408
Hiti-Schuch , Atelier Wilma , A-8863 Predlitz, Pirming, Y1 AUSTRIA / 0353418278
Hobson Precision Mfg. Co., 210 Big Oak Ln, Brent, AL 35034 / 205-926-4662; FAX: 205-926-3193 cahobbob@dbtech.net
Hoch Custom Bullet Moulds (*See Colorado Shooter's)*
Hodgdon Powder Co., 6231 Robinson, Shawnee Mission, KS 66202 / 913-362-9455; FAX: 913-362-1307
Hoehn Sales, Inc., 2045 Kohn Road, Wright City, MO 63390 / 636-745-8144; FAX: 636-745-8144 hoehnsal@usmo.com
Hoelscher , Virgil , 1804 S. Valley View Blvd., Las Vegas, NV 89102 / 310-631-8545
Hoenig & Rodman, 6521 Morton Dr., Boise, ID 83704 / 208-375-1116
Hofer Jagdwaffen, P., Buchsenmachermeister, Kirchgasse 24, A-9170 Ferlach, AUSTRIA / 43 4227 3683; FAX: 43 4227 368330 peterhofer@hoferwaffen.com www.hoferwaffen.com
Hogue Grips, P.O. Box 1138, Paso Robles, CA 93447 / 800-438-4747; or 805-239-1440; FAX: 805-239-2553
Holland's Gunsmithing, P.O. Box 69, Powers, OR 97466 / 541-439-5155; FAX: 541-439-5155
Hollinger, Jon. *(See Aspen Outfitting Co.)*

Hollywood Engineering, 10642 Arminta St., Sun Valley, CA 91352 / 818-842-8376; FAX: 818-504-4168
Home Shop Machinist The Village Press Publications, PO Box 1810, Traverse City, MI 49685 / 800-447-7367; FAX: 616-946-3289
Hondo Ind., 510 S. 52nd St., 104, Tempe, AZ 85281
Hoppe's Div. Penguin Industries, Inc., Airport Industrial Mall, Coatesville, PA 19320 / 610-384-6000
Horizons Unlimited, P.O. Box 426, Warm Springs, GA 31830 / 706-655-3603; FAX: 706-655-3603
Hornady Mfg. Co., P.O. Box 1848, Grand Island, NE 68802 / 800-338-3220; or 308-382-1390; FAX: 308-382-5761
Howell Machine, 815 1/2 D St., Lewiston, ID 83501 / 208-743-7418
H-S Precision, Inc., 1301 Turbine Dr., Rapid City, SD 57701 / 605-341-3006; FAX: 605-342-8964
HT Bullets, 244 Belleville Rd., New Bedford, MA 02745 / 508-999-3338
Huebner , Corey O. , PO Box 564, Frenchtown, MT 59834 / 406-721-7168
Hungry Horse Books, 4605 Hwy. 93 South, Whitefish, MT 59937 / 406-862-7997
Hunterjohn, PO Box 771457, St. Louis, MO 63177 / 314-531-7250
Hunters Supply, Inc., PO Box 313, Tioga, TX 76271 / 940-437-2458; FAX: 940-437-2228 hunterssupply@hotmail.com hunterssupply.net
Huntington Die Specialties, 601 Oro Dam Blvd., Oroville, CA 95965 / 530-534-1210; FAX: 530-534-1212
Hutton Rifle Ranch, P.O. Box 45236, Boise, ID 83711 / 208-345-8781

I

I.D.S.A. Books, 1324 Stratford Drive, Piqua, OH 45356 / 937-773-4203; FAX: 937-778-1922
Image Ind. Inc., 382 Balm Court, Wood Dale, IL 60191 / 630-766-2402; FAX: 630-766-7373
Impact Case Co., P.O. Box 9912, Spokane, WA 99209-0912 / 800-262-3322; or 509-467-3303; FAX: 509-326-5436 info@kkair.com www.kkair.com
Imperial *(See E-Z-Way Systems)*, PO Box 4310, Newark, OH 43058-4310 / 614-345-6645; FAX: 614-345-6600 ezway@infinet.com www.jcunald.com
Imperial Magnum Corp., P.O. Box 249, Oroville, WA 98844 / 604-495-3131; FAX: 604-495-2816
IMR Powder Co., 1080 Military Turnpike, Suite 2, Plattsburgh, NY 12901 / 518-563-2253; FAX: 518-563-6916
IMX, LLC, 2169 Greenville Rd., La Grange, GA 30241 / 706-812-9841; or 877-519-3473; FAX: 706-882-9050 mpatillo@crossfirellc.com
Info-Arm, P.O. Box 1262, Champlain, NY 12919 / 514-955-0355; FAX: 514-955-0357
Innovative Weaponry Inc., 2513 E. Loop 820 N., Fort Worth, TX 76118 / 817-284-0099; or 800-334-3573
INTEC International, Inc., P.O. Box 5708, Scottsdale, AZ 85261 / 602-483-1708
Intercontinental Distributors, Ltd., PO Box 815, Beulah, ND 58523
Intrac Arms International, 5005 Chapman Hwy., Knoxville, TN 37920
Ion Industries, Inc, 3508 E Allerton Ave, Cudahy, WI 53110 / 414-486-2007; FAX: 414-486-2017
Iosso Products, 1485 Lively Blvd., Elk Grove Village, IL 60007 / 847-437-8400; FAX: 847-437-8478
Ironside International Publishers, Inc., 3000 S. Eaos St., Arlington, VA 22202 / 703-684-6111; FAX: 703-683-5486
Ironsighter Co., PO Box 85070, Westland, MI 48185 / 734-326-8731; FAX: 734-326-3378 www.ironsighter.com
Island Pond Gun Shop, Cross St., Island Pond, VT 05846 / 802-723-4546
Israel Arms International, Inc., 1085 Gessner Rd., Ste. F, Houston, TX 77055 / 713-789-0745; FAX: 713-914-9515 iaipro@wt.net www.israelarms.com
Ivanoff, Thomas G *(See Tom's Gun Repair)*

J

J&D Components, 75 East 350 North, Orem, UT 84057-4719 / 801-225-7007
J&J Products, Inc., 9240 Whitmore, El Monte, CA 91731 / 818-571-5228; FAX: 800-927-8361
J&L Superior Bullets *(See Huntington Die Special)*
J.G. Dapkus Co., Inc., Commerce Circle, P.O. Box 293, Durham, CT 06422
J.G. Anschutz GmbH & Co. KG, Daimlerstr. 12, D-89079 Ulm, Ulm, GERMANY / 49 731 40120; FAX: 49 731 4012700 JGA-info@anschuetz-sport.com anschuetz-sport.com
J.I.T. Ltd., P.O. Box 230, Freedom, WY 83120 / 708-494-0937
J.P. Enterprises Inc., P.O. Box 378, Hugo, MN 55110 / 612-486-9064; FAX: 612-482-0970
J.P. Gunstocks, Inc., 4508 San Miguel Ave., North Las Vegas, NV 89030 / 702-645-0718
J.R. Williams Bullet Co., 2008 Tucker Rd., Perry, GA 31069 / 912-987-0274
Jackalope Gun Shop, 1048 S. 5th St., Douglas, WY 82633 / 307-358-3441
Jaffin, Harry. *(See Bridgeman Products)*
Jagdwaffen, P. *(See Bushenmachermeister)*
James Calhoon Mfg., Shambo Rte. 304, Havre, MT 59501 / 406-395-4079 www.jamescalhoon.com
James Calhoon Varmint Bullets, Shambo Rt., 304, Havre, MT 59501 / 406-395-4079 www.jamescalhoon.com
Jantz Supply, 309 West Main Dept HD, Davis, OK 73030-0584 / 580-369-2316; FAX: 580-369-3082 jantz@brightok.net www.knifemaking.com
Jarrett Rifles, Inc., 383 Brown Rd., Jackson, SC 29831 / 803-471-3616 www.jarrettrifles.com
Javelina Lube Products, PO Box 337, San Bernardino, CA 92402 / 714-882-5847; FAX: 714-434-6937
Jay McCament Custom Gunmaker, Jay McCament , 1730-134th St. Ct. S., Tacoma, WA 98444 / 253-531-8832
Jeffredo Gunsight, P.O. Box 669, San Marcos, CA 92079 / 760-728-2695
Jena Eur, PO Box 319, Dunmore, PA 18512
Jensen Bullets, RR 1 Box 187, Arco, ID 83213 / 208-785-5590
Jensen's Custom Ammunition, 5146 E. Pima, Tucson, AZ 85712 / 602-325-3346; FAX: 602-322-5704
Jensen's Firearms Academy, 1280 W. Prince, Tucson, AZ 85705 / 602-293-8516
Jericho Tool & Die Co., Inc., 2917 St. Hwy. 7, Bainbridge, NY 13733 / 607-563-8222; FAX: 607-563-8560 jerichotool.com www.jerichotool.com
Jerry Phillips Optics, P.O. Box L632, Langhorne, PA 19047 / 215-757-5037; FAX: 215-757-7097
Jester Bullets, Rt. 1 Box 27, Orienta, OK 73737
Jewell Triggers, Inc., 3620 Hwy. 123, San Marcos, TX 78666 / 512-353-2999; FAX: 512-392-0543
JGS Precision Tool Mfg., 100 Main Sumner, Coos Bay, OR 97420 / 541-267-4331; FAX: 541-267-5996
Jim Norman Custom Gunstocks, 14281 Cane Rd., Valley Center, CA 92082 / 619-749-6252
JLK Bullets, 414 Turner Rd., Dover, AR 72837 / 501-331-4194
John Masen Co. Inc., 1305 Jelmak, Grand Prairie, TX 75050 / 817-430-8732; FAX: 817-430-1715
John's Custom Leather, 523 S. Liberty St., Blairsville, PA 15717 / 724-459-6802; FAX: 724-459-5996
Johnson Wood Products, 34897 Crystal Road, Strawberry Point, IA 52076 / 563-933-6504 johnsonwoodproducts@yahoo.com
Jonad Corp., 2091 Lakeland Ave., Lakewood, OH 44107 / 216-226-3161
Jones Custom Products, Neil A., 17217 Brookhouser Rd., Saegertown, PA 16433 / 814-763-2769; FAX: 814-763-4228
Jones, J. *(See SSK Industries)*
Jones Moulds, Paul, 4901 Telegraph Rd, Los Angeles, CA 90022 / 213-262-1510
JRP Custom Bullets, RR2 2233 Carlton Rd., Whitehall, NY 12887 / 518-282-0084 or 802-438-5548
Jurras, L. *(See L E Jurras & Assoc.)*

K

K&M Services, 5430 Salmon Run Rd., Dover, PA 17315 / 717-292-3175; FAX: 717-292-3175
K. Eversull Co., Inc., 1 Tracemont, Boyce, LA 71409 / 318-793-8728;FAX: 318-793-5483 bestguns@aol.com
K.B.I. Inc, PO Box 6625, Harrisburg, PA 17112 / 717-540-8518; FAX: 717-540-8567
Ka Pu Kapili, P.O. Box 745, Honokaa, HI 96727 / 808-776-1644; FAX: 808-776-1731
Kahles A Swarovski Company, 2 Slater Rd., Cranston, RI 02920 / 401-946-2220; FAX: 401-946-2587
Kalispel Case Line, P.O. Box 267, Cusick, WA 99119 / 509-445-1121
Kapro Mfg.Co. Inc. *(See R.E.I.)*
Kaswer Custom, Inc., 13 Surrey Drive, Brookfield, CT 06804 / 203-775-0564; FAX: 203-775-6872
KDF, Inc., 2485 Hwy. 46 N., Seguin, TX 78155 / 830-379-8141; FAX: 830-379-5420
Keeler , R. H. , 817 "N" St., Port Angeles, WA 98362 / 206-457-4702
Keith's Bullets, 942 Twisted Oak, Algonquin, IL 60102 / 708-658-3520
Keith's Custom Gunstocks, Keith M. Heppler , 540 Banyan Circle, Walnut Creek, CA 94598 / 925-934-3509; FAX: 925-934-3143 kmheppler@hotmail.com
Kelbly, Inc., 7222 Dalton Fox Lake Rd., North Lawrence, OH 44666 / 216-683-4674; FAX: 216-683-7349
Kelley's, P.O. Box 125, Woburn, MA 01801-0125 / 800-879-7273; FAX: 781-272-7077 kels@star.net www.kelsmilitary.com
Keng's Firearms Specialty, Inc. / US Tactical Systems, 875 Wharton Dr., P.O. Box 44405, Atlanta, GA 30336-1405 / 404-691-7611; FAX: 404-505-8445
Kennebec Journal, 274 Western Ave., Augusta, ME 04330 / 207-622-6288
KenPatable Ent., Inc., PO Box 19422, Louisville, KY 40259 / 502-239-5447
Ken's Kustom Kartridges, 331 Jacobs Rd., Hubbard, OH 44425 / 216-534-4595
Kent Cartridge America, Inc, PO Box 849, 1000 Zigor Rd, Kearneysville, WV 25430
Kent Cartridge Mfg. Co. Ltd., Unit 16 Branbridges Industrial Esta, Tonbridge, Kent, ENGLAND / 622-872255; FAX: 622-872645
Kesselring Gun Shop, 4024 Old Hwy. 99N, Burlington, WA 98233 / 360-724-3113; FAX: 360-724-7003 info@kesselrings.com kesselrings.com
Kilham & Co., Main St., P.O. Box 37, Lyme, NH 03768 / 603-795-4112
Kimber of America, Inc., 1 Lawton St., Yonkers, NY 10705 / 800-880-2418; FAX: 914-964-9340
King & Co., PO Box 1242, Bloomington, IL 61702 / 309-473-2161
KK Air International *(See Impact Case Co.)*

KLA Enterprises, P.O. Box 2028, Eaton Park, FL 33840 / 941-682-2829; FAX: 941-682-2829
Kleen-Bore,Inc., 16 Industrial Pkwy., Easthampton, MA 01027 / 413-527-0300; FAX: 413-527-2522 info@kleen-bore.com www.kleen-bore.com
Klein Custom Guns, Don, 433 Murray Park Dr, Ripon, WI 54971 / 920-748-2931 daklein@charter.net
Klingler Woodcarving, P.O. Box 141, Thistle Hill, Cabot, VT 05647 / 802-426-3811
Knight Rifles, 21852 hwy j46, P.O. Box 130, Centerville, IA 52544 / 515-856-2626; FAX: 515-856-2628
Knight Rifles *(See Modern Muzzle Loading, Inc.)*
Knight's Mfg. Co., 7750 Ninth St. SW, Vero Beach, FL 32968 / 561-562-5697; FAX: 561-569-2955
Knippel, Richard, 500 Gayle Ave Apt 213, Modesto, CA 95350-4241 / 209-869-1469
Knoell , Doug , 9737 McCardle Way, Santee, CA 92071 / 619-449-5189
Kokolus , Michael M. *(See Custom Riflestocks)*
Kolpin Mfg., Inc., P.O. Box 107, 205 Depot St., Fox Lake, WI 53933 / 414-928-3118; FAX: 414-928-3687
Korzinek Riflesmith, J., RD 2 Box 73D, Canton, PA 17724 / 717-673-8512
Koval Knives, 5819 Zarley St., Suite A, New Albany, OH 43054 / 614-855-0777; FAX: 614-855-0945
Kowa Optimed, Inc., 20001 S. Vermont Ave., Torrance, CA 90502 / 310-327-1913; FAX: 310-327-4177
Kramer Designs, P.O. Box 129, Clancy, MT 59634 / 406-933-8658; FAX: 406-933-8658
Krause Publications, Inc., 700 E. State St., Iola, WI 54990 / 715-445-2214; FAX: 715-445-4087
Krieger Barrels, Inc., N114 W18697 Clinton Dr., Germantown, WI 53022 / 414-255-9593; FAX: 414-255-9586
KSN Industries Ltd *(See U.S. Importer-Israel Arms)*
Kukowski, Ed. *(See Ed's Gun House)*
KVH Industries, Inc., 110 Enterprise Center, Middletown, RI 02842 / 401-847-3327; FAX: 401-849-0045
Kwik-Site Co., 5555 Treadwell St., Wayne, MI 48184 / 734-326-1500; FAX: 734-326-4120 kwiksiteco@aol.com

L

L E Jurras & Assoc., L. E. Jurras , PO Box 680, Washington, IN 47501 / 812-254-6170; FAX: 812-254-6170 jurasgun@rtcc.net
L&R Lock Co., 1137 Pocalla Rd., Sumter, SC 29150 / 803-775-6127; FAX: 803-775-5171
L&S Technologies Inc *(See Aimtech Mount Systems)*
L.A.R. Mfg., Inc., 4133 W. Farm Rd., West Jordan, UT 84088 / 801-280-3505; FAX: 801-280-1972
L.B.T., Judy Smith , HCR 62, Box 145, Moyie Springs, ID 83845 / 208-267-3588
L.E. Wilson, Inc., Box 324, 404 Pioneer Ave., Cashmere, WA 98815 / 509-782-1328; FAX: 509-782-7200
L.P.A. Snc, Via Alfieri 26, Gardone V.T., Brescia, ITALY / 30-891-14-81; FAX: 30-891-09-51
Lakefield Arms Ltd *(See Savage Arms Inc.)*
Lapua Ltd., P.O. Box 5, Lapua, FINLAND / 6-310111; FAX: 6-4388991
Laser Devices, Inc., 2 Harris Ct. A-4, Monterey, CA 93940 / 408-373-0701; FAX: 408-373-0903
Laseraim Technologies, Inc., P.O. Box 3548, Little Rock, AR 72203 / 501-375-2227
LaserMax, Inc., 3495 Winton Place, Bldg. B, Rochester, NY 14623-2807 / 800-527-3703; FAX: 716-272-5427
Lawrence Brand Shot *(See Precision Reloading)*
Lawson Co., Harry, 3328 N Richey Blvd., Tucson, AZ 85716 / 520-326-1117; FAX: 520-326-1117
Le Clear Industries *(See E-Z-Way Systems)*, PO Box 4310, Newark, OH 43058-4310 / 614-345-6645; FAX: 614-345-6600
Leapers, Inc., 7675 Five Mile Rd., Northville, MI 48167 / 248-486-1231; FAX: 248-486-1430
Lee Co., T. K., 1282 Branchwater Ln, Birmingham, AL 35216 / 205-913-5222 odonmich@aol.com www.scopedot.com
Lee Precision, Inc., 4275 Hwy. U, Hartford, WI 53027 / 262-673-3075; FAX: 262-673-9273 info@leeprecision.com www.leeprecision.com
Legend Products Corp., 21218 Saint Andrews Blvd., Boca Raton, FL 33433-2435
Leica USA, Inc., 156 Ludlow Ave., Northvale, NJ 07647 / 201-767-7500; FAX: 201-767-8666
LEM Gun Specialties Inc. The Lewis Lead Remover, PO Box 2855, Peachtree City, GA 30269-2024 / 770-487-0556
Lethal Force Institute *(See Police Bookshelf)*, PO Box 122, Concord, NH 03301 / 603-224-6814; FAX: 603-226-3554
Leupold & Stevens, Inc., 14400 NW Greenbrier Pky., Beaverton, OR 97006 / 503-646-9171; FAX: 503-526-1455
Liberty Metals, 2233 East 16th St., Los Angeles, CA 90021 / 213-581-9171; FAX: 213-581-9351
Liberty Shooting Supplies, P.O. Box 357, Hillsboro, OR 97123 / 503-640-5518; FAX: 503-640-5518 info@libertyshootingsupplies.com www.libertyshootingsupplies.com
Lightforce U.S.A. Inc., 19226 66th Ave. So., L-103, Kent, WA 98032 / 208-476-9814; FAX: 208-476-9814
Lightning Performance Innovations, Inc., RD1 Box 555, Mohawk, NY 13407 / 315-866-8819; FAX: 315-867-5701
Lilja Precision Rifle Barrels, PO Box 372, Plains, MT 59859 / 406-826-3084; FAX: 406-826-3083 lilja@riflebarrels.com www.riflebarrels.com
Lind Custom Guns, Al, 7821 76th Ave SW, Lakewood, WA 98498 / 253-584-6361 lindcustguns@worldnot.att.net
Lindsley Arms Cartridge Co., P.O. Box 757, 20 College Hill Rd., Henniker, NH 03242 / 603-428-3127
Linebaugh Custom Sixguns, P.O. Box 455, Cody, WY 82414 / 307-645-3332 sitgunner.com
List Precision Engineering, Unit 1 Ingley Works, 13 River Road, Barking, ENGLAND / 011-081-594-1686
Lithi Bee Bullet Lube, 1728 Carr Rd., Muskegon, MI 49442 / 616-788-4479
Littler Sales Co., 20815 W. Chicago, Detroit, MI 48228 / 313-273-6889; FAX: 313-273-1099 littlerptg@aol.com
Littleton , J. F. , 275 Pinedale Ave., Oroville, CA 95966 / 916-533-6084
Loch Leven Industries / Convert-A-Pell, PO Box 2751, Santa Rosa, CA 95405 / 707-573-8735; FAX: 707-573-0369
Lock's Philadelphia Gun Exchange, 6700 Rowland Ave., Philadelphia, PA 19149 / 215-332-6225; FAX: 215-332-4800
Lohman Mfg. Co., Inc., 4500 Doniphan Dr., P.O. Box 220, Neosho, MO 64850 / 417-451-4438; FAX: 417-451-2576
Lomont Precision Bullets, 278 Sandy Creek Rd, Salmon, ID 83467 / 208-756-6819; FAX: 208-756-6824 klomont.com
London Guns Ltd., Box 3750, Santa Barbara, CA 93130 / 805-683-4141; FAX: 805-683-1712
Lortone Inc., 2856 NW Market St., Seattle, WA 98107
Lothar Walther Precision Tool Inc., 3425 Hutchinson Rd., Cumming, GA 30040 / 770-889-9998; FAX: 770-889-4919 lotharwalther@mindspring.com www.lothar-walther.com
Loweth , Richard H.R. , 29 Hedgegrow Lane, Kirby Muxloe, Leics, LE9 2BN ENGLAND / (0) 116 238 6295
Lupton, Keith. *(See Pawling Mountain Club)*
Lyman Instant Targets, Inc. *(See Lyman Products)*
Lyman Products Corp., 475 Smith Street, Middletown, CT 06457-1541 / 860-632-2020; or 800-225-9626; FAX: 860-632-1699 lymansales@cshore.com www.lymanproducts.com

M

M.H. Canjar Co., 6510 Raleigh St., Arvada, CO 80003 / 303-295-2638; FAX: 303-295-2638
MA Systems, P.O. Box 1143, Chouteau, OK 74337 / 918-479-6378
Mac-1 Airgun Distributors, 13974 Van Ness Ave., Gardena, CA 90249 / 310-327-3581; FAX: 310-327-0238 mac1@maclairgun.com maclairgun.com
Madis Books, 2453 West Five Mile Pkwy., Dallas, TX 75233 / 214-330-7168
Madis, George. *(See Winchester Consultants)*
Magma Engineering Co., P.O. Box 161, 20955 E. Ocotillo Rd., Queen Creek, AZ 85242 / 602-987-9008; FAX: 602-987-0148
Mag-Na-Port International, Inc., 41302 Executive Dr., Harrison Twp., MI 48045-1306 / 586-469-6727; FAX: 586-469-0425 email@magnaport.com www.magnaport.com
Magnum Research, Inc., 7110 University Ave. NE, Minneapolis, MN 55432 / 800-772-6168; or 763-574-1868; FAX: 763-574-0109 magnumresearch.com
Magnus Bullets, P.O. Box 239, Toney, AL 35773 / 256-420-8359; FAX: 256-420-8360
MagSafe Ammo Co., 4700 S US Highway 17/92, Casselberry, FL 32707-3814 / 407-834-9966; FAX: 407-834-8185
Magtech Ammunition Co. Inc., 837 Boston Rd #12, Madison, CT 06443 / 203-245-8983; FAX: 203-245-2883 rfine@mactechammunition.com www.mactech.com.br
Mahony , Philip Bruce , 67 White Hollow Rd., Lime Rock, CT 06039-2418 / 203-435-9341
Maine Custom Bullets, RFD 1, Box 1755, Brooks, ME 04921
Maionchi-L.M.I., Via Di Coselli-Zona, Industriale Di Guamo 55060, Lucca, ITALY / 011 39-583 94291
Mandall Shooting Supplies Inc., 3616 N. Scottsdale Rd., Scottsdale, AZ 85251 / 480-945-2553; FAX: 480-949-0734
Marble Arms *(See CRR, Inc./Marble's Inc.)*
Marchmon Bullets, 8191 Woodland Shore Dr., Brighton, MI 48116
Markell,Inc., 422 Larkfield Center 235, Santa Rosa, CA 95403 / 707-573-0792; FAX: 707-573-9867
Markesbery Muzzle Loaders, Inc., 7785 Foundation Dr., Ste. 6, Florence, KY 41042 / 606-342-5553; or 606-342-2380
Marksman Products, 5482 Argosy Dr., Huntington Beach, CA 92649 / 714-898-7535; or 800-822-8005; FAX: 714-891-0782
MarMik, Inc., 2116 S. Woodland Ave., Michigan City, IN 46360 / 219-872-7231; FAX: 219-872-7231
Marquart Precision Co., P.O. Box 1740, Prescott, AZ 86302 / 520-445-5646
MAST Technology, P.O. Box 60969, Boulder City, NV 89006
Master Lock Co., 2600 N. 32nd St., Milwaukee, WI 53245 / 414-444-2800
Match Prep--Doyle Gracey, P.O. Box 155, Tehachapi, CA 93581 / 661-822-5383; FAX: 661-823-8680
Maxi-Mount Inc., P.O. Box 291, Willoughby Hills, OH 44096-0291 / 440-944-9456; FAX: 440-944-9456 maximount454@yahoo.com

DIRECTORY OF THE HANDLOADER'S TRADE

Mayville Engineering Co. *(See MEC, Inc.)*
McBros Rifle Co., P.O. Box 86549, Phoenix, AZ 85080 / 602-582-3713; FAX: 602-581-3825
McCament, Jay. *(See Jay McCament Custom Gunmaker)*
McCann's Machine & Gun Shop, P.O. Box 641, Spanaway, WA 98387 / 253-537-6919; FAX: 253-537-6993 mccann.machine@worldnet.att.net www.mccannindustries.com
McDonald , Dennis , 8359 Brady St., Peosta, IA 52068 / 319-556-7940
McGowen Rifle Barrels, 5961 Spruce Lane, St. Anne, IL 60964 / 815-937-9816; FAX: 815-937-4024
McKinney, R.P. *(See Schuetzen Gun Co.)*
McMillan Fiberglass Stocks, Inc., 1638 W. Knudsen Dr. #102, Phoenix, AZ 85027 / 602-582-9635; FAX: 602-581-3825
McMillan Optical Gunsight Co., 28638 N. 42nd St., Cave Creek, AZ 85331 / 602-585-7868; FAX: 602-585-7872
McMillan Rifle Barrels, P.O. Box 3427, Bryan, TX 77805 / 409-690-3456; FAX: 409-690-0156
McMurdo, Lynn *(See Specialty Gunsmithing)*, PO Box 404, Afton, WY 83110 / 307-886-5535
MCS, Inc., 34 Delmar Dr., Brookfield, CT 06804 / 203-775-1013; FAX: 203-775-9462
MDS, P.O. Box 1441, Brandon, FL 33509-1441 / 813-653-1180; FAX: 813-684-5953
MEC, Inc., 715 South St., Mayville, WI 53050 / 414-387-4500; FAX: 414-387-5802 reloaders@mayul.com www.mayvl.com
MEC-Gar S.r.l., Via Madonnina 64, Gardone V.T. Brescia, ITALY / 39-30-8912687; FAX: 39-30-8910065
Meister Bullets *(See Gander Mountain)*
Mendez , John A. , P.O. Box 620984, Orlando, FL 32862 / 407-344-2791
Men-Metallwerk Elisenhuette GmbH, P.O. Box 1263, Nassau/Lahn, D-56372 GERMANY / 2604-7819
Meprolight *(See Hesco-Meprolight)*
Merit Corp., PO Box 9044, Schenectady, NY 12309 / 518-346-1420 sales@meritcorporation.com www.meritcorporation.com
Merkuria Ltd., Argentinska 38, 17005, Praha 7 CZECH, REPUBLIC / 422-875117; FAX: 422-809152
Michael's Antiques, Box 591, Waldoboro, ME 04572
Michaels Of Oregon, PO Box 1690, Oregon City, OR 97045 www.michaels-oregon.com
Mid-America Recreation, Inc., 1328 5th Ave., Moline, IL 61265 / 309-764-5089; FAX: 309-764-2722
Middlebrooks Custom Shop, 7366 Colonial Trail East, Surry, VA 23883 / 757-357-0881; FAX: 757-365-0442
Midway Arms, Inc., 5875 W. Van Horn Tavern Rd., Columbia, MO 65203 / 800-243-3220; or 573-445-6363; FAX: 573-446-1018
Military Armament Corp., P.O. Box 120, Mt. Zion Rd., Lingleville, TX 76461 / 817-965-3253
Miller Arms, Inc., P.O. Box 260 Purl St., St. Onge, SD 57779 / 605-642-5160; FAX: 605-642-5160
Miller Single Trigger Mfg. Co., Rt. 209, Box 1275, Millersburg, PA 17061 / 717-692-3704
Millett Sights, 7275 Murdy Circle, Adm. Office, Huntington Beach, CA 92647 / 714-842-5575; or 800-645-5388; FAX: 714-843-5707
Milstor Corp., 80-975 Indio Blvd., Indio, CA 92201 / 760-775-9998; FAX: 760-775-5229 milstor@webtv.net
Mirador Optical Corp., P.O. Box 11614, Marina Del Rey, CA 90295-7614 / 310-821-5587; FAX: 310-305-0386
Mitchell , Jack , c/o Geoff Gaebe, Addieville East Farm, 200 Pheasant Dr, Mapleville, RI 02839 / 401-568-3185
Mitchell Bullets, R.F., 430 Walnut St, Westernport, MD 21562
Mitchell Optics, Inc., 2072 CR 1100 N, Sidney, IL 61877 / 217-688-2219; or 217-621-3018; FAX: 217-688-2505 mitche1@attglobal.net
MI-TE Bullets, 1396 Ave. K, Ellsworth, KS 67439 / 785-472-4575; FAX: 785-472-5579
MMC, 5050 E. Belknap St., Haltom City, TX 76117 / 817-831-9557; FAX: 817-834-5508
Modern Gun Repair School, PO Box 846, Saint Albans, VT 05478 / 802-524-2223; FAX: 802-524-2053 jfwp@dlilearn.com www.mgsinfoadlifearn.com
Modern Muzzleloading, Inc, PO Box 130, Centerville, IA 52544 / 515-856-2626
Montana Armory, Inc *(See C. Sharps Arms Co. Inc.)*, 100 Centennial Dr., PO Box 885, Big Timber, MT 59011 / 406-932-4353; FAX: 406-932-4443
Montana Outfitters, Lewis E. Yearout, 308 Riverview Dr. E., Great Falls, MT 59404 / 406-761-0859
Montana Precision Swaging, PO Box 4746, Butte, MT 59702 / 406-494-0600; FAX: 406-494-0600
Montana Vintage Arms, 2354 Bear Canyon Rd., Bozeman, MT 59715
Morrison Custom Rifles, J. W., 4015 W Sharon, Phoenix, AZ 85029 / 602-978-3754
Morrison Precision, 6719 Calle Mango, Hereford, AZ 85615 / 520-378-6207 morprec@c2i2.com
Mo's Competitor Supplies *(See MCS Inc)*
Mountain Plains Industries, 244 Glass Hollow Rd., Alton, VA 22920 / 800-687-3000; FAX: 540-456-8134
Mountain South, P.O. Box 381, Barnwell, SC 29812 / FAX: 803-259-3227
Mountain State Muzzleloading Supplies, Inc., Box 154-1, Rt. 2, Williamstown, WV 26187 / 304-375-7842; FAX: 304-375-3737
MPI Stocks, PO Box 83266, Portland, OR 97283 / 503-226-1215; FAX: 503-226-2661
MSR Targets, P.O. Box 1042, West Covina, CA 91793 / 818-331-7840
MTM Molded Products Co., Inc., 3370 Obco Ct., Dayton, OH 45414 / 937-890-7461; FAX: 937-890-1747
Mulberry House Publishing, P.O. Box 2180, Apache Junction, AZ 85217 / 888-738-1567; FAX: 480-671-1015
Mulhern , Rick , Rt. 5, Box 152, Rayville, LA 71269 / 318-728-2688
Mullins Ammunition, Rt. 2, Box 304K, Clintwood, VA 24228 / 540-926-6772; FAX: 540-926-6092
Multiplex International, 26 S. Main St., Concord, NH 03301 FAX: 603-796-2223
Multi-Scale Charge Ltd., 3269 Niagara Falls Blvd., N. Tonawanda, NY 14120 / 905-566-1255; FAX: 905-276-6295
Murmur Corp., 2823 N. Westmoreland Ave., Dallas, TX 75222 / 214-630-5400
Muscle Products Corp., 112 Fennell Dr., Butler, PA 16002 / 800-227-7049; or 724-283-0567; FAX: 724-283-8310 mpc@mpc_home.com www.mpc_home.com
MWG Co., P.O. Box 971202, Miami, FL 33197 / 800-428-9394; or 305-253-8393; FAX: 305-232-1247

N

N.B.B., Inc., 24 Elliot Rd., Sterling, MA 01564 / 508-422-7538; or 800-942-9444
Nagel's Custom Bullets, 100 Scott St., Baytown, TX 77520-2849
National Bullet Co., 1585 E. 361 St., Eastlake, OH 44095 / 216-951-1854; FAX: 216-951-7761
National Target Co., 4690 Wyaconda Rd., Rockville, MD 20852 / 800-827-7060; or 301-770-7060; FAX: 301-770-7892
Naval Ordnance Works, Rt. 2, Box 919, Sheperdstown, WV 25443 / 304-876-0998
Navy Arms Company, Valmore J. Forgett Jr., 815 22nd Street, Union City, NJ 07087 / 201-863-7100; FAX: 201-863-8770 info@navyarms.com www.navyarms.com
NCP Products, Inc., 3500 12th St. N.W., Canton, OH 44708 / 330-456-5130; FAX: 330-456-5234
Necromancer Industries, Inc., 14 Communications Way, West Newton, PA 15089 / 412-872-8722
NEI Handtools, Inc., 51583 Columbia River Hwy., Scappoose, OR 97056 / 503-543-6776; FAX: 503-543-7865 nei@columbia-center.com www.neihandtools.com
Neil A. Jones Custom Products, 17217 Brookhouser Road, Saegertown, PA 16433 / 814-763-2769; FAX: 814-763-4228
Nelson, Stephen. *(See Nelson's Custom Guns, Inc)*.
Nelson's Custom Guns, Inc., Stephen Nelson , 7430 Valley View Dr. N.W., Corvallis, OR 97330 / 541-745-5232 nelsons-custom@home.com
New England Ammunition Co., 1771 Post Rd. East, Suite 223, Westport, CT 06880 / 203-254-8048
New England Arms Co., Box 278, Lawrence Lane, Kittery Point, ME 03905 / 207-439-0593; FAX: 207-439-0525 info@newenglandarms.com www.newenglandarms.com
New England Custom Gun Service, 438 Willow Brook Rd., Plainfield, NH 03781 / 603-469-3450; FAX: 603-469-3471 bestguns@cyborportal.net www.newenglandcustom.com
Newman Gunshop, 119 Miller Rd., Agency, IA 52530 / 515-937-5775
Nickels , Paul R. , 4328 Seville St., Las Vegas, NV 89121 / 702-435-5318
Niemi Engineering, W. B., Box 126 Center Rd, Greensboro, VT 05841 / 802-533-7180; FAX: 802-533-7141
Nightforce *(See Lightforce USA Inc)*
Nikon, Inc., 1300 Walt Whitman Rd., Melville, NY 11747 / 516-547-8623; FAX: 516-547-0309
Norincoptics *(See BEC, Inc.)*
North American Shooting Systems, P.O. Box 306, Osoyoos, BC V0H 1V0 CANADA / 604-495-3131; FAX: 604-495-2816
North Devon Firearms Services, 3 North St., Braunton, EX33 1AJ ENGLAND / 01271 813624; FAX: 01271 813624
North Pass, 1418 Webster Ave, Fort Collins, CO 80524 / 970-407-0426
North Specialty Products, 10091 Stageline St., Corona, CA 92883 / 714-524-1665
Northern Precision Custom Swaged Bullets, 329 S. James St., Carthage, NY 13619 / 315-493-1711
Northwest Arms, 26884 Pearl Rd., Parma, ID 83660 / 208-722-6771; FAX: 208-722-1062
Nosler, Inc., P.O. Box 671, Bend, OR 97709 / 800-285-3701; or 541-382-3921; FAX: 541-388-4667
Novak's, Inc., 1206 1/2 30th St., P.O. Box 4045, Parkersburg, WV 26101 / 304-485-9295; FAX: 304-428-6722
Nowlin Mfg. Co., 20622 S 4092 Rd, Claremore, OK 74017 / 918-342-0689; FAX: 918-342-0624 nowlinguns@msn.com nowlinguns.com

O

Oakland Custom Arms,Inc., 4690 W. Walton Blvd., Waterford, MI 48329 / 810-674-8261
Obermeyer Rifled Barrels, 23122 60th St., Bristol, WI 53104 / 262-843-3537; FAX: 262-843-2129
October Country Muzzleloading, P.O. Box 969, Dept. GD, Hayden, ID 83835 / 208-772-2068; FAX: 208-772-9230 ocinfo@octobercountry.com www.octobercountry.com

MANUFACTURER'S DIRECTORY

Oehler Research,Inc., PO Box 9135, Austin, TX 78766 / 512-327-6900; or 800-531-5125; FAX: 512-327-6903
Oil Rod and Gun Shop, 69 Oak St., East Douglas, MA 01516 / 508-476-3687
OK Weber,Inc., P.O. Box 7485, Eugene, OR 97401 / 541-747-0458; FAX: 541-747-5927 okweber@pacinfo okweber.com
Oklahoma Ammunition Co., 3701A S. Harvard Ave., No. 367, Tulsa, OK 74135-2265 / 918-396-3187; FAX: 918-396-4270
Old Wagon Bullets, 32 Old Wagon Rd., Wilton, CT 06897
Old West Bullet Moulds, J Ken Chapman , P.O. Box 519, Flora Vista, NM 87415 / 505-334-6970
Old Western Scrounger,Inc., 12924 Hwy. A-12, Montague, CA 96064 / 916-459-5445; FAX: 916-459-3944
Old World Gunsmithing, 2901 SE 122nd St., Portland, OR 97236 / 503-760-7681
Olympic Arms Inc., 620-626 Old Pacific Hwy. SE, Olympia, WA 98513 / 360-456-3471; FAX: 360-491-3447
Olympic Optical Co., P.O. Box 752377, Memphis, TN 38175-2377 / 901-794-3890; or 800-238-7120; FAX: 901-794-0676 80
Omark Industries,Div. of Blount,Inc., 2299 Snake River Ave., P.O. Box 856, Lewiston, ID 83501 / 800-627-3640; or 208-746-2351
One Of A Kind, 15610 Purple Sage, San Antonio, TX 78255 / 512-695-3364
One Ragged Hole, P.O. Box 13624, Tallahassee, FL 32317-3624
Optical Services Co., P.O. Box 1174, Santa Teresa, NM 88008-1174 / 505-589-3833
Orchard Park Enterprise, P.O. Box 563, Orchard Park, NY 14127 / 616-656-0356
Oregon Arms, Inc. *(See Rogue Rifle Co., Inc.)*
Oregon Trail Bullet Company, PO Box 529, Dept. P, Baker City, OR 97814 / 800-811-0548; FAX: 514-523-1803
Original Box, Inc., 700 Linden Ave., York, PA 17404 / 717-854-2897; FAX: 717-845-4276
Orion Rifle Barrel Co., RR2, 137 Cobler Village, Kalispell, MT 59901 / 406-257-5649
Ottmar , Maurice , Box 657, 113 E. Fir, Coulee City, WA 99115 / 509-632-5717
Outdoor Sports Headquarters, Inc., 967 Watertower Ln., West Carrollton, OH 45449 / 513-865-5855; FAX: 513-865-5962
Outers Laboratories, Route 2, P.O. Box 39, Onalaska, WI 54650 / 608-781-5800; FAX: 608-781-0368
Ox-Yoke Originals, Inc., 34 Main St., Milo, ME 04463 / 800-231-8313; or 207-943-7351; FAX: 207-943-2416
Ozark Gun Works, 11830 Cemetery Rd., Rogers, AR 72756 / 479-631-1024; FAX: 479-631-1024 ogw@hotmail.com www.eocities.com/ocarkgunworks

P

P.A.C.T., Inc., P.O. Box 531525, Grand Prairie, TX 75053 / 214-641-0049
P.M. Enterprises, Inc. / Precise Metalsmithing, 146 Curtis Hill Rd., Chehalis, WA 98532 / 360-748-3743; FAX: 360-748-1802 precise1@quik.com
P.S.M.G. Gun Co., 10 Park Ave., Arlington, MA 02174 / 617-646-8845; FAX: 617-646-2133
Pacific Cartridge, Inc., 2425 Salashan Loop Road, Ferndale, WA 98248 / 360-366-4444; FAX: 360-366-4445
Pacific Research Laboratories, Inc. *(See Rimrock)*
Pacific Rifle Co., PO Box 1473, Lake Oswego, OR 97035 / 503-538-7437
Pac-Nor Barreling, 99299 Overlook Rd., PO Box 6188, Brookings, OR 97415 / 503-469-7330; FAX: 503-469-7331
Paco's *(See Small Custom Mould & Bullet Co)*
Page Custom Bullets, P.O. Box 25, Port Moresby, NEW GUINEA
Pagel Gun Works, Inc., 1407 4th St. NW, Grand Rapids, MN 55744 / 218-326-3003
Paintball Games International Magazine Aceville, Castle House 97 High St., Essex, ENGLAND / 011-44-206-564840
Palsa Outdoor Products, P.O. Box 81336, Lincoln, NE 68501 / 402-488-5288; FAX: 402-488-2321
Paragon Sales & Services, Inc., 2501 Theodore St, Crest Hill, IL 60435-1613 / 815-725-9212; FAX: 815-725-8974
Parker & Sons Shooting Supply, 9337 Smoky Row Road, Strawberry Plains, TN 37871 / 865-933-3286; FAX: 865-932-8586
Parsons Optical Mfg. Co., PO Box 192, Ross, OH 45061 / 513-867-0820; FAX: 513-867-8380 psscopes@concentric.net
Pasadena Gun Center, 206 E. Shaw, Pasadena, TX 77506 / 713-472-0417; FAX: 713-472-1322
Passive Bullet Traps, Inc. *(See Savage Range)*
Paterson Gunsmithing, 438 Main St., Paterson, NJ 07502 / 201-345-4100
Paul and Sharon Dressel, 209 N. 92nd Ave., Yakima, WA 98908 / 509-966-9233; FAX: 509-966-3365 dressels@nwinfo.net www.dressels.com
Paul D. Hillmer Custom Gunstocks, 7251 Hudson Heights, Hudson, IA 50643 / 319-988-3941
Paulsen Gunstocks, Rt. 71, Box 11, Chinook, MT 59523 / 406-357-3403
Pawling Mountain Club, Keith Lupton , PO Box 573, Pawling, NY 12564 / 914-855-3825
Pease Accuracy, Bob , P.O. Box 310787, New Braunfels, TX 78131 / 210-625-1342
PECAR Herbert Schwarz GmbH, Kreuzbergstrasse 6, 10965, Berlin, GERMANY / 004930-785-7383; FAX: 004930-785-1934 michael.schwart@pecar-berlin.de www.pecar-berlin.de
Pecatonica River Longrifle, 5205 Nottingham Dr., Rockford, IL 61111 / 815-968-1995; FAX: 815-968-1996
Pejsa Ballistics, 1314 Marquette Ave., Apt 807, Minneapolis, MN 55403 / 612-374-3337; FAX: 612-374-5383
Pell, John T. *(See KOGOT)*
Peltor, Inc. *(See Aero Peltor)*
PEM's Mfg. Co., 5063 Waterloo Rd., Atwater, OH 44201 / 216-947-3721
Pence Precision Barrels, 7567 E. 900 S., S. Whitley, IN 46787 / 219-839-4745
Pendleton Royal, c/o Swingler Buckland Ltd., 4/7 Highgate St., Birmingham, ENGLAND / 44 121 440 3060; or 44 121 446 5898; FAX: 44 121 446 4165
Penn Bullets, P.O. Box 756, Indianola, PA 15051
Penrod Precision, 312 College Ave., PO Box 307, N. Manchester, IN 46962 / 260-982-8385; FAX: 260-982-1819
Pentax Corp., 35 Inverness Dr. E., Englewood, CO 80112 / 303-799-8000; FAX: 303-790-1131
Perazone-Gunsmith, Brian, Cold Spring Rd, Roxbury, NY 12474 / 607-326-4088; FAX: 607-326-3140
Peter Dyson & Son Ltd., 3 Cuckoo Lane, Honley Huddersfield, Yorkshire, HD7 2BR ENGLAND / 44-1484-661062; FAX: 44-1484-663709 info@peterdyson.co.uk www.peterdyson.com
Petersen Publishing Co. *(See Emap USA)*, 6420 Wilshire Blvd., Los Angeles, CA 90048 / 213-782-2000; FAX: 213-782-2867
Peterson Gun Shop, Inc., A.W., 4255 W. Old U.S. 441, Mt. Dora, FL 32757-3299 / 352-383-4258; FAX: 352-735-1001
Petro-Explo Inc., 7650 U.S. Hwy. 287, Suite 100, Arlington, TX 76017 / 817-478-8888
Pettinger Books, Gerald, Rt. 2, Box 125, Russell, IA 50238 / 641-535-2239 gpettinger@lisco.com
PFRB Co., PO Box 1242, Bloomington, IL 61702 / 309-473-3964; FAX: 309-473-2161
Phillippi Custom Bullets, Justin, P.O. Box 773, Ligonier, PA 15658 / 724-238-2962; FAX: 724-238-9671 jrp@wpa.net http://www.wpa.net~jrphil
Pinetree Bullets, 133 Skeena St., Kitimat, BC V8C 1Z1 CANADA / 604-632-3768; FAX: 604-632-3768
Plum City Ballistic Range, N2162 80th St., Plum City, WI 54761 / 715-647-2539
PlumFire Press, Inc., 30-A Grove Ave., Patchogue, NY 11772-4112 / 800-695-7246; FAX: 516-758-4071
PMC / Eldorado Cartridge Corp., PO Box 62508, 12801 U.S. Hwy. 95 S., Boulder City, NV 89005 / 702-294-0025; FAX: 702-294-0121 kbauer@pmcammo.com pmcammo.com
Pohl , Henry A. *(See Great American Gun Co.)*
Police Bookshelf, PO Box 122, Concord, NH 03301 / 603-224-6814; FAX: 603-226-3554
Polywad, Inc., P.O. Box 7916, Macon, GA 31209 / 912-477-0669 polywadmpb@aol.com www.polywad.com
Ponsness/Warren, P.O. Box 8, Rathdrum, ID 83858 / 208-687-2231; FAX: 208-687-2233
Pony Express Reloaders, 608 E. Co. Rd. D, Suite 3, St. Paul, MN 55117 / 612-483-9406; FAX: 612-483-9884
Powell & Son (Gunmakers) Ltd., William, 35-37 Carrs Lane, Birmingham, B4 7SX ENGLAND / 121-643-0689; FAX: 121-631-3504
Power Plus Enterprises, Inc., PO Box 38, Warm Springs, GA 31830 / 706-655-2132
Powley Computer *(See Hutton Rifle Ranch)*
Prairie River Arms, 1220 N. Sixth St., Princeton, IL 61356 / 815-875-1616; or 800-445-1541; FAX: 815-875-1402
Precise Metalsmithing Enterprises / P.M. Enterprises, 146 Curtis Hill Rd., Chehalis, WA 98532 / 360-748-3743; FAX: 360-748-8102 precise1@quik.com
Precision Airgun Sales, Inc., 5247 Warrensville Ctr Rd, Maple Hts., OH 44137 / 216-587-5005; FAX: 216-587-5005
Precision Delta Corp., PO Box 128, Ruleville, MS 38771 / 662-756-2810; FAX: 662-756-2590
Precision Gun Works, 104 Sierra Rd Dept. GD, Kerrville, TX 78028 / 830-367-4587
Precision Munitions, Inc., P.O. Box 326, Jasper, IN 47547
Precision Reloading, Inc., PO Box 122, Stafford Springs, CT 06076 / 860-684-7979; FAX: 860-684-6788 info@precisionreloading.com www.precisionreloading.com
Precision Shooting, Inc., 222 McKee St., Manchester, CT 06040 / 860-645-8776; FAX: 860-643-8215 www.precisionshooting.com
Precision Sport Optics, 15571 Producer Lane, Unit G, Huntington Beach, CA 92649 / 714-891-1309; FAX: 714-892-6920
Premier Reticles, 920 Breckinridge Lane, Winchester, VA 22601-6707 / 540-722-0601; FAX: 540-722-3522
Prescott Projectile Co., 1808 Meadowbrook Road, Prescott, AZ 86303
Price Bullets, Patrick W., 16520 Worthley Dr., San Lorenzo, CA 94580 / 510-278-1547
Prime Reloading, 30 Chiswick End, Meldreth, ROYSTON UK / 0763-260636
PRL Bullets, c/o Blackburn Enterprises, 114 Stuart Rd., Ste. 110, Cleveland, TN 37312 / 423-559-0340
Pro Load Ammunition, Inc., 5180 E. Seltice Way, Post Falls, ID 83854 / 208-773-9444; FAX: 208-773-9441
Professional Hunter Supplies *(See Star Custom Bull)*, PO Box 608, 468 Main St, Ferndale, CA 95536 / 707-786-9140; FAX: 707-786-9117 wmebride@humboldt.com

ProlixrÆ Lubricants, PO Box 1348, Victorville, CA 92393 / 760-243-3129; FAX: 760-241-0148 prolix@accex.net prolixlubricant.com
Proofmark Corp., PO Box 610, Burgess, VA 22432 / 804-453-4337; FAX: 804-453-4337 proofmark@rivnet.net
Pro-Shot Products, Inc., P.O. Box 763, Taylorville, IL 62568 / 217-824-9133; FAX: 217-824-8861
Protektor Model, 1-11 Bridge St., Galeton, PA 16922 / 814-435-2442 hrk@penn.com www.protektormodel.com

Q

Quack Decoy & Sporting Clays, 4 Ann & Hope Way, P.O. Box 98, Cumberland, RI 02864 / 401-723-8202; FAX: 401-722-5910

R

R&J Gun Shop, 337 S. Humbolt St., Canyon City, OR 97820 / 541-575-2130 rjgunshop@highdestertnet.com
R&S Industries Corp., 8255 Brentwood Industrial Dr., St. Louis, MO 63144 / 314-781-5400 polishingcloth.com
R.A. Wells Custom Gunsmith, 3452 1st Ave., Racine, WI 53402 / 414-639-5223
R.E.I., P.O. Box 88, Tallevast, FL 34270 / 813-755-0085
R.E.T. Enterprises, 2608 S. Chestnut, Broken Arrow, OK 74012 / 918-251-GUNS; FAX: 918-251-0587
R.I.S. Co., Inc., 718 Timberlake Circle, Richardson, TX 75080 / 214-235-0933
Rainier Ballistics Corp., 4500 15th St. East, Tacoma, WA 98424 / 800-638-8722; or 206-922-7589; FAX: 206-922-7854
Ram-Line Blount, Inc., P.O. Box 39, Onalaska, WI 54650
Ramon B. Gonzalez Guns, PO Box 370, 93 St. Joseph's Hill Road, Monticello, NY 12701 / 914-794-4515
Rampart International, 2781 W. MacArthur Blvd., B-283, Santa Ana, CA 92704 / 800-976-7240; or 714-557-6405
Ranch Products, P.O. Box 145, Malinta, OH 43535 / 313-277-3118; FAX: 313-565-8536
Randolph Engineering Inc., 26 Thomas Patten Dr., Randolph, MA 02368 / 781-961-6070; FAX: 781-961-0337
Ransom International Corp., 1027 Spire Dr, Prescott, AZ 86302 / 520-778-7899; FAX: 520-778-7993 ransom@primenet.com www.ransom-intl.com
Rapine Bullet Mould Mfg. Co., 9503 Landis Lane, East Greenville, PA 18041 / 215-679-5413; FAX: 215-679-9795
Raptor Arms Co., Inc., 273 Canal St, #179, Shelton, CT 06484 / 203-924-7618; FAX: 203-924-7624
Ravell Ltd., 289 Diputacion St., 08009, Barcelona, SPAIN / 34(3) 4874486; FAX: 34(3) 4881394
Ray Riling Arms Books Co., 6844 Gorsten St., Philadelphia, PA 19119 / 215-438-2456; FAX: 215-438-5395 sales@rayrilingarmsbooks.com www.rayrilings.com
Raytech Div. of Lyman Products Corp., 475 Smith Street, Middletown, CT 06457-1541 / 860-632-2020; or 800-225-9626; FAX: 860-632-1699 lymansales@cshore.com www.lymanproducts.com
RCBS Div. of Blount, 605 Oro Dam Blvd., Oroville, CA 95965 / 800-533-5000; or 916-533-5191; FAX: 916-533-1647 www.rcbs.com
Reagent Chemical & Research, Inc. *(See Calico Hard)*
Reardon Products, P.O. Box 126, Morrison, IL 61270 / 815-772-3155
Redding Reloading Equipment, 1089 Starr Rd., Cortland, NY 13045 / 607-753-3331; FAX: 607-756-8445 techline@redding-reloading.com www.redding-reloading.com
Redwood Bullet Works, 3559 Bay Rd., Redwood City, CA 94063 / 415-367-6741
Reiswig , Wallace E. *(See Claro Walnut Gunstock)*
Reloading Specialties, Inc., Box 1130, Pine Island, MN 55463 / 507-356-8500; FAX: 507-356-8800
Remington Arms Co., Inc., 870 Remington Drive, P.O. Box 700, Madison, NC 27025-0700 / 800-243-9700; FAX: 910-548-8700
Remington Double Shotguns, 7885 Cyd Dr., Denver, CO 80221 / 303-429-6947
Rhino, P.O. Box 787, Locust, NC 28097 / 704-753-2198
Rice, Keith *(See White Rock Tool & Die)*
Richards Micro-Fit Stocks, 8331 N. San Fernando Ave., Sun Valley, CA 91352 / 818-767-6097; FAX: 818-767-7121
Ridgeline, Inc, Bruce Sheldon , PO Box 930, Dewey, AZ 86327-0930 / 800-632-5900; FAX: 520-632-5900
RMS Custom Gunsmithing, 4120 N. Bitterwell, Prescott Valley, AZ 86314 / 520-772-7626
Robinson , Don , Pennsylvaia Hse, 36 Fairfax Crescent, W Yorkshire, ENGLAND / 0422-364458
Robinson Armament Co., PO Box 16776, Salt Lake City, UT 84116 / 801-355-0401; FAX: 801-355-0402 zdf@robarm.com www.robarm.com
Robinson Firearms Mfg. Ltd., 1699 Blondeaux Crescent, Kelowna, BC V1Y 4J8 CANADA / 604-868-9596
Robinson H.V. Bullets, 3145 Church St., Zachary, LA 70791 / 504-654-4029
Rochester Lead Works, 76 Anderson Ave., Rochester, NY 14607 / 716-442-8500; FAX: 716-442-4712
Rockwood Corp., Speedwell Division, 136 Lincoln Blvd., Middlesex, NJ 08846 / 800-243-8274; FAX: 980-560-7475
Rocky Mountain Target Co., 3 Aloe Way, Leesburg, FL 34788 / 352-365-9598
Rogue Rifle Co., Inc., P.O. Box 20, Prospect, OR 97536 / 541-560-4040; FAX: 541-560-4041
Romain's Custom Guns, Inc., RD 1, Whetstone Rd., Brockport, PA 15823 / 814-265-1948 romwhetstone@penn.com
Ron Frank Custom Classic Arms, 7131 Richland Rd., Ft. Worth, TX 76118 / 817-284-9300; FAX: 817-284-9300 rfrank3974@aol.com
Rooster Laboratories, P.O. Box 412514, Kansas City, MO 64141 / 816-474-1622; FAX: 816-474-1307
Rorschach Precision Products, 417 Keats Cir., Irving, TX 75061 / 214-790-3487
Roto Carve, 2754 Garden Ave., Janesville, IA 50647
Royal Arms Gunstocks, 919 8th Ave. NW, Great Falls, MT 59404 / 406-453-1149; FAX: 406-453-1194 royalarms@lmt.net lmt.net/~royalarms
RPM, 15481 N. Twin Lakes Dr., Tucson, AZ 85739 / 520-825-1233; FAX: 520-825-3333
Rubright Bullets, 1008 S. Quince Rd., Walnutport, PA 18088 / 215-767-1339
Rucker Dist. Inc., P.O. Box 479, Terrell, TX 75160 / 214-563-2094
Rupert's Gun Shop, 2202 Dick Rd., Suite B, Fenwick, MI 48834 / 517-248-3252
Russ Haydon Shooters' Supply, 15018 Goodrich Dr. NW, Gig Harbor, WA 98329 / 253-857-7557; FAX: 253-857-7884
Rutgers Book Center, 127 Raritan Ave., Highland Park, NJ 08904 / 908-545-4344; FAX: 908-545-6686
RWS *(See US Importer-Dynamit Nobel-RWS, Inc.)*, 81 Ruckman Rd, Closter, NJ 07624 / 201-767-7971; FAX: 201-767-1589

S

S&K Scope Mounts, RD 2 Box 72E, Sugar Grove, PA 16350 / 814-489-3091; or 800-578-9862; FAX: 814-489-5466 comments@scopemounts.com www.scopemounts.com
S&S Firearms, 74-11 Myrtle Ave., Glendale, NY 11385 / 718-497-1100; FAX: 718-497-1105
Sabatti S.r.l., via Alessandro Volta 90, 25063 Gardone V.T., Brescia, ITALY / 030-8912207-831312; FAX: 030-8912059
SAECO (See Redding Reloading Equipment)
Safari Press, Inc., 15621 Chemical Lane B, Huntington Beach, CA 92649 / 714-894-9080; FAX: 714-894-4949
Samco Global Arms, Inc., 6995 NW 43rd St., Miami, FL 33166 / 305-593-9782; FAX: 305-593-1014 samco@samcoglobal.com www.samcoglobal.com
Sanders Custom Gun Service, 2358 Tyler Lane, Louisville, KY 40205 / 502-454-3338; FAX: 502-451-8857
Sanders Gun and Machine Shop, 145 Delhi Road, Manchester, IA 52057
Sandia Die & Cartridge Co., 37 Atancacio Rd. NE, Auquerque, NM 87123 / 505-298-5729
Saunders Gun & Machine Shop, R.R. 2, Delhi Road, Manchester, IA 52057
Savage Arms, Inc., 100 Springdale Rd., Westfield, MA 01085 / 413-568-7001; FAX: 413-562-7764
Savage Range Systems, Inc., 100 Springdale RD., Westfield, MA 01085 / 413-568-7001; FAX: 413-562-1152
Saville Iron Co. *(See Greenwood Precision)*
Schaefer Shooting Sports, P.O. Box 1515, Melville, NY 11747-0515 / 516-643-5466; FAX: 516-643-2426 rschaefe@optonline.net www.schaefershooting.com
Scharch Mfg., Inc., 10325 Co. Rd. 120, Salida, CO 81201 / 719-539-7242; or 800-836-4683; FAX: 719-539-3021 scharch@chaffee.net www.scharch.com
Schiffman , Curt , 3017 Kevin Cr., Idaho Falls, ID 83402 / 208-524-4684
Schiffman , Mike , 8233 S. Crystal Springs, McCammon, ID 83250 / 208-254-9114
Schiffman , Norman , 3017 Kevin Cr., Idaho Falls, ID 83402 / 208-524-4684
Schmidt & Bender, Inc., PO Box 134, Meriden, NH 03770 / 603-469-3565; FAX: 603-469-3471 scopes@cyberportal.net schmidtbender.com
Schneider Bullets, 3655 West 214th St., Fairview Park, OH 44126
Schneider Rifle Barrels, Inc, Gary, 12202 N 62nd Pl, Scottsdale, AZ 85254 / 602-948-2525
Schroeder Bullets, 1421 Thermal Ave., San Diego, CA 92154 / 619-423-3523; FAX: 619-423-8124
Schumakers Gun Shop, 512 Prouty Corner Lp. A, Colville, WA 99114 / 509-684-4848
Scope Control, Inc., 5775 Co. Rd. 23 SE, Alexandria, MN 56308 / 612-762-7295
ScopLevel, 151 Lindbergh Ave., Suite C, Livermore, CA 94550 / 925-449-5052; FAX: 925-373-0861
Score High Gunsmithing, 9812-A, Cochiti SE, Albuquerque, NM 087123 / 800-326-5632; or 505-292-5532; FAX: 505-292-2592
Scot Powder, Rt.1 Box 167, McEwen, TN 37101 / 800-416-3006; FAX: 615-729-4211
Scot Powder Co. of Ohio, Inc., Box GD96, Only, TN 37140 / 615-729-4207; or 800-416-3006; FAX: 615-729-4217
Seebeck Assoc., R.E., P. O. Box 59752, Dallas, TX 75229
Seecamp Co. Inc., L. W., PO Box 255, New Haven, CT 06502 / 203-877-3429; FAX: 203-877-3429
Segway Industries, P.O. Box 783, Suffern, NY 10901-0783 / 914-357-5510
Seligman Shooting Products, Box 133, Seligman, AZ 86337 / 602-422-3607
Sellier & Bellot, USA Inc, PO Box 27006, Shawnee Mission, KS 66225 / 913-685-0916; FAX: 913-685-0917
Selsi Co., Inc., P.O. Box 10, Midland Park, NJ 07432-0010 / 201-935-0388; FAX: 201-935-5851

Manufacturer's Directory

Semmer, Charles *(See Remington Double Shotguns)*, 7885 Cyd Dr, Denver, CO 80221 / 303-429-6947
Sentinel Arms, P.O. Box 57, Detroit, MI 48231 / 313-331-1951; FAX: 313-331-1456
Shappy Bullets, 76 Milldale Ave., Plantsville, CT 06479 / 203-621-3704
Sharp Shooter Supply, 4970 Lehman Road, Delphos, OH 45833 / 419-695-3179
Sharps Arms Co., Inc., C., 100 Centennial, Box 885, Big Timber, MT 59011 / 406-932-4353
Shaw, Inc., E. R. *(See Small Arms Mfg. Co.)*
Shay's Gunsmithing, 931 Marvin Ave., Lebanon, PA 17042
Sheffield Knifemakers Supply, Inc., PO Box 741107, Orange City, FL 32774-1107 / 386-775-6453; FAX: 386-774-5754
Sheldon, Bruce. *(See Ridgeline, Inc)*
Shepherd Enterprises, Inc., Box 189, Waterloo, NE 68069 / 402-779-2424; FAX: 402-779-4010 sshepherd@shepherdscopes.com www.shepherdscopes.com
Shilen, Inc., 205 Metro Park Blvd., Ennis, TX 75119 / 972-875-5318; FAX: 972-875-5402
Shiloh Creek, Box 357, Cottleville, MO 63338 / 314-925-1842; FAX: 314-925-1842
Shiloh Rifle Mfg., 201 Centennial Dr., Big Timber, MT 59011 / 406-932-4454; FAX: 406-932-5627
Shooter's Choice Gun Care, 15050 Berkshire Ind. Pky., Middlefield, OH 44062 / 440-834-8888; FAX: 440-834-3388 www.shooterschoice.com
Shooters Supply, 1120 Tieton Dr., Yakima, WA 98902 / 509-452-1181
Shooting Chrony, Inc., 3269 Niagara Falls Blvd., N. Tonawanda, NY 14120 / 905-276-6292; FAX: 416-276-6295
Shoot-N-C Targets *(See Birchwood Casey)*
Shotgun Sports Magazine, dba Shootin' Accessories Ltd., P.O. Box 6810, Auburn, CA 95604 / 916-889-2220
Sierra Bullets, 1400 W. Henry St., Sedalia, MO 65301 / 816-827-6300; FAX: 816-827-6300
Sierra Specialty Prod. Co., 1344 Oakhurst Ave., Los Altos, CA 94024 FAX: 415-965-1536
Sightron, Inc., 1672B Hwy. 96, Franklinton, NC 27525 / 919-528-8783; FAX: 919-528-0995 info@sightron.com www.sightron.com
Silencio/Safety Direct, 56 Coney Island Dr., Sparks, NV 89431 / 800-648-1812; or 702-354-4451; FAX: 702-359-1074
Silver Eagle Machining, 18007 N. 69th Ave., Glendale, AZ 85308
Simmons , Jerry , 715 Middlebury St., Goshen, IN 46528-2717 / 574-533-8546
Simmons Gun Repair, Inc., 700 S. Rogers Rd., Olathe, KS 66062 / 913-782-3131; FAX: 913-782-4189
Simmons Outdoor Corp., PO Box 217, Heflin, AL 36264
Sinclair International, Inc., 2330 Wayne Haven St., Fort Wayne, IN 46803 / 260-493-1858; FAX: 260-493-2530 sales@sinclairintl.com www.sinclairintl.com
Siskiyou Gun Works *(See Donnelly, C. P.)*
Six Enterprises, 320-D Turtle Creek Ct., San Jose, CA 95125 / 408-999-0201; FAX: 408-999-0216
Skip's Machine, 364 29 Road, Grand Junction, CO 81501 / 303-245-5417
Slug Site, Ozark Wilds, 21300 Hwy. 5, Versailles, MO 65084 / 573-378-6430 john.ebeling.com
Small Arms Mfg. Co., 5312 Thoms Run Rd., Bridgeville, PA 15017 / 412-221-4343; FAX: 412-221-4303
Small Custom Mould & Bullet Co., Box 17211, Tucson, AZ 85731
Smith, Judy. See: L.B.T.
Sno-Seal, Inc. *(See Atsko/Sno-Seal)*
SOS Products Co. *(See Buck Stix-SOS Products Co.)*, Box 3, Neenah, WI 54956
Sound Technology, Box 391, Pelham, AL 35124 / 205-664-5860; or 907-486-2825 rem700P@sprintmail.com www.soundtechsilencers.com
Southern Ammunition Co., Inc., 4232 Meadow St., Loris, SC 29569-3124 / 803-756-3262; FAX: 803-756-3583
Southern Bloomer Mfg. Co., P.O. Box 1621, Bristol, TN 37620 / 615-878-6660; FAX: 615-878-8761
Specialty Gunsmithing, Lynn McMurdo, P.O. Box 404, Afton, WY 83110 / 307-886-5535
Specialty Shooters Supply, Inc., 3325 Griffin Rd., Suite 9mm, Fort Lauderdale, FL 33317
Speer Bullets, PO Box 856, Lewiston, ID 83501 / 208-746-2351; www.speer-bullets.com
Speiser , Fred D. , 2229 Dearborn, Missoula, MT 59801 / 406-549-8133
Spencer's Custom Guns, 4107 Jacobs Creek Dr, Scottsville, VA 24590 / 804-293-6836; FAX: 804-293-6836
SPG LLC, PO Box 1625, Cody, WY 82414 / 307-587-7621; FAX: 307-587-7695
Splitfire Sporting Goods, L.L.C., P.O. Box 1044, Orem, UT 84059-1044 / 801-932-7950; FAX: 801-932-7959 www.splitfireguns.com
Sport Flite Manufacturing Co., PO Box 1082, Bloomfield Hills, MI 48303 / 248-647-3747
Sportsman Supply Co., 714 E. Eastwood, P.O. Box 650, Marshall, MO 65340 / 816-886-9393
Sportsmatch U.K. Ltd., 16 Summer St., Leighton, Buzzard Beds, Bedfordshire, LU7 8HT ENGLAND / 01525-381638; FAX: 01525-851236 info@sportsmatch-uk.com www.sportsmatch-uk.com
Springfield, Inc., 420 W. Main St., Geneseo, IL 61254 / 309-944-5631; FAX: 309-944-3676
SSK Industries, J. D. Jones , 590 Woodvue Lane, Wintersville, OH 43953 / 740-264-0176; FAX: 740-264-2257
Stackpole Books, 5067 Ritter Rd., Mechanicsburg, PA 17055-6921 / 717-796-0411; FAX: 717-796-0412
Stalwart Corporation, PO Box 46, Evanston, WY 82931 / 307-789-7687; FAX: 307-789-7688
Stan De Treville & Co., 4129 Normal St., San Diego, CA 92103 / 619-298-3393
Stanley Bullets, 2085 Heatheridge Ln., Reno, NV 89509
Star Ammunition, Inc., 5520 Rock Hampton Ct., Indianapolis, IN 46268 / 800-221-5927; FAX: 317-872-5847
Star Custom Bullets, PO Box 608, 468 Main St., Ferndale, CA 95536 / 707-786-9140; FAX: 707-786-9117 wmebridge@humboldt.com
Starke Bullet Company, P.O. Box 400, 605 6th St. NW, Cooperstown, ND 58425 / 888-797-3431
Starline, Inc., 1300 W. Henry St., Sedalia, MO 65301 / 660-827-6640; FAX: 660-827-6650 info@starlinebrass.com http://www.starlinebrass.com
Starr Trading Co., Jedediah, PO Box 2007, Farmington Hills, MI 48333 / 810-683-4343; FAX: 810-683-3282
Starrett Co., L. S., 121 Crescent St, Athol, MA 01331 / 978-249-3551; FAX: 978-249-8495
State Arms Gun Co., 815 S. Division St., Waunakee, WI 53597 / 608-849-5800
Stewart Game Calls, Inc., Johnny, PO Box 7954, 5100 Fort Ave, Waco, TX 76714 / 817-772-3261; FAX: 817-772-3670
Stewart's Gunsmithing, P.O. Box 5854, Pietersburg North 0750, Transvaal, SOUTH AFRICA / 01521-89401
STI International, 114 Halmar Cove, Georgetown, TX 78628 / 800-959-8201; FAX: 512-819-0465 www.stiguns.com
Stiles Custom Guns, 76 Cherry Run Rd, Box 1605, Homer City, PA 15748 / 712-479-9945
Stillwell , Robert , 421 Judith Ann Dr., Schertz, TX 78154
Stoeger Industries, 17603 Indian Head Hwy., Suite 200, Accokeek, MD 20607-2501 / 301-283-6300; FAX: 301-283-6986 www.stoegerindustries.com
Stoeger Publishing Co. *(See Stoeger Industries)*
Stone Enterprises Ltd., 426 Harveys Neck Rd., PO Box 335, Wicomico Church, VA 22579 / 804-580-5114; FAX: 804-580-8421
Stoney Point Products, Inc., PO Box 234, 1822 N Minnesota St, New Ulm, MN 56073-0234 / 507-354-3360; FAX: 507-354-7236 stoney@newulmtel.net www.stoneypoint.com
Storey, Dale A. *(See DGS Inc.)*
Stratco, Inc., P.O. Box 2270, Kalispell, MT 59901 / 406-755-1221; FAX: 406-755-1226
Strutz Rifle Barrels, Inc., W. C., PO Box 611, Eagle River, WI 54521 / 715-479-4766
Sturm Ruger & Co. Inc., 200 Ruger Rd., Prescott, AZ 86301 / 928-541-8820; FAX: 520-541-8850 www.ruger.com
Sunny Hill Enterprises, Inc., W1790 Cty. HHH, Malone, WI 53049 / 920-795-4722; FAX: 920-795-4822
Swann , D. J. , 5 Orsova Close, Eltham North Vic., 3095 AUSTRALIA / 03-431-0323
Swarovski Optik North America Ltd., 2 Slater Rd., Cranston, RI 02920 / 401-946-2220; or 800-426-3089; FAX: 401-946-2587
Swift Bullet Co., P.O. Box 27, 201 Main St., Quinter, KS 67752 / 913-754-3959; FAX: 913-754-2359
Swift Instruments, Inc., 952 Dorchester Ave., Boston, MA 02125 / 617-436-2960; FAX: 617-436-3232
Swift River Gunworks, 450 State St., Belchertown, MA 01007 / 413-323-4052
Szweda, Robert *(See RMS Custom Gunsmithing)*

T

T&S Industries, Inc., 1027 Skyview Dr., W. Carrollton, OH 45449 / 513-859-8414
T.F.C. S.p.A., Via G. Marconi 118, B, Villa Carcina 25069, ITALY / 030-881271; FAX: 030-881826
T.H.U. Enterprises, Inc., P.O. Box 418, Lederach, PA 19450 / 215-256-1665; FAX: 215-256-9718
T.K. Lee Co., 1282 Branchwater Ln., Birmingham, AL 35216 / 205-913-5222 odonmich@aol.com www.scopedot.com
TacStar, PO Box 547, Cottonwood, AZ 86326-0547 / 602-639-0072; FAX: 602-634-8781
Tactical Defense Institute, 574 Miami Bluff Ct., Loveland, OH 45140 / 513-677-8229; FAX: 513-677-0447
Talley , Dave , P.O. Box 821, Glenrock, WY 82637 / 307-436-8724; or 307-436-9315
Talmage , William G. , 10208 N. County Rd. 425 W., Brazil, IN 47834 / 812-442-0804
Tamarack Products, Inc., PO Box 625, Wauconda, IL 60084 / 708-526-9333; FAX: 708-526-9353
Tank's Rifle Shop, PO Box 474, Fremont, NE 68026-0474 / 402-727-1317; FAX: 402-721-2573 jtank@mitec.net www.tanksrifleshop.com
Taracorp Industries, Inc., 1200 Sixteenth St., Granite City, IL 62040 / 618-451-4400
Target Shooting, Inc., PO Box 773, Watertown, SD 57201 / 605-882-6955; FAX: 605-882-8840
Tar-Hunt Custom Rifles, Inc., 101 Dogtown Rd., Bloomsburg, PA 17815 / 570-784-6368; FAX: 570-784-6368 www.tar-hunt.com
Tasco Sales, Inc., 2889 Commerce Pky., Miramar, FL 33025
TCCI, P.O. Box 302, Phoenix, AZ 85001 / 602-237-3823; FAX: 602-237-3858
TCSR, 3998 Hoffman Rd., White Bear Lake, MN 55110-4626 / 800-328-5323; FAX: 612-429-0526

Directory of the Handloader's Trade

TDP Industries, Inc., 606 Airport Blvd., Doylestown, PA 18901 / 215-345-8687; FAX: 215-345-6057
Tecnolegno S.p.A., Via A. Locatelli, 6 10, 24019 Zogno, I ITALY / 0345-55111; FAX: 0345-55155
Tele-Optics, 630 E. Rockland Rd., PO Box 6313, Libertyville, IL 60048 / 847-362-7757
Tepeco, P.O. Box 342, Friendswood, TX 77546 / 713-482-2702
Terry K. Kopp Professional Gunsmithing, Rt 1 Box 224, Lexington, MO 64067 / 816-259-2636
Tetra Gun Lubricants *(See FTI, Inc.)*
The A.W. Peterson Gun Shop, Inc., 4255 West Old U.S. 441, Mount Dora, FL 32757-3299 / 352-383-4258
The Ballistic Program Co., Inc., 2417 N. Patterson St., Thomasville, GA 31792 / 912-228-5739; or 800-368-0835
The BulletMakers Workshop, RFD 1 Box 1755, Brooks, ME 04921
The Country Armourer, P.O. Box 308, Ashby, MA 01431-0308 / 508-827-6797; FAX: 508-827-4845
The Gun Doctor, 435 East Maple, Roselle, IL 60172 / 708-894-0668
The Gun Parts Corp., 226 Williams Lane, West Hurley, NY 12491 / 914-679-2417; FAX: 914-679-5849
The Gun Room Press, 127 Raritan Ave., Highland Park, NJ 08904 / 732-545-4344; FAX: 732-545-6686 gunbooks@rutgersgunbooks.com www.rutgersgunbooks.com
The Gun Shop, 5550 S. 900 East, Salt Lake City, UT 84117 / 801-263-3633
The Gun Works, 247 S. 2nd St., Springfield, OR 97477 / 541-741-4118; FAX: 541-988-1097 gunworks@worldnet.att.net www.thegunworks.com
The Hanned Line, P.O. Box 2387, Cupertino, CA 95015-2387 smith@hanned.com www.hanned.com
The NgraveR Co., 67 Wawecus Hill Rd., Bozrah, CT 06334 / 860-823-1533
The Ordnance Works, 2969 Pidgeon Point Road, Eureka, CA 95501 / 707-443-3252
The Orvis Co., Rt. 7, Manchester, VT 05254 / 802-362-3622; FAX: 802-362-3525
The Outdoor Connection,Inc., 7901 Panther Way, Waco, TX 76712-6556 / 800-533-6076; or 254-772-5575; FAX: 254-776-3553 floyd@outdoorconnection.com www.outdoorconnection.com
The Paul Co., 27385 Pressonville Rd., Wellsville, KS 66092 / 785-883-4444; FAX: 785-883-2525
The Protector Mfg. Co., Inc., 443 Ashwood Place, Boca Raton, FL 33431 / 407-394-6011
The Wilson Arms Co., 63 Leetes Island Rd., Branford, CT 06405 / 203-488-7297; FAX: 203-488-0135
Thomas , Charles C. , 2600 S. First St., Springfield, IL 62794 / 217-789-8980; FAX: 217-789-9130
Thompson / Center Arms, P.O. Box 5002, Rochester, NH 03866 / 603-332-2394; FAX: 603-332-5133 tech@tcarms.com www.tcarms.com
Thompson Bullet Lube Co., PO Box 409, Wills Point, TX 75169 / 866-476-1500; FAX: 866-476-1500 thomlube@flash.net www.thompsonbulletlube.com
Thompson Precision, 110 Mary St., P.O. Box 251, Warren, IL 61087 / 815-745-3625
Thompson Target Technology, 4804 Sherman Church Ave. S.W., Canton, OH 44710 / 330-484-6480; FAX: 330-491-1087 www.thompsontarget.com
Thompson Tool Mount, 1550 Solomon Rd., Santa Maria, CA 93455 / 805-934-1281 ttm@pronet.net thompsontoolmount.com
Tiger-Hunt Gunstocks, Box 379, Beaverdale, PA 15921 / 814-472-5161 tigerhunt4@aol.com www.gunstockwood.com
Timber Heirloom Products, 618 Roslyn Ave. SW, Canton, OH 44710 / 216-453-7707; FAX: 216-478-4723
Time Precision, 640 Federal Rd., Brookfield, CT 06804 / 203-775-8343
Tioga Engineering Co., Inc., PO Box 913, 13 Cone St., Wellsboro, PA 16901 / 570-724-3533; FAX: 570-724-3895 tiogaeng@epix.net
Tirelli, Snc Di Tirelli Primo E.C., Via Matteotti No. 359, Gardone V.T. Brescia, I ITALY / 030-8912819; FAX: 030-832240
TMI Products *(See Haselbauer Products, Jerry)*
Tom's Gun Repair, Thomas G. Ivanoff, 76-6 Rt. Southfork Rd., Cody, WY 82414 / 307-587-6949
Tonoloway Tack Drives, HCR 81, Box 100, Needmore, PA 17238
Track of the Wolf, Inc., P.O. Box 6, Osseo, MN 55369-0006 / 612-424-2500; FAX: 612-424-9860
Traditions Performance Firearms, P.O. Box 776, 1375 Boston Post Rd., Old Saybrook, CT 06475 / 860-388-4656; FAX: 860-388-4657 trad@ctz.nai.net www.traditionsmuzzle.com
Trafalgar Square, P.O. Box 257, N. Pomfret, VT 05053 / 802-457-1911
Trevallion Gunstocks, 9 Old Mountain Rd., Cape Neddick, ME 03902 / 207-361-1130
Trico Plastics, 28061 Diaz Rd., Temecula, CA 92590 / 909-676-7714; FAX: 909-676-0267 ustinfo@ustplastics.com www.tricoplastics.com
Trijicon, Inc., 49385 Shafer Ave., P.O. Box 930059, Wixom, MI 48393-0059 / 810-960-7700; FAX: 810-960-7725
Trinidad St. Jr Col Gunsmith Dept., 600 Prospect St., Trinidad, CO 81082 / 719-846-5631; FAX: 719-846-5667
Triple-K Mfg. Co., Inc., 2222 Commercial St., San Diego, CA 92113 / 619-232-2066; FAX: 619-232-7675 sales@triplek.com www.triplek.com
Trius Traps, Inc., P.O. Box 25, 221 S. Miami Ave., Cleves, OH 45002 / 513-941-5682; FAX: 513-941-7970 triustraps@fuse.net triustraps.com
Trotman , Ken , 135 Ditton Walk, Unit 11, Cambridge, CB5 8PY ENGLAND / 01223-211030; FAX: 01223-212317
Tru-Balance Knife Co., P.O. Box 140555, Grand Rapids, MI 49514 / 616-453-3679
True Flight Bullet Co., 5581 Roosevelt St., Whitehall, PA 18052 / 610-262-7630; FAX: 610-262-7806
Truglo, Inc, PO Box 1612, McKinna, TX 75070 / 972-774-0300; FAX: 972-774-0323 www.truglosights.com
Tru-Square Metal Products Inc., 640 First St. SW, P.O. Box 585, Auburn, WA 98071 / 253-833-2310; or 800-225-1017; FAX: 253-83-2349 t-tumbler@qwest.net
Tucson Mold, Inc., 930 S. Plumer Ave., Tucson, AZ 85719 / 520-792-1075; FAX: 520-792-1075
Turnbull Restoration, Doug, 6680 Rt. 5 & 20, PO Box 471, Bloomfield, NY 14469 / 585-657-6338; FAX: 585-657-6338 turnbullrest@mindspring.com www.turnbullrestoration.com
Tuttle , Dale , 4046 Russell Rd., Muskegon, MI 49445 / 616-766-2250

U

Ultra Dot Distribution, 2316 N.E. 8th Rd., Ocala, FL 34470
Uncle Mike's *(See Michaels of Oregon Co.)*
Unertl Optical Co., Inc., 103 Grand Avenue, P.O. Box 895, Mars, PA 16046-0895 / 724-625-3810; FAX: 724-625-3819 unertl@nauticom.net
United Binocular Co., 9043 S. Western Ave., Chicago, IL 60620
United States Optics Technologies, Inc., 5900 Dale St., Buena Park, CA 90621 / 714-994-4901; FAX: 714-994-4904 www.usoptics.com
United States Products Co., 518 Melwood Ave., Pittsburgh, PA 15213-1136 / 412-621-2130; FAX: 412-621-8740 sales@us-products.com www.us-products.com
Universal Sports, PO Box 532, Vincennes, IN 47591 / 812-882-8680; FAX: 812-882-8680
Unmussig Bullets, D. L., 7862 Brentford Dr., Richmond, VA 23225 / 804-320-1165
USAC, 4500-15th St. East, Tacoma, WA 98424 / 206-922-7589

V

Valor Corp., 5555 NW 36th Ave., Miami, FL 33142 / 305-633-0127; FAX: 305-634-4536
VAM Distribution Co LLC, 1141-B Mechanicsburg Rd, Wooster, OH 44691 www.rex10.com
Vancini , Carl *(See Bestload, Inc.)*
Vann Custom Bullets, 330 Grandview Ave., Novato, CA 94947
Varmint Masters, LLC, Rick Vecqueray , PO Box 6724, Bend, OR 97708 / 541-318-7306; FAX: 541-318-7306 varmintmasters@bendcable.com www.varmintmasters.net
Vecqueray, Rick. *(See Varment Masters, LLC)*
Vega Tool Co., c/o T.R. Ross, 4865 Tanglewood Ct., Boulder, CO 80301 / 303-530-0174
Venco Industries, Inc. *(See Shooter's Choice)*
Verney-Carron, B.P. 72, 54 Boulevard Thiers, 42002, FRANCE / 33-477791500; FAX: 33-477790702
VibraShine, Inc., PO Box 577, Taylorsville, MS 39168 / 601-785-9854; FAX: 601-785-9874
Vibra-Tek Co., 1844 Arroya Rd., Colorado Springs, CO 80906 / 719-634-8611; FAX: 719-634-6886
Vic's Gun Refinishing, 6 Pineview Dr., Dover, NH 03820-6422 / 603-742-0013
Victory Ammunition, PO Box 1022, Milford, PA 18337 / 717-296-5768; FAX: 717-296-9298
Victory USA, P.O. Box 1021, Pine Bush, NY 12566 / 914-744-2060; FAX: 914-744-5181
Vihtavuori Oy/Kaltron-Pettibone, 1241 Ellis St., Bensenville, IL 60106 / 708-350-1116; FAX: 708-350-1606
Vincent's Shop, 210 Antoinette, Fairbanks, AK 99701
Vintage Industries, Inc., 781 Big Tree Dr., Longwood, FL 32750 / 407-831-8949; FAX: 407-831-5346
Viper Bullet and Brass Works, 11 Brock St., Box 582, Norwich, ON N0J 1P0 CANADA
Virgin Valley Custom Guns, 450 E 800 N #20, Hurricane, UT 84737 / 435-635-8941; FAX: 435-635-8943 vvcguns@infowest.com www.virginvalleyguns.com
Visible Impact Targets, Rts. 5 & 20, E. Bloomfield, NY 14443 / 716-657-6161; FAX: 716-657-5405
Vitt/Boos, 1195 Buck Hill Rd., Townshend, VT 05353 / 802-365-9232
Voere-KGH m.b.H., PO Box 416, A-6333 Kufstein, Tirol, AUSTRIA / 0043-5372-62547; FAX: 0043-5372-65752
Volquartsen Custom Ltd., 24276 240th Street, PO Box 397, Carroll, IA 51401 / 712-792-4238; FAX: 712-792-2542 vcl@netins.net www.volquartsen.com
Vom Hoffe *(See Old Western Scrounger, Inc., The)*, 12924 Hwy A-12, Montague, CA 96064 / 916-459-5445; FAX: 916-459-3944
VSP Publishers *(See Heritage/VSP Gun Books)*, PO Box 887, McCall, ID 83638 / 208-634-4104; FAX: 208-634-3101
Vulpes Ventures, Inc. Fox Cartridge Division, PO Box 1363, Bolingbrook, IL 60440-7363 / 630-759-1229; FAX: 815-439-3945

W

W. Square Enterprises, 9826 Sagedale Dr., Houston, TX 77089 / 281-484-0935; FAX: 281-464-9940 lfdwcpdq.net www.loadammo.co,
W.B. Niemi Engineering, Box 126 Center Road, Greensboro, VT 05841 / 802-533-7180 or 802-533-7141
W.C. Strutz Rifle Barrels, Inc., PO Box 611, Eagle River, WI 54521 / 715-479-4766
W.E. Brownell Checkering Tools, 9390 Twin Mountain Cir, San Diego, CA 92126 / 858-695-2479; FAX: 858-695-2479
W.J. Riebe Co., 3434 Tucker Rd., Boise, ID 83703
Waechter, 43 W. South St. #1FL, Nanticoke, PA 18634 / 717-864-3967; FAX: 717-864-2669
Walker Arms Co., Inc., 499 County Rd. 820, Selma, AL 36701 / 334-872-6231; FAX: 334-872-6262
Walters, John. *(See Walters Wads)*
Walters Wads, John Walters , 500 N. Avery Dr., Moore, OK 73160 / 405-799-0376; FAX: 405-799-7727 www.tinwadman@cs.com
WAMCO--New Mexico, P.O. Box 205, Peralta, NM 87042-0205 / 505-869-0826
Ward & Van Valkenburg, 114 32nd Ave. N., Fargo, ND 58102 / 701-232-2351
Warne Manufacturing Co., 9039 SE Jannsen Rd., Clackamas, OR 97015 / 503-657-5590 or 800-683-5590; FAX: 503-657-5695
Warren Muzzleloading Co., Inc., Hwy. 21 North, P.O. Box 100, Ozone, AR 72854 / 501-292-3268
WASP Shooting Systems, Rt. 1, Box 147, Lakeview, AR 72642 / 501-431-5606
Watson Trophy Match Bullets, 467 Pine Loop, Frostproof, FL 33843 / 863-635-7948; or 864-244-7948 cbestbullet@aol.com
WD-40 Co., 1061 Cudahy Pl., San Diego, CA 92110 / 619-275-1400; FAX: 619-275-5823
Weatherby, Inc., 3100 El Camino Real, Atascadero, CA 93422 / 805-466-1767; FAX: 805-466-2527 weatherby.com
Weaver Arms Corp. Gun Shop, RR 3, P.O. Box 266, Bloomfield, MO 63825-9528
Weaver Products, P.O. Box 39, Onalaska, WI 54650 / 800-648-9624; or 608-781-5800; FAX: 608-781-0368
Weaver Scope Repair Service, 1121 Larry Mahan Dr., Suite B, El Paso, TX 79925 / 915-593-1005
Weber & Markin Custom Gunsmiths, 4-1691 Powick Rd., Kelowna, BC V1X 4L1 CANADA / 250-762-7575; FAX: 250-861-3655 www.weberandmarkinguns.com
Webster Scale Mfg. Co., P.O. Box 188, Sebring, FL 33870 / 813-385-6362
Weems , Cecil , 510 W Hubbard St, Mineral Wells, TX 76067-4847 / 817-325-1462
Weigand Combat Handguns, Inc., 685 South Main Rd., Mountain Top, PA 18707 / 570-868-8358; FAX: 570-868-5218 sales@jackweigand.com www.scopemount.com
Wells Creek Knife & Gun Works, 32956 State Hwy. 38, Scottsburg, OR 97473 / 541-587-4202; FAX: 541-587-4223
Welsh, Bud. *(See High Precision)*
Wenig Custom Gunstocks, 103 N. Market St., PO Box 249, Lincoln, MO 65338 / 660-547-3334; FAX: 660-547-2881 gustock@wenig.com www.wenig.com
Werth , T. W. , 1203 Woodlawn Rd., Lincoln, IL 62656 / 217-732-1300
Wessinger Custom Guns & Engraving, 268 Limestone Rd., Chapin, SC 29036 / 803-345-5677
Western Mfg. Co., 550 Valencia School Rd., Aptos, CA 95003 / 831-688-5884 lotsabears@eathlink.net
Western Nevada West Coast Bullets, PO BOX 2270, DAYTON, NV 89403-2270 / 702-246-3941; FAX: 702-246-0836
Westley Richards & Co., 40 Grange Rd., Birmingham, ENGLAND / 010-214722953
White Rock Tool & Die, 6400 N. Brighton Ave., Kansas City, MO 64119 / 816-454-0478
White Shooting Systems, Inc. *(See White Muzzleload)*
Whitestone Lumber Corp., 148-02 14th Ave., Whitestone, NY 11357 / 718-746-4400; FAX: 718-767-1748
Wichita Arms, Inc., 923 E. Gilbert, P.O. Box 11371, Wichita, KS 67211 / 316-265-0661; FAX: 316-265-0760
Widener's Reloading & Shooting Supply, Inc., P.O. Box 3009 CRS, Johnson City, TN 37602 / 615-282-6786; FAX: 615-282-6651
Wideview Scope Mount Corp., 13535 S. Hwy. 16, Rapid City, SD 57701 / 605-341-3220; FAX: 605-341-9142 wvdon@rapidnet.com ww.jii.to
Wilcox Industries Corp, Robert F Guarasi , 53 Durham St, Portsmouth, NH 03801 / 603-431-1331; FAX: 603-431-1221
Wild West Guns, 7521 Old Seward Hwy, Unit A, Anchorage, AK 99518 / 800-992-4570; or 907-344-4500; FAX: 907-344-4005
Wilderness Sound Products Ltd., 4015 Main St. A, Springfield, OR 97478 / 800-47-0006; FAX: 541-741-0263
Wilhelm Brenneke KG, PO Box 1646, 30837 Langenhagen, Langenhagen, GERMANY / 0511/97262-0; FAX: 0511/97262-62 info@brenneke.de www.brenneke.com
Williams Gun Sight Co., 7389 Lapeer Rd., Box 329, Davison, MI 48423 / 810-653-2131; or 800-530-9028; FAX: 810-658-2140 williamsgunsight.com
Wilson Safety Prods. Div., PO Box 622, Reading, PA 19603-0622 / 610-376-6161; FAX: 610-371-7725
Wilson Combat, 2234 CR 719, Berryville, AR 72616-4573 / 800-955-4856; FAX: 870-545-3310
Winchester Consultants, George Madis , P.O. Box 545, Brownsboro, TX 75756 / 903-852-6480; FAX: 903-852-3045 gmadis@prodigy.com
Winchester Div. Olin Corp., 427 N. Shamrock, E. Alton, IL 62024 / 618-258-3566; FAX: 618-258-3599
Windish , Jim , 2510 Dawn Dr., Alexandria, VA 22306 / 703-765-1994
Winkle Bullets, R.R. 1, Box 316, Heyworth, IL 61745
Winter , Robert M. , PO Box 484, 42975-287th St., Menno, SD 57045 / 605-387-5322
Wise Custom Guns, 1402 Blanco Rd, San Antonio, TX 78212-2716 / 210-828-3388
Wiseman and Co., Bill, PO Box 3427, Bryan, TX 77805 / 409-690-3456; FAX: 409-690-0156
Wolfe Publishing Co., 2626 Stearman Rd. Ste A, Prescott, AZ 86301 / 520-445-7810; or 800-899-7810; FAX: 520-778-5124
Wolf's Western Traders, 1250 Santa Cora Ave. #613, Chula Vista, CA 91913 / 619-482-1701 patwolf4570book@aol.com
Woodleigh *(See Huntington Die Specialties)*
Woods Wise Products, P.O. Box 681552, Franklin, TN 37068 / 800-735-8182; FAX: 615-726-2637
Working Guns, Jim Coffin , 1224 NW Fernwood Cir, Corvallis, OR 97330-2909 / 541-928-4391
World of Targets *(See Birchwood Casey)*
Worthy Products, Inc., RR 1, P.O. Box 213, Martville, NY 13111 / 315-324-5298
Wright's Gunstock Blanks, 8540 SE Kane Rd., Gresham, OR 97080 / 503-666-1705 doyal@wrightsguns.com www.wrightsguns.com
WTA Manufacturing, PO Box 164, Kit Carson, CO 80825 / 800-700-3054; FAX: 719-962-3570
Wyant Bullets, Gen. Del., Swan Lake, MT 59911
Wyoming Custom Bullets, 1626 21st St., Cody, WY 82414

X

X-Spand Target Systems, 26-10th St. SE, Medicine Hat, AB T1A 1P7 CANADA / 403-526-7997; FAX: 403-528-2362

Y

Yearout, Lewis E. *(See Montana Outfitters)*, 308 Riverview Dr E, Great Falls, MT 59404 / 406-761-0859
Yesteryear Armory & Supply, P.O. Box 408, Carthage, TN 37030
York M-1 Conversions, 12145 Mill Creek Run, Plantersville, TX 77363 / 936-894-2397; FAX: 936-894-2397
Young Country Arms, William , 1409 Kuehner Dr #13, Simi Valley, CA 93063-4478

Z

Zanotti Armor, Inc., 123 W. Lone Tree Rd., Cedar Falls, IA 50613 / 319-232-9650
Zeeryp , Russ , 1601 Foard Dr., Lynn Ross Manor, Morristown, TN 37814 / 615-586-2357
Zero Ammunition Co., Inc., 1601 22nd St. SE, PO Box 1188, Cullman, AL 35056-1188 / 800-545-9376; FAX: 205-739-4683
Ziegel Engineering, 2108 Lomina Ave., Long Beach, CA 90815 / 562-596-9481; FAX: 562-598-4734 ziegel@aol.com www.ziegeleng.com
Zriny's Metal Targets *(See Z's Metal Targets)*

Annual Favorites From Krause Publications and DBI Books

Gun Digest® 2003
The World's Greatest Gun Book, 57th Annual Edition
edited by Ken Ramage

Commercial sporting rifle, pistol, shotgun, and airgun models currently marketed in the U.S. are listed with specifications, factory options, and retail prices. This heavily illustrated arms catalog also covers scopes, metallic sights, ammunition, and reloading presses. Top firearms writers offer authoritative articles and new product reports. Ballistics and prices are given for rifle and handgun cartridges, while shotshells are listed with loads and prices. The Arms Trade and Arms Library are completely updated to help you locate additional information.

Softcover • 8½x11 • 560 pages • 2,000 b&w photos • 16-page color section
Item# GD2003 • $27.95

2003 Standard Catalog of® Firearms
The Collector's Price & Reference Guide, 13th Edition
by Ned Schwing

Find more guns packed in this firearms identification and price reference than all other competing volumes combined. This updated 13th edition is clearly the largest and most comprehensive firearms reference available with more than 25,000 guns and 110,000 prices. Identify and price nearly every firearm manufactured since 1835 with the heavily illustrated listings. Prices are listed in up to six grades of condition for each gun. Discover the original firearms manufacturer by cross-referencing more than 550 trade names, and use the detailed indexes to easily locate specific guns. The updated 16-page color section showcases rare and notable guns recently sold at auction.

Softcover • 8¼x10⅞ • 1,396 pages • 6,000+ b&w photos • 16-page color section
Item# GG13 • $34.95

Guns Illustrated® 2003
The Standard Reference for Today's Firearms, 35th Edition
edited by Ken Ramage

The sporting firearms industry's standard reference features the latest, greatest rifles, shotguns, and handguns available with exciting new product reports and a heavily illustrated, updated, and expanded catalog section. Feature articles examine emerging arms and sporting knives trends, while new product reports cover developments in handguns, rifles, shotguns, muzzleloaders, sporting knives, and ammunition. See the latest rifles, handguns, shotguns, and muzzleloaders in this highly illustrated, expanded, and updated firearms catalog.

Softcover • 8½x11 • 336 pages • 1,500 b&w photos
Item# GI2003 • $22.95

Knives 2003
23rd Edition
edited by Joe Kertzman

See what top custom knifemakers can do with a piece of steel and a hammer. Hundreds of examples of ornate works of art and working tools are displayed and discussed, including the "best of the best" in a color section. See current custom knife designs and style trends and read the best knife articles on antique pocketknives, Roman swords, safari steel, how to assemble kit knives, and much more. Also features completely updated directories and custom knifemaking club membership

Softcover • 8½x11 • 312 pages
1,000+ b&w photos
8-page color section
Item# KN2003 • $22.95

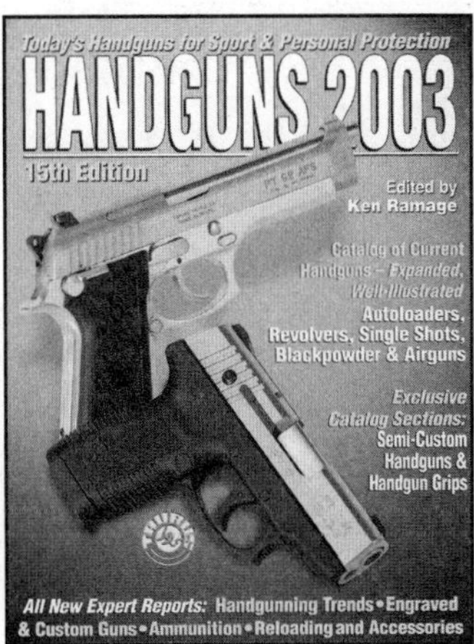

Handguns 2003
15th Edition
edited by Ken Ramage

See what's new from the handgun industry including extensive coverage of available commercial and semi-custom pistols, trends, and accessories. The semi-custom handguns and handgun grips catalog section is expanded and revised to include currently available products. Pistol coverage includes centerfire, rimfire, and blackpowder pistols, plus airguns. Also included are essential references such as the NRA Compendium of Firearms Laws, the NRA Right-to-Carry Reciprocity Guide, and a directory of the handgunning trade.

Softcover • 8½x11 • 320 pages
500+ b&w photos
Item# H2003 • $22.95

2003 Sporting Knives
2nd Edition
edited by Joe Kertzman

More than 60 cutlery companies reveal over 300 models of available sporting knives, complete with large, clear photos and detailed specifications and retail prices. The catalog covers knives from commercial sporting cutlery companies such as Browning, Buck, Case, Columbia River, and Spyderco. Enjoy new feature articles and reports from the field on knife trends, the latest blade materials, and the newest commercial knife designs. An updated reference directory lets you directly contact manufacturers and dealers.

Softcover • 8½x11
256 pages • 700 b&w photos
Item# DGK02 • $22.95

To order call **800-258-0929**
Offer GNB2
M-F 7am - 8pm • Sat 8am - 2pm, CST

Krause Publications, Offer GNB2
P.O. Box 5009, Iola WI 54945-5009
www.krausebooks.com

DBI BOOKS
a division of Krause Publications

Shipping & Handling: $4.00 first book, $2.25 each additional. Non-US addresses $20.95 first book, $5.95 each additional.

Sales Tax: CA, IA, IL, NJ, PA, TN, VA, WI residents please add appropriate sales tax.

Satisfaction Guarantee: If for any reason you are not completely satisfied with your purchase, simply return it within 14 days of receipt and receive a full refund, less shipping charges.